Let's Go

CITY GUIDES

the world's best selling
budget travel series

New York City

D0033847

COMPLETELY
REVISED FOR **2001** NEW! PHOTOS & MORE MAPS

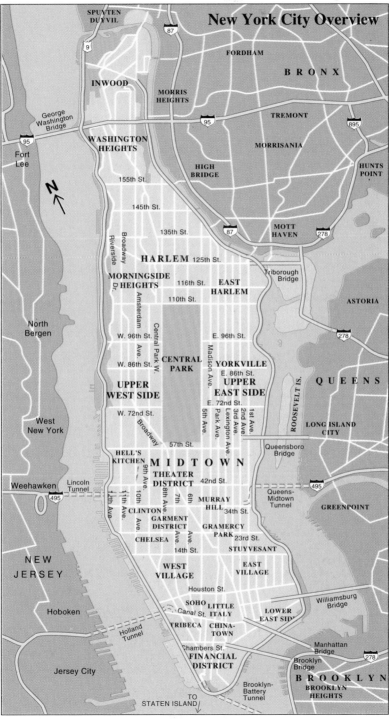

New York City Overview

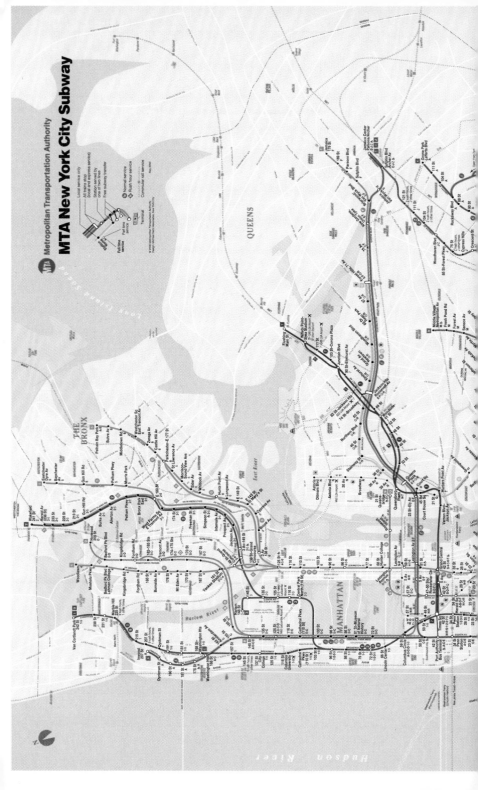

MTA New York City Subway

Metropolitan Transportation Authority

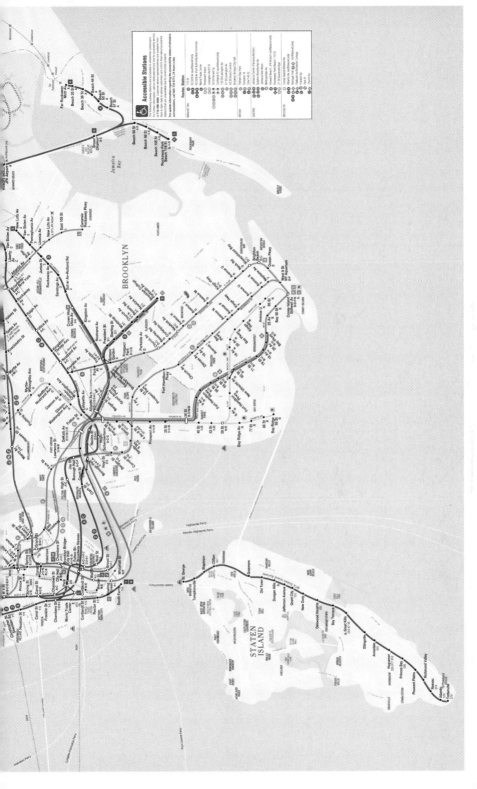

Downtown Manhattan

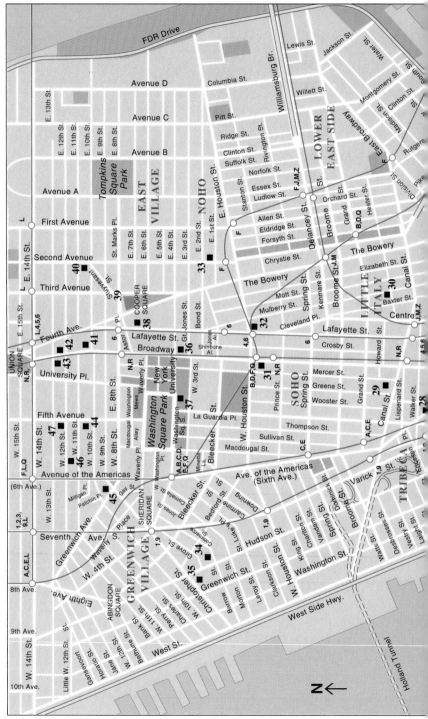

Downtown Manhattan

Midtown Manhattan

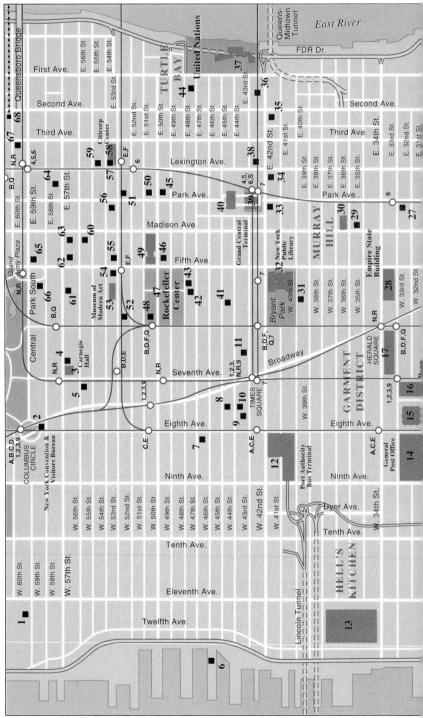

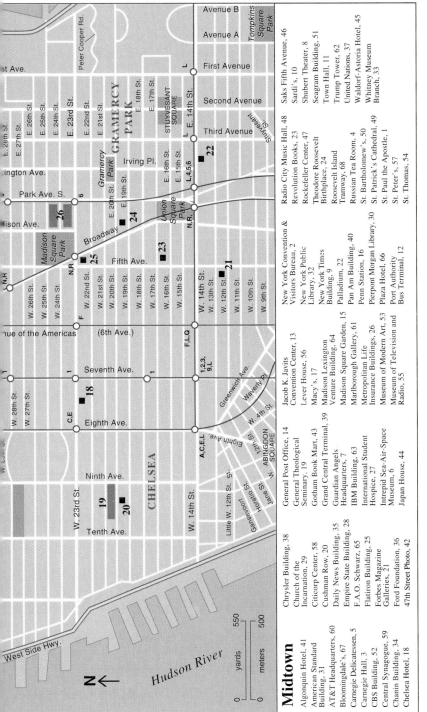

Uptown

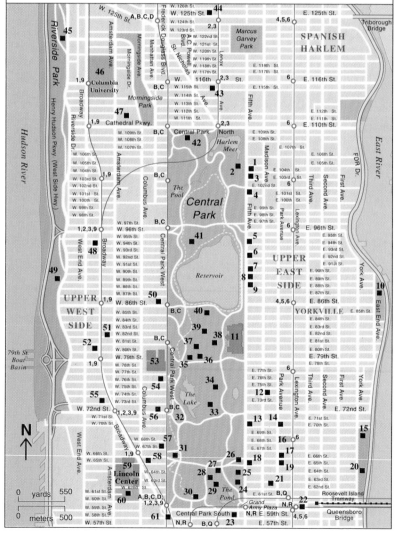

🖊 Let's Go writers travel on your budget.

"Guides that penetrate the veneer of the holiday brochures and mine the grit of real life."

—The Economist

"The writers seem to have experienced every rooster-packed bus and lunar-surfaced mattress about which they write."

—The New York Times

"All the dirt, dirt cheap."

—People

🖊 Great for independent travelers.

"The guides are aimed not only at young budget travelers but at the independent traveler; a sort of streetwise cookbook for traveling alone."

—The New York Times

"Flush with candor and irreverence, chock full of budget travel advice."

—The Des Moines Register

"An indispensible resource, *Let's Go*'s practical information can be used by every traveler."

—The Chattanooga Free Press

🖊 Let's Go is completely revised each year.

"Only *Let's Go* has the zeal to annually update every title on its list."

—The Boston Globe

"Unbeatable: good sightseeing advice; up-to-date info on restaurants, hotels, and inns; a commitment to money-saving travel; and a wry style that brightens nearly every page."

—The Washington Post

🖊 All the important information you need.

"*Let's Go* authors provide a comedic element while still providing concise information and thorough coverage of the country. Anything you need to know about budget traveling is detailed in this book."

—The Chicago Sun-Times

"Value-packed, unbeatable, accurate, and comprehensive."

—Los Angeles Times

Let's Go Publications

Let's Go: Alaska & the Pacific Northwest 2001
Let's Go: Australia 2001
Let's Go: Austria & Switzerland 2001
Let's Go: Boston 2001 **New Title!**
Let's Go: Britain & Ireland 2001
Let's Go: California 2001
Let's Go: Central America 2001
Let's Go: China 2001
Let's Go: Eastern Europe 2001
Let's Go: Europe 2001
Let's Go: France 2001
Let's Go: Germany 2001
Let's Go: Greece 2001
Let's Go: India & Nepal 2001
Let's Go: Ireland 2001
Let's Go: Israel 2001
Let's Go: Italy 2001
Let's Go: London 2001
Let's Go: Mexico 2001
Let's Go: Middle East 2001
Let's Go: New York City 2001
Let's Go: New Zealand 2001
Let's Go: Paris 2001
Let's Go: Peru, Bolivia & Ecuador 2001 **New Title!**
Let's Go: Rome 2001
Let's Go: San Francisco 2001 **New Title!**
Let's Go: South Africa 2001
Let's Go: Southeast Asia 2001
Let's Go: Spain & Portugal 2001
Let's Go: Turkey 2001
Let's Go: USA 2001
Let's Go: Washington, D.C. 2001
Let's Go: Western Europe 2001 **New Title!**

Let's Go *Map Guides*

Amsterdam	New Orleans
Berlin	New York City
Boston	Paris
Chicago	Prague
Florence	Rome
Hong Kong	San Francisco
London	Seattle
Los Angeles	Sydney
Madrid	Washington, D.C.

Coming Soon: *Dublin* and *Venice*

Let's Go

New York City

2001

Valerie de Charette editor

researcher-writers
Yayoi Shionoiri
Thandi O. Parris
Christian Lorentzen, Daniel Levi,
Matthew Murray, Bart St. Claire,
Joseph Turian, Matt Daniels,
Ian Pervil, T.J. Kelleher

John Fiore map editor
Luke Marion photographer

St. Martin's Press ♒ New York

HELPING LET'S GO If you want to share your discoveries, suggestions, or corrections, please drop us a line. We read every piece of correspondence, whether a postcard, a 10-page email, or a coconut. Please note that mail received after May 2001 may be too late for the 2002 book, but will be kept for future editions. **Address mail to:**

> Let's Go: New York City
> 67 Mount Auburn Street
> Cambridge, MA 02138
> USA

Visit Let's Go at **http://www.letsgo.com,** or send email to:

> feedback@letsgo.com
> Subject: "Let's Go: New York City"

In addition to the invaluable travel advice our readers share with us, many are kind enough to offer their services as researchers or editors. Unfortunately, our charter enables us to employ only currently enrolled Harvard students.

ABOUT LET'S GO

FORTY-ONE YEARS OF WISDOM

As a new millennium arrives, *Let's Go: Europe*, now in its 41st edition and translated into seven languages, reigns as the world's bestselling international travel guide. For over four decades, travelers criss-crossing the Continent have relied on *Let's Go* for inside information on the hippest backstreet cafes, the most pristine secluded beaches, and the best routes from border to border. In the last 20 years, our rugged researchers have stretched the frontiers of backpacking and expanded our coverage into Asia, Africa, Australia, and the Americas. This year, we've introduced a new city guide series with titles to San Francisco and our hometown, Boston. Now, our seven city guides feature sharp photos, more maps, and an overall more user-friendly design. We've also returned to our roots with the inaugural edition of *Let's Go: Western Europe*.

It all started in 1960 when a handful of well-traveled students at Harvard University handed out a 20-page mimeographed pamphlet offering a collection of their tips on budget travel to passengers on student charter flights to Europe. The following year, in response to the instant popularity of the first volume, students traveling to Europe researched the first full-fledged edition of *Let's Go: Europe*, a pocket-sized book featuring honest, practical advice, witty writing, and a decidedly youthful slant on the world. Throughout the 60s and 70s, our guides reflected the times. In 1969 we taught travelers how to get from Paris to Prague on "no dollars a day" by singing in the street. In the 80s and 90s, we looked beyond Europe and North America and set off to all corners of the earth. Meanwhile, we focused in on the world's most exciting urban areas to produce in-depth, fold-out map guides. Our new guides bring the total number of titles to 51, each infused with the spirit of adventure and voice of opinion that travelers around the world have come to count on. But some things never change: our guides are still researched, written, and produced entirely by students who know first-hand how to see the world on the cheap.

HOW WE DO IT

Each guide is completely revised and thoroughly updated every year by a well-traveled set of nearly 300 students. Every spring, we recruit over 200 researchers and 90 editors to overhaul every book. After several months of training, researcher-writers hit the road for seven weeks of exploration, from Anchorage to Adelaide, Estonia to El Salvador, Iceland to Indonesia. Hired for their rare combination of budget travel sense, writing ability, stamina, and courage, these adventurous travelers know that train strikes, stolen luggage, food poisoning, and marriage proposals are all part of a day's work. Back at our offices, editors work from spring to fall, massaging copy written on Himalayan bus rides into witty, informative prose. A student staff of typesetters, cartographers, publicists, and managers keeps our lively team together. In September, the collected efforts of the summer are delivered to our printer, who turns them into books in record time, so that you have the most up-to-date information available for your vacation. Even as you read this, work on next year's editions is well underway.

WHY WE DO IT

We don't think of budget travel as the last recourse of the destitute; we believe that it's the only way to travel. Living cheaply and simply brings you closer to the people and places you've been saving up to visit. Our books will ease your anxieties and answer your questions about the basics—so you can get off the beaten track and explore. Once you learn the ropes, we encourage you to put *Let's Go* down now and then to strike out on your own. You know as well as we that the best discoveries are often those you make yourself. When you find something worth sharing, please drop us a line. We're Let's Go Publications, 67 Mount Auburn St., Cambridge, MA 02138, USA (email: feedback@letsgo.com). For more info, visit our website, www.letsgo.com.

Contents

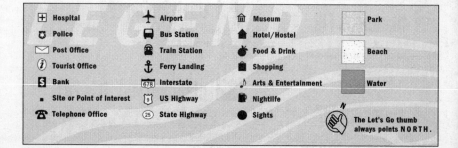

Hospital	Airport	Museum	Park
Police	Bus Station	Hotel/Hostel	
Post Office	Train Station	Food & Drink	Beach
Tourist Office	Ferry Landing	Shopping	
Bank	Interstate	Arts & Entertainment	Water
Site or Point of Interest	US Highway	Nightlife	
Telephone Office	State Highway	Sights	The Let's Go thumb always points NORTH.

HOW TO USE THIS BOOK

How to use this book? Ideally, you should read it cover to cover and memorize everything. In reality, we know this **brand-new, redesigned** (complete with **photos!**) guide to is just too irresistible to put down. So go ahead, bring it with you and join in-the-know tourists exploring the mesmerizing, never-ending streets and sights of NYC. Know, however, that you are carrying the savviest guide available to all that is hip, cutting-edge, and not-to-be-missed in the City that Never Sleeps.

Start planning your big city escapade with **Discover NYC,** which breaks down the city's top 25 sights, annual festivals, **suggested itineraries,** and **Let's Go Picks,** the best (and weirdest) of NYC. The **Life and Times** chapter is like Cliff's Notes to NYC history and culture, condensing Algonquin tribes and Rudy Giuliani into an oh-so-witty survey course on NYC. Before you completely lose yourself in the city's wonders, however, read through **Planning Your Trip,** which has info on everything you need to plan your urban sojourn, from visas and plane tickets to bank cards and insurance. For those spending months (or even years) in NYC, **Living in NYC** breaks down everything from finding housing and procuring long-term visas to community centers and where to work out.

Once in New York City, **Once in NYC** will be your best friend, dishing the dirt on the city's neighborhoods, public transport, and even how to act like a true New Yorker. The neighborhood breakdown here mirrors that of the rest of the book. **Sights, Museums & Galleries, Shopping, Food,** and **Accommodations** are all organized in the same geographical order: Manhattan is listed first, with its neighborhoods moving uptown from Lower Manhattan to Washington Heights; the other boroughs follow. If you don't know exactly where that chic sushi bar or super-budget hostel is, these chapters all feature break downs of listings by type and by price. All neighborhoods—complete with their hotels, museums, monuments, restaurants, bars, and subway stops—are plotted in the **map appendix** at the end of the book. The **Queer Apple** is a comprehensive guide for gay and lesbian travelers to New York, with information on communities, resources, and NYC's most fabulous parties. Finally, the **Service Directory** is a quick reference to any phone number that you could possibly need; if you want to get your hair cut, visit an embassy, or call a taxi, find that info here. Should you, for some reason, want to leave the city, **Daytripping** will guide you around the greater metropolitan area. Including New Jersey.

Scattered throughout this oh-so-informative, well-organized guide are tips on how best to explore NYC. Entries with a ▧ are our favorite favorites; they're either super cheap, super hip, or just plain super duper. If you really want to be budget, look for **On the Cheap,** sidebars that highlight everything from seeing Lady Liberty for free to how get a Kate Spade for less than $10. Or, if you want to live large, seek out **The Big Splurge** sidebars. For travelers with children, **Kids in the City** will help you keep those tiny tots appeased. Absolute essentials—such as avoiding the West Nile virus—is highlighted in white **Read Me!** boxes. Plain old **black sidebars** give the low-down on all that is quirky, interesting, and fab about NYC; whether you want to know about brownstones or the numerous garbage dump parks, you'll find the details here. Our *ultimate* insider's scoop, however, is detailed in one of our many **walking tours.** Let us plan out an entire day for you, including which museums to visit to where to chow and drink; you'll find these tours on map spreads in the Sights chapter.

And remember, anything you can't find is probably in the **index.**

A NOTE TO OUR READERS The information for this book was gathered by *Let's Go* researchers from May through August of 2000. Each listing is based on one researcher's opinion, formed during his or her visit at a particular time. Those traveling at other times may have different experiences since prices, dates, hours, and conditions are always subject to change. You are urged to check the facts presented in this book beforehand to avoid inconvenience and surprises.

RESEARCHER-WRITERS

Yayoi Shionoiri

Pakng mre punch thn peepl twce hr height, ths shining str made it thru evn the Slums of the cIty and the BacKwoods of the boros wth hr sense of humor stll intct. A Toronto native, but clearly too cool to be tied to any one locale, Yayoi never broke a sweat, sipping cool lattes, eating yummy snacks, and basking in ambiance. Pulling far ahead of the race, this dancing queen never let anyone down, except the patrons at Clit Club.

Thandi O. Parris

Too hot to handle, Thandi Sparked her way through NYC. So thorough, she insisted on doing nothing unless it was half-speed, double marginalia. And were we excited to get what she did—perfect in everyway, with the intros to match, this New Yorker knows the city inside and out (or, at least, the UES).

Christian Lorentzen

The office couch misses this hunk'o'lovin', but this lanky hep cat worked even more magic on the road then on Frame (inconceivable!). Leaving a trail of love-struck waitresses in his wake, this smooth talkin' explorer wafted his way through Manhattan, managing to juggle a job, perfect his prose, and party all in the same puff.

Daniel Levi

Perfect in every way, we only regret that this efficient *Let's Go* weapon was not available for exploitation sooner. Who else but the cheery-faced, blue-eyed receptionist could have seen every cockroach in Queens and still stand by the borough faithfully? So loyal, so quick, so devout, such a baritone, Dan's a pleasure in the office and in the Science Center.

Matthew Murray

A former Lampoon writer, and boy does it show(!), Matt was another NYC resident/SWAT team member, and 2001 saviour. A day-crawler, he balanced out the hard partiers on the team and scoured *Let's Go* for write-ups that were not to his humorific standards. The Indians fell for "pretty sweet beads?"—Wesley Willis would tip his hat.

Bart St. Claire

No disco was too loud, no drink too strong, as Bart braved bar after bar in his fervent quest to skim the cream and taste the dregs of gay New York. Bart would particularly like to blow a kiss to those he met "on the road"—Bob, Daniel, Frank, André, Larry, Buck, Dennis, Heriberto, Richard, Michael, and Sven. You were all wonderful.

Ian Pervil

This hardened veteran of the pop mag circuit--he's done time in the offices of *Time Out: New York, Entertainment Weekly*, and *Us Weekly*--trekked only a few blocks from his Christopher St. flat, but that saved the Village.

Joseph Turian

Short, maybe, but sweet.

Matthew Daniels

A hardy traveling companion to our Xian, he saw to it that neither of them was ravished on the dangerous hike through the woods and over the Heights.

T.J. Kelleher

This *Let's Go* nostalgic, for all his efforts, does not have much of an appreciation for musicals.

ACKNOWLEDGMENTS

VALERIE DE CHARETTE THANKS:
Melissa Gibson, for doing way more than she had to (and praise the lord she did); John Fiore for the best maps yet seen between these covers; Melissa Rudolph for keeping my pesky bookfile in check; all three of them again for the Sound of Music and 80s marathons; Luke Marion and Dara Cho for pictures; my researchers Yayoi, Thand-o-rama, Xian Lorentzen (you are Prince Charming), Bart and Anne Chisholm, Dan Levi, Matt Murray, Matt Daniels, Ian Pervil, TJ, Joseph, Semra, and Cody for their time and writing; my parents, Guenolé de Charette and Young Kim de Charette, for their invaluable research, love, support, money, I could list everything under the sun; Team Let's Go, especially Olivia, Nora, Aarup, Anup, Nick Grossman, Kaya, Mica, Western Europe and Europe (Kate Douglas, Dan Barnes, Carla, Karen, Becky...), Chris Russell, Mike Murakami, Johs, Alice, China Podlings, Bede, Dawid, still my favorite editor—none of you had to, thank you; all the City Guides, because we're that dope—props to us for going through with this crazy redesign; Chris Murphy for helping and not helping at the same time; and the USA/A&P pod (and the entire 4th floor) for loving my crystal-clear soprano. This book is dedicated to my NYC boys and girls—Dena, Alison, Kaitlin, Avery, and many others—you're what this city means to me.

LET'S GO: NYC 2001 THANKS:
Bob Lambert; Mark Trompeter; Yayoi's "mama and papa for cooking and chauffeuring;" Jstar for his companionship, (mjs) communication, and complaints about the heat; Tchaiko Parris and the Parris family; and everyone who was nice on the road.

Editor
Valerie de Charette
Managing Editor
Melissa Gibson
Map Editor
John Fiore

Publishing Director
Kaya Stone
Editor-in-Chief
Kate McCarthy
Production Manager
Melissa Rudolph
Cartography Manager
John Fiore
Editorial Managers
Alice Farmer, Ankur Ghosh,
Aarup Kubal, Anup Kubal
Financial Manager
Bede Sheppard
Low-Season Manager
Melissa Gibson
Marketing & Publicity Managers
Olivia L. Cowley, Esti Iturralde
New Media Manager
Jonathan Dawid
Personnel Manager
Nicholas Grossman
Photo Editor
Dara Cho
Production Associates
Sanjay Mavinkurve, Nicholas Murphy, Rosa Rosalez,
Matthew Daniels, Rachel Mason,
Daniel Visel
(re)Designer
Matthew Daniels
Office Coordinators
Sarah Jacoby, Chris Russell

Director of Advertising Sales
Cindy Rodriguez
Senior Advertising Associates
Adam Grant, Rebecca Rendell
Advertising Artwork Editor
Palmer Truelson

President
Andrew M. Murphy
General Manager
Robert B. Rombauer
Assistant General Manager
Anne E. Chisholm

Discover NYC

Immensity, diversity, and a tradition of defying tradition characterize the city known as "the Crossroads of the World." Since its earliest days, New York has scoffed at the timid offerings of other American cities. It boasts the most immigrants, the tallest skyscrapers, the biggest museum in the Western Hemisphere, and the largest landfill ever (otherwise refered to as Staten Island). Even the vast blocks of concrete have their own gritty charm. Returning from a dull vacation in rural Westchester, talespinner O. Henry noted, "there was too much fresh scenery and fresh air. What I need is a steam-heated flat and no vacation or exercise."

New York City is full of folks. The stars are shielded by a blanket of pollution. The buildings are tall, the subway smelly, the people rushed, the beggars everywhere. But for every inch of grime, there's a yard of silver lining. Countless people mean countless pockets of culture—you can find every kind of ethnicity, food, art, language, attitude. It's possible to be alone, but that's not the point—plunge into the fray and you'll find 8 million stories, curmudgeonly humor, innovative ideas, and a fair share of madness. The architecture, from colonial to Art Deco, reveals the stratae of history that NYC embodies. Meanwhile, there's flamenco at an outdoor cafe, jazz in historic speakeasies, jungle/illbient under a bridge, Eurotechno at a flashy club—whatever the question, New York has the answer.

INTRODUCING NEW YORK

Since it *is* the center of the world, NYC has sights catering to even the most specific of interests. Here are some suggested sights by theme that are sure to excite.

LITERARY NEW YORK

The city has inspired innumerable authors' greatest achievements. **Herman Melville** and **Washington Irving** were both born in Lower Manhattan at 6 Pearl St. and 131 William St.,

👆 LET'S GO PICKS

BEST PLACE TO SMOKE.
Puff to your heart's content at **Circa Tabac** (p. 208), the city's only cigarette lounge.

BEST CHOLESTEROL-LADEN SNACK. A **Krispy Kreme** (p. 192) donut, of course.

BEST PLACES TO FISH DRUNK. The Bronx's City Island. Rowboats, bait, tackle, and accessories are available at **The Boat Livery, Inc.** (p. 115) in the Bronx's City Island. Or, just slam vodka shots while dancing to Russian disco at **Primorski Restaurant** (p. 202) then go flap your arms about in the translucent waters of Brighton Beach. *Let's Go* does not recommend drunken swimming.

BEST QUICKIE MALE SEX.
Meet your partner at the **Meat Rack** or **Dick Dock** on **Fire Island** (p. 227).

BEST PARK ON TOP OF A GARBAGE DUMP. It's a tie. **Great Kills** (p. 110) Staten Island's beautiful park, might be on top of the Island's not-so-beautiful garbage dump. And while it's not technically a garbage dump, the **Riverside Park** (p. 100) in Harlem, is a surprisingly clean and pleasant park atop a sewage treatment plant.

BEST PLACE TO GET A NOSE JOB. Long Island (p. 232).

BEST PLACE TO BUY TRASHY CLOTHES AND ACCESSORIES. Girl-props.com (p. 141) specializes in all that is glittered, rhinestoned, and day-glo.

BEST BATHROOMS. Enter the unisex stalls at **Bar 89** (p. 209) and watch the glass door fog as you make stinky.

respectively (see p. 67). Irving, in fact, gave New York its ever-enduring pen- (and movie-) name, **Gotham City**. **Walt Whitman,** born in South Huntington, Long Island (one wonders how he became so cultured), edited the controversial **Brooklyn Eagle** newspaper (see p. 236). **Edgar Allen Poe,** living uptown in the rural Bronx, was so brutally poor that he sent his aging mother-in-law out to scour the area for edible roots (seep. 113). Starving artists filled **Greenwich Village** in the early 20th century—**Willa Cather, John Reed,** and **Theodore Dreiser** parented the American novel in its streets (see p. 74). Over time, the Village came to prevail as the city's literary center; **e.e. cummings** and **Djuna Barnes** both lived off 10th St. at **Patchin' Place** (see p. 76). **Edna St. Vincent Millay** lived in the same neighborhood, at Bedford St. (see p. 76), where she founded the **Cherry Lane Theater** (see p. 156). Harlem residents soon spoke up, too: **Langston Hughes,** a principle voice of the **Harlem Renaissance,** lived at 20 E. 127th St. and attended **Columbia University** (see p. 98); **Ralph Ellison** and **W.E.B. DuBois** lived on **Sugar Hill** (see p. 102). Drink at the former speakeasy that once served **John Steinbeck** and **Ernest Hemingway, Chumley's** (see p. 76). On Bleecker and MacDougal Sts., you'll find some of the coffee houses that the **Beats** made famous (see p. 74). **Thomas Wolfe** lived at 263 W. 11th St. **Dylan Thomas** wasn't the only one of the lot who tanked up at the **White Horse Tavern** on Hudson St. (although he was the unlucky one who lapsed into a fatal coma after a purported 18 shots of whiskey). And the final word in literary criticism, **Robert Benchley** and **Dorothy Parker's Round Table,** held court at the **Algonquin Hotel** (see p. 89).

NEUROTIC NEW YORK

Kibbitz with others in line for bagels and lox at **Zabar's** (see p. 197) and complain about nothing with **Jerry Seinfeld** and friends at **Tom's Restaurant** on the Upper West Side (see p. 198). Jerry's real-life ex, Shoshana Lonstein, graduate of NYC's exclusive Nightingale-Banford High School, now designs clothing for big-breasted women at **Shoshana's Place** in the East Village. **Erasmus Hall Academy** in **Flatbush, Brooklyn** (see p. 105) bred the Jewish-American princess herself, **"Babs" Streisand;** she broke the first face of her mirror while singing in the high school's chorus with Neil Diamond. Flatbush was also the birth place of Allen Stuart Konigsberg, the sardonic voice of Jewish NY, better known as **Woody Allen.** Classic New York scenes from Woody's movies are as common as virgins in a convent. The famous "bridge scene" from *Manhattan* is a shot of the **59th Street Bridge** (see p. 90); Woody sits with Diane Keaton at 57th St., just west of Sutton Place in Queens. Young Alvy Singer of *Annie Hall* grew up in the house under the **Coney Island Rollercoaster;** the house still

A PRETTY SWEET FRUIT

Many a folklorist has wondered the origin of the "Big Apple" moniker. Some would tell you that a happy marriage between jazz and capitalism produced this popular name for New York. In the 1920s and 30s when jazz musicians bragged about playing New York, they'd say they were playing "the Big Apple," meaning they had reached the height of success. Charles Gillett, the past president of the New York Convention and Visitors Bureau, popularized the name with his Big Apple Campaign in 1971. His P.R. ploy hit onto something inexplicably catchy.

rattles underneath (see **Coney Island,** p. 26). Since 1997, Woody toots his **clarinet** Monday nights at **Cafe Carlyle** in the Carlyle Hotel on Madison Ave. and 76th St. You can soothe your own neuroses with a reuben at **Katz's Delicatessen** on the Lower East Side (see p. 186), and taste what Meg Ryan was moaning about in *When Harry Met Sally.*

SWANK NEW YORK

Paris may have the Opera, London may have the Queen Mother, but no city does elitism like New York. Bid for the most-recently available Bauhaus construct at **Sotheby's,** 334 York Ave. (see p. 134), but first make sure you've procured the latest pastel pouch **Vuitton** is exhibiting at their flagship at 49 E. 57th St.—you can't show up at Sotheby's with any old Coach. And of course, you can't walk the streets of the Upper East Side without the newest heel from **Manolo,** 15 W. 55th St., right off Fifth Ave. While you're in the area, pick up a little 24-karat something at **Tiffany's & Co.** (see p. 149); it'll compliment those new shoes. Eat alongside the ladies who lunch at the **Russian Tea Room.** That's right, "tea": you can't eat, you have to wear that unforgiving Missoni knit tonight to the **Metropolitan Opera** (see p. 159). Don't worry, though, Henri at **Barney's New York** (see p. 149) said you looked smashing in it, and he wouldn't lie, would he? The final touch to your carefully cultivated image? A vintage shawl from one of those *darling* used clothing stores in **Alphabet City** (see p. 144)—but make sure it's pashmina.

DANCE AMONG THE STARS, HIS WAY

The "Chairman of the Board," **Frank Sinatra,** was a major cultural force in NYC in the mid-20th century. Born in **Hoboken, NJ** (see p. 229) Frank now has a park and a main street in town dedicated to his memory. When he was in his first musical on **Broadway** (see p. 153) in 1942, at the **Paramount Theater,** it only took a few weeks until 42nd St. Midtown traffic was brought to a standstill because of all the squirming young (and not-so-young) girls trying to get a glimpse of the "Sultan of Swoon." **Mare Chiaro,** a 90-year-old bar in Little Italy on Mulberry St., is better known to locals as "Frank's Bar" (see p. 72). He became so popular that when Republican presidential candidate Governor Dewey was talking outside the **Waldorf-Astoria Hotel** (see p. 88), devout Democrat Sinatra walked by and led the entire crowd away with him like a naughty Pied Piper. In NYC he drank, sang, and debauched with the rest of the Rat Pack, had affairs with numerous resident starlets, hobknobbed with everyone from **President Kennedy** to the **Capones,** and garnered a following so devout that even today there are places like **Grimaldi's,** a restaurant fully devoted to Ol' Blue Eyes (see p. 200).

SUGGESTED ITINERARIES
THREE-DAY NEW YORK JAUNT

DAY 1. Start your tour of NYC in **Greenwich Village** (see p. 74), the area that defines the city for most. A small neighborhood, the best idea is to walk aimlessly around its streets; buy a hoochie top for clubbing (see p. 142), get a **tatoo** or **body piercing** (see p. 142), make like an **NYU** film student, and challenge one of the chess players in **Washington Square Park** (see p. 74). If you tire of the trendy, visit the Village's cooler sibling in **Chelsea** (see p. 82). Home to the *avant* avant-garde, you can catch a few of its **galleries** (see p. 133) for free before night falls and its **bars and lounges** (see p. 207) pull you away to follow less intellectual pursuits.

DAY 2. Now it's time to get to business—you can't go home without embarrassing tourist photos. Walk around **East Midtown** (see p. 86) to see the NY you've always heard about. Walk the red carpet to the gilded **Trump Plaza** (see p. 89), take a tour of **Carnegie Hall** (see p. 90), pass by **St. Patrick's Cathedral** (see p. 89), one of the city's most recognizable buildings, and go uptown on Museum Mile. No trip to the city would be complete without a visit to the **Metropolitan Museum of Art** (see p. 120) and Frank Lloyd Wright's stunning **Guggenheim** (see p. 122). If you're not feeling too out-of-place against this privileged backdrop, hit up the stores along Fifth Avenue and 57th Street—**Tiffany's & Co.** (see p. 149), **Chanel**, and **Henri Bendel**—to get a full picture of the NYC's Upper East Side. After this stifling day, head to the bars of the **Upper West Side** (along Amsterdam Ave. between 72nd and 86th Sts.) to unwind in their *very* unpretentious company (see p. 95).

DAY 3. To make up for last night, wake up early and make the trek to the medieval **Cloisters** (see p. 126) in Washington Heights and lunch in the beautiful gardens. Instead of running right back to charted lands, stroll around neighboring **Harlem** (see p. 98), home of **Langston Hughes** and **Martin Luther King, Jr.** Harlem's residential side include its historical **brownstones** (see p. 102), which are Harlem's *thing*. When that gets boring, walking along **125th Street** should give you all the bustle you crave. Stop in at one of the million sports clothing stores or get some collard greens at **Sylvia's** (see p. 199).

FIVE DAYS IN THE CITY THAT NEVER SLEEPS

DAY 4. If you're staying this long you'll have to see the **Statue of Liberty** (see p. 61)—no buts about it. Get yourself to the **Staten Island Ferry** Terminal (don't start screaming yet, we're not going to send you there) to get the cheapest, if not closest, view of Lady Liberty (see p. 64); make sure you stay on the ferry until it's back safely onto Manhattan shores. From your southern-most vantage point of the island, you can either take the relaxing path through **Battery Park** (see p. 66) to get to the **Stock Exchange** (see p. 67) and **Twin Towers** (see p. 66), or detour through active **South Street Seaport**. Once you've reached the looming skyscrapers of the nation's financial ground zero, move on to **Chinatown** (see p. 71) for dinner and *lichee* ice cream.

DAY 5. After four days in the city, it's time to get over your Manhattan-centrism and make a foray into the Big Bad Boroughs. If it's **Brooklyn** you desire, take our Walking Tour (**Sights**, p. 61) for a taste of its unique flavor. But if its **Queens** you've wanted to visit ever since you saw *Coming to America*, join us on the **International Express** (more commonly known as the 7 train). Get off right at the entrance to the borough, near Queensboro, and pick a street to follow for the day. **Astoria Boulevard** (see p. 107) will bring you through Greece (Astoria), India (Jackson Heights), then, on Northern Blvd., to Korea (Flushing). If you choose the less commercial but still very active **Queens Boulevard** (see p. 107), you can visit Ireland (Woodside), sample a United Nations summit (Elmhurst), get lost in a Tudor wonderland (Forest Hills), and end up in the steamy West Indies (St. Albans). If you liked your World Tour that much, stay in Queens for the nightlife it offers in **Bayside**.

SEVEN-DAY SLICE OF THE APPLE

DAY 6. The **Lower East Side** (see p. 73) is the perfect follow-up to Manhattan's touristy side. Start off with an early lunch (that'll stay in your stomach all day) at one of the neighborhood's **delis** (see p. 186). Walk off that pastrami and see old, gritty NYC as it butts heads with that tireless monster, gentrification. You'll get addicted to the no-name **boutiques** and **antique stores** (see p. 140), so keep shopping just next-door in the hip-and-happening **East Village** (see p. 144). While you're there, see the remains of the old, turbulent East Village in the **murals** documenting the neighborhood's **drug wars** (see p. 79) and in **Tompkins Square Park** (see p. 79), the sight of one of the first recorded instances of police brutality. As a respite from the brutal realities of the city, take the ferry to pristine, surburban **Hoboken** (see p. 229) for a night of mindless fun at its small-town bars.

DAY 7. It's your last day—quick, there are still some things you *have* to see before you leave! Jog through **Central Park** (see p. 92) with the other New Yorkers—or rest on the beautiful **carousel** with their children—and rush to the **Museum of Natural History** (see p. 121). By the time you're out of there you'll be just in time to walk down to **Times Square** (see p. 85) to see the lights of Broadway. Since it's the end of your sojourn in the Big City, take the splurge and see a **Broadway show** (see p. 153) or eat a good dinner among the actors at **Sardi's** (see p. 192). "New York, New York, it's a hell of a town!"

HOLIDAYS AND FESTIVALS IN 2001

DATE	FESTIVAL	INFORMATION
November 23, 2000	Thanksgiving Day	Find a family; eat their turkey. Or attend Macy's Thanksgiving Day Parade, a 75-year tradition that begins at E. 77th St., runs along Central Park West, and goes south on Broadway to 34th St. Ogle the huge balloon floats assembled the night before at 79th St. and Central Park West, and see yourself on television!
Late-November to January	*Nutcracker* Season	The New York City Ballet performs its timeless classic. See p. 160 for ticket information.
December 2	Tree Lighting	At Rockefeller Center. ☎332-6868.
December 22	Channukah	Jewish celebration lasts 8 days.
December 25	Christmas	Businesses closed.
December 31	New Year's Eve Celebrations	Thousands gather around 42nd St. to glimpse the famous dropping of the Times Square ball—you'll get a better view on TV, without the drunkards and tourists.
January 1, 2001	New Year's Day	Massive hangovers, massive confetti clean-up. Businesses closed.
January 17	Martin Luther King, Jr.'s Birthday	City offices closed.
February 14	Valentine's Day	Snuggle up to that sweetie in your hostel or eat a candlelit dinner by the Hudson River.
February 21	President's Day	Businesses closed.
April 8-16	Passover	Jewish holiday celebrating freedom.
April 15	Easter Sunday	Businesses closed, bunny.
March 17	St. Patrick's Day Parade	Along Fifth Avenue, everything's green—even the bagels.
April 3-11	International Auto Show	At the Jacob Javits Convention Center.
May 6	Bike New York	A 2-decade springtime tradition—bike all 5 boroughs on traffic-free roads with 28,000 other cyclists. ☎932-2453.
May 28	Memorial Day	Concerts and fireworks at the South Street Seaport. Businesses closed.
June	Music in the Anchorage	Rock concert series at the base of the Brooklyn Bridge. ☎206-6674, ext. 252.
June to August	World Financial Center Festival	A full entertainment schedule throughout the summer. Mostly outdoors, mostly free. ☎945-0505.

DATE	FESTIVAL	INFORMATION
June to August	Summerstage	Performances in Central Park. Top acts, free! ☎360-2777; www.summerstage.org.
Mid-June to Mid-August	Celebrate Brooklyn	Outdoor performing arts festival at the Park Slope Bandshell. Free.
Mid-June	Welcome Back to Brooklyn Homecoming Festival	Festival celebrating the borough. Brooklyn natives who've made it big return home to the fanfare of bands, writers' readings, and family activities. Starts at Grand Army Plaza. Free. ☎718-855-7882, ext. 54; www.brooklynX.org/welcome.
Late June to Late July	Midsummer Night Swing	Dance under the stars at Lincoln Center to live music. See p. 160 for more information.
Late June to August	Shakespeare in the Park	Quality Shakespeare in Central Park's Delacorte Theater. Free. See p. 157 for more information.
June	Museum Mile Festival	Fifth Avenue closes from 82nd to 104th Sts. from 6-9pm; museums along the strip give free entertainments.
June	JVC Jazz Festival	Prestigious jazz festival with venues across the city. ☎496-9000 for annual dates and schedule.
June 25	Puerto Rican Independence Day	Parade along Fifth Ave. and festivities in El Barrio (Spanish Harlem).
June 26	Mermaid Parade	At Coney Island. A festival of fabulous fishies. See p. 26.
Late June	New York Restaurant Week	New York City's top restaurants allow you to partake of their fine eats for the mere price of the year (i.e., $21.00 in the year 2001). See p. 180.
July 4	Independence Day	Macy's fireworks display around Lower Manhattan and some over the river at the Battery Park esplanade.
Late July to August	Mostly Mozart	A celebration of Mozart. See p. 161.
Late August	Tap-A-Mania	Sponsored by Macy's, thousands of tap dancers congregate on 34th St. and Broadway. ☎695-4400.
September 3	Labor Day	Businesses closed. Also the rambunctious West Indian Parade along Eastern Parkway, from East New York to Flatbush Avenue, in Brooklyn.
Last weekend in August	US Open	Tennis championship held in the USTA's center in Flushing Meadows, Queens. ☎718-760-6200.
September 6	Labor Day/West Indian Day Parade	Labor Day honors US workers. Caribbean festival, Children's Carnival at St. John's Place in Brooklyn, and a West Indian Day Parade starting at Eastern Parkway in Brooklyn. Free. ☎718-625-15115 or 773-4052.
October 9	Columbus Day	Businesses closed.
Mid-October	Ice Skating begins	Rockefeller Center. ☎332-6868. See p. 173.
October 31	Halloween Parade	Oooh...inventive costumes and debauched fun. Sixth Ave. from Spring St. to 23rd St. See p. 22.
November 11	New York City Marathon (Election Day)	See skinny people sweat. NY Roadrunner's Club ☎423-2233. See p. 170.
November 11	Veterans' Day observed	Businesses closed.

SIGHTSEEING TOURS

WALKING TOURS

Adventure on a Shoestring, 300 W. 53rd St. (☎265-2663). See the city with veteran guide and budget connoisseur Howard Goldberg. Detailed 1½hr. tours incorporate chats with members of the various communities. Excursions reveal some of New York's better-kept secrets; Mr. Goldberg is a

THE 411 ON NEW YAUWK SLANG

A'ight
expression of agreement

to Ax
(v.) to ask

da Bomb
(n.) something excellent; (adj.) without the "da," meaning excellent

to Book
(v.) to hightail it out of there

Boricua
(adj., n.) Puerto Rican woman

to Bounce/to roll
(v.) to be out, to leave

the D.L.
(n.) the down-low, the low-down, the scoop; adj. "on the D.L tip"

Dope
(adj.) excellent; good looking

Ecksetera
et cetera

Esscuse Me?
"you better not have said what I think you said."

Fly
(adj.) Dope

Front
(v.) to feign; to affront

Gimme
"May I please have a..."

Hype
(adj.) Dope

I'm sayin'
expression of agreement

Keep it real
what true New Yorkers do

walking treasure trove of information on budget eats and accommodations. Themed tours run on holidays, like the Valentine's Day Big Apple Lovers' Tour, and fascinating tours like the Haunted Greenwich Village tour run year-round. Most tours cost $5; the price has never increased during the organization's 36 years of existence.

Big Onion Walking Tours (☎439-1090; www.bigonion.com). Graduate students in American history from Columbia or NYU lead tours of historic districts and ethnic neighborhoods. Themed excursions include "Central Park at Twilight," "Immigrant New York," "Historic Harlem," and the "Multi-Ethnic Eating Tour," which explores the gastronomical delights of places such as Chinatown and Little Italy. Tours average 2-2½hr. Adults $12-15, students and seniors $10-13. "Show-up" tours are Th-Su. Group tours and bus tours also available.

Heritage Trails New York, starting at Federal Hall, between Wall and Broad St. Mayor Giuliani recently helped organize 4 walking paths exploring the history and culture of Lower Manhattan. Maps and info for the trails (red, blue, green, and orange) can be found in the free trail maps available at numerous tourist stops, including visitor centers and at some sites along the trails.

Joyce Gold's Tours (☎242-5762). Ms. Gold has read over 900 books on Manhattan, the subject she teaches at NYU and at the New School. On 45 pre-set days each year she and a company of adventurers give tours focusing on architecture, history, and ethnic groups within the city. Tours last approximately 3hr., depending on the subject, and cost around $12.

Lower East Side Tenement Museum Walking Tours, 90 Orchard St. (☎431-0233). Neighborhood heritage tour strolls through the Lower East Side and examines how different immigrant groups shaped and continue to shape the area. 1hr. Sa and Su in summer at 1:30pm and 2:30pm. $9 adults, $7 students and seniors; combination tickets available for walking tour and tenement tours. (See **Museums,** p. 128; and **Sights,** p. 73.)

Municipal Art Society (☎935-3960, tour info ☎439-1049). Guided walking tours ($10-15); destinations change with the seasons but include most major districts of Manhattan, such as SoHo and Times Square. Their free tour of Grand Central Station Wed. 12:30pm, at the info booth on the main concourse. Call in advance.

Museum of the City of New York, 1220 Fifth Ave., and 103rd St. (☎534-1672). The museum sponsors popular walking tours Apr.-Oct. on Sa afternoons, lasting a leisurely 1-2hr. ($10). Areas covered include Chelsea, the Lower East Side, and Greenwich Village, with a focus on the history and architecture of the particular district. Call to sign up a few days beforehand.

Radical Walking Tours (☎718-492-0069). Historian/activist Bruce Kayton leads tours that cover the alternative history of NYC. For example, tours of Greenwich Village highlight radicals and revolutionaries like John Reed and Emma Goldman, as well as artistic and theatrical movements that flourished around them. Other tours include trips to Chelsea, Wall Street, the Lower East Side, and Central Park. Even lifelong locals will learn fascinating details about the city's history. No reservations required. Call for schedule and departure sites. All tours $10. 2-3hr.

92nd Street Y, 1395 Lexington Ave. (☎996-1100). The Y leads an astounding variety of walking tours covering all boroughs and many aspects of New York life, from the Garment District, SoHo artists, and the brownstones of Brooklyn to literary tours, museum visits, and even an all-night candlelight tour. Tours vary in length and cost $15-55. Call for the latest tours.

BOAT TOURS

Circle Line Tours, W. 42nd St., at the Hudson River, Pier 83 (☎563-3200; www.circleline.com). Another location at Pier 16 on the South Street Seaport. 3hr., 2hr. semi-circle and "Harbor Lights" tours, and 30min. speedboat rides. The 2hr. tours are worthwhile and relaxing. Semi-circle cruises the southern part of Manhattan at 11am, 2pm, and 4:30pm; only twice daily in the off-season (call ahead); $20, children $10, seniors $16. Evening "Harbor Lights" cruises daily at 7pm; M-F only in off season; $18, seniors $16, under 12 $10; light snacks and cocktails served. No reservations necessary; arrive 30-45min. early.

BUS TOURS

Brooklyn Attitude, 224 W. 35th St., between Seventh and Eighth Aves. (☎718-398-0939). Bus tour with several walking excursions through ethnic and historic neighborhoods in Brooklyn. Departure points in both mid-Manhattan and Brooklyn. $21-31.

Gray Line Sight-Seeing, 42nd St. and Eighth Ave., at the Port Authority Terminal (☎397-2600). Huge bus-tour company offering many trips, including jaunts through Manhattan and gambling junkets to Atlantic City. Conducted in English, French, German, Italian, Spanish among other languages. The Downtown tour (hourly 8am-5pm; $25, children $16) and Uptown tour (hourly 9am-5pm; $25, children $16) allow you to get on and off the bus at points to explore on your own. The 6hr. Night on the Town tour ($68, children $48) covers many sights (including the Statue of Liberty and World Trade Center observatories). Reservations aren't required for in-city tours, but arrive at the terminal 30min. early.

Harlem Spirituals, 690 Eighth Ave., between 43rd and 44th Sts. (☎391-0900). Offers tours of Manhattan, Brooklyn, and the Bronx. Tours of upper Manhattan, such as the "Spirituals and Gospel" tour, includes trips to historic homes and participation in a Baptist service (4hr.; Su 9:30am, W 9am; $35, with lunch $65). The "Soul Food and Jazz" tour (M, Th, Sa 7pm-midnight; $85) features a tour of Harlem, a filling meal at a Harlem restaurant (usually Sylvia's), and an evening at a jazz club. Reserve in advance.

New York Kool Tours (☎831-4440; www.kooltours.com). Day (2pm) and night tours (7pm and 11pm) of Chelsea and the East Village. Tours include free drinks and transportation. Must have over 21 ID. $20/person.

THE 411 ON NEW YAUWK SLANG

Lox and Shmear
(n.) a bagel with smoked salmon and cream cheese

Mami
(n.) exclamation remarking a woman's hotness

Not Tryin' To
don't want to

Peep
(v.) to look at

Phat; Phatty-Phat
(adj.) axcellent; most excellent

Pie
(n.) a pizza

Putz
(n.) a small member; a wimpy jerk

Schmuck
(n.) a jerk

Spot Blower
(n.) someone who spills the beans at an inopportune moment

Tar Beach
(n.) a rooftop for sunbathing

The City
(proper n.) the five boroughs

Tight
(adj.) Dope

True Dat
I'm sayin'

Wack
(adj.) bad; the opposite of dope

Word
True Dat

Yous
much like the French second person plural of "y'all"

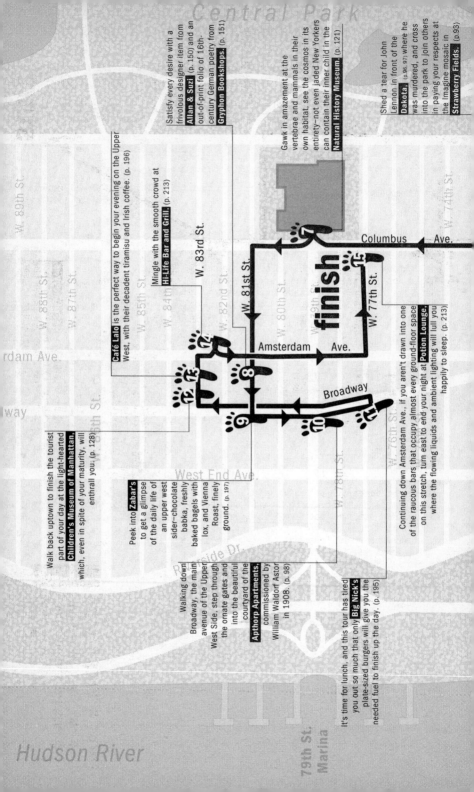

Central Park

Hudson River

Satisfy every desire with a frivolous designer item from **Allan & Suzi** (p. 150) and an out-of-print folio of 16th-century German poetry from **Gryphon Bookshops**. (p. 151)

Gawk in amazement at the vertebrae and mammals in their own habitat, see the cosmos in its entirety—not even jaded New Yorkers can contain their inner child in the **Natural History Museum**. (p. 121)

Shed a tear for John Lennon in front of the **Dakota**, (p. 96-97) where he was murdered, and cross into the park to join others in paying your respects at the Imagine mosaic in the **Strawberry Fields**. (p.93)

Walk back uptown to finish the tourist part of your day at the light-hearted **Children's Museum of Manhattan.** which, even in spite of your maturity, will enthrall you. (p. 128)

Café Lalo is the perfect way to begin your evening on the Upper West, with their decadent tiramisu and Irish coffee. (p. 196)

Mingle with the smooth crowd at **Hi-Life Bar and Grill.** (p. 213)

Peek into **Zabar's** to get a glimpse of the daily life of an upper west sider—chocolate babka, freshly baked bagels with lox, and Vienna Roast, finely ground. (p. 197)

Walking down Broadway, the main avenue of the Upper West Side, step through the ornate gates and into the beautiful courtyard of the **Apthorp Apartments,** commissioned by William Waldorf Astor in 1908. (p. 98)

It's time for lunch, and this tour has tired you out so much that only **Big Nick's** plate-sized burgers will give you the needed fuel to finish up the day. (p.195)

Continuing down Amsterdam Ave., if you aren't drawn into one of the raucous bars that occupy almost every ground-floor space on this stretch, turn east to end your night at **Potion Lounge**, where the flowing liquids and ambient lighting will lull you happily to sleep. (p. 213)

finish

W. 89th St.
W. 88th St.
W. 87th St.
W. 85th St.
W. 84th St.
W. 83rd St.
W. 82nd St.
W. 81st St.
W. 80th St.
W. 79th St.
W. 78th St.
W. 77th St.
W. 76th St.

Columbus Ave.
Amsterdam Ave.
Broadway
West End Ave.
Riverside Dr.
rdam Ave.
lway

79th St. Marina

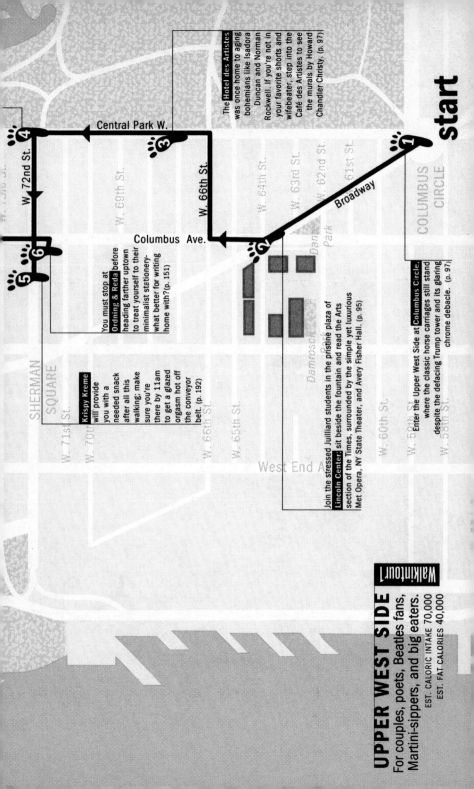

start

1 Enter the Upper West Side at **Columbus Circle**, where the classic horse carriages still stand despite the defacing Trump tower and its glaring chrome debacle. (p. 97)

2 Join the stressed Juilliard students in the pristine plaza of **Lincoln Center**; sit beside the fountain and read the Arts section of the Times, surrounded by the simple yet luxurious Met Opera, NY State Theater, and Avery Fisher Hall. (p. 95)

3 The **Hotel des Artistes** was once home to aging bohemians like Isadora Duncan and Norman Rockwell. If you're not in your favorite shorts and wifebeater, step into the Café des Artistes to see the murals by Howard Chandler Christy. (p. 97)

You must stop at **Ording & Reda** before heading farther uptown to treat yourself to their minimalist stationery— what better for writing home with? (p. 151)

Krispy Kreme will provide you with a needed snack after all this walking; make sure you're there by 11am to get a glazed orgasm hot off the conveyor belt. (p. 192)

COLUMBUS CIRCLE

Broadway

Central Park W.

W. 72nd St.

W. 69th St.

W. 66th St.

Columbus Ave.

W. 64th St.

W. 63rd St.

W. 62nd St.

W. 61st St.

W. 60th St.

W. 59th St.

W. 58th St.

W. 71st St.

W. 70th St.

W. 66th St.

W. 65th St.

SHERMAN SQUARE

Damrosch Park

West End Ave.

UPPER WEST SIDE
For couples, poets, Beatles fans,
Martini-sippers, and big eaters.

EST. CALORIC INTAKE 70,000
EST. FAT CALORIES 40,000

Walkintour!

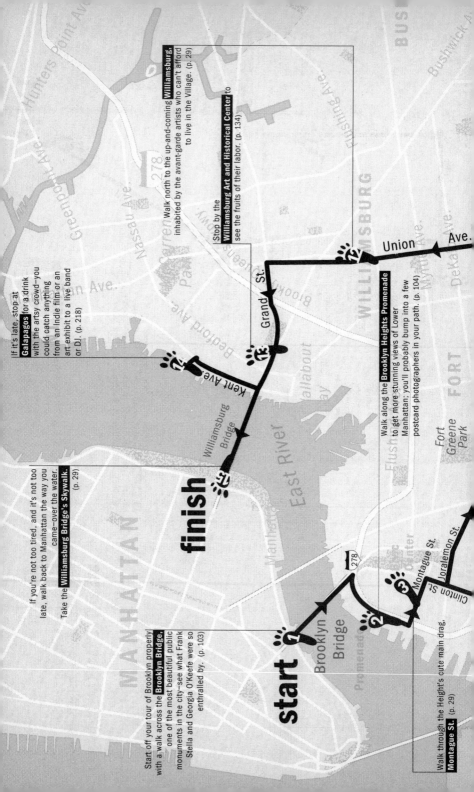

If it's late, stop at **Galapagos** for a drink with the artsy crowd—you could catch anything from an indie film or an art exhibit to a live band or DJ. (p. 218)

Walk north to the up-and-coming **Williamsburg**, inhabited by the avant-garde artists who can't afford to live in the Village. (p. 29)

Stop by the **Williamsburg Art and Historical Center** to see the fruits of their labor. (p. 134)

If you're not too tired, and it's not too late, walk back to Manhattan the way you came—over the water. Take the **Williamsburg Bridge's Skywalk.** (p. 29)

Start off your tour of Brooklyn properly with a walk across the **Brooklyn Bridge,** one of the most beautiful public monuments in the city—see what Frank Stella and Georgia O'Keefe were so enthralled by. (p. 103)

Walk along the **Brooklyn Heights Promenade** to get more stunning views of Lower Manhattan; you'll probably bump into a few postcard photographers in your path. (p. 104)

Walk through the Height's cute main drag, **Montague St.** (p. 29)

start

finish

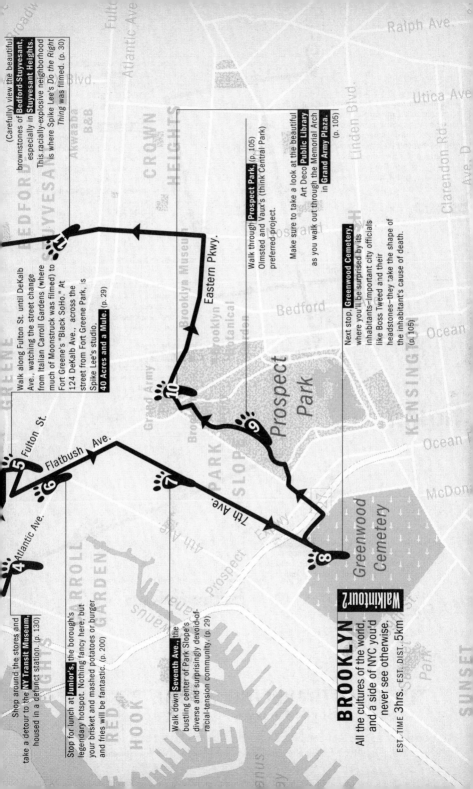

(Carefully) view the beautiful brownstones of **Bedford-Stuyvesant,** especially in **Stuyvesant Heights.** This racially-explosive neighborhood is where Spike Lee's *Do the Right Thing* was filmed. (p. 30)

Walk along Fulton St. until DeKalb Ave., watching the street change from Italian Carroll Gardens (where much of Moonstruck was filmed) to Fort Greene's "Black SoHo." At 124 DeKalb Ave., across the street from Fort Greene Park, is Spike Lee's studio, **40 Acres and a Mule.** (p. 29)

Walk through **Prospect Park,** (p. 105) Olmsted and Vaux's (think Central Park) preferred project.

Make sure to take a look at the beautiful Art Deco **Public Library** as you walk out through the Memorial Arch in **Grand Army Plaza.** (p. 105)

Next stop, **Greenwood Cemetery,** where you'll be surprised by its inhabitants–important city officials like Boss Tweed and their headstones–they take the shape of the inhabitant's cause of death. (p. 105)

Shop around the stores and take a detour to the **NY Transit Museum,** housed in a defunct station. (p. 130)

Stop for lunch at **Junior's,** the borough's legendary hotspot. Nothing fancy here, but your brisket and mashed potatoes or burger and fries will be fantastic. (p. 200)

Walk down **Seventh Ave.,** the bustling center of Park Slope's diverse and surprisingly devoid-of-racial-tension community. (p. 29)

Walkintour2

BROOKLYN

All the cultures of the world, and a side of NYC you'd never see otherwise.

EST. TIME 3hrs. EST. DIST .5km

Atlantic Ave.

Fulton St.

Flatbush Ave.

7th Ave.

Eastern Pkwy.

Prospect Park

Greenwood Cemetery

CROWN HEIGHTS

BEDFORD STUYVESANT

GREENE

PARK SLOPE

CARROLL GARDENS

RED HOOK

KENSINGTON

SUNSET

Bedford

Ocean

Grand Army

Brooklyn Museum

Brooklyn Botanical Garden

Atlantic Ave.

Ralph Ave.

Utica Ave.

Linden Blvd.

Clarendon Rd.

Broadway

Fulton

Blvd

4
5
6
7
8
9
10
11

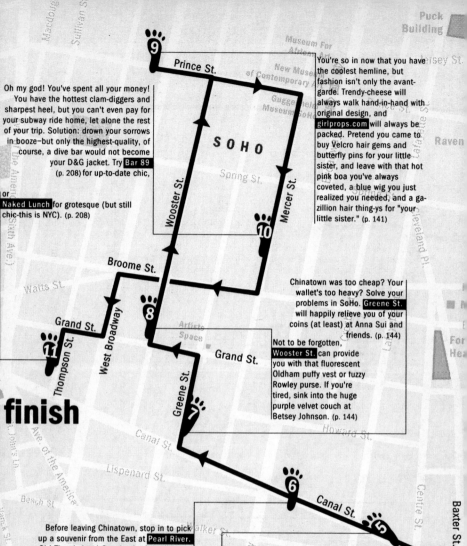

9

Prince St.

Oh my god! You've spent all your money! You have the hottest clam-diggers and sharpest heel, but you can't even pay for your subway ride home, let alone the rest of your trip. Solution: drown your sorrows in booze–but only the highest-quality, of course, a dive bar would not become your D&G jacket. Try Bar 89 (p. 208) for up-to-date chic,

or Naked Lunch for grotesque (but still chic–this is NYC). (p. 208)

You're so in now that you have the coolest hemline, but fashion isn't only the avant-garde. Trendy-cheese will always walk hand-in-hand with original design, and girlprops.com will always be packed. Pretend you came to buy Velcro hair gems and butterfly pins for your little sister, and leave with that hot pink boa you've always coveted, a blue wig you just realized you needed, and a ga-zillion hair thing-ys for "your little sister." (p. 141)

S O H O

Spring St.

Wooster St.

Mercer St.

10

Broome St.

Chinatown was too cheap? Your wallet's too heavy? Solve your problems in SoHo. Greene St. will happily relieve you of your coins (at least) at Anna Sui and friends. (p. 144)

8

Grand St.

West Broadway

Artists Space

Grand St.

Not to be forgotten, Wooster St. can provide you with that fluorescent Oldham puffy vest or fuzzy Rowley purse. If you're tired, sink into the huge purple velvet couch at Betsey Johnson. (p. 144)

Thompson St.

11

Greene St.

7

finish

Canal St.

Lispenard St.

6

Canal St.

5

Baxter St.

Before leaving Chinatown, stop in to pick up a souvenir from the East at Pearl River. Oh! The choices! Sequined velvet slippers, paper lanterns, bamboo mats, parasols, spicy wasabi peas–you'll never be able to pull yourself away from this temple to uselessness. (p. 140)

Pick up the newest Prada bag or Britney (hee hee!) CD for a fraction of their usual prices at the "boutiques" along Canal St. (p. 140)

T I B E C A

Franklin St.

Leonard St.

Knitting Factory

Hogan Pl.

TIRED OF TRAVELING BUDGET?
Voilà! Le Spend-Money-All-Day-Long Tour

EST. EXPENDITURE Well, that depends on whether they have that skirt in your size, that feathered necklace in ostrich...

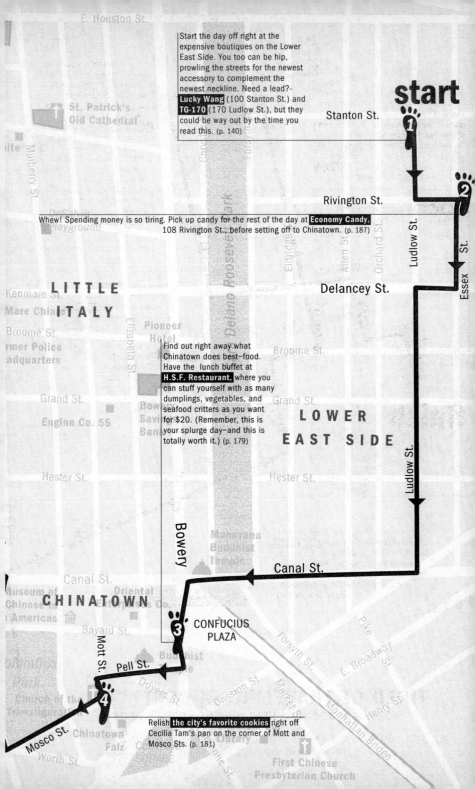

Start the day off right at the expensive boutiques on the Lower East Side. You too can be hip, prowling the streets for the newest accessory to complement the newest neckline. Need a lead?- **Lucky Wang** (100 Stanton St.) and **TG-170** (170 Ludlow St.), but they could be way out by the time you read this. (p. 140)

start

Stanton St.

Rivington St.

Whew! Spending money is so tiring. Pick up candy for the rest of the day at **Economy Candy**, 108 Rivington St., before setting off to Chinatown. (p. 187)

Delancey St.

LITTLE ITALY

Find out right away what Chinatown does best—food. Have the lunch buffet at **H.S.F. Restaurant,** where you can stuff yourself with as many dumplings, vegetables, and seafood critters as you want for $20. (Remember, this is your splurge day—and this is totally worth it.) (p. 179)

LOWER EAST SIDE

Canal St.

CHINATOWN

CONFUCIUS PLAZA

Relish **the city's favorite cookies** right off Cecilia Tam's pan on the corner of Mott and Mosco Sts. (p. 181)

Once in NYC

GETTING TO KNOW NEW YORK: NEIGHBORHOODS

Ah, New York City. You've just arrived—now what to do? Where to start? How to act? Perhaps you have your first run-in with the New York attitude as you're pushed out of the way a few times so that the real natives (who obviously have better places to be than you do) can get the first taxis from the airport. You finally snag the last one and arrive in Manhattan, the center of it all. But the New Yorkers around you are going so fast; they all appear to have important plans—at least, too important to stop and help a *tourist* (hide that camera!). No need to fear: you have come prepared. Whip out your ultra-cool-yet-unintimidating tour guide, *Let's Go: NYC*, and set to work making your own plans. Learn all the secrets to NYC's neighborhood cocktail—find a place to sleep, a place to spend the day, and, most importantly, a place to party.

Contrary to popular belief, **five boroughs** compose NYC: Brooklyn, the Bronx, Queens, Staten Island, and Manhattan. Pervading Manhattan-centrism has deep historical roots. The island's original inhabitants, the Algonquin, called it "Man-a-hat-ta" or "Heavenly Land." The British were the first to call the island "New York," after James, Duke of York, the brother of Charles II. Only in 1898 did the other four boroughs join the city's government. Flanked on the east by the "East River" (actually a strait) and on the west by the Hudson River, **Manhattan** is a sliver of an island, measuring only 13 mi. long and 2½ mi. wide. Sizeable **Queens** and **Brooklyn** are on the other side of the East River, and large **Staten Island** is to the south. North of Manhattan sits the **Bronx,** the only borough connected by land to the rest of the US.

1 7

MANHATTAN

LOWER MANHATTAN

⚇Subway: *1, 9 to South Ferry lands you at the southeastern tip of Battery Park; 4, 5 to Bowling Green. For a detailed **walking tour** of Lower Manhattan, call Heritage Trails at* ☎ *888-487-2457.* **Sights:** *p. 66.* **Food:** *p. 179.*

see map
pp. 316–317

The Southern tip of Manhattan is the financial hub of the city and, quite possibly, the entire world. With sleek office buildings rising above cobblestone streets and antiquated edifices, you can almost feel the "Invisible Hand" guiding you along your route. And while the bull markets of the later part of the 20th century have caused an unprecedented boom in real estate development in this part of the city, valiant efforts are being made to preserve the region's vast historical strata.

Lower Manhattan was the first part of the island settled by Europeans, and it subsequently set the stage for many US firsts, including the first Presidential inauguration, the first stock exchange, and the first instance of a cabbie giving a pedestrian the finger. The area's crooked streets remain as a reminder of New York's chaotic youth, before it got its act together and came up with the grid system used in its more northern parts. Omnipresent Heritage Trail markers indicate the most significant spots and provide historical information and anecdotes about the sites.

BATTERY PARK

The most southern point on the island, known today as Battery Park, once housed only fish and the men who loved them. The spot earned its nickname from the forts constructed by the American military on the shallow coastal banks. These forts were necessary well into the 19th century, as the British had a nasty habit of attacking American ships and cities. When the mammoth World Trade Center was being constructed in the 1970s, the millions of tons of soil dug up were deposited west of West St., and the residential Battery Park City apartments, some of New York's newest and glitziest digs, were built upon the landfill. Sculptures by artists such as Ned Smyth and Mary Miss line the esplanade, while the words of New York poets Walt Whitman and Frank O'Hara have been set into the gate bordering the harbor. If you want to go to Hoboken you can catch the ferry here (see p. 229). Just inside the north gate of Battery Park, Hope Garden, an AIDS memorial, holds 100,000 roses in memory of those who have died. The park contains numerous other memorials to veterans and immigrants who risked everything for the United States.

FINANCIAL DISTRICT

The Financial District, located roughly between Battery Park City and the civic center, is a supply-side economist's vision of heaven. Money, money, everywhere, and it shows. Pearl St., now one of the richest streets in the whole world, was once a dock where oyster harvesters shucked their catches for the day. The street's name comes from the fact that passers-by would often find pearls amid the empty husks. Broad St., northeast of Pearl, was once the site of an ill-fated attempt by Dutch colonists to recreate the canal systems of their homeland. The canal quickly became putrid and was filled shortly thereafter to become Broad St. Why they chose the name Broad St. and not Putrid Canal St. is a question that they probably had to deal with seriously. On Wall St., the cornerstone of both the district and the entire financial universe, men are bought and sold, fortunes are made and lost, and trillions of dollars are exchanged every day. Once the northern border to the New Amsterdam settlement, the street takes its name from the wall built in 1653 to shield the Dutch from those invasion-happy British. By the early 19th century, it had already become the financial capital that it is today, although without the hassle of those annoying day-traders.

CITY HALL AND THE CIVIC CENTER

The last remnants of turn-of-the-century New York reside in the civic center and City Hall, the nexus of city government. Most of the neighborhood's buildings are products of the late 19th-century "City Beautiful" campaign that paid homage to grandiose Classical architecture, with oversized columns and sculptures adorning most of the original structures. Nearly all of the buildings here house some branch of city, state, or federal government, and most of them sit atop a huge flight of lime steps.

SOUTH STREET SEAPORT

Walking east on Fulton St. leads you past a large strip of moderately priced, yet entirely mediocre, restaurants that ends at South St. Seaport. The shipping industry thrived here for most of the 19th century, when this was the most important port in the entire US. After the Civil War, South St. Seaport's shipping industry flourished, giving rise to bars, brothels, crime, and chain restaurants, only one of which, sadly, still remains to this day. In an aggressive campaign to clean up the place, politicians decided to build the Brooklyn Bridge right on top of it all. Unfortunately, this did not dissuade the riff-raff, especially the restaurateurs. In the mid-1980s, the Seaport Museum teamed up with the Rouse Corporation, which built Boston's Quincy Market, the St. Louis Union Station, and Baltimore's Harborplace, to design the 12-block "museum without walls." After 5pm, masses of professionals, attired in sneakers and skirts or trailing ties, descend upon the area for a well-deserved happy hour. It is up to you whether this is a reason to stay or get the heck out of here. The Seaport also offers museums with walls, shopping, sightseeing cruises, and street performers. Be warned, however: the Seaport, as well as most of lower Manhattan, is virtually deserted by 10pm, as most of the people who work here like to get away as soon as they can.

CHINATOWN

🚇*Subway:* 6, J, M, N, R, Z to Canal St.; walk east on Canal St. to get to Mott St., follow the curved street to get to the Bowery, Confucius Plaza, and E. Broadway. **Sights:** p. 71. **Food:** p. 191.

see map
pp. 318–319

North of the Neoclassical mammoths of the city government and the skyscrapers of the financial district, the streets begin to fill with exotic produce, fresh fish, and herbal medicine, spilling out of stores and onto sidewalk vending tables. Chinatown is loosely bounded by Worth Street to the south and Canal Street to the north, Broadway to the west and the Bowery to the east. The streets are dotted with pagoda-topped phone booths and filled with tourists, while McDonald's stands proud under its Chinese-charactered sign. But this is not a cultural front for tourism's sake. A vibrant community that maintains seven Chinese newspapers, over 300 garment factories, and innumerable food shops, New York's Chinatown contains the largest Asian community in the US outside San Francisco (over 300,000 estimated residents, comprising about half of the city's Asian population). Despite strict quotas on immigration, Chinatown grew up in the 1870s as Chinese-Americans fled anti-Chinese violence in the West. Although Chinese neighborhoods have since grown up in Queens' Flushing and Elmhurst and Brooklyn's Sunset Park and Bay Ridge, Chinatown continues to grow into the surrounding streets every year, especially up through Little Italy.

During the Chinese New Year, the area's frenetic pace accelerates to a fever pitch. The Fourth of July brings dangers of its own kind. Of the numerous brands of fireworks sold, few are legal, and of their dealers, most are intimidating. In case you need further discouragement, Mayor Giuliani's "Quality of Life" crime crackdown has made many fireworks even *more* illegal.

Mott and Pell Streets, the unofficial centers of Chinatown, boil over with Chinese restaurants and commercial activity. Every inch of the old red and green awnings lining the storefronts are decorated with Chinese-style baby jackets, bamboo hats, stuffed Hello Kittys, and miniature Buddhas. Their neighbors display dried ginseng roots, bucketfuls of glistening baby turtles, and delectable baked sweets. If it's labels you're into, Canal is the street for you; every inch of the sidewalk is used for commercial space, from the tiny closet-stores that spill half-way across the street to the bootleg video and CD peddlers on the sidewalk. Don't let the low-priced merchandise snooker you, though—creative labeling abounds in several stores and those are *not* Rolexes.

LITTLE ITALY

Subway: *4, 5, 6, N, R, J, M, Z to Canal St., B, D, F, Q to Broadway-Lafayette.* **Sights:** *p. 72.* **Food:** *p. 181.* **Accommodations:** *p. 269.*

see map
pp. 318–319

The name Little Italy conjures up a set of stock images culled from history books and movies: laundry hanging out of windows over streets clogged with people and pushcarts and implacable *padrones* whispering orders to hot-headed wiseguys. In truth, the Little Italy experience has less to do with sights and more with tastes (for more information, see **Restaurants**, p. 91). Pasta aside, the Little Italy of the public imagination has pretty much disappeared around these parts. Even at the turn of the century, the noisy, festive parades and street fairs drew revelers from uptown. Since the 1960s, however, the neighborhood's borders have receded in the face of an aggressively expanding Chinatown, and much of its authenticity has disappeared to the temptation of tourism. A small patch of restaurants and gift shops remains, frequented by visiting throngs. Once a year, however, Manhattan's Little Italy conjures up the old atmosphere; beginning the second Thursday in September, Mulberry Street goes wild during the raucous 10-day Feast of San Gennaro in celebration of the Neopolitan saint.

Mulberry Street remains the heart of the neighborhood. The reds, whites, and greens of the Italian flag flutter above it between Broome and Canal Streets. Come here for your very own "Kiss me, I'm Italian" t-shirt or *The Godfather* poster. The gift shop on the corner of Grand and Mulberry Streets, however, bears looking into even if you don't want to take home a souvenir. Instead of a tourist bureau, in here you can find Mr. Rossi, the store's proprietor, who may honor you with an exposition of the neighborhood's history.

Fleeing the tentacles of commercialization that have introduced J. Crew and Victoria's Secret to once-avant-garde SoHo, some of the area's most tragically hip galleries and boutiques—and the beautiful people who love them—have established a toehold in an area that used to belong to Little Italy and is now more a part of the Lower East Side. Some pseudo-hipsters call this region—extending roughly down from Houston to Spring Streets and over from Lafayette to the Bowery—**NoLIta** (**No**rth of **Li**ttle **Ita**ly), but most natives wouldn't be caught dead blaspheming Nabokov. Whatever your syntactical tastes, come here to view a scene in the making, still at the tender stage before the hipper-than-thou pioneer class has moved on. The vagaries of urban fashion are on full display at the small cafes, restaurants, and bars along upper Mott and Elizabeth Streets.

LOWER EAST SIDE

Everybody ought to have a Lower East Side in their life.
—Irving Berlin

Subway: *G, M, E, J, Z to Essex/Delandey St., near the Wiliamsburg Bridge.* **Sights:** *p. 73.* **Food:** *p. 186.* **Bars:** *p. 210.*

see map
pp. 326–327

Down below East Houston and east of the Bowery lurks the trendily seedy Lower East Side, where old-timers rub shoulders with heroin dealers, where kids riding kickboards share the streets with men in suits riding skateboards, and twenty-somethings emulate *la vie bohème* in what might be the new up-and-coming East Village. The history of the Lower East Side reflects America's history of immigration. The Lower East Side was once the most densely settled area in New York; 240,000 immigrants fleeing their homelands in search of a new life co-existed in one square mile. Initially populated by Irish immigrants in the mid-1800s, the area saw a large influx of Italians, Jews, Czechs, Slovaks, Poles, Romanians, Ukrainians, Russians, and Chinese from the 50 years preceding WWI. Post-WWII migrants to the area were mostly African-Americans and Puerto Ricans, and the 1980s and 90s have seen an influx of Latin Americans and Asians.

Main thoroughfares such as East Broadway continue to reflect the multicultural aspect of the neighborhood. Buddhist prayer centers have Jewish religious supply stores as their neighbors. Traces of the Jewish ghetto also persist on Orchard St., a historical shopping area that continues to fill up on Sundays with salesmen hawking discount goods in vacuum-sealed bags to multitudes of potential customers. Although the neighborhood retains its multicultural flavor, it is slowly shedding its working-class clothes for what is young, hip, and chic. For better or for worse, the neighborhood is being reborn from an historic ghetto to a happening, ghetto-fabulous place.

Well-established delis and stores offer pastrami, pickles, and pierogi alongside newer Pan-Asian cafes and bistros. A thriving alternative theater scene (like the Immigrants' Theatre Project or Todo Con Nada; see **Entertainment,** p. 161) and art studios (see **Sights,** p. 73) crowd out the old Jewish merchants. With small designers displaying their wares in sparse, futuristic spaces (often at to-covet-for boutique prices), the Lower East Side is posing a strong challenge for the title of hot spot of the moment. Still, it is relatively unpopulated by tourists, and cool hangouts (spanning the spectrum from cheap-but-good deli food to interesting theater and swanky lounges) are often hard to find on one's own. So, read up, make like you're a local (put away this guide), and venture out to the hidden gems of the Lower East Side. If you need guidance, visit the **Lower East Side Visitors Center,** 261 Broome St. between Orchard and Allen. (☎888-VALUES-4-U. Open Su-F 10am-4pm.)

EAST VILLAGE AND ALPHABET CITY

🚇Subway: 6 to Astor Pl. **Sights:** p. 76. **Food:** p. 188. **Bars:** p. 210.

see map
pp. 326–327

The East Village—section east of Broadway and north of East Houston—was carved out of the Bowery and the Lower East Side in the early 1960s, as artists and writers moved here to escape high rents in the West Village. Today, the East Village population represents greater diversity than its western neighbor; older Eastern European immigrants live alongside newer Hispanic and Asian arrivals. East Village residents embody a diverse spectrum of people, with punks, hippies, ravers, rastas, guppies, goths, beatniks, and virtually every other imaginable group coexisting among the variety of cafes, bars, clubs, shops, theaters, and community centers that fill this neighborhood. This multicultural coexistance has not come easily; many poorer residents of the East Village feel that wealthier newcomers have pushed them out by raising rents. These tensions, however, have forged the East Village into one of the most overtly politicized regions of New York City. Residents here need little coaxing to wax poetic about the protests of the 1960s, the evils of speculating landlords, or their hatred of (soon to be ex-) Mayor Giuliani.

Heterogeneity and rising rents are not the only hallmarks of this area. Not only is it the basis for the hit musical, *Rent,* the East Village also keeps alive a vigorous tradition of creativity in the everyday. Billie Holiday sang here, and, more recently, the East Village provided early audiences for Sonic Youth, the Talking Heads, Blondie, and Frank Zappa. The fashion world provides the East Village with its newest art of choice: here lurks style's avant-garde. For a more in-depth guide and map of both villages, pick up *The Village* guide available free at select stores.

Be sure to also head toward Alphabet City. East of First Avenue, south of 14th Street, and north of Houston St., the avenues give up on numbers and adopt letters. In its 1960s heyday, Jimi Hendrix and the Fugs would play open-air shows to bright-eyed love children. You'll still find East Village "deadbeatniks" and hard-core anarchists, as well as artists and students, hanging out in local cafes and shops. However, the area has also found itself squarely in the growing path of New York's wave of gentrification, manifest in the increasing numbers of boutiques and chic eateries. The area is generally safe during the day. Addictive nightlife on Avenues A and B ensure some protection, but use caution east of Avenue B after dark. For information on current issues and events in Alphabet City, check for free local papers at St. Mark's Bookshop and other stores in the area. Neighborhood posters can also let you in on current happenings.

TRIBECA

🚇Subway: 1, 9 to Franklin St. **Sights:** p. 74. **Food:** p. 184. **Nightlife:** p. 208.

see map
p. 321

Just twenty years ago, **Tri**angle **Be**low **Ca**nal Street, full of loading docks, warehouses, factories, and back alleys, was an industrial wastleland. By the early 80s, however, many of these manufacturing and real estate development companies had left the area, providing the perfect refuge for artists who were being slowly pushed out of Soho. The 70s and 80s saw the population of TriBeCa drastically increase as buildings were converted into gallery, performance, and living spaces. Recently, TriBeCa, like Soho years before it, was hit very hard by the indiscriminate machine of gentrification, and although many of the performance spaces and galleries have been saved, sky-rocketing rents and expensive restaurants and stores have forced most of the artists to abandon their living spaces to those who can afford it. Some of the area's wealthy residents include Robert DeNiro, Christopher Walken, and the late John F. Kennedy, Jr.

Hidden among hulking 19th-century cast-iron warehouses, you'll find pockets of restaurants, bars, specialty shops, and galleries, often maintaining SoHo's trendiness without the upscale airs. TriBeCa residents take great pride in their neighborhood, and consequently, streets and community facilities are under constant renewal and improvement. Southeast TriBeCa, along Broadway and Chambers Street, has a more commercial feel than the rest of the area. Discount stores and cheap restaurants of all types line these streets, and with City Hall and the Financial District nearby, the area tends to get pretty busy during the day. Don't leave TriBeCa without strolling along the quieter streets, like Hudson and West Broadway, where you'll find quite a few second-hand stores selling everything from furniture to vintage clothing.

SOHO

Subway: C, E to Spring St.; N, R to Prince St.; 1, 9 to Houston St. **Food:** p. 199. **Shopping:** p. 141. **Nightlife:** p. 208

see map p. 321

SoHo, the district **So**uth of **Ho**uston St. ("HOW-ston"), holds court between TriBeCa and Greenwich Village. Over the past 10 years, SoHo has solidified into a saucy dish of artsy, commercial-chic. The story of SoHo's evolution is that of an increasing number of New York neighborhoods. In the earlier part of the century, SoHo was a dark industrial zone operating factories and warehouses between its alleyways. In the mid-1940s, however, charmed by low rents and airy lofts, artists moved in; the trickle roared to a full-scale waterfall of immigration by the 1960s. Until the mid-1980s, SoHo's scene, led by Jean-Michel Basquiat, Keith Haring, and Kenny Scharf, blossomed as the hotbed of NYC artistic innovation, but as the 90s brought Victoria's Secret and J. Crew, the cutting-edge dulled. SoHo may no longer cradle the truly avant-garde, but it still boasts pockets of off-beat culture, high fashion, and meticulous design. Spurred on more now by capitalism than the muses, those who run the restaurants, bars, shops, and galleries of SoHo put great care into the appearance and ambience; come here to reap the benefits.

GREENWICH VILLAGE AND THE WEST VILLAGE

Subway: A, C, E, to W. 4th St. or 8th St. for the West Village; N, R to 8th St. for Greenwich Village. **Sights:** p. 74. **Food:** p. 181. **Accommodations:** p. 269.

see map pp. 322–323

Greenwich Village, the area between Chelsea and SoHo on the lower West Side, has emerged from a relentless process of cultural ferment that has layered grime, activism, and artistry atop a tangle of quaint, meandering streets. In this counter-cultural capital of the East Coast, transgressions are a way of life, and very little—neither dyed hair, nor pierced foreheads, nor the rantings of Washington Square Park's soapbox prophets—seems to faze weathered "Villagers." As alternative living bleeds into the mainstream, Greenwich Village has settled into the inevitable, comfortable maturity of iconoclasm. These bustling streets take the shocking and offbeat in stride.

The area, once covered in farms and hills, developed in the mid-19th century into a staid high society playground that fostered literary creativity. Herman Melville and James Fenimore Cooper wrote American masterworks here, and Mark Twain and Willa Cather regarded the U.S. heartland from their adopted homes near Washington Square. Henry James captured the debonair spirit of the Village in his novel *Washington Square*.

Real estate values plummeted at the turn of the century as German, Irish, and Italian immigrants found work in the industries along the Hudson River and in pockets of the Village. Cheaper rents prompted more marginal characters to set up shop and do their own thing: John Reed, John Dos Passos, e.e. cummings, and James Agee came here to begin their writing careers in relative obscurity. The Beat movement crystallized in the Village in the 1950s, and the 60s saw the growth of a homosexual community around Christopher St.

The Village's nonconformist ethos felt the city's intrusion in the late 60s. Violent clashes between police and homosexuals resulted in the Stonewall Riots of 1969, a powerful moment of awakening in the gay rights movement. In the 1970s the punk scene exploded and added mohawked and be-spiked rockers to the Village's diverse cast of characters. The 1980s saw the beginnings of the gentrification process that has continued through the 1990s and has made the Village a fashionable and comfortable settlement for those wealthier New Yorkers with a bit more spunk than their Uptown counterparts.

Today, with rising rents and the truly marginal heading eastward or to Brooklyn, many would argue that true "Village" life has shifted eastward. Still, in Greenwich, no matter what the hour, there's always a good time going on somewhere. If nothing else, there are few areas in the city so prime for people-watching. The Village comes out in all of its (non)traditional glory for the wild Village **Halloween Parade.** This is your chance to see people dressed as toilets or condoms. Slap on your own wig, strap on your appendage of choice, and join the crowd—no one will blink a rhinestoned eyelash.

Grand Central Terminal

LOWER MIDTOWN

GRAMERCY PARK, UNION SQUARE, AND MURRAY HILL

see map
pp. 326–327

⑦Subway: N, R, or 6 to 23rd St. **Sights:** p. 79. **Food:** p. 199. **Accommodations:** p. 269.

An area of historic interest, past financial district glory, and current residential chic-ness, lower Midtown is a hidden gem, an area yet to be trampled by most tourists. A burgeoning population of young professionals calls this end of Midtown home, as do hip cafes and restaurants that have sprung up in the past 10 years; a variety of ethnic cuisines reflect the recent expansion of this neighborhood.

Gramercy Park includes Madison Square, Union Square, and Stuyvesant Square, and fills the area bounded by Sixth Avenue and FDR Drive, and East 14th and 28th Streets. This neighborhood is organized around cultivated green plots, resembling residential areas of London, and offers picturesque walks unlike other parts of Manhattan.

Between this and the ruckus of East Midtown lies the sedate residential area of **Murray Hill.** Lined with streets of warm brownstones and condominiums—such as East 35th Street between Madison Avenue and Park Avenue South—this area is a reminder of a more genteel era when it was home to the 19th-century "robber barons."

I Love NY

CHELSEA

⑦Subway: C, E, 1, 9 to 23rd st. **Sights:** p. 82. **Food:** p. 179. **Accommodations:** p. 271. **Bars:** p. 212.

Extending west from Sixth Avenue to the Hudson River, and between 14th and 28th Streets, Chelsea is probably best known today for its very visible and vocal gay community. While the gay community of New York might shop for leather and lace on Christopher Street, this is where it does its living. Chelsea, especially around **Eighth Avenue** between 20th and 23rd Streets, is home to a large number of cafes and restaurants where the clientele is mostly fashionable men dining in couples. Boutiques interspersed throughout Eighth Avenue and **Seventh Avenue** between 18th and 23rd Streets offer unique objects for the home and outrageously fabulous clubwear. It's

View from Empire State Building

not only the cafes and boutiques, however, that sport the rainbow flag. Chelsea has achieved the enormous feat of normalizing the gay community while at the same time unifying it; the rainbow coalition flag can be seen fluttering over street lamps, laundromats, taxi cab dispatch companies, and travel agencies. Many of these local businesses are gay-owned and help to foster the feeling that Chelsea is a community like any other, just a bit more colorful. Unity is perhaps most visibly flaunted during **Pride Weekend** (usually the last weekend in June), a series of fesitivities culminating in the Gay Pride Parade up Fifth Ave. and ending in various tea dances throughout the neighborhood. During this weekend, the collective (very well-toned) chest of this area swells with a radiant pride.

Chelsea has more than just a large gay community, however. The neighborhood is an enclave for all sorts of lifestyles and backgrounds. The area is home to a large South and Latin American population; you'll hear Spanish as often as English here. The restaurants serve up a plethora of ethnic foods, from Chinese, Tex-Mex, and Spanish, to other cultural combinations emblematic of the melting-pot of Manhattan.

This welcoming area, with its old factories and warehouses by the water from a bygone industrial era is the chosen locale for SoHo artists fleeing uptown for cheaper rents. The area by the water (west of Ninth Avenue) retains a gritty, somewhat deserted feel that has seen growing numbers of artistic spaces and underground hangouts. Street level garages, entire buildings, and old warehouses have subsequently been transformed into **galleries** that exist beside still-functioning commercial firms. The superb galleries around **Tenth** and **Eleventh Avenues** and **22nd Street** house some of the most cutting-edge art in the city. These wide streets eventually reach the water and **Chelsea Piers** (☎ 336-6666), a tremendous sports and entertainment complex that offers everything from spectator sports and mini-golf to ice-skating and rock climbing.

EAST MIDTOWN

see map
pp. 332–333

🚇Subway: 6 to 59th St., 51st St., or 42ndSt./Grand Central Terminal; 4, 5 to 59th St. or 42nd St./Grand Central Terminal; E,F to Fifth Ave.; N,R to 50th St. **Sights:** p. 24. **Food:** p. 191. **Bars:** p. 212.

East of Sixth Avenue, from about 34th Street to 59th Street, lies the bulk of East Midtown. To many, this part of Manhattan represents New York at its New Yorkiest, with impossibly rich and beautiful business types and ingenues battling for sidewalk space with camera-toting, fanny-packed tourists. Mammoth office buildings and posh hotels dominate the skies of this particular landscape, while the streets are lined with fancy stores whose names most normal Americans have difficulty pronouncing. Of particular note is the section of Fifth Avenue between 42nd and 59th Streets—once the most desirable residential area among New York's social elite—which has been slowly transformed into a Socialist's worst nightmare, with high-end boutiques lining both sides of the street. Nevertheless, this stretch seems to be the choice for most of New York's larger protests and parades. From Gay Pride to Puerto Rican Day, New Yorkers and tourists alike seem to flock to this area to observe the eccentricities of New York at its finest. Here, *Let's Go* hopes to demystify the area immortalized in *Breakfast at Tiffany's*, so that you may explore the streets with all the nonchalance of a young Truman Capote.

WEST MIDTOWN

see map
pp. 332–333

🚇Subway: 1, 2, 3, 9 to Penn Station; A, C, E to 34th/Eighth Ave.; N, R to 34th St.; or B, D, F, Q to 33rd St. for Herald Sq. and Garment DIstrict. 1, 2, 3, 9, A, C, E, 7, S to Times Sq. for Times Sq. and Theater District. **Sights:** p. 82. **Food:** p. 194.

West Midtown has undergone a bit of a revival. Neon signs and gilt window frames formerly covered with grime have renewed luster. Big companies have snatched up and renovated the old Broadway theaters, now showcasing their shiny marble stairways between 31st and 59th St. on the West Side. Although some sections of West Midtown have become one large tourist attraction, some parts of the neighborhood retain its gritty character. The remnants of the **Garment District** can be found in the myriad of wholesale/retail stores along Broadway (upper 20s/lower 30s). **Herald Square,** at the convergence of Broadway and Sixth Ave. on 34th St., offers mainstream shopping in one busily trafficked area; it is named after the newspaper "Herald" that used to be located here.

Between Herald Square and the Hudson River is **Hell's Kitchen,** until very recently a violent area inhabited by immigrant gangs with misleading names such as "Battle Row Annie's Ladies' Social and Athletic Club." Indeed, the area once ranked among the most dangerous areas in North America; policemen would only patrol it in groups of four or more. As the story goes, the area was named during a conversation among a group of these policemen. After a particularly brutal night, one officer told the others, "We truly are in hell's kitchen." After two children were killed by crossfire in 1959, fed-up locals tried to improve the area's reputation by renaming it **Clinton,** which, as historical irony would have it, is now an equally loaded term. Then much of the housing in Hell's Kitchen was razed to build Lincoln Center and related projects. In recent years, a heterogeneous population has soaked Ninth and Tenth Avenue with restaurants, delis, and pubs; because of a recent economic upswing, the neighborhood has become one of New York's best areas for inexpensive ethnic food.

But it's at **Times Square** that you find the Big Apple's, er, core. At 42nd St., Seventh Ave., and Broadway, the city offers up one of the largest electronic extravaganzas in the world. In the past, admiring visitors remained completely oblivious as petty thieves stole their wallets. Indeed, Times Square may have given New York its reputation as a dark metropolis covered with strip clubs, neon, and filth, which have frightened away so many would-be tourists and residents. Perhaps after a few too many people saw *Blade Runner*, the Square's laces straightened. 50 cherry-red-jumpsuited sanitation workers have been put on the streets daily, with 40 public safety officers. Robberies, purse snatchings, and the number of porn shops in the area have plummetted. Large companies helped the campaign by inventing a brilliant yet succinct slogan, "New 42." The completion of Disney's entertainment complex in and around the New Amsterdam Theater, once home to the Ziegfield Follies, has brought us a pink-and-gold wonderland in which you may see the Tony Award-winning musical, the *Lion King*. Across the street, Madame Tussaud's and AMC united to rebuild the Liberty, Empire, and Harris theaters into a wax museum and 29-screen movie megaplex. The historic Victory Theater, where Abbot met Costello and Houdini made an elephant disappear, is now the eerily Orwellian "New Victory" Theater.

Still, Times Square has not strayed *too* far from its decadent past. A recent city ordinance required new offices to cover their facades with electronic and neon glitz, which would explain the enormous stock ticker atop the Morgan Stanley building. Teens continue to roam about in search of fake IDs and, as ever, hustlers cheat suckers. One-and-a-half million people pass through Times Square every day. Theater-goers, tourists, and wanderers crowd the streets well into the night. This neighborhood's theatricality extends beyond the walls of its venues, however, with world-renowned ads plastering skyscrapers. Marky Mark dropped his drawers before millions for Calvin Klein, Dave Letterman broadcast segments of his show on the Sony Jumbotron, and several superheroes have hurtled into the spiraling neon Coca Cola advertisement. You'll feel a part of something extraordinary just walking the streets of the Great White Way.

see map
pp. 334–335

UPPER EAST SIDE

Subway: *4, 5, 6 to 86th St. or 5, 6 to 77th or 96th St.* **Sights:** *p. 90.* **Food:** *p. 199.* **Accommodations:** *p. 274.* **Bars:** *p. 214.*

When walking through the Upper East Side, it is impossible not to notice its particular scent. It's in the clothing of the ladies, in the walk of the men; as a matter of fact, it's in the very air itself. And no, it's not the scent of Chanel No. 5 or any other ridiculously expensive perfume, although those also permeate the air. It's the smell of money. From the ostentatiously dressed, gloved doormen who still hail cabs on Park Avenue to the service entrances and nannies out walking the kids, the Upper East Side can be summed up in two words: privilege and wealth. Consisting of immaculately clean streets, a plethora of private schools that groom the country's elite for their inheritance, celebrity spottings, and opulent stores where the number of nose jobs are as ridiculous as the price tags, this fantasy land (from 59th Street to 110th Street and East End Avenue to Fifth Avenue) is definitely the Horn of Plenty.

The Upper East Side has held this reputation ever since the days of the late 19th and early 20th centuries, when some of New York's wealthiest citizens, such as the Fricks, the Vanderbilts, the Carnegies, the Tiffanies, and the Astors, decided to put the "upper" in

ON THE KITSCH

Part of South Brooklyn, **Coney Island** still retains the nostalgic feel of summer captured in the watercolors of painter and *New York Times Books Review* cartoonist David Levine. In the early 20th century, only the rich could afford to journey here. The introduction of nickel-fare subway rides made Coney Island accessible to all, and by the late 1940s the area became run down, clearing the way for housing projects.

A neighborhood of legend and olden-days cheesy charm, Coney Island is at its best on the last Saturday in June, during the traditional **Coney Island Mermaid Parade.** Wacky floats, costumes, and music go from Surf Ave. and W. 10th St. to Steeplechase Park. Queen Latifah was the Mermaid Queen in 1999—you too can register from 10am-noon on the day of the parade. For info, call ☎718-372-5159.

Upper East Side, by building elaborate mansions along Fifth Avenue. Today, of these parkside luxuries, the Frick and Carnegie mansions survive as the Frick Collection and the Cooper-Hewitt Museum, respectively. They are just two of the world-famous, fascinating nine museums—including the Metropolitan, the Guggenheim, the Museum of the City of New York, and (until this year) the International Center of Photography—that line **Museum Mile.** By the 1920s, with the demolition of the above-ground tracks of the New York Central Railway and as private homes became increasingly high maintenance, luxurious and elegant apartment houses, many of which still stand, were erected along both Fifth and Park Avenues. At the same time that the apartment houses were being constructed, **Madison Avenue,** previously a residential district, was being transformed into a fashion mecca. The wealthy inhabitants attracted high-end, elegant boutiques to the ground floors of the old row houses. Today some of the top designers, including Ralph Lauren, Vera Wang, Gucci, Dolce and Gabbana, Max Azaria, and Versace, line this expensive walkway (see **Shopping,** p. 149). Madison Avenue, where you might not even be able to afford to window shop, is also home to some of the most exclusive social clubs and expensive restaurants New York has to offer.

But there is also a more ethnically diverse (and cheap) face to the Upper East Side. In 1878, the opening of the Third Avenue elevated Railway attracted a great number of Eastern European, German, and Irish immigrants to an area that would later become known as Yorkville. **Yorkville** (beyond Third Avenue between 75th and 96th Streets), although it has been somewhat diluted in the wake of newer chain stores and pizza parlors, still retains a strong Hungarian and German flavor through its residents, old-style delis, and ethnic restaurants. In general, as you move east across Lexington Avenue, everything—including food—becomes more affordable.

Unfazed by the conspicuous extravagance, people fill the Upper East Side with activity. Hordes of tourists line the 50s (from Lexington to Sixth Avenues), and the urban young heat up the bars on **First and Second Avenues** (especially in the mid-80s and mid-70s) by night and the commercial **86th Street** (especially between Lexington and Third Avenues) by day.

see map pp. 338–339

UPPER WEST SIDE

Subway: *1, 9, 2, 3 to 96th or 66th Sts.; B, C to 81st St.* ***Sights:*** *p. 95.* ***Food:*** *p. 195.* ***Accommodations:*** *p. 275.* ***Bars:*** *p. 213.*

New York's frontier land of wealthy-yet-earnest types, the Upper West Side is perhaps one of the friendliest areas of Manhattan. Upper West Siders value a prep school education, but of a more liberal bent than that of their neighbors across Central Park. Two representative institutions delineate its borders—**Lincoln Center** and **Columbia University.** A recent surge of West Indian immigrants has revitalized the Upper West Side's intelligentsia. West Siders believe in midwifery and public television, freshly cut lilies, and comfortable shoes. Many a West Sider's ardent leftist past has given way to the more tempered passion of shopping for spinach ravioli at Zabar's. Women let their hair go gray while their partners just *love* them for it, and many treat their writer's block in a "safe-zone workshop." From posh Central Park West to the Hudson views of Riverside Drive, a non-stop sidewalk scene thrives, while nightlife and cultural options abound. The gods of organic fruit and progressive politics will reward you for wandering their domain. The large Jewish community of the Upper West Side fans out from 72nd Street between Broadway and West End Avenue; this area seems to be the residential spot of choice for the younger generation, whose ancestors began as immigrants in the Lower East Side.

While Central Park West and Riverside Drive flank the Upper West with residential quietude, **Columbus Avenue, Amsterdam Avenue,** and **Broadway** offer exciting dining, shopping, sites of artistic and cultural activity, and people-watching at all hours. Although originally conceived as residential thoroughfares, these three colorful and energetic avenues are crammed with eateries serving foods of various cultures, theaters of all kinds, and shops peddling everything from music scores to mobile phones. Because of the continuous bustle, Broadway feels safe even late at night, although *Let's Go* can't say the same of the side streets that intersect it or Amsterdam and Columbus Avenues above 98th Street. To learn more about the long history of this former enclave of the "red diaper baby," read *Upper West Side Story: A History and Guide* (Abbeville Press, 1989).

HARLEM

Harlem is a place where I like to eat, sleep, drink, and be in love.
-Langston Hughes

🚇*Morningside Heights subway:* 1, 9 to 110th or 116th St. **Central Harlem subway:** 2, 3, A, B, C, D to 125th St. **Spanish Harlem subway:** 6 to 116th or 125th St.

see map pp. 340–341 **Sights:** p. 98. Morningside Heights **food:** p. 194. Harlem **food:** p. 198. **Shopping:** p. 148.

Harlem, the largest neighborhood in all of Manhattan, extends from 110th Street to the 150s, between the Hudson and East Rivers, was founded by Dutch settlers in 1658. With the spreading of elevated railroads came a change in the area's population—wealthy country estates were replaced by downtown residents. A real estate collapse at the beginning of the 20th century induced the abandonment of many buildings and landlords, eager to find tenants, allowed blacks leaving the hostile South to move in. Between 1910 and 1920, Harlem began its transformation into a black neighborhood; as the number of blacks rapidly increased, the number of whites steadily declined.

The 1920s brought prosperity to Harlem and an artistic and literary movement known as the Harlem Renaissance was launched (see **Life & Times,** p. 56). The area was a mecca for Black artists and intellectuals such as Langston Hughes, Countee Cullen, and Zora Neale Hurston. The atmosphere was also ripe for rising jazz legends Louis Armstrong, Duke Ellington, Bessie Smith, Charles Mingus, and Billie Holliday. The clubs they played at still stand as monuments to their talent—the Lenox Lounge, Apollo Theater, and Cotton Club.

The Great Depression hit Harlem severely, but after World War II the area flourished culturally again. In the 1960s, riding the tidal wave of the Civil Rights movement, the radical Black Power movement thrived here. LeRoi Jones's The Revolutionary Theater performed consciousness-raising one-act plays in the streets, and Malcolm X, Stokely Carmichael, and H. Rap Brown spoke eloquently against racism and injustice. But Harlem's population was declining rapidly due to social and economic problems. In the 1970s and 80s, members of the community, recognizing the need for economic revitalization as a route to empowerment, began the attempt at redevelopment that continues today as the city pumps money into the area. Successful blacks are returning to their Harlem homes, trying to reinvest in the community. This urban renewal is evident in the restoration of many of the neighborhood's beautiful brownstones.

The dangerous and poor Harlem of urban legend exists largely in the area south of 125th Street in the Manhattan Valley, particularly along Frederick Douglass Avenue and Adam Clayton Powell Boulevard; avoid this area after dark. Over the years Harlem has entered the popular psyche as the archetype of America's frayed edges, but you won't believe the hype once you've actually visited the place. Although poorer than many areas, Harlem possesses great cultural and historical wealth. In recent years Harlem has also become a major tourist attraction, with a resurgence in popularity of its nightclubs, churches, and restaurants.

MORNINGSIDE HEIGHTS. Above 110th Street and below 125th, this area, caught between the chaos of Harlem and the color of the Upper West Side, is often overlooked. Cheap, unassuming restaurants dot this active collegiate neighborhood dominated by students from Barnard and Columbia University.

CENTRAL HARLEM. Although this area should be explored with caution, it also features some of the most affordable shopping the city has to offer, concentrated on Central Harlem's main thoroughfare, 125th Street. Honoring Harlem's great history, many of this neighborhood's streets have been renamed for past black leaders: Sixth/Lenox Avenue is also referred to as Malcolm X. Boulevard; 125th Street is also Martin Luther King Boulevard; and Eighth Avenue is Frederick Douglass Boulevard.

EAST HARLEM. Better known as Spanish Harlem, or El Barrio, its main artery, East 116th Street, rocks to a salsa beat and overflows with fruit stands, Puerto Rican eateries, and men vending flavored crushed ice on scorching summer days. Anti-crack murals and memorials to the drug's victims adorn the walls of projects and abandoned buildings as testimony to the neighborhood's chronic plight of poverty and crime. On your way up the East Side, you will notice Fifth and Park Avenues displaying up-close-and-personal social and cultural stratification: at East 96th Street a world of uniformed doormen suddenly becomes a world of bedraggled men sleeping in doorways. There is still beauty within this poverty, however, as displayed by the constantly changing Graffitti Wall of Fame at 106th Street and Park Avenue. El Barrio is at its best on Puerto Rican Independence Day, June 20, when streets close off for some serious festivity.

WASHINGTON HEIGHTS

🚇Subway: A, 1, 9 to 168th St.-Washington Heights. **Sights:** p. 101.

North of 155th St., Manhattan Island's curves eluded the leveling eye of the postmodern architect and the demolishing hand of the corporate contractor that rendered downtown neighborhoods so many clusters of flattened blocks. Washington Heights out-slopes Park Slope, and its several parks make it one of the greenest neighborhoods in the five

see map pp. 340–341

boroughs. Buildings perched atop high ridges peer down hundreds of feet onto their next-door neighbors. The demarcation of ethnic enclaves can appear just as suddenly as these cliffs. Once predominantly Irish, Washington Heights now joins large Latino, black, Greek, Armenian, and Jewish communities, and has had to deal with its share of cultural clashes. Recently, however, with crime decreasing and fewer crack dealers on the streets, the residents of Washington Heights take more pride in their neighborhood. You may want to bargain-shop along trinket-filled St. Nicholas Avenue or Broadway, where vendors sell swimwear, household items, and electronics for half the original price.

BROOKLYN

Our story begins, as all great stories do, in Brooklyn.
-Jon Kalish

When the Dutch settled this area in the 17th century, they called it Brooklyn, or "Broken Land." When asked to join New York in 1833, the City of Brooklyn refused, in its typical fashion, saying that the two cities shared no interests except common waterways. Not until 1898 did the citizenry decide, in a close vote, to join New York City's boroughs.

see map pp. 342–343

In the early 20th century, European immigrants flowed into the borough in great numbers, and after the Great Depression black Southerners also sought haven in Brooklyn. Many visitors experience Manhattan via shopping and consuming, but folks *live* in Brooklyn.

Each of Brooklyn's neighborhoods boasts a unique flavor, but despite their seemingly endless ethnic and religious differences, Brooklynites all share an indomitable pride in their home. Aged natives, even long after they've moved, still wail the Dodgers' defection to L.A. Old-timers remember Brooklyn as Woody Allen depicted it in Annie Hall, full of romantic images like that of protagonist Alvy Singer in his rickety home underneath a Coney Island roller coaster. Although such nostalgia is based in truth (someone still lives in the house under Coney Island's now-defunct Thunderbolt Rollercoaster), Brooklyn has many diverse faces, including some of the city's most artistically and culturally forward-looking. As New York's most populous borough, Brooklyn holds its own against Manhattan. It's a place to explore at a leisurely pace, getting a feel for the tempo and pulse of each neighborhood.

NORTH BROOKLYN. Brooklyn Heights, a uniformly preserved 19th-century residential area, sprang up with the development of steamboat transportation between Brooklyn and Manhattan in 1814. Rows of posh Greek Revival and Italianate houses in this area essentially created New York's first suburb. Montague Street, the neighborhood's main drag, has the stores, cafes, and mid-priced restaurants of a cute college town. Arthur Miller and W.H. Auden called this area home in the 1940s and 50s. Young, upwardly mobile types make this area home, while Atlantic Ave. has a thriving Middle Eastern community. **DUMBO** (Down Under the Manhattan Bridge Overpass), at Old Fulton Street, is its up-and-coming artistic underground community. To the east, vibrant **Fort Greene,** along DeKalb Avenue, is the hub of black artistic and cultural activity. Trees, hip hangouts, and elegant brownstones line the streets of "Black SoHo," as does filmmaker Spike Lee's production company, 40 Acres and a Mule (124 DeKalb Avenue). A number of other powerful art and entertainment residents fuel Fort Greene's pan-ethnic renaissance. Home to a growing number of artists since the last decade, **Williamsburg** has a wonderfully funky feel to it that centers around Bedford Avenue and Berry Street's cafes and shopping. In the south side of town, along Broadway, Heyward Wythe Street, and Bedford Avenue, thrives a Hassidic Jewish community, where men wear long black coats and hats that recall the garb of the Polish nobility of Eastern Europe. North of Broadway is predominatly Latino. **Greenpoint** is Brooklyn's northernmost border with Queens and home to a large Polish population. Manhattan Avenue is the heart of the neighborhood's business district. Just south of Atlantic Avenue lies the quiet Italian neighborhood of **Cobble Hill,** whose gorgeous brownstone-lined sidestreets segue into **Carroll Gardens.** The large Italian population is evidenced by the many pasta and pastry shops and the old *padrones* sitting in lawn chairs talking with their hands. The ground floors of Smith and Court Streets' buildings are crowded with thrift stores, antique vendors, artist cooperatives, and craft shops where restaurants leave space. On the other side of the Brooklyn-Queens Expressway (BQE) is the industrial waterfront area of **Red Hook.** Cobblestone streets and Atlantic Avenue lead to warehouses and docks, where there are wonderful views of the Statue of Liberty. Following Bay Street north brings you to the enormous Red Hook housing projects.

CENTRAL BROOKLYN. Sunset Park was named for this little stretch of green; here you'll find a sloping lawn criss-crossed by paths and an extraordinary view of Upper New York Bay, the Statue of Liberty, and Lower Manhattan. Avid consumers flock to the area's Fifth Avenue, which is lined with discount stores and hybrid restaurants. If you're traveling by car, you can head down to First Avenue and explore the trolley-scarred streets that were the setting for Uli Wedel's *Last Exit to Brooklyn.* This district has recently begun reflecting other ethnic influences with its growing Chinese and Middle Eastern populations. The nearby Shore Road of **Bay Ridge** is lined with mansions overlooking the Verrazano-Narrows Bridge and New York Harbor. Bay Ridge was the scene of John Travolta's strutting in the classic *Saturday Night Fever.* **Bensonhurst,** centered around Stillwell and Park Avenues, became a household word and rallying cry in the fight against racism following the brutal murder of Yusef Hawkins in 1989. Although the 2001 Odyssey disco is no longer operational, the predominantly Italian neighborhood centers around 86th Street, and is chock full of Italian bakeries, pizza joints, rowdy youths, and discount stores, especially around 17th Avenue. **Borough Park** is the largest Hassidic Jewish neighborhood in Brooklyn. In contrast to the more visible Crown Heights Lubavitchers, the Bobovers of Borough Park prefer to maintain an insular community. As in the other Hassidic neighborhoods of Brooklyn, visitors will feel more welcome if they are dressed conservatively. **Park Slope's** attitude, more than its sights and architecture, sets it apart from other areas. The neighborhood's extraordinary level of ethnic diversity seems exempt from the tensions of other

Brooklyn neighborhoods. Doctors, academics, opera singers, and writers—living with their new families on 7th Avenue or their twentysomething roommates on 5th Avenue—inhabit its charming brownstones. Restaurants and stores line the north-south avenues; Seventh Avenue has long been the neighborhood's main drag, but Fifth Avenue's budding thrift stores, gay bars, and even an art gallery or two, give it a hipper edge. Just southeast of Prospect Park is the neighborhood of **Flatbush,** where Manhattan's turn-of-the-century aristocracy maintained summer homes; you can wander around Argyle Street and Ditmas Avenue to see some of their old mansions. The area's socio-economic well-being, however, has long since deteriorated. Once a predominantly Jewish immigrant neighborhood, Flatbush is now home to significant Jamaican and other West Indian populations. Reggae music and exotic fruit stands fill major thoroughfares like Nostrand Avenue on summer days. Those venturing southeast into the neighborhoods of **Bushwick, Bedford-Stuyvesant (Bed-Stuy),** and **Brownsville** should be cautious. Low public funding, high unemployment, and inadequate public works have created burnt-out buildings, patches of undeveloped land, and stagnant commercial zones. Still, social consciousness and political activism emerge from every pothole in these neglected streets. Wall murals portraying Malcolm X, slogans urging patronage of black businesses, and Puerto Rican flags all testify to a growing sense of racial and cultural empowerment. Bed-Stuy also boasts an historic district called **Stuyvesant Heights,** containing, you guessed it, beautiful brownstones.

SOUTH BROOKLYN. Once the home of the largest Sephardic Jewish community outside of Israel, **Midwood** has lately seen increasing numbers of Arabs, Italians, and non-Sephardic Jews. Nonetheless, kosher eateries still dot major arteries like Kings Highway and Ocean Avenue, along with halal markets and pizza joints. In nearby **Sheepshead Bay** you can go after some blues (the fish, not the music) on any of the boats docked along Emmons Avenue. Traditionally, the passengers pool their bucks as a prize for the person who lands the biggest fish. Emmons Avenue runs along the bay and faces **Manhattan Beach,** a wealthy residential area of doctors and mafiosi (shh!). Beyond Ocean Parkway lies **Brighton Beach,** or "Little Odessa by the Sea," an area populated heavily by Eastern European immigrants and written about in Neil Simon's *Brighton Beach Memoirs*. By day it is home to Eastern-European delis, grocery stores, and shops; at night, Russian music, from disco to folk, livens up the neighborhood.

ORIENTATION

Brooklyn's main avenues dissect the borough. The **Brooklyn-Queens Expressway (BQE)** pours into the **Belt Parkway** and circumscribes Brooklyn. Ocean Parkway, Ocean Avenue, Coney Island Avenue, and diagonal Flatbush Avenue run from the beaches of southern Brooklyn to Prospect Park in the heart of the borough. The streets of western Brooklyn (including those in Sunset Park, Bensonhurst, Borough Park, and Park Slope) are aligned with the western shore and thus collide at a 45-degree angle with central Brooklyn's main arteries. In northern Brooklyn, several avenues—Atlantic Avenue, Eastern Parkway, and Flushing Avenue—travel from downtown east into Queens.

Brooklyn is also spliced by **subway lines.** Most lines serving the borough pass through the Atlantic Avenue Station downtown. The D and Q lines continue southeast through Prospect Park and Flatbush to Brighton Beach. The #2 and 5 trains head east to Brooklyn College in Flatbush. The B and N trains travel south through Bensonhurst, terminating at Coney Island. The J, M, and Z trains serve Williamsburg and Bushwick and continue east and north into Queens. The Brooklyn-Queens crosstown G train shuttles from southern Brooklyn through Greenpoint into Queens.

QUEENS

see map pp. 346–347

The borough of Queens, a true melting pot (and a big one—it comprises one-third of the city), affords the opportunity for around-the-world travel with only the help of a Metrocard and a pair of walking shoes. With an over 50% foreign-born population, Queens is the most ethnically diverse of the five boroughs. Its immigrant population overlaps in space: Elmhurst apartment buildings where Pakistani, Portuguese, and Ecuadorian families share the hall; generations: the children, grand-children, and great-grandchildren—spreading outward to residential neighborhoods and eventually to Long Island's suburbia; and culture: visit a Chinese Taco restaurant in Middle Village. While exploring Queens' interesting quilt of customs, a traveler could go the whole day without hearing a word of English spoken.

Queens has always warmly welcomed a wide spectrum of peoples—from 17th-century Dutch and English farmers to recent Greek immigrant families—all in search of a secure place in the New World. This rural colony, named in honor of Queen Catherine of Braganza, wife of England's Charles II, was seized from the Algonquin Indians in 1683. At the beginning of the 19th century, small farms began to give way to industry, making western Queens the busy production center it is now. Queens officially became a part of the City of New York in 1898, and the construction of the Long Island Railroad under the East River in 1910 fostered urban growth. Between 1910 and 1930, the borough's population quadrupled to one million, as immigrants poured in via Ellis Island. A 1950s building boom effectively completed the urbanization of Queens.

HUNTER'S POINT AND LONG ISLAND CITY. Home to Queens's industrial powerhouses for many years; in the 1930s, 80% of all industry in the borough was based here—Newtown Creek saw as much freight traffic as the Mississippi River.

ASTORIA AND STEINWAY. Astoria, known as "Little Athens," has by some estimates the largest Greek community in the world after Greece. Italian, Spanish, and Hindi are also spoken in the active markets, cafes, and bakeries of these middle-class neighborhoods. With low rent and easy access to Manhattan, Astoria and Steinway have lately become a center for artists, although the more elite avant-garde seems reluctant to cross the river.

WOODSIDE AND SUNNYSIDE. Here, new Irish immigrants join their established countrymen. Sunnyside, a remarkable "garden community" built in the 1920s, commands international recognition as a model of middle-income housing.

RIDGEWOOD. Founded by Eastern European and German immigrants a century ago, more than 2000 of its distinctively European brownstones are landmarks.

MIDDLE VILLAGE AND GLENDALE. Known for their old Italian and Greek families, a stroll around these communities offers visitors a time-warp to the old Mediterranean.

FOREST HILLS, KEW GARDENS, AND REGO PARK. These tudor houses are some of the most expensive real estate in NYC; they even have their own gardens and garages. The Real Good Construction Co. developed "Rego" Park—hence the name. Kew Gardens, the administrative center of Queens, has brought in big-city political bureaucracy.

JACKSON HEIGHTS, CORONA, ELMHURST. These neighborhoods congregate around the #7 subway line, which some have dubbed the "International Express." Elmhurst is said to have the most diverse concentration of nationalities in the world, with over 120 different ethnic groups in a few square miles. Jackson Heights has a significant, traditional Indian population: grandparents often never learn English and arranged marriages still permeate the dating scene. Corona, formerly West Flushing, has become home to a variety of Spanish-speaking communities.

FLUSHING. Continuing east on the "International Express," Flushing is "Little Asia," with large Korean and Chinese populations. Flushing, which begun as the Dutch settlement Vlissingen, is known as the supposed birthplace of religious freedom in the US. It was here that the Quakers successfully fought Governor Peter Stuyvesant's 1657 ban on their religion. Pre-American Revolution landmarks mingle with storefronts and outdoor food vendors.

COLLEGE POINT, WHITESTONE, BAYSIDE, AND BAY TERRACE. Second- and third-generation immigrants have settled into these neighborhoods, developing them into strong middle-class enclaves. Bay Terrace boasts real American shopping malls and ten-screen movie theaters. Bayside is a popular spot for dining and bar-hopping.

JAMAICA AND HOLLIS. Jamaica, named for the Jameco Indians, is the heart of the borough's African-American and West Indian communities. After WWII, St. Albans, centered on Linden Blvd., became home to newly well-off African-Americans. In the 1950s, this area recalled 1920s Harlem; jazz greats Count Basie, Fats Waller, and James P. Johnson, as well as baseball stars like Jackie Robinson and Roy Campanella, all lived in the Addisleigh Park area of St. Albans. Today, wealthier blacks have moved to communities like Laurelton while West Indian bakeries and restaurants flourish in the lively shopping district along Linden Blvd.

THE ROCKAWAYS. The southernmost part of Queens, their main draw is beaches.

ROOSEVELT ISLAND. Bought from the Dutch in 1828, this island was used as a dumping ground for unwanted people—jails, hospitals, quarantines, and a lunatic asylum were established on it. Boss Tweed of the politically murky Tammany Hall (see **Life and Times,** p. 48) was jailed here, as was Mae West (for her role, prefiguring Madonna, in a play called *Sex*). In 1969, architects Phillip Johnson and John Burgee redesigned the island as a state-sponsored utopia of mixed-income housing, security watch, and handicap-accessibility. In 1973, the island's name was changed from Welfare Island to Roosevelt Island in an attempt to clean up its image.

Since that time, the island has been run by a socialist-oriented local government that oversees activities and processes the list of applicants, over 10,000 long, who wish to move onto the island. The committees choose based on how the individual will contribute to the overall community; they have an intensely diverse set of individuals—ethnically, racially, physically, and economically. Many people, UN-affiliated, live not even 300 yards away from the hustle and bustle of East Midtown and the United Nations.

ORIENTATION

The streets of Queens are neither like the orderly grid of Upper Manhattan nor the haphazard angles of the Village; instead, a mixed bag of urban planning techniques has resulted in a logical—but extremely complicated—system. Streets generally run north-south and are numbered from east to west, from 1st St. in Astoria to 271st St. in Glen Oaks. Avenues run perpendicular to streets and are numbered from north to south, from Second Ave. to 165th Ave. The address of an establishment or residence often tells you the closest cross-street (for example, 45-07 32nd Ave. is cleverly near the intersection with 45th St.). The challenging parts of Queens's geography are its numbered drives, roads, and places set randomly amid the streets and avenues. Use a map; pick up the very useful Queens Bus Map (free) available on most Queens buses. The borough has a **tourism council** (☎718-647-3387), but lacks a central office .

THE BRONX

see map pp. 348–349

Thirty fires a night raged unchecked in the South Bronx during the 1970s (addicts torched buildings so they could collect and sell the plumbing fixtures; landlords torched buildings so they could collect insurance), and the borough seemed as far away as possible from its past of broad shopping promenades and vibrant, close-knit communities. Yet some sought creativity from within this world of negligence and decay. They reappropriated scratched-up, abandoned records, beginning the new way of life called hip-hop, made up of five elements: the musical genres of rapping (emceeing) and DJing (turntabling), breakdancing (b-boying and b-girling), and graffiti art (bombing). This indomitable spirit drives the Bronx's ongoing resurgence from the neglect of decades past. Educational outreach programs, clean-up patrols, and citizens' advocacy groups continually spring up, as Bronx residents take charge of their condition. Furthermore, influential natives, such as Jennifer Lopez and Rosie Perez, give back to the community with a message of empowerment.

While community art galleries around the borough attest to the continuation of a tradition of renewal, they also represent the Bronx's propensity to preserve everything from Revolutionary War-era homes to New York City's only virgin forest. Many only pass over the Bronx, viewing the borough's barbed buildings through the windows of elevated subways. Descending to street level, however, reveals a much less intimidating land that has persevered for generations. Until the turn of the 19th century, the area consisted largely of cottages, farmlands, and wild marshes. Then, in the 1840s, the tide of immigration swelled, bringing scores of Italian and Irish settlers. Since then, the flow of immigrants (now mostly Hispanic and Russian) has never stopped. This relentless stream has created vibrant ethnic neighborhoods (including a Little Italy to shame its Manhattan counterpart), quirky museums, a great zoo, a classic baseball stadium, lively shopping strips, and salsa/mambo dance clubs. The Bronx will give any visitor insight into the dynamics of burgeoning urban life, not to mention a peak at numerous attractions.

STATEN ISLAND

see map p. 350

*️⃣*Transportation:* The **Staten Island Ferry** (☎ 718-390-5253 or 718-815-BOAT) from the Manhattan Whitehall terminal to the Island. In Manhattan: 1, 9 train to South Ferry; N, R to Whitehall. In Staten Island: all buses and the SI railway. (Ferry: 30min.; from 6am-midnight, every hour on the hour from SI, on the ½-hr. from Manhattan; from 6am-12:30am runs at least every 30min. Free; cars $3.) **Sights:** p. 116. **Food:** p. 184.

In 1524, 32 years after Columbus "patented" the New World, a Florentine named Giovanni da Verrazano sailed into New York Harbor to get some fresh water. He refilled his casks off a chunk of land, unwittingly stepping into history as the godfather of Staten Island. The name (originally Staaten Eylandt) comes courtesy of Henry Hudson, who sailed through nearby waters on a 1609 voyage with the Dutch East India Company.

In 1964, builder Othmar "George Washington Bridge" Ammann spanned the gap between Staten Island and Brooklyn with a 4260-foot-long suspension number, the Verrazano-Narrows Bridge. (Until then it had only been traversable by private boat or the SI Ferry; see **Sail-by Shooting,** p. 64) Visible from virtually everywhere on the island, the bridge is the world's second-longest suspension bridge, outspanned only by the Humber Bridge in England.

Although traffic now flows more easily between Manhattan and Staten Island (via Brooklyn) these days, Staten Islanders continue to stubbornly resist the civilizing influence of the City. When visiting, expect grating accents reminiscent of 80s valley girls and a style taken mostly from 90s Kriss Kross videos. Many Manhattanites would link these unfortunate attributes to Fresh Kills, the landfill under a large part of Staten Island. Keeper of New York City's trash since 1948, it is the world's largest landfill and, when it closes on December 31st, 2001, will have created the tallest hill on the Eastern Seabord. While the commercial parts of the island look much like the inside of a landfill, perhaps it is also Fresh Kills that adds the suspiciously ominous air to SI's quiet residential areas.

Still, for no clear reason, Staten Islanders continue to be unsuccessful in their lobbies to borough, city, and state governments for independent municipality. Manhattanites, for their part, don't really understand why the city government won't let the island go (especially after December 31st); most only go there in order to ride the free ferry round-trip (without getting off) or to take driving tests (the waiting list is shorter than in Manhattan). Famous Staten Islanders past and present include: the architect Frederick Law Olmsted, Mr. Clean of Proctor & Gamble fame, Method Man and the rest of the Wu-Tang Clan, and popstar/cultural vanguard of the 21st century Christina Aguilera. Pick up much needed maps of Staten Island's bus routes as well as other pamphlets at the Staten Island **Chamber of Commerce,** 130 Bay St., bear left from the ferry station onto Bay St. (☎ 718-727-1900. Open M-F 9am-5pm.)

GETTING INTO NEW YORK
TO AND FROM THE AIRPORTS

Travel between the airports and New York City is a choice between inconvenience and money. **Public transportation** is cheap (no more than two tokens needed—$3, $4 in the case of Newark), but you will almost definitely have to transfer from bus to subway, subway to bus, or subway to subway at least twice (with all your luggage). **Private bus companies** (shuttles) charge slightly more, but will take you directly from the airport to any one of many Manhattan destinations: Grand Central Station (42nd St. and Park Ave.), the Port Authority Bus Terminal (41st St. and Eighth Ave.), or the World Trade Center (1 West St.), along with several prominent hotels. (But you will still probably need to take a taxi or public transportation from there to get to your final destination.) Most private services peter out or vanish entirely between midnight and 6am. A **taxi** is the most comfortable way of getting to the city, if you're willing to pay. Heavy traffic makes the trip more expensive; traveling during rush hour (7:30-10am and 4-7:30pm) can be hard on your wallet. Passengers are responsible for paying bridge and tunnel tolls.

The best resource for ground transportation to the airports is the Port Authority of NJ & NY's website, **http://www.panynj.gov**. If you make lodging reservations ahead of time, be sure to ask about **limousine services**—some hostels offer transportation from the airports for reasonable fares. (Note: limousine doesn't necessarily mean a 15-foot luxury car with TV and VCR. Limousine companies are usually just unmarked taxis that charge flat rates for airport commutes, making traffic a non-issue.)

JFK AIRPORT

▶30-60min. from Manhattan. Taxi around $30 (plus tolls and tip).

BY SUBWAY. Catch a free yellow-white-blue JFK Long-Term Parking bus from any airport terminal (every 15min., 24hr.) to the **Howard Beach-JFK Airport subway station.** You can take the **A train** from there to several points in the city ($1.50, exact change only; 1hr.). Heading from Manhattan to JFK, take the Far Rockaway A train.

BY BUS. Local **bus** Q10 ($1.50, exact change only) stops at the airport and connects to the A, E, J, L, F, and R subway lines, which in turn go to Manhattan; tell the driver what subway line you want, and ask him to tell you where to get off. Although these routes are safe during the day, nighttime travelers should check with the information desk to find the safest way into the city.

BY SHUTTLE. The **New York Airport Service Express Bus** (☎718-875-8200), is a private line that runs between JFK and Grand Central Terminal, Penn Station, and Port Authority ($13-15; every 15-30min., 6am-midnight). The **Gray Line Air Shuttle** (☎800-451-0455) will drop you off anywhere in Manhattan between 21st and 103rd. Sts. ($14-19; on demand 6am-11:30pm). The **SuperShuttle** (☎258-3826) will drop you anywhere in Manhattan between Battery Park and 227th St. ($13.50-14.50; on demand 24hr.). Inquire about all three at the Ground Transportation Center in JFK. All services take 40-70min.

LAGUARDIA AIRPORT

▶15-30min. away from Manhattan. Taxi $16-20 (plus tolls and tip).

BY BUS AND SUBWAY. The **M60 bus** (daily 4:50am-1am; $1.50) connects to the following subways in Manhattan: 1, 9 at 116th St. and Broadway; 2, 3 at 125th St. and Lenox Ave.; 4, 5, 6 at 125th St. and Lexington Ave. In Queens, catch the N at Astoria Blvd. and 31st St. Or, take the MTA **Q33 bus** (from the Marine Air Terminal) or the **Q47 bus** (everywhere else; both $1.50). Transfer to the 7, E, F, G, R ($1.50) at the 74th St./Broadway-Roosevelt Ave./Jackson Hts. **subway** stop in Queens. Takes at least 1½hr. Be especially careful traveling these routes at night.

BY SHUTTLE. The **New York Airport Service Express Bus** (☎718-875-8200) runs from LaGuardia to Grand Central Terminal, Penn Station, and Port Authority ($8-10; every 15-30min. 6:40am-11:40pm). The **Gray Line Air Shuttle** (☎800-451-0455) runs from LaGuardia to anywhere between 23rd and 96th Sts. ($13; on demand 7am-11pm). **Super-Shuttle** (☎258-3826) will drop you anywhere in Manhattan between Battery Park and 227th St. ($13.50-16.50; on demand 24hr.). All services take 30-60min.

NEWARK AIRPORT

▶30-60min. from Manhattan. Taxi $34-51, including tolls.

BY BUS. New Jersey Transit Authority, NJTA (☎973-762-5100), runs **Air Link bus #302** from the airport and Newark's Penn Station (not Manhattan's; $4). From there **bus #108** ($3.25, exact change) goes to Port Authority. Takes at least 1½hr.

BY TRAIN. **PATH trains** (☎800-234-PATH) also run from Newark Penn Station to Manhattan, stopping at Christopher St., Sixth Ave., 9th St., 14th St., 23rd St., and 33rd St. ($1). **NJT** (☎800-772-2222) runs from Newark Penn Station to Manhattan's Penn Station ($2.50). **Amtrak** (☎800-USA-RAIL) also travels from Penn to Penn ($7). Takes at least 1½hr.

BY SHUTTLE. **Olympia Airport Express** (☎964-6233) run from the airport to Port Authority, Grand Central Terminal, and Penn Station ($11; every 20-30min. 6am-midnight). **Gray Line Air Shuttle** (☎800-451-0455) runs from the airport to anywhere between 23rd and 63rd Sts. ($14; on demand 7am-11pm; takes 30-60min). **SuperShuttle** (☎258-3826) runs from Newark to anywhere between Battery Park and 227th St. ($17.50-22.50; on demand 24hr.; takes 30-60min.).

GETTING AROUND NYC
MANHATTAN'S STREET PLAN

The city of right angles and tough, damaged people.
—Pete Hamill

Most of Manhattan's street plan was the result of an organized expansion scheme adopted in 1811; from then on, the city mostly grew in straight lines and at right angles.

Above 14th St., avenues run north-south and their numbers increase from east to west (ie: First Ave. is on the East Side, Eleventh Ave. is on the West Side), except that named avenues are placed randomly in between (i.e., Columbus or Madison Aves.). For quick reference, Fifth Ave. or Central Park are usually considered the midpoints of the city, separating it into east and west. The consecutively-numbered streets run east-west. Most avenues are one-way, and streets usually run east if they're even-numbered and west if they're odd-numbered. Big avenues (like Broadway or Park Ave.) and big transverse streets (like 86th, 34th, and 14th Sts.) are two-way. One particularity: Sixth Ave. becomes Ave. of the Americas below Central Park, but few natives acknowledge this moniker.

Below 14th St., the city dissolves into a charming but confusing tangle of old, narrow streets. **Broadway,** which follows an old Algonquin trail, cavalierly defies the rectangular pattern and cuts diagonally across the island, veering east of Fifth Ave. below 23rd St. The **Financial District/Wall St. area,** set over the original Dutch layout, is full of narrow, winding, one-way streets. **Chinatown** has no organization, but Canal St. is usually considered its major thruway. **The Village,** only slightly less confusing, is where 10th, 4th, and 11th Sts. manage to form one intersection. The **East Village and Alphabet City** are grid-like, with named streets filling in the void after the numbers wind down to 1st St., and the avenues going from Ave. A to Ave. D east of First Ave.

The best thing to do when setting off to find something is to find out not only its **address** (ie: 230 Riverside Dr.), but also its **cross-street** (in this case, 95th St.).

BY SUBWAY

Operated by **New York City Transit** (English speakers ☎ 718-330-1234; non-English ☎ 718-330-4847; open daily 6am-9pm), the 238-mile New York subway system operates 24 hours a day, 365 days a year. It moves 3.5 million people daily, and has 468 stations. The fare for Metropolitan Transit Authority (MTA) subways is a hefty $1.50, so groups of four may find a cab ride to be cheaper and more expedient for short distances. Long distances are best traveled by subway, since once inside a passenger may transfer onto any of the other trains without restrictions. Free, extremely useful subway maps are available at any subway token booth, and additional copies are posted directly downstairs in any station and in every subway car.

The biggest **subway hubs** are 42nd St.-Grand Central on the east side and 42nd St.-Times Square on the west side. From these two, most trains can be connected to, and the two are connected by the 7 and S trains.

Although by far the quickest means of transportation in Manhattan, **the subways are much more useful for traveling north-south** than east-west, as there are only two crosstown shuttle trains (42nd and 14th St.). In upper Manhattan and in Queens, Brooklyn, and the Bronx, some lines run above ground.

Express trains stop only at certain major stations; **locals** stop everywhere. Be sure to **check the letter or number and the destination of each train,** since trains with different destinations often use the same track. When in doubt, ask a friendly passenger or the conductor, who usually sits near the middle of the train. Once you're on the train, **pay attention to the garbled announcements**—trains occasionally change mid-route from local to express or vice-versa, especially when entering or leaving Manhattan.

You'll see lit glass globes outside most subway entrances. Green means that the entrance is staffed 24hr. a day. Red indicates that the entrance is closed or restricted in some way, usually during off (night) hours; read the sign posted above the stairs.

FARES: METROCARD. The **MetroCard** now serves as the dominant form of currency for transit in New York. The card, containing a magnetic strip, can be used at all subway stations and on all public buses. Subway and bus fare is $1.50 per ride with the MetroCard, but purchasing a $15 card gets you one free ride ($30 gets you 2 free rides, etc.). Even more importantly, MetroCards can be used for subway-bus, bus-subway, and bus-bus transfers. When you swipe the card on the initial ride, a free transfer is electronically stored on your MetroCard and is good for up to 2hrs. **Without the MetroCard, bus-subway or subway-bus transfers are not free.** A single MetroCard can store up to four transfers, good for people traveling in a group. There are certain restrictions on bus-bus transfers (i.e. passengers on a north-south bus can generally only transfer to a bus going east-west).

UNLIMITED METROCARDS. "Unlimited Rides" MetroCards (as opposed to "Pay-Per-Ride" cards) are sold in 1-day ($4), 7-day ($17) and 30-day ($63) denominations and is good for unlimited use of the subway and bus systems during the specified period. **The Unlimited Rides Card is highly recommended for tourists who plan on visiting many sights.** Those with disabilities or over 65 qualify for a Reduced Fare card; call 878-7294 (TDD ☎878-0165) for information. The card can be purchased in all subway stations and at any newsstand, pharmacy, or grocery store bearing a MetroCard sticker in the storefront window. The 1-day "Fun Pass" can only be bought at stores or stands, not subway stations. The city has set up a helpful information line (☎800-638-7622; in NYC ☎638-7622) to answer any questions about this new technology.

SAFETY. The subway is the best example of public city transportation if the proper cautions are taken. Open 24hr., it isn't the cleanest, and there are homeless people living in stations and even subway cars themselves, but since everyone uses it all the time, it is generally safe, at least around central Manhattan. Nighttime is not necessarily a dangerous time to travel as long as you are taking a popular subway line and are not going to one of the outer boroughs. Try to be in the same subway car as other people, or at least one person who you think is safe—as always, your attitude is the key to your safety—and stay near the middle to be close to the conductor (you'll see his face from the platform). During rush hour and in crowded stations (like 42nd St.), try to keep your bag in front of you to avoid falling prey to quick-fingered pickpockets. A real concern for women specifically is sexual molestation—there are quite a few crazies who ride the subways to brush up or grope others. If this happens, be *loud* in your indignation.

BY BUS

Because buses are often mired in traffic, they can take twice as long as subways, but they are almost always safer, cleaner, and quieter. They'll also get you closer to your destination, since they stop every two blocks or so and run crosstown (east-west), as well as uptown and downtown (north-south). For long-distance travel (over 40 north-south blocks), buses can be a nightmare (except at night and on weekends, when traffic is manageable), but for shorter—and especially crosstown—trips, buses are often as quick as, and more convenient than, trains. The MTA transfer system provides north-south travelers with a paper slip, valid for a free ride east-west, or vice-versa, but you must ask the driver for a transfer when you board and pay your fare. Make sure you ring when you want to get off.

Bus stops are indicated by a yellow-painted curb, but you're better off looking for the blue sign post announcing the bus number or for a glass-walled shelter displaying a map of the bus's route and a schedule of arrival times (they are surprisingly on-point). A flat fare of $1.50 is charged at all times when you board; either a MetroCard (see above for more information), exact change, or a subway token is required—dollar bills are not accepted. If you use a MetroCard, within two hours you can transfer without charge from the bus to the subway or from a bus to another bus.

Ask for outer borough bus maps at any outer borough subway station; different restrictions apply to them as many are operated by private companies.

BY TAXI

With drivers cruising at warp speed along near-deserted avenues or dodging through bumper-to-bumper traffic, cab rides can give you painful ulcers. Even if your stomach survives the ride, your budget may not. But taxis are the most convenient and safest form of travel. The meter starts at $2 and clicks 30¢ for about every four street blocks or one long avenue block; 30¢ is also tacked on for every 75 seconds spent in slow or stopped traffic, a 50¢ surcharge is levied from 8pm to 6am, and passengers pay for all tolls. Don't forget to tip 15%; cabbies expect the dough. Before you leave the cab, ask for a receipt, which will have the taxi's identification number (either its meter number or its medallion). This number is necessary to trace lost articles or to make a complaint to the **Taxi Commission** (☎221-8294; open M-F 9am-5pm). Some drivers may illegally try to show the naive visitor the "scenic route"; quickly glance at a street map before embarking so you'll have some clue if you're being taken to your destination, or just being taken for a ride. Use only yellow cabs—they're licensed by the state of New York. Cabs of other colors are unlicensed "gypsy" cabs and are illegal in NYC. When hailing a cab: if the center light on the cab's roof is lit, then the cabbie is picking up fares; if it is dark, the cab is already taken. If you can't find anything on the street, commandeer a radio-dispatched cab (see **Service Directory**, p. 294, for phone numbers). Use common sense to make rides cheaper—catch a cab going your direction and get off at a nearby street corner. When shared with friends a cab can be the cheapest, safest, and most convenient option, especially late at night. You can't, however, cram more than four people into a cab.

BY CAR

What do New Yorkers know about driving? Don't do it in the city. Some never learn to drive at all, terrified by the prospect of wide right turns in midtown traffic (worst between 34th and 57th Sts.). When behind the wheel in New York, you are locked in combat with aggressive taxis, careless pedestrians, and lunatic bicycle couriers.

The even greater hassle of parking joins in to make having a car nothing but a nuisance. Expect to circle an area for up to 40min. looking for a **free spot** on the street, and don't be surprised if you have to park many blocks from your destination. Read the signs carefully; a space is usually legal only on certain days of the week. The city has never been squeamish about towing, and recovering your car once it's towed will cost $100 or more. Some streets have parking meters, that cost 25¢ per 15min., with a limit of one or two hours. **Parking lots** are the easiest but the most expensive option. In Midtown lots, expect to pay at least $25 per day and up to $15 for two hours. The cheapest parking lots are downtown— try the far west end of Houston St.—but make sure you feel comfortable with the area.

Break-ins and car theft happen often, particularly if you have a radio. The wailing of a car alarm is such a familiar tune to New Yorkers that you may hear them sing along. Never leave anything visible inside your car, and, if it is removable, hide your radio also.

INTERNATIONAL DRIVING PERMIT

For information on how to obtain the **International Driving Permit (IDP),** contact the one of the following organizations in your home country:

Australia: Contact your local Royal Automobile Club (RAC) or the National Royal Motorist Association (NRMA) if in NSW or the ACT (☎08 9421 4298; www.rac.com.au/travel). Permits AUS$15.

Canada: Contact any Canadian Automobile Association (CAA) branch office in Canada, or write to CAA, 1145 Hunt Club Rd., Suite 200, K1V 0Y3 Canada. (☎613-247-0117; fax 247-0118; www.caa.ca/ CAAInternet/travelservices/internationaldocumentation/idptravel.htm).Permits CDN$10.

Ireland: Contact the nearest Automobile Association (AA) office or write: The Automobile Association, International Documents, Fanum House, Erskine, Renfrewshire PA8 6BW (☎990 500 600). Permits IR£4.

New Zealand: Contact your local Automobile Association (AA) or their main office at Auckland Central, 99 Albert St. (☎9 377 4660; fax 302 2037; www.nzaa.co.nz.). Permits NZ$8.

South Africa: Contact your local Automobile Association of South Africa office or the head office at P.O. Box 596, 2000 Johannesburg (☎11 799 1000; fax 799 1010). Permits SAR28.50.

U.K.: Visit your local Automobile Association (AA) Shop. To find the location nearest you that issues the IDP, call ☎0990 50 06 00. More information available at www.theaa.co.uk/motoring/ idp.asp). Permits UK£4.

U.S.: Visit any American Automobile Association (AAA) office or write to AAA Florida, Travel Related Services, 1000 AAA Drive (mail stop 100), Heathrow, FL 32746 (☎407-444-7000; fax 444-7380). You do not have to be a member of AAA to receive an (IDP/IADP). Permits $10.

CAR INSURANCE

Most credit cards cover standard insurance. If you rent, lease, or borrow a car, you will need a **green card,** or **International Insurance Certificate,** to prove that you have liability insurance. Obtain it through the car rental agency; most include coverage in their prices. If you lease a car, you can obtain a green card from the dealer. Some travel agents offer the card. Verify whether your auto insurance applies abroad. If you have a collision abroad, the accident will show up on your domestic records if you report it to your insurance company. Rental agencies may require you to purchase theft insurance in countries that they consider to have a high risk of auto theft.

CAR RENTAL

All agencies maintain varying minimum-age requirements and require proof of age as well as a security deposit. Agencies in Queens and Yonkers are often less expensive than their Manhattan counterparts, especially for one-day rentals. Most auto insurance policies will cover rented cars, and some credit cards like American Express and Chase Visa take care of your rental insurance costs if you've charged the vehicle to their card (but be sure to ask about all the particulars from the companies themselves; as always, "restrictions apply"). Many smaller local rental car companies allow drivers 21 years or older (most companies only rent to customers 25 or older); some even allow drivers 18 years or older. Most require a young driver surcharge in these cases, so check first.

Dollar: at JFK, ☎718-656-2400; at LaGuardia, ☎718-244-1235.

Enterprise: In the US and Canada, ☎800-566-9249; in French-speaking Canada, ☎800-Loc-Auto; in the UK, ☎0-800-800227, to verify that your desired location rents to younger drivers. To check for locations near you in the US, ☎800-566-9249.

Nationwide, 1338 44th St., between 13th and 14th Aves., in Brooklyn (☎718-435-6000). Reputable nationwide chain. Mid-sized domestic sedan $50 per day, $289 per week; 299 free mi. per day, 1200 per week. Great weekend specials. Open M-Th 8am-6:30pm, F 8am-6pm, Sa 10am-11pm, Su 8am-noon. Vehicle return 24hr. Must be 23 with a major credit card.

AAMCAR Rent-a-Car, 315 W. 96th St. (☎222-8500), between West End Ave. and Riverside Dr. Compacts $50 per day, M-Th 200 free mi., 25¢ each additional mi.; $330 per week with 1000 free mi. Ask about weekend specials. Must be 23 to rent; $10 surcharge for drivers under 25. Open M-F 7:30am-7pm, Sa 9am-5pm, Su 9am-7pm. No one-day rentals June-Aug. Sa-Su.

BY BICYCLE

Weekday biking in commuter traffic poses a mortal challenge even for veterans. But on weekends, when the traffic thins, cyclists who use helmets and caution can tour the Big Apple on two wheels. See **Sports,** p. 171, for routes and rentals.

BY FOOT

Walking is the cheapest, arguably the most entertaining, and often the fastest way to get around town. During rush hours the sidewalks are packed with suited and sneakered commuters. In between rush hours, sidewalks are still full of street life. Twenty street blocks (north-south) make up a mile; one east-west block from one avenue to the next is about triple the distance of a north-south, street-to-street block. New York distances are short: a walk from the south end of Central Park to the World Trade Center, through all of Midtown and downtown Manhattan, for example, should take under 90min.

WHEN IN NEW YORK
BLENDING IN

Acting like a tried-and-true New Yorker is your best defense. The New Yorker walks briskly; tourists wander absently. Be discreet with street maps and cameras; address requests for directions to police officers or store-owners. Consider covering your flagrant *Let's Go* guide with plain paper. Stay out of public bathrooms if you can; they tend to be filthy and unsafe. Instead, try department stores, hotels, or restaurants; even those with a "Restrooms for Patrons Only" sign on the door will usually allow you in if you look enough like a customer (Barnes & Noble bookstores are a great place for bathroom stops). If, despite your confident swagger, you suspect you're being followed, duck into a nearby store or restaurant.

ELECTRIC CURRENT AND FILM

CONVERTERS AND ADAPTERS. In the US and Canada, electricity is 110V; 220V electrical appliances don't like 110V current. Visit a hardware store for an adapter (changes the shape of the plug) and a converter (changes the voltage). Don't make the mistake of using only an adapter (unless appliance instructions explicitly state otherwise).

FILM. Despite disclaimers, airport security X-rays *can* fog film, so if you're bringing film with speeds over 800, the best idea is to either buy a lead-lined pouch, sold at camera stores, or ask the security to hand inspect it. Always pack it in your carry-on luggage, since higher-intensity X-rays are used on checked luggage. All types of film for all types of cameras are available in NYC, but the most often seen kind, available in all drug, grocery, and convenience stores, is 35mm.

LAWS

You cannot buy **tobacco products** in NYC (or elsewhere in the US) if you are under the age of 18; the age for **alcohol** is 21. Many restaurants that have active bars will become 21+ after a certain time of night and will not let people under 21 enter even just to eat dinner.

Smoking is prohibited in most restaurants, some have smoking sections that you need to request, and very few are open smoking everywhere. All outdoor seating, unless labeled otherwise, is fine to smoke in legally, but you may very well get looks from the surrounding patrons, especially in more family-oriented restaurants and cafes.

MEASUREMENTS

Although the metric system has made considerable inroads into American business and science, the British system of weights and measures continues to prevail in the US. The following is a list of US units and their metric equivalents:.

MEASUREMENT CONVERSIONS

1 inch (in.) = 25.4 millimeters (mm)	1 millimeter (mm) = 0.039 in.
1 foot (ft.) = 0.30 m	1 meter (m) = 3.28 ft.
1 yard (yd.) = 0.914m	1 meter (m) = 1.09 yd.
1 mile = 1.61km	1 kilometer (km) = 0.62 mi.
1 ounce (oz.) = 28.35g	1 gram (g) = 0.035 oz.
1 pound (lb.) = 0.454kg	1 kilogram (kg) = 2.202 lb.
1 fluid ounce (fl. oz.) = 29.57ml	1 milliliter (ml) = 0.034 fl. oz.
1 gallon (gal.) = 3.785L	1 liter (L) = 0.264 gal.
1 acre (ac.) = 0.405ha	1 hectare (ha) = 2.47 ac.
1 square mile (sq. mi.) = 2.59km^2	1 square kilometer (km^2) = 0.386 sq. mi.

NEWSPAPERS

Today, New York supports over 100 different newspapers, reflecting the diversity of its urban landscape. Weekly ethnic papers cater to the black, Hispanic, Irish, Japanese, Chinese, Indian, Korean, and Greek communities, among others.

EL DIARIA/LA PRENSA

The highly political El Diario/La Prensa has been stirring up controversy since 1914. Founded originally with Puerto Ricans (or Nuyoricans) in mind, the journal reaches over 53,000 Spanish-speaking New Yorkers from a vast array of Latin-American origins.

THE NEW YORK POST AND THE DAILY NEWS

The city's two major tabloid dailies infamously flaunt less-than-demure sensibilities. The *Daily News*, recently "rescued" by the late Robert Maxwell, has slightly better taste—it doesn't use red ink, and it reports fewer grisly murders. Both papers have editorial opinions more conservative than their headlines, as well as comics, advice pages, gossip columns, and horoscopes. The *Post* has a great sports section, and both have good metropolitan coverage.

THE NEW YORK TIMES AND NEWSDAY

The *Times* still soberly claims to be the authority on "all the news that's fit to print." Its editorial page provides a nationally respected forum for policy debates, coveted political endorsements, and the rantings of demi-celebrity columnists such as Maureen Dowd, William Safire, and Frank Rich. Praise from its Book Review section can revitalize living authors and immortalize dead ones, and its Sunday crossword puzzles enliven brunches from Fresno to Tallahassee. Although it is successfully circulated nationally, the paper remains staunchly centered on New York; theater directors, nervous politicians, and other fervent readers often make late-night Saturday newsstand runs to buy the hefty, definitive Sunday *Times*. *Newsday* offers local coverage by a youngish staff, some entertaining columnists, and a special Sunday section for the kids.

THE VILLAGE VOICE AND THE NEW YORK PRESS

The Village Voice, the largest weekly newspaper in the country, captures a spirit of the city each Wednesday that you won't find in the dailies. The left-leaning *Voice* prefers to stage lively political debates and print quirky reflections on New York life. It also sponsors some excellent investigative city reporting—and the city's most intriguing set of personal ads. The real estate and nightlife listings are legendary and indispensable to visitors and natives alike. Best of all, it is free to Manhattanites and can be picked up at any street corner midweek. The *New York Press*, another free weekly, also has good club and nightlife listings, in addition to entertaining articles on politics and culture.

THE WALL STREET JOURNAL AND NEW YORK OBSERVER

The *Journal* gives a quick world-news summary in the left-most column of page one for breakfasting brokers more interested in the market pages. With its pen-and-ink drawings, conservative bent, market strategies, and continual obsession with the price of gold, the *Journal* offers to all a Wall Street insider's world perspective. The Upper East Side's *Observer* prints commentary on city politics on its dapper pink pages.

MAGAZINES

On the glossy side, New York is undoubtedly the magazine publishing capital of the country; most national periodicals have their headquarters somewhere in the city. While old staples like **Time, Newsweek,** and **Rolling Stone** have resided here for decades, other New York mainstays have not always been so venerable. **Vanity Fair** originally made its fame by publishing content that was considered by some to be scandalous by the standards of the time, and **Vogue** was a weekly digest of the trivialities and whims of New York's high society before it became *the* fashion arbiter. A bastion of respectability, the **New Yorker** publishes fiction and poetry by well known authors and the occasional fledgling. During former *Vanity Fair* editor Tina Brown's short-lived reign as *New Yorker* editor-in-chief, she brought the magazine a new style, with bimonthly articles by black intellectual Henry Louis Gates, Jr., occasional cartoons by Art Spiegelman, photographs by Annie Leibowitz, and themed issues. The editorial fate of the magazine is now in the hands of David Remnick.

New York magazine prints extensive entertainment listings and focuses more on the city's "wealthy" lifestyle. The amazingly fast-selling *Best of New York* issue, which comes out in late spring, is a definitive guide to the city's hippest new spots. **Time Out: New York** is the most recent weekly player in the local newsprint rivalry. Read primarily for its vastly helpful entertainment listings, rumor has it that *Time Out* includes colorful, well-written articles, too.

RADIO

In New York City, the radio spectrum serves up everything from soulless elevator instrumentals (WLTW 106.7 FM) to pirate radio broadcasts of underground sounds and community activism. As with most American radio, the lower on the dial, the less-commercial (and more innovative) the sounds will be. Columbia's WKCR 89.9 FM has "Out to Lunch" weekdays from noon to 3pm, when a spectrum of jazz is played by those knowledgeable about the current scene. For independent hip-hop and underground rap, check out Stretch and Bobbito's show on KCR (Th 1-5am). WQHT 97.1 FM sends out more commercial styles, beginning each weekday with Dr. Dre and Ed Lover's morning show of phat beats, dope rhymes, and fast-paced talk. In the evenings QHT brings in DJs to cut, scratch, and mix on the last major label wax.

The following stations are FM unless otherwise noted:

TYPE	DIAL POSITION
Classical	WNYC 93.9, WQXR 96.3
Jazz	WBGO 88.3, WCWP 88.1, WQCD 101.9
College/Indie/Alternative/Popular	WNYU 89.1, WKCR 89.9, WSOU 89.5, WFMU 91.1, WDRE 92.7, WHTZ 100.3, WAXQ 104.3, WXRK 92.3 102.7
Classic Rock	WQXR 104.3, WNEW 102.7
Top 40	WPSC 88.7, WRKS 98.7, WPLJ 95.5, WRCN 103.9, WMXV 105.1
Hip-Hop/R&B/Soul	WQHT 97.1, WBLS 107.5, WWRL 1600AM
Oldies	WRTN 93.5, WCBS 101.1
Foreign-Language Programming	WADO 1280AM, WWRV 1330AM, WKDM 1380AM, WZRC 1480AM, WNWK 105.9
News	WABC 770AM, WCBS 880AM, WINS 1010AM, WBBR 1130AM
Public Radio	WNYC 93.9, WNYC 820AM, WBAI 99.5
Sports	WFAN 660AM
Pirate	103.9 (Sunday in Williamsburg), 88.7 Steal This Radio (Lower East Side)

TAXES AND TIPPING

The prices quoted throughout *Let's Go* do not include New York sales tax, which is 8.25%. Hotel tax is also 8.25%.

Remember that service is never included on a New York bill, unless you're in a large party at a restaurant (seven or more people), and then it is noted. Tip cab drivers and waiters 15%. For waiters, New Yorkers usually just "double the tax"; exceptional waiters—or those who work at exceptional restaurants—are more often tipped 20% of the tab. Tip hairdressers 10% and bellhops around $1 per bag. Bartenders usually expect between 50¢ and $1 per drink, depending on what type of environment you're in.

KEEPING IN TOUCH

MAIL

SENDING MAIL

Stamps for a normal letter envelope costs 33¢ for domestic mail, 50¢ for international. **Aerogrammes,** printed sheets that fold into envelopes ready to be air mailed, are sold at post offices for 45¢. Most US post offices offer an **International Express Mail** service, which is the fastest way to send an item overseas. (A package under 8oz. can be sent to most foreign destinations in 40-72 hr. for around $13.)

If you have questions concerning services, post office branch locations, or hours, call the Customer Service Assistance Center (☎967-8585; open M-F 8:30am-6pm). For speedier service at any time, dial ☎800-725-2161 for the 24hr. info line which provides information on branch hours and locations, postal rates, and zip codes and addresses. For major post office branches in NY, see **Service Directory,** p. 293.

RECEIVING MAIL

Depending on how neurotic your family and friends are, consider making arrangements for them to get in touch with you. Mail can be sent **General Delivery** to New York's **central post office branch,** 421 Eighth Ave. (☎330-2902; open 24hr.), occupying the block between Eighth and Ninth Ave. and 33rd and 32nd St. General Delivery mail should be sent to 390 Ninth Ave.; you must collect your General Delivery mail at the Ninth Ave. entrance. General Delivery letters to you should be labeled like this:

Buttah <u>CUTS</u> (capitalize & underline last name for accurate filing)
c/o General Delivery
Main Post Office
James A. Farley Building
390 Ninth Ave.
New York City, NY 10001
USA (if from another country)
HOLD FOR 30 DAYS

When you claim your mail, you'll have to present ID; if you don't claim a letter within two to four weeks, it will be returned to its sender.

Throughout the US, **American Express** acts as a mail service for cardholders if you contact them in advance. Under this free **Client Letter Service,** they will hold mail for 30 days, forward upon request, and accept telegrams. Address the envelope the same as you would for General Delivery. Some offices offer these services to non-cardholders (especially those who have purchased AmEx Travelers Cheques), but you must call ahead to make sure. For a complete explanation, call ☎800-528-4800.

TELEPHONES

Most of the information you will need about telephones—including area codes for the US, foreign country codes, and rates—is in the front of the local **white pages** telephone directory. The **yellow pages,** published at the end of the white pages or in a separate book, is used to look up the phone numbers of businesses and other services. Federal, state, and local government listings are provided in the blue pages at the back of the directory. To obtain local phone numbers or area codes of other cities, call **directory assistance** at 411. **All phone numbers listed without an area code are Manhattan numbers with the area code (212).**

To accommodate NYC's exploding number of cell phones (it's the ultimate necessity for socialites), **new area codes** have been added in the last year. 646 joined 212 and 917 to represent Manhattan, 347 joined the 718 of the outer boroughs, 973 joined 201 for New Jersey, and 631 is the Suffolk area code, leaving 516 solely for Nassau. In order to avoid the confusion of changing the area codes of already-existing numbers, these new area codes (with the exception of Long Island), are being given to new phones—they do not represent any sort of geographic area.

AREA CODES

TELEPHONE CODES			
Manhattan	212, 917, 646	Staten Island	718, 347
Brooklyn	718, 347	Hoboken/NJ	201, 973
The Bronx	718, 347	Long Island	516 (Nassau)
Queens	718, 347		631 (Suffolk)

CALLING NYC FROM HOME

1. The international access code of your home country, unless calling from the US or Canada. **International access codes** include: Australia 0011; Ireland 00; New Zealand 00; South Africa 09; UK 00.

2. 1 (US country code).

3. The appropriate New York area code. If no area code is listed in *Let's Go,* assume 212.

4. Local number, always seven digits.

CALLING HOME FROM NYC

You can place **international calls** from any telephone. To call direct, dial the universal international access code (011) followed by the country code, the city/area code, and the local number. Drop the first zeros of country codes and city codes if they are listed (ie: 033 is 011-33).

COUNTRY CODES			
Australia	61	Ireland	353
Austria	43	New Zealand	64
Canada	1	South Africa	13
Italy	39	United Kingdom	44
		United States	1

A calling card is probably your best and cheapest bet. Calls are billed either collect or to your account. MCI WorldPhone also provides access to MCI's Traveler's Assist, which gives legal and medical advice, exchange rate information, and translation services. Other phone companies provide similar services to travelers. To **obtain a calling card** from your national telecommunications service before you leave home, contact the appropriate company below.

US: AT&T (☎888-288-4685; www.att.com/traveler); **Sprint/Global One** (☎800-877-4646; www.globalone.net/calling.html); **MCI/Worldphone** (☎800-444-4141; from abroad dial the country's MCI access number; www.mci.com/worldphone/english/accessnoalpha/shtml).

Canada: Bell Canada **Canada Direct** (☎800-565-4708; www.stentor.ca/canada_direct/eng/travel/cardform.htm).

UK: British Telecom **BT Direct** (☎800 34 51 44; www.chargecard.bt.com/html/access.htm).

Ireland: Telecom Éireann (becomes Eircom in September 1999) **Ireland Direct** (☎800 250 250; www.telecom.ie/eircom).

Australia: Telstra **Australia Direct** (☎13 22 00).

New Zealand: Telecom New Zealand (☎800 000 000; www.telecom.xtra.co.nz/cgi).

South Africa: Telkom South Africa (☎09 03; www.telkom.co.za/international/sadirect/access.htm).

To **call home** with a **calling card,** contact the North American operator for your service provider by dialing:

BT Direct: ☎800-445-5667 AT&T, ☎800-444-2162 MCI, ☎800-800-0008 Sprint.

Australia Direct: ☎800-682-2878 AT&T, ☎800-937-6822 MCI, ☎800-676-0061 Sprint.

Telkom South Africa Direct: ☎800-949-7027.

Wherever possible, use a calling card for international phone calls, as the long-distance rates for national phone services are often exorbitant. You can usually make direct international calls from pay phones, but if you aren't using a calling card you will have to drop your coins as quickly as your words. Where available, prepaid phone cards and, occasionally, major credit cards can be used for direct international calls, but they are still less cost-efficient. Although incredibly convenient, in-room hotel calls invariably include an arbitrary and sky-high surcharge (as much as $10).

The expensive alternative to dialing direct or using a calling card is using an international operator to place a **collect call.** An English-speaking operator from your home nation can be reached by dialing the appropriate service provider listed above, and they will typically place a collect call even if you don't possess one of their phone cards.

CALLING WITHIN THE US

Telephone numbers in the US consist of a three-digit area code followed by seven digits, written as 123-456-7890. Only the last seven digits are used in a **local call. Calls outside the area code** from which you are dialing require a "1" and the area code and number. In NYC, a call to another borough will be local in terms of price, but you'll still need to dial a "1" and the area code and number. For example, to call the Brooklyn Museum from Manhattan, you would dial 1-718-638-5000, but it would only cost $0.25. Generally, discount rates apply after 5pm on weekdays and Sunday and economy rates every day between 11pm and 8am; on Saturday and on Sunday until 5pm, economy rates are also in effect. Numbers beginning with area code 800 or 888 are **toll-free calls** requiring no coin deposit. Numbers beginning with 900 are **toll calls** and charge you (often exorbitantly) for whatever "service" they provide.

Pay phones are plentiful, most often stationed on street corners and in public areas. Be wary of private, more expensive pay phones—the rate they charge per call should be printed on the phone. Put your coins (25¢ for a local call in NYC) into the slot and listen for a dial tone before dialing. If there is no answer or if you get a busy signal, you will get your money back after hanging up, unless you connect to an answering machine.

The simplest way to call within the country is to use a coin-operated phone. You can also buy **prepaid phone cards,** which carry a certain amount of phone time depending on the card's denomination. The card usually has a toll-free access telephone number and a personal identification number (PIN), both of which you need to place a call. A computer tells you how much time or how many units you have left on your card. Be very careful as to the type of card you buy; some operate with a PIN number you must know beforehand, while others contain the PIN on the card itself. You can purchase these cards at any pharmacy, grocery, or convenience store, usually at the cashier.

EMAIL (ELECTRONIC MAIL)

For lists of cyber cafes in NY, see **Service Directory,** p. 292. You may want to consult www.cyberiacafe.net/cyberia/guide/ccafe.htm where you can find a list of **cybercafes** to call your own. **Public libraries** offer free Internet connections; however, there is often a wait and you are limited to 15-30min. (see **Service Directory,** p. 293).

SAFETY AND SECURITY

PERSONAL SAFETY

Despite the recent dramatic decreases in crime levels throughout the city, personal safety should always be a consideration when visiting the Big Apple.

EXPLORING. Pay attention to the neighborhood that surrounds you. A district can change character dramatically in the course of a single block (e.g., 96th St. and Park Ave.). Many notoriously dangerous districts have safe sections; look for children playing, women walking in the open, and other signs of an active community. If you feel uncomfortable, leave as quickly and directly as you can, but don't allow your wariness to close off whole worlds to you. Careful, persistent exploration will build confidence, strengthen your emerging New York attitude, and make your stay in the city that much more rewarding.

GETTING AROUND NEW YORK BY NIGHT. Terrible freak accidents can happen in the securest of neighborhoods, and you can get safely home in the worst of neighborhoods every day. Don't let NYC's reputation discourage you from exploring—it's not as scary as people imagine. Some quick guidelines:

Stay out of Central Park when it's dark; by the same token stay away from all large public parks and less-traversed, secluded areas like the Brooklyn Heights Promenade at night.

During the day everything is relatively safe, even "bad" neighborhoods; at night, stay away from under-frequented places if you are alone or in a small group of women or young kids. *Let's Go* mentions neighborhoods that are slightly shadier during the night; be careful, but don't let it take over your vacation.

SELF-DEFENSE . A good self-defense course will give you more concrete ways to react to different types of aggression. **Impact, Prepare, and Model Mugging** can refer you to local self-defense courses in the United States (☎ 800-345-5425). Workshops (2-3hr.) start at $50 and full courses run $350-500. Both women and men are welcome.

FINANCIAL SECURITY

PROTECTING YOUR VALUABLES

Rip-off artists seek the wealthy as well as the unwary, so hide your riches, especially in neighborhoods where you feel uncomfortable. Carrying a shoulder bag is better than having a backpack; in the midst of a crowd, it is easy for pickpockets to quietly unzip backpack pockets and remove items. Wear your shoulderbag diagonally across your chest so it cannot be pulled off.

Tourists make especially juicy prey because they tend to carry large quantities of cash—hence *Let's Go*'s advocacy of traveler's checks. Don't count your money in public or use large bills. Tuck your wallet into a less-accessible pocket and keep an extra ten bucks or so in a more obvious one (this is "Mugging Money," a NYC tradition—it appeases the criminals and you aren't left destitute). Keep an extra bill for emergencies in an unlikely place, such as your shoe or sock.

If you take a car into the city, do not leave *anything* visible inside the car—put it all in the trunk, and if your tape deck/radio is removeable, remove it and put it in the trunk also. You should never sleep in your car, no matter how low on cash you are.

PICKPOCKETS AND CON ARTISTS

Con artists run rampant on New York's streets. Beware of hustlers working in groups. If someone spills ketchup on you, someone else may be picking your pocket. Be distrustful of sob stories that require a donation from you. (And remember that no one ever wins at three-card monte.

DRUGS AND ALCOHOL

You must be 21 years old to purchase alcoholic beverages legally in New York State. The more popular drinking spots, as well as more upscale liquor stores, are likely to card—and ruthlessly. Smaller convenience stores and liquor stores in poorer neighborhoods will usually accept any type of ID, but few stores will let you get away with no proof of age whatsoever, even though it may be fake.

Possession of marijuana, cocaine, crack, heroin, methamphetamines, MDMA ("ecstasy"), hallucinogens, and most opiate derivatives (among many other chemicals) is punishable by stiff fines and imprisonment. But that doesn't stop New York's thriving **drug trade,** whose marketplaces are street corners, club bathrooms, and city parks throughout the city, most conspicuously the Village's Washington Square Park. Whiffs of marijuana smoke are commonplace throughout the city, for this drug is low on the NYPD's list of problems. Trying to acquire drugs brings increasing levels of personal danger (both from the police and sketchy dealers). Often people risk their necks buying "heroin" to discover that they've purchased powdered soap. Attempting to purchase illegal drugs of any sort is a **very bad idea.** Out-of-towners seeking (or on) a high are walking targets—not just for cops, but for thieves, as well.

If you carry **prescription drugs** when you travel, it is vital to have a copy of the prescriptions themselves readily accessible at US Customs. Check with the US Customs Service before your trip for more information on questionable drugs.

Life & Times

HISTORY AND POLITICS

THE EARLY YEARS: 1624-1811

The **Dutch West Indies Company** founded the colony of **New Amsterdam** on the southern-most tip of Manhattan in 1624 as a trading post, but England soon asserted rival claims to the land. While the mother countries squabbled, the colonists went about their burgeoning business, trading beaver skins, colorful *wampum* (beads made of white or violet seashells), and silver with the neighboring Native Americans. In 1626, New York's tradition of great bargains began when Peter Minuit bought the island from "natives" for 60 guilders, or just under US$24. However, the men he assumed were locals were actually Canarsee Delawares visiting the island and didn't even own the property they sold.

The rich and fertile land made light work for European settlers. "Children and pigs multiply here rapidly," gloated one colonist. When the Dutch West Indies Company tried to interfere, the settlers resented it. Calvinist **Peter Stuyvesant,** the Dutch governor at the middle of the 17th century, enforced strict rules on the happy-go-lucky settlement. He shot hogs, closed taverns, and whipped Quakers, sparking protest and anger among the citizenry. Inexplicably, the draconian Stuyvesant has since become a local folk hero. New York schools, businesses—even several neighborhoods (see Bedford-Stuyvesant in Brooklyn, **Once in NYC,** p. 28)—bear his name.

Unhappy with Dutch rule, early colonists refused to back Stuyvesant in resisting the English, and the Brits took over the settlement in 1664. The new British governors were slightly less offending, if only because they were less effective: between 1664 and 1776, New York experienced 22 suspensions of governance.

Left to its own devices, the city continued to mature. The city's first newspaper, the **Gazette,** appeared in 1725. Ten years later, **John Peter Zenger,** editor of the *New York Weekly Journal,* was charged with libel for satirizing public officials. The governor of New York threw Zenger into jail and publicly burned copies of his paper. Zenger's aquittal set a precedent for a great US tradition—freedom of the press. In 1754, higher education came to New York in the form of **King's College** (later renamed **Columbia University,** p. 98). By the late 1770s, the city was a major port with a population of 20,000. Early success made New Yorkers preoccupied with prosperity and uninterested in the first whiffs of revolution. British rule was good for business—and, true to its reputation, money ruled even then in the soon-to-be capital of capitalism.

Understandably, the new American army made no great efforts to protect the ungrateful city, and New York was held by the British throughout the war. As a result, the **American Revolution** was a rough time for the metropolis. Fire destroyed a quarter of the city in 1776, and the rest was pillaged and deserted. By the time the defeated British left in 1783, most New Yorkers were relieved.

With its buildings in heaps of rubble and one-third of its population off roaming Canada, New York made a valiant effort to rebuild; it began a tradition of resilience. "The progress of the city is, as usual, beyond all calculations," wrote one enraptured citizen. New York's post-Revolution comeback entailed briefly serving as the nation's capital, acquiring a bank, and establishing the **first stock exchange,** which met under a buttonwood tree on Wall Street (p. 67). Indeed, much of America's federal framework harks back to the centralizing fiscal policies of the first Secretary of the Treasury, New Yorker and Federalist **Alexander Hamilton.** Meanwhile, **The 1811 Commissioner's Plan** established Manhattan's rectilinear street grid with characteristic New York ambition—at the time, the island consisted primarily of marshes and open fields, and boasted fewer than 100,000 residents. Merchants built mansions on the new streets, along with tenements for the increasing numbers of immigrants from Eastern and Northern Europe.

GREASY PALMS: 1811-1900

Administration and services continued to lag behind irrepressible growth. By the early 19th century, New York was the largest US city, but pigs, dogs, and chickens continued to run freely. Fires and riots made streetlife precarious, while the foul water supply precipitated a cholera epidemic. The notorious corruption of **Tammany Hall** (in the original ConEd building in Battery Park City, p. 66), the center of city government, reached its peak in the 1850s under Democrat **"Boss" William Tweed,** who promised money and jobs to people, often immigrants, who agreed to vote for his candidates. Under Tweed's thumb, embezzlement and kickbacks were routine. He robbed the city of somewhere between 100 and 200 million dollars. When citizens complained, Tweed said defiantly, "Well, what are you going to do about it?" A *New York Times* exposé finally led to Tweed's arrest in 1875, and although perennial complainer George Templeton Strong cracked, "The New Yorker belongs to a community governed by lower and baser scum than any city in Western Christendom," some say that Tammany Hall during this time made great strides in city population growth and work reform under the pro-union and anti-aristocratic Democrats.

Either way, New Yorkers remained loyal to the city, often neglecting national concerns in favor of local interests. New York initially opposed the **Civil War,** as its desire to protect trade with the South outweighed abolitionist and constitutional principles. The attack on South Carolina's Fort Sumter rallied New York to the Northern side, but a class-biased conscription act in July of 1863 led to the infamous **New York City Draft Riots,** which cost over a thousand lives.

After the war, the city entered a half-century of prosperity, during which New York developed the elements of urban modernity that now distinguish it. Horace Greeley's **New York Tribune** became the first nationally-distributed paper. Home to the *Tribune* and its rivals, Nassau Street was dubbed **"Newspaper Row"** in the middle of the century (in Battery Park City, p. 66). The latter part of the 19th century also saw the competition between Joseph Pulitzer's *New York World* and William Randolph Hearst's *New York Journal,* which resorted to sensationalist reporting later called **"Yellow Journalism."**

New York characteristically led the vanguard of both the naught and the nice. The **Metropolitan Museum of Art** (p. 120) was founded in 1870, and **Bloomingdale's** (p. 148) opened its now-venerable doors in 1872. In 1883, the **Brooklyn Bridge** (p. 103), an engineering marvel, was completed; many considered it the world's most beautiful bridge. The project cost the lives of many immigrant laborers. The new transportation gateway allowed the incorporation of the **Outer Boroughs**—the Bronx (p. 32), Brooklyn (p. 28), Queens (p. 30), and Staten Island (p. 33)—into the City of New York in 1898. During this period of rapid change, **Teddy Roosevelt** headed the police department, reforming New York in time for the turn of the century. He sallied forth at night dressed in a cape, searching for policemen who were sleeping on the job or consorting with prostitutes. At the tail end of the century, **Frederick Law Olmsted** and **Calvin Vaux** created **Central Park** (p. 92) on 843 rolling acres, and the **Flatiron Building** (p. 80), the first skyscraper, was erected in 1902. With 2000 farms still in New York and a speed limit of nine miles per hour, the city began to spread out, both horizontally and vertically. "It'll be a great place if they ever finish it," O. Henry quipped.

THE "NEW METROPOLIS": 1900-1930

Despite entrepreneurial optimism among the powers-that-were, 70% of New York's population dwelled in substandard tenement housing in 1900; a turn-of-the-century war on slums was swept into a new stage of renewal. **Colonel George E. Waring**'s army of "White Wings" put "a man instead of a voter behind every broom," thus creating the double benefit of jobs and cleaner streets. New York's most famed photographer of the era, **Jacob Riis** (p. 110 to his park), elegized, "It was Colonel Waring's broom that first let light into the slum." The first thirty years of the century saw a Beaux-Arts construction boom, the building of the **Williamsburg Bridge** (p. 105)—then the longest suspension bridge in the world—and a brand new infrastructure. Perhaps the city's greatest development during this era was the opening of its world-renowned **subway** (p. 35) system.

New York's innovations reached such glamorous proportions that the city began to feature prominently in the young art form of cinema. Early films, with such apt titles as "The Cheat" (1915), portrayed the city as the "new" or "great" metropolis, emphasizing a booming business world that foreshadowed the **Roaring Twenties.**

During the 1920s, New York City revitalized still other media. After the 1917 **NAACP** protest—during which thousands of African-Americans marched down Fifth Avenue, crying out against lynchings and countless other denials of rights— the "New Negro" appeared. In the 1920s, the **Harlem Renaissance** (p. 56) reached full swing, its books and music announcing a changing world.

MID-CENTURY REFORM: 1930-1990

Bent on healing New York's social ills, **Fiorello LaGuardia,** the city's immensely popular mayor from 1933-45, said, "Nobody wants me but the people," as he reorganized the government and revitalized the city. LaGuardia's leadership engendered a fierce civic pride that saw New Yorkers through the **The Great Depression,** kicked off in 1929 when the over-inflated stock market of the **New York Stock Exchange** crashed. Post-World War II prosperity brought more immigrants and businesses to the city. In this era, **Robert Moses** became the most powerful official in New York. As chief of staff of the New York State Reconstruction Commission, this urban planner steamrolled over dissenting politicians and councils to create the physical landscape of New York as we now know it. He created 36 parks and a network of roads (parkways) to make them accessible to the public, added 12 bridges and tunnels, and built Lincoln Center (p. 95), Shea Stadium (p. 169), and numerous housing projects (see **Go Down Moses,** p. 230). But even as the world celebrated New York as the capital of the 20th century, cracks in the city's foundations became apparent. By the 1960s, crises in public transportation, education, and housing exacerbated racial tensions and fostered criminal activity.

John V. Lindsay ran for mayor in 1965 with the slogan, "He is fresh and everyone else is tired," but even his freshness wilted under the barrage of crime, racial problems, labor unrest, and drought. City officials raised taxes to provide more services, but higher taxes drove middle-class residents and corporations out of the city. As a series of recessions and budget crises swamped the government, critics deplored **Mayor Robert Wagner's** "dedicated inactivity." By 1975, the city was pleading with the federal government to rescue it from impending bankruptcy, but was rebuffed. *The Daily News* headline the next day read "Ford to New York: Drop Dead."

However, resilient NYC rebounded on an attitude of streetwise hope. The city's massive (if goofy) **"I Love New York" campaign** spread cheer via bumper stickers. Large manufacturing, which had gone south and west of New York, was supplanted by fresh money from high finance and infotech, the big growth industries fueled by President Ronald Reagan's Reagonomics. In the 1980s, **Wall Street** (p. 67) was hip again (or at least grotesquely profitable), and the upper middle class face of the city recovered some of its lost vitality. In poorer areas, meanwhile, discontent pervaded, manifesting itself in waves of crime and vandalism that scared off potential tourists. With a New Yorker's armor of curmudgeonly humor, **Ed Koch** defended his city's declining reputation, becoming America's most visible mayor. Koch appeared on Saturday Night Live, providing an endless stream of quotables, most notably his catchphrase, "How'm I doing?"

THE LAST DECADE: 1990-2001

The financial flurry of the 1980s faded into the gray recession of the early 1990s, aggravating class tensions. Racial conflict, in particular, reached an all-time high in the late 80s and early 90s, when bigoted beatings erupted in the boroughs. A nationally publicized riot in **Crown Heights, Brooklyn** (p. 28) was sparked by a hit-and-run incident, in which an Orthodox Jewish man killed a young West Indian boy. **David Dinkins,** the city's first black mayor, elected in 1989 on a democratic platform that glorified New York's "Gorgeous Mosaic," fought hard to encourage unity between the city's ethnic groups and dismantle bureaucratic corruption. Dinkins's term saw the abolition of the **Board of Estimate** system of municipal government, under which each borough's president had one vote. (This system was blatantly unfair, as borough populations differ vastly.) An expanded 35-member City Council, in which each borough can initiate zoning, propose legislation, and deal with contractors independently, replaced the old system.

Mounting fiscal crises and a persistent crime rate, however, led to Dinkins's defeat at the hands of **Rudy Guiliani** in the 1993 mayoral election. The election was strongly divided along racial lines. Many moderate whites who had supported Dinkins in 1989 defected to the side of the Republican Guiliani, who addressed a number of intertwining fears with a campaign that could be summed up in two words: Safety First. Some New Yorkers adore Mayor Guiliani for cracking down on crime and cleaning up formerly murky areas, such as Times Square. Critics believe the Mayor cares only about beautifying tourist-heavy Manhattan, at the expense of "the Boroughs" and their large minority populations. Some say his budget cuts have damaged **The New York City Board of Education,** formerly headed by the more charismatic of the two Rudies, **Rudy Crew,** until Guiliani ousted him in December 1999. Now NYC is desperately seeking its 12th Chancellor in the last 20 years. Still others assert that Guiliani's war on crime has translated into an overzealous police force. Accusations of police brutality reached a fever pitch in 1997-98, when the story of **Abner Louima** broke, revealing how Officer Volpe, aided by colleagues, sexually assaulted an innocent Haitian man with a toilet plunger. Federal prosecutors concluded a 20-month investigation of the New York City Police Department's indulgent attitude toward the violence of its officers with Volpe's plea of guilty in June 1999. But the February 1999 murder of **Amadou Diallo** by four officers who claimed he fit the description of a persued serial rapist—firing 41 times in five seconds while Diallo stood unarmed in his apartment building's vestibule—sparked renewed public protest. The policemen were indicted two months later for second-degree murder, but New Yorkers are still up in arms, this time aiming at Guiliani, his immoderate police strategies, and his "no-apologies" stance.

Priding himself on never taking a vacation and resting only five hours a night, tenacious Rudy Guiliani pursues his anti-crime campaign and Quality of Life Initiative with increasing vigor. No doubt he hoped his hard-line attitude would earn voters' confidence in his 2000 Senate campaign against US First Lady, democrat **Hillary Rodham Clinton,** but cancer finally overtook him, forcing him to drop out of the race.

ETHNIC NEW YORK

IMMIGRANTS

New Yorkers have always claimed a wide range of national origins. A Jesuit missionary described one lively New Amsterdam fort in which artisans, soldiers, trappers, sailors, and slaves all mingled together, speaking no fewer than 18 languages. The slave-owning Dutch had a sizeable African population with them, and the first black settlement began in today's SoHo in 1644. Germans and Irish came over in droves between 1840 and 1860; in 1855, European-born immigrants constituted nearly half of New York's population.

After the Civil War, a massive wave of immigration began, cresting around the turn of the century. Europeans left famine, religious persecution, and political unrest in their native lands for the promise of America. Beginning in 1890, Italians, Lithuanians, Russians, Poles, and Greeks joined German and Irish immigrants *en masse*.

European immigrants worked long hours in detestable and unsafe conditions for meager wages; only the **Triangle Shirtwaist Fire** of 1911, which killed 145 female factory workers, brought about enough public protest to force stricter regulations on working conditions (see **Neighborhoods**, p.151). Meanwhile, Tammany Hall-based "ward bosses" took the confused new arrivals under their wing, helping them find jobs and housing and providing them with funds in case of illness or accident—in exchange for votes. The US Congress restricted immigration in the 1920s, and the 1929 Great Depression brought the influx to a halt. The encroaching terrors in Europe in the late 1930s, however, brought new waves of immigrants, particularly Jews seeking escape from Hitler's persecution.

HARLEM

An influx of rural Southern blacks during and after World War I led to the creation of **Harlem.** In the early 20th century, real estate mavericks built hundreds of Harlem tenements in the hope of renting to whites once the subway arrived; the plan backfired as whites bypassed Harlem and moved farther uptown. Working at a failing real estate office, black janitor **Philip Payton** realized the business African-Americans would bring and transformed himself into the entrepreneur who created modern Harlem by convincing renters to open their buildings to blacks. The cultural and literary **Harlem Renaissance** of the 1920s stands as testament to the vitality and creativity that the new settlement brought. Nevertheless, people of color were charged more than their white counterparts for the unhealthy tenement rooms, and the **Cotton Club,** Harlem's famous jazz nightclub, didn't even allow blacks inside, unless they were performing (see **Neighborhoods**, p.195).

THE MODERN MELTING POT

Today the melting pot simmers with over seven million people speaking over 80 languages. New York boasts more Italians than Rome, more Irish than Dublin, and more Jews than Jerusalem. The cultural diversity resulting from immigration has made whites a minority in the city. In the early 1990s, immigration was 32% higher than it was in the 1980s, with the top sources being the Dominican Republic, the former Soviet Union, China, Jamaica, and Guyana. While immigration policies were criticized nationwide, Mayor Guiliani staunchly defended immigrants, calling them the lifeblood of New York.

But this saturation of cultures has not led to racial harmony. Ethnic divisions cause much of the city's strife, dating as far back as the 17th century. In the last decades, ethnic conflict has led to, and been the result of, extreme segregation and distrust across communities. The 1960s saw riots in Harlem, Bedford-Stuyvesant, and the South Bronx, as angry African-Americans railed against governmental and police injustices. In the late 1980s, racially related deaths in Bensonhurst and Crown Heights in Brooklyn, and Howard Beach in Queens, demonstrated the lethal potential of ethnic tensions.

Despite these inherent conflicts, New York's lasting cultural ferment reflects how the city symbolizes opportunity to thousands of immigrants. And, while it takes years or lifetimes to assimilate into other cities, newcomers become New Yorkers almost instantly.

NEIGHBORHOODS

Harlem, Chinatown, Little Italy, and the Jewish Lower East Side spring to mind as the most reputed ethnic enclaves of New York. However, lesser-known ethnic communities thrive throughout the five boroughs. In Queens, Astoria (especially along Ditmars and 23rd Ave., p. 31) hosts a large **Greek** community; at Flushing's Main St. (p. 31), you could be stepping into **Korea; Israeli** eateries pepper Queens Blvd. in Forest Hills (p. 31); and Jackson Heights (p. 31) bustles with large **Indian** and **South American** populations. In Brooklyn, an **Arab** community centers around Atlantic Ave. in Brooklyn Heights (p. 28); **West Indians** and **Hassidim** rub elbows in Crown Heights (p. 28); Brighton Beach (p. 28), dubbed "Little Odessa," boasts a lively **Russian** enclave; and Bensonhurst (p. 28) presents a more vivid portrait of **Italian-American** life than does Manhattan's Little Italy. In the Bronx, Belmont (p. 32) also hosts an **Italian** community; the South Bronx (p. 32), the birthplace of hip-hop, is home to many **African-Americans** and **Latinos.**

ARCHITECTURE

A hundred times have I thought "New York is a catastrophe" and fifty times: "It is a beautiful catastrophe."
—Le Corbusier, architect

Capricious New York has always warmed to the latest trends in architecture, hastily demolishing old buildings to make way for their stylistic successors. In the 19th century, the surging rhythm of endless destruction and renewal seemed to attest to the city's vigor and enthusiasm. Walt Whitman praised New York's "pull-down-and-build-over-again spirit," and *The Daily Mirror* was an isolated voice when, in 1831, it criticized the city's "irreverence for antiquity."

EARLY YEARS AND EUROPEAN INFLUENCE

Traces of Colonial New York are hard to find. The **original Dutch settlement** consisted mostly of traditional homes with gables and stoops. One example from 1699, the restored **Vechte-Cortelyou House,** stands near Fifth Avenue and 3rd St. in Brooklyn. The British, however, built over most of these Dutch structures with imposing, Greek-influenced, **Federal-style** buildings like **St. Paul's Church** (p. 69) on Broadway.

Even after the British had been forced out, their architectural tastes lingered, influencing the townhouses built by their prosperous colonists. Through the early 19th century, American architects continued to incorporate such Federal details as dormer windows, stoops, doors with columns, and fan lights. Federal houses still line Charlton St., Vandam St., and the South St. Seaport area (p. 70). The old **City Hall,** built by D.C. mastermind Pierre L'Enfant in 1802, employs Federal detailing on a public building (p. 68).

The **Greek Revival** of the 1820s and 30s added porticoes and iron laurel wreaths to New York's streets. Greek Revival prevails on **Washington Square North,** Lafayette St., and W. 20th St. (p. 74). Gray granite **St. Peter's,** built in 1838 with high, vaulted ceilings pointing to the heavens, was the first **Gothic Revival** church in America (p. 82).

While learning from the old country and the classical tradition, Americans did manage to introduce some architectural innovations. Beginning in the 1850s, thousands of brownstones made from cheap stone quarried in New Jersey sprang up all over New York. Next to skyscrapers, the **brownstone townhouse** may be New York's most characteristic structure. Although beyond most people's means today, the houses were once middle-class residences—the rich lived in block-long mansions on Fifth Avenue, while apartments were for the poor. Brownstones sport an essential element of a New Yorker's lifestyle—the raised **stoop.** An innovation brought over by the Dutch in the 17th century to elevate the best rooms in the house above street-level, the stoop today has its own urban culture of "stoop ball," checker-playing, and intense neighbor-watching.

In 1884, New York's architectural hierarchy was disrupted with the building of luxurious apartment houses like the **Dakota** (later John Lennon's home, see p. 97) and the **Ansonia** (p. 97), both on the Upper West Side.

In the 1890s, American architects studying abroad brought the **Beaux-Arts** style from France and captivated the nation. Beaux-Arts, a blend of Classical detail and lavish decoration, stamped itself on structures built through the 1930s. Memorable examples are the **US Customs House** (p. 67) and the **New York Public Library** (p. 86).

THE SKYSCRAPER: AN AMERICAN AESTHETIC

Flatiron Building

Made possible by combining new technologies—the elevator and the steel frame—skyscrapers allowed the city to explode upward and assuaged the growing pains engendered by New York's spectaclar commercial and human growth. The first skyscraper, the **Flatiron Building**, sprouted up on 23rd Street in 1902 (p. 80). Tall buildings like it proved a useful idea in a city forever short on space, and other monoliths soon appeared.

In 1913, Cass Gilbert gilded the 55-story **Woolworth Building** with Gothic flourishes, piling on antique "W"s and dubbing it "Cathedral of Commerce" (p. 68). The **Empire State Building** (p. 82) and the **Chrysler Building** (p. 87), fashioned from stone and steel and built like rockets, stand testimony to America's romance with science and space.

Just 14 years after the first skyscraper came the nation's first zoning resolution, which restricted the height and bulk of the dizzying buildings. Knowledge of the changes in the zoning codes throughout the decades is the key to understanding and dating the city's architectural quirks. Does the building have a stepped, pyramidal roof? Look like a wedding cake? Zoning restrictions of the late 1940s stipulated that tall buildings had to be set back at the summit. New York's first curtain of pure glass was the 1950 **United Nations Secretariat Building**, a nightmare to air-condition (p. 87). Then, in 1958, Ludwig Mies Van der Rohe and Philip Johnson created the **Seagram Building**, a glass tower set behind a plaza on Park Avenue. Crowds soon gathered to mingle, sunbathe, and picnic, much to the surprise of planners and builders. A delighted planning commission began offering financial incentives to every builder who offset a highrise with public open space. Over the next decade, many architects stuck empty plazas next to their towering office complexes. Some of them looked a little too empty to the picky planning commission, which changed the rules in 1975 to stipulate that every plaza should provide public seating. By the late 70s, plazas moved indoors, when high-tech atriums with gurgling fountains and pricey cafes began to flourish.

Algonquin Hotel

The leaner skyscrapers date from the early 1980s, when shrewd developers realized they could get office space, bypass zoning regulations, *and* receive a bonus from the commission if they hoisted up "sliver" buildings. Composed largely of elevators and stairs, the disturbingly anorexic newcomers provoked city-wide grumbles. Those tired of living in the shadow

Woolworth Building

HIP-HOP (R)EVOLU-TION

In 1973, Bronx DJ Kool Herc began prolonging songs' funky drum "break" sections by using two turntables and two copies of the same record, switching to the start of the second copy when the first one ended and then doubling back. Dancers took up the rhythm's challenge, by 1975 evolving break-dancing in response to similar turntable manipulations by Afrika Bambaataa, Grandmaster Flash, Kool, and other denizens of the 174th St. area by the Bronx River. Thus, the Bronx birthed the art of DJing, an acrobatic dance style, and a musical genre known as hip-hop/rap that would shape the sound of the new millennium. For the phatty-phat 411, hit Davey D's exhaustive web page at www.daveyd.com

of shafts altered zoning policy in 1983 so that structural planning would encourage more room for air and sun.

Builders have finally recognized the overcrowding problem in East Midtown and expanded their horizons somewhat. New residential complexes have risen on the Upper East Side above 95th St., while Donald Trump, the city's most notorious real-estate guru, recently erected the second of his muscular and gaudy towers in Columbus Circle near the Upper West Side; some developers have even ventured into the outer boroughs. The planning commission that oversees the beautiful catastrophe now takes overcrowding and environmental issues into account when making decisions.

Throughout this continual modernization, concern has arisen that New York's history might be quickly disappearing. Mounting public concern climaxed when developers destroyed gracious **Penn Station** in 1965; the **Landmarks Preservation Commission** was created in response. Since then, the LPC has successfully claimed and protected 21,000 individual sites as "landmarks." However, developers seek loopholes and air-rights (the rights to scrape a specific plot of sky) to expand the skyline.

Closer to the ground, efforts in the past few years to revitalize old theaters in **Times Square** and to rid the area of its once pornographic motif have aroused anger in those who resent the "Disney-fication" of this gritty area and the subsequent hike in local rents.

NEW YORK IN MUSIC

I lay puzzle as I backtrack to earlier times
Nothing's equivalent, to the New York state of mind
—Nas, "N.Y. State of Mind"

Between the extremes of Nas' rap lyrics and Frank Sinatra's crooning plea that "It's Up to You New York," lies a world of quick cadence, lyrical meandering, and pleasing dissonance all of that owe their inspiration to New York City. **Leonard Bernstein** captured the bleeding heart of the city in his musicals *West Side Story*, while **George Gershwin** used the rhythms of his train rolling into New York for the musical skeleton of his *Rhapsody in Blue*.

From sweet vibrations to killer beats, New York is *the* place to catch new music. Nearly every performer who comes to the States plays here, and thousands of local bands and DJs compete to make a statement and win an audience. Venues range from stadiums to concert halls to back-alley sound-systems. Every day of the year, clubs, bars, and smaller venues serve up sounds from open-mic folk singers to "eclectronic" DJ recombination. Annual festivals abound, such as summertime's **Next Wave Festival** that takes over the Brooklyn Academy of Music with spectacular, offbeat happenings, crackpot fusions of classical music, theater, and performance art. Whatever your inclination, New York's expansive musical scene should be able to satisfy it. (See **Arts and Entertainment,** p. 161 to p. 169.)

JAZZ

From the beginning, Jazz has expressed the sound of the big city. The Big Band sound thrived here in the 1920s and 30s, when Duke Ellington set the trend in clubs around the city. **Minton's Playhouse** in Harlem was home to **Thelonious Monk** and one of the birthplaces of bebop, a highly sophisticated jazz variant. Miles Davis, Charlie Parker, Dizzy Gillespie, Max Roach, Tommy Potter, Bud Powell, and many others contributed to the New York sound of the late 1940s and 1950s, when beatniks, hepcats, and poor old souls filled 52nd St. clubs. Today, at the Fez Cafe, one can tap into the legacy of this revolutionary era with the **Mingus Big Band,** dedicated to playing the works of the virtuoso bassist and band-leader of the 1940s, Charles Mingus. Free-jazz pioneer Cecil Taylor and spaceman Sun Ra set up shop in NYC during the 1960s and 70s. Today, skilled experimentalists like John Zorn and James Blood Ulmer destroy musical conventions at clubs like the **Knitting Factory.**

PUNK AND POST-PUNK

True to the grit of city living, the New York rock sound has always had a harder edge than its West Coast or Southern counterparts. The **Velvet Underground,** Andy Warhol's favorite band and a seminal 1960s rock group, combined jangling guitars with disconcerting lyrics on sex, drugs, and violence that deeply influenced the next generation of bands. In 1976, ambitious avant-garde poets and sometime musicians took over the campy glam-rock scene in downtown barroom clubs like **CBGB's** and Max's Kansas City. Bands and performers like the Ramones, Patti Smith, Blondie, and the Talking Heads brought venom, wit, and a calculated stupidity to the emerging **punk** scene. Ever since, New York has convulsed with musical shocks. In the 1980s, angry kids imported **straight-edge** from Washington, D.C.: a bevy of fast-rocking, non-drinking, non-smoking bands packed Sunday all-ages shows at CBGB's. In the 1980s and early 1990s the **post-punk** scene crystallized around bands such as Sonic Youth and Pavement. Obscure vinyl can be found in the city's many used record stores; prices can be absurd, but the selection surpasses that of any other North American city (see **Shopping,** p. 137). As the millennium approaches, **post-rock** proliferates. Locals Bowery Electric and Ui incorporate drum machines and dub techniques in efforts to keep rock radical, while native Brooklynites and indie-rockers extraordinaire, Lady Bug Transistor, make effete rock sexy with flutes, organs, and trumpets.

STREET POETS

Rap and **hip-hop** also began on New York's streets, and the list of NYC artists reads like a History of Urban Music, including such heavyweight emcees as KRS-1, Chuck D, LL Cool J, Run-DMC, EPMD, and Queen Latifah (who leapt across the river from Jersey). Bronx DJs **Grandmaster Flash** and **Afrika Bambaataa** laid the foundations in the late 70s and early 80s with records rooted deeply in electronic processing, scratching, and sampling. In 1979, the **Sugarhill Gang** released *Rapper's Delight*, widely considered the first true rap record.

Predominant in the East Coast hip-hop hierarchy are the **Native Tongues,** a loose collection of New York (OK—some are Long Islanders) acts which includes A Tribe Called Quest, De La Soul, and Black Sheep. Straight outta Staten Island came the ol' dirty Wu-tang Clan, whose dense, brooding beats and clever use of kung-fu samples have made names for several of its coterie, including **Method Man** and the **GZA.** Pampered young funsters like the Beastie Boys and Luscious Jackson transcended racial lines to broaden the national appeal of the hip-hop genre, incorporating jazz loops, hardcore thrash, and funk samples into their stylistic repertoire. Other recent NYC area acts to climb the charts include Nas, Mobb Deep, and the Fugees (including Wyclef Jean and 1999 Grammy winner, **Lauryn Hill,** who also have powerful solo personas). And, although too commercial, Puff Daddy's protégé, Mase, put Harlem back on the map with his 1998 release, "Harlem World," before retiring to devote himself to his new-found commitment to Christianity.

For a clearer glimpse of the hip-hop scene in New York (and across the country) pick up a copy of New York-based *The Source*, the genre's premier publication, or check out Davey D's Hip Hop Corner on the web (www.daveyd.com). In Brooklyn, the **Crooklyn Dub Consortium** eschews commercial success to create otherworldly dubhop where crooked beats fuse with third world instrumentation and Jamaican dub styles. Williamsburg record label and guerrilla think tank **Wordsound** acts as the Consortium's subterranean base. As the litany of the city's hip-hop greats reveals, Gotham's soundtrack is laid to a fat beat. At the same time, the beat itself echoes New Yorkers' feet pounding pavement.

THE ELECTRONIC WAVE

Although the Big Apple may have pioneered the hip-hop sound, it lags a bit behind Europe on the **techno** frontier. Nevertheless, New York City serves as ground zero for the east coast stage of the **rave** revolution that took hold of European and L.A. club culture. Deeelite and Moby first got the city grooving where **disco** left off with their toe-tapping amalgamation of ambient and techno-funk, and now home-grown superstar DJs like Junior Vasquez, Frankie Bones, and DB keep the crowds dancing to the newest **house, trance, jungle,** and **trip-hop.** Downtown's kitsch-hungry partygoers now groove to "loungecore," a sexy, shmaltzy revival of 1970s soft porn soundtracks and exotica records that goes great with polyester.

The newest aural concoction New York has to offer is **illbient,** a mix attitude that values sonic experiments over smooth dance mixes. At an illbient happening you might hear a hardcore rock single spliced with a minimalist piano piece, or a DJ cutup of two identical Sherlock Holmes records which fades into Moroccan *gnawa* music. Illbient sessions often incorporate video, performance art, and dance in a commitment to "cultural alchemy." Illbient resonates with the density of cultures that only New York City can provide, and can be heard at **SoundLab** (☎ 212-726-1724). Illbient performers to watch out for include Lloop, DJ Olive, the Bedouin, **/rupture,** We, Sub Dub, Byzar, and media soluble DJ Spooky.

LITERARY NEW YORK

Since **William Bradford** was appointed America's first public printer in 1698 and went on to found the country's first newspaper, the *New York Gazette*, New York City has been the literary capital of the Americas. The epicenter of the city's literary vanguard changed with each successive movement, but the Big Apple has never lacked prolific pens.

Midtown contains the legendary **Algonquin Hotel,** 59 W. 44th St. (p. 89). In 1919 the wits of the **Round Table**—writers like Robert Benchley, Dorothy Parker, Alexander Wollcott, and Edna Ferber—adopted this hotel for their famous weekly lunch meetings, making the Algonquin the site of inspiration for much of the *New Yorker* magazine.

The area surrounding Columbia University witnessed one of the most vibrant and important moments in American literary history, the **Harlem Renaissance,** which took place in the 1920s. Novels like George Schuyler's *Black No More* and Claude McKay's *Home to Harlem* are tales of the exoticized underworld of speakeasies and nightclubs that white folks found so fascinating. **Zora Neale Hurston,** then a Columbia anthropology student, helped create the buzz up in Harlem with her novel, *Their Eyes Were Watching God.* Poet **Langston Hughes** and his circle founded radical journals that proposed the idea of a "New Negro." The next generation of black talent, including **Ralph Ellison** and **James Baldwin,** expanded the scope of African-American literature, dealing with issues of whiteness and idea of America. Ellison's *Invisible Man* offers an epic excursion into the complexities of black and white life in Manhattan, while Baldwin's work, such as *Go Tell It On The Mountain*, wields a grittier edge.

Columbia University continued to be the intellectual magnet of the Upper West Side. The roving Beat crowd swamped the area in the late 1940s when **Allen Ginsberg** and **Jack Kerouac** studied at the college. During the controversial late 60s, Brooklyn resident Paul Auster also honed his writing chops there. **Public School #6**, also on the Upper West Side, boasts such prestigious alums as *Catcher in the Rye* author, **J.D. Salinger.**

Later in the 20th century, the **East Village** became America's literary headquarters when the nomadic Kerouac and Ginsberg moved in next to neighbors Amiri Baraka **(Le Roi Jones)** and **W.H. Auden** (who spent many years at 77 St. Mark's Place, basement entrance).

The **Gotham Book Mart,** 41 W. 47th St., established in 1920, has long been one of New York's most important literary digs. The store, famous for its second-story readings, has hosted some of the biggest writers of the century and once attracted all of literary New York. During the years when **Ulysses** was banned in the US, those in the know came to Gotham to buy imported copies of Joyce's magnum opus under the counter. Check out the memorabilia and old photographs that document the bookstore's history (p. 147).

Farther downtown, many a writer whiled away his or her dying days in relative obscurity at the **Chelsea Hotel,** on 23rd St. between Seventh and Eighth Ave (p. 82). Among the surviving tenants are **Arthur Miller** and **Vladimir Nabokov.**

Some **must-reads** involving the city of dreams:

The Age of Innocence and **The House of Mirth,** Edith Wharton. Two tales of turn-of-the-century romance and woe among the New York gentry.

Another Country, James Baldwin. Interracial lovers and same-sex couples uncover beauty and tremendous pain trying to relate to one another in 60s Manhattan.

A Tree Grows In Brooklyn, Betty Smith. An Irish woman's coming-of-age in early 20th-century Brooklyn. Also a 1945 film by Elia Kazan.

The Bonfire of the Vanities, Tom Wolfe. A Wall Street financier takes a wrong turn off the TriBoro Bridge. Hijinks ensue. For your own sake, miss the movie.

Bright Lights, Big City, Jay MacInerney. 1980s New York. A columnist for the *New Yorker* divides his time between clubs and cocaine. Michael J. Fox starred in the film. Also see *Story of My Life*, another tale of Manhattan self-indulgence.

The Catcher in the Rye, J.D. Salinger. A now-classic fable of alienated youth. Prep-schooler Holden Caulfield visits the city and falls from innocence.

Eloise, Kay Thompson. A classic children's book. Young Eloise lives in the Plaza Hotel, wreaking havoc on every elegant floor and combing her hair with a fork.

The Great Gatsby, F. Scott Fitzgerald. An incisive commentary on the American Dream, vis-à-vis the rise and fall of would-be New Yorker Jay Gatsby.

Jazz, Toni Morrison. This Nobel prize-winning novel is written in jazz form: sensual, cerebral, and experimental. It examines love, murder, and the magical potency of the city in 1920s Harlem.

New York Trilogy, Paul Auster. Three playfully literary short stories set in Brooklyn Heights and Manhattan, riff on the conventions of detective fiction.

LIGHTS, CAMERA, NEW YORK!

Always a ham, the Big Apple has shown off its pretty face on the silver screen since the birth of the genre. It's not unusual, on your mid-morning stroll down Fifth Avenue, to encounter production assistants and camera crews in mirrored sunglasses waving their hands and shouting in California-ese. The city encourages film production by granting free permits to those filmmakers who want to shoot on location; there is even a special police task force—the New York Police Movie and Television Unit—to assist with traffic re-routing and scenes involving guns or uniformed police officers. As a testament to how seriously this city takes its film industry, Mayor Guiliani proclaimed May 18, 1998 "Godzilla Day" in honor of the opening of the gargantuan flick that was shot in New York. "The industry," in turn, has rewarded Gotham well; in 1997, 213 films were shot in New York with anywhere between 60 to 90 productions on location in a given day.

If your stay in New York inspires you to create your very own urban movie cityscape, contact **The Mayor's Office of Film, Theater, and Broadcasting**, 1697 Broadway #602 (489-6710; www.ci.nyc.ny.us/html/filmcom). Their website provides a daily schedule of the films being shot in the city. If you want to catch a flick on screen instead, call 777-FILM for movie listings—you can even order tickets. However, you might want to VCR it, as most theaters here have hiked their prices to a whopping $9.50.

Here is a smattering of quintessential New York films:

Annie Hall (1977). Woody Allen and Diane Keaton play tennis, flirt, and squabble in this funny, romantic ode to the city, crystallizing Allen's image as a neurotic Upper West Side intellectual.

Basquiat (1996). Chronicles the tragic rise to fame of Gotham street artist Jean-Michele Basquiat, protege of an aging Andy Warhol (played with great nuance by David Bowie).

Breakfast at Tiffany's (1961). Audrey Hepburn frolics through Upper East Side society.

Brighton Beach Memoirs (1986). Neil Simon's—imagine it—semi-autobiographical comedy about growing up Jewish in Brooklyn with baseball and sex on the brain.

A Bronx Tale (1993). Robert DeNiro's directing debut: a tale of a boy torn between his Pop and the temptations of mob life. Shot in Brooklyn and Queens.

Coming to America (1988). Eddie Murphy emerges from his utopian jungle community in search of independence in Queens.

The Daytrippers (1997). A clan of Long Islanders trek into the Big City to confront a philandering husband. Or is he?

Desperately Seeking Susan (1985). A bored housewife finds excitement when she assumes the identity of that hippest of East Village hipsters, Madonna.

Do the Right Thing (1989). Spike Lee's explosive look at one very hot day in the life of Brooklyn's Bed-Stuy. Colorful, stylized cinematography. Racial tensions at the boiling point.

Empire (1968). Master icon-manipulator Andy Warhol brings you eight hours of the Empire State Building, shot from dawn to dusk on a stationary camera.

The Fisher King (1991). Shock-jock Jeff Bridges and homeless dude Robin Williams seek redemption in the fantastical dimension of New York.

The French Connection (1971). An all-time great chase scene: Gene Hackman vs. the B train.

Ghostbusters (1984). Bill Murray and Dan Ackroyd try to rid the city (and Sigourney Weaver) of ghosts. Note the New York Public Library, among other landmarks.

The Godfather I, II, and III (1972-1990). Coppola's searing study of one immigrant family and the price of the American Dream. Based on a bestseller by Mario Puzo.

Goodfellas (1990). Scorsese's look at true-life gangster Henry Hill. Great location shots in the city, especially the Bamboo Lounge in Canarsie.

Hair (1979). The love-child musical brought to the screen, complete with hippies tripping in Sheep Meadow in Central Park. Nell Carter sings a solo.

Kids (1995). Larry Clark's study of some baaaaaad NY kids. Not for the queasy.

King Kong (1933). Single giant ape seeks female atop symbol of phallic power.

Little Odessa (1995). Tim Roth in a thriller about the emerging Russian-American mafia in Brooklyn's Brighton Beach. From the book by Joseph Koenig.

Manhattan (1979). Woody Allen's hysterically funny love note to New York. Glimmering skyline, to the tune of Gershwin's *Rhapsody in Blue*.

Mean Streets (1973). Harvey Keitel and Robert DeNiro cruise around Little Italy looking for trouble. This film put Scorsese on the map.

Men In Black (1997). Aliens among us? Intergalactic roaches, baby extraterrestrials? Will Smith and Tommy Lee Jones save the world at the Unisphere in Queens?

Metropolitan (1990). Whit Stillman chronicles the dying Park Avenue debutante scene: a tale of east (side) meets west (side), conversation, and cocktails.

Midnight Cowboy (1969). Jon Voight as a would-be hustler, and Dustin Hoffman as street rodent Ratso Rizzo, star in this devastating look at the seedy side of NY.

Moonstruck (1987). Cher falls in love with baker Nicholas Cage in this romantic comedy set in Carroll Gardens. Watch for the scene in Lincoln Center.

Newsies (1992). A Disney musical chronicling the 1899 newspaper boys' strike against Pulitzer and Hearst. A teenyboppers dream.

New York Stories (1989). Martin Scorsese, Francis Ford Coppola, and Woody Allen grind their cinematic axes on the Big Apple, to varying success.

On the Town (1949). Start spreading the news—Gene Kelly and Frank Sinatra are sailors with time and money to burn in New York City.

Saturday Night Fever (1977). John Travolta shakes his polyester-clad booty.

Serpico (1973). Al Pacino fights the power in this true tale of NYPD corruption.

The Seven-Year Itch (1955). Marilyn Monroe and subway grates—perfect together.

Taxi Driver (1976). DeNiro is Travis Bickle, a taxi driver with issues. Don't look him in the eye...and tip him well.

West Side Story (1961). Romeo and Juliet retold à la fire escape.

When Harry Met Sally (1989). Meg Ryan and Billy Crystal continually emote about their foibles against a New York backdrop. The ultimate date movie.

Sights

Yikes! Where to begin? You'll get a crick in your neck if you keep looking up at the skyscrapers without the proper guidance. An idea hits you—just pull out that friend of friends, *Let's Go: NYC!* Ah, here it is. Hmm... You could go on a tour, maybe on a boat, a double-decker bus, or even on foot (See **Tours**, p. 7). But look here—you could also walk around yourself, without those other embarrassing tourists decked out in their Hawaiian-print shirts, camcorders, and oh-so-last-decade haircuts. Just follow our sights writeups, listed by neighborhood, perfect for a relaxed but informed stroll through the Big City. Shed your insecurities, get into your walking shoes (the strappy python ones, please, this is New York, after all), swing your Armani jacket over your shoulder, and get to know everything, from the packed and famous to the quiet and tucked away.

MANHATTAN

THE STATUE OF LIBERTY

Give me your tired, your poor,
Your huddled masses yearning to breathe free,
The wretched refuse of your teeming shore.
Send these, the homeless, the tempest-tossed to me.
I lift my lamp beside the golden door!
—Emma Lazarus

🖪 *Contact: 363-3200; www.nps.gov/stli. Constantly updated **video snapshot** of Miss Liberty: www.sccorp.com/cam/. **Ferries** leave for Liberty Island from the piers at Battery Park, 9:00am-3:45am every 30min. weekdays, 8:30am-4:10am every 20min. Sa-Su; call for winter hours and frequency. Visi-*

Yankee Stadium in the Bronx. Where the best baseball team in the world continues to represent for the best city in the world (p. 115).

Cathedral of St. John the Divine. Europe may have the oldest cathedral, but NYC made sure it had the biggest. Thankfully, this massive structure is also fantastically beautiful (p. 99).

Columbia University. One of the Ivy League and a festering nest of New England architecture, you'll forget you're in NYC when you walk through the gates and into this cobblestoned incubator for hatching CEOs (p. 98).

The Cloisters. This original medieval structure was brought overseas in its complete form and placed on divine grounds just for you (p. 126).

Central Park. A huge garden paradise in the middle of all the bustle of NYC? You have to see it to believe it (p. 92).

Museum Mile. Don't know which museum you want to visit? Hit most of the big ones in NYC with a walk down Fifth Ave. With the **Metropolitan Museum of Art** and Wright's **Guggenheim,** among many others, you will not be disappointed (p. 26).

American Museum of Natural History. This museum is so fun and interesting, you won't even realize you're learning. Hurry up, a 90-ft. whale and brand-new planetarium await you (p. 121).

Lincoln Center. Dress up and make like the cultured elite as you promenade through this sprawling arts complex; go at night, when the buildings and fountain glitter with lights (p. 95).

Times Square. Forget Hollywood; this is **Broadway,** baby. The epitome of action, excitement, and neon. Cross your fingers and pray that they extend the longest-running show in Broadway history (*Cats* at the Winter Garden Theater), so that you can still see it in 2001 (p. 85).

Rockefeller Center. Profit from the rober baron's fortune; see Prometheus bring the mortals fire, ice skate outdoors, and see the Rockettes kick at this complex (p. 86).

Flushing Meadows-Corona Park in Queens. Site of two World Fairs, the relics are amazing even in their deterioration (p. 109).

Tiffany & Co. Gawk and gaze at the glittering baubles in this **Fifth Avenue** museum of glamour; putting on one of their necklaces will magically turn you into Audrey, we promise (p. 149).

St. Patrick's Cathedral. You'll recognize the largest Catholic cathedral in the US from a billion postcards—it's even better in 3D (p. 89).

United Nations. Well, technically, this isn't NYC; it's independent from city jurisdiction. All the more reason to go and mail yourself an internationally-stamped letter (p. 87).

Waldorf-Astoria Hotel. On elegant **Park Avenue,** this gorgeous hotel is a vestige of old upper crust NYC in all its gilded, luxurious splendor (p. 88).

Grand Central Terminal. Recently renovated, this tremendous terminal is back to its original

QUEENS

Roosevelt Island

QUEENSBORO BRIDGE

QUEENS-MIDTOWN TUN.

FDR

1st Ave.

E. 57th St.

3rd Ave.

E. 34th St.

Park Ave.

E. 42nd St.

5th Ave.

Broadway

6th Ave.

7th Ave.

E. 23rd St.

W. 23rd St.

8th Ave.

9th Ave.

10th Ave.

W. 57th St.

W. 42nd St.

12th Ave.

W. 34th St.

(West

Amsterdam Ave.

11th Ave.

Broadway

W. 72nd St.

W. 86th St.

W. 96th St.

Columbus Ave.

Central Park West

Central Pk. S.

Central Pk. N.

CENTRAL PARK

5th Ave.

Madison Ave.

Lexington Ave.

2nd Ave.

E. 86th St.

E. 96th St.

E. 110th St.

E. 72nd St.

West End Ave.

Riverside Dr.

Cathedral Pkwy.

Henry Hudson Parkway

Chrysler Building. Designed after the front of the car it's named for, this is a staple of the NYC skyline (p. 87).

NY Public Library. The Main Branch, backed by beautiful **Bryant Park**, and guarded by a pair of great lions, is an old-school library, with marble staircases and immense rooms lined by floors of books and filled with long dark-wood tables and green-shaded lamps (p. 86).

Empire State Building. Smack in the middle of Manhattan, you can't miss this monument to our technological achievement and one of the most recognizable buildings in the world (p. 82).

Macy's in Herald Square. Until the last few years the biggest store in the world, come to buy your very own exorbitantly-priced skirt or bag (p. 84); or elbow your way through the crowds of Herald Sq. to the cheap-o stores of 34th St. and Eighth Ave. and (the cheapest option) the fabric vendors of the neighboring **Garment District** (p. 85).

Washington Square Park. The epicenter of The Village, filled with NY cool kids and drug dealers, surrounded by **New York University,** and in one of the hippest areas of the city (p. 74).

Chinatown. Bustling with activity, this is an ethnic enclave (p. 19). Buy asian imports at their real prices, designer (sort of) duds not at their real prices, and eat eat eat.

Brooklyn Bridge. It's so cliché, but even locals make it a practice to walk/jog/skate/bike across this suspended masterpiece—it's beautiful (p. 103).

New York Stock Exchange. Where the world's markets try to make it big, under the long shadow of their Financial District neighbors, the **Twin Towers** (p. 67).

Lady Liberty and Ellis Island. The symbol of freedom and the US—worth a look just for its fame (p. 61–65). Take the **Staten Island ferry** to see this paramour for free and without the 3-hr. climb.

BROOKLYN

E. Houston St.

WILLIAMSBURG BRIDGE

4th Ave.

Broadway

Delancey

MANHATTAN BRIDGE

BROOKLYN BRIDGE

Americas)

Lafayette St.

Bowery

Grand St.

St. James Pl.

Broadway

Wall St.

W. Houston St.

Canal St.

West St.

HOLLAND TUNNEL

BROOKLYN-BATTERY TUNNEL

sights

on the cheap

sail-by shooting

Completely free if you don't disembark, the Staten Island ferry may very well offer the world's premier sightseeing bargain. Wave Manhattan goodbye as you pass **Ellis Island**, the **Statue of Liberty**, and Governor's Island en route to Staten Island. The ferry began shuttling commuters in 1810 thanks to the entrepreneurial Cornelius Vanderbilt and his mother's money. It turned public in 1905, but the city charged up to 25¢ for the scenic view until 1997. Postcard photographers flock here for some of the most marketable shots of the city. The ride is particularly exhilarating at sunset or night. (See orientation under Staten Island in **Once in NYC**, p. 33.)

tors wishing to go all the way up to the crown must leave on the first ferry. **Ferry Information:** 269-5755. **Tickets:** $7, seniors $6, ages 3-17 $3, under 3 free. Buy ferry tickets at Castle Clinton or across Battery Park from the South ferry terminal (see **Lower Manhattan,** p. 66). **Summer wait** to climb Liberty 1-2hr. Gift shop with essential items like $1.85 foam Liberty crowns. Cafeteria's greasy fried things $4.25.

For over a century, the Statue of Liberty has represented the most noble elements of the American Dream. She has also made appearances in countless novels, television shows, and films, including *Splash, Planet of the Apes,* and alien epic *Independence Day.* For all these reasons, the Statue of Liberty has become a world-renowned tourist draw with lines as long as the green lady is tall.

Lady Liberty began in the 1870s as French sculptor's Frederic-Auguste Bartholdi's large-scale tribute to Franco-American relations. The new statue commemorated the victory of the Union in the Civil War and the constitutional extension of liberty to black slaves; more pragmatically, the gift encouraged America to oppose the decidedly liberty-less government of Napoleon III in France. While his countrymen plotted against the establishment in 1870s Paris, Bartholdi, with President Grant and others, plotted production of the biggest statue the world had ever seen, *Liberty Enlightening the World.*

The monument soon acquired a new significance: its location made it an immigrant's first sight upon pulling into the harbor. The statue became a symbol of immigration, the foundation of American culture. Joseph Pulitzer, a millionaire Hungarian immigrant who realized the American Dream with his publishing empire, raised money for the 89 ft. pedestal by guilt-tripping ordinary New Yorkers into giving what they could. Once complete, the pedestal received its finishing touch, the now-famous words of welcome by poet Emma Lazarus.

A group of determined suffragettes chartered a boat and sailed themselves over to the statue's 1886 opening ceremonies, interrupting speakers by pointing out the irony of a female embodiment of Liberty in a country where women could neither vote nor attend the statue's inauguration. 1965 saw a more extreme protest, as four terrorists tried to sever the Lady's head and arm it with explosives.

An ideal trip to Liberty Island will entail fewer fireworks. Ferries run in a Battery Park-Liberty-Ellis loop. The ticket costs the same no matter how long you stay and regardless of whether you want to see only the statue or the immigration station, so you might as well do both. The ferry ride is one long, tourist-pleasing photo-op, with jaw-dropping views of the Lower Manhattan skyline, the Brooklyn Bridge, and, of course, Miss Liberty.

Once you're on the island, head quickly for the statue's back entrance, where you'll choose one of two lines. The significantly faster line on the right leads to the elevator carting folks to the observation decks atop **Richard Morris Hunt's pedestal.** The line on the left offers the only route to the crown. It's all stairs: 22 narrow, spiraling stories' worth, the last leg a precipitous staircase with lines that move at a snail's pace. Air-conditioned? No way. There are only two reasons to go to the crown: (1) like Mt. Everest, because it's there; or (2) to glimpse Gustave Eiffel's (yes, *that* Eiffel) internal support-system. Beware—the view boasts little splendor: tiny, airplane-type windows look out not on Manhattan but on the Brooklyn dockyards. Senior citizens, young children, and anyone impatient should avoid the climb.

Some of the artifacts on display over the second entrance doors include an actual-size mold of Liberty's face, various artists' renderings of the sculpture, and evidence of Miss Liberty's lasting influence, such as the cover of Supertramp's *Breakfast in America* LP. A third-floor immigration exhibit should whet your appetite for the much more fascinating Ellis Island. Tours are sporadic and depend on staffing availability.

Bring food—Liberty's costs a bundle and the climb to her crown is strenuous.

City Hall

ELLIS ISLAND

➐ *For instructions on how to get to Ellis Island, see **Liberty Island,** above. **Video documentary:** "Island of Hope, Island of Tears." 30min. Shown in 2 theaters, 1 with a preceding 15min. talk by a ranger. **Play:** "Ellis Island Stories," based on oral histories of those who passed through Ellis Island; performed in spring, summer, and fall. The film is free (call for play prices), but you must get **tickets** at the **info desk** near the entrance in advance of the showing. **Audio-Tour:** 1¼hr. $4, seniors $3.50, students and under 17 $2.50. **Restaurant** prices expensive (fish and fries $4).*

While the Statue of Liberty embodies the American Dream, Ellis Island chronicles the harsh realities of starting over in the New World. The island re-opened as a museum in 1990, after multi-million dollar renovations. From 1892-1954, 12 million immigrants were processed here, many winding up with new names in their new *patria*. During its peak (1892-1920), Ellis Island ushered 5000 people per day into the US In the spring of 1998, the island legally became New Jersey territory; the Supreme Court settled the dispute between the neighbor states based on a 160-year-old claim. Ellis Island's exhibits alternate between the site's history and that of the peopling of America.

World Trade Center

The museum houses: a computer to help track immigration records (for those whose ancestors passed through Ellis); the overwhelming **Registry Room,** where most of the processing took place; a computer that tests your citizenship knowledge (it's harder than you think); and a collection of artifacts and clothing that immigrants brought from the Old World. There aren't any musty piles of genealogical records here, but librarians can recommend institutions that can help with tracing long-lost genetic kin.

One of the Liberty and Ellis Island Foundation's fundraisers is the **American Immigrant Wall Of Honor.** This stainless steel, 6-foot wall lists the names of anyone who donated $100. The names, which include George Washington, loosely symbolize how immigrants are fundamental to the American experience.

Esplanade sculpture in Battery Park City

LOWER MANHATTAN

WORLD TRADE CENTER

*Subway: 1, 9, R, N to Cortlandt St.; A, C, E to Chambers St. **Observation Deck**, 2 World Trade Center (☎ 323-2340). Ticket booth on mezzanine. Open daily June-Aug. 9:30am-11:30pm; Sept.-May 9:30am-9:30pm. $12.50; students $10.75; seniors $9.50; ages 6-12 $6.25; under 6 free. **Branch of the Visitor Information Center** on the mezzanine. Open M-Sa 9am-5pm; off season M-F 9am-5pm. **TKTS Booth** also on mezzanine (see p. 250).*

see map
pp. 316-317

One good thing about the World Trade Center is that it acts as the perfect compass for the directionally-handicapped. Visible from almost everywhere at least as far up as midtown, it means South. The main plaza, on Church and Dey St., contains sculpture, a fountain, and ample seating space for checking out Wall St. types in all their material glory. During the summer, the plaza plays host to daily lunchtime entertainment, such as public theater, dance, and musical (☎ 435-6600; www.panynj.gov/onstage).

The Twin Towers are actually fraternal. One stands 1372-feet tall, four feet taller than its sibling, and will never let him forget it. This dynamic duo was completed in 1973 by the New York Port Authority and was, for a time, the tallest structure in the world. The bombing of the complex in 1993 left no scars other than the "All visitors must carry ID" signs, the security checkpoints, and the guards' complete loss of a sense of humor.

If you want to get to the 107th floor observatory, skip the boring exhibits on commerce and history and get in line for tickets. When you get there, you'll notice that the building's exposed skeleton does not allow for an uninterrupted view, but let's see you try to build a 1372-feet tall building. Weather permitting, the rooftop observation deck on the 110th floor offers a better view. It's even romantic when the city lights up at night. Telescopes (25¢) on the roof allow you to see if any naked people have left their curtains open.

BATTERY PARK CITY

CASTLE CLINTON

*20min. **walking tours** daily every hr. 10:05am-4:05pm. Free. Castle open daily 8:30am-5pm.*
This fort was originally 200 feet offshore on an artificial island and served as a defense against the marauding, bloodthirsty British during the War of 1812. The only shots ever fired were during target practice, so by 1824 the city figured it was safe to lease out the Castle for public entertainment. Over the course of the next few decades, massive construction efforts resulted in a magical bridge made of waste that connected the island to Manhattan. Soon it became New York's main immigrant landing depot, and between 1855 and 1889, more than 8 million immigrants passed through its walls. When Ellis Island took over this function, Castle Clinton became the New York Aquarium. After a while, the Aquarium moved to its current location in Coney Island, leaving this place the boring ticket booth that it is now.

THE WORLD FINANCIAL CENTER

☎ 945-0505.
This building, adjacent to the Twin Towers, boards many of the major companies we know and owe. The four granite-and-glass 40-story towers are covered by distinctive geometric copper roofs. The main public space, the glass-enclosed **Winter Garden,** is a stunning galleria replete with a sprawling marble staircase and sixteen 40-foot-tall palm trees imported all the way from California. The garden, which faces the river esplanade, features over 40 prohibitively expensive shops and restaurants, and hosts year-round festivals and performances that are open to the public.

STATE STREET

On the northeast border of Battery Park lies State St. This was the site of the most glamorous shore front residences of wealthy merchants and their wealthy families, but today the shore is nowhere to be found. Landfills have a tendency to dull an area's grandeur, but two brick-and-wood ghosts of a bygone era remain.

SHRINE OF ST. ELIZABETH ANN SETON. Originally named the James Watson House in 1792, the shrine was once the home of Elizabeth Ann Seton, who became the first US-born saint in 1975. The adjoining **Church of Our Lady of the Rosary** dates from 1883, when it was a shelter for Irish immigrant women. *(7-8 State St. ☎ 269-6865.)*

NEW YORK UNEARTHED. This urban archaeology museum is north on State St., at the rear of the courtyard adjacent to the church. It houses a large collection of stuff that used to be buried in the ground. *(19 State St. ☎ 748-8628.)*

17 STATE STREET. Right next to the museum stands the sheer, elegant, and largely empty wedge of 17 State St. Built in 1989, this great white whale of a building stands on the site of the house in which Herman Melville was born in 1819. Melville went on to pen works such as *Moby Dick* and "Bartleby the Scrivener," but is best known for being the great-great-uncle of dance music sensation Moby.

FINANCIAL DISTRICT

NEW YORK STOCK EXCHANGE

🄵 *20 Broad St. between Wall St. and Exchange Pl. ☎ 656-5168 or 656-5165. Open M-F 9am-4:30pm*

More than 3100 companies compete on the Stock Exchange, which handles billions of shares daily. Once inside, you can check your portfolio, ask questions at any of a number of interactive computer stations, or watch a film on the functions and high tech features of the exchange. Or, you can do what you came here to do: head to the observation gallery to watch hundreds of dot-coms lose millions by the minute. The gallery has been enclosed in glass ever since the 1960s, when Abbie Hoffman and his merry band of Yippies threw dollar bills at the traders, who stopped trading to chase after the money, perfectly acting out the role the anti-capitalist protestors had anticipated. The only trace of Red Communism you'll find here today are the free tickets to get inside, which are handed out on a first-come, first-serve basis beginning at 8:45am.

US CUSTOMS HOUSE

🄵 *1 Bowling Green.*

Completed in 1907, when the city still derived most of its revenue from customs, this building now houses the Smithsonian's **National Museum of the American Indian** (see p. 130). The Customs House sits on the original Algonquin trading ground, which later became the site of the Dutch Fort Amsterdam in 1626. The magnificent Beaux-Arts building sits behind Baroque sculptures representing the supposed four continents and six races, and Mercury, the Roman god of commerce, whose face crowns each of 40 columns. Daniel Chester French, the same artist who sculpted the Lincoln Memorial in Washington, D.C., created these sculptures.

BOWLING GREEN

The Museum of the American Indian looks over the site of the city's first mugging—Peter Minuit's purchase of Manhattan for the equivalent of $24 in beads. This spot eventually became the city's first park, used for the playing of bowls, an ancestor of

Trinity Church

Peking Ship

Lower East Side Tenement Museum

US bowling, except without the snack bar. The green's controversy continued in the 18th century, as colonists rioted here to protest King George III's Stamp Act. When it was repealed, the fickle crowd built an enormous statue of him in 1770. The honeymoon was over, however, when the Declaration of Independence was read and the crowd tore down their gift and melted it to make anti-British munitions for the Revolutionary War.

TRINITY CHURCH

🛈 74 Trinity Pl. Open M-F 7am–6pm, Sa 8am-4pm, Su 7am-4pm. Welcome center open daily 10-11:45am and 1-3pm.

Around the corner from the NYSE, on Broadway, this Neo-Gothic creation has the last laugh over its towering, billion-dollar neighbors. Trinity Church owns much of the land on which these monoliths reside, thereby ensuring that this church won't be needing to take any second collections any time soon. When it was first built in 1846, its Gothic spire made it the tallest structure in the city. The Episcopal congregation itself dates from 1696. The 2½-acre yard, created in 1681, houses the grave of Alexander Hamilton.

FEDERAL HALL

🛈 26 Wall St. Disabled entrance: 15 Pine St. ☎825-6888. Open M-F 9am-5pm; in summer also Sa-Su 9am-5pm. Free tours on request.

A tight-pantsed George Washington stands guard in front of this Parthenon lookalike, which housed the original City Hall after 1793. It was here that the 1735 trial of John Peter Zenger was held to help establish freedom of the press. Also, in roughly the same spot that his likeness stands, a living Washington was sworn in as President. After that, it served as the nation's first seat of government; James Madison first presented the Bill of Rights to Congress at this spot. The original structure was demolished in 1812 and later rebuilt to house numerous federal agencies including the Customs House, the Sub-Treasury, and the FBI. Exhibits now include the illustrated Bible used to swear in Washington, a 10-min, animated program called "Journey to Federal Hall," and activities for kids.

CITY HALL AND THE CIVIC CENTER

CITY HALL

🛈 Broadway at Murray St., off Park Row. ☎788-6879. Open to tourists M-F 10am-4pm. Public meetings often run later and can be interesting to watch. Market open Tu and F 8am-6pm; Jan.-Mar. F only.

For the past few years, Mayor Rudy Guiliani has had his way with New York City from this John McComb Jr. and Francois Mangin-designed edifice. It is unclear whether McComb and Mangin (who also helped design St. Patrick's cathedral) would approve of Guiliani's removal of the Times Square strip clubs. In 1865, thousands of mourners paid their respects to the body of Abraham Lincoln under the hall's vaulted rotunda. City Hall sits, strangely enough, in City Hall Park, once home to a jail, a public execution ground, and a barracks for British soldiers. A recent renovation has left the park looking as good as new, and a small farmer's market flourishes here during the day. Here, in 1774, Alexander Hamilton led a protest against the British-imposed tea tax. On July 9, 1776, George Washington and his troops camped here before the reading of the Declaration of Independence. The area along Park Row, now inhabited by a statue of journalist Horace Greeley, was formerly known as **"Newspaper Row,"** because most of New York's newspapers were published near the one place they were guaranteed to find scandal.

AFRICAN BURIAL GROUND

As recently as 1991, archaeologists found the remains of over 20,000 slaves buried only 20 feet underground at the corner of Duane and Elk Sts. This is the largest known excavated African cemetery in the world. Congress declared it a national landmark, in response to protests against a new Federal Court building slated to be built over the site. The space now stands undisturbed with plans in the works for an elaborate memorial.

THE FEDERAL RESERVE BANK OF NEW YORK

🛈 33 Liberty St. ☎720-6130. Free 40min. tours M-F 9:30, 10:30, 11:30am, 1:30, and 2:30pm, but 7 days advance notice required. Must be 16+. 30 people per group max. limit.

South on Nassau St. and across Maiden Lane, this neo-Renaissance building occupies an entire city block. Built in 1924 and modeled after the Palazzo Strozzi, the home of a 15th-century Florentine banking family, the grave facade is designed to keep you away from one-fourth of the world's gold bullion. No, this gold does not belong to the US; all but 2% of that is kept at Fort Knox, KY. Most of it belongs to other countries, who store their precious metals in a vault 5 stories below ground, with 121 triple-locked compartments.

FEDERAL OFFICE BUILDING

🚩 *290 Broadway, off Reade St., a block north of City Hall.*

Here, a new lobby holds breathtaking public art installations including Clyde Lynd's sculpture "America Song" and Roger Brown's commemorative mosaic depicting legions of AIDS-stricken faces descending into a sea of skulls. On the floor of the central rotunda, a work entitled "The New Ring Shout" commemorates the African burial ground. The title of this 40-foot-wide work of terrazzo and polished brass derives from a historical dance of celebration.

WOOLWORTH BUILDING

🚩 *233 Broadway, south of the Federal Office Building.*

You can't miss this deliciously ornate 1913 construction. F.W. Woolworth purportedly paid millions in cash to house the offices of his five-and-dime store empire in what was known as the "Cathedral of Commerce." The Chrysler Building replaced it as the world's tallest structure in 1930. Its lobby boasts Gothic arches and flourishes that vault over glittering mosaics, gold painted mailboxes, and imported marble designs and carved caricatures; note the one of Woolworth himself counting change and the one of architect Cass Gilbert holding a model of the building.

ST. PAUL'S CHAPEL

🚩 *A block and a half south of the Woolworth Building, near Fulton St.* ☎ *602-0773. Chapel open M-F 9am-3pm, Su 7am-3pm.*

Inspired by the design of London's St. Martin-in-the-Fields, this chapel was built in 1766, with the clock tower and spire added in 1794. It is Manhattan's oldest public building in continuous use, not missing any action since George Washington prayed here in his personal pew on Inauguration Day.

SURROGATE'S COURT

🚩 *31 Chambers St., near Center St.* ☎ *374-8244.*

Two sculpture groups—*New York in Its Infancy* and *New York in Revolutionary Times*—grace the Beaux-Arts exterior of this former Hall of Records. Meanwhile, 24 statues of notable New Yorkers enliven the building's interior. In the strangely pagan lobby, Egyptian tile mosaics and the 12 signs of the Zodiac cover the ceiling. A trip up to the balcony will give you a closer look. The court also boasts a library and a garden.

TWEED COURTHOUSE

🚩 *Next to City Hall.*

Named after the infamous Boss Tweed of the **Tammany Hall** scandals, this Victorian interpretation courthouse took ten years and $14 million to build. That's $14 million in the 1860s, which translates roughly to one hundred trillion dollars or something. Rumor has it that $10 million went to Tweed himself, setting off a public outcry that marked the beginning of the end for Boss Tweed and his embezzling ways.

OTHER SIGHTS

THE BROAD FINANCIAL CENTER. At Whitehall and Pearl St., on the east side of Bowling Green, this center contains one of NYC's craziest lobbies.

UNITED STATES COURTHOUSE. North on Center St. lies the plain and pillared United States Courthouse, built in 1936 and crowned by its designer with a golden roof.

WHO KNOWS WHY THE CAGED BIRD SINGS?

Early rising ornithologists will want to take a sunrise stroll to **Sara Delano Roosevelt Park**, west of the Bowery, at the corner of Chrystie and Delancey Sts. There, between about 7am and 9am, a group of older Chinese men gather each morning from spring to fall to give sun to the songbirds.

The men arrive at the small garden at the park's northern edge with beautiful wooden bird cages covered in cloth so that their occupants don't wake too early. After positioning the cages, the men gingerly remove the coverings and bid their songbirds good morning. The men do some stretching excercises as they wait for their birds to awake from the night's slumber and warm to the sun. Once sufficiently bathed in light, the birds give fanfare to the day. The songs are amazingly loud and melodic, and are easily heard over the roar of early morning traffic. This is an old Chinese tradition intended as a distraction from vice, but, as one of the men remarked, it's more "like walking your dog."

Yoga groups practice to the morning song of the birds, including members of **Falun Xiulian Dafa**, a semi-religious yoga group that is growing rapidly in China and is currently the victim of political oppression from the Chinese government, who sees a potential threat in them.

SOUTH STREET SEAPORT

SEAPORT MUSEUM VISITOR'S CENTER

12-14 Fulton St. ☎748-8600. $6, students $4, seniors $5, ages 4-12 $3. Separate ship ticket $3.

Your first stop at the Seaport, the pretty visitor's center provides information on and sells passes to any of the galleries, ships, or other sites that constitute the museum.

FULTON FISH MARKET

End of Fulton St. at South Street Seaport. ☎748-8786. Tours May-Oct. 1st and 3rd Th of each month; 1¾hr.; 6am; $10. Reservations required one week in advance.

The largest fresh fish market in the country, the Fulton Market has repeatedly clashed with the city, but continues to open at 4am as it has for over 160 years. After a suspicious fire, Mayor Guiliani went to town on the organized crime influences that allegedly controlled the market. Nevertheless, New York's store and restaurant owners continue to buy their fresh fish here, as they have done since the Dutch colonial period. Between midnight and 8am you can see buyers surveying the still-gasping catch of the day, which have just been trucked in via refrigerated vehicle.

PEKING

On the Hudson River off Fulton St. and next to Pier 17. For a sample of this rich history, catch the 15min. 1929 film of the ship during an actual passage around Cape Horn, shown daily 10am-6pm.

In 1911, a Hamburg-based company constructed the *Peking*, the second-largest sailing ship ever launched. It spent most of its career on the "nitrate run" to Chile, a route that passes around Cape Horn, one of the most dangerous stretches of water in the world. Help the current crew raise one of the ship's 32 sails or simply take a half-hour tour.

OTHER SIGHTS

SEAPORT SHIPS. Some ships docked at the seaport ain't going anywhere, like the smaller *Wavertree*, an iron-hulled, three-masted ship built in 1885. You can also see the *Ambrose*, a floating lighthouse built in 1907 to mark an entrance to New York Harbor. The *Pioneer* sailing ship offers the wonderful two- and dreaded three-hour tours on which you can assist in the sailing duties.

TITANIC MEMORIAL LIGHTHOUSE. Ironically named, the diminutive lighthouse features neither Leo, nor Kate Winslet, nor the vocal stylings of Canada's own Celine Dion. What gives? *(Corner of Fulton and Water Sts.)*

BOWNE & CO. To the left on Water St., a number of 18th-century buildings have been restored for commercial use. Bowne & Co., a restored 18th-century printing shop, offers demonstrations on working the letterpress. *(211 Water St. ☎ 748-8660. M-Sa 10am-5pm.)*

PIER 17. If you thought you were getting out of this area without seeing a mall, you couldn't be more wrong. You cannot escape the Pier 17 Pavilion, a shopping mall and restaurant arcade near the river on Fulton St.

SCHERMERHORN ROW. In the main square, you may spy Schermerhorn Row, the oldest complete block of buildings in Manhattan, constructed between 1811 and 1812.

CHINATOWN

see map
pp. 318–319

BUDDHIST TEMPLE

🏠 *4 Pell St., off Mott St.*

Inside this red-and-gold theological treat, the devout are invited to kneel and give offerings in front of a porcelain statue, while the less devout can browse through the gift shop in the rear of the same room.

Mahayana Buddhist Temple

THE MUSEUM OF THE CHINESE IN THE AMERICAS

🏠 *70 Mulberry St., at Bayard St. ☎ 619-4785. Open Tu-Sa noon-5pm. $3, students and seniors $1.*

The first museum ever dedicated to the history of the Chinese-American experience, its two small rooms contain a fascinating collection of writing, images, and artifacts.

MAHAYANA BUDDHIST TEMPLE

🏠 *133 Canal St., near the Manhattan Bridge.*

This brand-new space, with its TV screens, spotlights, and state-of-the-art sound system, might be jarring for those who think of Buddhism as a religion practiced in musty old monasteries in ancient Tibet; maybe this is the new wave.

Chinese Lanterns

FIRST SHEARITH ISRAEL GRAVEYARD

🏠 *South side of Chatham Sq., at St. James Pl., between James and Oliver Sts.*

This historical site attests to the neighborhood's previous guise as part of the Jewish Lower East Side. The cemetery served NYC's first Jewish congregation, the Spanish-Portuguese Shearith Israel Synagogue. Some gravestones date from as early as 1683.

LIN ZE XI

🏠 *NE corner of Chatham Sq.*

Here stands a statue of this Chinese official who, for his efforts in the Opium Wars, is honored as a forefather of the "Just Say No to Drugs" campaign.

COLUMBUS PARK

At Columbus Park, near the Museum of the Chinese in the Americas, children play on the basketball courts while elderly residents vie for bench space with jurors and lawyers on recess from the nearby Federal and State courthouses.

Chinatown street scene

MANHATTAN BRIDGE

Walking northeast toward where the Bowery and East Broadway meet will bring you past the grand arch and flanking colonnades that mark the entrance to the **Manhattan Bridge.** These were designed by Carrère and Hastings, the same firm that designed the New York Public Library (p. 86) and the Frick Mansion (p. 123).

LITTLE ITALY

see map
pp. 318–319

MARE CHIARO

▪ *Mulberry St., just below Kenmare St.*

Better known as "Frank's Bar," the haunt of Ol' Blue Eyes Sinatra himself, this 90-year-old bar has hosted everyone from Gene Kelly to Madonna. As owner Tony Tenneriello will tell you, Mare Chiaro's tin walls and wood paneling have appeared in several movies, including *The Godfather III* and the steamy *9½ Weeks.*

BOWERY SAVINGS BANK

▪ *130 Bowery St., at Grand St.*

This restored bank is an anomaly of un-touristed, un-Italian elegance. Designed by Stanford White, who also designed the arch in Washington Square Park and the original Madison Square Garden, and built in 1894, the building still houses the bank. It is one of the first examples of White's Neoclassical style, featuring a cavernous ceiling, immense pillars, stained glass, and gold leaf.

POLICE HEADQUARTERS

▪ *Corner of Broome and Centre Sts.*

Well, former police headquarters: since the 1970s this domed Beaux-Arts giant has been a luxury co-op apartment building. Built in 1909, this elegantly refurbished lobby, complete with marble columns and massive chandelier, makes it hard to imagine a more pleasant place to get booked.

RAVENITE

▪ *Corner of Mulberry and Prince Sts.*

This red brick storefront reflects this area's recent conversion of old-world grit to nouveau gritty chic; it once masked "Dapper Don" John Gotti's club, the Ravenite. The powerful head of the Gambino crime family held court here until his 1992 conviction. Now the expensive fabrics of designer **Amy Chan** dust the original floor and line the exposed brick walls of the club.

ST. PATRICK'S OLD CATHEDRAL

▪ *264 Mulberry St., near Prince St. ☎ 226-8075.*

Not to be confused with the newer uptown cathedral of the same name, Catholic St. Patrick's facade, completed in 1815 and damaged in an 1866 fire, completes the neighborhood's old-world Italian image. Sadly, reconstruction tamed the quirky architecture of America's second oldest Gothic Revival building into a blander form.

PUCK BUILDING

▪ *Corner of Lafayette and E. Houston, at the northern fringe of Little Italy.*

This beautiful red-brick building was built in 1885 to house the satirical *Puck* magazine. After the magazine's demise in 1916, the building served for a while as the headquarters of the magazine's descendant, *Spy.* Today, some floors are office space while others are rented out for parties and photo shoots. The building honors its namesake with a cute golden Puck grinning mischievously from his roost over the Lafayette St. door.

OTHER SIGHTS

ENGINE CO. 55. If old-fashioned fire stations set you aflame, the still-active Engine Co. dates from 1898. *(363 Broome St. between Mott and Elizabeth Sts.)*

DESALVIO PLAYGROUND. Here is the neighborhood feeling of Little Italy; old-timers square off over checkers while children clamber over the jungle gym. *(Corner of Spring and Mulberry Sts.)*

NOLITA SIGHTS

SHOPPING. Too expensive to be anything but sights, NoLIta's stores are the place for avant-garde spending. Browse the area around Mulberry and Elizabeth Sts. to see antique Amazonian feather masks or Bella Freud designs (daughter of Lucien) at **Language,** 238 Mulberry St.

SCULPTURE GARDEN. On a swath of grass between Spring and Prince Sts. is the striking Elizabeth Street Company's sculpture garden.

MANHATTAN CASTLES AND PROPS. Weather permitting, see this company spread its enormous display of...er...junk? Old bathtubs, street signs, traffic lights, furniture, billboards, gargoyles—if it's manmade and old, they've got it. This company also rents items to movies. *(76 E. Houston between Bowery and Elizabeth St. ☎ 505-8699. Open daily 9:30am-6pm.)*

Knitting Factory

LOWER EAST SIDE

see map
pp. 326–327

LOWER EAST SIDE TENEMENT MUSEUM

*✦ 90 Orchard St. between Broome and Delancey Sts. ☎ 431-0233. See **Museums,** p. 128 and **Walking Tours,** p. 73 for info on tours.*

Between 1863-1935, some 7,000 immigrants from 20 countries made this tenement, built in 1863 by a German immigrant tailor, their home. Houses a museum and offers tours.

SCHAPIRO'S HOUSE OF KOSHER WINES

✦ 126 Rivington St., off Essex St. ☎ 674-4404. Tours Su 11am-4pm. Open for buying and tasting Su-Th 11am-5pm, F 11am-3pm.

Tour the only operational winery left in NYC, famous for once giving a bottle of "the wine you can cut with a knife" to every immigrant family. Look for the beautiful graffiti advertising the store on the sides of the building.

Wetlands

ART FIEND FOUNDATION

✦ 123 Ludlow St. between Rivington and Delancey Sts. ☎ 420-1033. Open Th-Su 1-7pm.

This art studio exemplifies the Loaisaid's up-and-coming-ness.

SYNAGOGUES

CONGREGATION ANSHE CHESED. New York's oldest synagogue, the red-painted Gothic Revival structure was built in 1849 to seat 1500. It now houses the Jose Oresanz Foundation as well as a converted gallery space. *(172-176 Norfolk St., off Stanton St. ☎ 780-0175.)*

ELDRIDGE ST. SYNAGOGUE. This synagogue recently completed a multi-million dollar renovation that birthed a Lower East Side historical museum. The synagogue was built in the Moorish style in 1886. *(12 Eldridge St., near Canal St. ☎ 219-0903. Museum open Su and Tu-Th noon-4pm. Tours $4; children, students, and seniors $2. Tours available with advance notice.)*

Naked Lunch Bar

NYU NEWS

NYU Information: 50 W. 4th St. ☎998-4636. Has free maps.

NYU is the country's largest private university. It is most notable for hip students, top-of-the-line communications and film departments, and some of the least appealing contemporary architecture in the Village. Many desperately functional-looking buildings around the Square proudly display the flaming purple NYU flag.

On the southeast side of the park, where Washington Sq. South meets LaGuardia Pl., you'll find NYU's **Loeb Student Center,** garnished with pieces of scrap metal that purportedly represent birds in flight.

Mere steps away sits **Gould Plaza** in front of NYU's Stern School of Business and the Courant Institute of Mathematical Sciences. The plaza is home to a shiny aluminum Dadaist sculpture by Jean Arp.

At Green Street and Waverly Place lies NYU's **Brown Building,** the former site of the **Triangle Shirtwaist Company** where a 1911 fire killed most of the primarily female staff—the doors had been chained shut to prevent the workers from taking too many breaks. The ensuing uproar led to new workplace regulations and a rejuvenated worker safety movement.

Across the street looms another rust-colored bulk, the **Elmer Holmes Bobst Library,** designed by architects with the idea of unifying the severely disjointed campus through red-sandstone facades. Unfortunately the money ran out before the project was complete, so NYU opted for the purple flags instead.

TRIBECA

see map
p. 321

FIREHOUSE

∏ *114 Moore St., near White St.*
As you near this building when shopping in this area, you'll be surprised at how familiar it is. It is from this firehouse that Bill Murray, Dan Ackroyd, and fellow **Ghostbusters** helped rid NYC of unwanted paranormal activity in two 1980s films.

TRIBECA GRILL

∏ *Corner of Franklin and Greenwich Sts.*
Robert DeNiro's **TriBeCa Grill** is on the ground floor of the TriBeCa films building, in which Miramax and several other production companies work their cinematic magic. The actor-cum-entrepreneur has also opened the TriBeCa Bakery in the middle of the block, and the deeply chic, expensive, and surprisingly friendly Nobu (on the corner of Franklin St. and Hudson St.), a "fusion cuisine" restaurant that attracts all types of celebrities. Rumor has it that several other neighborhood institutions belong to Mr. "You Lookin' at Me?"—but you didn't hear it here.

WASHINGTON MARKET PARK

∏ *Triangle bounded by Greenwich, Chambers, and West Sts.*
☎ *408-0100 for info, or bulletin board schedule by main gate.*
This surprisingly big spread of grass hosts Thursday evening concerts each week from late June to early August in its charming blue-and-white gazebo. Performances include every type of music, from jazz to R&B to country. The park has a funky playground that attracts kids of all ages.

GREENWICH VILLAGE

see map
pp. 322–323

∏ *Subway: To **West Village,** A, C, E to W. 4th St. or 8th St.; 1, 9 to Christopher St./Sheridan Sq. or 14th St. To **East Village,** 6 to Astor Pl. To **Central Village,** N, R to 8th St.*

WASHINGTON SQUARE PARK AREA

I know not whether it is owing to the tenderness of early associations, but this portion of New York appears to many persons the most delectable.

—Henry James, *Washington Square*

Washington Square Park has stood at the center of Village life for most of this century. Native Americans once inhabited the marshland here, and by the mid-17th century it had become home to black slaves freed by the Dutch. The latter half of the 18th century saw the area converted into a potter's field for the burial of the poor and unknown (around 15,000 bodies lie buried here) and then as a hanging-grounds during the Revolutionary War. In the 1820s the area metamorphosed into a park and parade ground. Soon, high-toned residences made the area the center of New York's social scene.

In the late 1970s and early 80s, Washington Square Park became a base for low-level drug dealers. The mid-80s saw a noisy clean-up campaign that has made the park fairly safe, though its drug traffic has not altogether vanished. After $900,000 worth of renovations were completed in 1995, the park today hosts musicians, misunderstood teenagers, muttering homeless people, and romping children.

At the north end of the Park stands the **Washington Memorial Arch,** built in 1889 to commemorate the centennial of George Washington's inauguration. Until 1964, Fifth Ave. actually ran through the arch; residents, however, complained of the noisy traffic.

THE ROW
🚩 *On the north side of the park.*
Built largely in the 1830s, this stretch of stately Federal-style brick residences soon became an urban center populated by 19th-century professionals, dandies, and novelists. **Number 18,** now demolished, housed Henry James's grandmother and provided the setting for his novel *Washington Square*.

PICASSO
🚩 *On the corner of Bleeker St. and LaGuardia Pl.*
Proclaimed by the *New York Times* as the ugliest piece of public art in the city, this masterpiece stands almost unoticed in all the hubbub of the area.

WEATHERMEN
🚩 *18 W. 11th St., at Fifth Ave.*
Here is the site of the 1970 explosion that had esteemed actor Dustin Hoffman scrambling to save his possessions when next-door neighbors and local radicals, The Weathermen, had a bomb-making mishap at 18 W. 11th St. The townhouse currently at this site has a unique front window designed to commemorate the shape of the explosion.

THE NEW SCHOOL
🚩 *66 W. 12th St.*
Formerly the New School for Social Research, past faculty of this school include John Dewey and W.E.B. DuBois. During World War II, the New School made itself famous by offering positions to European intellectuals fleeing the Nazis; now, it continues its tradition of progressive-minded thinking and even generates the popular Bravo cable show *Inside the Actor's Studio*, hosted by Professor James Lipton.

GRACE CHURCH
🚩 *800 Broadway, between 10th and 11th Sts.*
This church was constructed in 1845 using white marble mined by prisoners of the notorious New York State prison Sing Sing. Despite its dark medieval interior and creepy Gothic exterior, the church used to be *the* place for weddings and still holds a lovely Passion of St. Matthew at Easter. It shares its site with an affiliated private grammar and middle school, aptly called the Grace Church School.

WEST OF SIXTH AVENUE (WEST VILLAGE)
JEFFERSON MARKET LIBRARY
🚩 *425 Sixth Ave. ☎ 243-4334. Open M and Th 10am-6pm, Tu and F noon-6pm, W noon-8pm, Sa 10am-5pm.*
Built as a courthouse in 1876, this cross between a castle and a church has detailed brickwork, stained-glass windows, and a turreted clock tower. It occupies the triangle formed by the intersection of W. 10th St., Sixth Ave., and Greenwich Ave. The remarkable structure faced and beat a demolition plot in the early 1960s, and was once voted the fifth most beautiful building in the country.

SHERIDAN SQUARE

Intersection of Seventh Ave., Christopher St., and W. 4th St.

Rioters against the Civil War draft gathered here in 1863 for some of the darkest days in NYC's history; protesters brutally murdered hundreds of free blacks. Since then, the area has become much more tolerant, as evidenced by Christopher St.'s large gay community. The area of the street near Sheridan Sq. has been renamed **Stonewall Pl.,** alluding to the Stonewall Inn, site of the 60s police raid that sparked the gay rights movement. (See **The Queer Apple,** p. 221 and p. 224.) Within Sheridan Sq., two sculptures of same-sex couples stand locked in embraces, a tribute to the neighborhood's history. An unhitched General Sheridan stands nearby, love's looker-on.

CHUMLEY'S

86 Bedford St. between Grove and Barrow Sts. ☎675-4449. Open Su-Th 4pm-midnight, F-Sa 4pm-2am.

This bar and restaurant became a speakeasy in Prohibition days, serving to literary Johns (Dos Passos and Steinbeck), Ernest Hemingway, and Thornton Wilder. William Faulkner, Dylan Thomas, Lillian Hellman, and J.D. Salinger have also raised a glass here. Partly in homage to its clandestine history (and because it's just *so* cool), no sign indicates that this cream-colored building with a brown door might be a bar.

OTHER SIGHTS

MEAT-PACKING DISTRICT. Walking up Hudson St. will lead you to the meat-packing district, a super trendy area for those who love the grit of the city. Lofts have sprung up in old factories, cafes in old garages, and clubs in old stockyards. This urban renewal, however, has had little effect on the shady weekend sidewalk late-night scene. *(Around W. 12th and Gansevoort Sts.)*

PATCHIN PLACE. Off 10th St. and Sixth Ave. you'll see an iron gate and a street sign that reads "Patchin Place." The 145-year-old buildings that line the modest path housed writers e.e. cummings, Theodore Dreiser, and Djuna Barnes during their Village sojourns.

75½ BEDFORD STREET. Near the corner of Commerce St., at 75½ Bedford St., is **the narrowest building in the Village,** measuring 9½ft. across. The writer Edna St. Vincent Millay lived here in 1923 and 1924, during which she founded the **Cherry Lane Theater,** which has showcased Off-Broadway theater ever since. *(38 Commerce St. ☎989-2020. See Entertainment,* p. 156.) Actors Lionel Barrymore and Cary Grant also liked cramped quarters; each lived at 75½ Bedford after her departure.

EAST VILLAGE

see map
pp. 326–327

ST. MARK'S PLACE

Where E. 8th St. would be, between Cooper Sq. E. and Ave. A.

Full of pot-smoking flower children and musicians in the 1960s, this street gave Haight-Ashbury a run for its hashish. In the late 1970s, it taught London's Kings Road how to do punk, as mohawked youths hassled passersby from the brownstone steps off Astor Pl. Nowadays, those '60s and '70s youths still line the street—in their old-tattooed-geezer incarnations. The '90s St. Mark's Pl. is a drag full of tiny ethnic eateries, street level shops, sidewalk vendors selling trinkets of all kinds—from plastic bug-eye sunglasses to polyvinyl chloride fetish wear—music shops, and, of course, tattoo shops. In a way, St. Mark's resembles a small-town Main Street—a small town with a bad-ass history. Although many more-obscure-than-thou types now shun the commercialized and crowded areas of the street, St. Mark's remains the hub of East Village life and *the* place to start your tour of the neighborhood.

ASTOR PLACE

At the junction of Lafayette, Fourth Ave., and E. 8th St.

Simultaneously a small road and a large cultural intersection, this western border of the East Village simmers with street life. Check out the ever-popular **Beaver Murals** at the Astor Subway Stop—they pay homage to John Jacob Astor's prolific fur trade. Upstairs from the murals, the subway kiosk, a cast-iron Beaux-Arts beauty, was built in 1985 as part of a reconstruction of the station. A **large black cube** balanced on its corner distinguishes Astor Place's position. If you and your friends push hard enough the cube will rotate, but you may disturb Astor Pl.'s various denizens sitting (or sleeping) underneath it. "The Cube," or "the Alamo," provides a meeting point for countless rallies, marches, and demonstrations, as well as a space for impromptu performances and asphalt for hordes of prepubescent skaters.

Double Happiness Bar

THE COOPER UNION FOUNDATION BUILDING

7 E. 7th St., at Cooper Sq. in Astor Pl. ☎ 353-4199. Gallery open M-Th 11am-7pm.

Peter Cooper, the self-educated industrialist, founded the Cooper Union for the Advancement of Science and Art in 1859 as a tuition-free technical and design school. Cooper Union helped to forge a uniquely American approach toward education—as the first college intended for the underprivileged, one of the first coeducational, the first racially open college, and the first college to offer free adult-education classes. Both the American Red Cross and the NAACP began here. And if that's not enough history for you, Cooper Union also stands as the oldest building in the US to incorporate steel beams (made of old railroad rails). The second floor **Houghton Gallery** hosts changing exhibits on design and American history as well as displays by the talented and stylish student body, but not during the summer.

Sonnabend Gallery

THE JOSEPH PAPP PUBLIC THEATER

425 Lafayette St. ☎ 539-8750; www.publictheater.org.

This grand brownstone structure was constructed by John Jacob Astor in 1853 to serve as the city's first public library. After its collection moved uptown, the building became headquarters to the Hebrew Immigrant Aid Society, an organization that assisted thousands of poor Jewish immigrants in the early 1900s. In 1967, Joseph Papp's **New York Shakespeare Festival** converted the building. The Public Theater also hosts premieres of new plays. Look for long lines of people waiting for free tickets to **Shakespeare in the Park** (see **Entertainment,** p. 157).

ST. MARK'S IN THE BOWERY CHURCH

*131 E. 10th St. ☎ 674-6377. See **Entertainment,** p. 164, for Theater and Projects info.*

Erected in 1799, St. Mark's Church stands on the site of Peter Stuyvesant's estate chapel; the Dutch governor lies buried in the small cobblestone graveyard. Restored in the mid-1970s but burned in a 1978 fire, the building was repaired by 1986. St.

Soho Shopping

COLOR ME GREEN

Before the flagships of hipness moved into the East Village and Alphabet City, they were home to debris-ridden abandoned lots. In 1973, Liz Christy and the **"Green Guerrillas"** began planting neighborhood window boxes and tree pits and throwing water balloons filled with seeds into lots. By 1986 they had transformed the northeast corner of Bowery and Houston into a flowering oasis they named the **Liz Christy Bowery-Houston Garden.** (Open Sa noon-4pm; growing season Tu 6pm-dusk.) Recently, the Green Guerrillas encountered a new enemy—Mayor Giuliani, whose administration sought to sell the lots. Luckily, **Bette Midler** has bought these municipal lots in order to preserve the gardens. To find out more about the Green Guerrillas, call ☎674-8124 or check out www.greenguerilla.org.

Other spectacular community gardens in the area include:

Sixth Street and Avenue B Garden. The must-see mother of all community gardens; a fantasy jungle. Open daily in summer 8am-8pm.

Miracle Garden, E. 3rd St. at Ave. B. Small but tall and lush.

Campos Garden, E. 12th St. between Aves. B and C. A plethora of fruits and veggies. Open Mar.-Oct. Su 3-5pm and intermittently during the week.

El Sol Brillante, 12th St. between Aves. A and B.

Community Garden, Ave. C (Loisaida Ave.) between 8th and 9th St.

Mark's has a long history of political activism and involvement in the arts. It hosts several community companies, including the **Ontological Theater,** which continues to produce some of the better off-Broadway plays, as well as the **Danspace Project** and the **Poetry Project.**

COLONNADE ROW

◪ *428-434 Lafayette and 4th Sts.*

New York's most famous 19th-century millionaires—John Jacob Astor, Cornelius "Commodore" Vanderbilt, and the Franklin Delano Roosevelt family dwelled in three of these four-columned houses, built in 1833. There used to be nine of these houses; the remaining ones are unfortunately the worse for wear.

THE 2ND AVE. DELI

◪ *156 Second Ave., at 10th St. See* **Food,** *p. 189.*

This famous Jewish landmark is all that remains of the "Yiddish Rialto," the stretch of Second Ave. between Houston and 14th Sts. that comprised the Yiddish theater district in the early part of the 20th century. Stars of David in the sidewalk out front contain the names of actors and actresses who spent their lives entertaining Jewish immigrants. While this community no longer remains the Jewish enclave it once was, the historic deli stands as a loyal mainstay; it still serves up the meanest pastrami sandwich in town.

ABE LEBEWOHL PARK

◪ *E. 10th St. and Second Ave. To find out other Greenmarket locations in the city, call ☎477-3220.*

On March 4, 1996, Abe Lebewohl, founder of the 2nd Ave. Deli and leading member of the Lower East Side/East Village community, was murdered as he deposited his daily receipts into his bank account late at night. The city renamed the small plot of land in front of St. Mark's Church in his honor. Every Tuesday from 7am-6pm, Abe Lebewohl Park holds a **Farmer's Market** as part of the Greenmarket program supporting regional farming.

OTHER SIGHTS

NEW YORK MARBLE CEMETERIES. The New York Marble Cemeteries gave the city its first two non-sectarian graveyards. *(Second Ave. between 2nd and 3rd Sts. and 2nd St. just east of Second Ave.)*

ST. GEORGE UKRAINIAN CATHOLIC CHURCH. Ukrainian-American life centers on 7th St., with cafes and several churches. The most remarkable is St. George Ukrainian Catholic Church. The artwork inside, visible only if you stop by Sunday after mass, eclipses even the haunting icons that ornament the outer doors. *(On Taras Sevchenko Pl., near Cooper Sq. E.)*

ALPHABET CITY

TOMPKINS SQUARE PARK

🚩 *Located between Aves. A and B and E. 7th and 10th Sts.*

A few years ago, police officers precipitated a riot when they attempted to forcibly evict a band of the homeless and their supporters from this park. An aspiring video artist recorded scenes of police brutality, setting off public outcry and further police-inspired violence. The park has only recently reopened after several years' hiatus, but it still reflects the collective psyche of its environs' churlish misfits. "East Side Anarchists," who hoofed down to Tompkins Sq. after tearing through St. Mark's Pl., incited one of many riots that erupted in New York City following the Rodney King verdict in 1992. In addition, much to the city's chagrin, several five-foot-tall marijuana plants were found growing in the park in 1997. Officials promptly rooted out such pesky foliage. Basketball courts and a playground in the northwest section of the park have gained popularity with the younger, less activist East Village set; you can almost always happen upon a pickup soccer game. The **dog run** in the park, a designated area for letting man's best friend romp about, provides marvelous canine-watching. In the summer, you're bound to stumble upon **impromptu concerts** here.

Washington Square Park

OTHER SIGHTS

MEMORIAL MURALS. East of the park, countless memorial murals attest to the scars left by the drug war. Many other murals—most of them attributed to local legend "Chico"—celebrate the neighborhood. Other altruistic projects include the community gardens (see **Color Me Green**, p. 78).

SPACE 2B. At the corner of Ave. B and 2nd St., a fence made of pipes and car parts surrounds Space 2B, an outdoor gallery and performance space.

LOWER MIDTOWN

see map
pp. 328–329

GRAMERCY PARK AND UNION SQUARE

To escape the roar of the Midtown crowds, walk downtown from the Empire State Building area. Move swiftly, as there's nothing to see where **Andy Warhol's Factory**—studio, production offices, freakhouse—once churned out Pop Art with mechanical speed at the now desolate 19 E. 32nd St., between Fifth and Madison Aves. The surrounding neighborhoods, however, have plenty to offer.

New School

CHURCH OF THE TRANSFIGURATION

🚩 *29th St. between Fifth and Madison Aves.* ☎ *684-6770. www.little-church.org. Open daily 8am-6pm.*

Better known as "The Little Church Around the Corner," this national landmark has been the home parish of New York's theater world ever since a liberal pastor agreed to bury Shakespearean actor George Holland here in 1870, when comic actors were considered low-lifes. The charming Gothic cottage-esque

Bleecker and McDougal Sts.

structure features peculiar green roofs, cherub-like gargoyles, and a pleasantly manicured garden with a bubbling fountain out front. Check out the stained glass windows: they may look like a scene from the Bible, but look again—the vignette is from *Hamlet*.

MADISON SQUARE PARK

Southern end of Madison Ave. Call Parks Dept. for info: ☎ *361-8111.*

Before the park's opening, it was in this public space that a game formerly known as "New York ball" was played by a group called the Knickerbockers. This game evolved to become America's favorite pasttime—baseball. Officially opened as a park in 1847, it originally served as a public cemetery. Around it stand statues of famous Civil War generals. The park is currently being reconstructed to preserve its original design and is expected to reopen in the spring of 2001.

NEW YORK LIFE INSURANCE BUILDING

51 Madison Ave. between 26th and 27th Sts.

Built by Cass Gilbert (of Woolworth Building fame) in 1928, this multi-tiered structure is topped by a golden pyramid-shaped roof. The building is located on the former site of P.T. Barnum's "Hippodrome," which was rebuilt by Stanford White and served as the original Madison Square Garden from 1890 to 1925. It soon became the premier spot for New York's trademark entertainment spectacles. Star architect and man-about-town White was fatally shot here in 1906 by the unstable husband of a former mistress (the story was later fictionalized in E.L. Doctorow's *Ragtime*).

METROPOLITAN LIFE INSURANCE TOWER

Corner of Madison Ave. and 23rd St.

Surveying Madison Sq. Park from 700 ft. above ground, the rather unaesthetic-looking tower, a 1909 addition to an 1893 building, once made this building a member of New York's tallest-building-in-the-world club. The minute hands of the clocks (one on each of the building's four faces) weigh 1,000 pounds each, while the hour hands are reputed to be only 700 pounds. The annex on 24th St., connected by a walkway, features an eye-catching neo-Gothic facade.

69TH REGIMENT ARMORY

68 Lexington Ave., at 26th St. Open W-M 11am-7pm.

The armory is notable only for having hosted the infamous art exhibition in 1913 that brought Picasso, Matisse, and Duchamp—who Teddy Roosevelt called "a bunch of lunatics"—to the shores of America. Perhaps in homage to its history of exhibiting art, temporary installations can sometimes still be found in its old basketball courts. The National Guard currently calls this imposing eyesore of a building home—it was designed to be a menace during riots.

FLATIRON BUILDING

175 Fifth Ave., off the southwest corner of Madison Sq. Park.

Eminently photogenic, this historic site is yet another ex-tallest building. The intersection of Broadway, Fifth Ave., and 23rd St. forced the construction of its dramatic wedge shape (only 6-feet wide at its point). In 1902, the Fuller Building, as it was originally named, was the city's first skyscraper with more than 20 stories to its glory; it was one of the first buildings in which exterior walls were hung on a steel frame. The building acquired its name because of its resemblance to the clothes-pressing device. (See **Architecture,** p. 52.)

THE THEODORE ROOSEVELT BIRTHPLACE

28 E. 20th St. between Broadway and Park Ave. South. ☎ *260-1616. Open W-Su 9am-5pm. 30min. guided tours 9am-4pm; $2.*

Until he was 15, Teddy Roosevelt lived in this brownstone, a typical example of 1840s style. The museum now consists of five elegant period rooms from Teddy's childhood. E. 20th St. is actually called Theodore Roosevelt Way. The free exhibit downstairs offers a self-guided tour through the events of the 26th president's life.

GRAMERCY PARK

⚑ *Lexington Ave. between 20th and 21st Sts.*

This gorgeous and gated private park, built in 1831, was the brainchild of Samuel B. Ruggles, a developer fond of greenery. He drained an old marsh and then laid out 66 building lots around the periphery of the central space. Buyers of his lots received keys to enter the private park; for many years, the keys were made of solid gold. Over 150 years later, little has changed; the park, with its wide gravel paths, remains the only private park in New York, immaculately kept by its owners (and left open for daytime visitors!). The surrounding real estate is some of the choicest in the city, sporting a London-esque flair of Greek Revival and Victorian Gothic-style townhouses.

ARTS CLUBS

PLAYERS CLUB. Actor Edwin Booth (brother to Lincoln's assassin) established The Players Club, an exclusive social club where actors and actresses (then considered social outcasts) could congregate. Members have included Mark Twain, Sir Laurence Olivier, Frank Sinatra, Walter Cronkite, and Richard Gere. *(16 Gramercy Park South. Groups of 10 or more can call the library, ☎ 228-7611, for tours. Suggested contribution $5, students and seniors $3.)*

NATIONAL ARTS CLUB. Created in 1898, the National Arts Club boasts past members such as artist Robert Henri, Woodrow Wilson, and Theodore Roosevelt. They have a free gallery open usually every day noon-5pm, but visitors are advised to call ahead. *(15 Gramercy Park South. ☎ 475-3424.)*

STUYVESANT SQUARE

Stuyvesant Sq. is named after Governor Peter Stuyvesant (see **Life and Times,** p. 47) who owned farm property there, in the 17th century. The statue of the Governor in the square was created by Gertrude Vanderbilt Whitney, later the founder of the Whitney Museum (see **Museums and Galleries,** p. 123). On Rutherford Pl. is **St. George's Church,** created in 1856 in the style of Romanesque Revival; another Quaker **Friends Meeting House,** created in 1860 in Greek Revival style, can also be seen on the same street.

UNION SQUARE

⚑ *Between Broadway and Park Ave. South, and 17th and 14th Sts. Market open M, W, F-Sa 7am-6pm; F-Sa are biggest market days.*

So named because it was a "union" of two main roads, Union Square and the surrounding area sizzled with High Society aristocrats before the Civil War. Early in this century, the name gained dual significance when the neighborhood became a focal point of New York's large Socialist movement, which held its popular May Day celebrations in the park. Later, it was abandoned to drug dealers and derelicts, but in 1989 the city attempted to reclaim it. The park is now pleasant and generally safe, although not pristine; denizens run the gamut from homeless people and sunbathers to pigeons. The scent of herbs and fresh bread wafts through the park, courtesy of the **Union Square Greenmarket;** farmers, fisherman, and bakers from all over the region come to hawk their fresh produce, jellies, and baked goods.

UNION SQUARE SAVINGS BANK

⚑ *20 Union Sq. East. ☎ 239-6200.*

Although designed by Henry Bacon, architect of the Lincoln Memorial in Washington, D.C., this old neoclassical building was never declared a historical landmark. The bank is now the site of the Daryl Roth Theatre, currently home of the much talked-about De La Guarda (see **Entertainment,** p. 160).

MURRAY HILL

With few claims to fame, residential Murray Hill remains virgin to hard-core tourism.

CHURCH OF THE INCARNATION

◪ *209 Madison Ave. between 35th and 36th Sts. Open M-F about 11:30am-2pm, but times vary.*

Built in 1864, this is the "landmark church" of Murray Hill. Features stained glass by Tiffany, sculptures by Augustus Saint-Gaudens, and memorials by Daniel Chester French.

PIERPONT MORGAN LIBRARY

◪ *29 E. 36th St., at Madison Ave. ☎ 685-0610.*

The original library building was completed in 1906 and designed by Charles McKim. In the style of a Renaissance *palazzo*, the library is both understated and elegant; it is definitely worth a visit for both architectural beauty and its collection devoted to the printed word (see **Museums,** p. 124).

CHELSEA

HOTEL CHELSEA

◪ *222 W. 23rd St. between Seventh and Eighth Aves. ☎ 243-3700.*

This historical hotel has housed and continues to house some of the more interesting American literati and cultural figures. In this cavernous 400-room complex, of which 250 rooms have been permanently rented out, some 150 books have been penned, including works by such esteemed authors as Arthur C. Clarke, Arthur Miller, William Burroughs, Mark Twain, Eugene O'Neill, Vladimir Nabokov, Thomas Wolfe, and Dylan Thomas. Joni Mitchell, John Lennon, and Jasper Johns all called this hotel home at some point in their careers. Yet, despite the hype surrounding it, the hotel is discreet and maintains a charming seediness. Ethan Hawke is rumored to live here periodically, but the doorpeople aren't telling secrets. (Singles $175-275; doubles $185-285. Reservations definitely recommended.)

FLOWER DISTRICT

◪ *Blooms on 28th St. between Sixth and Seventh Aves.*

Here wholesale distributors and buyers of flora congregate each morning to stock the city's florists and garden centers. The district turns your average commercial block into a fragrant and stunning oasis.

OTHER SIGHTS

ST. PETER'S CHURCH. Many of Chelsea's buildings date back to the mid-1800s when Clement Clark Moore (the clergyman/scholar who is perhaps most known for writing the poem *'Twas the Night Before Christmas*) owned and developed this area. St. Peter's Church, the oldest Gothic revival church in the US, towers silently over the neighborhood. *(346 W. 20th St. between Eighth and Ninth Aves. ☎ 929-2390.)*

CUSHMAN ROW. An example of Clement Moore's architectural work lives on at Cushman Row, a terrace of brownstones complete with wrought-iron railings. *(404-418 W. 20th St.)*

GENERAL THEOLOGICAL SEMINARY. These posh homes face the brick cathedral and grounds of the General Theological Seminary, a serene, peaceful oasis that blooms with roses in the summer. If you're lucky, you may catch some aspiring monks playing tennis. The calming, Old World grounds are open to the public. *(125 Ninth Ave., between 20th and 21st Sts. ☎ 243-5150. Open M-F noon-3pm, Sa 11am-3pm.)*

see map
pp. 332-333

WEST MIDTOWN

THE EMPIRE STATE BUILDING

> New York impressed me tremendously because, more than any other city in the world, it is the fullest expression of our modern age.
> —Leo Trotsky

*350 Fifth Ave and 34th St. Subway: N, R to 34th St./Herald Sq.; B, D, F, Q to 33rd St.. Walk east one long block on 33rd or 34th St. to Fifth Ave. www.esbnyc.com. **Observatory:** ☎ 736-3100. Open daily 9:30am-midnight (last elevator up at 11:30pm); tickets sold until 11:30pm. $9; seniors $7; children under 12 $4. **Skyride:** ☎ 279-9777. Open daily 10am-10pm. $11.50; ages 4-12 and seniors $8.50. Combination Pass $17; seniors $13; children $10.*

Ever since King Kong first climbed the Empire State Building with his main squeeze in 1933, the world-renowned landmark has attracted scores of tourists. The observatories welcome nearly 4 million visitors each year. Even alien "tourists" chose the landmark as the epicenter of their destruction in *Independence Day*. Completed in 1931, the building has become synonymous with the New York skyline and as integral to the city's image as yellow cabs, bagels, and the Statue of Liberty. Although no longer the tallest building in the world (the Petronas Twin Towers in Malaysia wins) or even the tallest in New York (the Twin Towers have several floors on it), the towering spire still dominates postcards, movies, and the hearts of city residents.

Herald Square

Built on the site of the original Waldorf and Astoria hotels, the limestone, granite, and stainless-steel-sheathed structure pioneered Art Deco design. It stretches 1454 feet into the sky and contains 2 miles of shafts for its 73 elevators. Only 20 months elapsed from the day the contract was signed to the day the building opened; the building is a monolithic example of industrialization during the booming '30s.

The lobby stands as a gleaming shrine to Art Deco interior decorating, right down to its mail drops and elevator doors. Follow arrows on the wall to the concourse level, where you can purchase tickets to the observatory. Note the sign indicating visibility level—a day with perfect visibility offers views for 80 miles in any direction, but even on a day with a visibility of only 5 miles, one can still spot the Statue of Liberty. Prepare to wait up to an hour during peak visiting times in the summer.

As if the view didn't inspire enough awe, the Empire State offers the **New York Skyride**, a simulation of a spaceship journey through the city (stick to the Observatory).

Washington Square Park

HELL'S KITCHEN
JACOB K. JAVITS CONVENTION CENTER

Along Twelfth Ave. between 34th and 38th Sts.

The Javits Center hosts some of the grandest-scale events in the world, including international boat, car, and motorcycle shows. The convention center sits at the beginning of Hell's Kitchen, the neighborhood that fostered the "Westies"—the gangs that inspired Leonard Bernstein's 1957 *West Side Story* and Marvel Comic's crimefighter Daredevil.

JOHN JAY COLLEGE OF CRIMINAL JUSTICE

899 Tenth Ave. at 58th St.

Student protests over tuition hikes culminated in a two-week takeover of this CUNY in May 1990. The turmoil ended in a violent reinstatement of power by administration officials. Renovations have given the 1903 neo-Victorian building, formerly the DeWitt Clinton High School (attended by Calvin Klein), a postmodern atrium and extension.

The Cage

ALL LIT UP

The Empire State Building's tower is illuminated in various colors throughout the year. Usually green and red, during Channukah the tower is draped in blue and silver colors, in homage to the Jewish holiday; when Frank Sinatra died, the tower was illuminated in blue tones in reverence of "Old Blue Eyes." The tower has also had its series of random adornments: one foggy night on July 28, 1945, a US Army B-25 bomber crashed into the 79th floor of the building. Burning debris hurled for blocks, although the steel frame swayed less than two inches. Fourteen people lost their lives in the bizarre accident, but many survived thanks to New York Fire Department heroes like John Coletti of the 34th St. Hook and Ladder. In other incidents, two blimps docked there in 1931 and, in the same year, King Kong, the giant ape, fought army planes from atop the famous tower.

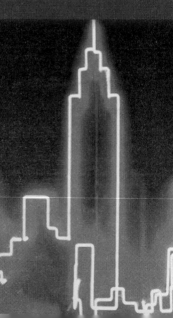

HERALD SQUARE AREA AND THE GARMENT DISTRICT

PENNSYLVANIA STATION

◪ Corner of 33rd St. and Lexington Ave.

The interior of Penn Station has been refurbished over the past few years; curved metal panels have replaced ceiling tiles formerly covered with dripping limestone stalagmites, and antiseptic French bakeries vending rosemary bread have replaced truant-officer-filled videogame arcades. The original Penn Station was created in 1910; modeled on the Roman baths of Caracalla, it featured a 150-foot high glass ceiling and wrought iron. It was demolished in the 1960s in favor of more practical space 50 feet below.

MADISON SQUARE GARDEN

◪ Seventh Ave. between 31st and 33rd Sts. ☎ 465-5800. Tours every hour on the hour M-Sa 10am-3pm, Su and holidays 11am-3pm; 1hr.; $14, children under 12 $12.

The railway tracks leading in and out of Penn Station are covered by "The Garden." Built in 1968 in its fourth incarnation, it is New York's premier entertainment complex, hosting a wide array of top acts, including the Knicks, Yankees, and Rangers. A visit behind the scenes includes glimpses of the locker rooms, the arena and concert stage, backstage access, and luxury boxes.

THE JAMES A. FARLEY BUILDING

◪ 421 Eighth Ave.

New York's immense main post office faces Madison Square Garden with its 53-foot Corinthian columns. Completed in 1913, the broad portico of this monumental neoclassical building bears a quotation from Herodotus and now the adopted motto of the US Postal Service: "Neither snow nor rain nor heat nor gloom of night stays these couriers from the swift completion of their appointed rounds." Inside one can see the small poster of mugshots and fingerprints of the real-life "America's Most Wanted," or look around the one-room **Post Office Museum** that proudly displays such items as postal clerk ties, scales, and hats of decades past.

MACY'S

◪ 151 W. 34th St. between Broadway and Seventh Ave.

This titan of materialism, occupying a full city block, recently relinquished its title as the "World's Largest Department Store" and changed its billing to the "World's Finest Department Store" when a new store in Germany was built one square foot larger. With 10 floors and some two million square feet of merchandise, Macy's has come a long way from its beginnings in 1857, when it grossed $11.06 on its first day of business. No longer in top form as seen in *Miracle on 34th St.*, the store retains some touches of old; check

Call the USA

"feel free to call"

1-800-COLLECT

1 8 0 0
COLLECT

When in Ireland
Dial: 1-800-COLLECT (265 5328)

When in N. Ireland, UK & Europe
Dial: 00-800-COLLECT USA (265 5328 872)

Member of
Dublin Tourism

Australia	0011	800 265 5328 872
Finland	990	800 265 5328 872
Hong Kong	001	800 265 5328 872
Israel	014	800 265 5328 872
Japan	0061	800 265 5328 872
New Zealand	0011	800 265 5328 872

out the wooden escalators on the higher floors. The store sponsors the **Macy's Thanksgiving Day Parade,** a New York tradition buoyed by helium-filled, 10-story Snoopy's and Barneys, as well as marching bands, floats, and general hoopla. Other annual Macy-sponsored events include the **4th of July fireworks** extravaganza on the East River, the annual Flower Show, and "Tapamania," when hundreds of tap-dancers cut loose on the sidewalks of 34th St. in late August (call ☎ 695-4400 for info).

Nuyorican Poets Café

GARMENT DISTRICT

▣ *West 30s between Broadway and Eighth Avenue.*

The Garment District was once a redlight district known as the Tenderloin. By the 1930s, it was reputed to have the largest concentration of apparel manufacturers in the world. Today, a small statue named *The Garment Worker,* depicting an aged man huddled over a sewing machine, sits near the corner of 39th St. and Seventh Ave. to commemorate the formative era. Curious to find out the accoutrements of the latest fashion trends (both current and trickling down to the masses)? Walk along Broadway from the upper 20s and lower 30s for wholesale and retail fabric, jewelry, clothing, perfume, accessory, and leather stores.

TIMES SQUARE AND THE THEATER DISTRICT

THE NEW YORK TIMES

▣ *229 W. 43rd St., just west of Times Sq.*

Here are the offices, founded in 1851, that the square was named for in 1904. At that time the *Times* inhabited One Times Square—the big, triangular building at the head of the Square).

Empire State Building

THEATER DISTRICT

The nearby **Theater District** stretches from 41st to 57th St. along Broadway, Eighth Ave., and the streets that connect them. Some of the theaters have been converted into movie houses or simply left to rot as the cost of live productions has skyrocketed. Approximately 40 theaters remain active (most of them grouped around 45th St.), 22 of which have been declared historical landmarks.

SHUBERT ALLEY. Originally built as a fire exit between the Booth and Shubert Theaters, the alley now serves as a private street for pedestrians (a half-block west of Broadway between 44th and 45th St.). After shows, fans often hover at stage doors to get their playbills signed.

THEATER ROW. This block of renovated Broadway theaters occupies 42nd St. between Ninth and Tenth Ave.

THE DRAMATISTS GUILD. This group protects the playwrights, composers, and lyricists behind the scenes of every show. Members of the guild include luminaries Stephen Sondheim, Peter Stone, and Mary Rodgers. According to their charter, "producers, directors, agents, students, academicians, and patrons of the arts" can all become members for $50 per year. Autograph hunters prowl outside. *(1501 Broadway, suite 701.)*

Union Square

CITY CENTER THEATER

🚩 *130 W. 55th St. between Sixth and Seventh Ave.*

Up several blocks from the Times Square area, City Center Theater replaced a mosque in 1943. Sickles and crescents still adorn each doorway, four tiny windows face Mecca (or at least the East Side) from the limestone upper stories, and a Moorish dome caps the roof. Venture inside the lobby to see the elaborate tile mosaics that surround the elevators.

EAST MIDTOWN

see map
pp. 332–333

ROCKEFELLER CENTER

🚩 *Between 48th and 51st Sts. and Fifth and Sixth Aves.* **Subway:** *B, D, F, Q to 50th St./ Sixth Ave.*

In the American tradition of "bigger is better," Rockefeller Center is the world's largest privately owned business and entertainment complex. Occupying 22 acres, it includes a two-mile-long underground concourse, dozens of restaurants, plaza shops, and other amenities for the few hundred-thousand people who work and play here.

TOWER PLAZA. The sunken plaza, topped by the famous gold-leafed statue of Prometheus, is surrounded by over 100 flags of UN members. During summer and spring the world-famous **ice-skating rink** lies dormant underneath an overpriced cafe; it reopens for fall and winter just in time for the annual lighting of the Christmas tree. In front of the International Building on Fifth Ave., between 50th and 51st Sts., stands the bronze six-pack totin' **Atlas** upholding the weight of the world with his triceps.

G.E. BUILDING. This 70-story tower on Sixth Ave., once home to RCA, remains the jewel of the complex. Note the limestone pylons marking the 49th St. entrance and the mural of hulking workers (and, oddly enough, Lincoln) heaving and straining deep inside the lobby. Now, G.E. subsidiary **NBC** has its headquarters here. The network offers an hour-long tour that traces the history of NBC, from their first radio broadcast in 1926 through the heyday of TV programming in the 1950s and 60s to that knee-slapping episode of *Will and Grace* last week. The tour visits the studios of Conan O'Brien and the infamous 8H studio, home of *Saturday Night Live. (Entrance Fifth Ave and 49th St.)*

RADIO CITY MUSIC HALL. Narrowly escaping demolition in 1979, this New York landmark received a complete interior restoration shortly thereafter. Though it was built in 1932, the 5874-seat theater remains the largest in the world. It fuctioned as a movie theater between 1933 and 1975, premiering films like *King Kong* and *Breakfast at Tiffany's.* Now it is being used mostly for its original purpose: live performance. Acts ranging from Tony Bennett to Phish to Oasis have all graced the stage in the past year alone. Of course, you can always catch Radio City's main attraction, the Rockettes. *(Corner of Sixth Ave. and 51st St.)*

NEW YORK PUBLIC LIBRARY

🚩 *42nd St. and Fifth Ave.* ☎ *869-8089. Open M and Th-Sa 10am-6pm, Tu-W 11am-7:30pm. Free **tours** Tu-Sa at 11am and 2pm, leaving from the Friends Desk in Astor Hall.*

On sunny afternoons, throngs of people recline on the NYPL's marble steps. Featured in the hit 80s film *Ghostbusters,* two marble lions, Patience and Fortitude, dutifully guard the library from ghosts, goblins, spooks, Rick Moranis, and illiteracy. The impressive main reading room is a hit with both bookish introverts and indigent New Yorkers seeking shelter from the elements. Unfortunately, if any vagants plan on checking out the latest Stephen King page-turner, they'll have to do it across the street at the Mid-Manhattan branch; this library is for research purposes only.

BRYANT PARK

🚩 *Park open daily 7am-9pm. The New York Convention and Visitors Bureau,* ☎ *484-1222 or 517-5700, provides a schedule of events.*

Behind the library, this park is home to trees, squirrels, pigeons, and hormonally-charged youngsters. Fresh off the success of the World's Fair that was held there in 1853, Bryant Park attracts secretaries on their lunch breaks and sunbathers with a little too much confidence in their figures. The stage at the head of the park's open field plays host to a variety of free cultural events throughout the summer, including screening of classic films, jazz concerts, and amateur comedy.

GRAND CENTRAL TERMINAL

◪ E. 42nd St. between Madison and Lexington Aves, where Park Ave. should be.

Grand Central was once the main transportation hub for out-of-town visitors and commuting New Yorkers. While today its importance has been partially eclipsed by Penn Station and the airplane, Grand Central is still a sight to see. The majestic "lobby" or Main Concourse, renovated to its original splendor, has been known to add a little spice to the drudgery of commuting; occasional jazz and classical musicians and innovative art exhibits are featured throughout the year.

PAN AM BUILDING

◪ Looms over Park Ave. and 44th and 45th Sts.

Growing out of the back of Grand Central, this monolith slices Park Ave. in half. Although the once-familiar Pan Am logo atop the building has been replaced by that of Met Life, the skyscraper retains its old name and vaguely aerodynamic shape. Also, the Pan Am building is huge. How huge? Well, how does the world's largest commercial office space ever built sound to you? Contained within this space are 2.4 million sq. ft. of corporate cubicles and all the pink marble you can handle. Deep inside the lobby, right above the escalators, hangs an immense red-and-white Josef Albers mural.

THE CHRYSLER BUILDING

◪ 42nd St. and Lexington Ave.

A spire influenced by radiator grille design tops this Art Deco palace of industry—one of many details meant to evoke the romance of the automobile in the Chrysler Automobile Company's "Golden Age." Other monuments to motoring include a frieze of idealized cars in white and gray brick on the 26th floor, flared gargoyles near the top styled after 1929 hood ornaments and hubcaps, and stylized lightning-bolt designs symbolizing the energy of the new machine. During construction in 1929, the Chrysler Building engaged in a race with the Bank of Manhattan building for the title of the world's tallest structure. Work on the bank stopped when it appeared to have won. But with capitalist ingenuity, devious Chrysler machinists then brought out and added the spire that had been secretly assembled inside. While many consider it to be the most eye-pleasing in New York, it ruined architect William Van Alen's career: Chrysler, unsatisfied with the final product, accused Alen of bribery and refused to pay him.

THE UNITED NATIONS BUILDING

◪ First Ave. between 42nd and 48th Sts. ☎963-4475; General Assembly ☎963-7713. Tours, in 20 languages, depart from the UN visitor's entrance at First Ave. and 46th St. $7.50, students $4.50, grades 1-8 $3.50, over 60 $5.50; disabled 20% discount. Children under 5 not admitted on tour. 45min.; every 15min.; daily 9:15am-4:45pm.

Though located along what would be New York's First Ave., this area is international territory and not subject to the laws and jurisdiction of the US—as evinced by the 184 flags flying outside at equal height, in flagrant violation of American custom. An understated skyscraper and expansive lobby compose the bulk of the structure, while outside a rose garden and statuary park provide a lovely view of the multi-hued East River and the industrial wastelands of western Queens. Note the statue depicting a muscle-bound man beating a sword into a plowshare; the buff Socialist was a gift to the UN by the former USSR in 1959. The only way to view the imposing **General Assembly** is by a guided tour.

UNICEF HOUSE

Up First Ave. from the UN.

This building houses the headquarters of UNICEF, the international organization devoted to advocacy for children. The **Danny Kaye Visitors Center** opened in July 1994 with exhibits and explanations of UNICEF's mission. Recent displays included an exhibit on children's rights.

THE WALDORF-ASTORIA HOTEL

301 Park Ave., between 49th and 50th Sts.

Ritzier than the Ritz itself, the Waldorf-Astoria is the crème de la crème of Park Avenue hotels. Cole Porter's piano sits in the front lounge, a huge chandelier dominates the lobby, and the carpeting ensures that every person who enters received the red carpet treatment. The Duchess of Windsor, King Faisal of Saudi Arabia, and the Emperors Hirohito and Akihito of Japan all stayed here. Unfortunately, unless you are carrying around this book for kitsch value, you probably can't afford the rooms here.

SONY PLAZA

530 Madison Ave. between 55th and 56th Sts. ☎833-8830. Lab open Tu-Sa 10am-6pm, Su noon-6pm. Free.

On its way to buying everything buyable, the Sony Corporation recently bought Philip Johnson's postmodern masterpiece, the erstwhile AT&T Building, and renamed it. It now features two massive superstores offering hands-on interaction with state-of-the-art products and free movie screenings of releases by Sony-owned Columbia Pictures. Sony has also answered its charge to provide free education for the children of New York with its new **Sony Wonder** technology lab, a most worthwhile interactive introduction to communications technology.

CITICORP CENTER

The corner of 53rd St. and Lexington Ave.

What do you do when you need to build a skyscraper, but pesky zoning laws prevent you from razing an historic temple? Easy. Just do what Mr. Drummond did in that episode of *Diff'rent Strokes*, when one of his buildings was going to be built on a Native American burial ground: Stilts! The distinctive 45-degree angled roof was intended to be a solar collector; today instead the roof supports an intriguing gadget, the so-called TMD, or Tuned Mass Damper, which senses and records the tremors of the earth and warns of earthquakes—an important feature for a building on stilts.

ST. BARTHOLOMEW'S CHURCH

Between 50th and 51st Sts. ☎378-0200.

This Byzantine church draws heavily upon medieval European religious architecture for its inspiration. Completed in 1919, the temple features a large mosaic of the Resurrection. The life-sized marble angel in the devotional area left of the altar has been a favorite of visitors and worshippers for years. St. Bart's hosts a summer festival of classical music on Sundays at 11am. Outside of the church is Cafe St. Bart's, a lovely but sinfully expensive, outdoor cafe.

CENTRAL SYNAGOGUE

652 Lexington Ave. and 55th St.

In 1870, Henry Fernbach built what stands today as the oldest continuously operating synagogue in the city. Its Moorish-revival architecture combines a lavish facade of onion domes and intricate trim with an exquisite display of stained glass within.

MADISON LEXINGTON VENTURE BUILDING

135 E. 57th St.

Barely eight years old, this stylish building has already garnered praise for its design. The fountain out front is its most conspicuous feature, encircled by Italian marble columns.

THE ALGONQUIN HOTEL

▰ 44th St., between Fifth and Sixth Aves.

Alexander Woollcott's "Round Table," a regular gathering of the 1920s' brightest theatrical and literary luminaries, made this hotel famous. The Algonquin's proximity to the offices of *The New Yorker* attracted the "vicious circle" of Robert Benchley, Dorothy Parker, and Edna Ferber, among other barbed tongues. The **Oak Room** still serves tea every afternoon, and folks say that, for better or for worse, the restaurant's menu and decor have not changed in 50 years.

ST. PATRICK'S CATHEDRAL

▰ Southeast corner of Fifth Ave. and 51st St. ☎ 753-2261.

New York's most famous church and America's largest Catholic cathedral was completed in 1879 after 21 years of labor. The twin spires on the Fifth Ave. facade, captured in countless photos and postcards, streak 330 feet into the air. Here, F. Scott Fitzgerald, author of *The Great Gatsby*, exchanged vows with his sweetheart Zelda.

NY Public Library

UNIVERSITY CLUB

▰ NW corner of Fifth Ave. and 54th St.

This turn-of-the-century granite palace accommodates aging, rich white guys, and since 1987, aging rich white women. As indicated by its name, this organization was among the first men's clubs that required its members to hold college degrees. Twenty prestigious university crests adorn its facade, which is as close as you'll get to the interior; entrance to the club is for members and guests only.

PLAZA HOTEL

▰ Fifth Ave. and 59th St. at Central Park South.

This Henry J. Hardenberg French Renaissance style luxury hotel and historical landmark was opened in 1907. Splendid in its carved marble fireplaces and crystal chandeliers, The Plaza consists of Specialty Suites (with names such as Louis XVI and the Vanderbilt), costing up to $15,000 per night, and houses four world-renowned restaurants, including the Oak Room and the Oak Bar. Past guests have included Frank Lloyd Wright, the Beatles, Mark Twain, F. Scott Fitzgerald, and Kay Thompson's fictional character, Eloise (whose portrait hangs downstairs just off the main lobby). The Plaza, which was sold in 1995 by Donald Trump to Prince Walid bin Tala, owner of Fairmont Hotels, for an astounding $325 million (although less than Trump shelled out for it), has been a celebrity in its own right, featured in such films as *Home Alone II*, *Scent of a Woman*, *The Way We Were*, *Crocodile Dundee*, and Alfred Hitchcock's *North by Northwest*.

Trump Tower

OTHER SIGHTS

GRAND ARMY PLAZA. Inspired by the Parisian style and divided by 59th St., Grand Army Plaza lies on Fifth Ave. in front of the Plaza Hotel, serving also as an entrance to Central Park. The Pulitzer Fountain, with Karl Bitter's bronze statue of Pomona, the goddess of abundance, is set to one side, while directly across from it sits Saint-Gaudens' gilt equestrian statue of Union General William Tecumseh Sherman.

Rockefeller Center

CROWN BUILDING. Originally designed by Warren and Wetmore and completed in 1919, the Crown Building was topped with a 6-foot copper goddess who was donated to be melted down for the World War II effort. In 1978 (while owned by Ferdinand and Imelda Marcos) the upper tier was overlaid with 24½-carat gold leaf and embedded with colored glass to represent set jewels. As the sun sets, the reflected light creates a magnificent crown that is upstaged only by the gold-plated windows. Now it houses, among others, Playboy Enterprises. *(730 Fifth Ave., at 57th St.)*

TRUMP TOWER. One block away, Trump Tower shines like a beacon to excess. Inside, a ludicrous 80-foot waterfall washes down upon an atrium of orange, pink, and brown marble. Expensive stores selling suits Hillary Clinton would wear or dresses reminiscent of *Dynasty* fill the first floor "mall." The result is tacky with a capital Trump. *(Fifth Ave. and 56th St.)*

UPPER EAST SIDE

CARL SCHURZ PARK

see map
pp. 334–335

🚶 *Between 84th and 90th St. along East End Ave. Closes at 1am. 50-min. tours of the Mansion by reservation only;* ☎ *570-4751; Mar. to mid-Nov. W at 10 and 11am, and 1 and 2pm. Suggested donation $4; seniors $3.*

Carl Schurz Park is named for the German immigrant who served as a Civil War general, a Missouri senator, President Rutherford B. Hayes's Secretary of the Interior, and finally as editor of the *Tribune*. Built in 1910, the park overlooks the turbulent waters of Hell's Gate. **John Finley Walk,** which begins at E. 82nd St., forms a border on the eastern side of the park. Perfect for a romantic stroll, this strip also provides a spectacular view of the East River and of the Triboro and 59th St. Bridges. **Gracie Mansion,** at the northern end of the park (E. 88th St.), has been the official home of the mayor of New York City since 1942, when Fiorello LaGuardia set the precedent. Rudy Giuliani presently occupies this historical landmark, built between 1799 and 1804.

HOUSES OF WORSHIP

The Upper East Side is filled with large and beautiful sanctuaries, such as **Christ Church, United Methodist,** 520 Park Ave. (☎838-3036). **Temple Emanu-El,** 1 E. 65th St. at Fifth Ave. (☎744-1400), is the largest Reform Jewish House of Worship in the world. The multi-domed Catholic **Church of St. Jean Baptiste,** at the corner of Lexington Ave. and 76th St. (☎472-2853), is splendid with its paired towers and Corinthian porticoes. The **Church of the Holy Trinity,** 316 E. 88th St. between First and Second Aves. (☎289-4100), French Gothic-inspired and possessing a spectacular tower, was originally built to minister episcopalian services to the poorer residents of Yorkville. The **Church of the Heavenly Rest,** at the corner of Fifth Ave. and 90th St., possesses breathtaking stained glass windows by J. Gordon Guthrie and offers episcopal services. The **Russian Orthodox Church Outside Russia,** 75 E. 93rd St., at Park Ave. (☎534-1601), is a neo-federal style complex with an interior courtyard, designed by Delano and Aldrich and now a landmark building. New York's most prominent mosque, the **Islamic Cultural Center,** Third Ave. and 96th St. (☎722-5234), was precisely oriented by computer to face the holy city of Mecca. The striking and unusual **St. Nicholas Russian Orthodox Cathedral,** 15 E. 97th St. (☎289-1915), with its five onion domes and its Baroque design that evolved in 17th-century Moscow, is the only one of its style in NY.

CARNEGIE HALL

🚶 *881 Seventh Avenue, at 57th St. Subway: N, R to 57th St.; B, D, E to Seventh Ave.* ☎ *903-9790 for tours. 1hr. tours M-Tu and Th-F at 11:30am, 2pm, and 3pm; $6, students and seniors $5, under 12 $3. Museum, displaying artifacts and memorabilia, open M-Th and Th-F 11am-4:30pm; free. See **Entertainment,** p. 162, for concert information.*

How do you get to Carnegie Hall? Practice, practice, practice. Carnegie Hall, home of the New York Philharmonic and host to every other genre of performers, has become synonymous with musical excellence since its beginning in 1891. In its illustrious and eclectic career, which began with the American debut of Tchaikovsky, "the Hall" has hosted such artists as Caruso, Toscanini, and Bernstein; jazz greats like Dizzy, Ella, and Billie; and Bob Dylan, the Beatles, and the Rolling Stones. Other notable events from Carnegie's playlist include Marion Anderson (after she was denied a performance at the nation's capital because of her race), the world premiere of Dvořák's Symphony No. 9 *(From the New World)*, political landmarks such as Winston Churchill's lecture on the Boer War in 1901, and speeches by Booker T. Washington, Albert Einstein, and Martin Luther King, Jr.'s (his last) on February 23, 1968.

In the late 1950s, the threat of Carnegie Hall's replacement by a skyscraper generated a citywide campaign, led by violinist Isaac Stern, to save the building. In 1960, the campaign convinced the City of New York to purchase the Hall for $5 million. Decades of patchwork maintenance and periodic face-lifts had left the building in various stages of disrepair, leading to a $60 million renovation and restoration program in 1985, in commemoration of the 25th anniversary of the rescue. Legend has it that, before it was repaired, the hole in the ceiling gave Carnegie Hall better-than-perfect acoustics.

Bryant Park

"OLD BOYS" CLUBS

Glide over to the 60s to see where the sons of privilege cavort and establish networks of power.

METROPOLITAN AND UNION CLUBS. Designed by Stanford White and built by David H. King Jr. to perfectly resemble a 16th-century Italian palazzo, **The Metropolitan Club,** 1 E. 60th St. (first president: J.P. Morgan), was founded in 1891 by a group of distinguished gentlemen who were disgruntled with the rejection of some of their friends from the very exclusive **Union Club,** 101 E. 69th St.

KNICKERBOCKER CLUB. Inversely, The Knickerbocker Club was founded in 1871 by Union men who believed that the club's admissions policies had become *too* lax and liberal. Member names you might recognize: Hamilton, Eisenhower, Roosevelt, Rockefeller, dare we continue? *(2 E. 62nd St.)*

Sothebys's

GROLIER CLUB. The Grolier Club, an organization of book collectors, was founded in 1884 and named in honor of Jean Grolier, prominent bibliophile during the Renaissance. Completed in 1917, this Georgian structure houses a collection of fine bookbindings, quarterly exhibitions, and a specialized research library open by appointment. *(47 E. 60th St., between Madison and Park Aves. ☎838-6690.)*

LOTOS CLUB. The French Renaissance style, Richard Hunt-designed Lotos Club, an organization of actors, musicians, and journalists, was founded in 1870. *(E. 66th St. between Fifth and Madison Aves.)*

OTHER SIGHTS

FRANK E. CAMPBELL FUNERAL CHAPEL. A prestigious funeral chapel, the Frank E. Campbell Funeral Chapel has buried the best: Robert Kennedy, John Lennon, Elizabeth Arden, James Cagney, Jack Dempsey, Tommy Dorsey, Judy Garland, Howard Johnson, Mae West, Arturo Toscanini, Jaclyn Onassis, and, most recently, Cardinal John O' Connor of NY. *(1076 Madison Ave., at 81st St. ☎288-3800.)*

F.A.O. Schwarz

MADISON LEXINGTON VENTURE BUILDING. Beautiful fountains encircled by Italian marble colums in front of the stylish Madison Lexington Venture Building offer a relaxing place of rest on your urban journey. *(135 E. 57th St.)*

HENDERSON PLACE HISTORIC DISTRICT. Near 87th St., along East End Ave., are the remaining 24 of the original 32 connected, Queen Anne-style inspired houses of the Henderson Place Historic District. Completed in 1882 and intended for "persons of moderate means," they flaunt beautiful gables, dormers, mansards, and, some say, ghosts.

HUNTER COLLEGE. Founded in 1870 as a teacher's training school for women, Hunter College became coeducational in 1964. *(695 Park Ave., at 68th St. ☎ 772-4242.)*

CENTRAL PARK

see map   see map
p. 336   p. 337

There is no greenery; it is enough to make a stone sad.
—Nikita Khrushchev, on New York, 1960

🔲 *General Information:* ☎ *360-3444; for parks and recreation info call ☎ 360-8111 (M-F 9am-5pm). Main entrance:* **subway** *1, 9 to 59th St.-Columbus Circle; N to 59th St.-Fifth Ave. The Central Park Conservancy, which runs the park and offers public programs, has four visitors centers that offer brochures, calendars of events, and* **free park maps,** *at* **Belvedere Castle** *(☎ 772-0210), located mid-park at 79th St.; the* **Charles A. Dana Discovery Center** *(☎ 860-1370), at 110th St. near 5th Ave.; the* **North Meadow Recreation Center** *(☎ 348-4867), mid-park at 97th St.; and the* **Dairy,** *mid-park near 65th St. The Dairy also showcases exhibits, books, and other collectibles reflecting the history of the park; open Apr.-Oct. Tu-Su 10am-5pm, Nov.-Mar. Tu-Su 10am-4pm.*

If you miss one thing in New York, make it the Statue of Liberty. But for crying out loud, visit Central Park. The first landscaped public park in the US, Central Park was not always the beautiful oasis in the midst of an urban jungle that it is today. Until the mid-1800s, these 843 acres were considered a social and geographical wasteland. Consisting of swamps, bluffs, bogs, cliffs, glacial leftovers, and garbage dumps, this area was home to over 1600 of the city's poorest residents, including Irish pig farmers, German gardeners, and the black Seneca Village population, all squatters, who occupied shantytowns, huts, and caves on the site. Around 1850, some of New York's wealthiest citizens began to advocate for the creation of a park, claiming that, in terms of social reform, a public park would offer a respectable source of leisure and recreation. In truth, the upper class had long envied the public grounds of London and Paris and now sought a comparable establishment. In 1857, a contest was held to choose the best landscape design for the park. The winning idea was Frederick Law Olmsted's collaboration with Calvert Vaux, the "Greensward Plan," inspired by the English romantic tradition, which has both formal and picturequeue components. It required over 20,000 workers, today's equivalent of $20 million, 15 years, and the planting of over 270,000 trees and shrubs. The plan also called for the sinking of road, eight feet below the park's surface in order to carry crosstown traffic, creating the atmosphere of uninterrupted expanse and rural isolation upon which even those pesky skyscapers lining the fringe of the park cannot intrude.

If Central Park's foliage could talk, it would recount countless stories of celebrity concerts and marathons, of "happenings" and "be-ins" in the 60s, and the controversial gay and lesbian rallies of the past two decades. When you explore its tree-lined paths, you become lost in that rich history. In order not to get geographically lost, however, look to the nearest aluminum lamppost for guidance; its small metal plaque's first two digits tell you what street you're nearest (e.g., E89 = East 89th St.). In order to navigate from East to West, or vice versa, you can use one of the four transverses, spaced out conveniently at 65th St., 79th St., 85th St., and 97th St. The 72nd St. East and West entrances also afford a less direct east-west navigation route. In addition, East Dr. and West Dr. both run north-south on either side of the park, from Central Park South/59th St. to Central Park North/110th St. (both between Central Park West and Fifth Ave.). Finally, it is very important to mention that, like many other parts of the city, the park can be a dangerous place even during the day and should be avoided after dark.

CENTRAL PARK WILDLIFE CENTER. Formerly the Central Park Zoo, don't miss the **Delacorte Musical Clock,** just north of the main area, spring to life every half-hour. Beyond the clock lies the **Tisch Children's Zoo,** a petting zoo. *(E. 64th St. and Fifth Ave. ☎439-6500. Apr.-Oct. M-F 10am-5pm, Sa-Su 10:30am-5:30pm; Nov.-Mar. daily 10am-4:30pm. Last entry 30min. before closing. Combined admission $3.50, seniors $1.25, ages 3-12 50¢, under 2 free.)*

CHILDREN'S DISTRICT. Vaux and Olmsted designated the area south of the 65th St. Transverse as a place for the young to frolic and receive affordable nourishment. Then, the Dairy distributed food and purity-tested milk to poor families susceptible to food poisoning. Next door, Olmsted and Vaux's **Kinderberg** (Children's Mountain) has become a visitor's center. (See **Wee Ones' Wonderland,** p. 94.)

THE ARSENAL. The ivy-covered Arsenal was originally built in 1814 to protect against the British in the War of 1812. It is home to the Park's administrative offices, including the Central Park Conservancy. The 3rd-floor Arsenal Gallery hosts free park-related exhibitions. *(At Fifth Ave. and E. 64th St. ☎360-8111. Open M-F 9am-4pm.)*

SHEEP MEADOW. Named for the sheep who grazed there until lawnmowers put the flock out of work in 1934, A popular spot for love-ins and drug fests in the 60s and 70s; today this area still hosts the occasional alterna-teen trying to get high alongside the frisbee-tossers and picnicking families. On summer days, so many tanning bodies cover it that some locals morbidly call the spot "Gettysburg." *(Meadow extends from about 66th to 69th St. on the western side of Central Park, directly north of the Carousel.)*

THE LAKE. Spreading out to the west from underneath Bow Bridge, you can watch rowers awkwardly maneuver their boats around the lake. More fun yet, rent one yourself at the **Loeb Boathouse** (mid-park at 75th St.); for prices, see **Entertainment,** p. 171.

CONSERVATORY WATER. To the east of the Terrace and the Lake, competitive model-yachters gather to race, even observing Olympic yachting regulations. From the Conservatory Sailboats cart, less serious yachters can rent remote-control sailboats. *(At 74th St., off Fifth Ave. Races Sa at 10am late-March to mid-November. Conservatory boats ☎673-1102; $10 per hr. with license or credit card deposit.)*

STRAWBERRY FIELDS. Yoko Ono's memorial to her late husband stands directly across from the Dakota Apartments where John Lennon was assassinated and where Ono still lives. Ono battled for this space against city-council members who had planned a Bing Crosby memorial on the same spot. Picnickers and 161 varieties of plants now adorn the hills around the circular **"Imagine" mosaic.** On John Lennon's birthday, October 9th, thousands gather here to remember the legend. *(West of the Lake at 72nd St. and West Dr.)*

BELVEDERE CASTLE. In 1869 Vaux designed this whimsical fancy. The castle rises from Vista Rock, like something out of a fairy tale, commanding a view of the legendary Ramble to the south and the Great Lawn to the north. For many years a weather station, Belvedere Castle has been reincarnated as an education and information center. *(Mid-park, just off the 79th St. Transverse. Observatory open Tu–Su 11am-5pm.)*

THE GREAT LAWN. Here, near the Delacorte Theater, Paul Simon crooned and the Stonewall 25 marchers rallied. The New York Philharmonic and the Metropolitan Opera Company hold summer performances here (see **Classical Music,** p. 161). On normal days the Great Lawn hosts pickup softball, touch football, and soccer games.

HARLEM MEER. Sundays from late May to early September, this 11-acre lake holds the **Harlem Meer Performance Festival** that brings free jazz, reggae, and Latin music, dance, and theater performances. The **Charles A. Dana Discovery Center** features exhibitions and activities presenting Central Park as an environmental space to be explored by amateur and professional biologists alike. The Center also leads tours and loans out free fishing rods and bait for use in the Meer; carp, largemouth bass, and chain pickerel abound, but there is a catch-and-release policy in effect. *(110th St. near Fifth Ave., at the northeast corner of the park. ☎860-1370. Open Tu-Su Apr.-Oct. 10am-5pm; Nov.-Mar. 10am-4pm.)*

kids in the city

wee ones' wonderland

Kids love Central Park; these are some of the tots' favorites.

The Friedsam Memorial **Carousel,** brought from Coney Island and restored in 1893, stands at 65th St., west of Center Dr., with its 58 hand-carved horses. (Open M-Sa 10am-6pm, Su 10am-6:30pm, weather permitting; Thanksgiving to mid-Mar. Sa-Su 10am-4:30pm. $1.)

Alice in Wonderland and her friends live at 74th St. off Fifth Ave. A statue of **Hans Christian Andersen,** a gift from Copenhagen in 1956, depicts him with the Ugly Duckling. Children scramble over the statues, sitting in Andersen's lap or clinging precariously to the Mad Hatter's oversized *chapeau*. The NY Public Library sponsors summer storytelling at the Andersen statue, usually Sa 11am; call ☎340-0849 for info.

Formerly a Swedish 19th-century schoolhouse placed in the park in 1876, the **Swedish Cottage Marionette Theater,** at 81st St. mid-park, puts on regular puppet shows. (☎988-9093. Reservations required. Shows usually Tu-F 10:30am and noon, Sa 1pm. Adults $5, children $4.)

With a $20 deposit and valid ID, older children can rent equipment at the Dairy and square off at the nearby **Chess and Checkers House.**

CLEOPATRA'S NEEDLE. This Egyptian obelisk was first erected at Heliopolis in 1600 BC and whisked away to Alexandria in 12 BC by the theiving Romans. NYC got hold of the ancient pylon in 1881, courtesy of the Egyptian government and William Vanderbilt, who footed the $100,000 shipping bill. Among other inconveniences, moving this 71ft. granite needle required the construction of a railroad track from the Hudson River. *(Just north of Turtle Pond and east of the Great Lawn, near 81st St.)*

TAVERN ON THE GREEN. Built in 1870, this rural Victorian Gothic structure orignally was home to the sheep who grazed in Sheep Meadow. Launched as a restaurant in 1934, Tavern has established a reputation for prestige and wealth. Even if you can't afford a meal, drop by in order to gape at the chandeliers, antique prints, paintings, and stained glass. *(West of Sheep Meadow, between 66th and 67th Sts. ☎873-3200. On average, lunch $11-26, dinner $15-37 . Open M-F noon-3:30pm and 5:30-11:30pm, Sa-Su 10am-3:30pm and 5-11:30pm.)*

CONSERVATORY GARDEN. Inspired by the European tradition of formal landscaping, this romantic haven is full of neat paths and colorful flowers. The Burnett Fountain, located in the center of the south (English) section, depicts Mary and Dickon, from Frances Hodgson Burnett's classic novel *The Secret Garden*. *(105th St., near Fifth Ave. ☎860-1382. Free tours of the Garden summer Sa at 11am. Gates open spring-fall daily 8am-dusk.)*

OTHER SIGHTS. Off the eastern shore of the Lake and the 72nd St. transverse, **Bethesda Fountain** presides over the end of the long **Mall.** Emma Stebins sculpted the fountain's 1865 statue, **Angel of the Waters,** in Rome. One of the benches on the northwest shore of the Conservatory Water stars in Edward Albee's play *The Park Bench* and actors occasionally perform it here. The **Shakespeare Garden,** containing every plant, flower, and herb mentioned in the Bard's works, sits near the Cottage. The recently re-opened **Turtle Pond** stretches out adjacent to the Delacorte theater. Joggers circle the shiny, placid **Jacqueline Kennedy Onassis Reservoir** (the track around it is 1.58 miles). North of the Reservoir, at the 97th St. Transverse, ballers will find the basketball courts of the **North Meadow Recreation Center** (☎348-4867), which sponsors such activities as boardgames, pool, and wall climbing. Most of these are free, but some that require equipment have a small fee.

ACTIVITIES. Central Park is where city folk shed their high-heels and briefcases on weekends and turn into Extreme Sports Diehards. West Dr. and 67th St., near Tavern on the Green, has a **slalom course,** sponsored by the NYRSA, for pros and amateurs alike. Usually dominated by showoffs, it might seem intimidating, but watching them fall can be just as entertaining. **Wollman Rink** and **Lasker Rink** host ice-skaters in the winter; call for times and prices. *(Wollman: ☎396-1010; near 64th St. Lasker: ☎396-0388; 106th St., mid-park.)* Watch the outstanding skate dancers at the **Bandshell** for free. There are various courts, including **tennis** and **basketball,** located throughout the park, and ball field permits can be obtained by calling ☎408-0209. You can also catch sight of people **horseback riding** in the park (see **Participatory Sports,** p. 171). **Bikes** and **rowboats** are available on the northeast shore of the lake at Loeb Boathouse. There are a plethora of tours offered by the Park, such as the **free walking tours** that take you on adventures throughout the park, telling you the secrets behind the statues and teaching you the name of the flowers in the gardens (☎360-2726). Along 59th St. at Grand Army Plaza, **trolley tours** will take you on 90min. tours of the park, and slow-moving, oat-chomping horses lead romantic **carriage tours** of the park. *(Trolley tours ☎397-3809. May 1st-Nov. M-F 10:30am, 1pm, and 3pm. Carriage tours ☎246-0520. $34 for first 20min., $10 each additional 15min.)* You may find Central Park **Bicycle Tour** a healthier, more humane choice. *(☎541-8759. Tours leave daily at 10am, 1pm, and 4pm from 2 Columbus Circle. $30 for 2hr., under 16 $20.)* For those adept on in-line skates, **New York Skateout** offers tours of the park with a historical slant. They also offer **in-line skating classes.** *(Reservations ☎486-1919. Tours daily 9am and 5pm. $25 for 1½hr.)*

Belvedere Castle

UPPER WEST SIDE

see map
pp. 334–335

LINCOLN CENTER

🄵 *Columbus Ave. between 62nd and 66th Sts.* ☎*LINCOLN.* **Subway:** *1, 9 to 66th St.* 1hr. **tours** *of theaters and galleries daily at 10:30am, 12:30pm, 2:30pm, 4:30pm. Adults $9.50; students and seniors $8. Backstage Met Opera House tours M-F 3:45pm, Sa 10am;* ☎*769-7020 to reserve.*

The seven facilities that constitute Lincoln Center—*the* cultural Mecca of established art—accommodate over 13,000 spectators. When Carnegie Hall seemed fated for destruction in 1955, power broker Robert Moses masterminded this project (see **Go Down, Moses,** p. 230). The ensuing construction forced the eviction of thousands and erased a major part of the Hell's Kitchen area (see p. 83). Lincoln Center also knocked out most of Manhattan's capacity for receiving large passenger ships, thereby increasing the need for trans-continental air travel. The complex was designed as a modern version of the public plazas of Rome and Venice, and despite its critics (the *Times* called it "a hulking disgrace"), the spacious, uncluttered architecture—as well as the cultural performances that take place here—have made it one of New York's most admired locales.

When facing away from Columbus Ave., the Plaza is bounded by the Metropolitan Opera House straight ahead, with the Beaumont Theater to the right of it; the New York State Theater to the left, with Damrosch Park to its left; and Avery Fisher Hall to the right, with Juilliard and the Reade Theater to its right and slightly behind it. The Library is entered from the back (Amsterdam Ave. side) of the complex.

Strawberyy Fields

Merry-Go-Round

THE FRONTIER OF LUXURY

Roberta Flack, Lauren Bacall, Boris Karloff, and Leonard Bernstein are just a few of the famous past residents of the Dakota. Music publisher Gustave Schirmer held salons attended by Mark Twain, Herman Melville, and Peter Tchaikovsky. John Lennon made this luxury apartment his home, and was assassinated outside it on December 8, 1980. When constructed in 1884, the complex was surrounded by open land and shanties. So far removed from the city was the site that someone remarked, "It might as well be in the Dakota Territory." The name stuck, and architect Henry Hardenbergh even gave it a frontier flare—look for the bas-relief Native American head and the stone garnish of corn and arrowheads that adorn the "territory."

THE PLAZA. Hopeful young dancers glide across the plaza on their way to rehearsal and student musicians mill about carrying their cumbersome instrument cases. Tourists and lovers favor the plaza's impressive fountain for rendez-vous. There, Cher and Nicholas Cage were *Moonstruck* and the cast of *Fame* danced at the beginning of each show. Near Avery Fisher Hall's main entrance, you'll find an automated **info booth.**

THE METROPOLITAN OPERA HOUSE. Lincoln Center's 1966 centerpiece by Wallace K. Harrison has a Mondrian-inspired glass facade. Chagall murals grace the plaza and lobby, where a grand, many-tiered staircase curves down to the humble opera buff. See **Entertainment,** p. 159.

VIVIAN BEAUMONT THEATER. In 1965, Eero Saarinen built this theater, a tidy glass box under a heavy cement helmet. Theatrical premieres here have included *Six Degrees of Separation* and *Arcadia.* In front, Henri Moore's 1965 *Lincoln Center Reclining Figure* lolls in the reflecting pool.

NEW YORK STATE THEATER. This wonder of modern architecture houses the New York City Ballet—founded by George Balanchine and now run by former *premier danseur* Peter Martins—and the New York City Opera. December promises the City Ballet's *Nutcracker,* a yearly ritual for many New Yorkers. See **Entertainment,** p. 159 and p. 160.

DAMROSCH PARK. Hosts frequent outdoor concerts and the perennially popular Big Apple Circus in its Guggenheim Bandshell. (☎ 875-5593.) See **Entertainment,** p. 166.

AVERY FISHER HALL. This hall, designed in 1966 by Max Abramovitz, houses the New York Philharmonic under the direction of Kurt Masur. Previous Philharmonic directors include Leonard Bernstein, Arturo Toscanini, and Leopold Stokowski (see **Classical Music,** p. 161). Every July and August, Avery Fisher Hall hosts the **Mostly Mozart Festival,** featuring world-class musicians playing—you guessed it—Mozart.

JUILLIARD SCHOOL. Prodigies eat deli sandwiches on the combined terrace and bridge leading across 66th St. from the Vivian Beaumont plaza to the halls of this prestigious school. Here Itzhak Perlman and Pinchas Zukerman fine-tuned their skills, Robin Williams tried out his first comedy routines, and Christopher Reeve and Val Kilmer learned how to act. Juilliard is considered one of the best performing arts schools in the US and is notoriously difficult to get into. The school is considering lowering admission numbers even further, making all future students scholarship fellows. Within the Juilliard building complex you'll find the intimate **Alice Tully Hall,** home to the Chamber Music Society of Lincoln Center (see **Classical Music,** p. 161).

WALTER E. READE THEATER. Lincoln Center's newest offering, the theater features foreign films and special festivals (see **Film,** p. 157); scan the schedule in the window.

NEW YORK PUBLIC LIBRARY FOR THE PERFORMING ARTS. Over eight million items, from videotapes to manuscripts, are all available for loan to anyone with a NYC library card. (Performing Arts Branch ☎870-1630.) To accommodate renovations, the collections will temporarily reside in the Mid-Manhattan Library, Fifth Ave. and 40th St., and the Library Annex, 521 W. 43rd St. (see **Service Directory,** p. 293).

COLUMBUS CIRCLE

🖪 *Intersection of Broadway and 59th St. Subway: A, B, C, D, 1, 9 to 59th St.*

This bustling nexus of pedestrian and automobile traffic is where Midtown ends and the Upper West Side begins; it is also the beginning of Central Park West. On the west side of the circle you'll see the **New York Coliseum,** built in 1954 by the TriBoro Bridge and Tunnel Authority to serve as the city's convention center. Although the building seems to be the permanent home of the Columbus Circle Marketplace and Amish exposition, its front has become an unofficial shelter for the homeless, protecting them from the winds whipping across the circle.

Harmony Atrium

DAKOTA APARTMENTS

🖪 *1 W. 72nd St., at the corner of Central Park W. See **The Frontier of Luxury,** p. 96.*

As Manhattan's urbanization peaked downtown in the late 19th century, wealthy residents sought tranquility in the blossoming Upper West Side. This elegant building was immortalized in Roman Polanski's film *Rosemary's Baby.* (See **Life and Times,** p. 52)

ANSONIA HOTEL

🖪 *2109 Broadway between 73rd and 74th Sts.*

The *grande dame* of *belle* apartments bristles with ornaments, curved Veronese balconies, and towers. Constructed in 1904, it has 2,500 rooms as well as various cafes, tea rooms, writing rooms, and a dining room seating 550. Its soundproof walls and thick floors enticed illustrious tenants like Enrico Caruso, Arturo Toscanini, and Igor Stravinsky. Theodore Dreiser did his own composing here, and Babe Ruth stayed just a few doors away. William Stokes, the developer of the Ansonia, used the building for an entirely different purpose—he raised chickens, ducks, and a pet bear on its roof.

Zabar's

HOTEL DES ARTISTES

🖪 *1 W. 67th St. between Central Park W. and Columbus Ave.*

A stately mass of luxury co-ops originally designed to house bohemians who had moved beyond their romantic garret stage. Built by George Mort Pollard in 1913, the building has housed Isadora Duncan, Alexander Wollcott, Norman Rockwell, and Noel Coward. Here you will also find the notoriously romantic **Café des Artistes.** The menu is a little on the *cher* side, but the pastoral murals of reclining nudes, painted in 1934 by Howard Chandler Christy, deserve a peek. Proper dress required for entrance to the restaurant.

Columbus Circle

THE NEW YORK SOCIETY FOR ETHICAL CULTURE

🏛 *2 W. 64th St., at Central Park W. ☎ 874-5210.*

Local illuminati convene here for weekly lectures, readings, and classical recitals. This venerable organization helped found many others, including the American Civil Liberties Union. The building, constructed in 1910, has gargoyle water spouts atop its roof.

BIBLE HOUSE

🏛 *1865 Broadway, near 61st St. ☎ 408-1200. Gallery open M-W and F 10am-6pm, Th 10am-7pm, Sa 10am-5pm. Library open M-F 10am-5pm. Free.*

The American Bible Society distributes the Good Book in nearly every tongue. Its exhibition gallery showcases JudeoChristian art, as well as rare and unorthodox Bibles, plus a smattering of Guttenberg pages and an online Bible.

APTHORP APARTMENTS

🏛 *2211 Broadway, at 79th St.*

Its ornate iron gates and a spacious interior courtyard, complete with beautiful fountain, have starred in a number of New York-based films: *The Cotton Club*, *Heartburn*, *Network*, *Witness*, and *The Changeling*. Its simple marble facade features bas-relief vestal virgins. The apartments were built by Clinton and Russell in 1908 on commission from William Waldorf Astor, who named them after the man who owned the site in 1763. Ask the guard to let you check out the courtyard.

EL DORADO APARTMENTS

🏛 *Between 90th and 91st Sts., on Central Park W.*

This appropriately named residence on Central Park W. showcases flashy Art Deco detailing in a full array of golds. The El Dorado lobby is a national landmark, and well worth a stop if you can convince the numerous security guards that you won't sneak a visit to the stars who reside there.

OTHER SIGHTS

TRUMP INTERNATIONAL HOTEL AND TOWERS. Donald Trump has laid his newest gargantuan monstrosity, Trump International Hotel and Towers, atop Columbus Circle. A shiny, silver globe adorns the Towers' facade, perhaps as a prediction of Trump's next real estate acquisition.

RIVERSIDE PARK. The bow-tie of Sherman Square knots at 72nd St. and Broadway. To the west, by the river, begins Riverside Park, where a statue of **Eleanor Roosevelt** greets locals walking their pooches. The park is quite desolate at night, but provides wonderful views and impressive architecture. *(West of Riverside Dr., from 72nd St. to the GW Bridge/ 175th St.)*

WEST SIDE COMMUNITY GARDEN. The West Side Community Garden is a sweet-smelling sanctuary with flowers, benches, and vegetable plots maintained by community volunteers. *(Between 89th and 90th Sts. and Columbus and Amsterdam Aves.)*

LOTUS GARDEN. Especially verdant and bright is the Lotus Garden; you can sit on benches and admire the fat tulips. *(97th St. between Broadway and West End Ave. Open Su 1-4pm.)*

HARLEM

see map pp. 340–341

MORNINGSIDE HEIGHTS

COLUMBIA UNIVERSITY

🏛 *Morningside Dr. and Broadway, from 114th to 120th Sts. Group tours for prospective students late fall through spring, but no regularly scheduled public tours.*

New York City's member of the Ivy League was chartered in 1754. Now co-ed, Columbia also has cross-registration with all-female **Barnard College,** across Broadway. The campus, like a good portion of the city, was designed by McKim, Mead & White. Its centerpiece, the magisterial **Low Library,** is named after former Columbia president Seth Low. The statue of **Alma Mater** in front of the building was a rallying point during the riots of 1968. Resilient and proud, Alma survived a bomb during student protests in 1970.

CATHEDRAL OF ST. JOHN THE DIVINE

Amsterdam Ave. between 110th and 113th Sts. ☎316-7540; tours ☎932-7347. Open M-Sa 7am-6pm, Su 7am-8pm. Suggested donation $2, students and seniors $1. Vertical tours (you go up 124ft.) noon and 2pm on 1st and 3rd Sa of month; $10; reservations necessary. Regular horizontal tours Tu-Sa 11am, Su 1pm; $3.

Already the world's largest cathedral, unfinished St. John's breaks its own record with every stone added. Its construction, begun in 1892, isn't expected to be completed any time soon. A "living cathedral," St. John's features altars and bays dedicated not only to the sufferings of Christ, but also to such things as the experiences of immigrants and victims of genocide and AIDS. The central nave contains a 100-million-year-old nautilus fossil, a modern sculpture for 12 firefighters who died in 1966, a 2000lb. natural quartz crystal, the world's most powerful organ stop, appropriately titled the Great Organ, which consists of some 8035 pipes, and a "Poet's Corner" honoring writers such as Nathaniel Hawthorne and Edith Wharton. An extensive secular schedule complements Episcopal services with concerts, art exhibitions, poetry readings, lectures, theater, and dance events. The complex also contains a homeless shelter, a school, music and dance studios, a gymnasium, a Greek amphitheater (still under construction), a wonderful children's sculpture garden, and a beautiful Biblical Garden.

GRANT'S TOMB

Near the intersection of Riverside Dr. and 122nd St. ☎666-1640. Open daily 9am-5pm. Free. Informal ranger-guided tours on request; 5-90min., depending on how many questions you ask; free.

This massive granite mausoleum—the largest of its kind in America—rests atop a hill overlooking the river. Once covered with graffiti, it is now a pristine monument worthy of Civil War general and 18th US President Ulysses S. Grant and his wife Julia. Bronze casts of the general's cronies surround the tomb. Rest on the funkadelic mosaic tile benches around the monument, inspired by Antonio Gaudí and added in the mid-1970s.

RIVERSIDE CHURCH

120th St. and Riverside Dr. ☎870-6792. Bell tower open Tu-Sa 10:30am-5pm, Su 9:45-10:45am and noon-4pm. Admission to observation deck Tu-Sa $2, students and seniors $1. Free tours Su 12:30pm.

This steel-framed knock-off of France's Chartres sprang up in only two years, thanks to John D. Rockefeller, Jr.'s deep pockets. The tower observation deck commands an amazing view both of the bells within and the expanse of the Hudson River and Riverside Park below. Best heard from the parks around the church, **concerts** on the world's largest carillon (74 bells) resonate on Sundays at 10:30am, 12:30pm, and 3pm.

CENTRAL HARLEM

TERESA HOTEL

Northwest corner of 125th St. and Powell Ave.

The Teresa Hotel once housed Malcolm X and Fidel Castro. An unconventional tourist, Castro felt safer in Harlem than in other parts of NYC; still, charmingly paranoid, he brought along live Cuban chickens for his meals. Now housing office buildings, the Teresa, after its segregation policy was dropped in 1940, reigned for some years as what *Ebony* referred to as the "Waldorf of Harlem."

NATURAL NEW YORK

Due to its size and residential nature, Harlem has many parks perfect for a relaxing picnic or stroll after the bustle of Midtown. Visit one of the following if NYC is getting too stifling for your suburban sensibilities.

Morningside Park. You too can discuss your sexual fantasies in this strolling park, just like Meg Ryan in *When Harry Met Sally.* *(Along the Hudson River, between 110th and 123rd Sts.)*

Sakura Park. Japanese for "cherry blossoms," the sakura were a gift to the city in 1912. Features a statue of General Daniel Butterfield, best known for composing "Taps." *(Across the street from Grant's Tomb.)*

Riverbank State Park. The state resolved to put a sewage plant here in 1993, an act many considered racist, so Gov. Cuomo built a state-run park over it. Ice and roller rinks, pool, tennis, tracks, baseball diamonds, and picnic fields make up for the sewage. The officials have vanquished the odor ("really, it's tidewater") problem—the park is surprisingly clean. *(Off the West Side Highway, enter at 135th St. ☎ 693-3654.)*

Jackie Robinson Park. Originally Colonial Park, these 12.8 acres were renamed in 1978; the hero himself stands in bronze at its center. *(145th-152nd St. between Edgecombe and Bradhurst Aves.)*

Marcus Garvey Park. Named after the "Back-to-Africa" movement advocate, this park features huge canopy trees and sloping rocks. *(120th-124th Sts. between Fifth and Madison Aves.)*

THE SCHOMBURG CENTER FOR RESEARCH IN BLACK CULTURE

🚇 *135th St. and Lenox Ave. ☎ 491-2265 or 491-2200. Open M-Sa 10am-6pm, Su 1-5pm. Free.*

This branch of the public library houses the city's archives on black history and culture. The center's namesake, avid black history scholar Arturo Schomburg, collected photographs, oral histories, and artwork, all of which appear on exhibit here. The center also houses the **American Negro Theater,** a venue for a wide range of entertainment including concerts and plays featuring local talent and celebrities. Year-round, the center features impressive exhibits of photographs and artwork by black New Yorkers and provides a wealth of information to minority travelers (see **Living in NYC,** p. 286). In celebration of its 75th Anniversary, the Center will present a year-long series of programs and events through May 2001. Along the front of the center, a year-round exhibit features brief biographies of 100 notable black New Yorkers.

HALE HOUSE

🚇 *152 W. 122nd St. between Powell and Lenox. For tours or to volunteer: ☎ 663-0700. Open M-F 9am-5pm.*

The center's founder, the legendary "Mother" Clara Hale (1905-1992), pioneered the care of children born HIV-positive for over 30 years. Her selfless and extensive work earned the support of such influential people as Yoko Ono, Donald Trump, and Patrick Ewing. Today her daughter Dr. Lorraine Hale runs the House, which now boasts a monument to the original Ms. Hale.

THE ABYSSINIAN BAPTIST CHURCH

🚇 *132 W. 138th St. between Malcolm X and Powell Blvds. ☎ 862-7474. Su services 9am and 11am.*

Adam Clayton Powell, Jr. presided over the pulpit here in 1930 before becoming NYC's first black congressman. His father, Adam Clayton Powell, Sr., a legendary figure credited with catalyzing the black migration to Harlem, preceded his son at this church in 1908. The pastor, Calvin Butts, a well-known local political leader, administers to the over 5,000-member congregation.

OTHER SIGHTS

CITY COLLEGE. Hidden away behind its gates, this sloping campus is incredibly beautiful. Founded in 1847 by Townsend-Harris, City College is the nation's first public college. Woody Allen graduated from here. *(Convent Ave. from 135th to 41st St., enter at 138th St.)*

HAMILTON HEIGHTS. Walk down Hamilton Terrace, between Convent and St. Nicholas Aves., for an example of this area's intricately designed brownstones. The two-story Colonial-style **Hamilton Grange,** 287 Convent Ave., was built by Alexander Hamilton. The National Parks Service wants to restore the house, make it a bona fide national landmark, and move it to the nearby St. Nicholas Park.

MASJID MALCOLM SHABAZZ. The silver dome of this mosque, named for its first minister, Malcolm X, glitters on 116th St. at Lenox Ave. (☎662-2200. Services F 1pm.)

WASHINGTON HEIGHTS

see map pp. 340–341

MORRIS-JUMEL MANSION

🔝 65 Jumel Terrace between 160th and 162nd Sts. ☎923-8008. Subway: C to 163rd St. Open W-Su 10am-4pm. $3; seniors and students $2. Accompanied children under 12 free. Guided tours by appointment; add 50¢ to admission, $1.50 for children under 12.

The Georgian Morris-Jumel Mansion was built in 1765 and is Manhattan's oldest existing house. Washington lived here while planning his successful (but little-known) Battle of Harlem Heights in the autumn of 1776. In 1810, Stephen and Eliza Jumel purchased the house, and after Stephen died in 1832, Eliza married Aaron Burr in the front room in 1833. Don't be afraid to knock if the house seems closed. The gardens are exceptional, with a great view of the Harlem River. Nearby, at St. Nicholas Ave. and 161st St., more brownstones with architecturally varied facades vie for attention on **Sylvan Terrace.**

AUDUBON BALLROOM

🔝 165th St. between Broadway and St. Nicholas Ave. Subway: C to 163rd St.

On February 21, 1965, militant black leader Malcolm X was assassinated on these grounds by three of his own supporters during a rally. Long abandoned, the 1912 structure faced demolition more than once in the 1970s and 80s, when the city was bombarded with protests for its destructive designs on the building. The Audubon was rededicated by Mayor Giuliani in 1997, partly as a memorial to Malcolm X and primarily as a medical research center.

GEORGE WASHINGTON BRIDGE

🔝 Best view from the corner of 181st St. and Riverside Dr. Subway: A to 181st St.

The construction of this 14-lane, 3500-foot suspension bridge coincided with the beginning of the Great Depression and the ensuing purse-tightening left the bridge's two towers without the granite sheathing that designer Othmar Amman had intended. The naked steelwork creates the precociously postmodern, erector-set look that so excited Le Corbusier, who pronounced it "the most beautiful bridge in the world."

Apollo Theater

Fort Tyron Park

125th Street

SUGAR DADDY

Perhaps Harlem's most prized possessions are its historic buildings, especially its beautiful brownstones. Below are the most famous of the neighborhood.

SUGAR HILL. In the 1920s and 30s, African-Americans with "sugar" (a.k.a. money) moved here. In addition to leaders W.E.B. DuBois and Thurgood Marshall—both of whom lived at 409 Edgecombe—and musical legends Duke Ellington and W.C. Handy, some of the city's most notable gangsters operated here. (Wesley Snipes starred as one in the film *Sugar Hill*.) The area is also the birthplace of Sugarhill Records, the rap label that created the Sugarhill Gang, whose 1979 "Rapper's Delight" became the first hip-hop song to reach the Top 40. *(143rd to 155th St. between St. Nicholas and Edgecombe Aves.)*

STRIVER'S ROW. A group of impressive 1891 brownstones presents a combination of architectures, from neo-Colonial to Stanford White's Italian Renaissance-inspired style. Originally envisioned as a "model housing project" for middle-class whites, legend says Striver's Row acquired its nickname from lower class Harlemites who felt their neighbors were "striving" to attain "uppity" middle-class status. Now part of the St. Nicholas Historic District, the neighborhood appears in Spike Lee's *Jungle Fever. (138th and 139th Sts. between Powell and Fredrick Douglass Blvds.)*

LITTLE RED LIGHTHOUSE

⌗ *Just beneath the bridge, in Fort Washington Pk. Subway: A to 181st. St.*

Originally constructed to steer barges away from Jeffrey's Hook, you may remember the lighthouse best from Hildegarde Hoyt Swift's children's book *The Little Red Lighthouse and the Great Grey Bridge*. To get there, go the intersection of Riverside Dr. and 181st St., then go west across the suspended walkway. From there, go south along Riverside Dr. (keeping the Hudson River to your right) and follow the path as it curves down the hill and to your right. The trail eventually comes out right at the edge of the water. The trail is a little spooky; please don't travel it alone or at night.

YESHIVA UNIVERSITY

⌗ *Amsterdam Ave. from 182nd to 186th Sts. Subway: 1, 9 to 181st St. YUM main galleries: Center for Jewish History, 15 W. 16th St., at Fifth Ave.*

Surrounded by kosher bakeries and butcher shops, Yeshiva—founded in 1886, the oldest Jewish-studies center in the US—stands in a bustling Hispanic neighborhood. On 186th St., the **Samuel H. & Rachel Golding Building,** formerly known as Tannenbaum Hall, provides the centerpiece of the campus, featuring Romanesque windows and colorful minarets that contrast with the drab, institutional architecture of the rest of the campus. A branch of the Yeshiva University Museum (The main galleries are downtown) here features exhibits focusing on the Jewish community.

OVERLOOK TERRACE

⌗ *Take stairs up from east side of 187th St. Subway: A to 190th St.*

On the west side of the island, Ft. Washington Ave. rises steeply to command a wide vista of the Hudson River on one side and the central valley of the island on the other. The journey north along Ft. Washington Ave. takes you past a succession of mid-rise apartment buildings (c. 1920), home to many Jewish and Hispanic families.

FORT TRYON PARK

⌗ *The official (and safest) entrance is at Margaret Corbin Circle. Subway: 1 to 190th St. Conservancy instructors take people to climb about twice a month; ☎ 342-4865.*

Central Park's Frederick Law Olmsted lovingly landscaped this park, which was donated to the city by John D. Rockefeller in exchange for permission to construct Rockefeller University. You can still see the crumbling remains of Fort Tryon, a Revolutionary War bulwark. The park also contains a path along the west side that offers views of the Washington Bridge and the Palisades, and The

Cloisters, the Met's sanctuary for medieval art (see **Museums,** p. 126). This is one of the most peaceful sights in Manhattan and is worth the trip even if you don't have a taste for medieval art. If you're an experienced climber you can register to climb up and rappel down the 50-ft. face of the cliff on the eastern side to Ft. Tryon Park.

see map pp. 342–343

BROOKLYN

BROOKLYN BRIDGE

🚇 *Subway: 4, 5, 6 to Brooklyn Bridge. In Brooklyn: 2, 3 to Clark St.; A, C to High St.*

Cathedral of St. John the Divine

Walking across the Brooklyn Bridge at sunrise or sunset is one of the most exhilarating strolls New York City has to offer—especially when you're dodging the cyclists on the pedestrian path. Gracefully spanning the gap between Lower Manhattan's dense cluster of skyscrapers and Brooklyn's less intimidating shore, it offers an escape from the business of Manhattan and a regal entrance to the more residential, uniquely-flavored neighborhoods of Brooklyn. Widely considered the world's most beautiful bridge, Georgia O'Keefe and Joseph Stella have memorialized this technological and aesthetic triumph on canvas, while Hart Crane and Walt Whitman expressed their admiration in verse.

Completed in 1883, the bridge is a result of careful, elegant calculation and design, as well as human effort. After chief architect John Augustus Roebling crushed his foot in a surveying accident and died of gangrene, his son Washington (and subsequently Washington's wife Emily Warren, after he succumbed to the bends) took over. The trio achieved a combination of delicacy and power that imbues the whole borough with irrepressible pride. Plaques at either end of the walkway commemorate the Roeblings and the 20 workers who died in the bridge's underwater chambers during construction.

El Museo del Barrio

CENTRAL BROOKLYN

DOWNTOWN BROOKLYN

DUMBO ART COMMUNITY

Some old warehouse spaces in this growing artistic area have already been made into galleries by Brooklyn's volunteer artist militias.

135 PLYMOUTH ST. This holds several makeshift galleries, including the **Ammo Exhibitions Space.** *(At Anchorage St.)*

BROOKLYN BRIDGE ANCHORAGE. A gallery is housed within the bridge's cavernous suspension cable storage chambers; it features cutting-edge, multi-media installations that make good use of the vaulted, 80-foot ceilings. **Creative Time** also shares the under-bridge space with Anchorage. *(Corner of Hicks and Old Fulton St. ☎ 718-802-1215. Open mid-May to mid-Oct. Th-Tu noon-8pm, W noon-7pm. Creative Time open Th-F 3-8pm, Sa-Su 1-6pm.)*

Columbia University

THE EAGLE WAREHOUSE AND STORAGE CO.

🏠 *28 Old Fulton St., at Front St.*

The *Brooklyn Eagle* newspaper was once produced in this building. Its editor, Brooklyn poet-laureate Walt Whitman, was fired due to either laziness or his bold anti-slavery views, depending upon the slant of your source. The company now houses apartments.

BOROUGH HALL

🏠 *209 Joralemon St., at the southern end of Fulton Mall. Free* **tours** *Tu 1pm.*

Built in 1851, this beautiful Greek temple-inspired edifice once housed the city hall of an independent Brooklyn. It is the borough's oldest building and now houses the Borough President's office. At the opposite side of the building, Columbus Park has a statue of Justice, standing firmly with scales and sword on top of the hall *without* a blindfold.

BROOKLYN HEIGHTS

🏠 *Subway: N, R, 2, 3, 4, 5 to Court St./Borough Hall.*

PROMENADE

🏠 *Spans between Remsen and Orange Sts.*

The view of lower Manhattan from this waterfront walkway is one of *the* New York sights to see—even if it doubles as the roof of the toxic Brooklyn-Queens Expressway (BQE). To the left, Lady Liberty peeps from behind Staten Island, and in fair weather, Ellis Island appears in full view.

ST. ANN AND THE HOLY TRINITY EPISCOPAL CHURCH

🏠 *Montague St., on the corner of Clinton St.* ☎ *718-834-8794. Arts:* ☎ *718-858-2424.*

One of the more impressive landmarks on Montague St., St. Ann's contains over 4000 square feet of stained glass. An alternative and illustrious **private school** operates on the church grounds, as does the **Arts at St. Ann's,** an acoustically superb cultural center that attracts performers like Lou Reed and Marianne Faithfull. The church hosts weekly free organ concerts (W; 1:10pm).

BROOKLYN HISTORICAL SOCIETY

🏠 *128 Pierrepont St.* ☎ *718-624-0890. Take a right on Clinton St. to get to Pierrepont St., parallel to Montague and Remsen Sts. Open M and Th-Sa noon-5pm.*

This striking building, lined with gargoyle-busts of Shakespeare, Beethoven, and others, houses both the very informative historical society and a museum. The research library is closed indefinitely for renovations.

WILLOW STREET

🏠 *Willow St. between Clark and Pierrepont Sts.*

To see the Heights' potpourri of 19th-century styles, explore the Federal-style Willow Street. Numbers 155-159 were the earliest houses here (c. 1825), with dormer windows punctuating the sloping roofs.

INSTITUTE PARK

🏠 *Subway: 2, 3 to Eastern Pkwy/Brooklyn Museum.*

THE BROOKLYN BOTANIC GARDEN

🏠 *1000 Washington Ave.* ☎ *718-622-4433. Open Apr.-Sept. Tu-F 8am-6pm, Sa-Su and holidays 10am-6pm; Oct.-Mar. Tu-F 8am-4:30pm, Sa-Su and holidays 10am-4:30pm. $3; students and seniors $1.50; ages 5-15 50¢; free Tuesdays*

This 52-acre fairyland was founded in 1910 on a reclaimed waste dump by the Brooklyn Institute of Art and Sciences. If you've gotten over that traumatic bee stinging in grade school, the **Fragrance Garden for the Blind** is an olfactory carnival—with mint, lemon, violet, and more appetizing aromas. The more formal **Cranford Rose Garden** crams in over 100 blooming varieties of roses. Every spring, visitors can take part in the **Sakura Matsuri** (Japanese cherry blossom festival) at the Cherry Walk and Cherry Esplanade. The woodsy **Japanese Garden** contains weeping willows and a viewing pavilion over a pond. The artificial scenery's authenticity fools the many water birds that flock to the site. The **Shakespeare Garden** displays 80 plants mentioned in Will's works. Toward the rear of the gardens two cement pools blossom with lily pads. You should not miss the 100 varieties of tropical water-lilies and sacred lotus that radiate in the summer in the **Lily Pool Terrace,** as well as the rainbow assortment of flowering annuals in the **Annual Border**—both just outside of the conservatory.

THE BROOKLYN PUBLIC LIBRARY

◪ *Corner of Eastern Pkwy. and Flatbush Ave. ☎ 718-780-7700. Open M 10am-6pm, Tu-Th 9am-8pm, F-Sa 10am-6pm, Su 1-5pm; closed Su June-Sept.*

Its striking Art Deco main branch building stands majestically on the Grand Army Plaza. The library has spawned 53 branches and contains 1,600,000 volumes. There are changing exhibitions on the second floor.

FLATBUSH

◪ *Subway: D to Church Ave.; 2, 5 to Flatbush Ave./Brooklyn College.*

EBBETS FIELD. This is where the long-mourned Brooklyn Dodgers used to play. It's demolished now, but don't mention that in front of a native.

ERASMUS HALL ACADEMY. The second-oldest high school in North America, Barbra Streisand and New York Jets' football great Joe Namath matriculated here. Constructed with the participation of Aaron Burr, John Jay, and Alexander Hamilton, no brick can be moved from the school's central building or, according to some antiquated charter, a neighboring Dutch Reform Church will repossess it. *(At Flatbush and Church Aves.)*

PROSPECT PARK

◪ *Subway: 2, 3 to Grand Army Plaza. To climb arch: Sa-Su noon-4pm. ☎ 718-965-8951. Free.*

Enter the park at Grand Army Plaza, passing through the Memorial Arch, built in the 1890s to commemorate the North's Civil War victory. The charioteer atop the arch is an emblem of the maiden Columbia, the symbol of the victorious Union. Frederick Law Olmsted and Calvert Vaux designed the park in the mid-1800s and supposedly liked it better than their Manhattan project, Central Park. Many Brooklynites share this sentiment towards the 526-acre urban oasis. Head to **Prospect Lake,** south of **Long Meadow,** or **Lookout Hill** for peaceful views of glacial pools and the manmade lake below.

LEFFERT'S HOMESTEAD. At the eastern part of the park, this preserved Dutch farmhouse was burned by George Washington's troops and rebuilt in 1777. The Children's Historic House Museum is inside, and there is a horse taken from Coney Island's 1912 carousel nearby who pipes an odd version of "Ob-La-Di, Ob-La-Da." *(At Flatbush and Ocean Ave. ☎ 718-965-6505. Open Sa-Su and holidays noon-5pm. Free.)*

ACTIVITIES. In summer, concerts are held at the Bandshell in the northwestern corner of the park—enter at Prospect Park W. and 9th St. *(☎ 718-965-8999.)* Paddle boats and horses are available for rent at Wollman Rink. *(Daily noon-5pm. $10 per hr.; horses $25-30 per hr.)*

GREENWOOD CEMETERY

◪ *Fifth Ave. and 25th St. ☎ 718-469-5277. Open daily 8am-4pm.* **Tours:** *2hr.; Su 1pm; $6.*

coney island

This is Brooklyn the way it was during its Golden Era, except that it's not that exciting in our highly-technological age. Still, this is a good place for kids if they're bored of brownstones.

Take a 100-second-long, rickety, screaming whirl on the legendary **Cyclone,** built in 1927. It's a historic place according to the National Register, and couples have been married on it. (834 Surf Ave, and W. 10th St. Open daily mid-June to Sept. noon-midnight; Easter weekend to mid-June F-Su noon-midnight. $5.)

The **Wonder Wheel,** at 150feet, was the world's tallest when it was built. (In Deno's, on Surf Ave. $3.)

The Ghost Hall is as scary as the *Munsters,* but it's pure Coney Island camp. (12th St., off Bowery. $2.50.)

For the extra small, **Deno's,** right next to Astroland, has rides kiddie-sized, like the Sea Serpent roller coaster. ($2 per ride, $15 for 10.)

The real spirit of Coney Island, however, is at the **Coney Island Circus Sideshow,** which has sword swallowers, snake charmers, jugglers, and "freaks." (12th St., at Surf Ave. Open F 2-10pm, Sa-Su 1pm-midnight. $3, children $2.)

This vast, hilly kingdom of ornate mausoleums and tombstones sits directly south of Park Slope and makes for a pleasant, if morbid, walk. Samuel Morse, Horace Greeley, and Boss Tweed slumber at this "Victorian Necropolis." Headstones here take the form of sinking ships, wrecked trains, empty beds and chairs, and fire hydrants in a macabre reminder of how each grave's occupant died.

NORTH BROOKLYN

GREENPOINT HISTORIC DISTRICT

🚩 *Bounded by Java St. to the north, Meserole St. to the south, and Franklin St. to the west.*

The Italianate and Grecian houses here were built in the 1850s, when Greenpoint was home to a booming shipbuilding industry. The Union's iron-clad **Monitor,** which stalemated the Confederacy's Merrimac, was built here.

BROOKLYN BREWERY

🚩 *79 N. 11th St.* ☎ *718-486-7422. Go south on Bedford Ave. until N. 11th St. Tap room open F 6-10pm, Sa noon-5pm; tours and tastings Sa noon-4:30pm.*

This is the Brewery that produces the Brooklyn Lager and Brooklyn Brown Ale on tap at all the local bars.

SOUTH BROOKLYN

CONEY ISLAND

Walk on the boardwalk along the white beach. Buy a frank (hot dog, $2) at Gregory and Paul's (by Astroland Amusement Park) and head into the midway. Surf Ave., across from the amusement parks, has some interesting antique shops (825 Surf Ave.) Fireworks are held on the boardwalk every summer Friday (W. 12th-10th Sts.) at 9pm.

ABANDONED RIDES. Head west on Surf Ave. or take the boardwalk to the corner of W. 16th St., where the deceased **Thunderbolt** coaster stands in majestic ruins—relentless greenery has grown over its base. The tall, rusted skeleton of the **Parachute Jump** is also there. Once a year, on Puerto Rican National Day, a flag somehow gets tied to the top.

NEW YORK AQUARIUM. Home to the first beluga whale born in captivity, the aquarium has all the regular denizens here, from penguins and piranhas to sharks and jellyfish. They even have some coneys, the fish that gave Coney Island its name. An outdoor theater showcases dolphins. (*At Surf and W. 8th Sts.* ☎ *718-265-3474. Open M-F 10am-5pm, Sa-Su 10am-6pm. $9.75; children 2-12 and seniors $6.*)

see map pp. 342–343

QUEENS

Less a borough of famous sights or museums, Queens is about its ethnic communities. Follow our walking tour guidelines below or get lost on your own—Queens will reward you at every turn.

ASTORIA AND LONG ISLAND CITY

⚐ Subway: N to Broadway and 31st St.; G, R to Steinway St.

This area densely packs an average block with a number of delis, a Greek bakery, and an Italian grocery. Avid shoppers head east on Broadway to Steinway St. "Little Athens" is located in the blocks surrounding the N subway line's last stop, Ditmars Blvd. Various places on Vernon Blvd. have pleasant boardwalk sections along the water that end near the Sculpture Park (see below).

Brooklyn Heights Promenade

THE STEINWAY PIANO FACTORY. The world-famous Steinway pianos have been manufactured in the same spot, in the same way, since the 1870s. The 12,000 parts of a typical Steinway include a 340lb. plate of cast iron and tiny bits of Brazilian deer skin. Over 95% of piano performances in the US are played on Steinway grands. *(19th Rd. and 77th St. ☎ 718-721-2600. Open M-F 9am-5pm. No tour; office for business only.)*

⊠THE SOCRATES SCULPTURE PARK. Sculptor Mark di Suvero created this curiosity, located just across from the building labeled "Adirondack Office Furniture." Thirty-five stunning, if unnerving, day-glo and rusted metal abstractions cluster on the site of what was once an illegal dump. Nearby, the Sound Observatory challenges the viewer's interpretive skills—you can spend hours figuring out how to trigger rhythms and sounds on the interactive audio-sculptural apparatus. *(At the end of Broadway, across the Vernon Blvd. intersection. ☎ 718-956-1819. Open daily 10am-sunset. Free.)*

Brooklyn Bridge

KAUFMAN-ASTORIA STUDIO. The US's largest studio outside of Los Angeles sits on a 13-acre plot with 8 sound stages. Paramount Pictures used these facilities to make such major motion pictures as *Scent of a Woman* and *The Secret of My Success.* Television's *The Cosby Show* was taped here as well. The studios are closed to the public, but next door is the **American Museum of the Moving Image** (see **Museums,** p. 125).

JACKSON HEIGHTS, ELMHURST, AND CORONA

⚐ Subway: 7, E, F, G, R to Roosevelt Blvd.

A great day can be spent walking through these neighborhoods. Exit the subway at Roosevelt Ave. and peruse the shops on the blocks surrounding it. This area, particularly 74th and 73rd Sts., is home to many of the city's Indians, Pakistanis, Nepalese, and Iranians. Return to Roosevelt

Brooklyn brownstones

Ave. and walk east past the myriad shops and signs that slowly change from Hindi to Spanish. Turn right on Hampton St. or Ithaca St. to detour into the neighborhood of Elmhurst. Turn left on Elmhurst Ave. to return to Roosevelt Blvd.; continuing on Roosevelt will bring you to the more hispanic Corona.

FLUSHING

🚇 *Subway: 7 to Main St.*

Most signs around Main St. are penned in Korean or Chinese characters, not English, and ducks and dumplings adorn shop windows. Main St. is the commercial hub of the neighborhood. Walk north and turn right on Northern Blvd. to get a sense of "Little Asia."

THE KINGSLAND HOMESTEAD. Built in 1775, the Homestead was a typical home of the time, but few similar structures remain today. It holds a permanent collection of antique china and memorabilia that belonged to early trader Captain Joseph King. There is also a permanent collection of antique dolls and a fully-furnished "Victorian Room," depicting the typical furnishings of a middle-class citizen of the time. As home of the **Queens Historical Society,** the Homestead also displays three or four temporary exhibits each year concerning aspects of the borough's history. *(143-35 37th Ave. ☎ 718-939-0647. Open Tu and Sa-Su 2:30-4:30pm. $2, students and seniors $1. Historical Society open M-F 9:30am-5pm. Free tours. Academic adventurers can use the archival and genealogical research center by appointment.)*

QUEENS BOTANICAL GARDEN. An exhibition for the 1939 World's Fair in nearby Flushing Meadows-Corona Park (see p. 109), the garden had to move when the park was redesigned for the 1964 World's Fair. At its present site it boasts a 5000-bush rose garden, a 23-acre arboretum, more than nine acres of "theme gardens," and a new home compost demonstration site. On weekends, the Garden plays host to a cavalcade of wedding parties, each competing for gazebos, fountains, and the home compost demonstration site as a backdrop for commemorative photos. *(☎ 718-886-3800. Walk from the station or take the Q44 bus toward Jamaica. Open Tu-Su Apr.-Oct. 8am-7pm; Nov.-Mar. 8am-4:30pm. Free.)*

FLUSHING TOWN HALL. Built in 1862, it was recently restored in the Romanesque tradition. Local art and historical exhibitions await inside. Live jazz and classical concerts F, except in the summer; call ahead. *(137-35 Northern Blvd. ☎ 718-463-7700. Suggested donation $3; students and seniors $2, under 12 $1. Concerts $20, students and seniors $15.)*

BOWNE HOUSE. This low, unassuming house, built in 1661, is the oldest remaining residence in Queens and is filled with interesting antiques. Here, John Bowne defied Dutch governor Peter Stuyvesant's 1657 ban on Quaker meetings and was exiled for his efforts. *(37-01 Bowne St. ☎ 718-359-0528. Open Tu and Sa-Su 2:30-4:30pm. $2, seniors and under 14 $1.)*

CENTRAL QUEENS

🚇 *Jamaica: E, J, Z to Jamaica Center. The Q44, Q34, and Q25 also go to and from Flushing.* **St. Albans:** *E, J, Z to Jamaica Center, then bus Q4 to Linden Blvd.*

The main strip on Jamaica Ave., stretching from 150th to 168th St., constantly roars with activity. Restaurants selling succulent Jamaican beef patties, stores peddling African clothing and braids, and mobs of local shoppers rushing to get a deal crowd the brick-lined **pedestrian mall** on 165th St. Saint Albans can best be explored by a walk down Linden Blvd. The West Indian culture congregates on both sides of Hillside Ave. eastward.

JAMAICA ARTS CENTER. This gallery offers workshops and powerful art exhibits by local and international artists. Past exhibitions have included the photographic collection "The Many Faces of Queens Women," a collection of quilts including patchworks made of Wonder Bread and condoms, and an installation of bamboo stick sculptures. *(161-04 Jamaica Ave., at 161st St. ☎ 718-658-7400. Open M-Tu and F-Sa 9am-6pm, W-Th 9am-8pm. Free.)*

KING MANOR MUSEUM. This recently-renovated colonial residence was once that of Rufus King, an early abolitionist, signer of the Constitution, one of New York's first senators, and an ambassador to Great Britain. The house, set in 11-acre **King Park,** dates back to the 1750s and combines Georgian and Federal architecture. The period rooms downstairs give you an idea of how they lived back in the day. The museum offers year-round public programs for children and adults, and the park hosts the "Jazz Under the Stars" summer concert series on F nights. *(At Jamaica Ave. and 150th St. ☎ 718-206-0545. Open Sa-Su noon-4pm; second and last Tu of the month 12:15-2pm. $2, students and seniors $1.)*

FOREST PARK. A densely wooded area with miles of park trails, a bandshell, a golf course, a carousel ($1), baseball diamonds, tennis courts, and horseback riding. If you like horses, **Lynne's Riding School** and **Dixie Dew Riding Academy** will oblige you with a guided trail ride. *(☎ 718-235-4100; events info ☎ 718-520-5941; golf ☎ 718-296-0999. Subway: J, Z to Woodhaven Blvd.; L, M to Myrtle/Wyckoff; then board bus Q55. Forest Park open daily 6am-9pm. Riding School: 88-03 70th Rd.; ☎ 718-261-7679; open daily 10am-6pm. Academy: 88-11 70th Rd.; ☎ 718-263-3500; open daily 8am-7pm. Both $25 per hr.)*

▊FLUSHING MEADOWS-CORONA PARK

🛈 *Subway: 7 to 111th St. or Shea Stadium.*

From the Van Wyck Expressway, motorists gaze upon the ruins of a more glamorous past. Rusting towers and half-eaten buildings punctuate the serene trees of Flushing Meadows-Corona Park, home to the 1939 and 1964 World's Fairs. The 1255-acre swamp, nestled between Corona and Flushing, became a huge rubbish dump until city planners decided to turn the area into fairgrounds. The remnants from the first fair are long gone, and the monuments from the second fast deteriorating. Yet behind the trees hide several excellent attractions, sculptured gardens, and one or two well-kept monuments. The grounds are worth a visit, not only for these hidden gems, but for the old steel and concrete dinosaurs themselves. On weekends and throughout the summer, the park comes alive as local families come here to play frisbee and let off steam. Conveniently located signs guide visitors around the spacious grounds.

NEW YORK HALL OF SCIENCE. Futuristic when it was constructed in 1964, the hall now stands flanked by rusty rockets. Its vision of the future may not have aged well on the outside, but a recent renovation and expansion have made the exhibitions inside current and engaging. Although largely oriented for children, this museum will keep visitors of all ages occupied with over 150 hands-on displays. *(111th St. and 48th Ave. ☎ 718-699-0005, ext 365. Open Sept.-June Tu-W 9:30am-2pm, Th-Su 9:30am-5pm; July-Aug. M 9:30am-2pm, Tu-Su 9:30am-5pm. $7.50, seniors and under 15 $5. Free Sept.-June Th-F 2-5pm.)*

THE QUEENS WILDLIFE CENTER AND ZOO. Features North American animals as well as more exotic species. A petting zoo features sheep, goats, cows, and other cuddly creatures. *(☎ 718-271-7761. Open M-F 10am-5pm, Sa-Su 10am-5:30pm. Tickets sold until 30min. before closing. $2.50, seniors $1.25, under 12 50¢.)*

NEW YORK STATE PAVILION. The original center of the 1964 Fair. The architect Philip Johnson probably never envisioned the towers as hide-outs for alien spacecraft as they were used in *Men In Black.* A new expansion has turned a part of the old pavilion into the new **Queens Theater in the Park** (see **Arts and Entertainment,** p. 157). South of the Pavilion, across the expressway overpass and behind the Planet of the Apes Fountain, is a restored **Coney Island carousel** that pipes out silly chipmunk tunes. *(Open daily 10:30am-8:30pm. $1 per ride.)*

THE UNISPHERE. A 380-ton steel globe tilts in retro-futuristic glory over a fountain. Constructed by the steel industry for the 1964 World's Fair, the Unisphere dramatically symbolizes "man's aspirations toward peace and his achievements in an expanding universe." Rings encircling the globe represent the three manmade satellites then in orbit. On sweltering summer afternoons you may be tempted to romp around the fountain with everyone else despite the "No Wading" signs.

THE NEW YORK CITY BUILDING. The south wing houses the **World's Fair Ice Skating Ring** (☎ 718-271-1996; open Oct.-Mar.), the north wing the **Queens Museum of Art** (☎718-

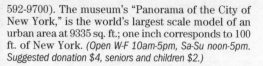

PHUN PHACTORY

A graffiti-ed yellow brick road on the sidewalk leads up to the entrance of the superintendent's office. Inside sits Pat Delillo, doling out permission to young street artists to "write" their colorful drawings on the outer walls, roof top, polls, and inner sanctuary of this old factory warehouse. In 1993 he initiated the first not-for-profit organization for graffiti writers, encouraging them move off the streets and focus their talents in legal locations. In general, the colorful murals turn over every few months, except for the ones dedicated to writers killed in street violence. Pat encourages visitors as he wants to spread the word for his cause. *(Phun Phactory. ☎ 718-482-7486; www.phunphactory.org. Subway: E, F to 23rd St.; 7 to 45th Rd in Hunter's Point. Open daily 9am-6pm. Suggested donation $5.)*

592-9700). The museum's "Panorama of the City of New York," is the world's largest scale model of an urban area at 9335 sq. ft.; one inch corresponds to 100 ft. of New York. *(Open W-F 10am-5pm, Sa-Su noon-5pm. Suggested donation $4, seniors and children $2.)*

OTHER SIGHTS. While in the park, you can also cavort in a playground accessible to disabled children or try your hand at a full course of **pitch 'n' putt golf,** which has 18 par-three holes. (☎718-271-8182. Open daily 8am-7pm. Greens fee Sa-Su $7.25, M-F $8.25. Club rental $1 each.) In the southern part of the park, **Meadow Lake** offers paddle- and row-boating, while **Willow Lake Nature Area** hosts an occasional free tour. **Shea Stadium** (☎718-507-8499), to the north of the park, was built for the 1964 Fair; it is now home to the Mets (see **Sports,** p. 169). Nearby, the **USTA National Tennis Center** and **Arthur Ashe Stadium** (☎718-760-6200) host the US Open.

SOUTHERN QUEENS

🚇 *Subway: A (marked Rockaways) to Broad Channel for **wildlife refuge**. Walk west along Noel Rd., which is just in front of the station, to Crossbay Blvd., then turn right and walk to the center. A (marked Far Rockaway) for **Rockaway Beach;** stop at 67th St., 60th St, or 44th St. A (marked Rockaways) for **Jacob Riis Park;** stop at Rockaway Pk., then transfer to Q22 westward. Or, take the E, F, G, R line to 74th St./Roosevelt Ave. in Jackson Heights, then the Q53 express bus to Broad Channel, which cruises past the front entrance of the refuge and the park. Car trip is much easier.*

THE JAMAICA BAY WILDLIFE REFUGE. Roughly the size of Manhattan and 10 times larger than Flushing Meadows-Corona Park, this park constitutes one of the most important urban wildlife refuges in the US, harboring more than 325 species of birds and small animals. Environmental slide shows and tours are held on weekends. *(☎718-318-4340. Park open daily dawn to dusk. Visitor/Nature Center open daily 8:30am-5pm. Free, but pick up map and permit at visitors center.)*

ROCKAWAY BEACH. Immortalized by the Ramones in one of their pop-punk tributes, the 10-mile-long public beach is lined by a **boardwalk.** Between Beach 126th St. and Beach 149th St., the beach has divisions between public and private waterfront areas. There is limited street parking during the summer. *(From Beach 3rd St. in Far Rockaway to Beach 149th St. in the west. ☎718-318-4000.)*

JACOB RIIS PARK. Part of the 26,000-acre Gateway National Recreation Area that extends into Brooklyn, Staten Island, and New Jersey. The park was named for Jacob Riis, a photojournalist and activist in the early 1900s. He persuaded the city to turn this overgrown beach into a public park. Today, the area is lined with its own gorgeous beach and boardwalk, as well as basketball and handball courts and a golf course. The former nude beach is at the eastern end; in the 1980s the beach decided to "clean up its act" and now only allows you to go topless. *(Just west of Rockaway Beach, separated from it by a huge chain-link fence. ☎ 718-318-4300. Parking $3.25.)*

ROOSEVELT ISLAND

🚇 *Subway: B, Q to Roosevelt Island; 4, 5, 6, N, R to 59th St. (at Lexington Ave.), then walk to 59th St. and Second Ave. and hop the tram.*

THE TRAM. A bright red tram shuttles residents and tourists across the East River. At the 59th St. tram stop you can pick up a handy walking tour map of the island for 25¢. The tram ride allows a grand view of the East Side as you hover 250 ft. above the United Nations complex and the distinctive visages of the Chrysler and Empire State Buildings. One of the few publicly operated commuter cable cars in the world, it generates an annual loss of $1 million, and its future has become uncertain since the subway opened to the island about 10 years ago. *(☎ 832-4555. Every 15min. Su-Th 6am-2am, F-Sa 6am-3:30am; twice as frequently at rush hour. One-way $1.50; no metro cards accepted. 6min. each way.)*

Flushing Meadows (Unisphere)

ISLAND LIFE. Once on the island, walk north or take the mini-bus (25¢) up **Main St.** and roam around a bit. A **walking/skating path** encircles the island, and gardens and playgrounds abound on the northern half. The southern tip of the island is currently off-limits while the city restores the ruins of the asylum and hospital. **Lighthouse Park,** at the northernmost tip of the island, is a pleasant retreat with views of the swirling East River.

The atmosphere on the island is small-town and friendly. The community runs a **communal garden** (open May-Sept. Sa-Su 8am-6pm) and keeps fit on the plentiful running tracks, tennis courts, soccer fields, and softball diamonds. Other than these options, little entertainment exists—there's no movie theater, record store, or even bowling alley.

Little Asia (Flushing)

see map pp. 348–349

THE BRONX

CENTRAL BRONX

BRONX ZOO/WILDLIFE CONSERVATION PARK

🚇 **Subway:** *2 to Pelham Parkway; walk two blocks west to Boston Rd., turn left, cross the intersection and follow Boston Rd., bearing right.* **Bus:** *Express Bx12; $1.25-1.40; ☎ 718-330-1234 for info. Liberty Lines bus leaves from Madison Ave. in Midtown for the Bronxdale entrance to the zoo ($3 each way); ☎ 718-652-8400 for info.* **Telephone:** *☎ 718-367-1010 or 718-220-5100.* **Open** *daily M-F 10am-5pm, Sa-Su and holidays 10am-5:30pm. Parts of the zoo* **close** *Nov.-Apr.* **Admission:** *$9, seniors and children 2-12 $5; W free.* **Disabled-access:** *☎ 718-220-5188.* **Food:** *African Market, Flamingo Pub, and Zoo Terrace.*

The Bronx Zoo/Wildlife Conservation Park, also known as the New York Zoological Society, is perhaps the borough's

Shea Stadium

biggest attraction next to Yankee stadium. The largest urban zoo in the United States, it provides a home for over 4000 animals. While the odd building dots the zoo, this newly environmentally conscious park prefers to showcase its stars within the 265-acre expanse of natural habitats created for each species' dwelling pleasure. The timber rattlesnake and Samantha the python (the largest snake in the US) serve life in the **Reptile House,** but more benign beasts wander free in the Park's "protected sanctuary," occasionally allowing for startlingly close interaction between inhabitant and visitor. Indian elephants frolic unfettered in a **Wild Asia** while white-cheeked gibbons tree-hop in the **JungleWorld.**

Other noteworthy habitats include the **Himalayan Highlands, South America,** and the **World of Darkness.** Kids imitate animals at the hands-on **Children's Zoo,** where they can climb a spider's web or try on a turtle shell. If you tire of the kids, the crocodiles are fed Mondays and Thursdays at 2pm, sea lions daily at 3pm.

If you're tired, take the **Safari Train,** which runs between the elephant house and Wild Asia ($2). Or soar into the air for a Tarzan's-eye view of the park from the **Skyfari aerial tramway** that runs between Wild Asia and the Children's Zoo ($2). The **Bengali Express Monorail** glides around Wild Asia (20min., $2). On free Wednesdays, lengthy lines for this ride accurately simulate the experience of waiting for a train in India. If you find the pace too hurried, saddle up a **camel** in the Wild Asia area ($3).

NEW YORK BOTANICAL GARDENS

🚇 Subway: *4, D to Bedford Park Blvd. Walk 8 blocks east or take the Bx26, Bx12, or Bx19 bus.* **Train:** *Metro-North Harlem line goes from Grand Central Terminal to Botanical Garden Station, which is right outside the main gate.* ☎ *212-532-4900 for info.* **Telephone:** *☎718-817-8700.* **Open** *Apr.-Oct. Tu-Su 10am-6pm; July-Aug. Th and Sa grounds open until 8pm; Nov.-Mar. Tu-Su 10am-4pm.* **Admission** *$3; students and seniors $2; children 2-12 $1; W all day and Sa 10am-noon free. Certain exhibits throughout garden incur an additional charge; "passports" ($4-10) available for all garden displays. Various* **tours** *(both paid and free) depart daily; inquire at the Visitor's Information Center.*

North across East Fordham Rd. from the zoo sprawls the labyrinthine New York Botanical Garden. Here, urban captives cavort amid such oddities as trees, flowers, and the open sky. Snatches of forest and waterways attempt to recreate the area's original landscape. The 250-acre garden, an outstanding horticultural preserve, serves as both a research laboratory and a plant and tree museum. One can scope out the 40-acre hemlock forest kept in its natural state, the Peggy Rockefeller Rose Garden, the T.H. Everett Rock Garden and waterfall, and a hands-on children's adventure garden. Although it costs an extra few dollars to enter, the **Conservatory** deserves a visit; the gorgeous domed greenhouse contains a few different ecosystems of exquisite plant life. If you go exploring by yourself, get a garden map; it's a jungle out there. The crowded 30-minute **tram ride** ($1) skirts most of the major sights.

🏛 EAST FORDHAM ROAD

🚇 *E. Fordham Rd. from Webster Ave. to University Ave. Subway: 4, C, D to Fordham Rd.*

If you prefer urban bustle to bucolic greenery, this street is the busiest shopping district in New York City. Influenced mainly by black and Hispanic cultures, the strip is one long, bargain-filled marketplace. Music blaring from storefront speakers attracts customers. Street vendors vie with department and specialty stores, while wizened women dish out *helado* alongside bargain beepers and gold figurines of the Madonna.

FORDHAM UNIVERSITY

🚇 *Webster Ave. between E. Fordham Rd. and Dr. Theodore Kazimiroff Blvd.* ☎ *718-817-1000.*

Begun in 1841 by John Hughes as St. John's College, 80-acre Fordham has matured into one of the nation's foremost Jesuit schools. Robert S. Riley built the campus in classic collegiate Gothic style in 1936—so Gothic, in fact, that *The Exorcist* was filmed here. The college's photogenic history doesn't end there—Denzel Washington studied here.

BELMONT

🚇 *Subway: 4 to Fordham Rd,; then Bx12 to Arthur Ave. MetroNorth also runs a shuttle bus on weekends and holidays that stops at the Bronx Zoo; see **Bronx Zoo**, p. 111.*

This uptown "Little Italy," with its two-story rowhouses and byzantine alleyways, cooks up some of the best Italian food west of Naples. **Arthur Ave.** is home to some wonderful homestyle southern Italian cooking. At **Dominick's,** between 186th and 187th Sts., boisterous crowds blindly put away pasta. (see **Food,** p. 204). To get a concentrated sense of the area, stop into **Arthur Avenue Retail Market,** 2334 Arthur Ave. between 186th and Crescent Sts. This indoor market is indeed a Little Italy onto itself, with *caffè*, a butcher, a grocer, a cheese shop, and other stalls selling Italian necessities. Meanwhile, outside the **Church of Our Lady of Mt. Carmel,** 627 187th St., at Belmont Ave., stands a pair of ecclesiastical shops where you can buy a statuette of your favorite saint. The portable martyrs come in all sizes and in every color of the rainbow. The church holds high mass in Italian daily at 10:15am, 12:45, and 7:30pm. The church lights up the street and the neighborhood every July 15th with its **festival** of the Lady of Mt. Carmel. Across and up the street is the **Belmont Italian-American Playhouse,** 2385 Arthur Ave. between 186th and 187th Sts. (☎718-364-4700). The theater also puts on Italian language productions, ranging from *Filumena* to the satires of wacky Nobel Prize-winner Dario Fo. The theater is usually closed during the summer. Recently a large **Kosovar** population has left its mark on the Arthur Ave. area; the Kosovar flag with its red background and spidery bird is hung in the window fronts of many stores, private "men's clubs," and eateries.

EDGAR ALLAN POE COTTAGE

🚇 *E. Kingsbridge Rd. and Grand Concourse, five blocks west of Fordham University. ☎718-881-8900. Subway: 4, D to Kingsbridge Rd. Open Sa 10am-4pm, Su 1-5pm. $2.*

The morbid writer and his tubercular cousin/wife lived spartanly in the cottage from 1846 until 1848. Here Poe wrote *Annabel Lee*, *Eureka*, and *The Bells*, a tale of the neighboring Fordham bells. The museum displays a slew of Poe's manuscripts and macabrabilia.

HERBERT H. LEHMAN COLLEGE

🚇 *Jerome Ave. and E. 198th St. ☎718-960-8000. Subway: 4 to Bedford Park Blvd./Lehman College. Ticket office open Sept.-May M-F 10am-5pm; closed in summer.*

Founded in 1931 as Hunter College, Lehman is a fiefdom in the CUNY empire. The UN Security Council met in the gymnasium building in 1946. In 1980, the Lehmans endowed the first cultural center in the Bronx, the **Lehman Center for the Performing Arts,** on the Bedford Park Blvd. side of campus. One block up through Harris Park, the **Bronx High School of Science** is an established center of academic excellence, as evidenced by the Nobel Prize winners who matriculated here.

NORTHERN BRONX

VAN CORTLANDT PARK

🚇 *Subway: 1, 9 to 242nd St. ☎718-430-1890. The park's **special events office** (☎718-430-1848) offers info about the many concerts and sports activities that take place during the warmer months.*

Van Cortlandt Park spreads across 1146 acres of ridges and valleys in the northwest Bronx. The slightly grungy park has two golf courses, new tennis courts, baseball diamonds, soccer, football, and cricket fields, kiddie recreation areas, a large swimming pool, and barbecue facilities. While children of all ages swarm the various ball fields, nearby Van Cortlandt Lake teems with fish. Hikers have plenty of clambering options: the **Cass Gallagher Nature Trail** in the park's northwestern section leads to rock outcroppings from the last ice age and to what is arguably the most untamed wilderness in the city; the **Old Putnam Railroad Track,** once the city's first rail link to Boston, now leads past the quarry that supplied marble for Grand Central Terminal. Ballplayers have a choice between the baseball and softball diamonds of the **Indian Field recreation area** (laid atop the burial grounds of pro-rebel Stockbridge Indians who were ambushed and massacred by British troops during the Revolutionary War) or the **Parade Grounds,** where you can play tennis, soccer, and cricket.

VAN CORTLANDT HOUSE. In the southwest section of the park, just below the Parade Ground, stands this national landmark, built in 1748 by the prominent political clan of the same name. The house is the oldest building in the Bronx. George Washington held his 1781 meeting with Rochambeau to determine his strategy in the last days of the Revolutionary War here. He also began his triumphal march into NYC from here in 1783. Besides featuring the oldest dollhouse in the US, the house also sports a colonial-era garden and sundial. *(At 246th St. ☎ 718-543-3344. Open Tu-F 10am-3pm, Sa-Su 11am-4pm. Small fee to enter.)*

WOODLAWN CEMETERY

🚺 *East of Van Cortlandt Park. Subway: 4 to Woodlawn. Open daily 9am-4:30pm.*

Music lovers pay tribute at the resting place of jazz legends Miles Davis, Duke Ellington, and Lionel Hampton. Other famous individuals, such as Herman Melville, are buried here, some of them in impressive mausoleums.

MANHATTAN COLLEGE

🚺 *From corner of Broadway and 242nd St.., take 242nd uphill all the way. ☎ 718-862-8000.*

You'll see the red-brick buildings and chapel of this 139-year-old private liberal arts institution that began as a high school as you walk up 242nd St. The campus sprawls over stairs, squares, and plateaus like a life-sized game of Chutes and Ladders. The second staircase on campus brings you to a sheer granite bluff crowned with a kitsch plaster Madonna, a likely kidnapping victim from a suburban garden. Hardy souls who ascend the campus's peaks can take in a cinemascopic view of the Bronx. In direct contrast to much of the poverty-stricken borough, this area (Riverdale) features some extremely wealthy residences and a triumvirate of esteemed private schools—Fieldston School (featured in Francis Ford Coppola's short film in *New York Stories*), Horace Mann, and Riverdale.

🏛 WAVE HILL

🚺 *675 W. 252nd St. ☎ 718-549-3200. Subway: 1, 9 to 231st St., then bus Bx7 or Bx10 to 252nd St. Walk across Pkwy. Bridge and turn left; walk to 249th St., turn right and walk to Wave Hill Gate. Open June to mid-Oct. Tu-Th and Sa-Su 9am-5:30pm, W 9:30am-dusk; mid-Oct. to May Tu-Su 10am-4:30pm. $4, students and seniors $2; Tu free, Sa free until noon.*

This pastoral estate in Riverdale commands a broad view of the Hudson and the Palisades. Samuel Clemens Longhorn (a.k.a. Mark Twain), Arturo Toscanini, and Teddy Roosevelt all resided in this impressive mansion. Donated to the city over 20 years ago, the estate currently offers concerts and dance amid its greenhouses and spectacular formal gardens that are free with the price of admission to the grounds.

VALENTINE-VARIAN HOUSE

🚺 *Bainbridge Ave. and 208th St. ☎ 718-881-8900. Subway: D to 205th St., then walk north 2 blocks. Open Sa 10am-4pm, Su 1-5pm, otherwise by appointment. Call before visiting to ensure it's open. $2.*

The second-oldest building in the Bronx (built in 1758) saw light action during the Revolution. It has since become the site of the **Museum of Bronx History,** which is run by the Bronx County Historical Society and functions as the borough archive.

PELHAM BAY PARK

🚺 *Subway: 6 to Pelham Bay Park, the bus Bx29 to stables. Rangers: ☎ 718-430-1890. Stables: Shore Rd. at City Island Dr. ☎ 718-885-0551. Open daily 9am-dusk. $25 per hr. Museum: Shore Rd., opposite the golf courses. ☎ 718-885-1461. Open W and Sa-Su noon-4pm. Closed in Aug. $2.50; students and seniors $1.25, under 12 free.*

New York City's largest park, **Pelham Bay Park** boasts over 2100 acres of green saturated with playing fields, tennis courts, golf courses, picnic spaces, wildlife sanctuaries, a beach, and even training grounds for the city's mounted police force. The deeply knowledgeable **park rangers** lead a variety of history- and nature-oriented walks for creatures great and small. From the **Pelham Bay stables,** you can take a guided ride around the park on horseback. Inside the park, the Empire/Greek Revival **Federalist Bartow-Pell Mansion Museum** sits among a prize-winning formal herb garden landscaped in 1915. The house's wonders include a free-standing spiral staircase and an herb garden arranged around a pond complete with goldfish and spouting cherub. Just down the road find **Orchard Beach,** which gets mobbed on hot summer days. Snack stands feed the sun-seeking throngs, and the lifeguards watch over them from Memorial Day to Labor Day (daily 10am-7pm).

CITY ISLAND

🚇 *Subway: 6 to Pelham Bay Park; board bus Bx29 outside the station; get off at the first stop on City Island.*

NY Botanical Gardens

For a whiff of New England in New York, visit **City Island,** a community of century-old houses, sailboats, and a shipyard. Aquatic life can be sampled in the many seafood restaurants lining City Island Ave.; they're pricier than those in the Bronx proper, but a careful search will yield the elusive $10 lobster. The food chain stops dead in its tracks at the nearby **Pelham Cemetery** on the west end of Reville Rd. Emblazoned on the gate is: "Lives are commemorated...deaths are recorded...love is undisguised...this is a cemetery." Hmmm. Thoughts to ponder as you wait for the #29 bus, which leaves every 30 minutes.

SOUTH BRONX

This is not the part of town to meander in search of out-of-the-way places. It does, however, offer up a few morsels to the directed traveler.

YANKEE STADIUM

🚇 *E. 161st St., at River Ave. ☎ 718-293-4300. Subway: 4, C, D to 161st St.*

Bronx Zoo

Sports fans will enjoy a visit to this historic arena, built in 1923. The aging stadium's frequent face-lifts have kept it on par with younger structures. The Yankees played the first night game here in 1946, and the first message scoreboard tallied runs here in 1954. Inside the 11.6-acre park (the field measures only 3.5 acres), monuments honor Yankee greats like Lou Gehrig, Joe DiMaggio, and Babe Ruth. Yankee Stadium injects the South Bronx's economy with much-needed income. Controversial Yankees owner George Steinbrenner has announced a possible abandonment of "The House That Ruth Built" for the more tourist-friendly confines of Midtown Manhattan. Ouch. (See **Baseball,** p. 169.)

Yankee Stadium

THE BRONX MUSEUM OF THE ARTS

🚇 *1040 Grand Concourse, at 165th St. ☎ 718-681-6000, ext. 141 for events. Open W 3-9pm, Th-F 10am-5pm, Sa-Su noon-6pm. Suggested donation $3, students and seniors $2; W free.*

Set in the rotunda of the Bronx Courthouse, the museum's two small galleries exhibit works by contemporary masters as well as local talent, with a focus on Latino, African-American, and women artists. The museum encourages the community to create textual and visual responses to the permanent collection and mounts the (often nutty) viewer feedback alongside the original work.

THE LONGWOOD HISTORIC DISTRICT

🖪 *Bronx Council on the Arts at ☎ 718-931-9500. Subway: 6 train to Longwood Ave.; then walk two blocks away from the overpass up Longwood Ave. Open Th-F noon-5pm, Sa noon-4pm. Free.*

This neighborhood with stately brownstones is reminiscent of Harlem's Striver's Row. The **Longwood Arts Gallery,** located on the third floor of a former public school building, houses art studios and often features work from its artist-in-residence program.

STATEN ISLAND

Unless a specific site from the following list particularly piques a personal interest, Staten Island is, on the whole, not worth the trek. But perhaps, to some, the few fine attractions may seem better for their mystique, away from the bustle of Manhattan, patiently waiting to be discovered. Because of the hills and the distances (and some dangerous neighborhoods in between), it's a bad idea to *walk* from one site to the

see map p. 350

next. **Make sure to plan your excursion with the bus schedule in mind.**

SNUG HARBOR CULTURAL CENTER

🖪 *Cultural Center: 1000 Richmond Terrace. Bus S40 or S52. ☎ 718-448-2500. Free tours of the grounds offered Sa-Su 2pm, starting at the Visitors Center. Botanical Garden: ☎ 718-273-8200; www.sibg.org. Open daily dawn-dusk. Scholar's Garden: Open Apr. to mid-Nov. Tu-Su 10am-5pm. $5. Tours W, Sa, Su on the hour noon-4pm. Newhouse Center: ☎ 718-448-2500 ext. 260. Open W-Su noon-5pm. Suggested donation $2. Noble collection: ☎ 718-447-6490. Open M-F 9am-2pm. Children's Museum: ☎ 718-273-2060. Open Tu-Su 11am-5pm. $4; under 2 free.*

Founded in 1801, Sailors' Snug Harbor originally served as a home for retired sailors in the US (the iron fence that barricades it originally kept old salts from quenching their thirst at nearby bars). Purchased by the city and opened in 1976 as a cultural center, it now includes 28 historic buildings scattered over wonderfully placid, unpopulated parkland—83 sprawling, green, and amazingly well-kept acres of national historic landmark. Gardens of various styles are cultivated throughout the grounds of the Center as part of the **Staten Island Botanical Garden:** the **Connie Gretz Secret Garden, the New York Chinese Scholar's Garden,** and the **White Garden** (which offers tea every other Su) are a few. The Center provides various spaces as resources for the arts. The **Newhouse Center for Contemporary Art** shows revolving exhibits of contemporary art; the **John A. Noble collection** houses Noble's artwork that focuses on NY's working waterfront. The **Children's Museum** features funky, interactive exhibits. Plays, recitals, and concerts occur often. Snug Harbor also offers free summer concerts Su on the North Lawn.

HISTORIC RICHMOND TOWN

🖪 *441 Clarke Ave. Bus S74 to Richmond Rd. and St. Patrick's Pl.; 30min. ☎ 718-351-1611. Open July-Aug. W-F 10am-5pm, Sa-Su 1-5pm; Sept.-Dec. W-Su 1-5pm. $4; students, seniors, and 6-18 $2.50.*

A huge, recreated village complex documenting three centuries of Staten Island's culture and history, Historic Richmond Town features reconstructed 17th- to 19th-century dwellings exhibiting artifacts as well as authentic "inhabitants" (costumed master craftspeople and their apprentices). Thanks to budget cuts, only 10 of these buildings, spread over 100 acres, remain permanently open to the public. Head for the **Voorlezer's House,** the oldest surviving elementary school in the US (built in 1695). Call in advance to find out what you can see and for info about the summertime "living history" events.

MORAVIAN CEMETERY

▶ *On Richmond Rd., at Todt Hill Rd., in Dongan Hills. Bus S74 to Todt Hill Rd. Open daily 8am-6pm.*

Commodore Cornelius Vanderbilt, the creator of the ferry, and his monied clan lie in this ornate crypt, built in 1886 by Richard Morris Hunt. Central Park creator Frederick Law Olmsted landscaped this park-like cemetery with beautiful winding paths and gentle hillsides that sacriligiously tempt a picnic.

STATEN ISLAND CONFERENCE HOUSE

▶ *Bus S78 to Craig Ave.; walk one block south to Satterlee, make a right, and walk half a block.* ☎ *718-984-6046. Open F-Su 1-4pm. $2; seniors and under 12 $1. Guided tours by appointment.*

The only peace conference ever held between British forces and American rebels was here. At the summit on September 11, 1776, British commander Admiral Lord Howe engaged in an attempt to forestall the American Revolution with three Continental Congress representatives—Benjamin Franklin, John Adams, and Edward Rutledge. A national landmark, the site houses period furnishings and Revolutionary War minutiae.

Museums

MUSEUMS

Witness a culture collecting itself. Swoon under a life-sized replica of a great blue whale at the American Museum of Natural History. Control a 900-foot aircraft carrier at the Intrepid Sea-Air-Space Museum. Slip into the world of the 2000-year-old Egyptian Temple of Dendur or of Van Gogh's 100-year-old *Café at Arles* at the Metropolitan Museum of Art. Relax alongside Monet's *Water Lilies* at the Museum of Modern Art. Or analyze the question of racialized space in the contemporary art at the Whitney. New York has accumulated more stuff in more museums than any other city in the New World, and it doesn't seem to be letting up. From the famous to the community-oriented, every museum here will hold your interest.

During the annual **Museum Mile Festival** in mid-June, Fifth Ave. museums keep their doors open until late at night, stage engaging exhibits, involve city kids in mural painting, and fill the streets with music. Most museums also sponsor film series and live concerts throughout the year (see **Entertainment,** p. 157).

MUSEUMS BY NEIGHBORHOOD

MUSEUM DIRECTORY

METROPOLITAN MUSEUM OF ART

◪ *1000 Fifth Ave., at 82nd St.* ☎ *Recorded info* ☎ *535-7710, upcoming concerts and lectures* ☎ *570-3949.* **Open:** *Su and Tu-Th 9:30am-5:15pm, F-Sa 9:30am-8:45pm.* **Suggested donation:** *$10; students and seniors $5; members and children under 12 (with an adult) free. Foreign Visitors Desk: Maps, bro-chures, and assistance in a number of languages; call* ☎ *650-2987.* **Gallery Tours:** *Free. Daily. Inquire at the main info desk for schedules, topics, and meeting places, or call* ☎ *570-3930. Key to the Met Audio Guides: $5, $4.50 for members, discounts for groups.* **Disabled Access:** ☎ *535-7710. Wheelchairs at the coat-check areas; enter through the 81st St. entrance.* **TTY:** ☎ *396-5057.*

Founded in 1870 by a group of distinguished art collectors, philanthropists, civic lead-ers, and artists, the Met, whose collection includes more than two million works of art spanning over 5,000 years, is one of the largest and (we think) *the* finest museum in the world. The sheer volume of superior artwork at this museum inspires awe. Don't rush the Metropolitan experience; you could camp out here for a month—in fact, two chil-dren did live here in the children's book *From the Mixed-up Files of Mrs. Basil E. Frankweiler*. But never fear, tour and audio guide information is listed above.

If you decide to brave this museum on your own, here is one suggested strategy: focus on examining a limited number of collections in depth. The **European paintings** col-lection, for instance, which contains over 3,000 works, forms the greatest collection of its kind in the world. Here you will find an extensive ensemble of instantly recognizable masterpieces by Manet, van Gogh, Cézanne, Vermeer, and Monet, not to mention such works as van Eyck's *The Crucifixion* and *The Last Judgement*, El Greco's *View of Toledo*, and Botticelli's *The Last Communion of Saint Jerome*. The Met's most pop-ular and unique exhibition, however, is definitely its **Egyptian Art** collection. Art in this department dates from the Prehistoric Period (before 1300 BC) to the Byzantine Period (8th century AD) and includes fascinating artifacts of this ancient culture such as jewelry and the fully intact **Temple of Dendur.** If Egypt isn't your style, travel over to Asia, where you'll find the largest and most comprehensive collection of **Asian art** in the West, from monumental Chinese Buddhist sculptures to Japanese prints, not to mention a beautiful re-creation of a Ming scholar's garden. One exhibition that should not be over-looked, however, is the world-renowned **Costume Institute** located on the Ground Floor of the museum. This collection houses over 75,000 costumes and accessories from five continents from the 17th century to the present and offers interesting rotating exhibits like the 1998 memorial to Gianni Versace.

The impressive list continues from there. Other collections include the **American Art** exhibition, which possesses such classics as Sargent's *Madame X;* the **Greek and Roman Galleries; Art of Africa, Oceania, and the Americas,** with its superb examples of wood and bronze sculptures; and the collection of **20th-century art,** featuring such works as Picasso's *Gertrude Stein*, Matisse's *Dance*, and Pollock's *Autumn Rhythm*.

Not to be missed: the annual Christmas tree that goes up at the end of November on the first floor, covered with the Met's stunning collection of papier-mâché angels and accompanied by their Neopolitan crêche (nativity).

MUSEUM OF MODERN ART (MOMA)

◪11 W. 53rd St. between Fifth and Sixth Aves. ☎ 708-9400; info and film schedules 708-9480. **Admission:** $10, students and seniors $6.50, under 16 free. Pay-what-you-wish F 4:30-8:30pm. Extra fee for some special exhibitions; audio guide rental $4. **Open** Sa-Tu and Th 10:30am-5:45pm, F 10:30am-8:15pm. Free brochures and film tickets at information desk.

MoMA commands one of the world's most impressive collections of post-Impressionist, late 19th- and 20th-century art. Founded in 1929 by scholar Alfred Barr in response to the Met's refusal to display cutting-edge work, the museum's first exhibit, held in an office building, displayed then unknowns Cézanne, Gauguin, Seurat, and van Gogh. But as the ground-breaking works of 1900 to 1950 moved from cult to masterpiece status, MoMA, in turn, shifted from revolution to institution. In 2000, the museum reclaimed its innovative edge by commissioning award-winning Japanese architect Yoshio Taniguchi to expand and renovate the museum—a 650-million-dollar project lasting until 2005. Temporary exhibits partially compensate for the interim closure of parts of the permanent collection. Whatever its state of outward polish, however, MoMA always promises to stun and inspire the visitor with one of the most impressive art collections in the world.

MoMA's impressive facilities and collection include the **Abby Aldrich Rockefeller Sculpture Garden,** an expansive courtyard adorned with a world-class assemblage of modern sculpture, often featuring works by Matisse, Picasso, and Henry Moore, as well as temporary exhibitions. However, the most stunning aspect of the museum are its **uptairs galleries.** Some of the collection's most renowned works are Rodin's *John the Baptist;* van Gogh's *The Starry Night;* Duchamp's dadaist *To Be Looked at (from the Other Side of the Glass) with One Eye, Close To, for Almost an Hour; White on White* by the Russian Constructivist Malevich; Henri Matisse's *Dance (First Version);* Mark Rothko's *Red, Brown, and Black,* and Andy Warhol's signature pieces, the gold *Marilyn Monroe* and the *Campbell Soup Cans.* However, MoMA owns much more 20th-century art than it will ever have space to display. An ever-changing assortment of works lurks behind the third-floor stairwell, in a chamber full of the museum's recent acquisitions.

AMERICAN MUSEUM OF NATURAL HISTORY

◪Central Park W., 79th-81st Sts. ☎ 769-5100; www.amnh.org. **Open:** Su-Th 10am-5:45pm, F-Sa 10am-8:45pm. **Suggested Donation:** $10; students and seniors $7.50; children $6. **Highlight Tours:** 6 per day, usually leaving 15min. past the hr. ☎ 769-5200 for reservations. **Discovery Room:** Open Tu-F 2-4:30pm, Sa-Su 1-4:30pm. Closed Sept. Call ahead to check hours. **Imax:** ☎ 769-5034. Combo-ticket (Museum and Imax) $15, students and seniors $11, children 2-12 $9. **Double Feature:** F-Sa at 9pm $21, students and seniors $15.50, children $12.50. **Rose Center Hayden Planetarium** (Museum and Space Show): $19, students and seniors $14, children $11.50. **Wheelchair access.** Video displays **captioned** for hearing-impaired.

REST YER BONES

If you aim to see the Met in its entirety, you'll need place to rest. Many charming courts and gardens offer a romantic setting for foot relief. Try the **Charles Engelhardt court** in the American Wing, or the **European Sculpture Garden** between the Wrightsman Galleries and the Kravis Wing. Do a little meditating in the **Astor Court**, a Chinese scholar's garden complete with goldfish in the Asian Art wing. The **Temple of Dendur** offers an area upon which you can sit like a Nubian bird on a wire, while enormous windows grant a splendid view of Central Park. On cool summer days, the **Gerald and Iris B. Cantor Roof Garden** (6th floor) allows you suntan amidst sculpture, while a view of the skyline proves that most gardens in the world lack a little attitude.

You're never too old for the Natural History Museum. One of the largest science museums in the world, it organizes displays around the theme of "evolution" and chronicles natural environments and cultural histories. An active, world-renowned learning and research facility, the Museum of Natural History sends out over 100 expeditions of scientists and explorers throughout the world each year.

The museum's greatest draw is its **dinosaur halls,** which display real fossils in 85% of its exhibits (most museums use fossil casts). If you're not into prehistory, chart the development of the human race and world cultures displayed in life-sized dioramas, get dazzled by two-inch iridescent butterflies, five-foot crustaceans, roaring lions, and the famous 90-foot whale suspended from the ceiling.

The **Alexander White Natural Science Center,** the museum's only room holding *live* animals, explains the ecology of New York City to kids, while the **Discovery Room** gives them artifacts they can touch. During the academic year, **The People Center,** open weekends only, schedules scholarly talks and demonstrations of various cultures' folk arts. The museum also houses an **Imax** cinematic extravaganza on one of New York's largest movie screens—four stories high and 66 feet wide.

The newest addition to the museum is the sparkling **Hayden Plantarium** within the **Rose Center for Earth and Space.** The museum turns its eyes heavenward with this space-age wing focusing on innovative exhibits about the evolution and history of the universe. Friday 6-8pm is "Starry Nights," a music event.

GUGGENHEIM MUSEUM

◪1071 Fifth Ave., at 89th St. ☎423-3500. **Open:** Su-W 9am-6pm, F-Sa 9am-8pm. **Admission:** $12; students and seniors $7; under 12 free; F 6-8pm "pay-what-you-wish." **Another Branch:** Guggenheim Museum SoHo (see p. 126). **Wheelchair accessible:** ☎423-3539.

The Guggenheim's most famous exhibit? The building itself, surely. Designed by Frank Lloyd Wright, this inverted ziggurat, which is a stepped or winding pyramidal temple of Babylonian origin, is a modern architectural masterpiece. In his attempt to embrace Nature and emphasize its plasticity, Wright produced a spiral design reminiscent of a nautilus shell, with interdependent spaces and the divisions of the galleries similar to the membranes of a citrus fruit.

The Guggenheim contains a large collection of abstract, ultra-modern, non-objective paintings, including significant works in the fields of cubism, surrealism, American minimalism, and abstract expressionism. Each spin of the museum's spiral holds one sequence or exhibit, while a portion of the **Tower Galleries** exhibits the **Thannhauser Collection.** Donated by Justin K. Thannhauser in 1976, the group of 19th- and 20th-century works includes several by Picasso, Matisse, van Gogh, Gaugin, Manet, and Cézanne. The rest of the permanent collection features geometric art, including that of Mondrian and his Dutch De Stijl school, the Bauhaus experiments of German Josef Albers, and the Russian modernists. The collection also holds several Degas sculptures and works by such artists as Kandinsky and Klee, and German Expressionists such as Kirchner.

WHITNEY MUSEUM

⑦1945 Madison Ave., at 75th St. ☎570-3676. **Open:** Tu-W and F-Su 11am-6pm, Th 1-9pm. **Admission:** $10; students and seniors $8; children under 12 free; Th 6-9pm pay-what-you-wish and free cocktails. **Another branch** is located in the Philip Morris building (120 Park Ave., at 42nd St.; subway 4, 5, 6 to 42nd St.; ☎917-663-2453), where a sculpture court features a changing array of installation pieces. Admission and frequent gallery talks (M, W, F at 1pm) free. **Wheelchair accessible.**

When the Metropolitan Museum declined a donation of over 600 works from Gertrude Vanderbilt Whitney in 1929, the wealthy patron and sculptor formed her own museum within the walls of a futuristic fortress-style building designed by Marcel Breuer.

This museum, the only one with a historical mandate to champion the works of living American artists, has assembled the largest collection, consisting of 12,000 objects, of 20th- and 21st-century American art in the world. Even the modern art skeptic will not be able to refrain from being impressed by Jasper John's *Three Flags*, Frank Stella's *Brooklyn Bridge*, Ad Reinhardt's *Abstract Painting, Number 33*, Willem De Kooning's *Woman on Bicycle*, and Georgia O'Keefe's Flower Collection.

COOPER-HEWITT NATIONAL DESIGN MUSEUM

⑦2 E. 91st St., at Fifth Ave. ☎849-8400. **Open:** Tu 10am-9pm, W-Sa 10am-5pm, Su noon-5pm. **Admission:** adults $8; students and seniors $5; under 12 free; Tu 5-9pm free. **Library:** ☎849-8330. Open by appointment until 5:30pm daily. **Wheelchair accessible.**

Founded in 1897 by the Hewitt sisters, the National Design Museum was the first—and remains the only—museum in the US devoted exclusively to historical and contemporary design and to the advancement of Science and the Arts. Housed in the historic Carnegie Mansion since 1967, this museum contains over 250,000 objects—one of the largest collections of design in the world—organized mainly into the categories of applied arts and industrial designs, drawings and prints, textiles, and wall-coverings. In addition, this Smithsonian-owned institution possesses an extensive library collection and a beautiful garden that is a place for exhibits and summer concerts (see **Entertainment,** p. 162).

FRICK COLLECTION

⑦1 E. 70th St., at Fifth Avenue. ☎288-0700. **Open:** Tu-Sa 10am-6pm, Su 1-6pm. **Admission:** $7; students and seniors $5. No children under 10 admitted; children under 16 must be accompanied by an adult. Group visits by appointment only. Free **audio guides. Wheelchair accessible.**

Designed by Thomas Hastings in the style of 18th-century European domestic architecture, the former residence of Henry Clay Frick, the Pittsburgh coke and steel industrialist, is now home to one of the most magnificent ensembles of fine art. This extraordinary collection of works, two-thirds of which belonged to the private collection of Frick himself, consists of impressive Western masterpieces of the early Renaissance through the late 19th century. The world's greatest Old Masters are displayed here, not to mention exquisite vases, 18th-century French sculptures, Renaissance bronzes, furniture, and porcelains.

The distinguished list of artists on view at the Frick include Renoir, Rembrandt, van Eyck, Goya, Velasquez, Vermeer, Turner, Whistler, Bellini, El Greco, Holbein, Gainsborough, Constable, Corot, Titian, Fragonard, Veronese, and Boucher; all seen within the intimate ambiance achieved by the setting of a private house. Free audio guides or guide books ($1) will help you through the tangled web of art works that are on display in mixed historical periods. The Garden Court, where Frick's favorite organ music sometimes plays, is very relaxing (see **Entertainment,** p. 162). The Frick Collection also operates an art reference library at 10 E. 71st St., which is one of the leading institutions for research in the history of art.

PIERPONT MORGAN LIBRARY

▶29 E. 36th St,. at Madison Ave. ☎685-0610. www.morganlibrary.org. **Open** Tu-F 10:30am-5pm, Sa 10:30am-6pm, Su noon-6pm. **Admission** $8; students and seniors $6; under 12 free.

The Pierpont Morgan Library contains a stunning collection of rare books, sculptures, and paintings gathered by banker J.P. Morgan and his son. Completed in 1907, the library remained private until 1924, when J.P. Morgan opened it to the public. In 1991, the museum doubled its size with the acquisition of Morgan's former townhouse. Its permanent collection, not always on display, includes drawings and prints by Blake and Dürer, illuminated Renaissance manuscripts, Thoreau's journals, a manuscript copy of Dickens's *A Christmas Carol*, and sheet music handwritten by Beethoven and Mozart. In 1999 the library acquired the archives of *The Paris Review*.

Impressive changing exhibitions compete with the beauty of the library itself. The **West Room,** Morgan Sr.'s sumptuous former office, has a carved ceiling made during the Italian Renaissance and stained glass from 15th- and 17th-century Switzerland. The heart of the library, the **East Room,** features stacks of mahogany-toned, hand-bound volumes encircled by two balconies. Among the more notable items in the room are one of three existing likenesses of John Milton, a fabulous 12th-century jewel-encrusted triptych believed to contain fragments from the Holy Cross, and one of 11 surviving copies of the Gutenberg Bible, the first printed book.

If you have time for a spot of tea ($2.50), you can travel back in time in the enclosed marble courtyard of the Morgan Court Café, with its vaulted sun roof and graceful trees; or you can rest your feet for free by the fountain.

OTHER MAJOR COLLECTIONS

ALICE AUSTEN HOUSE MUSEUM AND GARDEN

▶2 Hylan Blvd., in Staten Island. **Bus** S51 to Hylan Blvd. Walk one block toward the water. ☎ 718-816-4506. **Open** Mar.-Dec. Th-Su noon-5pm; grounds open daily until dusk. $2; children free.

The 18th-century cottage was home of photographer Alice Austen, who took more than 8,000 photographs of her upper-middle-class life. After the 1929 stock market crash, Austen languished in the poorhouse until the Staten Island Historical Society discovered her work and published it in *Life* months before her death. This quiet museum displays Austen's photos and has a garden with great Verrazano-Narrows views.

THE ASIA SOCIETY

▶Uptown: 725 Park Ave., at 70th St.; subway: 6 to 68th St. **Midtown:** 502 Park Ave., at 59th St.; subway: 4, 5, 6 to 59th St., N, R to Lexington Ave. ☎517-ASIA or 288-6400. **Open** M-Sa 10am-6pm. $4; students/seniors $2; free noon-2pm daily. Tours: Sa 12:30pm.

Exhibitions of Asian art, from Iran and Japan to Yemen and Mongolia and including Asian-American works. Also presents symposia, musical performances, film screenings, and an acclaimed "Meet the Author" series. Scheduled for 2001: *Monks and Merchants: Silk Road Treasures from Northwest China, 4th-7th Century* (Fall 2001).

AMERICAN CRAFT MUSEUM

▶40 W. 53rd St. ☎956-3535. **Open** Tu-W and F-Su 10am-6pm, Th 10am-8pm. $5; students and seniors $2.50; Th 6-8pm pay-what-you-wish. Wheelchair accessible.

Not the old-fashioned quilts and Shaker furniture you might expect. No wooden *chachkas* here—this museum redefines the concept of crafts. Three floors of exhibits change every 3 months and feature large, elaborate installations, in diverse media, by contemporary (one might even say avant garde) American craftsmen.

AMERICAN MUSEUM OF THE MOVING IMAGE

*35th Ave., at 36th St., in Astoria, Queens. ☎718-784-0077; **Subway:** N to Broadway in Astoria. Walk along Broadway to 36th St., turn right, go to 35th Ave.; museum is on the right. **Open** Tu-F noon-5pm, Sa-Su 11am-6pm. $8.50; students and seniors $5.50; children $4.50; under 4 free. Screening tickets free with admission.*

Unfortunately, this museum isn't half as exciting as it sounds. The best it has to offer is on the third floor, where you can create your own digitally animated film sequence, dub your voice into scenes from *Taxi Driver*, or alter sound effects from movies like *Terminator 2*. Go to watch vintage films Saturday and Sunday; see a double feature for the price of museum admission.

AUDUBON TERRACE MUSEUM GROUP

*613 W. 155th St. between Broadway and Riverside Dr. **Hispanic:** ☎926-2234. **Open** M-Sa 10am-4:30pm, Su 1-4pm. Free. **Numismatic Society:** ☎234-3130. **Open** Tu-Sa 9am-4:30pm, Su 1-4pm. Free. **Academy:** ☎368-5900.*

Cloisters

Once part of John James Audubon's estate and game preserve, the terrace now contains the following museums and societies: **Hispanic Society of America,** devoted to Spanish and Portuguese arts and culture, including mosaics, ceramics, and paintings by El Greco, Velázquez, and Goya. Students of Hispanic culture will enjoy the 100,000-volume research library. The **American Numismatic Society** presents…the fascinating history of the penny! (Who knew?) An extraordinary collection of coinage and paper money from prehistoric times to the present is on display in the exhibition room. The **American Academy of Arts and Letters** honors American artists, writers, and composers. There are also occasional exhibits of manuscripts, paintings, sculptures, and first editions.

BROOKLYN MUSEUM

*200 Eastern Pkwy. at Washington Ave. **Subway:** 2, 3 to Eastern Pkwy. ☎718-638-5000. **Open** W-F 10am-5pm, Sa 10am-9pm, Su 11am-6pm. **Suggested donation** $4, students $2, seniors $1.50, under 12 free.*

Guggenheim

For lovers of all things ancient, the Metropolitan Museum of Art's sibling merits a trip to Brooklyn. You'll find outstanding Ancient Greek, Roman, Middle Eastern, and Egyptian galleries on the third floor; only London's British Museum and Cairo's Egyptian Museum itself have larger Egyptian collections. John Singer Sargent and the Hudson River School grace the American Collection on the fifth floor. Nearby, the contemporary gallery contains noteworthy work by Alfredo Jaar and Francis Bacon. European art from the early Renaissance to Post-Impressionism, including works by Rodin, Renoir, and Monet also appear on the fifth floor. Meanwhile, multimedia Asian art fills the second floor. The enormous Oceanic and New World art collection takes up the central two-story space on the first floor—the towering totem poles covered with human/animal hybrids could fit nowhere else. The impressive African art collection here was the first of its kind in an American museum when it opened in 1923.

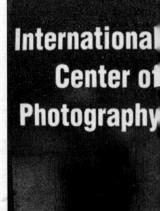

International Center of Photography

THE CLOISTERS

*Fort Tryon Park in Washington Heights. ☎923-3700. **Open** Mar.-Oct. Tu-Su 9:30am-5:15pm; Nov.-Feb. 9:30am-4:45pm. Museum **tours** Mar.-Oct. Tu-F 3pm, Su noon. Suggested donation $10; students and seniors $5. Includes same day admission to the Met's main building in Central Park.*

Charles Collen brought the High Middle Ages to Manhattan in 1938, erecting this tranquil branch of the Metropolitan Museum of Art from pieces of 12th- and 13th-century French monasteries. John D. Rockefeller donated the site (now Ft. Tryon Park) and many of the works that make up the Cloister's incredibly rich collection of medieval art, including frescoes, panel paintings, and stained glass. During the summer, retreat to the air-conditioned Treasury to admire the most fragile offerings, including incredibly intricate illuminated manuscripts and carvings in miniature. Enjoy the sublimely detailed work of the world-famous Unicorn Tapestries, and rest in either of two small gardens planned according to the symbolism and aesthetic sensibilities of medieval horticulture.

FORBES MAGAZINE GALLERIES

*62 Fifth Ave. at 12th St. ☎206-5548. **Open** Tu-Sa 10am-4pm; hours subject to change. Free. Children under 16 must be accompanied by an adult. Th reserved for group tours; call in advance.*

Just one more multi-millionaire financier who turned over his personal collection to the public. The late Malcolm Forbes's irrepressible penchant for the offbeat permeates this collection of eclectic exhibits. Some of the more interesting include the world's largest private collection of Fabergé *objets d'art* and a Monopoly exhibit featuring versions of the game in its various stages of evolution.

GUGGENHEIM MUSEUM SOHO

575 Broadway, at Prince St. ☎423-3500. Open Th-M 11am-6pm. Wheelchair accessible.

This branch of the Guggenheim fills two floors of a historic 19th-century building with selections from the museum's mammoth permanent modern collection. The current exhibit "Andy Warhol: The Last Supper" is expected to continue indefinitely. The gallery store peddles artsy trinkets perfect for browsing.

HALL OF FAME FOR GREAT AMERICANS

*181st St. and Martin Luther King Jr. Blvd. CUNY: ☎718-289-5100. **Subway:** 4 to Burnside Ave. Walk 6 blocks west on Burnside Ave. as it becomes 179th St., then 1 block north. **Open** daily 10am-5pm. Free.*

Located on the grounds of City University of New York (CUNY) in the Bronx, this poignant yet decrepit hall features over 100 bronze busts of America's immortals solemnly whiling away the years, among them Alexander Graham Bell, Abraham Lincoln, Booker T. Washington, and the Wright brothers.

INTERNATIONAL CENTER OF PHOTOGRAPHY

*1133 Ave. of the Americas, at 43rd St. ☎860-1777; ext. 160 for darkroom rental. **Open** Tu-Th 10am-5pm, F 10am-8pm, Sa-Su 10am-6pm. $6; students and seniors $4; under 12 $1.*

Housed in a landmark townhouse built in 1914 for *New Republic* founder Willard Straight, ICP is New York City's only museum of photography. Historical, thematic, and contemporary works, running from fine art to photo-journalism to celebrity portraits, are showcased. Home to one of the world's largest schools of photography, the ICP also offers use of their darkroom for $8 per hour.

INTREPID SEA-AIR-SPACE MUSEUM

*Pier 86 at 46th St. and Twelfth Ave. ☎245-0072. **Open** May 1-Sept. 30 M-F 10am-5pm, Sa-Su 10am-6pm; Oct. 1-Apr. 30 W-Su 10am-5pm. Last admission 1hr. before closing. $12, seniors, students, ages 12-17, and veterans $9, ages 6-11 $6, ages 2-5 $2, active duty servicemen, and children under 2 free, wheelchair patrons half price.*

One ticket admits you to the veteran World War II and Vietnam War aircraft carrier *Intrepid*, the Vietnam War destroyer *Edson*, the only publicly displayed guided-missile submarine *Growler*, and the lightship *Nantucket*. Pioneer's Hall displays models, antiques, and film shorts of flying devices from the turn of the century to the 1930s. You can also climb aboard the Intrepid's 900 ft. flight deck to view old and new warbirds— including a declassified CIA A-12 Blackbird, the world's fastest spy plane. Don't miss the Iraqi tanks parked near the gift shop; they were captured in the Gulf War. There are a number of guided tours of the museum and its different attractions, which range from 10min. to 3hr. in length. The museum offers a schedule of temporary and new exhibits and events; call for details. New exhibits in 2000: "Flying Machines," in which you may participate in simulations of the first machines of aviation.

ISAMU NOGUCHI GARDEN MUSEUM

32-37 Vernon Blvd., at 10th St. and 33rd Rd., in Long Island City, Queens. ☎718-721-1932. **Subway:** N to Broadway. Walk along Broadway toward Manhattan until the end, then turn left on Vernon Blvd. On weekends, **$5 shuttle bus** leaves from the Asia Society, 70th St. and Park Ave. in Manhattan, every 30min. 11:30am-3:30pm; return trips every hr. noon-5pm. **Open** Apr.-Oct. W-F 10am-5pm, Sa-Su 11am-6pm. **Suggested donation** $4; students and seniors $2. Lengthy free tour at 2pm. Wheelchair accessible.

Fourteen galleries were established here in 1985, next to Isamu Noguchi's studio. His breathtaking sculptures stand around the shimmmering water of *The Well*. Among designs of lamps, Italian playground slides, and gardens, the world-renowned sculptor also conceived *Sculpture to Be Seen From Mars*, a 2-mile-long face carved in the dirt next to Newark International Airport as a monument to man in the post-atomic age.

JAPAN SOCIETY

333 E. 47th St. and First Ave. ☎832-1155. **Open** Sept.-June Tu, Th, Sa, Su 11am-6pm, W and F 11am-6:30pm; in May M-F 11am-6pm. Suggested donation $5.

Behold the first example of contemporary Japanese design in New York City. Junzo Yoshimura juxtaposes a plain, western facade with an entirely Asian interior, sought to embody the society's aim to bring the people of Japan and the US closer together. In the spirit of a traditional Japanese home, there is an interior pool garden on the first floor, complete with stones and bamboo trees. The gallery on the second floor exhibits traditional and contemporary Japanese art. The Society also sponsors Japanese language courses, lectures, meetings with notable leaders, a film series, and performances.

JACQUES MARCHAIS MUSEUM OF TIBETAN ART

*338 Lighthouse Ave., in Staten Island. **Bus** S74 to Richmond Rd. & Lighthouse Ave.; turn right and walk up the fairly steep hill.* ☎718-987-3500. **Open** Apr.-Nov. W-Su 1-5pm; Dec.-Mar. W-F 1-5pm. $3; seniors and students $2.50; under 12 $1.

One of the largest private collections of Tibetan art in the West; bronzes, paintings, and sculpture from Tibet and other Buddhist cultures are found in this hilltop museum, fashioned after a Himalayan mountain temple. Its terraced sculpture gardens look down on the distant Lower Bay. Programs on Asian culture (fees vary) cover topics ranging from mask making to meditation—call for information.

THE JEWISH MUSEUM

1109 Fifth Ave., at 92nd St. ☎423-3200. **Open** Su-M and W-Th 11am-5:45pm, Tu 11am-8pm. $8; students and seniors $5.50; Tu 5-8pm pay-what-you-wish. Wheelchair access info: ☎423-3225.

The permanent collection of over 14,000 works, *Culture and Continuity: The Jewish Journey*, details the Jewish experience throughout history, ranging from ancient Biblical artifacts and ceremonial objects to contemporary masterpieces by Marc Chagall, Frank Stella, and George Segal. Popular rotating exhibits usually emphasize the interpretation of art through the lens of social history. Summer Nights movie and sitcom programs run through July and August.

child's play

Founded in 1973 by Harlem and Upper West Side artists and educators in response to the elimination of music and cultural programs in public schools, **The Children's Museum of New York** has a sound studio, media center, and interactive exhibits. Fun characters like Dr. Seuss' cat and Snoopy and friends (coming Oct. 2000) act as guides throughout the museum. Check out the "Body Odyssey" exhibit that allows you and your child to crawl through, climb on, and pedal through the gears of creaky machines. *(212 W. 83rd St., off Amsterdam Ave. ☎ 721-1223. Subway: 1, 9 to 86th St. Open Tu-Su 10am-5pm; winter W-Su 10am-5pm. Adults and children $6; seniors $3; under 1 free. Wheelchair accessible.)*

Housed in a renovated 1904 firehouse, **The New York City Fire Museum** is for kids who want to be firemen when they grow up. See a hand-pulled truck from when George Washington was a volunteer NYC firefighter. Big moments in NYC history are honored, like the P.T. Barnum Museum fire, in which several firemen were injured rescuing the 400lb. fat lady. *(278 Spring St. between Varick and Hudson Sts. ☎ 691-1303. Subway: 1. 9 to Houston St. Open Tu-Su 10am-4pm. Suggested donation $4; students and seniors $2; under 12 $1.)*

◼ LOWER EAST SIDE TENEMENT MUSEUM

⌂*90 Orchard St., near Broome and Delancy Sts. ☎431-0233. **Visitors center** open Tu-Su 11am-5pm. 1hr. tours of the tenement Tu-F every ½hr. 1-3pm and 4pm; in summer M every hr. 1-4pm, Th 6pm and 7pm, Sa-Su every ½hr. 11am-4:30pm. $9, students and seniors $7. See Walking Tours in **Sights**, p. 73.*

The visitors center offers exhibits and photographs documenting Jewish life on the Lower East Side. Two main tours are offered: the Tenement Tour, which views one apartment in ruin, and a tour that views three meticulously restored apartments to recreate specific moments in the lives of three immigrant families who actually lived there (the Gumpertzes in the 1870s, the Rogarshevskys in 1918, and the Baldizzis in 1939). The tenement inspires tourists to share their own families' immigrant experiences.

EL MUSEO DEL BARRIO

⌂*1230 Fifth Ave., at 104th St. ☎831-7272. **Open** W-Su 11am-5pm. Suggested contribution $4; students and seniors $2.*

Founded in 1969, and originally housed in an East Harlem classroom, this museum has evolved into a respectable Latino cultural institution. Representing art and culture from the Caribbean and Latin America, El Museo features video, painting, sculpture, photography, theater, and film projects. The permanent collection includes pre-Columbian art and Santos de Palo, hand-crafted wooden saint figures from Latin America. Rotating exhibits involve contemporary Latin American artists confronting the issues affecting the Hispanic-American community.

THE MUSEUM FOR AFRICAN ART

⌂*593 Broadway between Houston and Prince Sts. ☎966-1313. Subway: N, R to Prince St.; 6 to Spring St. **Open** Tu-F 10:30am-5:30pm; Sa-Su noon-6pm. $5; students and seniors $2.50.*

Features two major exhibits a year, along with several smaller exhibitions of stunning African and African-American art, often with special themes, such as storytelling, magic, religion, or mask-making. Objects on display span centuries, from ancient to contemporary, and come from all over Africa. Many hands-on family-oriented workshops on African culture offered.

◼ MUSEUM OF AMERICAN ILLUSTRATION

⌂*128 E. 63rd St. between Park and Lexington Aves. ☎838-2560. **Open** Tu 10am-8pm, W-F 10am-5pm, Sa noon-4pm. Free.*

Established in 1981 by the Society of Illustrators, this treasure of a museum has over 1,500 works by such legendary artists as Rockwell, Pyle, and Wyeth. Changing exhibitions focus on the link between past, present, and future in the field of illustration.

MUSEUM OF THE CITY OF NEW YORK

*1220 Fifth Ave., at 103rd St. ☎534-1672. **Open** W-Sa 10am-5pm, Su noon-5pm. Suggested contribution adults $7; seniors, students, and children $4. Also has booth that sells tickets to theaters, other museums, and various city attractions.*

This fascinating museum details the history of the Big Apple, from the construction of the Empire State Building to the history of Broadway theater. Collections include an extensive photography exhibit documenting the evolution of New York in the first half of the 20th century, an exhibit on the consolidation of the boroughs in 1898, a toy gallery, and a variety of spectacular and intriguing changing exhibits.

MUSEUM OF JEWISH HERITAGE: A LIVING MEMORIAL TO THE HOLOCAUST

*18 First Pl. ☎968-1800. **Open** Su-W 9am-5pm, Th 9am-8pm, F 9am-2pm, closed on Jewish holidays. $7; students and seniors $5; under 5 free.*

Inside MOMA

A simultaneously painful and uplifting tribute to the Jewish people. Housed in a sleek, new 6-sided building evocative of the 6-sided star of David. Collection of poignant personal artifacts combined with hours of personal narratives captured on video only begin to present a larger picture of Jewish life. While the exhibits on the Holocaust are inherently upsetting, they are tempered by the final exhibits which present a hopeful future.

MUSEUM OF TELEVISION AND RADIO

*25 W. 52nd St. between Fifth and Sixth Aves. ☎621-6600; daily activity schedule ☎621-6800. **Open** Tu-W and F-Su noon-6pm, Th noon-8pm. Open F until 9pm for theaters only. $6; students and seniors $4; under 13 $3.*

Despite its monumental title, this museum might better fit the description of an archive. With a collection of more than 95,000 TV and radio programs, the museum's library has a specially designed computerized cataloging system that allows you to find, say, every program starring Michael J. Fox in the database. Request an episode from a librarian, and privately watch or listen to it at one of the 96 TV and radio consoles. Serious scholars can request programs from the museum/library's archives held in a nuke-proof safe in upstate NY. Hosts a number of film series that focus on topics of social, historical, popular, or artistic interest (read: *Monty Python* marathons); daily schedule at the front counter.

Museum for Afican Art

NATIONAL ACADEMY MUSEUM

*1083 Fifth Ave. between 89th and 90th Sts. ☎369-4880. **Open** W-Su noon-5pm, F noon-6pm. $8; seniors, students, and children under 16 $4.50.*

Founded in 1825 to "promote the fine arts through exhibition and instruction" in America, this museum includes painting, sculpture, architecture, and graphic art. Currently the academy hosts exhibits, trains young artists, and serves as a fraternal organization for distinguished American artists. Such notables as Winslow Homer, Frederic Edwin Church, John Singer Sargent, and Thomas Eakins represent the 19th century in the permanent collection. The Academy also annually features America's oldest, continuously held juried art competition, scheduled to appear on exhibition in May 2001.

American Museum of Natural History

NATIONAL MUSEUM AND ARCHIVE OF LESBIAN AND GAY HISTORY

208 W. 13th St. between Seventh and Eighth Aves. ☎ *620-7310.* **Open** *daily 6-9pm.*

This musem is housed in the Lesbian and Gay Community Services Center (p. 222), which houses the bathroom where every surface was painted by Keith Haring.

NATIONAL MUSEUM OF THE AMERICAN INDIAN

1 Bowling Green. ☎ *668-6624. Subway: 4, 5 to Bowling Green.* **Open** *daily 10am-5pm, Th closes at 8pm. Free.*

Housed in the stunning Beaux-Arts Customs House, this excellent museum exhibits the best of the Smithsonian's vast collection of Native American artifacts, in galleries and exhibitions designed by Native American artists and craftsmen, who add beautiful personal strokes. The galleries are organized thematically, not by geographical area, and focus on personal stories and accounts.

NEW MUSEUM OF CONTEMPORARY ART

583 Broadway between Prince and Houston Sts. ☎ *219-1222; fax 431-5328.* **Open** *Su-W noon-6pm, Th-Sa noon-8pm. $6; artists, students, and seniors $3; under 18 free. Th 6-8pm free.*

Founded in 1977, the New Museum supports the hottest, the newest, and, usually, the most controversial in contemporary art, making it one of the premier and most important museums of modern art in the world. Three galleries feature innovative art in many media from around the world. You'll also find a free, spacious reading room, interactive exhibitions, and a bookstore. The museum sponsors free lectures, symposia, panel discussions, and film screenings that attempt to find connections between the art world and contemporary social issues. Most major exhibitions are complemented by "gallery talks" in which the artist holds court at the museum to discuss the work and answer questions.

NEW YORK HISTORICAL SOCIETY

2 W. 77th St., at Central Park W. ☎ *873-3400. Library and gallery* **open** *Tu-Su 11am-5pm; in summer library open Tu-F 11am-5pm. Suggested donation $5; children and seniors $3. Library free.*

The Society has a museum devoted to fascinating exhibits centered on the history of New York City. In their block-long Neoclassical building, the astute staff will help you uncover obscure facts about the city's past or provide trivia about the present. Founded in 1804, this is New York's oldest continuously operated museum. The Society's extensive collections include Tiffany lamps and Audubon watercolors. Kids should visit the permanent "Kid City" installation that delightfully chronicles the history of New York.

NEW YORK TRANSIT MUSEUM

130 Livingston St., at Schermerhorn and Boerum Pl. ☎ *718-243-3060.* **Subway:** *2, 3, 4, M, N, R to Borough Hall-Court St.; then walk down to Schermerhorn and take a left.* **Open** *Tu-F 10am-4pm, Sa-Su noon-5pm. $3, children and senior citizens $1.50, seniors free W afternoons.*

Housed in a defunct subway station, this newly renovated little museum describes the birth and evolution of every aspect of New York's mass transit system. Check out the walk-through exhibit, from subway maps to turnstiles to the trains themselves.

PARSONS EXHIBITION CENTER

2 W. 13th St., at Parsons School of Design on Fifth Ave. ☎ *229-8987.* **Open** *M-F 9am-6pm. Free.*

A variety of exhibitions, many of student and faculty work, including photography, computer art, painting, and sculpture.

STATEN ISLAND INSTITUTE OF ARTS AND SCIENCES

75 Stuyvesant Pl., on the far corner of Wall St. in Staten Island. ☎ *718-727-1135.* **Open** *M-Sa 9am-5pm, Su 1-5pm. Suggested donation $2.50; students, seniors, and under 12 $1.25.*

Open since 1885, its galleries feature rotating displays pertaining to the art, science, and history of the region, varying from portraits from their permanent collection to informative exhibits about "Famous People from Staten Island."

STUDIO MUSEUM IN HARLEM

◩144 W. 125th St. ☎864-4500. **Open** W-Th noon-6pm, F noon-8pm, Sa-Su 10am-6pm. Suggested donation $5; students and seniors $3; under 12 $1.

Founded in 1967 at the height of the Civil Rights movement, the Studio Museum is dedicated to the collection and exhibition of works by black artists. currently undergoing a major renovation and expansion, this museum features two exhibitions a year, both culled from the photographs, paintings, and sculptures in the museum's collection.

▨ WATERFRONT MUSEUM

◩Barge #79, 290 Conover St. at Pier 45, in Red Hook, Brooklyn. ☎718-624-4719. **Subway:** A, C, F, 2, 3, 4, 5 to Jay St./Borough Hall; M, N, R to Court St.; then bus #B61 to Beard St.; walk a block in the opposite direction from bus; left onto Conover St. and it's 2 blocks to the waterfront.

This is not your typical museum. First, it's on a barge floating in the New York Harbor. Second, the focus of the museum is the barge, the pier, the stunning view, and the waterfront area in addition to the exhibits themselves. The proprietor of the museum pulled the barge out of a muddy bank himself and took years to restore it to its present state; it is the only functional wooden barge left in New York Harbor. The museum hosts a great **Sunset Concert Series** Saturday evenings July-Aug. (free) and **Circus Sundays** in June when jugglers and acrobats come to entertain the kids (free, shows at 2pm and 4pm).

GALLERIES

New York's galleries are where contemporary art *goes down*. What's even better, gallery proprietors don't expect the sassy traveler (read: you with *Let's Go: NYC)* to buy anything (read: be able to afford anything on display); they don't even charge for entrance.

To start, ask for a free copy of *The Gallery Guide* (www.galleryguideonline.com) at a major museum or gallery. It lists the addresses, phone numbers, and hours of virtually every showplace in the city. It comes with several maps so that you can walk as surely as any designer-clad, stilleto-ed aesthete. Extensive gallery info is also in the "Choices" listings of the free *Village Voice*, the Art section of *Time Out* and *New York* magazines, the complimentary *The New York Art World* (www.thenewyorkartworld.com) available in select galleries, and *The New Yorker*'s "Goings On About Town."

SoHo is a gallery wonderland, with a particularly dense concentration of more than 40 different establishments showing in a variety of media. Other cutting-edge outposts have recently emerged in **Chelsea** in reclaimed industrial spaces. **Madison Avenue** in the 60s and 70s has a generous sampling of ritzy showplaces, and another group festoons **East 57th St.** The outer borough gallery scene is growing rapidly (like Brooklyn's Williamsburg), and often dwells on local themes.

The **Art Shuttle** transports gallery-goers between Soho, Chelsea, and beyond on Saturdays. (☎769-8100; www.artshuttle.org; Sa 11am-6pm.)

SOHO

SoHo galleries not only open and close with amazing rapidity, but many of them unfortunately have had to cut their losses and sell what they call "bread and butter" commercial art—a landscape that goes well with a sofa or a sunset dangerously verging on airbrush. Still, the avant-garde does make a stand here. The most cutting edge offerings have trouble making it to the ground-level, commercial galleries that line West Broadway and Broadway, so explore the second or third floors of gallery-packed buildings if you want to see SoHo's more experimental art. The addresses 560-594 Broadway are known as the **Broadway Gallery Buildings,** with many small galleries packed inside. The following is only a sampling of this packed neighborhood.

▨ **ARTISTS SPACE.** Non-profit gallery open since 1972. Its space often has several small but well-curated exhibits assembled by unique themes that are always interesting. Slide file of unaffiliated artists gives those without backing a chance to shine. (38 Greene St., at

Grand St., 3rd fl. ☎ 226-3970; www.artistsspace.org. Open Tu-Sa 10am-6pm; summer W-Sa noon-6pm. Slide file open by appointment, usually F-Sa. Frequent free evening performances.)

POP. One of the more commercial galleries, this space offers works by pop masters such as Warhol, Lichtenstein, and Haring. Go see real pop art for free. *(473 W. Broadway, below Houston St. www.popinternational.com. Open Tu-Sa 11am-6pm.)*

DRAWING CENTER. Specializing exclusively in original works on paper, this non-profit space manages to set up reliably high-quality exhibits. Both historical and contemporary works are on show—everything from Picasso to Kara Walker. *(35 Wooster St. ☎ 219-2166. Open Tu and Th-F 10am-6pm, W 10am-8pm, Sa 11am-6pm; closed Aug.)*

SHAKESPEARE'S FULCRUM. This is a gallery like no other; the owner wears transparent vixen-like clothing and shows Actual Art—art that requires the forces of nature for completion. Be sure to pick up the gallery's complimentary packet on its mission and gestalt. *(480 Broome St., at Wooster St. ☎ 966-6848. Open Tu-Sa 11am-6pm, Su 1-6pm.)*

EXIT ART/THE FIRST WORLD. A fun and happening "transcultural" and "transmedia" non-profit space, featuring experiments in the presentation of visual art, theater, film, and video. About as friendly and young as it gets in the NYC art scene. The **Café Cultura** (open F-Sa 11am-6pm) lets you pose with a beer. *(548 Broadway, between Prince and Spring Sts., 2nd fl. ☎ 966-7745. Open Tu-Th 11am-6pm; summer M-F 11am-6pm; closed Aug.)*

PRINTED MATTER, INC. Featuring the best artist books and magazines in the biz, this non-profit bookshop/gallery lets you peruse books on art as well as books that are art. Artists like John Baldessari, Cindy Sherman, and Kiki Smith are all associated with PM, but it is the commitment to displaying books by unknowns that makes Printed Matter such a valuable resource. *(77 Wooster St. ☎ 925-0325. Open Tu-F 10am-6pm, Sa 11am-7pm.)*

THREAD WAXING SPACE. An eclectic space that shows in various media. Mostly group shows with thematically curated exhibits, sometimes solo shows. *(476 Broadway between Broome and Grand Sts., 2nd fl. ☎ 966-9520; www.threadwaxing.org. Open Tu-Sa 10am-6pm.)*

TONY SHAFRAZI. A commercial highbrow gallery that boasts being one of the first to display art by 1980s masters such as Haring and Basquiat. *(119 Wooster St. between Prince and Spring Sts. ☎ 274-9300. Open Tu-Sa 10am-6pm.)*

ILLUSTRATION HOUSE. Devoted to exhibiting American illustration history. Works by Rockwell and Nyeth can be found here. *(96 Spring St. between Mercer and Broadway. ☎ 966-9444; www.illustration-house.com. Open Tu-Sa 10am-6pm.)*

DIA CENTER FOR THE ARTS. An extension of the Chelsea gallery (see below), it has been showing Walter De Maria's *The New York Earth Room* since 1980. *(141 Wooster St. between Houston and Prince Sts., 2nd fl. ☎ 473-8072. Open Sept.-July W-Sa noon-6pm.)*

THE WORK SPACE. A tiny space that shares property with other businesses (hence the regular business hours). Still, worth a look for their group shows often curated by theme. *(96 Spring St. between Mercer and Broadway, 8th fl. ☎ 219-2790. Open M-F 10am-5pm.)*

WOOSTER PROJECTS. Innovatively curated group shows that have great variety in showing both old masters and young artists. *(26 Wooster St. between Grand and Canal Sts. ☎ 226-7677; www.woosterprojects.com. Open Tu-Sa noon-6pm.)*

DEITCH PROJECTS. Any gallery that has a logo resembling the layout and font of a Brillo box deserves to be checked out. Often has group shows of up-and-coming artists. *(76 Grand St. between Greene and Wooster Sts. ☎ 343-7300. Open Tu-Sa noon-6pm.)*

STALEY-WISE. Found in one of the Broadway Gallery buildings, this space focuses on fashion photography—Louise Dahl-Wolfe, Helmut Newton, Man Ray, etc. *(560 Broadway, just south of Prince St., 3rd fl. ☎ 966-6223. Open Tu-Sa 11am-5pm.)*

CHELSEA

Many of the galleries originally in SoHo have been lured to the warehouses in Chelsea by cheaper rents. Be sure to check out the building at **529 W. 20th St.** between Tenth and Eleventh Aves.; with eleven floors, it is a treasure trove of contemporary art. The area between Fifth and Sixth Aves. and 17th and 21st Sts. is known as the **Photography District.** And if you happen to be clubbing at **Twilo,** there might be exhibits on the 2nd fl. (542 W. 27th St. between Tenth and Eleventh Aves. ☎ 268-1600.)

SONNABEND. Originally located in SoHo, this famous gallery has shown works by well-known American and European contemporary masters for 40 years. *(536 W. 22nd St. between Tenth and Eleventh Aves. ☎ 627-1018. Open Tu-Sa 10am-6pm.)*

DIA CENTER FOR THE ARTS. Museum-sized, but with a definite sensibility for catching the pulse of current art. Four-stories of changing exhibits covering a balanced range of media and styles. Don't leave without stopping by the permanent installation on the roof. *(548 W. 22nd St. between Tenth and Eleventh Aves. ☎ 989-5566; www.diacenter.org. Open W-Su noon-6pm; closed July-Aug. $6; students and seniors $3. See DIA above in SoHo.)*

Stuart Parr Gallery

THE MUSEUM AT FASHION INSTITUTE OF TECHNOLOGY. A heavenly place for all those fashionista-artsy crossover types. Several changing exhibits related to anything and everything fashionable—from photography and textiles to mannequin displays. *(Seventh Ave. and 27th St. ☎ 217-5800; www.fitnyc.suny.edu. Open Tu-F noon-8pm, Sa 10am-5pm.)*

TARANTO GALLERY. Near the photography district, this simplistic gallery features seasoned and young photographers in both group and solo shows. *(245 W. 19th St. between Seventh and Eighth Aves. ☎ 691-9040. Open M-F 9am-7pm, Sa 11am-5pm.)*

I-20. Open a silver warehouse door and step right into I-20, a gallery exhibiting high quality contemporary art displayed in a beautiful 11th-floor space. Also commands an exhilarating view of the river and piers below. *(529 W. 20th St., 11th fl. ☎ 645-1100; www.I-20.com. Open Tu-Sa 10:30am-6pm.)*

Exit Art

GAVIN BROWN'S ENTERPRISE CORP. An interactive space that is both a gallery and a social area. The bar, **Passerby,** has DJs Tu and Th. *(436 W. 15th St. between Ninth and Tenth Aves. ☎ 627-5258. Open Tu-Sa 10am-6pm.)*

MAX PROTETCH. Having started as an exhibition space for architectural drawings, Protetch now hosts impressive and intelligent contemporary shows of painting, sculpture, and all things in between. *(511 W. 22nd St. between Tenth and Eleventh Aves. ☎ 633-6999. Open Tu-Sa 10am-6pm; summer M-F 10am-6pm; closed Aug. Wheelchair accessible.)*

D'AMELIO TERRAS. Shows works in sculpture and photography. *(525 W. 22nd St. between Tenth and Eleventh Aves. ☎ 352-9460. Open Tu-Sa 10am-6pm; summer M-F 10am-5pm.)*

D'Amelio Terras

57TH STREET

FULLER BUILDING. This stylish Art Deco building harbors 12 floors of galleries with frequent turnover, featuring contemporary notables, ancient works like Frederick Schultz, and several modern works galleries. *(41 E. 57th St. between Madison and Park Aves. Most open M-Sa 10am-5:30pm, but call ahead to make sure; Oct.-May most closed M.)*

PACE GALLERY. Four floors dedicated to the promotion of widely disparate forms of art. Includes Pace Masterprints, the Pace African Art Gallery, Pace-MacGill photography, and Pace-Wildenstein contemporary prints. *(32 E. 57th St. between Park and Madison Aves. ☎421-3237, 421-3688, 759-7999, and 421-3292, respectively as listed. Open June-Sept. M-Th 9:30am-6pm, F 9:30am-4pm; Oct.-May Tu-Sa 9:30am-6pm. **Also at** 142 Greene St. between Prince and Houston Sts.; ☎431-9224.)*

UPPER EAST SIDE

SOTHEBY'S. One of the most respected auction houses in the city, offering everything from Degas to Disney. Auctions open to anyone, but some require a ticket (first come, first serve). Pop in and pretend you're an avid collector. *(1334 York Ave., at 72nd St. ☎606-7000; ticket office ☎606-7171. Both open M-Sa 10am-5pm, Su 1-5pm; closed Sa-Su in summer.)*

CHRISTIE'S. Flaunts its collection of valuable wares as one of the most well known international auction houses. Like Sotheby's, auctions are open to the public. *(20 Rockefeller Plaza at 49th St., between Fifth and Sixth Aves. ☎636-2000. Open M-Sa 10am-5pm, Su 1-5pm.)*

LEO CASTELLI. Showing a selection of contemporary masters such as Jasper Johns and Ed Ruscha. *(59 E. 79th St. between Park and Madison Aves. ☎249-4470. Open Tu-Sa 10am-6pm; summer Tu-F 10am-5pm.)*

GAGOSIAN. Represents an impressive group of artists such as Warhol, Yves Klein, and Richard Serra. *(980 Madison Ave., near 77th St. ☎744-2313. Open M-Sa 10am-6pm.)*

M. KNOEDLER & CO., INC. One of the oldest and most respected galleries in the city. Mounts exhibits such as "The Collector as Patron in the 20th Century." *(19 E. 70th St. between Madison and Fifth Aves. ☎794-0550. Open M-Th 9:30am-5pm; summer M-F 9:30am-5pm.)*

HIRSCHL AND ADLER GALLERIES. Two floors of selected art: on the 1st floor is a wide variety of 18th- and 19th-century European and American art; upstairs, at Hirschl and Adler Modern, more contemporary works are displayed. *(21 E. 70th St. between Fifth and Madison Aves. ☎535-8810; www.hirschlandandadler.com. Open Tu-F 9:30am-5:15pm, Sa 9:30am-4:45pm; summer M-F 9:30am-4:45pm.)*

ACQUAVELLA. This majestic building houses exhibitions specializing in post-Impressionist paintings, drawings, and sculpture. Big names such as Picasso, Degas, Cézanne, and Giacometti. *(18 E. 79th St. between Fifth and Madison Aves. ☎734-6300. Open M-F 10am-5pm; open Sa-Su for larger shows.)*

BROOKLYN

Mostly located in artistically vibrant **Williamsburg,** Brooklyn's galleries often provide space for cutting-edge artists who have yet to break into the commercialized world of downtown Manhattan. As a result, the art here is current and often fresh.

█ THE WILLIAMSBURG ART AND HISTORICAL CENTER. The official center of the Williamsburg arts scene, it exhibits local artists and has spaces for a variety of media such as theater, poetry, and music. The Center also sponsors **walking tours** of the area. *(135 Broadway between Bedford and Driggs. Subway: J, M, Z to Marcy Ave. and walk 3 blocks west on Broadway; L to Bedford Ave. and walk down Bedford to Broadway. ☎718-486-7372. Open Sa-Su noon-6pm.)*

█ PIEROGI 2000. Although it has shown bigger-name artists like Amy Sillman and Tom Nozkowski, what sets this Williamsburg gallery apart are its "front files," hundreds of affordable works by emerging artists. The files are kept on shelves and are meant to be perused by visitors. *(177 N. 9th St., between Bedford and Driggs Aves. Subway: L to Bedford Ave. ☎ 718-599-2144. Open F-M noon-6pm.)*

BROOKLYN WORKING ARTISTS COALITION (BWAC). Plans a series of interesting site-specific exhibits throughout Brooklyn. Summer 2000 saw "Between the Bridges Sculpture Show" at Empire Fulton Ferry State Park. *(☎ 718-596-2507; www.bwac.org.)*

EYEWASH. This little gem specializes in installations of photography and other media. *(143 N. 7th St. between Bedford and Berry St., 4th fl. Subway: L to Bedford Ave., then walk ½ block to N. 7th St. ☎ 718-387-2714. Open Sa-Su 1-6pm and by appointment.)*

THE BRONX

The community-oriented galleries here often showcase local talent and address issues of neighborhood and ethnic identity.

LEHMAN ART GALLERY. Housed in a building designed by Marcel Breuer, the gallery's past exhibitions have included artifacts from Papua New Guinea and a series of paintings commemorating Puerto Rican victims of domestic violence. Every June, Lehman holds a children's show displaying art made by local youngsters in the museum's education program. *(250 Bedford Park Blvd., at West and Goulden Aves. On the campus of Herbert Lehman College, in the Fine Arts Building. Subway: 4, D to Bedford Park. ☎ 718-960-8731; www.math240.lehman.cuny.edu/art/galleryinfo. Open M-Th 10am-4pm; Aug. by appointment only.)*

QUEENS

THE INSTITUTE FOR CONTEMPORARY ART/P.S. 1. At the site of New York's first public school, P.S.1 presents cutting-edge exhibitions and offers studio space to local artists; well known for its annual outdoor DJ party series. Long Island City also offers a fabulous view of Manhattan. *(22-25 Jackson Ave., LI City, Queens. Subway: E, F to 23rd St.-Ely Ave. ☎ 718-784-2084; www.ps1.org. Open W-Su noon-6pm. Suggested donation $4.)*

Shopping

There is perhaps no easier place to spend money than New York City. With everything you could ever imagine, from the (former) largest department store in the world to the hottest new boutique to the hardest-to-find underground used-clothing store, how can you, a mere first-time visitor, ever find what you want? Read on, loyal follower: this is your bible to the largest, the cutest, and the hippest. Find a department store; find a designer flagship store; find an out-of-print import CD; find the cheapest, tightest shirt for tonight; find $10 Prada bags and Rolex watches (ok, so maybe they're not always real, but, if you're lucky, you'll find the vendor with the stolen ones); even find hard-core mall shopping (although that's banished to Long Island; see **Daytrips,** p. 234).

SHOPPING BY TYPE

BR	Brooklyn	**GUM**	Gramercy, Union, and Murray	**SH**	SoHo
CH	Chelsea	**GV**	Greenwich Village	**SI**	Staten Island
CHI	Chinatown	**HWH**	Harlem & Washington Hts.	**UES**	Upper East Side
EM	East Midtown	**LI**	Little Italy	**UWS**	Upper West Side
EV	East Village	**LES**	Lower East Side	**WM**	West Midtown
		LM	Lower Manhattan		

ACCESSORIES		**ACCESSORIES, CONT.**	
Adorned (p. 144)	EV	Reminiscence (p. 146)	GUM
It's a Mod, Mod World (p. 145)	EV	Starfish & Jelli (p. 146)	EV
Lucky Wang (p. 140)	LES	Tiffany & Co. (p. 149)	EM
Manhattan Portage (p. 145)	EV		

PERIODICALS AND NEWSPAPERS
Universal News and Cafe Corp. (p.141)   SH

POSTERS AND COMICS
Anime Crash (p.142)   GV
Forbidden Planet (p.142)   GV
See Hear (p.146)   HWH
Village Comics (p.144)   GV

TOYS AND GAMES
▨ F.A.O. Schwarz
Game Show (p.150)   UES
Star Magic (p.150)   UES
Village Chess Shop (p.144)   GV

PETS
BJ Discount Pet Shop (p.140)   LES

REVOLUTIONARY BOOKSTORES
Black Out Books (p.144)   EV
Revolution Books (p.147)   CH

SEWING SUPPLIES
▨ K. Trimming (p.141)   SH
Tender Buttons (p.150)   UES

SEX (AND SEXUAL) SHOPS
Condomania (p.142)   GV
La Petite Coquette (p.143)   GV
Leather Man (p.143)   GV
Patricia Field (p.143)   GV
Religious Sex (p.145)   EV

SPECIALTY BOOKSTORES
Applause Theater & Cinema Books (p.150) UWS
Argosy Bookstore (p.149)   UES
Asahiya Bookstore (p.148)   EM
Books of Wonder (p.147)   CH
Complete Traveller Bookstore (p.146)   GUM
▨ The Drama Book Shop (p.147)   WM

SPECIALTY BOOKSTORES, CONT.
Ivy's Books (p.151)   UWS
Liberation Bookstore (p.148)   HWH
Murder Ink (p.151)   UWS
See Hear (p.146)   HWH

SPECIALTY SHOPS
Chick Darrow's Fun Antiques (p.150)   UES
Counter Spy Shop (p.149)   EM
Hammacher Schlemmer (p.149)   EM
Maxilla & Mandible (p.151)   UWS
Pop Shop (p.145)   EV
Reminiscence (p.146)   GUM
Rita Ford Music Boxes (p.150)   UES
Star Magic (p.150)   UES

VIDEOSTORES
▨ Kim's Audio and Video (p.145)   EV

VINTAGE CLOTHING
Andy's Chee-Pee's (p.142)   GV
Antique Boutique (p.142)   GV
▨ Canal Jean Co. (p.141)   SH
Cheap Jack's (p.142)   GV
▨ Domsey's (p.151)   BR
Encore (p.150)   UES
Honeymoon (p.145)   EV
Love Saves the Day (p.145)   EV
Metropolis (p.145)   EV
Michael's (p.150)   UES
NYC Mart (p.146)   EV
Physical Graffiti (p.146)   EV
Rags-A-Gogo (p.145)   EV
Reminiscence (p.146)   GUM
Shoshana's Place (p.146)   EV
▨ SoHo Flea Market (p.141)   SH
Tatiana (p.146)   EV
Treasure Trends (p.146)   EV

SHOPPING BY NEIGHBORHOOD

LOWER MANHATTAN

see map
pp. 316–317

▨ **Century 21,** 22 Cortlandt St. (227-9092), between Broadway and Church St., by the World Trade Center. A shopper's dream—department store with *very* discounted designer wares. Sift through the bargain basement duds to find that Armani suit you could never afford. Open Su 11am-6pm, M-W 7:45am-8pm, Th 7:45am-8:30pm, F 7:45am-8pm, Sa 10am-7:30pm.

J & R Music World, 23 Park Row (732-8600 or 238-9000), near City Hall. Subway: N, R, 4, 5, or 6 to City Hall. Will also meet most of your electronics needs with competitive prices. Open M-W and F-Sa 9am-7pm, Th 9am-7:30pm, Su 10:30am-6:30pm.

Nassau St. Pedestrian Mall, located west of City Hall, stores here offer discounted clothing, often for $10 or less. It's well worth the rummage, but don't head here past 6pm.

World Trade Center (435-4170), at West and Liberty St. Located in the concourse, this "mall" provides a sufficient variety of 40 shops and restaurants, its biggest drawback is its "basement" feel. Shops open M-F 7:30am-6:30pm, Sa 10am-5pm (see p. 66).

on the cheap

chinatown

You can find Asian imports, $5 burned Ds, and anything else under the sun here, including that wicker ate Spade you've been trying to convince yourself is worth the splurge. You don't have to think twice when it's "Too fuh ten dollah " And if the stores along anal don't have the nice black vinyl bag with the Prada logo, ask them to stick one on—they're in the back.

The Oriental Culture Enterprise, 13-17 Elizabeth St., 2nd fl. (☎226-8461). This bookstore specializes in hinese literature. Its extensive collection includes books, tapes, Ds, newspapers, calligraphy equipment, and musical instruments. Open daily 10am-7pm.

Pearl River, 277 anal St., at Broadway. (☎431-4770). This hinese department store sells all the basic necessities, along with a few hard-to-find luxuries. heap clothes, paper lanterns, the miraculous Japanese buckwheat pillow, and soft-core "male model" playing cards. All cheap, all under one roof. Open daily 10am-7:30pm.

LITTLE ITALY

see map
pp. 318–319

Find Outlet, 229 Mott St., between Prince and Spring Sts. (☎226-5167). Although most boutiques here boast high pricetags, this store is an outlet that sells wares from other NoLIta boutiques at cheaper prices. Often 50-80% off the original, Find makes fabulous New York labels available for the cheapskate in all of us. Longsleeve shirts $44 (originally $90). Open daily noon-7pm. **Other location:** 361 W. 17th St. (☎243-3177).

Language, 238 Mulberry St. (☎431-5566; www.language-nyc.com), between Prince and Spring St. Subway: 6 to Spring St.; N, R to Prince St.; B, D, F, Q to Broadway-Lafeyette. Exquisite (and unaffordable) clothing and furniture—some designed inhouse, some unbelievably vintage. Perhaps the most gracefully original urban gear around. Open M-W and Sa 11am-7pm, Th 11am-8pm, Su noon-7pm.

LOWER EAST SIDE

see map
pp. 326–327

Shopping in the Lower East Side is slowly becoming an expensive venture. Up-and-coming designers and select shops often display their handmade, cutting-edge wares in stores that look more like museums. Browse around Orchard, Stanton, and Ludlow Sts.

BJ Discount Pet Shop, 151 E. Houston St. (☎982-5310). This shop brings together the words "pet," "discount," and "bizarre." Their petite pets have made it rather big: the Madagascar hissing roaches appeared in *Men In Black,* a millipede was in a Showtime movie, and many other species have debuted on David Letterman. The owners have a sense of humor, evident in the South American Boa cage with a sign reading "Hug me." Open M-Sa 10am-6:30pm.

Lucky Wang, 100 Stanton St. (☎353-2850). A temple to nylon day-glo fur, the designers here focus on accessories made of this material they call "cyberfur." Pompom keychains ($2) and various types of bags (around $10). The store also stocks knitted products, apron bags made of oriental cloth ($40), and beaded jewelry. Open Tu-F noon-7pm, Sa 1-7pm, Su 1-6pm.

TG-170, 170 Ludlow St. (☎995-8660). One of the meccas of hip in the Lower East Side, this store has been around since 1995. Still very forward-thinking, it stocks smaller, hipper labels mostly for women. Skirts $85, *petit bateau* t-shirts $30, camisoles on sale $20. Open daily noon-8pm.

Zao, 175 Orchard St., between Stanton and Houston Sts. (☎505-0500). Flashy and truly chi-chi, this store is worth a browse. If you don't think the racks of Jeremy Scott and

Vexed Generation clothing is worth the pricetag, at least peruse the art, cutting edge fashion mags (*The Face* and other imports available), and the home goods in the mezzanine. Go farther into the depths of cool and discover an art gallery space and a beautiful garden complete with metallic waterfall installation in back. Open daily 11am-7pm.

SOHO

see map
p. 321

SoHo may be Valhalla for Japanese tourists, but you can still find some deals at the district's used clothing stores and streetside stands. Check out the daily "fair" that sets up shop in a lot on **Wooster and Spring Sts.** The bargain hunt continues on Broadway with a wide selection of used clothing stores, like **Alice Underground**. In addition, **Prince St.** between Broadway and West Broadway usually features the best jewelry, books, accessories, and inexpensive street art right on the sidewalk. Flea market devotees should check out the outdoor **Soho Flea Market** at the western end of Canal St., and the **Antiques Fair and Collectibles Market** (☎ 682-2000; open Sa-Su 9am-5pm), held year-round, hosting some 50-100 vendors on the corner of Broadway and Grand St. This is a very small neighborhood—you can walk it in less than an hour, so use that time to find bargains.

Canal Jean Co., 504 Broadway between Spring and Broome Sts. (☎ 226-3663). This original and enormous home of surplus bargains brims with neon ties, baggy pants, alterna-tees, and silk smoking jackets. Artsy hipsters can buy their black slim-fitting jeans here. Poke around bargain central in the basement. Open Su-Th 10:30am-8pm, F-Sa 10:30am-9pm; in summer daily 9:30am-9pm.

Sephora, 555 Broadway between Spring and Prince Sts. (☎ 625-1309). An overwhelming array of cosmetic products; they even have an organ of scents, where you can mix together your own personal scent. The tantalizing rainbow arrangements and the sheer magnitude of perfumes, powders, and exfoliaters at Sephora could convince even Snow White that she needed Shiseido's help. Prices run the gamut. Open M-Sa 11am-8:30pm, Su 11am-7pm.

Girlprops.com, 153 Prince St., off Broadway (☎ 505-7615). It must have been here that the Pilgrims got their $24 worth of bauble to buy Manhattan, because only girlprops.com can make the seriously cheap seem seriously attractive. Descend into this underground lair of accessorizing to see girls of all ages trying on, oggling at, and salivating over every kind of hair clip, boa, lariat, body glitter, jeweled item, rhinestone belt, make-up, bracelet, or tiara that is currently in style. Individually inexpensive—but beware, those sparkly bobby pins do add up. Most under $10. Open M-W 9am-11pm, Th and Su 10am-midnight, F-Sa 10pm-1am.

K. Trimming Co., 519 Broadway between Spring and Broome Sts. (☎ 431-8829). The world's largest trimming center, K. Trimming is a cavernous warehouse featuring every kind of sewing product you could ever want: doilies, swaths of colored fabrics, sequins, embroidered trimmings, pom-poms, ribbons, buttons, etc. It's a tempting sartorial jungle where amateur and aspiring SoHo designers come to find their wares. Open Su-Th 9am-7pm, F 9am-4pm.

Final Home, 241 Lafayette St. (☎ 343-0532). Japanamania has hit New York in the form of this very new, and very trendy, designer store. Subsidiary of Issey Miyake. Good location to find discount flyers for underground clubs and rave events. Open M-Sa 11am-7pm, Su noon-6pm.

A Photographer's Place, 133 Mercer St. between Prince and Spring Sts. (☎ 431-9358). Small, quiet store contains photography books aplenty—new, rare, and out of print—as well as a great postcards collection. Open M-Sa 11am-8pm, Su noon-6pm.

Universal News and Cafe Corp., 484 Broadway between Broome and Grand Sts. (☎ 965-9042). Over 7000 magazine titles (foreign and domestic) covering everything from fashion to fishing to politics. It'a also a cafe so you can munch and relax while you read. Open daily 5am-midnight.

Untitled, 159 Prince St. between Broadway and Thompson St. (☎ 982-2088). In SoHo since 1970, this fine arts store specializes in design and typography. Veritable library of postcards, catalogued for your convenience (each 75¢). Open M-Sa 10am-10pm, Su 11am-7pm.

GREENWICH VILLAGE

see map
pp. 322–323

Andy's Chee-pee's, 691 Broadway, between E. 4th St. and Great Jones St. (460-8488). Not really cheap at all, but worth a peek, if only for that vintage clothing aroma. Open M-Sa 11am-9pm, Su noon-8pm.

Anime Crash, 13 E. 4th St., between Broadway and Lafayette St. (254-4670). Japanese pop culture, from Akira to Zandor. Import comics, model sets, huge posters, and cool miscellany. CDs, videos, and laser discs also on sale. Open M-Th 11am-9pm, F-Sa 11am-9 pm, Su noon-7pm.

Antique Boutique, 712 Broadway, near Washington Pl. in Greenwich Village (460-8830). Blares better techno than many clubs, and sells both stunning vintage clothing and interesting new designs (both *very* expensive). As with most outfitters of club gear, expect a lot of shiny plastics and outrageous attitudes. A live DJ spins Saturday 3pm-9pm so you can shop *and* get your groove on. Open M-W 11am-9pm, Th-Sa 11am-10pm, Su noon-8pm.

☒ Astor Place Hair Stylists, 2 Astor Pl., at Broadway (☎ 475-9854). Complement your new Village wardrobe with a distinctive trim at the largest haircutting establishment in the world, famed for its low-priced production-line approach to style. One observer noted, "It's like Club MTV with clippers." Many of the employees, including the so-called Michelangelo of hair-shaving, have been in the press. Don't let the constant drone of mechanical clippers frighten you—this is no salon, but you can get a good haircut. John Malkovich, Run DMC, Adam Sandler, and Joan Rivers represent some of the celeb clientele that frequent this establishment. One hundred-ten people (including a DJ) work in this 3-story complex. Short hair cuts $11; long hair cuts $13; Su $1 extra. Open M-Sa 8am-8pm, Su 9am-6pm.

Bleecker St. Records, 239 Bleecker St. (☎ 255-7899). Subway: A, B, C, D, E, F, or Q to W. 4th St. The walls of this vintage shop are decorated with old vinyl platters. Heavy concentration of jazz LPs complement a formidable selection of old rock, blues, country, and soul. Open M-Th 11am-10pm, F-Sa 11am-1am, Su noon-10pm.

Biography Bookstore, 400 Bleecker St., at W. 11th St. (☎ 807-8655). Let us sit upon the ground and tell sad tales of the deaths of kings, presidents, rock idols, and other personalities. Biography-browsing at its best. Strong gay/lesbian section, as well as bestsellers. Open M-Th 11am-10pm, F-Sa 11am-11pm, Su 11am-7pm.

Cheap Jack's Vintage Clothing, 841 Broadway (☎ 995-0403), between 13th and 14th St. Subway: L, N, R or 4, 5, 6 to Union Sq. Yet another vintage store using the word "cheap" a bit too loosely. Jack, whoever he is, sells racks and racks of worn jeans, old flannels, leather jackets, and other vintage "gems." Open M-Sa 11am-7pm, Su noon-7pm. AmEx, V, MC.

Condomania, 351 Bleecker St., near W. 10th St. (☎ 691-9442). "America's first condom store" is basically just condoms, dental dams, and lube. Pick up some XXX-rated fortune cookies or a box of "Penis Pasta" with your order. Friendly staff answers all questions and gives safe-sex tips. Open Su-Th 11am-11pm, F-Sa 11am-midnight.

Disc-O-Rama, 186 W. 4th St., between Sixth and Seventh Aves. (☎ 206-8417). All CDs $10 or below. Strong alternative section in addition to more standard Top 40 choices. The CDs aren't in order, so be prepared for a search (only the top 200 are organized). DVDs, books, vinyl downstairs. Open M-Th 10:30am-11pm, F 10:30am-midnight, Sa 10:30am-1am, Su 11:30am-8:30pm. Call ☎ 260-8616 for their **annex** at 40 Union Sq. East and ☎ 477-9410 for their **classical and clearance store** at 146 W. 4th St.

Forbidden Planet, 840 Broadway, at 13th St. (☎ 473-1576). An amazing repository of all things sci-fi. Comics, posters, models, toys, Play Station games (to buy, sell, and trade), and art books (including how-to-draw books). Doesn't keep it as real as it used to now that it is under new management, but you can still get a reprinted copy of the first X-Men ($3) or Kiss action figures ($13). Unhealthily skinny boys and the death-goth girls who love them congregate here. Open M-Sa 10am-10pm, Su 11am-8pm.

☒ Generation Records, 210 Thompson St., between Bleecker and 3rd Sts. (☎ 254-1100). All kinds of alternative and underground rock on CD and vinyl; the hardcore and industrial/experimental selection is especially impressive. Fairly low prices (CDs $11-13) and the best assortment of hard-to-find imports in the Village. Great deals on used merchandise downstairs (CDs about $6).

Also carries videos, t-shirts, posters. Open Su-Th 11am-10pm, F-Sa 11am-1am.

La Petite Coquette, 51 University Pl. (473-2478), between 9th and 10th St., in Greenwich Village. The fulfillment of your bordello fantasies. This small shop offers all things beaded, embroidered, laced, fringed, and tied to add intrigue to your evenings and perfume your drawers. Celebrity photos on the walls testify that La Petite Coquette will elude your budget, but they won't drive away the true lingerie enthusiast. Come for their post-Valentine's Day sale (mid- to late Feb.) when most items are 40% off. Open M-W and Sa 11am-7pm, Th 11am-8pm, Su noon-6pm.

The Leather Man, 111 Christopher St. (243-5339), between Bleecker and Hudson St. Subway: 1, 9 to Christopher St. What a window display! Not for the timid—chains, leather, and, in the basement, all manner of sex toys, etc. Plenty of stuff for your folks...nudge, nudge, wink, wink. Friendly staff, helpful to all genders and orientations. Gift certificates available. Open M-Sa noon-1opm, Su noon-8pm.

Macy's in Herald Square

◙ **Other Music,** 15 E. 4th St., across from Tower Records (☎477-8150). Specializing in the alternative and avant-garde. Obscure stuff abounds, but you can avoid steep import prices with the sizeable used CD section. Posters and flyers keep the clientele updated on where to see their favorite performers, and the staff is an even better source of information. Open M-Th noon-9pm, F-Sa noon-10pm, Su noon-7pm.

Patricia Field, 10 E. 8th St., near Fifth Ave. (☎254-1699). Fabulous array of costly, kinky, hip gear with a perpetual "prostitute sale:" the fabric of choice is vinyl and the colors are neon. The sale rack offers excellent bargains (rubber short-shorts for $22). Pick up a new rider's crop ($34) for your collection. Extensive selection of "pasties" (nipple tassles, $12-18). Open M-Sa noon-8pm, Su 1-7pm. Sister store **Hotel Venus** at 38 W. Broadway (☎966-4066).

Second Coming Records, 231 and 235 Sullivan St., near W. 3rd St. (☎228-1313). Vinyl, and lots of it. An especially strong selection of underground 7-inches. Thanks to a recent expansion, the CD stock now accommodates a wide range of alternative and popular releases, both new and used. Also good for alternative imports and bootlegs. Open M-Th 11am-7pm; F, Sa 11am-9pm; Su nooon-7pm.

Garment Distrcit

◙ **Shakespeare and Company,** 716 Broadway at Washington Pl. (☎529-1330). A New York institution. Shakespeare & Co. carries high-quality literature, high-brow journals, a great selection of vintage crime, art, and theater books, and a huge periodical section. Too bad they closed the Upper West Side location; the bookstore scene in *When Harry Met Sally* was filmed there. Open Su-Th 10am-11pm, F-Sa 10am-midnight.

◙ **Strand,** 828 Broadway (☎473-1452), at 12th St. Subway: 4, 5, 6, or L, or N, R to 14th St. The world's largest used bookstore. A must-see, with 8 mi. of shelf space that holds nearly 2 million books including rare titles and first editions. 50% off review copies and paperbacks. Vast collection of art books. Check the outdoor carts for extreme bargains. Staffers will search out obscure titles at your bidding. Ask for a catalog, or better yet, get lost in the shelves on your own. Open M-Sa 9:30am-9:20pm, Su 11am-9:20pm.

Tower Records, 6921 Broadway (☎505-1500), at E. 4th St. Subway: F, B, D, Q to Broadway and Lafayette St.; or N, R to 8th St. One-stop music emporium, nearly a block long with 4 full floors of merchandise. Gadgets like the music-video computer let you preview select songs before purchasing them, while a touch-screen store

CDs and Music in the Bronx

the BIG $plurge

soho spending

When the urge to conspicuously consume begins to tug at your heartstrings, you can browse through So o's extensive selection of clothing boutiques, handmade stationers, and home furnishing stores. **Broadway** is lined with the likes of **Armani** (568 Broadway) and **Dolce and Gabbana** (532 Broadway). **Joseph** (115 Greene) and neighbor **Anna Sui** (113 Greene) are right off Broadway. Along **Prince St.**, you'll find the classic streamlined clothing of **Agnès B.** and Prada's more affordable and street-oriented sibling, **Miu Miu**. (Although, as if in response to the ever-increasing level of gentrification obvious in this neighborhood, **Prada** proper is moving in.) If you're looking for a store where the decor is as off-beat and luxurious as the clothing, **Betsey Johnson**, on Wooster St., might just be your bed of velvet. **Wooster St.** is also home to quirky but established designers like **Cythnia Rowley** and **Todd Oldham**. Caution to the uninitiated: these are not bargain designer boutiques. Some stores, like **INA** (21 Prince St.), which features top names like Prada and elmut ang at up to -off the original price, may be the next best thing, but they'll still run you a pretty penny.

directory makes tracking down that elusive album by your favorite mainstream artist a cinch.

 Uncle Sam's Army Navy, 37 W. 8th St., between Fifth and Sixth Aves., in Greenwich Village (☎674-2222). Eclectic and funky supply of military garb from around the world (we're talkin' *East* German uniform pants). Also houses good selection of less official wear for when you're at ease. Awesome selection of helmets. $14-19 (sometimes on sale for $12). Work pants "that will never tear" $15. No tax (Uncle Sam's pays it for you) and prices are negotiable. Very gay friendly. Open M-F 10am-9pm, Sa 10am-10pm, Su 11am-8pm.

Village Chess Shop, 230 Thompson St., between Bleecker and W. 3rd Sts. (☎475-9580). The Village's keenest intellects square off in rigorous strategic combat while sipping coffee ($1) and juice ($1.50). Play is $1 or $1.50 for clocked play per hour per person ($3 per hour to watch). Don't !@%* swear or you'll be penalized $1.25. Novices can get their game analyzed for $3. The shop also showcases several breathtaking antique chess sets, as well as more recent models based on Star Trek, Alice In Wonderland, Shakespearean characters, and Romans vs. Barbarians. Open daily noon-midnight.

Village Comics, 214 Sullivan St. (777-2770), between Bleecker and W. 3rd St. The requisite comics jostle for space amidst collectible figurines, sci-fi trinkets, horror-movie doodads, and, in the back, porn movies and magazines. For kids who love D&D and adults who've never stopped playing. Open M-Tu 10am-7:30pm, W-Sa 10am-8:30pm, Su 11am-7pm.

EAST VILLAGE

St. Mark's Pl. shops sell a fantastic assortment of silver jewelry and odd trinkets. Check out any of the boutiques selling handmade, fashionable one-of-a-kinds along 9th St. off Ave. A. Vintage clothing stores are liberally sprinkled throughout the area.

see map pp. 326-327

Accidental, 131 Ave. A, between St. Mark's and 9th St. (☎995-2224). If you crave the eerie lyric of that gritty DJ after clubbing, stop by Accidental to find it—this place *never* closes. Cluttered almost so you can't move, chock full of $8-10 CDs, $9 tapes and videos. Open 24hr.

Adorned, 47 Second Ave., between 2nd and 3rd Sts. (☎473-0007). Comfortable, safe, and friendly place to add bauble to your body. As they see it, they're here to "make you beautiful, not mutilated." Custom work available. Nose piercing $15; navel $20. Jewelry not included. Skilled, traditional *henna* work (hands and feet) $20 and up. Tattoos $75 and up. Open Su-Th noon-8pm, F-Sa noon-10pm.

Black Out Books, 50 Ave. B, between 3rd and 4th Sts. (☎777-1967; www.panix.com/~blackout). A self-described "meeting place/clearinghouse for activists and ideas," Black Out serves as a haven for East Village anarchists, activists, and those who love them. Sections on "Art as Resistance," "Imprisonment," and, surprisingly, "Erotica," fill the small store. Check windows for community political and social activities. Open daily 11am-10pm.

Downtown Music Gallery, 211 E. 5th St., between Second and Third Aves. (☎473-0043). Dense and diverse, the selection of CDs and records should please most non-mainstream music enthusiasts. A knowledgable and helpful staff. Open Su-Th noon-9pm, F-Sa noon-11pm.

Honeymoon, 105 Ave. B (☎477-8768). 40s to 80s vintage; from Pucci dresses ($650) to skirts ($3-5). Open daily 1-9pm. Another location at 620 E. 6th St. (☎473-4942). Open Tu-Su 2-8pm.

House of Trance, 122 St. Mark's Pl. (☎533-6700). Step into the shroom-induced, blacklight-lit ambiance of this store to chill with Goa-trancers, the 90s version of psychedelic flower children. Day-glo T-shirts with funky designs $17-20, camisoles $17. Open daily 11am-midnight.

It's a Mod, Mod World, 85 First Ave., between E. 3rd and 4th Sts. (☎460-8004). This store is a beaded day-glo-painted temple to the unnecessary but wonderful delights in life. An absolutely fabulous selection of gift items and jewelry. On display are *Barbie* doll installations (available for sale), as well as clocks made of cereal and candy boxes ($20). Open M-Th noon-10pm, F-Sa noon-11pm, Su noon-8pm.

▧ Kim's Video and Audio, 6 St. Mark's Pl. (☎598-9985). Upstairs holds new and used vinyl and a tremendous video showcase specializing in independent and foreign films; downstairs has a startlingly strong selection of independent and import CDs for reasonable prices. The supply of experimental beats—from 1970s Jamaican dub to avant jazz to futuristic jungle—is exhaustive. Open daily 9am-midnight.

Jammyland, 60 E. 3rd St., between First and Second Aves. (☎614-0185). Wide selection of reggae, dub, dance hall, ska, and other Jamaican innovations, along with a decent world music supply. Open M-Sa noon-midnight, Su noon-10pm.

Lancelotti, 66 Ave. A, between E. 4th and 5th Sts. (☎485-6851). A cute shop selling funky housewares for the kitchen, bathroom, and other rooms. Glass cups $2.50-9. Open M-F noon-8pm, Sa 11am-8pm, Su noon-7pm.

Love Saves the Day, 119 Second Ave., at E. 7th St. (☎228-3802). Since 1966, this store has been selling vintage clothing ($15 shirts) and fabulously random collectibles. Yes, one person's junk really can be another person's treasure. Open daily 1-8:30pm.

Manhattan Portage, 333 E. 9th St., between First and Second Aves. (☎995-5490; www.manhattanportageltd.com). You don't have to be a DJ or a bike messenger to carry these utility bags. Urban Outfitters sells them all over the country now, but here's where they started. $35-40. Open Su-Th noon-7pm, F-Sa noon-8pm.

Metropolis, 43 3rd Ave., between E. 9th and 10th Sts. (☎358-0795). A selection of new and vintage club wear and shoes, heavy on the funk and slightly cyber-y. Complete with a DJ booth; make sure to pick up flyers at the front of the store on the way out. Open M-Th noon-10pm, F-Sa noon-10pm.

Miracle on St. Mark's, 100 St. Mark's Pl., between First Ave. and Ave. A (☎614-7262). A tiny but wonderful selection of fashionable wear for women. Open W-Sa noon-8pm, Su 2-6pm.

The Pop Shop, 292 Lafayette St. (219-2784), at Houston St. 1980s pop artist Keith Haring's cartoonish, socially conscious artwork can be found on posters and postcards all over the city, but where else can you find Haring-decorated umbrellas ($40), t-shirts ($20), and practically anything else? You can get a full-sized Keith Haring poster for anywhere from $5 to $40. Opened in 1985, the shop was handpainted by the late artist in his distinctive style, and all proceeds benefit the Keith Haring Foundation. Open M-Sa noon-7pm, Su noon-6pm.

Rags-A-Gogo, 73-75 E. 7th St., between First and Second Aves. (☎254-4771). A well-organized selection of basic vintage gear: T-shirts $6 and the multi-purpose urban hoodie $12. Open M-Sa noon-8pm, Su noon-7pm.

Religious Sex, 7 St. Marks Pl. (☎477-9037; www.religioussex.com), between Second and Third Ave., in Greenwich Village. Specializing in the "beautiful and the unusual," Religious Sex supplies vinyl corsets, plush tigerskin cowboy hats, opulent boas, and tulle and sequined tutus to Village fetishists and luminaries such as Prince, Drew Barrymore, and Aerosmith. Amazing array of kinky outerwear that delights in the outlandish and dabbles in the gothic. Leave mom at home. 4" vinyl spike heels $125. Open M-W noon-8pm, Th-Sa noon-9pm, Su 1-8pm.

See Hear, 59 E. 7th St. between First and Second Aves. (☎505-9781). Dedicated to books, comics, 'zines, and rock mags, mostly of the underground variety. Open Tu-Su 2-10pm.

Starfish & Jelli, 96 St. Mark's Pl., between First Ave. and Ave. A (☎388-0007). Handmade jewelry with shiny beads and feathers. Delightfully feminine. Open daily 3-8pm, but times vary.

St. Mark's Bookshop, 31 Third Ave., at 9th St. (☎260-7853). The ultimate East Village bookstore. Excellent selection, with an emphasis on current literary theory, fiction, and poetry. Good selection of mainstream and avant-garde magazines. Helpful staff. Open daily 10am-midnight.

St. Mark's Pl. Record Stores, line both sides of St. Mark's Pl., mostly between Third Ave. and Ave. A. You'll be browsing barely-organized shelves/racks/drawers for hours, but you'll find the best price for used and new CDs here, as well as a huge variety of records. Especially good: **Sounds,** at 20 St. Mark's Pl. (☎677-3444). Open daily noon-11pm. **CD & Cassette Annex,** at 16 St. Mark's Pl. (☎677-2727). Open daily noon-usually 11pm.

Treasure Trends, 204 First Ave., between E. 12th and 13th Sts. (☎777-5514). Mainly 80s-90s vintage, but great selection at good prices. Sports jerseys ($15), polo shirts ($8), and logo t-shirts ($7) all organized by hues of the rainbow. $15 skirts and $25 platforms. Open Su-Th 11am-10pm, F-Sa 11am-11pm.

Vintage Stores: Physical Graffiti, 96 St. Mark's Pl. (☎477-7334). Open M-Sa 1pm-midnight, Su 1-10pm. **NYC Mart,** 22 St. Mark's Pl. (☎982-1822); open daily 2-10pm, their $3 sale rack is fab! **Tatiana,** 111 St. Mark's Pl. (☎717-7684); open daily noon-8pm. **Shoshana's Place,** 315 E. 9th St. (☎654-6594); open daily 1-9pm.

GRAMERCY PARK, UNION SQUARE, AND MURRAY HILL

The Complete Traveller Bookstore, 199 Madison Ave., at 35th St. (☎685-9007). Possibly the widest selection of guidebooks on the Eastern Seaboard. Also carries a well-kept selection of antique books and travelogues about distant lands. Most importantly, the store carries a full assortment of *Let's Go* guidebooks (priceless). Open M-F 9am-7pm, Sa 10am-6pm, Su 11am-5pm. AmEx, V, MC, Discover. Wheelchair accessible.

see map
pp. 328-329

Lord and Taylor, 424 Fifth Ave. (☎391-3344), between 38th and 39th St. Subway: B, D, F to 42nd St.; or N, R to 34th St. Courtly and claustrophobic. Features 10 floors of fashion frenzy. Scores of New Yorkers come to be shod at the acclaimed shoe department and treated like lords—caring service and free early morning coffee. Lord and Taylor also offers legendary Christmas displays. The first in history to use the picture window as a stage for anything other than merchandise, the store began this custom in 1905 during an unusually balmy December that failed to summon the appropriate meteorological garnish; Lord and Taylor filled its windows with mock blizzards, reviving the Christmas spirit for gloomy city-dwellers. Open M-Tu and Sa 10am-7pm, W 9am-8:30pm, Th-F 10am-8:30pm, Su 11am-7pm.

Reminiscence, 50 W. 23rd St., between Fifth and Sixth Aves., in Gramercy (☎243-2292). Happily stuck in a 1970s groove. Come check out this store's gifts (inflatable flamingo cups $5; plastic straw bags $3-10) and 70s jewelry. It even has its own brand that makes clothing such as Hawaiian shirts and tulle skirts ($36) from deadstock material. A selection of vintage gear (slips $10, jeans $12) available. Open M-Sa 11am-7:30pm, Su noon-7pm.

Rock and Soul, 462 Seventh Ave., between 35th and 36th Sts. (☎695-3953). Behind the storefront selling hi-fi electronics, DJ equipment, and gold jewelry is a pathway to full crates of vinyls. Great if you're looking for old-school classics or new releases in soul, R&B, reggae, or hip-hop. Open M-Sa 9:30am-7pm. AmEx, V, MC.

Throb, 211 E. 14th St., between 2nd and 3rd Aves. (☎533-2328). Jungle, trip-hop, house, loungecore, and more. Throb caters to folks who are serious about their beats. Wax for the DJs, CDs for the audiophiles, flyers for those looking to party, and a (cute) staff to assist the (gasp) unfamiliar. Open M-Sa noon-9pm, Su 1-9pm.

CHELSEA

see map pp. 328–329

Books of Wonder, 16 W. 18th St., between Fifth and Sixth Aves. (☎989-3270). Selected as one of NY's 50 Best, this is a jewel of a children's bookstore. The antique book section is amazing. The store hosts a variety of programs related to children's books. Open M-Sa 10am-7pm, Su noon-6pm.

Kikko Import, Inc., 825 Sixth Ave., between 28th and 29th Sts. (☎564-2693). A wholesaler of a fantastic array of wigs, in various natural and not-so-natural looking styles and colors. From $10 pieces to full "ready to wear wonders" for that upcoming costume party or fabulous night out. Open for retail, M-F 9am-6:30pm.

Midnight Records, 263 W. 23rd St., between Seventh and Eighth Aves., in Chelsea (☎675-2768). A mail-order and retail store specializing in hard-to-find rock records. Posters plaster the walls; every last nook is crammed with records—over 10,000 in stock. Lots of 60s and 70s titles. Most LPs $9-20. Open Tu and Th-Sa noon-6pm.

Revolution Books, 9 W. 19th St. between Fifth and Sixth Aves. (☎691-3345). Books on radical struggles from around the world in all languages. Large collection of works on Marx, Mao, and Malcolm X. From political science pieces to manifestos, posters to children's books, all things political and radical can be found here. Not-for-profit and mostly staffed by very clued-in volunteers. Open M-Sa 10am-7pm, Su noon-5pm.

Weiss and Mahoney, 142 Fifth Ave., at 19th St. (☎675-1915). A "peaceful" army/navy store, the fashion militant (not fashion police, mind you) can indulge in cargo pants ($25-30) and jungle boots ($20). Buy Carhartt at original (not designer) prices (denim jeans $20). Open M-F 9am-7pm, Sa 10am-6pm, Su 11am-5pm.

WEST MIDTOWN

SoHo Shopping

see map pp. 332–333

◼ **Coliseum Books,** 1771 Broadway, at 57th St. (☎757-8381). This alternative to big chain stores is just a stone's throw from Lincoln Center and Carnegie Hall. Fine selection of drama and music in addition to its main stock of new releases and poetry. Easily navigable. Open M 8am-10pm, Tu-Th 8am-11pm, F 8am-11:30pm, Sa 9am-11:30pm, Su noon-8pm.

◼ **The Drama Book Shop,** 723 Seventh Ave. (☎944-0595; fax: 730-8739; www.dramabookshop.com), at the corner of 48th St. Subway: 1, 9, 2, 3, N, R to Times Square. Take the elevator to the 2nd floor. If it ever appeared onstage, you'll find it in print here. Find half the aspiring actors in the city and the monologues they seek, all in one compact location. A necessary stop for any theater, film or plain ol' performing arts buff. Accepts AmEx, MC, V. Open M-F 9:30am-7pm, W 9:30am-8pm, Sa 10:30am-5:30pm, Su noon-5pm.

◼ **Gotham Book Mart,** 41 W. 47th St., between Fifth and Sixth Aves. (☎719-4448). Legendary and venerable, Gotham's renowned selection of new and used volumes of 20th-century writing has long made it a favorite among the New York literati. This little renegade store smuggled censored copies of works by Joyce, Lawrence, and Miller to America. Then-unknowns LeRoi Jones, Tennessee Williams, and Allen Ginsberg all worked here as clerks. The store boasts first editions with illustrations by the late Edward Gorey. An upstairs gallery features changing exhibits. Open M-F 9:30am-6:30pm, Sa 9:30am-6pm.

Shoe Heaven (West of 6th Avenue)

Tiffany & Co.

on the cheap

ghetto-fabulous

Yo, MTV Rap, yo yo. Harlem is the spot for dem old-school kicks you seen by Adidas. Yeah, yo, 125th St. has the dopest FUBU gear around, brother And those new vests by Hilfiger, damn, kid. Dat's not all hit da area up yo'self: **125th St., between Lenox Ave. and Adam Clayton Powell Blvd.**

125th is perfect for straight-up strolling, yo. But check out dese other places, dey hot too.

Liberation Bookstore, 421 Lenox Ave., at 131st St. (☎281-4615). This small store houses a great selection of African and African-American history, art, poetry, and fiction. Open Tu-F 3-7pm, Sa noon-4pm. Cash only.

Sugar Hill Thrift Shop, 409 W. 145th St. between St. Nicholas and Convent Aves. (☎281-2396). Ripe with quality vintage clothing and used household merchandise and antiques, this shop is definitely the sweet side of Sugar Hill. Come see what all the buzz is about. Open M-F 10am-6pm, Sa noon-5pm. V, MC.

Hacker Art Books, 45 W. 57th St. (☎688-7600), between Fifth and Sixth Ave. Subway: B, Q to 57th St. Five flights up from the rumble of the street, Hacker's volumes comprise one of the best art book selections anywhere. Catalogs of Picasso's ceramics stand alongside how-to books and the work of cutting-edge theorists. The selection here should satisfy art historians, birdhouse builders, and fans of prehistoric stoneware alike. MC, V. Open Sept.-June M-F 9:30am-6pm; July-Aug. M-Sa 9:30am-6pm.

Macy's, 151 W. 34th St., between Broadway and Seventh Ave. (☎695-4400). This department store can provide the most exhilarating or the most frustrating experience, depending on your mood. Take a whirl in its labyrinth-like interior, where you can purchase a book, grab a snack or an all-out meal, get a facial or a haircut, mail a letter, have your jewelry appraised, exchange currency, purchase theater tickets, and get lost. Open M-Sa 10am-8:30pm, Su 11am-7pm. (See **Sights,** p. 84.)

Manhattan Mall, at Sixth Ave. and 33rd St. (☎465-0500). Cheesy Malldom, USA to be found in 8 levels of commodity heaven. Provides ample anthropological specimens of all that is commercially mainstream, be it Express or Modell's. The top level, following the predictable architectural formula for the stripmall, is an entire floor of homogenized, multi-cultured fast food. Open M-Sa 10am-8pm, Su 11am-6pm.

Nobody Beats the Wiz, 871 Sixth Ave., at 31st St. (☎594-2300), and 17 Union Sq. W., at 15th St. (☎741-9500). In desperate need of a camcorder or camera to make memories of NYC permanent? Check out this chain store's selection of electronics, often at great value prices. If you bring in an advertisement for an item that is priced lower than N.B.T.W., they will discount the item 10% for you. Both locations open M-Sa 10am-8pm, Su 11am-7pm.

EAST MIDTOWN

see map pp. 332-333

Asahiya Bookstore, 52 Vanderbilt Ave. (☎883-0011), at E. 45th St. Subway: 4, 5, 6, 7, or S to 42nd St. Japanese books and periodical abound. Origami, stationery, and a few English-language books on Japan for the gaijín in all of us. Open daily 10am-8pm. AmEx, MC, V.

Bergdorff-Goodman, 745 and 754 Fifth Ave., between 57th and 58th Sts. (☎753-7300). In addition to housing all of the top designers of high fashion, this legendary mansion of clothing (and pomp), splendid in its marble and chandelier surroundings, is every celebrity's one-stop shopping choice when they want to be left alone. Open M-Sa 10am-7pm, Th 10am-8pm.

Bloomingdale's, 1000 Third Ave., at 59th St. (☎705-2000). Begun in 1872 by two brothers, Bloomie's is "not just a store, it's a destination." Not only was Bloomingdale's the *first* "department" store, it also invented the designer shopping bag in 1961 and made such designers as Ralph Lauren, Donna Karan, and Fendi. If you're lucky enough to survive the mob of perfume assailants, tourists, and casual shoppers, you'll find that it's fun to get lost in this colorful store. Open M-F 10am-8:30pm, Sa 10am-7pm, Su 11am-7pm.

The Counter Spy Shop, 444 Madison Ave. (☎688-8500), between 49th and 50th St. Subway: 6 to 51st St. James Bond fans and clinical paranoids will love this store, devoted to the technology of subterfuge and deception. Bullet-proof vests, hidden cameras, and domestic lie detectors share the racks with false-bottom cans ($20) and junior spy t-shirts ($10). One useful title: *How To Get Even with Anybody, Anytime*. Open M 9am-6pm, Tu-F 9am-7pm, Sa 10am-4pm, Su 11am-4pm. AmEx, V, MC, Discover.

Dollar Bills, 32 E. 42nd St. (☎867-0212), between Madison and Fifth Ave. Subway: 4, 5, 6, or S to Grand Central; or 1, 2, 3, 9, or N, R to Times Sq. and walk east on 42nd St. Do you have billionaire-Trump taste and a bankrupt-Trump budget? Fear no more, insolvent wayfarer, Dollar Bills has the couture labels at pret-a-porter prices. It usually takes some rummaging, but if you are patient, you just might find that Armani needle in the haystack. Open M-F 8am-7pm, Sa 10am-6pm, Su noon-5pm.

⊠ F.A.O. Schwarz, 767 Fifth Ave., at 58th St. (☎644-9400). A child's ultimate fantasy world: everything that whirs, flies, or begs to be assembled appears in this huge hands-on toy store. But, like Tom Hanks in *Big*, adults, too, can reclaim their inner spoiled brat. Come Christmas, with amusement-park-like lines that continue for miles outside, and jam-packed frenzied shoppers inside, the store celebrates the holiday season in a ritual that resembles the running of the bulls in Pamplona. Open Su-W 10am-7pm, Th-Sa 10am-8pm.

Fine Line, 954 Third Ave., between 57th and 58th Sts. (☎527-2603). This clothing company is one of the cheapest boutiques around, offering items from $10-$60. Open M-F 8am-8pm, Sa 10am-8pm, Su 11am-7pm.

Hammacher Schlemmer, 147 E. 57th St., between Third and Lexington Aves. (☎421-9000). Known for its unique and innovative products, Hammacher Schlemmer (named for the German immigrants who started it) has always been ahead of the future. This store was the first to carry such items as the steam iron, the electric razor, the microwave, and the cordless telephone (thank you Hammacher Schlemmer!). Open M-Sa 10am-6pm.

Nike Town, 6 E. 57th, between Fifth and Madison Aves. (☎891-6453). Nike's latest advance toward world domination, this sports museum/athletic department store shows that Nike knows just what to do when it comes to taking your money. Call for more info on their free running club (Tu 6-7:30pm). Open M-F 10am-8pm, Sa 10am-7pm, Su 11am-7pm.

Saks Fifth Avenue, 611 Fifth Ave. (☎753-4000), between 49th and 50th St. Subway: B, D, F, Q to 50th St. Subdued and chic. This institution has aged well and continues to combine inflated prices with smooth courtesy. At Saks you truly get what you pay for; in this case, it's expensive clothes Open M-W and F 10am-7pm, Th 10am-8pm, Sa 10am-6:30pm, Su noon-6pm.

Tiffany & Co., 727 Fifth Ave., at 57th St. (☎605-4222). *Breakfast,* anyone? Although you may not be able to afford any of the precious gemstones, there is still much to feast your eyes upon in this world-renowned jewel sanctuary. Donald Trump and Marla Maples named their daughter after this symbol of the nouveau-riche. Open M-Sa 10am-6pm, Th 10am-7pm. V, MC, AmEx.

Warner Bros. Studio Store, 1 E. 57th St., at Fifth Ave. (☎754-0300). Let Superman elevate you throughout these 8 floors of merchandise dedicated to Warner Bros.' most profitable icons, from the Looney Tunes and the Flintstones to Batman and Robin. That's *not* all folks...you can watch WB cartoons all day on the two-story screen. Open M-Sa 10am-8pm, Su 11am-7pm.

UPPER EAST SIDE

Argosy Bookstore, 116 E. 59th St., between Park and Lexington Aves. (☎753-4455). Specializes in old, rare, and out-of-print books, along with autographed editions, Americana, and antique maps and prints. Look for the racks of $1 books. Open M-F 10am-6pm; Oct.-Apr. also Sa 10am-5pm.

Barneys New York, 660 Madison Ave., at 61st St. (☎833-2466). Although you'll find neither Bedrock nor Wilma here, you might just spot some other celebrity shoppers in this exclusive store. This Barneys also boasts a concierge and cafe to complement your shopping experience. Open M-F 10am-8pm, Sa 10am-7pm, Su 11am-6pm.

see map
pp. 334–335

Chick Darrow's Fun Antiques & Collectibles, 1101 First Ave., between 60th and 61st Sts. (☎838-0730). Established in 1962, Chick Darrow's is the world's first antique toy shop. Possessing a wide variety of items, from 19th-century carpet toys to *Star Trek* memorabilia and *everything* in between, this store will definitely delight seekers of the usual and the unusual. Open Tu-F noon-7pm, Sa noon-5pm.

█ **Corner Bookstore,** 1313 Madison Ave., at 93rd St. (☎831-3554). Careful selection and a friendly staff make this cozy neighborhood bookstore a treasure for Upper East Side book lovers. Note the antique cash register and the *zaftig* cat named Murphy. Open M-Th 10am-8pm, F 10am-7pm, Sa-Su 11am-6pm.

█ **Crawford Doyle Booksellers,** 1082 Madison Ave. (☎288-6300), between 81st and 82nd St. Synthesizes computer technology and old-fashioned customer care to serve all your bookstore needs. Open M-Sa 10am-6pm, Su noon-5pm.

Diesel, 770 Lexington Ave., at 60th St. (☎308-0055). Known for its young, hip, and urban gear, this Diesel also boasts a DJ spinning the latest tunes F-Sa and a moderately priced cafe. Open M-Sa 10am-8pm, Su noon-6pm.

Encore, 1132 Madison Ave., at 84th St., 2nd fl. (☎879-2850). Second-hand designer clothes. Open M-W and F 10:30am-6:30pm, Th 10:30am-7:30pm, Sa 10:30am-6pm, Su noon-6pm; closed Su July to mid-Aug.

Game Show, 1240 Lexington Ave., at 83rd St. (☎472-8011). Classic games like Monopoly, Pictionary, Jeopardy, Price is Right, and Family Feud, not to mention the new hit Who Wants to be a Millionaire? Also carries adult games like Dirty Minds: Volumes I *and* II, although their downtown location is known for having the more "adult adult" games. Open M-W and F-Sa 11am-6pm, Th 11am-7pm; Sept.-May also Su noon-5pm. **Also at** 474 Ave. of the Americas between 11th and 12th Sts. (☎633-6328). Open M-W and F-Sa noon-7pm, Th noon-8pm, Su noon-7pm.

HMV, 1280 Lexington Ave., at 86th St. (☎348-0800). Looking for that lost *The Grind* workout video? Well, seek and ye shall find in this music megastore. Providing the latest in a wide range of DVDs and music, from pop and hip-hop to classical and jazz, His Master's Voice also houses a *Ticketmaster* outlet. Open M-Sa 9am-11pm, Su 10am-10pm. **Other locations:** 57 W. 34th St., at 6th Ave.; 234 W. 42nd St. between Seventh and Eighth Aves.; 565 Fifth Ave., at 46th St.; and 308 W. 125th St. between St. Nicholas and Eighth Aves.

Michael's, 1041 Madison Ave., between 79th and 80th Sts., 2nd fl. (☎737-7273). Peddles "gently-used" designer threads. Open M-W and F-Sa 9:30am-6pm, Th 9:30am-8pm; closed Sa July-Aug.

Star Magic, 1256 Lexington Ave., between 85th and 84th Sts. (☎988-0300). Specializing in "space age gifts," this store carries everything from telescopes to dried astronaut ice cream to triops—new-age fish pets. Satisfy the magician in you. **Also at** 745 Broadway, at 8th St. (☎228-7770). Open M-Sa 10am-8pm, Su 11am-7pm.

Rita Ford Music Boxes, 19 E. 65th St., between Madison and Fifth Aves. (☎535-6717). The first, and only, store in the US to service, repair, and sell both antique and contemporary music boxes, Rita Ford's has been winding up beautiful music since 1947 and has designed exclusive boxes for the White House, the State Department, and overseas royalty. Open M, W, and F-Sa 9am-5pm; Tu and Th 9am-6pm.

Tender Buttons, 143 E. 62nd St. (☎758-7004), near Lexington Ave. A treasure trove of billions of buttons. If you carelessly lost the button on your favorite Renaissance doublet, you will find a replacement here. Also has cuff links and buckles. The ladies-who-lunch shop here. Open M-F 10:30am-6pm, Sa 10:30am-5:30pm.

UPPER WEST SIDE

see map
pp. 338–339

Allan and Suzi, 416 Amsterdam Ave., at 80th St. (☎724-7445). RuPaul, Courtney Love, and Annie Lennox shop here. From new Gaultier Madonna-wear at 70% off to that coveted conservative Prada jacket, this store is *haute couture* discount (although still expensive) chaos. Helpful staff can find you just what you were dreaming of. A large assortment of fabulously authentic platform shoes and feather boas all colors of the synthetic, chemically-dyed rainbow surround the melée. Men's clothing includes Armani and Versace suits. Open daily noon-7pm.

Applause Theater and Cinema Books, 211 W. 71st St., between Broadway and West End Ave. (☎496-7511). Great selection of scripts, screenplays, and books on everything about theater and cinema, from John Wayne to tap dancing. Over 4000 titles. Look out for their intermittent $1 sale and the odd celebrity. Knowledgeable staff. Open M-Sa 10am-8pm, Su noon-6pm.

Gryphon Bookshops, 2246 Broadway, between 80th and 81st Sts. (☎362-0706). Open for 25 years and the sister shop to the Gryphon Record Shop, this sliver of a bookstore is filled from floor to ceiling with used and rare books. Sift through the LitCrit aisle, play scripts sorted by author, and cookbooks; you're bound to find something that'll catch your eye. Very knowledgeable staff. Frequent sales. Open daily 10am-midnight.

Gryphon Record Shop, 233 W. 72nd St., just off Broadway (☎874-1588). Wall-to-wall shelves of classical, Broadway, and Jazz LPs, many rare or out of print. Great books on music. Proprietor has the knowledge to match. Open M-Sa 11am-7pm, Su 12:30-6:30pm.

Maxilla & Mandible, 451 Columbus Ave. (☎724-6173), between 81st and 82nd St. Subway: 1 or 9 to 79th St. Shelves and boxes of well-displayed shells, fossils, eggs, preserved insects, and—most of all—bones from every imaginable vertebrate (including *Homo sapiens*). A giant walking-stick insect under glass and an 11ft. alligator skeleton stand out prominently among the merchandise. "Dinosaur dung" for the little ones ($3). Call for hours; they change constantly.

Canal Jeans and Co.

Murder Ink, 2486 Broadway, between 92nd and 93rd Sts. (☎362-8905). Decorated in the official colors of murder (red and black), this store is loaded with enough whodunits to have you looking over your shoulder for a lifetime. New and used books. The bookshop is located next to and linked internally with **Ivy's Books,** a bookshop specializing in rare books. Murder Ink is open daily 10:30am-7pm; Ivy's daily 10am-10pm.

Ordning & Reda, 253 Columbus Ave., between 71st and 72nd Sts. (☎799-0828). A minimalist-design addict's heaven. The Swedish stationer has finally come to the States in its primary (and secondary) color and simplistic glory. Pop into the store and drool at the paper, notebooks, and binders all organized by color. Notebooks a pricey $7-28. Open M-Sa 11am-8pm, Su 11am-6pm.

St. Mark's Place

BROOKLYN

see map pp. 342–343

Clovis Press, 229 Bedford Ave., in Williamsburg. (☎718-302-3751. Subway: L to Bedford Ave. An eclectic selection of 'zines, art, and printed matter straight from artists' studios. Interesting cultural magazines also available: everything from *The New Yorker* to *BUST*. Open daily noon-8pm.

▨ **Domsey's,** 431 Kent Ave., in Williamsburg (☎718-384-6000). Subway: J, M, Z to Marcy. Poorly-paid Manhattanites and hipsters alike head to Domsey's, rather far from the main drag of Williamsburg. Astounding bargains await the diligent shopper in this sprawling warehouse. Check out the tuxedos for $15 and corduroy Levi's in all sorts of colors ($5). The selection is vast. Open M-F 8am-5:30pm, Sa 8am-6:30pm, Su 11am-5:30pm.

▨ **Girdle Factory,** 218 Bedford Ave., in Williamsburg. Subway: L to Bedford Ave. A cavernous collective of small spaces, inhabited by artist's studios, cafes, a beauty salon **(Hello, Beautiful)** and shops. Check out **Mini Minimarket** (☎728-302-9337) for kitschy, nostalgic, Tokyo-inspired stuff. Open daily noon-9pm.

SoHo Shopping

Entertainment

In Manhattan, every flat surface is a potential stage and every inattentive waiter an unemployed, possibly unemployable, actor.
—Quentin Crisp

You could go to a rock show Monday, a NY Philharmonic concert Tuesday, a jazz bar and cabaret on Wednesday, the Metropolitan Opera on Thursday, an underground rap show on Friday, a matinee and evening musical on Saturday, and the ballet on Sunday, and you'd still be able to do it for every week after that for the rest of your life without having to see any thing twice. *Let's Go* lists New York's most essential venues and hot spots, but be sure to check local sources to find out about other places and get the scoop on current offerings. It's the shows that are good, not the venue. In each category we list a few known spots or groups, and under that simply a list of places that have had good events or shows in the past. Look through publications for the most up-to-date run-down on entertainment in the city: try *Time Out: New York*, the *Village Voice*, *New York* magazine, and *The New York Times* (particularly the Sunday edition). The monthly *Free Time* calendar ($2) lists free cultural events throughout Manhattan. Try the NYC Parks Department's **entertainment hotline** (☎360-3456; 24hr.) for the lowdown on special events in parks throughout the city. Call the **NYC/ON STAGE hotline** (768-1818) for a comprehensive listing of theater, dance, and music events taking place each week.

BROADWAY

Most Broadway theaters are located on the "Great White Way," north of Times Square, between Eighth Ave. and Broadway. Broadway theaters are open only when a play is in production, and most don't have phones; often phone numbers given for a theater

24244

on the cheap

CheapSeats

The Great White Way's major theatrical draws may seem locked away in gilded Broadway cages, but you *can* find cheap tickets. Should **Ticketmaster** (☎307-7171) not work, try the standby ticket distributor, **TKTS** (see p. 155), or any of the following options.

Rush Tickets: Some theaters distribute them on the morning of the performance; others make student rush tickets available 30 minutes before showtime. Lines can be extremely long, so get there *early*.

Cancellation Line: No rush luck? Some theaters redistribute returned or unclaimed tickets a few hours before curtain. You might have to sacrifice your afternoon—but, come on, Dame Edna is worth it!

Sold-out Shows: Even when a show is sold out to the public, theaters often have prime house seats reserved for VIPs which become available at showtime.

Standing-room Only: Sold on the day of show, tend to be around $15 or $20. Call first, as some theaters can't accommodate standing room.

Hit Show Club: 630 Ninth Ave. (☎581-4211), between 44th and 45th St. This free service distributes coupons redeemable at the box office for over 1/3 off regular ticket prices. Call for coupons via mail or pick them up them up at the club office.

box office are in fact handled by a larger ticket broker agency. Here's a list of some current Broadway blockbusters.

Annie Get Your Gun, Marquis Theatre, 1535 Broadway at 46th St. (www.anniegetyourgun.com). Starring Bernadette Peters. Tickets $35-75. Students get 50% off $60 seats.

Beauty and the Beast, Lunt-Fontanne Theatre, Broadway and 46th St. (☎307-4747 or 800-755-4000; www.disneyonbroadway.com). Tickets $25-80.

Cabaret, Studio 54, 254 W. 54th St. at Broadway. Was the hottest ticket on Broadway in the summer of 1998. Alan Cummings has left the cast, however.

Chicago, Shubert Theater, 225 W. 44th St. (www.chicagothemusical.com). An excellent revival, the choreography by Anne Reinking is well worth it. $20 tickets available at box office 10am day of performance. Tickets $37.50-85.

Fosse, Broadhurst Theater, 235 W. 44th St. Choreographed by Chet Walker and *Chicago*'s Ann Reinking, this 1999 Tony-Award-winning Bob Fosse tribute recreates the biggest numbers of the legendary choreographer's career.

Les Miserables, Imperial Theater, 249 W. 45th St. (www.lesmis.com).

Phantom of the Opera, Majestic Theater, 247 W. 44th St. (www.thephantomoftheopera.com).

Rent, Nederlander Theater, 208 W. 41st St. (www.siteforrent.com). A modern update of *La Bohème*, with wireless mikes strapped to their heads. $20 tickets available after 5:30pm line-up for 6pm lottery at the box office for evening shows Tu-F; 2 tickets per person, cash only.

The Lion King, New Amsterdam Theater, 216 W. 42nd St at Broadway (☎307-4747 or 800-755-4000; www.disneyonbroadway.com). The intricate costumes in this elaborate show combine an actor's body movements with those of the animal he controls. $20 rush tickets available 10am day of performance. Tickets $25-90. Long lines.

THEATER

Broadway warhorses like *The Phantom of the Opera* and *Les Misérables* have ushered armies of tourists, senior citizens, and suburbanites through the theater doors for interminable runs. Furthermore, the recent resurrection of Broadway has triggered an equally vibrant theater scene throughout the city—off-Broadway, off-off-Broadway, in dance and studio spaces, museums, cafes, parks, even in parking lots—cheaper and more accessible than anything along Shubert Alley.

INFORMATION

For listings of Broadway, off-Broadway, and off-off-Broadway shows, see *Listings*, a weekly guide to entertainment in Manhattan ($1). For info on shows in any of the five boroughs as well as ticket availability, you can also call the **New York City On Stage Hotline,** ☎768-1818.

DISCOUNT TICKETS

Though Broadway tickets usually run upwards of $50, many money-saving schemes exist. Some theaters have $20 seats in the farthest reaches of the balcony, though these seats are hard to come by. **TDF Vouchers** (Theatre Development Fund) is the nation's largest nonprofit service organization for the performing arts and offers discount vouchers for off-off-Broadway productions and other events sponsored by small, independent production companies. For those eligible—students, teachers, performing-arts professionals, retirees, union and armed forces members, and clergy—it's a great deal. *($28 buys four vouchers redeemable at the box office of any participating organization. 221-0885.)*

TKTS sells tickets at a 25-50% discount on the day of the performance of many Broadway and some larger off-Broadway shows. The board near the front of the line for each TKTS booth posts the names of the shows with available tickets. Expect a $2.50 service charge per ticket, and have cash or traveler's checks for payment. The lines begin to form an hour or so before the booths open, but move fairly quickly. More tickets become available as showtime approaches, so you may find fewer possibilities if you go too early. *(768-1818. Duffy Square, at 47th St. and Broadway. Tickets sold M-Sa 3-8pm for evening performances; W and Sa 10am-2pm for matinees; and Su 11am-7pm for matinees and evening performances. Less competitive lines form downtown, where TKTS has a branch in the mezzanine of 2 World Trade Center. Open M-F 11am-5:30pm, Sa 11am-3:30pm; Sunday matinee tickets sold on Saturday.)*

You can get a similar discount with **"twofer"** (i.e., two for the price of one) ticket coupons available at bookstores, libraries, and the Times Square Visitors Center. As they apply mostly to old Broadway standards that have been running strong for a very long time, you should never have to pay full price to see *Cats*. For more info on how to get cheap tickets, see **Cheap Seats**, right and left.

You may reserve full-price tickets over the phone and pay by credit card through: **Tele-Charge** (☎239-6200 or outside NYC 800-432-7250; 24hr.) for Broadway shows; **Ticket Central** (☎279-4200; open daily 1-8pm) for off-Broadway shows; **Ticketmaster** (☎307-4100 or outside NYC 800-755-4000; 24hr.) for all types of shows. All three services assess a per-ticket service charge; ask before purchasing. You can avoid these fees if you buy tickets directly from the box offices.

Off-Broadway theaters, by definition, feature less mainstream presentations for crowds of 499 or fewer. Runs are generally short; however, they occasionally jump to Broadway houses (as in the case of *Rent*). Many of the best off-Broadway houses huddle in the Sheridan Square area of the West Village. Eugene O'Neill got his break at the Provincetown Playhouse, and Elisa Loti made her American debut

MoreCheapSeats

High 5 Tickets to the Arts (☎445-8587): Through this program any junior high or high-school student between the ages of 13 and 18 can attend theater shows, concerts, and-museum exhibitions for only $5. Tickets are sold at all New York Ticketmaster locations; proof of age is required, and tickets must be purchased at least one day prior to the performance. For more details and a listing of available shows, see High 5's website.

Kids' Night on Broadway (☎563-2929): This annual program, sponsored by TDF and the League of American Theatres, gives children ages 6 to 18 free admission (with the purchase of one regularly priced ticket) on four specified nights. Kids' Night debuted in NY last year and was so successful that it has expanded to 20 cities. Tickets start selling in October; performances are Jan.-Feb.

CareTix (☎840-0770, ext. 230): Sponsored by Broadway Cares/Equity Fights AIDS, CareTix sells house seats for sold-out Broadway and off-Broadway shows, and for some non-theatrical events. Tickets are twice the regular box office price, but you can claim one-half of what you pay as a tax-deductible charitable contribution to BC/EFA.

Audience Extras (☎989-9550): A little-known program with a lot of leftover tickets (many for prime house seats) to theater shows, concerts, and dance performances. You must pay a one-time membership fee of $130; after that, however, each ticket will only cost you $3. Most tickets sold on a day-of-show basis.

at the Actors Playhouse. **Playwrights Horizons,** 416 W. 42nd St. (☎279-4200), between Ninth and Tenth Ave., and **Manhattan Theater Club,** 131 W. 55th St. (☎399-3000 or 581-1212), for instance, rank among the most prestigious launching pads for new American plays. Off-Broadway tickets cost $15-45; TKTS sells tickets to the larger off-Broadway houses. You may see shows for free by arranging to usher; this usually entails dressing neatly and showing up at the theater around 45 minutes ahead of curtain, helping to seat ticket-holders, and then staying for 10 minutes after the performance to help clean up. Call the theater after 5pm and speak with the house manager far in advance.

Many of the theaters listed below offer variety and eclecticism, and many host several different companies each year. Listings and reviews appear the first Wednesday of every month in **Simon Says,** a *Village Voice* guide tailored to unconventional theater happenings around the city. Other publications with theater listings include *New York* magazine, the *New York Press,* the *New Yorker, Time Out: New York.*

Whether it be an improvised opera, performance art, stand-up comedy, political commentary, theatrical monologue, music, dance, or video art, alternative theater thrives throughout the city. Here are some suggested theaters that have proven themselves in the past. But a good show has nothing to do with the theater; periodicals should be your first resource.

Actors Playhouse, Seventh Ave. between Christopher and Bleecker St. (☎463-0060). Tickets $35-45. Box office open 3-8pm on show days and Sa-Su noon-8pm.

Astor Place Theater, 436 Lafayette St., near Astor Pl. (☎800-BLUEMAN). Home to the infectious *Blue Man Group.* Tickets $45-55. Box office open daily noon-8pm or until 15min. before last show. Shows Tu-Th 8pm, F-Sa 7pm and 10pm, Su 4pm and 7pm.

Beacon Theatre, 2130 Broadway, at 74th St. (☎307-7171). The theater to the Beacon Hotel, this venue hosts music acts, as well as other performances and plays. In 2000, Tracy Chapman performed weeks after Ellen Degeneres put on a one-woman show. Tickets $30-50.

Cherry Lane, 38 Commerce St., at Grove St. (☎989-2020). Has hosted such American premieres as Beckett's *Waiting for Godot* and plays by Ionesco and Albee. Tickets $45. An alternative theater in the same building has even more experimental productions. Tickets $12. Box office open Tu-F 2-8pm, Sa 2-9pm, Su noon-7pm. (See **Sights,** p. 76.)

The Joseph Papp Public Theater, 425 Lafayette St. (☎539-8750). From 1957 until 1991, when Joseph Papp died, his theater epitomized its founder's determination and bold originality. Today, theater impresario and Tony-winning director of *Angels in America* on Broadway, George C. Wolfe, runs the show, so to speak. The Public's six venues present a wide variety of productions and have hosted a decade-long marathon of Shakespeare's every last work, right down to *Timon of Athens.* Ticket prices vary.

Lamb's, 130 W. 44th St. (☎997-1780 or 575-0300). One 349-seater, one 29-seater host family-oriented plays and musicals. Tickets $25-35.

New York Theatre Workshop, 79 E. 4th St. (☎460-5475). Box office open Tu-Sa 1-6pm.

Orpheum, 126 Second Ave. between E. 7th and 8th Sts., in the East Village (☎477-2477). Scored success with Mamet's *Oleanna.* Now playing the infectious, rhythmic *Stomp.* Tickets $30-50. Box office open daily 1-6pm. Shows Tu-F 8pm, Sa 7pm and 10:30pm, Su 3pm and 7pm.

Primary Stages, 354 W. 45th St. (☎333-4052), between Eighth and Ninth Ave. Has fostered the works of David Ives since 1989. Box office open M-Sa noon-6pm.

Samuel Beckett Theater, 410 W. 42nd St. (☎594-2826), between Ninth and Tenth Ave. Artsy productions of contemporary drama, sometimes including post-performance discussions with members of the cast. Tickets $45, students and seniors $35. Box office open 5-8pm.

SoHo Repertory Theatre, 46 Walker St. (☎941-8632; fax 941-7148), between Broadway and Church St. Tickets $10.

SoHo Think Tank Ohio Theater, 66 Wooster St. (☎966-4844), between Grand and Broome St. A theater that puts on deliberately intellectual and provoking pieces combining theater, performance art, dancing, sketch comedy, and music. In the summer of 1999 the theater hosted *The Ice Factory.* "Cafe Ohio" opens before shows at 6pm for "drinks and conversation." Shows usually W-Sa at 7pm. $10.

Sullivan Street Playhouse, 181 Sullivan St. (☎674-3838). Home to *The Fantasticks,* the longest running show in US history. The city has renamed that section of road "Fantasticks Lane." Grab a twofer pass. All seats Tu-Th and Su $37.50, F-Sa $40. Shows Tu-F 8pm, Sa 3 and 7pm, Su 3 and 7:30pm. Box office open Tu-Su noon-showtime.

Theater for the New City, 152 First Ave., in the East Village (☎254-1109). New avant-garde productions. Productions Th-Su 8pm. Tickets around $10. Dispatches a roving theater troupe throughout the city that performs in parks and streets (late July-Sept.). Open M-F 10am-6pm.

Union Square Theatre, 100 E. 17th St., near Union Sq. (☎505-0700). This respectable off-Broadway theatre currently houses *The Laramie Project,* an interview compilation piece based on the Wyoming murder of gay student Matthew Shepard. Box office open M and W-F 1-7pm, Tu 1-6pm, Sa noon-7pm, Su noon-6:30pm. Tickets $55. Validated parking on E. 16th St., $5.

Vineyard Theater Company's Dimson Theatre, 108 E. 15th St., between Union Sq. and Irving Pl. (☎353-3366). Currently under construction, the theatre is slated to re-open with its fall 2000 season of Craig Lucas' *Stranger.* Validated parking on E. 16th St., $5.

OUTDOOR THEATERS

Queens Theater in the Park, in Flushing Meadows-Corona Park (☎718-760-0064). Film and performing arts center that hosts an annual Latino arts festival (late-July to mid-Aug.), among other events. Call for dance and theater listings.

🔳 **Shakespeare in the Park** (☎539-8750), near the West 81st St. entrance of Central Park, just north of the 79th St. Transverse. This renowned series, founded by the same Papp of the Joseph Papp Public Theater, is a New York summer tradition. Two Shakespeare plays, one late June to mid-July and the second early August to September, bring outstanding actors and directors to the outdoor Delacorte amphitheatre in Central Park. The theater has witnessed the unforgettable performance of Al Pacino as Mark Anthony in *Julius Caesar* in 1988, the ovation-worthy kiss shared by Tracy Ullman and Morgan Freeman in 1990's production of *Taming of the Shrew,* not to mention performances by Denzel Washington and Patrick Stewart. Tickets available 1pm the day of performance at the Delacorte and 1-3pm at the Public Theatre at 425 Lafayette St.; try to get there by 10:30am. Stand-by line forms at 6pm. Limit 2 tickets per person. Doors open Tu-Su at 7:30pm; shows start at 8pm.

FILM

American Museum of the Moving Image, 35th Ave. at 36th St., Astoria, Queens (☎718-784-0077; see **Museums**). Three full theaters showing everything from silent classics to retrospectives of great directors. Recent programs have ranged from 50s *Father of the Bride* to *Fast Cars and Women.* Free with admission to museum: $8.50, seniors and students $5.50, children under 12 $4.50. Screenings Sa-Su; call for hours.

🔳 **Angelika Film Center,** 18 W. Houston St., at Mercer St. (☎995-2000; box office 995-2570). "K" is for *Kultur:* 8 screens of alternative, independent, and foreign cinema. Show up early on weekends; tickets frequently sell out far in advance. $9.50, seniors and under 12 $6.

Anthology Film Archives, 32 Second Ave., at E. 2nd St. (☎505-5181). A forum for independent filmmaking, focusing on the contemporary, offbeat, and avant-garde, chosen from US and foreign production. Has regular **New Filmmaker Series** and the annual **New York Underground Film Festival** (Mar.) and **Mix Festival** (Nov.), a les-bi-gay film festival. $8, students and seniors $5.

Cinema Village, 22 E. 12th St., just west of University Pl. (☎924-3363). Features independent documentaries and hard-to-find foreign films. Great seats that lean back. $8.50, students $6.50, children and seniors $5.50.

Film Forum, 209 W. Houston St., near Sixth Ave. and Varick St. (☎727-8110; box office ☎727-8112). Three theaters with a strong selection in classics, foreign films, and independent films. $9, seniors $5 (M-F before 5pm).

Iris and B. Gerald Cantor Film Center, 36 E. 8th St. between University and Greene Sts. (☎998-4100). Generally for student screenings; sometimes it shows off-beat films that are open to the public and free. Check postings or call for schedule.

The Kitchen, 512 W. 19th St. between Tenth and Eleventh Aves. (☎255-5793 ext. 11). Subway: C, E to 23rd St. World-renowned showcase for offbeat arts events in an unassuming location.

Features experimental and avant-garde film and video, as well as concerts, dance performances, and poetry readings. Season runs Sept.-May, but a summer talk series ($10 each talk) hosts such avant-garde artistic luminaries as Lee Breuer. Call for info. Ticket prices vary by event.

Millennium Film Workshop, 66 E. 4th St. between Bowery and Second Ave. (☎673-0090). Subway: F to Second Ave. More than just a theater, this media arts center presents an extensive program of experimental film and video Sept.-June and offers classes and workshops. Also has equipment available for use. Tickets $7.

Museum of Modern Art: Roy and Niuta Titus Theaters, 11 W. 53rd St. (☎708-9480; see **Museums,** p. 121). The MoMA serves up an unbeatable diet of great films daily in its 2 lower-level theaters. The film department holds what it claims to be "the strongest international collection of film in the United States," and it's hard to doubt them. Film tickets are included in the price of admission and are available upon request. Also ask about screenings in the video gallery on the 3rd floor.

New York Public Libraries: For a real deal, check out a library, any library. All show free films: documentaries, classics, and last year's blockbusters. Screening times may be a bit erratic, but you can't beat the price. (For complete info on New York libraries, see **Service Directory,** p. 293.)

Walter Reade Theater, at Lincoln Center (☎875-5600; box office 875-5601). Subway: 1, 9 to 66th St. New York's performing arts octopus flexes yet another cultural tentacle with this theater next to the Juilliard School. Foreign and critically acclaimed independent films dominate. Tickets $8.50. Box office open daily 30min. before start of first film, closes 15min. after start of last show.

Ziegfeld, 141 W. 54th St. (☎765-7600), between Sixth and Seventh Aves., one of the largest screens left in America, showing first-run films. A must-visit for big-screen aficionados. Consult newspapers for complete listings. Tickets run $9.50 for adults and $6 for seniors and under 11.

FESTIVALS

Anthology Film Archives (see above) has regular **New Filmmaker Series** and the annual **New York Underground Film Festival** (Mar.) and **Mix Festival** (Nov.), a les-bi-gay film festival.

Bryant Park Film Festival, Bryant Park (☎512-5700), at 42nd St. and Sixth Ave. Subway: B, D, F, Q, N, R, S or 1, 2, 3, 7, 9 to 42nd St. Running from late June to August, this free outdoor series features classic revivals such as *Mr. Smith Goes to Washington, Citizen Kane,* and *The Sound of Music.* Movies begin Mondays at sunset; rain date Tuesday nights.

NY Video Festival (☎875-5600; www.filmlinc.com.), sponsored by the Film Society of Lincoln Center. Runs in mid-July at the Walter Reade Theater in Lincoln Center. Tickets $8.50, seniors $4.50 at weekday matinees. Website has info on many film festivals organized by themes.

Symphony Space, 2537 Broadway (box office ☎864-5400), at 95th St. Subway: 1, 9 or 2, 3 to 96th St. Primarily a live performance space, but every July the Foreign Film Festival showcases the expanding canon of quality foreign films. $8. Box office open daily noon-7pm.

Walter Reade Theater (see above) hosts the **New York Video Festival** in July.

LIVE TELEVISION

You can bring those TV fantasies to life in the city of dreams. Ask Ricki Lake's guest that burning question: you're the boss. It's best to order your tickets two to three months in advance, although standby tickets often crop up. Read on for a sampler of what deals the big names offer and how to get on the ticket.

Late Show with David Letterman (CBS) at the Ed Sullivan Theater, 1697 Broadway (☎975-1003), at 53rd St. The cuddly-yet-acerbic host performs his antics in front of a studio audience. If you are lucky enough to get tickets, bring a sweater—the studio is notoriously cold. Order tickets for his *Late Show* well in advance by writing: Late Show Tickets, 1697 Broadway, NY, NY 10019. Tapings are M-Th 5:30pm and another Th 8pm. For standby tickets on the day of the show, call 247-6497 at 11am on tape days (M-Th). Tickets are no longer given out at the theater.

Late Night with Conan O'Brien (NBC) (☎664-3057) at the G.E. Building in Rockefeller Center. Tapings Tu-F 5:30-6:30pm. To order in advance call or send a postcard to NBC Tickets, 30 Rockefeller Plaza, NY, NY 10012. You may receive up to 5 tickets at a time, but must book a month and a half in advance. Standby tickets also available tape days (Tu-F) at 9am at the 49th St. entrance, but you must show up at 4:15pm to see if there is enough room. Active in summer. Must be 16 or older.

Live with Regis (WABC) (☎456-3537). Send a postcard with name, address, phone number, and your request for up to 4 tickets to: Live Tickets, Ansonia Station, P.O. Box 230-777, NY, NY 10023. Expect a year-long wait. For standby tickets, line up at the corner of 67th St. and Columbus Ave. at 7am or earlier on weekdays. Must be 10 or older.

Ricki Lake Show (WWOR) (☎352-8600). Tapings W, Th 3 and 5pm; F 1 and 3. Write to Ricki Lake, 401 Fifth Ave., NY, NY 10016, or go in person at least an hour before a taping.

Rosie O'Donnell (NBC) (☎664-3056). Send postcards March-June to NBC Tickets at Rockefeller Plaza (see **Conan,** above). A completely random lottery cares not for your desired dates or number of tickets. Standby tickets, available at 7:30am taping days (M-Th, Sa), are also based on a lottery (read: you don't have to break your neck to get in line by 4am) from 30 Rockefeller Plaza. Ages 6-16 must be accompanied by adult.

Saturday Night Live (NBC) (☎664-3056). *SNL* goes on hiatus June-Aug. and only accepts ticket requests in Aug. Order tickets by sending a postcard to Rockefeller Plaza (see **Conan,** above). Warning: they don't accept requests for a specific date or quantity of tickets. Standby: get in line on the mezzanine level of Rockefeller Center (49th St. side) at 9am the morning of the show. You must be at least 16. P.S. Don't hold your breath.

The View (ABC) (☎456-1000). Brainchild of brazen Barbara Walters, this new hit talk sow brings together 4 opinionated women (not including Barbara's occasional appearances) from different worlds to dish the dirt. Send a request for tickets at least 2-3 months in advance to Ticket Coordinator, 320 W. 66th St., NY, NY 10023. Standby tickets available on show days, in line at the same address. It's best to show up around 9am, as filming begins at 11am every weekday.

OPERA

Dicapo Opera Theatre, 184 East 76th St., between Third and Lexington Aves. (☎288-9438), has been earning great critical acclaim and standing ovations at *every* performance—it's easy to understand why tickets go very quickly (usually around $40, senior discounts available).

The Metropolitan Opera Company, at the Lincoln Center's Metropolitan Opera House (☎362-6000; www.metopera.org). Lincoln Center Plaza is on the Upper West Side at Broadway and Columbus Ave. (see **Sights,** p. 95). North America's premier opera outfit. Plays on a stage as big as a football field. Artistic Director, James Levine, directs the likes of Luciano Pavarotti, Frederica von Stade, and Placido Domingo in new productions and favorite repertory classics. Regular tickets run upwards of $250, so go for the upper balcony at around $50—the cheapest seats have an obstructed view. You can stand in the orchestra ($16) along with the opera freakazoids who've brought along the score, or all the way back in the Family Circle ($12). Season Sept.-Apr. M-Sa; box office open M-Sa 10am-8pm, Su noon-6pm. In summer, call ticket line at ☎362-6000 for info on free park concerts.

The New York City Opera, at Lincoln Center's New York State Theater (☎870-5570). See **Sights,** p. 95, for more on the Lincoln Center. This smaller opera company has come into its own under the direction of Christopher Keene, general director since 1989. "City" now has a split

Apollo Theater

Smalls

Lenox Lounge

season (Sept.-Nov. and Mar.-Apr.), and keeps its ticket prices low year-round ($25-92). Call M to check the availability of $10 rush tickets, then wait in line the next morning. Box office open M 10am-7:30pm, Tu-Sa 10am-8:30pm, Su 11:30am-7:30pm.

New York Grand Opera (☎360-2777; www.summerstage.org). Free performances at the Central Park Summerstage, every Wednesday night in July.

DANCE

American Ballet Theater, at the Metropolitan Opera House, Lincoln Center (☎477-3030; box office ☎362-6000). Celebrating its 60th anniversary season, puts on the opulent classics of ballet such as *Swan Lake* and *Sleeping Beauty;* also does some more contemporary works by established modern choreographers like Twyla Tharp. Tickets $17-75; available at the box office.

Dance Theater Workshop, 219 W. 19th St. between Seventh and Eighth Aves., in Chelsea (☎924-0077; www.dtw.org). Subway: 1, 9 to 18th St. Supports emerging dancers. Also hosts innovative dance performances throughout the year. Students get 1/3 off regular ticket prices for most shows. Box office open M-F 10am-6pm.

De La Guarda, 20 Union Sq. East (☎239-6200; www.dlgsite.com), an Argentinian performance art troupe whose show "Villa Villa" is described as a trip to the rain forest, a disco, and an air show. Tickets ($40-45) for standing room only are hot and pricey, but a limited number are sold for $20 two hours before each show. Box office open Tu-Su noon-showtime.

⊠ Joyce Theater, 175 Eighth Ave. between 18th and 19th Sts. (☎242-0800). Subway: 1, 9 to 18th St. *The* place to go for modern dance, the Joyce runs energetic, eclectic programming year-round. If you are in the city for a while it may be worth it to buy a series of tickets to get a 40% discount. Companies like the Parsons, Les Ballet Trockadero (all-male on pointe ballet) and Pilobolus have all been known to stage stints at the Joyce. Tickets $20-40.

New York City Ballet, at the New York State Theater, Lincoln Center (☎870-5570; www.nycballet.com). The company's most critically acclaimed works have been the more modern pieces like *Serenade and Apollo,* but they are most famous for that New York Christmas tradition—George Balanchine's **The Nutcracker.** Reserve early for this classic. Season Nov.-Feb. and May-June. Tickets $12-65. Tickets can be purchased at the NY State Theater (see **Lincoln Center,** p. 161).

Thalia Spanish Theater, 41-17 Greenpoint Ave. between 41st and 42nd Sts., in Sunnyside, Queens (☎718-729-3880). Subway: 7 to 40th St./Lowery St. Dedicated to the arts of Spanish-speaking cultures. Their dance performances are exquisite, and the theater was showcasing these dance forms long before they became popular. The mid-Nov. to Feb. season brings **flamenco.** In spring and summer, Thalia heats it up with **Tango Tango** and theater pieces. Throughout the year, Thalia also shows Mexican pieces featuring **folklorico** dance. Shows usually Th-Su evenings. Tickets $20, students $18. Call to find out which shows are in English and Spanish.

FESTIVALS AND SEASONAL EVENTS

⊠ Central Park Summerstage, at the Rumsey Playfield, at 72nd St, near Fifth Ave., in Central Park (☎360-2777; www.SummerStage.org). Mid-June to late Aug., Summerstage hosts spectacular free cultural events, like concerts, dance, and spoken word. Past performers have included everyone from the Fugees and the Rocksteady Crew to the Gypsy Kings and They Might Be Giants. Big names from all genres, but also an outstanding selection of smaller or foreign celebrities.

Dances for Wave Hill, W. 249th St. and Independence Ave., at Wave Hill in the Bronx (☎718-549-3200). Three annual performances in July, inspired by the Wave Hill landscape. Free with admission to Wave Hill. $4, students and seniors $2, under 6 and members free.

PARTICIPATORY EVENTS

⊠ Midsummer Night Swing, outdoors in Lincoln Center Plaza (☎875-5766). For the past two decades, some of the best names in jazz, big band, swing, latin, and even line-dance have been coming to play at this exuberant happenin' from late-June to late-July. Come with or without a partner to dance the night away, see great couples swishing around you, or merely to take in the ambiance. If access to the plaza dance floor is sold out, you can strut your stuff (along with other hapless dancing feet) anywhere on the plaza. Tickets go on sale at the plaza at 6pm, but the line often begins at 5pm. Dancing 8:15-11pm; free lessons 6:30pm. $11; 6-night pass $62.

Dancing on the Plaza, Dana Discovery Center, at Fifth Ave. and 110th St, in Central Park (☎860-1370). Free dancing under the stars to the sounds of salsa, classic disco, swing, and ballroom every Th in Aug. 6-8:30pm. The first 45min. are devoted to lessons for the toe-tied.

Dancing Through Sunset Parks (☎718-567-9620), throughout Brooklyn parks. Run by the Young Dancers in Repertory Center for Dance Studies this annual series offers twice weekly dance classes for kids and teenagers in local parks in the mornings. July-Aug. Call for details.

CLASSICAL MUSIC

Musicians advertise themselves vigorously in New York City, so you should have no trouble finding the notes. Free recitals are common, especially in smaller spaces; just look in *Time Out* and The *Free Time* calendar ($2) for listings of priceless events.

LINCOLN CENTER

Lincoln Center (☎LIN-COLN; www.lincolncenter.org, see **Sights,** p. 95) remains the great depot of New York's classical music establishment. Regular tickets are pricey, but student and rush rates exist for select performances. You can buy all Lincoln Center tickets through **CenterCharge.** (☎721-6500. Open M-Sa 10am-8pm, Su noon-8pm.) **Alice Tully Hall** box office hours are daily 11am to 6pm (opens Su at noon) and also until 30min. after the start of every performance. **Avery Fisher Hall** box office hours are daily 10am to 6pm (opens Su at noon) and 30min. after the start of every performance.

Chamber Symphony Orchestra, at Alice Tully Hall (☎875-5788; www.ChamberMusicSociety.org). Season Nov.-May. Most tickets $35; some $25 student tickets available.

Great Performers Series, at Alice Tully and Avery Fisher Halls (☎721-6500). Or call Avery Fisher Hall (☎875-5020, after 3pm ☎875-5030). Hosts a series of performances Oct.-May, and occasional discussions by guests such as Yo-Yo Ma, Itzhak Perlman, Emanuel Ax, Murray Perahia, and the Academy of St. Martin in the Fields. Tickets start at $28 for a series.

Mostly Mozart, at Alice Tully and Avery Fisher Halls (☎875-5766). In its 35th season, this summer festival (July-Aug.) is a NY staple. Tickets $15-50. A few free events. 50 tickets for every event are set aside for $10, available on the day of the event, at the box office.

National Chorale, at Avery Fisher Hall (☎333-5333). Choral music to make your soul soar. During the Christmas season, the Chorale puts on Handel's *Messiah;* look also for Mozart, Bach, and Schubert choir staples. Tickets from $21.

New York Philharmonic, at Avery Fisher Hall (☎875-5709; www.newyorkphilharmonic.org). Begins its regular season mid-Sept. Tickets $10-60. On the day of select performances students can get $10 tickets. Come early or call ahead.

MUSIC SCHOOLS

Visiting a music school promises low cost and high quality music—a panacea for a weary budget traveler's soul. Except for opera and ballet productions ($5-12), concerts at the following schools are free and frequent (especially Sept.-May): the **Juilliard School of Music,** Lincoln Center (see above); the **Mannes College of Music,** 150 W. 85th St. (☎580-0210), between Columbus and Amsterdam Ave.; the **Manhattan School of Music,** 120 Claremont Ave. (☎749-2802); and the **Bloomingdale School of Music,** 323 W. 108th St. (☎663-6021), near Broadway.

▨ **Brooklyn Academy of Music,** 30 Lafayette St. (☎718-636-4100; www.bam.org), between Felix and Ashland Pl. Subway: 2, 3 or 4, 5 or D, Q to Atlantic Ave.; or B, M or N, R to Pacific St. The oldest performing arts center in the country, the Brooklyn Academy of Music (BAM) has compiled a colorful history of magnificent performances: here Pavlova danced, Caruso sang, and Sarah Bernhardt played Camille. Now, it focuses on new non-traditional, multicultural programs—with the occasional classical music performance. Jazz, blues, performance art, opera, and dance take this stage. Late spring brings Dance Africa, featuring West African dancing as well as crafts. BAM's annual **Next Wave Festival,** Sept.-Dec., features contemporary music, dance, theater, and performance art; it helped start talent like Mark Morris and Laurie Anderson. Call about student rush. The **Brook-**

lyn **Philharmonic Orchestra,** which performs here Nov.-Mar. and hosts a brief opera season Feb.-June. Orchestra and opera tickets $30-50. Manhattan Express Bus ("BAM bus") departs round-trip from 120 Park Ave. at 42nd St. for each performance ($5, round-trip $10).

Juilliard School of Music (☎ 769-7406; www.juilliard.edu) is one of the world's leading factories of classical musicians. Juilliard's **Paul Recital Hall** hosts free student recitals almost daily Sept.-May; Alice Tully Hall holds larger student recitals, also free, most W Sept.-May at 1pm. Orchestral recitals, faculty performances, chamber music, and dance and theater events take place regularly at Juilliard and never cost more than $10—you may see the next generation's Yo-Yo Ma for a third of the cost of seeing this one's. Call for a complete schedule.

OTHER VENUES

Carnegie Hall, Seventh Ave., at 57th St. (CarnegieCharge: ☎247-7800). Subway: N, R to 57th St.; B, D, E to Seventh Ave. The New York Philharmonic's original home is still the favorite coming-out locale of musical debutantes. Top soloists and chamber groups are booked regularly. Box office open M-Sa 11am-6pm, Su noon-6pm. Some shows have $10 rush tickets—call for information. See **Carnegie Hall,** p. 90, for more about the hall.

Frick Collection, 1 East 70th St., at Fifth Ave. (☎288-0700). Subway: 6 to 68th St. From Sept. through May, the Frick Collection hosts free classical concerts Su 5pm (summer concerts in July and Aug.). Tickets limited to 2 per applicant; written requests must be received by the 3rd M before the concert, or show up 30min. before the show and try to steal seats of no-shows (see **Museums,** p. 123).

Metropolitan Museum of Art, 1000 Fifth Ave., at 82nd St. (☎570-3949). Subway: 4, 5, 6 to 86th St. The Met posts a schedule of performances covering the spectrum from traditional Japanese music and Russian balalaika to all-star classical music recitals Sept.-June. Call for more info. Chamber music in the bar and piano music in the cafeteria F-Sa evenings; free with museum admission (see **Museums,** p. 120).

FESTIVALS

⬛ Lincoln Center Out-of-Doors (☎875-5108), events throughout Lincoln Center and Damrosch Park. Celebrating its 30th anniversary, for 3 weeks in Aug., Lincoln Center sponsors a completely free performance arts festival. Dance by Parsons Dance Company, chamber music by groups from the world over, jazz by famed Mingus Big Band...the line-up is fantastic.

Lincoln Center Festival (☎875-5928). Cutting-edge and ethnic events spanning dance, theater, opera, and music throughout the Lincoln Center complex in mid-July. Tickets $15-85. Ask for student discounts at the Avery Fisher Hall box office.

Concerts in the Park (☎875-5709; www.newyorkphilharmonic.org), in parks throughout the five boroughs and Long Island July-Aug. The Philharmonic plays magnificent outdoor concerts in parks during July. Concerts 8pm, followed by fireworks. Some (great) things in life *are* free.

Cooper-Hewitt Museum, 2 E. 91st St., at Fifth Ave. (☎849-8400; see **Museums,** p. 123). Subway: 4, 5, 6 to 86th St.; 6 to 96th St. Free Cross-Currents concert series brings everything from classical to hip-hop to the garden of the museum from late June through July. Tu 6:30-8pm.

Museum of Modern Art (☎708-9491; for more info see **Museums,** p. 121). "Summergarden," an contemporary classical music series, features Juilliard students performing in the museum's Sculpture Garden. July and Aug. F-Sa at 8:30pm. On most weekends in July and Aug., Enter through the (normally locked) back gate at 14 W. 54th St. between 6 and 10pm. Free.

World Financial Center in Battery Park City (☎945-0505 or 528-2733). The Hudson River Festival has free performances daily throughout the summer in the Winter Garden (the main atrium), the Esplanade, and various locations throughout Battery Park City. The festival features dynamic theatre, dance, art exhibitions, and world music events such as West African storytelling and dance. Other free dance and music concerts appear at the nearby World Trade Center.

St. Paul's Chapel and Trinity Church Classical Music Festival. on Broadway between Church and Fulton St. (☎602-0874 or 602-0747). Host summer classical music festival (Th 1pm) and noon concert series (Sept.-June M and Th). Suggested donation $2. Trinity presents classical concerts Sept.-June Su at 4pm. Tickets $15-20, though there is a discount for students and seniors. Trinity also has free concerts in summer.

GENERAL ENTERTAINMENT VENUES

■ **Symphony Space,** 2537 Broadway, at 95th St. (☎864-5400; www.symphonyspace.org). Subway: 1, 9 to 96th St. This former skating rink distinguishes itself with brilliant programming, like "Wall to Wall Bach"and a birthday gala for the late composer John Cage. Every Bloomsday (June 16), Symphony Space celebrates James Joyce's *Ulysses* with readings, lectures, and parties. The performance season (Sept.-June) offers classical and traditional ethnic musical performances, plays, dance, and the "Selected Shorts" program of fiction read by famous actors. Sponsors an ambitious program of old and new foreign films every July. Open Tu-Sa 1-7pm. Tickets by phone Th-Sa noon-6pm. Most movies $8, other events up to $45.

■ **92nd Street Y,** 1395 Lexington Ave. (☎996-1100). The Upper East Side's cultural mecca. The Y's Kaufmann Concert Hall seats only 916 people and offers an intimate setting unmatched by New York's larger halls, with flawless acoustics and the oaken ambience of a Viennese salon. Once home to the **New York Chamber Symphony** under the fiery direction of Gerard Schwartz, the Y still plays host to a panoply of world-class visiting musicians. A distinguished artists series dating back to the late 1930s has featured all the big names from Segovia and Schnabel to Yo-Yo Ma, Alfred Brendel, and Schlomo Mintz. Also hosts an ongoing series of literary readings and some of the most engaging lectures in New York. $15-35 for all events. Closed in summer.

Theater District

Brooklyn Center for Performing Arts (☎718-951-4500 or 951-4522), 1 block west of the junction of Flatbush and Nostrand Ave. on the campus of Brooklyn College. Subway: 2 or 5 to Flatbush Ave. The Brooklyn Center for Performing Arts at Brooklyn College (BCBC) prides itself on presenting many exclusive events each year. In recent years it has showcased the Russian National Dance Company, André Watts, the kiddie-friendly Famous People Players, and the Garth Fagan Dance Company with Wynton Marsalis. Season Oct.-May. Tickets $20-40.

Cathedral of St. John the Divine, 1047 Amsterdam Ave., at 112th St. (☎662-2133). This beautiful church offers an impressive array of classical concerts, art exhibitions, lectures, plays, movies, and dance events. NY Philharmonic performs on occasion, and soprano saxaphonist Paul Winter gives annual Winter Solstice concert. Prices vary.

Village Vanguard

Colden Center for the Performing Arts, 65-30 Kissena Blvd., at Queens College in Flushing, Queens (☎718-793-8080). Subway: 7 to Main St.-Flushing; then bus Q17 or Q25-34 to the corner of Kissena Blvd. and the Long Island Expressway. Beautiful, 2143-seat theater hosts an excellent program of jazz, classical, and dance concerts Sept.-May. Special efforts made to feature emerging artists whose works reflect the borough's cultural diversity. Call for schedule and prices.

Cultural Institutes. These centers for expats are valuable for their libraries, small but interesting exhibits, classes, and lectures. Some of these services are only open to members, but all the institutes have highly useful lists of cultural events throughout the city.

Alliance Française, 22 E. 60th St. (☎355-6100), the cultural arm of the French Embassy, offers Gallic lectures, classes, programs, and

Swing 46

ꗊ ꗕ ꗕ ꗕ ꗕ ꗕ ꗕ ꗕ ꗕ ꗕ ꗕ ꗕ ꗕ ꗕ

films. (Open M-Th 9am-8pm, F 9am-6pm, Sa 9am-2pm; box office at 55 E. 59th St., ☎355-6160.)

Goethe Institute, 1014 Fifth Ave. between 82nd and 83rd Sts. (☎439-8700), imports Germanic culture also through the medium of films, concerts, classes, and lectures. (Open Tu and Th 9am-7pm, M, W, F 9am-5pm.)

Americas Society, the **Spanish Institute,** and the **Italian Cultural Institute** occupy three historically landmarked buildings on Park Ave. between 68th and 69th St. (680 Park Ave., ☎249-8950; 684 Park Ave., ☎628-0420; and 686 Park Ave., ☎879-4242; respectively.)

China Institute, 125 E. 65th St. between Park and Lexington Aves. (☎744-8181), aims to promote the understanding of Chinese culture and history through classes, lectures, performances, and film series; its gallery showcases a broad spectrum of Chinese art and architecture from the Neolithic period to the present. (Gallery hours: M-W, F-Sa 10am-5pm, Tu-Th 10am-8pm, Su 10am-5pm; $3, students and seniors $2, under 12 free, Tu and Th 6-8pm free.)

Asia Society, see **Museums,** p. 124, also has films from or about Asia. (Box office open: M-F 10am-5pm; adults $7, students and seniors $5.)

Merkin Concert Hall, 129 W. 67th St., between Broadway and Amsterdam Ave. (☎362-8719). Subway: 1, 9 to 66th St. This division of the Hebrew Arts School offers programs diverse in genres of music; a typical week at the Merkin might include love songs spanning 400 years, classical and modern Chinese music, or a gay chorus. This intimate theater is known as "the little hall with the big sound." Season Sept.-June. Tickets $8-50. Box office open M-Th noon-6pm, F noon-4pm.

St. Mark's Church in the Bowery, 131 E. 10th St., at Second Ave. Has performance spaces for the **Ontological Theater** (☎533-4650), **Danspace Project** (☎674-8194), and **Poetry Project** (☎674-0910). While the Ontological Theater pioneered the wackiness of playwright Richard Foreman, Danspace has provided a venue for emerging dancers and experimental styles of movement since the 1920s (Isadora Duncan danced in this space). Call for info on upcoming events, or check the board outside; you'll need to make reservations for theater tickets and arrive 15min. early for the show. Tickets for Danspace $10-15, Poetry Project $4-7.

JAZZ

Since its beginnings in the early 20th century, jazz has played a pivotal role in New York's music scene. Uptown at Minton's during the 50s, Charlie Parker, Dizzy Gillespie, and Thelonious Monk were overthrowing traditional swing and planting, arguably, the roots of new genres, such as R&B and Rock N' Roll. Today, New York remains a jazz capital, with a multitude of genres, from Big Band orchestras and traditional stylists to free, fusion, and avant-garde artists, thriving in venues throughout the city. Downtown's crowd is more young, funky, and commercialized whilst in Harlem you'll find a more intimate and smooth type of jazz. You can check out one of the many hazy dens that bred lingo like "cat" and "hip" (a "hippie" was originally someone on the fringes of jazz culture who talked the talk but was never really in the know), or more formal shows at Lincoln Center. Summer means open-air (often free) sets in parks and plazas. Throughout the year, many museums offer free jazz in their gardens and cafes.

JAZZ CLUBS

Expect high covers and drink minimums at the legendary jazz spots. Most crowd tables together and charge $6-9 per drink. While hearing the jazz gods costs an arm and a leg these days, a few bars supply reliable no-names free of charge. And, although some "classier" joints take credit cards, bring cash just in case.

Apollo Theater, 253 W. 125th St. between Frederick Douglass and Adam Clayton Powell Blvds. (☎749-5838; box office ☎531-5305). This historic Harlem landmark has heard Duke Ellington, Count Basie, Ella Fitzgerald, Lionel Hampton, Billie Holliday, and Sarah Vaughan. A young Malcolm X shone shoes here. Today, the Apollo continues to undergo its resurgence in popularity. A big draw is W's legendary Amateur Night, featuring shows ranging from "regular" to "show-off" and "top dog" ($13-30), where the audience assumes the starring role of judge, jury, and many times, executioner. Order through Ticketmaster (☎307-7171) or at the box office (Open M, Tu, Th, F 10am-6pm, W 10am-8:30pm, Sa noon-6pm).

Birdland, 315 W. 44th St. between Eighth and Ninth Aves. (☎581-3080). Said by Charlie Parker to be the "jazz corner of the world," this dinner club serves up cajun food and splendid jazz in a mellow, neon-accented, nouveau setting. The gumbo ($16) and the popcorn shrimp ($9) are as legendary as the club itself. Appetizers $6-10, entrees $12-19. Music charge, including a complimentary drink, $20-30. An additional $10 minimum food/drink. Open daily 5pm-2am; first set nightly at 9pm, 2nd at 11pm. Reservations recommended. AmEx, Discover, MC, V.

Blue Note, 131 W. 3rd St., near MacDougal St. (☎475-8592). The legendary jazz club is now more of a commercialized concert space. But the Blue Note still epitomizes splendid jazz and brings in many of today's all-stars, such as Take 6. Cover for big-name performers $20-70. $5 food/drink minimum. Students half-off cover Su-Th 11:30pm set only. For a great deal, go to the after hours, where the cover for late night jam sessions drops to $5 (F-Sa). Reasonable Sunday jazz brunch includes food, one drink, and jazz for $18.50 (noon-5pm, shows at 12:30 and 2:30pm; reservations recommended). Sets daily 9pm and 11:30pm. Open Su-Th 7pm-2am, F-Sa 7pm-4am. AmEx, Diner's Club, MC, V.

Cotton Club, 656 W. 125th St., on the corner of Riverside Dr. (☎663-7980). With performers such as Duke Ellington, Cab Calloway, and Cole Porter, the name Cotton Club was synonymous with exclusivity, sophistication, and splendid jazz. Today, more tourists than regulars appear at this jazz hall of the greats. Cover for brunch and Gospel Shows $25; jazz shows $32; no minimum, dinner included. Call ahead for reservations and information. MC, V.

Detour, 349 E. 13th St. between First and Second Aves. (☎533-6212). Great nightly jazz and no cover—a perfect mix. One-drink minimum. Happy hour M-F 4-7pm, drinks 2-for-1. Mixed drinks ($6), bottled beer ($4). Open M-Th 3pm-2am, F-Su 3pm-4am. Shows M-Th 9pm-midnight; F-Su 9:30pm-1:30am. Wheelchair accessible. AmEx, MC, V.

Fez, 380 Lafayette St. between 3rd and 4th Sts., under Time Café (☎533-2680). This lushly-appointed, Moroccan-decorated performance club draws an extremely photogenic crowd, especially on Thursday nights when the Mingus Big Band holds court (sets at 9:30pm and 11:30pm. $18, students pay $10 for second set. Reservations suggested.) Other nights vary: music ranges from jazz to alt-pop, hip-hop, and spoken word. Popular drag show on Su draws a huge gay clientele. Cover $5-30; 2-drink minimum. Open Su-Th 6pm-2am, F-Sa 6pm-4am. Cash only at the door but MC, V for food/drink.

❧ Knitting Factory, 74 Leonard St. between Broadway and Church St. (☎219-3055). Featuring several shows nightly, ranging from avant-garde and indy rock to jazz and hip-hop, this multi-level performance space is also great for late night loungin'. Sonic Youth played here every Th for years (alas, no more). Hosts rock acts and a summertime **jazz festival,** too. Cover $5-20; entry to the cozy bar up front free. Box office open M-F 10am-11pm, Sa-Su 2-11pm. Bar open M-F 4:30pm-2am, Sa-Su 6pm-2am. All age shows. Free live music every night in tap bar at 11pm.

Lenox Lounge, 288 Lenox Ave. between 124th and 125th Sts. (☎427-0253). Glorious in the days when Ella Fitzgerald, Billie Holiday, and Alvin Reed graced its stage, it remains "one of the hidden treasures of Harlem." Intimate, it still boasts the original 1939 decor. Jazz F, Sa. $10; M night jam session free. 2-drink minimum. First set 10pm; last set 1am. Open daily noon-4am.

❧ Small's, 183 W. 10th St., at Seventh Ave. (☎929-7565). Some of the best up-and-comers performing night after night with the occasional visit from luminaries. Yes, the fact that it doesn't serve alcohol allows it to stay open all night, often providing over 10hr. of great music, a splendid after-hours spot, and a late, late night showcase for musicians who still have chops left over from performances at other clubs. Cover $10. Free show Sa 6:30-9pm. Free non-alcoholic beverages. Open Su-Th 10pm-8am, F-Sa 6:30pm-8am. Call ahead for early bird specials (no cover).

Showman's Café, 375 W. 125th St. between St. Nicholas and Morningside Aves. (☎864-8941). A symbol of the original 1942 Showman's, which featured the likes of Lionel Hampton and Duke Ellington, this excellent jazz club attracts a largely local crowd. Showtimes: 8:30, 10:30pm and 12:30am. No cover. 2 drink minimum. Open M-Sa noon-4am.

St. Nick's Pub, 773 St. Nicholas Ave. between 148th and 149th Sts. (☎283-9728). A small, comfy bar with a dedicated crowd and the smoothest jazz. Su soul quartet show 6pm-midnight. M especially notable: Patience Higgins and the Sugar Hill Jazz Quartet. Cover $3, or 2 people for $5 with 2-drink minimum. Mixed drinks $5-6. If you're lucky enough to visit on the right day (usually M), soul food is free. Bar opens at 12:30pm, jazz shows M-Sa 9pm until 3 or 4am. Cash only.

Swing 46, 349 W. 46th St. between Eighth and Ninth Aves. (☎262-9554). Formerly the home of Red Blazer Too, this place has jumped on the big band wagon and delivers all kinds of smooth grooves like Swingtime M, Jump Tu, and Big Band Th. Pink and palmy decor helps get you in the Ipanema mood. Cover includes swing lessons at 9:15pm. Su-W $7, Th-Sa $12 with 2-drink minimum (drinks $10-16). Happy Hour, with half-price drinks, daily 5-8pm. Dinner ($14-24) served daily 5pm-midnight. Sets begin at 10:30pm. No smoking in main room. AmEx, MC, V.

Village Vanguard, 178 Seventh Ave. between W. 11th and Greenwich Sts. (☎255-4037). A windowless, wedge-shaped cavern, as old and hip as jazz itself. The walls are 65-years-thick with memories of Lenny Bruce, Leadbelly, Miles Davis, and Sonny Rollins. Every M the Vanguard Orchestra unleashes its torrential Big Band sound on sentimental journeymen at 9:30 and 11:30pm. Cover M-Sa $15, plus $10 minimum. Sets Su-Th 9:30 and 11:30pm, F-Sa 9:30, 11:30pm, and 1am. Doors open at 8:30pm. Reservations recommended. Cash and checks only.

Sweet Basil, 88 Seventh Ave. between Bleecker and Grove Sts. (☎242-1785). Traditional jazz with dinner. Lots of tourists, some regulars. Occasional star sets. Cover $17.50. No cover for jazz brunch (Sa-Su 2-6pm). Shows Su-Th 9 and 11pm (cover $17.50), F-Sa 9, 11pm, and 12:30am (cover $20). $10 food/drink minimum. Open daily noon-2am. AmEx, MC, V.

Londel's, 2620 Eighth Ave./Frederick Douglass Blvd. between 139th and 140th Sts. (☎234-6114). With its oak-wood flooring and high ceilings, this sophisticated supper club brings lots of class and nouveau Southern cuisine to Sugar Hill. Entrees $12-18. Drinks $7. F and Sa nights feature live jazz and blues from 8-11pm. Cover $5; $10 food/drink minimum. Open Tu-Sa 11:30am-midnight, Su brunch noon-5pm.

Arthur's Tavern, 57 Grove St. between Bleecker and Seventh Ave. S. (☎675-6879). Largely local crowd flocks to hear decent live jazz and blues played in this little joint. But the size makes you feel as if the band is playing just for you. Also features a full American Italian menu. Open Su-M 8pm-3am, Tu-Th 6:30pm-3am, F-Sa 6:30pm-4am. Sets begin at 7pm. No Cover. 1-drink minimum. Drinks $7. Cash only.

OTHER JAZZ VENUES

Guggenheim Museum (☎423-3500; see **Museums,** p. 122). Live jazz, Brazilian, and world beat music in its rotunda F and Sa 5-8pm year-round. Museum admission required, but F 6-8pm is pay-as-you-wish.

Museum of Modern Art (☎708-9480; see **Museums,** p. 121). From September to May MoMA features jazz in its Garden Cafe on F 5:30-7:45pm. Museum admission is required, but F 4:30-8:30pm is pay-what-you-wish.

Radio City Music Hall (☎247-4777; see **Sights,** p. 86) boasts a bill of great performers that reads like an invitation list to the Music Hall of Fame; Ella Fitzgerald, Frank Sinatra, Ringo Starr, Linda Ronstadt, and Sting, among others, have all performed at the legendary venue. Box office 50th St. and Sixth Ave. Open M-Sa 10am-8pm, Su 11am-8pm.

Saint Peter's, 619 Lexington Ave. (☎935-2200; see p. 82), at 52nd St. Su jazz vespers at 5pm, usually followed at 7pm or 8pm by a jazz concert ($5-10 donation for the concert). Informal jazz concerts often held W afternoons at 12:30pm. Oct. 8th, the annual All Night Soul session rocks 5pm-5am. In addition, the hippest ministry in town brings you art openings and exhibits, theater, lectures, and more. Dale R. Lind, Pastor to the Jazz Community, oversees tuneful deeds.

SUMMER JAZZ AND FESTIVALS

The **JVC Jazz Festival** blows into the city from June to July. All-star performances of past series have included Elvin Jones, Ray Charles, Tito Puente, and Mel Torme. Tickets go on sale in early May, but many events take place outdoors in the parks and are free. Check the newspaper for listings. **Bryant Park,** which has events all summer, also hosts a large number of these concerts, as does **Damrosch Park** at Lincoln Center. Call ☎501-1390 in the spring for info, or write to: JVC Jazz Festival New York, P.O. Box 1169, New York, NY 10023. Annual festivals sponsored by major corporations bring in local talent and industry giants on the forefront of innovation. The concerts take place throughout the city (some free) but center at TriBeCa's **Knitting Factory** (☎219-3055 in spring).

Central Park Summerstage, at 72nd St. in Central Park (☎ 360-2777), divides its attention among many performing arts, including jazz. Call or pick up Central Park's calendar of events, available at the Dairy in Central Park (see **Central Park,** p. 92). The free concerts run mid-June to early August.

The **World Financial Center Plaza** (☎ 945-0505) infrequently hosts free concerts between June and September, featuring jazz styles ranging from Little Jimmy Scott to the Kit McClure Big Band, an all-female jazz orchestra. The **World Trade Center** (☎ 435-4170), on Church St. at Dey St., hosts free R&B, blues, and jazz concerts in its plaza Wednesday to Friday after work and Tuesday to Friday at lunchtime from July until early September. Two performers are featured each week, one performing at noon and the other at 1pm. The **South Street Museum** (☎ 732-7678) sponsors a series of outdoor concerts from July to early September at Pier 17, Ambrose Stage, and the Atrium. Head to **Lincoln Center Plaza** and Damrosch Park's **Guggenheim Bandshell** to hear free jazz, salsa, and Big Band delights. **Alice Tully Hall,** also at Lincoln Center, presents a summer jazz series (☎ 875-5299). Guest soloist Wynton Marsalis trumpeted the inaugural season.

Swing 46

ROCK, POP, PUNK, FUNK

Combine the grit, heady anonymity, and super self-consciousness of New York with the rhythmic rattle of the subway and you have arrived at the perfect environment for musical inspiration. The Velvet Underground moaned to Gotham as the city flirted with heroin, languor, and insipid conversation, Patti Smith and Television layered poetry and guitar lines over a beat you couldn't dance to in the dark days of Disco, Sonic Youth drowned out an otherwise disposable decade in a riot of noise and feedback, Public Enemy fought the power before anybody had ever heard the name Giuliani, and the Wu-Tang Clan rose from the Staten slums (wow). Hit the newsstand Wednesday morning for comprehensive show listings in the *Village Voice* or *Time Out: New York.*

Carnegie Hall

The **CMJ Music Marathon** (☎ 877-6-FESTIVAL; www.cmj.com) runs for four nights in the fall and includes over 400 bands and workshops on alternative music culture and college radio production. **The Digital Club Festival** (☎ 677-3530), a newly reconfigured indie-fest, visits New York in late July. The **Macintosh New York Music Festival** presents over 350 bands over a week-long period. For more electronic experimental sounds, check out Creative Time's **Music in the Anchorage,** a June concert series happening in the massive stone chambers in the base of the Brooklyn Bridge. (☎ 206-6674, ext. 252 for info, or stop by **Other Music,** see p. 143, for tickets and a brochure.)

If arena rock is more your style, check out **Madison Square Garden** (☎ 465-6000), at Seventh Ave. and W. 33rd St., perhaps America's premier entertainment facility. MSG hosts over 600 events and nearly 6,000,000 spectators every year. **Radio City Music Hall** (☎ 247-4777) and **New Jersey's Meadowlands** (☎ 201-935-3900) also stage high-priced performances. From June to early September the **Coca-Cola Concert Series** (☎ 516-221-1000) brings rock, jazz, and reggae concerts to Jones Beach. (Tickets $15-40; See **Long Island,** p. 232, for transportation info.)

Joyce Theater (Hell's Kitchen)

Beacon Theater, 2124 Broadway between 74th and 75th Sts. (☎496-7070). Mid-sized concert hall featuring mid-sized alternative rock names, as well as world-beat concerts and multi media performance events. Long stands by road horses like Simon & Garfunkel or the Allman Brothers are not uncommon. Call for schedule; there's something almost every weekend. Tickets $25-100.

The Bitter End, 147 Bleecker St. between Thompson and LaGuardia Sts. (☎673-7030). Small space hosts folk, country, and roots rock acts; they claim artists like Billy Joel, Stevie Wonder, Woody Allen, and Rita Rudner performed here as unknowns. Look for their likenesses in the gaudy mural. Call for show times. Cover $5-12. Open Su-Th 7:30pm-2am, F-Sa 7:30pm-4am.

Bottom Line, 15 W. 4th St., at Mercer St. (☎228-7880 for info; ☎228-6300 for box office). A somber space with a mixed bag of music and entertainment—from jazz to kitsch to country to theater to old-time rock-and-roll by over-the-hill singers. Recent shows include Roger McGuinn and ex-Stones guitarist Mick Taylor. Double proof of age (21+) required, or come with a parent or guardian. Some all-ages performances. Cover $15-30. Shows nightly 7:30 and 10:30pm.

CBGB/OMFUG (CBGB's), 315 Bowery, at Bleecker St. (☎982-4052). The initials have stood for "country, bluegrass, blues, and other music for uplifting gourmandizers," since 1973, but the New York Dolls, Television, the Ramones, Patti Smith, and Talking Heads rendered the initials synonymous with punk. The music remains loud, raw, and hungry. Shows nightly around 8pm. Cover $3-10. Next door, **CB's Gallery** (☎677-0455) presents softer live music.

Continental, 25 Third Ave. between St. Mark's Pl. and Stuyvesant (☎529-6924; www.nytrash.com/continental). A dark club that hosts the loud set nightly. Come for noise, rock, and local punk. Iggy Pop, Debbie Harry, and Patti Smith have all played here—recently. Check lamp posts and fliers for shows and times. Happy Hour daily half-price drinks. Shot of anything $2 with a beer. Cover free-$7.

The Cooler, 416 W. 14th St., at Greenwich St. (☎229-0785). In the heart of the meat-packing district. The Cooler showcases non-mainstream alternative, dub, electronica, and illbient by some of the town's smartest DJs in a huge vault of a room. Randomly hosts good underground hip-hop shows as well. Cover varies. Free Mondays. Doors open Su-Th 8pm, F-Sa 9pm.

Irving Plaza, 17 Irving Pl., at 15th St. between Third Ave. and Union Sq. (☎777-6800 or 777-1224 for concert info). A mid-sized club decorated in a puzzling chinoiserie style. Rock, comedy, performance art, and other entertainment in its enormous space. Purchase tickets in advance for the bigger shows. Cover varies. Doors generally open at 8pm. Box office open M-F noon-6:30pm.

Knitting Factory, 74 Leonard St. between Broadway and Church St. (☎219-3055). Walk up Broadway to Leonard St. Several shows nightly. Sonic Youth played here every Thursday for years (alas, no more), and Lou Reed stopped in to show off new material from his album, *Ecstasy*, before its release last spring. Summertime brings the **What is Jazz festival.** Shows $20-30 for entrance to the back room/performance space only; entry to the cozy bar up front is always free, as is the downstairs jazz space some nights. Box office open M-F 10am-11pm, Sa-Su 2-11pm. Bar open M-F 4:30pm-2am, Sa-Su 6pm-2am.

Maxwell's, 1039 Washington St. (☎201-798-0406), in Hoboken. See **Daytrips,** p. 231.

Mercury Lounge, 217 E. Houston St., at Ave. A (☎260-4700). Once a gravestone parlor, the Mercury has attracted an amazing number of big-name acts to its fairly small-time room, running the gamut from folk to pop to noise. Past standouts: spoken-word artist Maggie Estep, Morphine, and Mary Lou Lord. Music nightly. Cover varies. Box office open M-F 11am-7pm, Sa noon-7pm.

Roseland, 239 W. 52nd St., at Eighth Ave. and Broadway. (☎777-6800). Decently priced concert club featuring major-label alt-rock, like Travis, and Hip Hop, like De La Soul. Tickets $20-30.

Wetlands Preserve, 161 Hudson St., near Laight St. in TriBeCa. (☎386-3600). A giant Summer of Love mural in the back room sets the tone, a Volkswagen bus curio shop swims in tie-dyes, and mood memorabilia harkens back to Woodstock in this 2-story whole-earth spectacular. Wetlands began the neo-hippie movement as a stomping ground for Phish, Dave Matthews, Blues Traveler and the Spin Doctors in the early '90s, has fallen on hard times booking acts like Big Frog, the Japanese Dead cover band. Cover $7-10. Shows begin 9 or 10pm.

Tonic, 107 Norfolk St. between Delancey and Rivington Sts. (☎358-7501; www.tonicnyc.com). Artists like Cibo Matto, MC Paul Barman, and the members of Sonic Youth have used this space to put on conceptual, experimental music programs. Unexpected combination, collaboration, and juxtaposition are its functional principles. Films every M. Cover free-$10.

Bowery Ballroom, 6 Delancey St., near the Bowery (☎ 533-2111). Where bands go when they've grown out of CBGB's but aren't exactly Talking Heads yet. Every once in a while a name like the Eels or Catherine Wheel comes and sells out a show. Tickets $10-20.

SPORTS

SPECTATOR SPORTS

There is nothing like a New York fan. They are loud, obnoxious, and deathly faithful, even if New York teams sometimes don't seem quite deserving—and that's when the fans become the biggest critics. Remember, however, that they are the first to exhibit pride, basking in the reflected glory when their teams do right, and although *they* can offend the players, out-of-towners absolutely cannot. While most cities would be content to field a major league team in each big-time sport, New York, ultimately excessive in all areas of life, opts for the Noah's Ark approach: two baseball teams, two NHL hockey teams, two NFL football teams (although the Giants and Jets are now quartered across the river in New Jersey), an NBA basketball team, a WNBA basketball team, and an MLS soccer squad. New York also hosts a number of celebrated world-class events such as the New York Marathon and the US Open. City papers overflow with info on upcoming events.

BASEBALL

YANKEES. The legendary **New York Yankees** (team of Joe DiMaggio, Mickey Mantle, Babe Ruth, and Lou Gehrig) was founded in 1901. Since then, they have won more championships than any other team in American sports. The Bombers, as they're affectionately known, led by such players as Bernie Williams and David Justice, play ball at **Yankee Stadium** in the South Bronx. (☎ 718-293-4300. Subway: 4, B, D, to Yankee Stadium.) In 1998, the Yankees won the most games in baseball history and overcame the San Diego Padres in the World Series, thus regaining their stature as the best team around. In 1999 they took the division title and won the Series again against the Atlanta Braves. Everyone waits hopefully for a three-peat in 2000. (Tickets usually available day of the game; $8 to $30; you can also find them on the web at www.tix.com.)

METS. Created in 1962 to replace the much-mourned Giants and Dodgers, the **National League Mets** (short for "Metropolitans") set the still-unbroken major league record for losses in a season during their first year. Seven years later, the "Miracle Mets" captured the World Series. They wound up deep in the cellar again, spawning a David Letterman catchphrase: "We're so close to spring you can almost hear the Mets suck." 1999, however, found the Mets first in their division, and in summer 2000, the Mets, led by Mike Piazza, Mike Bordick, and Robin Ventura were second in the Eastern Division. Watch them go to bat at **Shea Stadium** in Queens (☎ 718-507-6387. Subway: 7 to Willets Point/ Shea Stadium. Tickets $13-30.)

SUBWAY SERIES. The two teams face off every summer in the popular Subway Series. In 2000, the Yankees took the Mets 2-1.

BASKETBALL

KNICKS. Although they've been unable to regain the heights of their 1969 Championship Season, the New York Knickerbockers are still a force in the NBA. In 1999, the Knicks shocked the basketball world by becoming the worst regular season team to reach the championship series. 2000 saw the team, having been led by such greats as Latrell Sprewell, Allan Houston, and Patrick Ewing, miss the championship to the Indiana Pacers in the Conference finals. The Knicks do their dribbling at **Madison Square Garden** (☎ 465-5867) from November to late April. Tickets, which start at $22, need to be ordered well in advance. On the **collegiate level,** the Garden plays host to St. John's Red Storm during the winter and the NIT and Big East tournaments in March.

LIBERTY. Also playing at the Garden are the **New York Liberty** (☎564-9622) of the Women's National Basketball Association (WNBA). Star players Rebecca Lobo, Vickie Johnson, Tari Phillips, Teresa Weatherspoon, and Sophia Witherspoon have led the Liberty, currently leading the Eastern Conference, to the top of the league standings in each of the last four seasons. (Season June-Aug. Tickets start at $8.)

FOOTBALL

Although both New York teams once battled in the trenches at Shea Stadium, nowadays they play across the river at **Giants Stadium** in East Rutherford, New Jersey. The **Jets,** led by charismatic coach Bill Parcells, resurrected quarterback Vinny Testaverde, and loud-mouth wideout Keyshawn Johnson, have NY abuzz with talk of bringing home a third Super Bowl ring. (☎516-560-8200. Tickets start at $25; cash only at the Meadowlands box office.) Even after rebuilding their squad post-1998, the **Giants** (☎201-935-8222) placed a disappointing third in the 1999 NFC East Conference. Season ticket holders have booked all the games for the next 40 years, and the waiting list is over 15,000. See *Let's Go: New York City 2040* for details. Try a local sports bar for your best view of the action.

HOCKEY

The **New York Rangers** play at **Madison Square Garden** (MSG ☎465-6741; Rangers ☎308-6977) from October to April. After enduring 54 championship-less years, the Rangers finally captured the Stanley Cup in June 1994. With the recent reacquisition of Mark Messier to the squad, while still mourning the 1999 retirement of hockey's greatest player ever, Wayne Gretzky, they have their eyes set on the cup for this 2000-2001 season. (Ticket on sale Aug. They start at $25; reserve well in advance.) The **New York Islanders,** after winning four consecutive Stanley Cups in the early 1980s, are now one of the few teams worse than the Rangers. They hang their skates at the **Nassau Coliseum** in Uniondale, Long Island. (☎516-794-9300. Season also runs Oct.-Apr. Tickets $27-70.)

SOCCER

Buoyed by swelling youth interest and the 1994 World Cup in New York, soccer has undergone a meteoric rise in popularity in the past few years, culminating in the start of a new American league, **Major League Soccer (MLS).** New Yorkers have wasted no time learning what the rest of the world has known for decades: no other sport is like *fútbol*. Although they placed last in 1999, the **New York/New Jersey Metrostars,** with leaders like Adolfo Valencia and Tab Ramos, are shining in 2000. The Metrostars kick off at **Giants Stadium.** (☎888-4-METROTIX/463-8768. Season late Mar. to early Sept. Tickets $15-30.)

TENNIS

Tennis enthusiasts who get tickets three months in advance can attend the **US Open,** one of tennis's four Grand Slam events, in late August and early September at the United States Tennis Association's (USTA) Tennis Center in Flushing Meadows Park, Queens. (☎718-760-6200 Tickets $33-69. On sale by early June; call ☎888-673-6849 to buy.)

HORSERACING

Fans can watch the stallions at **Belmont Park** (☎718-641-4700) Wednesday to Sunday, May through July and September to mid-October, and may even catch a grand slam event. The **Belmont Stakes,** run the first Saturday in June, is one leg in the Triple Crown. ("Belmont Special" train leaves Penn Station twice per day. $8 round-trip, includes $1 off admission.) The **Aqueduct Racetrack,** next to JFK Airport (☎718-641-4700), has races from late October to early May, also Wednesday through Sunday. (Subway: A to Aqueduct.) Grandstand seating at both tracks $2.

THE NEW YORK CITY MARATHON

On the first Sunday in November, two million spectators line rooftops, sidewalks, and promenades to cheer 22,000 runners in the **New York City Marathon** (16,000 racers actually finish). The race begins on the Verrazano Bridge and ends at Central Park's Tavern on the Green. Call the NY Roadrunner's Club (☎860-4455) for info on signing up.

PARTICIPATORY SPORTS

Whether trying to slim down at the health club or commuting to work via bicycle, endless amateur and recreational athletes twist and flex in New York. Although space in much of the city is at a premium, the **City of New York Parks and Recreation Department** (☎ 800-201-PARK/7275 for a recording of park events) manages to maintain numerous playgrounds and parks in all boroughs, for everything from baseball and basketball to croquet and shuffleboard.

BEACHES

For non-city beaches, including the surprisingly easy-to-get-to Jones Beach, see **Long Island,** p. 234.

Manhattan Beach (¼ mi.-long), on the Atlantic Ocean. Ocean Ave. to Mackenzie St. in Brooklyn (☎ 718-946-1373). Subway: D to Brighton Beach; then bus B1.

Orchard Beach and Promenade (1¼ mi.-long), on Long Island Sound in Pelham Bay Park, Bronx (☎ 718-885-2275). Subway: 6 to Pelham Bay Park; then bus 12 to Orchard Beach.

Rockaway Beach and Boardwalk (7½ mi.-long), on the Atlantic Ocean (☎ 718-318-4000). Lifeguards Memorial Day-Labor Day daily 10am-6pm. Subway: A to "Broad Channel;" then "S" shuttle to Rockaway Park.

Staten Island: South Beach, Midland Beach, and **Franklin D. Roosevelt Boardwalk** (2½ mi.-long), on Lower New York Bay. South Beach is toted as one of NYC's "best beaches," and offers spectacular views of the Narrows. Bus S51 from the ferry terminal.

POOLS

Public pools exist in all the boroughs of New York, but isolated incidents of sexual assault have occurred in them in the past couple years. The NYC Parks Department has added security and is considering segregating some pools by sex. Some of the nicer (and safer) pools include **John Jay Pool** (☎ 794-6566), east of York Ave. at 77th St., and **Asser Levy Pool** (☎ 447-2020), at 23rd St. and Asser Levy Pl. (next to the East River). All outdoor pools are open early July through Labor Day, 11am or noon to 7pm, depending on the weather. Both pools listed above are free, although the latter's heated indoor pool is open only to members. Call ☎ 800-201-PARK/7275 for other locations.

BASKETBALL

Courts can be found in parks and playgrounds all over the city and are frequently occupied. **Pickup games** can be found in various parts of the city, each with its own rituals, rulers, and degree of intensity. **The Cage,** at W. 4th and Sixth Ave., is home to some of the city's best amateur players: rumor has it that scouts for college and pro teams occasionally drop by incognito to ferret out new talent. Other spots worth checking out (if you're any good) include **Central Park, 96th and Lexington Ave.,** and **76th and Columbus Ave.**

BICYCLING

From spring to fall, daily at dawn and dusk and throughout the weekend, packs of dedicated (and spandex-ed) cyclists navigate the trails and wide roads of **Central Park.** The circular drive is car-free Monday-Thursday 10am-3pm and 7-10pm, Friday 10am-3pm, and Friday 7pm until Monday 6am. On the West Side between 72nd and 110th Sts., along the Hudson bank, **Riverside Park** draws more laid-back riders. Other excellent places to cycle on the weekends include the deserted **Wall Street** area and the unadorned roads of Brooklyn's **Prospect Park.** If you must leave your bike unattended, use a strong "U" lock. Thieves laugh at (then cut through) chain locks. Don't leave quick-release items unattended; you will find them very quickly released.

Loeb Boathouse, mid-park at 75th St., in Central Park (☎ 861-4137; 717-9048). 3-speeds $8 per hr., 10-speeds $10, tandems $15. Valid ID and $100 cash or credit card deposit required. Open Apr.-Sept. daily 10am-5pm, weather permitting.

Metro Bicycle Stores, Lexington Ave. at 88th St. (☎ 427-4450). Seven convenient locations throughout the city. Entry-level mountain bikes and hybrids. $7 per hr., $35 per day, $45 over-

HELL ON WHEELS

The **in-line skating craze** has hit New York hard. Messengers careen through crowded streets on their skates, oblivious to the flow of traffic around them, and park paths are often clogged with talented (and not-so-talented) bladers. Some areas even have slalom courses and half-pipes set up similar to skateboarding courses. **New York Skateout** offers both in-line skating lessons and tours (☎486-1919). See **In-Line Skating**, p. 172, for rental info. The following open stretches feature good views and a skate-happy crowd:

Battery Park: Skate from the tip of Manhattan through Battery Park City. Great view of the harbor and skyline and an extremely flat skating surface.

West Street: The city has blocked off about ten blocks from Christopher to Horatio Sts. Lots of heavy-duty skaters and a view of the Hudson.

Chelsea Piers: Roller rink in a massive sports complex on the Hudson, at 23rd St. and 12th Ave. Very popular with in-line hockey players.

East River Promenade: Slightly narrow boardwalk from 60th St. to 81st St. The path is very low and close to the river, with great views of Roosevelt Island.

Central Park: The park has several roller-zones, including the self-descriptive Outer Loop, a slalom course near Tavern on the Green (67th St.).

night. Daily rentals due back 30min. before store closes and overnight rentals next day at 10am. $250 cash or credit card deposit and valid ID required. Helmet rental $2.50 per bike. Open F-Tu 9:30am-6:30pm, W-Th 9:30am-7:30pm.

Pedal Pushers, 1306 Second Ave. between 68th and 69th Sts. (☎288-5592). The best rates in the city. 3-speeds $4 per hr., $10 per day, $12 overnight; 10-speeds $5 per hr., $14 per day, $14 overnight; mountain bikes $6 per hr., $17 per day, $25 overnight. Overnight rentals require $150 deposit on a major credit card, but regular rentals only need major credit card, passport, or a NY state driver's license deposit. Open F-M 10am-6pm, W 10am-7pm, Th 10am-8pm. Rent a helmet for an extra $2 per day.

JOGGING

When running in **Central Park** during no-traffic hours (see **Bicycling,** above), stay in the right-hand lane to avoid being mowed down by the pedal-pushers. **Stay in populated areas and stay out of the park after dark.** Recommended courses include the 1.58mi. jaunt around the Reservoir (between 84th and 96th Sts.) and a 1.72 mi. route along West Dr., starting at Tavern on the Green, heading south to East Dr., and circling back west on 72nd St. Another beautiful place to run is **Riverside Park,** which stretches along the Hudson River bank from 72nd to 116th St.; **don't stray too far north.** For information on clubs and races around the city, call the **New York Roadrunner's Club,** 9 E. 89th St. between Madison and Fifth Aves. (☎860-4455). They host races in Central Park on summer weekends.

IN-LINE SKATING

For speed on wheels, there are many in-line skate rental locations throughout the city. For low prices and convenience, **Blades** (☎888-55-Blades) has over eight stores in the Metropolitan area. (Open M-Sa 11am-8pm, Su 11am-6pm. Flat rate $20; includes all protective gear. $200 deposit or credit is required.) Blades also has various sister stores that feature the same prices and conditions, like **Peck and Goodie Skates,** 917 Eighth Ave. (☎246-6123), between 54th and 55th St., where they'll also hold your shoes. They offer private lessons for a fee of $40/hr. (open M-Sa 10am-8pm, Su 10am-6pm).

BOWLING

Bowlmor Lane, 110 University Pl., near 13th St., offers bowling, lights, music, and alcohol all in one place; it just might be as close to heaven as you'll get. (☎255-8188. Imported beer $6-7, domestic $4. Open Tu-W 10am-1am, Th 10am-2am, F 10am-4am, Sa 11am-4am, Su 11am-1am. Shoe rental $3. M-Th and F before 5pm $6 per person per game, after 5pm F and all day Sa-Su, rates increase $1. After 6pm, becomes 21+)

GOLF
New Yorkers remain avid golfers, jamming all of the 13 well-manicured city courses during the weekends. Most are found in the Bronx or Queens, including **Pelham Bay Park** (☎718-885-1258), **Van Cortlandt Park** (☎718-543-4595), and **Forest Park** (☎718-296-0999). Greens fees are approximately $11-20 for NYC residents and $17-26 for non-NYC residents. Reserve at least one week in advance for summer weekends.

ICE SKATING
The first gust of cold winter air brings out droves of aspiring Paul Wylies and Tara Lipinskis. While each of the rinks in the city has its own character, nearly all have lockers, skate rentals, and a snack bar.

Rockefeller Center, Fifth Ave. and 50th St. (☎332-7654). Open only in the cold months and always crowded, with throngs of spectators around the outside edges. Call for prices.

Wollman Memorial Rink (☎396-1010) is located in a particularly scenic section of Central Park, near 64th St. $15 for 2hr., $25 all day; includes helmet and pads; $100 deposit required.

Sky Rink, at W. 21st St. and the Hudson River (☎336-6100). Boasts 2 full-sized indoor Olympic rinks. Usually open M 12:30-2:20pm and 4-9:20pm, Tu 12:30-2:20pm and 4-5:20pm, W and F 12:30-2:20pm and 4-6pm, Th 4-6:30pm, Sa 11:45am-6:20pm, and Su noon-5:50pm. Adults $11, 12 and under $8. Skate rentals $5.

HORSEBACK RIDING
Central Park horseback riding, for those well-versed in English saddle, operates out of **Claremont Stables,** 175 W. 89th St. (☎724-5100. Open M-F 6:30am-10pm, Sa-Su 8am-5pm. $40 per hr. Make reservations.) **Queens'** Forest Park has guided trail rides by **Dixie Do Stables.** (☎718-263-3500. Open M 8am-5pm, Tu-Su 8am-7pm. $25 per hr.)

CLIMBING
You can climb to your heart's content at the **ExtraVertical Climbing Center** in the Harmony Atrium, 61 W. 62nd St.; no experience necessary. (☎586-5382. Day pass $16, students $12, challenge climbs $9 for 2, equipment rental $6; lessons $55-110; monthly passes $75, students $50. Open summer M-F 1-10pm, Sa 10am-10pm, Su noon-8pm; winter M-F 5-10pm, Sa 10am-10pm, Su noon-8pm.) In addition, **North Meadow Recreation Center,** mid-park at 97th St. in **Central Park,** offers 4-week courses for $200 per person. (☎348-4867 for reservations. Every Su 10am.)

ROWBOATS
You can rent them at the **Loeb Boathouse** in Central Park. (☎517-2233; 517-3623. Open daily Apr.-Sept. 10am-6pm, weather permitting. $10 per hr.; refundable $30 deposit.)

Food

"What can I get for ten dollars?" "Anything you want." Yes, it's true. New York is home to every kind of food imaginable, and with our attitude good quality is a must. Besides the ethnic enclaves that dot the city, certain types of food pervade throughout. **Chinese food, pizza,** and **bagels** are the best examples—MSG reaches every borough through so many plates of beef and broccoli, neon "tomato sauce" (grease) fills the arteries of every self-respecting New Yorker, and no native could be *phklemped* after starting the day with cream cheese and lox on a bagel. But do not miss NYC's **street food:** sweet roasted nuts in the winter, mustard-slathered hot dogs and pretzels throughout the year, and a summer favorite: flavored ice in any color of the rainbow (find them at your ghetto's local Coco Helado man). Your stomach will beg you to stop after only a dollar or two of food.

ORGANIZATION

We have prefaced the neighborhood restaurant listings with a list of the same restaurants, categorized **by cuisine.** Restaurants that combine low prices and high quality are denoted by a thumb (☒). Every restaurant listed in the boxes is followed by an abbreviated neighborhood label, which directs you to the listings **By Neighborhood,** in which you'll find the restaurant's complete write-up.

   $ signifies the $5-10 entree range, **$$** the $10-15 range, and **$$$** the $15-20 range.

BX	Bronx	**EV**	East Village	**Q**	Queens
BC	Central Brooklyn	**GV**	Greenwich Village	**SH**	SoHo
BD	Downtown Brooklyn	**HWH**	Harlem & Washington Hts.	**SI**	Staten Island
BN	North Brooklyn	**LI**	Little Italy	**TBC**	TriBeCa
BS	South Brooklyn	**LES**	Lower East Side	**GUM**	Gramercy, Union and Murray
CH	Chelsea	**LM**	Lower Manhattan	**UES**	Upper East Side
CHI	Chinatown	**MH**	Morningside Heights	**UWS**	Upper West Side
EM	East Midtown	**NL**	NoLita	**WM**	West Midtown

BY TYPE OF FOOD

CAJUN, CARIBBEAN, CREOLE

Brisas del Caribe (p. 184)	SH
Hammond's Finger Lickin' Bakery (p. 200)	BC
Jamaican Hot Pot (p. 199)	HWH
La Caridad 78 Restaurant (p. 196)	UWS
National Café (p. 189)	EV
Negril (p. 191)	CH
Roy's Jerk Chicken (p. 200)	BC
Sisters (p. 199)	HWH
Two Boots Restaurant (p. 189)	EV

DELI

Carnegie Delicatessen (p. 193)	WM
⚑ Katz's Delicatessen (p. 186)	LES
Manganaro's (p. 193)	WM
2nd Ave. Delicatessen (p. 189)	EV

DESSERTS, SWEETS

Chinatown Ice Cream Factory (p. 181)	CHT
⚑ Economy Candy (p. 187)	LES
Eddie's Sweet Shop (p. 204)	Q
⚑ Galaxy Pastry Shop (p. 203)	Q
⚑ Hong Kong Egg Cake Co. (p. 181)	CHT
⚑ The Lemon Ice King of Corona (p. 203)	Q
Moishe's Bake Shop (p. 190)	EV
Philip's Confections (p. 202)	BS
Something Sweet (p. 190)	EV
Sweet-n-Tart Cafe (p. 180)	CHT
Teuscher Chocolatier (p. 194)	EM
Veniero's (p. 190)	EV

DINER

Bendix Diner (p. 190)	CH
Chat 'n' Chew (p. 191)	GUM
EJ's Luncheonette (p. 194)	UES
Jackson Hole Wyoming (p. 195)	UES
⚑ Jackson Diner (p. 203)	Q
Jerry's (p. 184)	SH
Moonstruck (p. 191)	GUM
Tom's Restaurant (p. 198)	MH

ETHIOPIAN

Massawa (p. 198)	MH

FAST FOOD

⚑ Big Nick's Pizza and Burger Joint (p. 195)	UWS
D+S Plaza (p. 196)	UWS
Europa (p. 179)	LM
McDonald's (p. 179)	LM
Papaya King (p. 195)	UES
⚑ Nathan's (p. 202)	BS

FRENCH

Elephant and Castle (p. 186)	GV
⚑ Le Gamin Cafe (p. 184)	SH

GREEK, MIDDLE EASTERN

Amir's Falafel (p. 197)	MH
Caesar's (p. 190)	CH
⚑ Caravan (p. 200)	BD
Damask Falafel (p. 188)	EV
⚑ Elias Corner (p. 202)	Q
Fountain Cafe (p. 200)	BD

GREEK, MIDDLE EASTERN, CONT.

Ferdinando's (p. 201)	BN
Moonstruck (p. 191)	GUM
Olive Tree Cafe (p. 186)	GV
⚑ Oznot's Dish (p. 201)	BN
Sahadi Importing Company (p. 201)	BD
Sahara East (p. 189)	EV
Uncle George's (p. 203)	Q
Uncle Nick's Greek Cuisine (p. 199)	WM

IBERIAN

Spain (p. 186)	GV
La Rosita Restaurant (p. 198)	MH

INDIAN, PAKISTANI, AND AFGHAN

Anand Bhavan (p. 203)	Q
⚑ Jackson Diner (p. 203)	Q
Khyber Pass Restaurant	EV
Rose of India (p. 189)	EV
Tamarind (p. 196)	UWS
Pakistan Tea House (p. 185)	TBC

ITALIAN

⚑ Basta Pasta (p. 191)	GUM
Becco (p. 193)	WM
Benito One (p. 181)	LI
Cucina di Pesce (p. 188)	GV
Cucina Stagionale (p. 185)	GV
Da Nico (p. 182)	LI
Dipalo Dairy (p. 182)	LI
⚑ Dominick's (p. 204)	BX
⚑ Emilia's (p. 204)	BX
Ferdinando's (p. 201)	BN
Intermezzo (p. 190)	CH
La Focacceria (p. 189)	EV
La Mela (p. 182)	LI
Latticini-Barese (p. 201)	BD
Lombardi's (p. 182)	LI
Manganaro's (p. 193)	WM
Pasquale's Rigoletto (p. 204)	BX
Rocky's Italian Restaurant (p. 182)	LI
Two Boots Restaurant (p. 189)	EV
Zigolini's (p. 179)	LM

JAPANESE AND KOREAN

⚑ Basta Pasta (p. 191)	GUM
Dojo (p. 188)	EV
⚑ Dosanko (p. 194)	EM
Kum Gang San (p. 203)	Q
Ivy's Cafe (p. 196)	UWS
Mill Korean Restaurant (p. 198)	MH
Miyako (p. 201)	BN
Mottsu (p. 183)	NL
Sapporo (p. 193)	WM
⚑ Yakitori Taisho (p. 188)	EV
Yoshi (p. 187)	LES

JUICE BARS

Lucky's Juice Joint (p. 184)	SH
Squeeze (p. 201)	BN
Uptown Juice Bar (p. 185)	TBC

BY NEIGHBORHOOD

Neighborhoods are listed in geographical order (as in the rest of the book), with Hoboken last, and restaurants within each area are in order of preference.

LOWER MANHATTAN

see map
pp. 316–317

Lower Manhattan eateries tailor their schedules to the lunch breaks of Wall St. brokers. This means fast food that is not always super-expensive. Browse **Broadway** near Dey and John Sts. In the summer, food **pushcarts** offer tempting deals on falafel, burritos, and gyros. You can always take your food purchased inside outside, and **Liberty Park,** across the street from the WTC, offers a perfect place to do so.

Zigolini's, 66 Pearl St., at Coenties Alley (☎425-7171). One of the few places in the area where you can get an indoor, air-conditioned seat most of the time, although there is more seating outside, if you're so inclined. Serving filling sandwiches ($5-7) and great pasta ($7-11), Zigolini's also offers the option of creating your own sandwich. Open M-F 7am-7pm.

Europa, 199 Water St., a block down from the Titanic Memorial at the South St. Seaport (☎422-0070). Smoothly decorated and high-ceilinged, this gourmet self-serve joint is a little more expensive than nearby fast-food options. Fortunately, you're paying for good taste. Grilled chicken breast sandwich on ciabatta bread with lettuce, tomatoes, and basil pesto ($6.50). Open daily 6:30am-8:30pm. Delivery until closing.

McDonald's, 160 Broadway, at Liberty St. (☎385-2063). Yeah, it's a McDonald's, but what a McDonald's! Step inside and witness one of New York's finest examples of postmodern shmaltz. Wall St.'s Mickey D's sports a door person in a tux, a pianist above the entrance, a stock ticker, and a McBoutique on the 2nd floor. They keep the ketchup packets in glass and brass bowls here—a little touch of McClass to justify the slightly inflated McPrice (but the same McFood). Open M-F 6am-9pm, Sa-Su 7:30am-9pm.

CHINATOWN

see map
pp. 318–319

The neighborhood's 300-plus restaurants cook up superfantastic Chinese, Thai, and Vietnamese cuisine, and they won't burn a hole through your wallet. Be prepared, however, for waiters with a poor grasp of English and little ambience. Many places are cash only (unless where noted) and don't serve alcohol, but allow you to bring your own. You can take an after-dinner stroll through technicolor streets, as you delight in Chinese ice cream or Vietnamese desserts—but bring a few friends, for safety's sake.

☒ **Hop Kee,** 21 Mott St., at the corner of Mosco St. (☎964-8365). Bare bones in the ambiance department, but this is *real* Chinese food. Their specialties are expensive—snails cantonese style ($10.25) and pineapple with roasted duck ($14.75)—but dishes like beef chow fun are only $4.10. Open daily 11am-4am.

☒ **New Silver Palace,** 52 Bowery St., at Canal St. (☎964-1204). This enormous restaurant is known for its excellent dimsum ($3-5; served 9am-4pm), but their shark fin soup is what they make their money on—it's $150 per table (serves 8-10 people). Open daily 9am-11pm. V, MC.

☒ **H.S.F. Restaurant,** 46 Bowery (☎374-1319). They have great dim sum ($3-5; served 11am-5pm), but order their buffet special, where they bring you a pot of boiling broth and you take as many vegetables, dumplings, etc. from their huge buffet and cook it at your table ($19.95 per person; served after 5). Open daily 8am-4:30pm.

Excellent Dumpling House, 111 Lafayette St., just south of Canal St. (☎219-0212). Small, unassuming, and perennially crowded with folks enjoying splendid food and fast service. Terrific veggie and meat dumplings fried, steamed, or boiled ($4 for 8 pieces). Huge bowls of noodle soups $3.50-4. Beer. Open daily 11am-9pm. **$**

the BIG $plurge

not quite a free lunch

Most budget travelers spend their sojourn in New York City without ever stepping foot into one of the city's swankier restaurants, but there are ways to treat yourself to an *extremely* fine meal without completely busting your wallet. Every summer, many restaurants participate in **NY Restaurant Week,** during which the price of lunch corresponds to the current year. For example, the 2001 price will be $21.00. While this still might seem like a lot, at ritzy places like Lutece, Gramercy Tavern, Peter Luger, and Le Cirque, it's quite a bargain. The program has begun expanding to include the entire summer, and reservations tend to go quickly. For a list of participating restaurants, send a stamped envelope to: NYC Restaurants, New York Convention and Visitors Bureau, 2 Columbus Circle, New York, NY 10019.

Harden & L.C. Corp., 43 Canal St., near Ludlow St. (☎966-5419). Maybe the best meal deal in Manhattan: a massive Malaysian dinner for only $2.50. There is a menu for this Malaysian greasy spoon, but nobody uses it: cruise in between 11am and 10:30pm, point to the 3 sides you want, and you'll get a huge plate of rice with a heaping portion of each side. While veggie dishes are available, strict vegetarians should opt elsewhere. Bright fluorescent lights and Chinese soap operas spice up the ambience. Bring your own alcohol. Open daily 7am-9pm. **$**

Wong Kee, 113 Mott St. between Canal and Hester Sts. (☎966-1160). Cheap, consistently good Cantonese food. For the best deals, go for the Cantonese noodles, the *lo mein,* or the fried rice dishes ($3-5). If you're willing to spend a bit more, try the bean curd with straw mushrooms ($6) or the specialty of the house, *wong kee* steak ($8.50). Open daily 11am-10pm. **$**

Joe's Shanghai, 9 Pell St. between Bowery and Mott St. (☎233-8888). From fried turnip cakes ($3.25) to crispy fried whole yellowfish ($13), this Chinatown branch of the Queens legend serves up all sorts of tasty Shanghai specialties. But the true source of Joe's acclaim is his *shiao lung bao* ($7), crab meat and pork dumplings in a savory soup. Be prepared for communal tables and long lines of *bao* addicts on weekends. Beer. Open daily 11am-11:15pm. **$-$$**

Shanghai Cuisine, 89-91 Bayard St., at Mulberry St. (☎ 732-8988). The house specialty, braised soy duck with 8 treasures ($34), must be ordered a day in advance and is the richest dish you will ever taste—attack this dish only in large groups. Less intense dishes exist, like spicy pepper salt prawns ($13), and mixed vegetables ($7). Beer and wine. Open daily 11am-10:30pm. **$$**

Bo-Ky, 78-80 Bayard St. between Mott and Mulberry Sts. (☎406-2292). Tourists rarely grace this quality Vietnamese joint specializing in soups (most under $5). The coconut-and-curry chicken soup ($5) will clear that nasty head cold instantly. *Pho,* the beef broth king of Vietnamese soups, will fill you up without emptying your wallet ($3-5). Open daily 8am-9:30pm. **$**

Sweet-n-Tart Cafe, 76 Mott St., at Canal St. (☎334-8088). Alongside inexpensive standard Chinese fare, this crowded little purple-and-white "cafe" offers *tong shui,* sweet Chinese "tonics" (soups), each believed to have medicinal value for a specific part of the body: dry bean curd with gingko for healthy skin ($2.25), lotus seeds in herbal tea with egg for the liver and kidneys ($2.60). Find out what snow frog with lotus seeds does for you. Open daily 9am-11:30pm. **$**

New York Noodle Town, 28½ Bowery, at Bayard St. (☎349-0923). Pan-fried or in soup, *lo mein* or the wider Cantonese-style, these noodles are incredible and cheap (most under $6.50). If you're willing to spend a bit more, try the barbecued duck ($9), or the salt-roasted flounder ($16). Often crowded; go early. Bring your own alcohol. Open daily 9am-4am. **$-$$**

House of Vegetarian, 24 Pell St. between Canal and Bayard Sts. (☎226-6572). All animals are ersatz on the huge menu of this small and appropriately green eatery; soy and wheat by-products, taro root, and mushroom disguise themselves as beef, chicken, and fish. Fantastic dumplings (3 for $2) should please both veggies and non-veggies alike. Most entrees $6-10. Ice-cold lotus-seed or lychee drink $2. Open daily 11am-11pm. **$**

Nyona, 194 Grand St. between Mulberry and Mott Sts. (☎334-3669). Popular, excellent Malay-sian dishes in a cool, wood-lined interior. The delectably spicy *nasi lemak* ($4) puts chili ancho-vies and curry chicken in a bed of coconut rice. For an unusual dessert, ask for the "ABC"—an indescribable treat that's not on the menu. Beer and wine. Open daily 11am-11:30pm. **$-$$**

Thailand Restaurant, 106 Bayard St. (☎349-3132). Chinatown's first Thai restaurant has dealt well with the mushrooming competition. Simple and quiet, but head and shoulders above the other joints. Taste the killer *pad thai* ($5.50) and roasted duck in curry with coconut milk, bam-boo shoots, onions, and bell peppers ($9.50). Known for homemade Thai desserts like sweet rice with egg custard and coconut milk ($1.50). AmEx. Open daily 11:30am-11pm. **$**

Vietnam, 11-13 Doyers St. between Bowery and Pell St. (☎693-0725). All of the standards—brittle spring rolls, shrimp on sugar cane, noodle soups—and then some. Try the tasty, filling Viet-namese crepes ($6) for a distinct, assertive flavor. Ask about the more innovative items on the menu like the stir-fried salmon with black bean sauce ($7). Beer. AmEx. Open daily 11am-9:30pm. **$**

SHOPS

🦀 **Hong Kong Egg Cake Co.,** on the corner of Mott and Mosco Sts., in a small red shack—just fol-low the line wrapped around the corner. Cecelia Tam will make you a dozen soft, sweet egg cakes fresh from the skillet ($1) that she's been at for 19 years. Open W-Th and Sa-Su 10:30am-5pm.

Chinatown Ice Cream Factory, 65 Bayard St., at Mott St. (☎608-4170). Satisfy your sweet-tooth with homemade lychee, taro, ginger, red bean, or green tea ice cream. One scoop $2, two $3.60, three $4.60. Open Su-Th noon-11:30pm, F-Sa 11:30am-11:30pm.

Ten Ren Tea and Ginseng Company, 75 Mott St. between Canal and Bayard Sts. (☎349-2286). Comfortable and classy, Ten Ren boasts a huge selection of rare, delectable teas rang-ing in price from the very cheap to hundreds of dollars a pound. To beat the heat in the sum-mer, get the Green Tea Powder ($4-7), and add a packet's worth to a cold bottle of water. Drop in some apple juice for sweetener, and you've got a very refreshing, very *green* caffeine drink. Open daily 10am-8pm.

Dynasty Supermarket Corp., 69 Elizabeth St., at Hester St. (☎966-4943). One of the most extensive markets in the area and provides an air-conditioned refuge from the tumult of the street. Find ginseng, sea cucumber, live mudskipper, chicken feet, and Hostess cupcakes all in one stop. Open daily 9:30am-8:30pm.

LITTLE ITALY

see map pp. 318–319

The three blocks of **Mulberry St.** between Grand and Canal St. are packed tight with the sidewalk tables of myriad *trattorie* and *caffè*, under the can-opy of Italian flags. At 7pm, the street comes to life; arrive a bit earlier for one of the better tables. On weekends, reservations are a must. For the sake of thrift and ambience, dine at a *ristorante* and then move to a *caffè* to sat-isfy your sweet tooth. While it isn't hard to find restaurants in Little Italy, it *is* hard to find stand-out cuisine. Most restaurants really milk their old world "charm." Save money with sizable appetizers *(antipasti)* or a snack at one of the many shops and groceries. Unless otherwise noted, all places take major credit cards.

Benito One, 174 Mulberry St. between Grand and Broome Sts. (☎226-9171). A small, friendly *trattoria* featuring a menu of excellent Sicilian fare. A favorite is *pollo scarpariello*, chicken on the bone with garlic, olive oil, and basil ($11). Pasta $7-13, veal $14.50, poultry $11-13, seafood $13-20. $6.50 lunch special until 4pm. Open Su-Th 11am-11pm, F-Sa 11am-midnight. **$-$$**

Da Nico, 164 Mulberry St. between Broome and Grand Sts. (☎343-1212). Cheap, tasty food in a lovely environment or tree-shaded garden in back—frequented by Al Pacino and Johnny Depp. *Pollo marsala* ($11.50) will sate an empty tummy. Lunch: pasta $6-10, entrees $6.50-12.50. Dinner: pasta $10-15, entrees $11-25. Open Su-Th 11am-11pm, F-Sa 11am-midnight. **$$**

La Mela, 167 Mulberry St. between Broome and Grand Sts. (☎431-9493). Plastered with photos and postcards, La Mela is the place to come for a raucous time. The chummy, boisterous waitstaff serve up generous portions "family style"—a sort of home-style *prix fixe* selection with the dishes of the day written on a sign outside the restaurant. The wine is cheap ($18 for 1.5L), but you can also bring your own. Pasta $6-8, entrees $11-15. Open daily noon-11pm. **$$**

Lombardi's, 32 Spring St. between Mott and Mulberry Sts. (☎941-7994). New York's oldest licensed pizzeria (1897), credited with creating the famous New York-style thin-crust, coal-oven pizza (for some reason they don't take credit for the grease). A large pie feeds 2 ($12.50). Toppings are pricey ($3 for one, $5 for two, $6 for three), as are the more creative assortments, like the fresh clam pie ($20 for a large)—but they're worth it. Reservations for groups of 6 or more. Cash only. Open M-Th 11am-11pm, F-Sa 11:30am-midnight, Su 11am-10pm. **$-$$**

Rocky's Italian Restaurant, 45 Spring St., at Mulberry St. (☎274-9756). A true neighborhood joint, Rocky's buzzes with strains of the Old Country. Their "homestyle cooking" boast means you can ask for things that aren't on the menu. For lunch, try a pizza hero ($4) or sandwich ($4-7), served until 5pm. Pasta $6.50-11, entrees $8-15. The chicken with garlic sauce ($12) is a treat. The wine is cheap ($14 for a carafe), but you can also bring your own. Open daily 11am-11pm; kitchen closes at 10:30pm. Jul.-Aug. closed M. **$-$$**

Mandalay Cuisine, 380 Broome St., at Mulberry St. (☎226-4218). A rare Burmese pearl washed up on the Italian shores of Mulberry St. Refined Burmese cuisine (a marriage of Indian and Thai food) served in a cozy setting. Start with the 1000-layered pancake (a delicate bread, $2.50). Entrees range from $8.50 (Burmese curry) to $12.75 (mixed seafood). Beer and wine available. Open M-F 4-11pm, Sa-Su noon-11pm. **$-$$**

CAFFÈS

Caffè Palermo, 148 Mulberry St. between Grand and Hester Sts. (☎431-4205). The best of the *caffè* offerings along Mulberry. Summers, Palermo opens onto the street with an espresso bar up front. Most pastries $3-5. The staff takes much pride in its tasty *tiramisù* ($5); the cannoli ($2.75) and cappuccino ($3.25) are also quite good. Open daily 10am-midnight.

La Bella Ferrara, 110 Mulberry St. (☎966-1488). The name is cribbed from the larger, factory-like Caffè Ferrara on Grand St. and basically means "better Ferrara." The local choice for after-dinner dessert. Pastries $2-2.50, cakes $4-5, cappuccino $3. Cash only. Open daily 9am-2am.

SHOPS

Dipalo Dairy, 206 Grand St., at Mott St. (☎226-1033). Even the toughest budget traveler cannot live on bread alone; enter Dipalo Dairy. The shop offers a selection of breads, meats, and pastas, but specializes in cheeses. The soft, fleshy mozzarella ($4.69 per lb.) is their mainstay, but the goat cheese and the *ricotta fresca* are also delicious. What's more...free samples! The proprietor insists: "You must not buy it unless you taste it first." Open daily 9am-6:30pm.

NOLITA

NoLIta, for lack of a better word, is a budding pocket of culinary action for the recently hip and fashionable. Since you'll pay the price for ambience around Elizabeth, Mott, and Mulberry Sts., you might want to go early for drinks and an appetizer or late for drinks and dessert. Major credit cards are accepted, unless otherwise noted.

see map
pp. 318–319

🗹 **Rice,** 227 Mott St. between Prince and Spring Sts. (☎226-5775). Fantastic food—and darn cheap. Standard favorites here—basmati, jasmine, sticky, Japanese. But do explore the more exotic Thai black or Bhutanese red ($1-4). The sauces range from mango chutney to Aleppo yogurt ($1). You can also add ratatouille, shrimp coconut curry, or chicken satay, among other enticing toppings ($3.50-8). Soups also available ($4.50). Crowds spill out into the street waiting for tables. Beer only. Open daily noon-midnight. No credit cards. **$**

Cafe Gitane, 242 Mott St., at Prince St. (☎334-9552). A focal point of NoLIta life, this cafe specializes in seeing and being seen. Always crowded, and a rack of glossy fashion mags invites all to linger. Salads $5-7, glass of wine $5-7, tasty dishes like the grilled eggplant with goatcheese and pesto on watercress $8, and tiramisu $4. Open daily 9am-midnight. Cash only. **$**

Cafe Colonial Restaurant, 276 Elizabeth St., at the corner of Houston St. (☎274-0044). Great entree options like the veggie burger ($8) and soft-shell crab sandwich ($12). Beers $4.50. Open Su-M 8am-11pm, Tu-Sa 8am-midnight. **$$**

M&R Bar, 264 Elizabeth St. between Houston and Prince Sts. (☎226-0559). Works the comfortable neighborhood bar appeal with just a bit of attitude. Weekend brunch 11:30am-4pm, $8-10. Sandwiches $9-12; appetizers $6. Happy Hour M-F 5-6:30pm, $3 beer. Late-night menu until 1am or 2am on weekends. Open M-Th 5pm-midnight, F 5pm-4am, Sa 11:30am-4pm and 5pm-midnight, Su 11:30am-4pm and 5pm-midnight. **$-$$**

Mottsu, 285 Mott St. between Prince and Houston Sts. (☎343-8017). Japanese eatery. Entrees are pricey (chicken teriyaki $14, lambchops $22), but the lunch box specials (tempura, noodles, sushi, or sashimi with rice and miso soup) are less expensive ($8-13). Open for lunch M-F noon-3pm; dinner Su-Th 5-11pm, F-Sa 5-11:30pm; Su brunch 3-5pm. **$$**

Cafe Habana, 229 Elizabeth St. between Prince and Houston Sts. (☎625-2002). Inexpensive but stylish. The chicken diablo (blackened chicken, mesclun, and black beans, $6.25) and Hawaiian (ham, cheddar, grilled pineapple, $6.25) are delightful options. Other entrees range from rice and beans ($4) to grilled steak ($10.50). Open daily noon-8pm. **$**

SOHO

see map
p. 321

Food is all about image in SoHo. Down with the diners that have been relegated to the fringes of town! Food here comes in a variety of exquisite and pricey forms, precious little of it fried or served over a counter. Often the best deal in SoHo is brunch, when the neighborhood shows its cozier, good-natured front (and puts the calorie-counter away). For more out-of-the way treasures, **W. Houston** between Macdougal and Thompson St. offers some tasty finds. Strolling along any one of the side streets, such as **Sullivan,** is always a good bet for great people-watching and latte-sipping.

▨ Space Untitled, 133 Greene St., near Houston St. (☎260-8962). The best of SoHo—huge, warehouse-like space with plenty of bar stools and chairs to make yourself comfortable. Black, white, brick, and art surround you while you eat, unless you choose gourmet to go. Sandwiches $3-7; fabulous desserts $1.75-4.50. Coffee $1.50-2; wine and beer $4.50. Open M-Th 8am-10pm, F-Sa 8am-11pm, Su 8am-9pm. **$**

▨ Penang, 109 Spring St. between Mercer and Greene Sts. (☎274-8883). Excellent Malaysian cuisine served in a beautiful and exotic setting. Check out the waterfall in the back while you savor the award-winning *roti canai* $4.25 or the tasty *poh-piah,* steamed

Hard Rock Cafe

Mare Chiaro

New York City Bagels

spring rolls $6. Vegetarians: the *kari sayur campur* ($12.50) will leave you elated. Entrees ($8-20) are generally pricey, but worth it. Cocktails $9, a little pricey, especially since you'll have a few while waiting for a table on weekends. Open M-Th noon-midnight, F-Sa noon-1am. **$$**

▨ Le Gamin Café, 50 MacDougal St. between Prince and Houston Sts. (☎254-4678). Always packed with locals, this very European cafe offers simple and tasty French-inspired fare. The *salade de chevre chaudaux noix* (goat cheese croutons, tomato, mesclun, and walnuts, $9) is a sumptuous dish. Cafe au lait $3. Crepes $3.50-8. Open daily 8am-midnight. **$$**

Lucky's Juice Joint, 75 W. Houston St, near W. Broadway (☎388-0300). Sunny stop specializes in fresh juice combinations. Exotic smoothies ($4-5) made with a whole banana and a choice of everything from soy milk to peaches; a variety of other additions—from ginseng to bee pollen—can be included for a dollar more. Fresh and tasty food for the weary gallery-goer available in the outdoor cafe area. Veggie sandwiches $4.50-5.50; chilled 1 oz. "shots" of wheat grass $1.50. Open M-Sa 9am-8pm, Su 10am-8pm. **$**

Brisas del Caribe, 489 Broadway, at Broome St. Latin-American food in a decidedly un-SoHo setting. During the day this dive is populated almost exclusively by men on break from crew-work here for the very cheap food (french fries $2; hot sandwiches $2.35-5) and roast pork that is rumored to be the best in town ($3.50). Open daily generally 6am-6pm. **$**

Jerry's, 101 Prince St. between Mercer and Greene Sts. (☎966-9464). The calimari salad ($7.50) will definitely add some spice to your life. Great selection of sandwiches, like the melted Vermont cheddar with bacon and tomato on seven-grain bread ($7.50). Beer $5. Open M-W 9am-11pm, Th-F 9am-11:30pm, Sa 10:30am-11:30pm, Su 10:30am-5pm. **$-$$**

Kelley and Ping Asian Grocery and Noodle Shop, 127 Greene St. between Houston and Prince Sts. (☎228-1212). In a hollowed-out SoHo warehouse space now decorated with its own sleek Asian food products and gorgeous deep wood, Kelly and Ping serves up tasty noodle dishes for $7. Wraps $4; soups $6-7; wok dishes under $7.50. Also has a tea counter for all things not Lipton. Open daily 11:30am-4pm and 6-11pm. **$**

Lupe's East L.A. Kitchen, 110 Sixth Ave., at Watts St. (☎966-1326). Lupe's is a small, downscale cantina: one of the cheaper and tastier spots around. Burritos and enchiladas ($8-10) with beer are extremely filling. The Super Vegetarian Burrito ($7.50) and the Taquito Platter ($7.50) are super-tasty, as are the *huevos cubanos*—eggs any style with black beans and sweet plantain ($6-7). 4 types of hot-pepper sauce provided for those who crave fire. Brunch ($4-8) served Sa-Su 11:30am-4pm; open Su-Tu 11:30am-11pm, W-Sa 11:30am-midnight. **$**

SHOPS

Gourmet Garage, 453 Broome St., at Mercer St. (☎941-5850). The Garage is organic-intensive, purveying pastas, fresh produce, salads, and teas. Shhh...the Garage's best kept secret is that you can sample olives here to your heart's content. Open daily 7am-9pm.

Dean and Deluca, 560 Broadway, at Prince St. (☎226-6800). This gourmet shop is more gallery than grocery. The colors, smells, packaging, and presentation here are all exquisite. You might be able to afford a lollipop. Open M-Sa 10am-8pm, Su 10am-7pm.

TRIBECA

While dining in TriBeCa may be funkier than the experience in SoHo, the prices have begun to match those of its northern counterpart. Most of the restaurants cater to a wealthier, *chic*-er adult set. For really cheap fare head to the borders of TriBeCa, especially around **Chambers and Church Sts.** (which have a handful of **halal** eateries).

see map p. 321
Bar Odeon, 138 W. Broadway between Thomas and Duane Sts. (☎233-6436). Tasty French-American served in a casual setting. Entrees $11-20. Open M-Th 11:30am-midnight, F-Su 11-12:30am. **$$**

Bubby's, 120 Hudson St., at N. Moore St. (☎219-0666). Rough brick walls, un-upholstered window seats, and two walls of windows add to this cafe's stylish simplicity. Scones, muffins, and pies keep this place, originally a pie company, packed with locals; entrees ($9-15) are a bit expensive, but great soups and salads ($5-10) can fill you up. Brunch Sa-Su 9am-4:45pm; expect a wait. Open M-Tu 8am-11pm, W-F 8am-3am, Sa 9am-3am, Su 9am-10pm. **$$-$$$**

El Teddy's, 219 W. Broadway between Franklin and White Sts. (☎941-7070). You'll definitely have no trouble finding it—the monstrous, stained-glass awning hangs over windows of light-up whirligigs. First-rate, creative Mexican cuisine with a strong dose of California health food. Soups and salads $6-7; quesadillas around $8. Open M-F noon-3pm and 6-11:30pm, Th-Sa 6pm-1am, Su 6-11pm. **$-$$**

Pakistan Tea House, 176 Church St. between Duane and Read Sts. (☎240-9800). Perennially busy hole-in-the-wall eatery simmers with Tandoori dishes and other traditional Pakistani favorites. Their combo plates ($4) are an amazing deal. All meat is **halal.** Open daily 11am-4:30pm. **$**

Uptown Juice Bar, 116 Chambers St. (☎964-4316). Vegetarian and vegan platters, burgers, sandwiches, salads and pastries all under $9 (most under $5). 10% off with student ID. Open M-F 7am-8pm, Sa 7am-6pm. **$**

Yaffa's Tea Room, 19 Harrison St. between Church St. and W. Broadway (☎274-9403). In an eclectic arrangement of used furniture and hipsters, Yaffa's serves a very cool high tea ($20, reservations required), from M-Sa 2-6pm; it includes cucumber, salmon, or watercress finger sandwiches, fresh-baked scones, a dessert sampler, and a pot of tea. Sandwiches $8.50-11; salads $6-11; entrees $9-15. "Couscous Night" Th 6:30pm-midnight. The attached bar/restaurant is less subdued, with a different menu (including tapas). Bar/restaurant open Su-Th noon-2am, F-Sa noon-4am; tea room open 8:30am-midnight. **$$-$$$**

GREENWICH VILLAGE

The West Village's free-floating, artistic spirit spawns many creative eateries and even makes stumbling around looking for food as much fun as dining. Take our suggestions into consideration, but you must walk the circuitous streets and look for yourself—you will be richly, deliciously rewarded.

see map
pp. 322–323 **Chez Brigitte,** 77 Greenwich Ave. between Seventh Ave. and Bank St. (☎929-6736). This hole-in-the-wall French diner-cum-bistro is the darling of the *New Yorker* for its $7.50-9 French entrées. Cash only. Open daily 11am-10pm. **$**

Home, 20 Cornelia St. between W. 4th and Bleecker Sts. (☎243-9579). American neighborhood cuisine served in an intimate brownstone dining room. Crispy potato wrapped grilled vegetables with roasted tomatoes and garlicky greens, $16. AmEx. Sa-Su brunch 11am-4pm. M-Sa dinner 6-11pm, Su 5:30-10:30pm. **$$**

John's Pizzeria, 278 Bleecker St. between Seventh Ave. S. and Morton St. (☎243-1680). They don't serve slices, and only have standard toppings like pepperoni, anchovies, mushrooms, and the like, but John's is widely regarded as Manhattan's best pizzeria. Two sizes, small and large, $9-19.50. Cash only. Open M-Th 11:30am-11:30pm, F-Sa 11:30am-12:30pm, Su noon-11:30pm. **$-$$**

Tartine, 253 W. 11th St., at W. 4th St. (☎229-2611). Bring your own wine to complement a fine Continental lunch, brunch or dinner in the serene sidewalk seating of this secluded West Village bistro. Entrées are delicately prepared and reasonably priced (chicken sautéd in lemon and sage, $13). *Prix-fixe* Su brunch $9.75. Cash only. Open M-Sa 9am-10:30pm, Su 9am-10pm. **$$**

Arturo's Pizza, 106 W. Houston St. at Thompson St. (☎677-3820). Arturo's has served up great, cheap pizza and divey class for decades now. The big, cheesey pies ($10-17) are divine. Entrees range from $11-28. Live jazz M-F 9pm-1am, Sa-Su 9pm-2am. Open M-Th 4pm-1am, F-Sa 4pm-2am, Su 3pm-midnight. **$**

Cucina Stagionale, 275 Bleecker St. (☎924-2707), at Jones St. Italian dining in a low-key, classy environment. Packed on weekends, lines reach the street. The *conchiglie* (shells and sauteed calamari in spicy red sauce, $8) or the spinach and cheese ravioli ($7) will tell you why. Pasta dishes $7-10; veal, chicken, and fish dishes $8-13. If you get dessert, the bill still won't exceed $15. Cash only. No alcohol, but you may bring your own. Open daily noon-midnight. **$**

Eva's, 11 W. 8th St. between MacDougal St. and Fifth Ave. (☎677-3496). Refreshing fast-ser-vice health food. Massive veggie plate with falafel, grape leaves, and eggplant salad $5.55. Vita-min store in back adds to the anti-ambience. Open M-Sa 11am-11pm, Su 11am-10pm. $

Olive Tree Cafe, 117 MacDougal St., north of Bleecker St. (☎254-3480). Standard Middle Eastern food offset by endless stimulation. If you get bored by the old movies on the wide screen, you can rent chess, backgammon, and Scrabble sets ($1), doodle with chalk on the slate tables, or sit on the patio and survey the Village nightlife. Falafel sandwich $2.75; chicken kebab platter with salad, rice pilaf, and vegetable $8.75; delicious egg creams $2. Open daily 11am-4am. $

Peanut Butter & Co., 240 Sullivan St. at 3rd St. (☎677-3995). This odd peanut-colored restau-rant aims to make you feel like a kid again. All sandwiches include fresh peanut butter (ground daily). Sandwiches $4-7. Open Su-W noon-9pm, Th noon-10pm, F-Sa noon-midnight.

The Pink Teacup, 42 Grove St. between Bleecker and Bedford St. (☎807-6755). Soul food in a small, pink, and friendly environment. As multiple Martin Luther King, Jrs. gaze at you from the walls, you can sit at the table of brotherhood and swoon over tasty fried chicken. Steep dinner prices, but the $6.25 lunch special (M-F 11am-2pm) includes choice of fried chicken or stew, soup and salad, two vegetables, and dessert. Coffee, eggs, and fritters can feed two for under $10. Cash only. Bring your own booze. Open Su-Th 8am-midnight, F-Sa 8am-1am. $-$$

Ray's Pizza, 465 Sixth Ave. at 11th St. (☎243-2253). Half the uptown joints claim the title of "Original Ray's," but here's the real McCoy. People have flown here from Europe just to bring back a few pies, while kids from neighboring P.S. 41 have had first dates here. Well worth braving lines and paying upwards of $1.90 for a cheese-heavy slice. Scant seating; get pizza to go. Open Su-Th 11am-2am, F-Sa 11am-3am. $

Spain, 113 W. 13th St. between Sixth and Seventh Aves. (☎929-9580). Enormous tureens of traditional Spanish food for $9-19. The entrees can easily satisfy 2 or even 3 people (sharing incurs an extra $2 charge). Try the *paellas* or anything with garlic. Tantalizing and *free* appetizers such as *chorizo*. Cash only. Open daily noon-1am. $$

Day-O, 103 Greenwich Ave. (☎924-3168), between Jane and W. 12th St. AmEx, MC, V. Spicy concoctions of Caribbean and Southern cuisine with the most soul on the West Village. Firebird Jerk Chicken Wings $8. BBQ Ribs $18. Open Su-W noon-10:30pm, Th-Sa noon-1am.

CAFES

Caffè Dante, 79 MacDougal St. south of Bleecker St. (☎982-5275). A Village staple, with black-and-white photos of the Old World and atmospheric lighting. *Frutta di bosco* (cream pastry with fruit) $5.25, coffee-based liquids $2-6, nice *gelati* and Italian ices around $5. You'll love the matchbooks. A great place to take Beatrice. Open daily 10am-3am.

Caffè Mona Lisa, 282 Bleecker St. near Jones St. (☎929-1262). Like the coffee here, *La Gio-conda*'s recurring image is strong but not overpowering. In addition to well-brewed beverages ($1.25-4.50) and other cafe fare, Mona Lisa's oversized mirrors, stuffed chairs, and eccentric fur-niture pieces will make you smile enigmatically. Open daily 11am-2am.

LOWER EAST SIDE

Essex St. has **delis** that are reminiscent of the area's Yiddish past. Many of the stores close in observance of the Sabbath, sundown Friday to sun-down Saturday, so make sure you stock up on your deli delectables during the week.

see map
pp. 326–327

☒ **El Sombrero,** 108 Stanton St., on the corner of Ludlow St. (☎254-4188). If the gods ate at a Mexican restaurant (and lived on a budget), they'd dine here. The crowd is animated and vibrant, eating large portions of excellent food. Vegetable enchiladas ($8) make a satisfying meal, but you'll marvel at the Fajitas Mexicana ($10). Quench your thirst with variously sized margaritas (small, a mere $3) and beer. Hours vary, but opens around noon and closes at midnight or slightly later. Cash only. $$

☒ **Katz's Delicatessen,** 205 E. Houston St., near Orchard St. (☎254-2246 or 800-4HOT-DOG). Since 1888, Katz's has remained an authentic Jewish deli. Katz's widened its appeal with its "Send a salami to your boy in the army" campaign during WWII. (Rumor has it that Katz's is considering updating their motto to "Send a salami to your boy in Armani" to reflect changes in the neighborhood.) Every president in the last 2 decades has proudly received a Katz salami. The food is orgasmic (as Meg Ryan confirmed, when she made a loud scene here in *When Harry Met Sally*), but you pay extra for the atmosphere. Heroes $5.10, knishes $2.25, franks $2.15, sandwiches around $9. Open Su-Tu 8am-10pm, W-Th 8am-11pm, F-Sa 8am-3am. **$-$$**

Grilled Cheese, 168 Ludlow St., south of Stanton St. (☎982-6600). Nothing complicated, this tiny sliver of a joint serves up freshly made sandwiches, homemade ice cream sandwiches ($4), and salads ($5-6), as well as delectable liquids (espresso milkshakes $4). Besides their regular sandwiches ($6), the grilled cheeses have various permutations, composed of choices of bread, cheeses, toppings, and spreads ($4). Pop in and savor the simple things in life. Open daily noon-midnight. **$**

Casa Mexicana, 133 Ludlow St., at Rivington St. (☎473-4100). Although this restaurant has oddly kitschy decor, the food is authentically Mexican. Try the *molcajete ranchero* (chicken $8, sirloin $9), a meat dish served with charred cactus and their homemade salsa. Open Su-Th 11am-5pm and 6pm-midnight, F-Sa 11am-5pm and 6pm-1am. **$-$$**

Yoshi, 201 E. Houston St., near Orchard St. (☎539-0225). Soothing green pastel and light wood interior sets the classy stage for Japanese food at a very reasonable price. Sushi-sashimi combo $13. Beer, wine, and sake available. Open daily 5pm-1am. **$$**

Tiengarden, 170 Allen St. (☎388-1364). A very Zen restaurant that goes beyond vegan cuisine, refraining from including any of the five impurities that could damage your *Chi*. Kosher...Asian style. The spicy organic tofu ($6.50) still has plenty of flavor. No alcohol. Open Su-F noon-4pm and 5-10pm. Cash only. **$**

CAFES

Rivington 99 Cafe, 99 Rivington St., at Ludlow St. (☎358-1191). Sometimes you want nothing more than a cup of coffee and a place to read the paper from cover-to-cover (or at least the Style section), and this locals' cafe is it. Open M-Sa 9am-7pm, Su 10am-6pm.

Pink Pony Café, 176 Ludlow St. between E. Houston and Stanton Sts. (☎253-1922). This self-consciously trendy cafe/ice cream parlor/performance space catering to the Lower East Side artistic set is decorated in a style that joins American retro and Las Vegas glam. Try their lemon-and-ginger drink ($1.50). Performance space in back lends itself to stand-up comedy and screenings; call for schedule. Comfy chairs and couches. Pick up flyers for local performance and music events. Open Su-Th 10:30am-midnight, F-Sa 10:30am-4am.

SHOPS

▩ **Economy Candy,** 108 Rivington St. (☎254-1531). Imported chocolates, jams, and countless confections fill this store, all at rock-bottom prices. Step into this sweet-tooth's heaven and treat yourself to a huge bag of gummi bears ($2) or a pound of chocolate-covered apricots ($5). They also have cotton candy ($2), and Turkish desserts, as well as a selection of spices. Open M-F 8:30am-6pm, Sa 10am-5pm, Su 8:30am-5pm.

▩ **Guss Lower East Side Pickle Corp.,** 35 Essex St., at Hester St. (☎254-4477 or 800-252-4877). Pickles and poultry used to be sold in pushcarts until 1938, when they were abolished for hygiene

Milady's Bar

Tom's Restaurant

Tavern on the Green

and health reasons. Tradition continues at Guss's, selling glorious gherkins straight out of vats, from super-sour to sweet (individual 50¢-$2; quart $4). They also offer cole slaw, pickled tomatoes, carrots, and t-shirts ($10). Open Su-Th 9am-6pm, F 9am-4pm.

Yonah Schimmel Knishery, 137 E. Houston St. (☎477-2858). Rabbi Schimmel's establishment since 1910, it makes the act of knishery an art. A dozen varieties available for $1.75. Try yogurt from the 88-year-old strain for $1.50. Open daily 8:30am-6pm except during the Sabbath.

EAST VILLAGE

see map
pp. 326–327

This is probably the best area in the city for the budget traveler to sample the world of New York food for under $10. **First and Second Aves.** have a top-notch restaurant selection in a variety of ethnicities. **St. Mark's Pl.** hosts a slew of inexpensive and popular village institutions. At night, **Avenue A** throbs with bars and sidewalk cafes. A whole row of Indian restaurants line **6th St.** between First and Second Aves.

🔳 **Yakitori Taisho,** 5 St. Mark's Pl. (☎228-5086). Look for the huge red paper lantern out front. This authentic dive serves good Japanese fare at wonderful prices. 10 skewers of chicken and vegetables $12, cold ramen $4, chicken teriyaki $7. Open daily 11am-11pm. **$**

🔳 **Frank's,** 88 Second Ave., at E. 5th St. (☎420-0202). An adorable sliver of a place with a friendly bistro feeling. Breakfasts are served in sets ($6 or $9); lunch menu centers around healthy sandwiches ($6-8) and pasta ($9-10). Dinner fare is more expensive. M-F 5:30-7pm is Aperitivo Hour—free antipasti until 6:30pm. Expect a wait for seats. Open for lunch daily 10:30am-4pm; dinner M-Th 5pm-1am, F-Sa 5pm-2am, Su 5pm-midnight. **$-$$**

Bulgin' Waffles Cafe, 49.5 First Ave., at E. 3rd St. (☎477-6555). Decorated in a Latin tone, this cute cafe encourages taking a *siesta* in between meal hours. Serves waffles ($4) and wafflettes (hazelnut $2). Drinks $1-4. Open Tu-F 8am-2pm and 4-10pm, Sa 10am-10pm, Su 10am-4pm. **$**

`**Cucina di Pesce,** 87 E. 4th St. between Second and Third Aves. (☎260-6800). Classic little Italian place with oil paintings, rosily-lit nooks, and sidewalk seating. Dishes are relatively inexpensive and large. Spinach penne (with asparagus, sundried tomatoes, and fontina cheese) $8; salmon with sauteed mushrooms and pasta $11. Free mussels at the bar as you wait for your table. Daily special M-F 4-6:30pm, Sa-Su 4-6pm: full dinner with bread, soup, entree, and glass of wine $10. Open Su-Th 4pm-midnight, F-Sa 4pm-1am. **$-$$**

Damask Falafel, 89 Ave. A between E. 5th and 6th Sts. (☎673-5016). This closet-sized stand serves the cheapest and best falafel in the area—$2.50 for a sandwich; $3.50 for a falafel platter with tabouli, chick peas, salad, and pita bread; $2.50 for two succulent stuffed grape leaves. Open M-F 11am-2am, Sa-Su 11am-4am. **$**

Dojo Restaurant, 24 St. Mark's Pl. between Second and Third Aves. (☎674-9821). One of the most popular restaurants and hangouts in the East Village, it offers an incredible variety of vegetarian and Japanese foods that combine the healthy with the cheap and inexplicably tasty. You can even take home a container of Dojo's renowned carrot dressing. Soyburgers with brown rice and salad $3.50. Dojo salad $5. Yakisoba $5-7. Beer $2.75-4; pitchers $12-15. Outdoor tables imbued with noisy St. Mark's ambience. Open Su-Th 11am-1am, F-Sa 11am-2am. **Also at** 14 W. 4th St. between Broadway and Mercer St. (☎505-8934). **$**

Elvie's Turo-Turo, 214 First Ave. between 12th and 13th Sts. (☎473-7785). Pan-asian food served cafeteria-style. There's no menu here—you just point to what you want. Choose from dishes like *pancit* (a stir-fried rice noodle dish), chicken adobo, and pork and chicken barbecue. One dish $4, two for $5.75. Open M-Sa 11am-9pm, Su 11am-8pm. **$**

Flor's Kitchen, 149 First Ave., at 9th St. (☎387-8949). Small Venezuelan restaurant serving up all sorts of *arepas* (filled corn cakes, $2.75-3.25) and *empanadas* ($2.75). The beet soup is quite good ($2.50-4). Open M-Th 11am-11pm, F-Sa 11am-midnight, Su 10am-10pm. **$**

Kate's Joint, 58 Ave. B between 4th and 5th Sts. (☎777-7059). Good vegan with a groovy flair. This couch-lined, chill eatery delivers veggie fare like tofu teriyaki ($10), unsausage patty ($1.25), and unturkey club ($7). Lunch special daily 9am-4pm for $5 (selections like vegan pancakes and cheese omelette). Pick up flyers of local events here. Open daily 9am-1am. **$**

The Kiev, 117 Second Ave., at 7th St. (☎674-4040). A funky Eastern European breakfast extravaganza. A cup of homemade soup comes with an inch-thick slab of challah ($2.50). Lengthy menu features sandwiches of all sorts, along with potato pancakes, *kasha varnishke,* and more *pierogi* than you could shake a schtick at. Open 24hr. **$**

La Focacceria, 128 First Ave. between St. Mark's Pl. and 7th St. (☎254-4946). Serving delectable Sicilian eats for 85 years. The *vesteddi* (fried ricotta and kashkaval cheese, $2) and Sicilian-style eggplant sandwiches ($5) are exceptional. Open M-Th 11am-10pm, F-Sa 1-11pm. **$**

Mama's Food Shop, 200 E. 3rd St. between Aves. A and B (☎777-4425). See laid-back Villagers obeying Mama's order to "Shut up and Eat." Fried chicken or salmon (each $7) with sides like honey-glazed sweet potatoes and broccoli or couscous ($1 each). Vegetarian dinner includes any 3 sides ($7). Bread pudding and cobbler come by the ½ pint ($3), if you have room left for dessert. Open M-Sa 11am-11pm. Mama has recently created a doppelganger for herself with **Step Mama's,** across the street at 199 E. 3rd St. (☎228-2663), which sells sandwiches, soups, and sides. The nourishment continues next door at **Mama's Milk,** a new, creative smoothie shop. **$**

National Café, 210 First Ave., at 13th St. (☎473-9354). Home cooking, Cuban style. It's hard to find a better Cuban lunch special in the city; from 10:30am-3pm the National serves an entree of the day, rice and beans or salad, plantain, a cup of soup, and bread for $4.25. Even without the specials, everything on this garlic-heavy menu is well under $10. Open M-Sa 11am-10pm. **$**

Rose of India, 308 E. 6th St. between First and Second Aves. (☎533-5011 or 473-9758). Decorated like a Christmas tree, the Rose of India demonstrates the difficulty of advertising on a block covered in Indian restaurants. The food, however, is a definite stand-out. Curries with rice, *dal,* and chutney $5-7. Nine different breads $1.75-3, samosas $2. Great lunch special ($5). Bring your own booze. Make reservations on weekends. Open daily noon-1am. **$**

Sahara East, 184 First Ave. between 11th and 12th Sts. (☎353-9000). The culinary fare here is standard Middle Eastern ($5 for salads, $11 for meat entrees), but the restaurant has other benefits: a hookah ($5) den in the back garden. Puff away at the fruity (legal) substance and make like you're the caterpillar from *Alice in Wonderland.* Belly dancing on Friday and Saturday nights. Open M-F 9am-3am, Sa-Su 9am-4am. **$-$$**

2nd Ave. Delicatessen, 156 Second Ave., at 10th St. (☎677-0606). Established in 1954, this is *the* definitive New York deli. The Lebewohl family has proudly maintained this strictly kosher joint since 1954. Meals served with an array of pickles. Try the chopped liver ($6.50), *babka* ($3.25), *kasha varnishkes* ($4), or mushroom barley ($4), all reputed to be among the best in the city. Open Su-Th 8am-midnight, F-Sa 8am-3am. (See **Sights,** p. 78.) **$**

St. Dymphna's, 118 St. Mark's Pl. between First Ave. and Ave. A (☎254-6636). Modern Irish food, a full bar, and a lush garden out back. The beef and Guinness casserole ($10) and chicken, smoky bacon, and wild mushroom pie ($12.50) shame average pies. Open for lunch M-F 10am-4pm; dinner daily 5pm-midnight; brunch Sa-Su 10am-5pm. Bar open daily until 4am. **$-$$**

Two Boots Restaurant, 37 Ave. A at 3rd St. (☎505-2276). Which 2 boots? Italy and Louisiana. A swinging East Village *mezcla* of Cajun and Italian, this establishment packs locals with its hybrid pizzas ($5.95-22) and po'boys ($5-6). Has a **video store** attached; daily pizza/video combo specials. **Den of Cin** (below the video store) is a screening room/performance space (☎254-1441). The recognizably colorful Two Boots also exists as **take-out on Bleecker St.** and Broadway (☎777-1033) and in the West Village (☎633-9096). Open daily noon-midnight. **$-$$**

Veselka, 144 Second Ave., at 9th St. (☎228-9682). "Traditional food served in a friendly, non-traditional setting" boasts the menu. Big, beautiful murals adorn everything, including the dumpster around the corner. Enormous menu includes 7 varieties of soups, as well as salads, blintzes, meats, and other Eastern European fare. Combination special gets you soup, salad, stuffed cabbage, and four melt-in-your-mouth *pierogi* ($8). Great breakfast specials: challah french toast, OJ, and coffee for $4.25 Open 24hr. **$**

Whole Earth Bakery and Kitchen, 130 St. Mark's Pl. between First Ave. and Ave. A (☎677-7597). Inspired by the owner's 87-year-old mother, Whole Earth gives home cooking a strictly vegan tweak. The baked goods are shockingly tasty *sans* eggs. Ask for flavorful tofu/garlic spread on other items. Cookies 50¢-$2; fruit cobbler $1.50; oil/sugar-free muffins $1.50; veggie burger $3.50. The owner also custom-designs vegan wedding cakes. Open daily 9am-12:30am. **$**

Yaffa Café, 97 St. Mark's Pl. between First Ave. and Ave. A (☎674-9302 or 677-9001). Cocktail garden party meets Indian disco lounge, this "open always" cafe has great food and fabulous ambience. All sorts of sandwiches ($4-7), salads (around $6), and a multitude of entrees. Beer $3.50. The outdoor garden is open all summer and is a work of art itself. Open 24hr. **$**

CAFES

Alt.Coffee, 139 Ave. A, at E. 9th St. (☎529-CAFE). This cafe is a haven for artists, anarchists, and alterna-types galore. Offering all sorts of (non-alcoholic) liquids ($1.50-3.75), sandwiches, and vegan cookies ($2.25), as well as internet access ($10/hour). Local art adorns the walls. And yes, you can smoke here. Open M-Th 8:30am-1:30am, F 8:30am-3am, Sa 10am-3am, Su 10am-1:30am.

SHOPS

Moishe's Bake Shop, 115 Second Ave. between 6th and 7th Sts. (☎505-8555). For 30 years this bake shop has served up strictly kosher, *geshmak* (that's Yiddish for tasty) breads and cookies. Challah $2.75. Open Su 7am-8pm, M-Th 7:30am-8:30pm, F 7am until 1hr. before sunset.

Something Sweet, 177 First Ave., at 11th St. (☎533-9986). Delectable and inventive sweets that give Veniero's a run for its money. Indulge in a tropical fruit tart ($2.25), a mousse tart ($2), or a *crème brulée* ($2.25). Open M-Sa 8am-8pm, Su 9:30am-5:30pm.

Veniero's, 342 E. 11th St. between First and Second Aves. (☎674-7070). Established in 1894, this Italian pastry shop has clogged the arteries of many sweets-lovers and packs in loyal patrons. Spacious cafe seating. Cannolis $1.25-1.50. Open Su-Th 8am-midnight, F-Sa 8am-1am.

CHELSEA

From 14th to 23rd Sts., restaurants combine Central American and Chinese cuisine, as well as varieties of Cajun and Creole specialties. The neighborhood's enthusiastic gay contingent has inspired many fashionable watering holes and diners. **Eighth Ave.** between provides stylish restaurants and cafes. (See also **Gay and Lesbian Life,** p. 221.)

see map
pp. 328–329

⊠ Kitchen, 218 Eighth Ave., near 21st St. (☎243-4433). Cooks Mexican food to go and hawks books, Mexican paraphenalia, and a large number of spices. Burrito stuffed with pinto beans, rice, and green salsa $6.25-6.50. $12.50 delivery min. Open M-Sa 9am-10:30pm, Su 11am-10:30pm. **$**

⊠ Soups on Seventeen, 307 W. 17th St., off Eighth Ave. (☎255-1505). This eatery will liquify your mind with the astounding things it does to soup. Daily rotations of soup, sandwich, or salad with bread, fruit, and cookie $5-7 for 16 oz., $9-13 for 32 oz. Open M-Sa 11am-7pm. **$**

Food Bar, 149 Eighth Ave. (☎243-2020). A truly fabulous eatery that features relatively cheap sandwiches ($7) and large-portioned entrees ($11). Sit at a window seat to people-watch. Take-out available. Open M-Th 11am-4pm and 5-11:30pm, F 11am-4pm and 5pm-midnight, Sa 5pm-midnight, Su 5-11:30pm. **$-$$**

Bendix Diner, 219 Eighth Ave., at 21st St. (☎366-0560). A successful new hybrid—the Thai greasy spoon—it features American grub and Thai chow, sporting "Get Fat!" as its motto. Entrees around $8, sandwiches $4-8, "Thai breakfast" $3-3.50. Breakfast available all day. Open M-W 8am-midnight, Th-Sa 8am-1am, Su 8am-11pm. **$**

Blue Moon Mexican Cafe, 150 Eighth Ave. between 17th and 18th Sts. (☎463-0560). A funky hangout, this cafe offers Happy Hour daily 4-7pm ($4 margaritas, $3 beer and sangria), as well as weekend brunch serving mimosas and other alcoholic beverages (around $8). Mexican fare entrees $11. Brunch 11:30am-4pm. Su-Th noon-11pm, F-Sa 11:30am-midnight. **$-$$**

Caesar's, 206 Seventh Ave. between 21st and 22nd Sts. (☎366-4865). No-frills Greek-Mediterranean-diner grub in an airy joint decorated in blues, cabaret-style. Advertises a "smoking section." Couch lounge in back; open front window onto the street in summer. Entrees around $6. Turkish coffee $2. Juice/smoothie bar $3-4. Open 24hr. **$**

Intermezzo, 202 Eighth Ave. between 20th and 21st Sts. (☎929-3433). Intimate, popular Italian restaurant offers ample, inventive antipasti and salads. If you want a full meal for dinner, your cheapest bet is the $9.95 *prix fixe* menu (M-F 4-6pm). The lunch menu also offers tasty dishes for $6-9 (M-F noon-4pm). Brunch ($6) served Sa-Su noon-4pm. Open Su-Th noon-11pm, F-Sa noon-midnight. **$-$$**

Mary Ann's, 116 Eighth Ave., at 16th St. (☎633-0877). Benevolent waiters serve up huge portions of inventive Mexican cuisine in this white-walled restaurant slung with lights. Entrees $8-12. $1 Corona with entree on Th. Open M-Tu noon-10:30pm, W-Th 11:30am-11pm, F-Sa 11:30am-11pm, Su noon-10pm. Cash only. **$-$$**

Negril, 362 W. 23rd St. between Eighth and Ninth Aves. (☎807-6411). Colorful decor and excellent Jamaican food in this gay-friendly eatery. Dinner options are mid-priced, but lunch is affordable—around $8. Open M 5pm-midnight, Tu-Th noon-midnight, F-Sa noon-1am. Lively bar open F-Sa until 2am. **$-$$**

Spring Joy, 172 Eighth Ave. between 18th and 19th Sts. (☎243-1688). Although the city seems to have fallen out of love with Chinese food, Spring Joy serves up good Chinese food at even more shocking prices. Numerous lunch options under $5; dinner $5.75-8.50. Design your own dish $7; diet options $6-8.50. *And* free white wine with your dinner. Open M-F 11:30am-midnight, Sa-Su noon-midnight. **$**

UNION SQUARE AND GRAMERCY PARK

see map
pp. 328–329

This slightly gentrified, ethnically diverse neighborhood provides visitors honest meals and reasonable prices. On Lexington and Third Ave., in the upper 20s and lower 30s, a small cluster of Pakistani and Indian restaurants and other ethnic cuisine restaurants battle for customers. The area around Union Square offers an equally diverse, albeit trendier, dining experience. Sprinkled throughout the area are Korean delis where you can fill up with prepared pastas, salads, and hot entrees.

▨ **Pete's Tavern,** 129 E. 18th St., at the corner of Irving Pl. (☎473-7676). "NY's oldest original bar," legend has it that O. Henry wrote *The Gift of the Magi* in one of its booths. Since 1864, this tavern continues to serve sandwiches ($7) and entrees (veal cutlet parmigiana $10) at modest prices, retaining its old pub atmosphere. Kitchen open daily 11am-1am. **$-$$**

▨ **Jai-Ya,** 396 Third Ave. between 28th and 29th Sts. (☎889-1330). Critics rave over the Thai (and other Asian) food, with three degrees of spiciness, from mild to "help-me-I'm-on-fire." The soothing interior tangoes with budget prices and a decidedly upscale look. Most dishes $7-11. Vegetarian options available. Lunch specials M-F 11:30am-3pm. Open M-F 11am-midnight, Sa 11:30am-midnight, Su 5pm-midnight. Also at 81-11 Broadway in Elmhurst, Queens (☎718-651-1330). **$$**

Candela, 116 E. 16th St. between Park Ave. South and Irving Pl. (☎254-1600). Cavernous and candlelit, this modern Gothic, stylish American eatery features expensive entrees and gracious service well worth the price. Dining outside in warmer weather can be a delight, but don't expect a view. Visit at lunchtime for moderately-priced meals (seared tuna salad $12.50, exotic mushroom ravioli $12.50). Promoters are known to throw parties on Friday nights—call ahead to inquire. Open M-F 11:30am-3pm, M-Su 5:30-11pm, Su brunch 11am-3pm. Bar opens at 5pm. **$$-$$$**

▨ **Basta Pasta,** 37 W. 17th St. between Fifth and Sixth Aves. (☎366-0888). A true fusion attempt, this eatery combines Japanese flavors with Italian dishes (spaghetti with flying fish roe and Japanese basil $12). *Prix fixe* lunch is available from noon-2:30pm for $14 or $26. Open M-F noon-2:30pm and 6-11pm, Sa 6-11pm. **$$**

Chat 'n' Chew, 10 E. 16th St. between Union Sq. and Fifth Ave. (☎243-1616). This 1920s ice cream parlour-esque diner serves up simple cuisine. Heaping plates of macaroni and cheese ($7.25), classic grilled cheese with tomato ($6), and "Not your Mother's Meatloaf" ($11.25). Open M-Th 11:30am-11:30pm, F-Sa 10:30am-11:30pm, Su 10:30am-11pm. AmEx, V, MC. **$-$$**

Moonstruck, 449 Third Ave., at 31st St. (☎213-1100). This updated diner offers an array of Greek and American fare. Gorge on a staggering array of sandwich options including the Moonstruck Burger ($7.85) and such traditional diner fare as Silver Dollar Griddlecakes ($5.90. Most entrees hover between $10-14, but pasta dishes are a bit cheaper ($9.75). Open Su-W 6am-12:30am, Th-Sa 24hr. **$-$$**

on the cheap

kreme of the krop

What's so amazing about **Krispy Kreme** donuts? Watch as the pale dough rings become a delightful golden-tan, ride a conveyor belt under a waterfall of glaze, and finally get picked up by the workers (who stick a straw through the middle so as not to flaw the masterpiece) to end up in your welcoming mouth. Absolutely get one straight off the belt (only glazed are made hot during the day) nothing compares to a rispy reme **(85¢).**

Harlem: 280 125th St., at Eighth Ave. (☎531-0111). Open daily 6am-10pm. Hot glazed every 10min. 6-11am and 4-8pm.

Upper West: 141 W. 72nd St. between Broadway and Columbus Ave. (☎724-1100). Open Su-Th 6am-10pm, F-Sa 6am-midnight. Hot glazed every 10min. 6-11am and 5pm-1hr. before closing.

Upper East: 1493 Third Ave. between 84th and 85th Sts. (☎879-9111). Open daily 6am-10pm. Hot glazed 6-11am and 5-9pm.

Chelsea: 265 W. 23rd St. between Seventh and Eighth Aves. (☎620-0111). Open Su-Th 6am-10pm, F-Sa 6am-midnight. Hot glazed every 10min. 6-11am and 5-9pm.

Tibetan Kitchen, 444 Third Ave. between 30th and 31st Sts. (☎679-6286). This tiny place serves excellent food true to its Tibetan roots—meatier than Chinese, with a dollop of Indian. *Momo* (beef dumplings, $7.50) and *bocha* (buttered, salted tea, $3.25) are both delicious. Veggie dishes are plentiful ($6.75-8). Open M-F noon-3pm and 5-11pm, Sa 5-11pm. **$**

Zen Palate, 34 E. Union Sq., across from Union Sq. Park (☎614-9291). *The* Asian-fusion chain for hipsters. Asian-inspired vegetarian/vegan cuisine, including soothing, healthy, and fabulously fresh treats like "Shredded Heaven" (assorted veggies and spring rolls with brown rice, $8.45), stir-fried rice fettuccini with mushrooms ($7.65), or other concoctions on brown rice/seaweed/kale. Fresh-squeezed juices or rice milkshakes $1.75-3. Open M-Th and Su 11am-10:45pm, F-Sa 11am-11:45pm. **Other locations:** 663 9th Ave., at 46th St. (☎582-1669) and 2170 Broadway, at 76th St. (☎501-7768). **$-$$**

CAFES

Sunburnt Espresso Bar, 206 Third Ave., at 18th St. (☎674-1702). Despite its strained attempt at decor trendiness, this bakery-smelling cafe truly represents the diversity of the area's locals. Impressive selection of liquids and solids ($5), dreamy shakes and smoothies ($3.25-5), and fat-free muffins ($1.75). Lunch specials $5 or $7. Open daily 7am-11pm. **$**

Coffee Shop Bar, 29 Union Sq. West facing Union Sq. Park (☎243-7969). Open 23hrs. a day, this hangout combines classic American diner fare with a Brazilian twist. Waifs abound, but Twiggy figures aren't a likely result of the delicious food like the tasty *media noche* sandwich ($9). Good for dessert ($5-6), a very late dinner ($8-17), or watching others have dinner. Beers $4-6. Open daily 7am-6am. They card (21+) in the wee hours. AmEx, V, MC.

Guy & Gallard, 120 E. 34th St., at Lexington Ave. A juice/coffee bar complete with small bakery and deli sections (☎684-3898). Come in for your *chai* fix (steamed or iced $1.50-3) or coffee drinks ($1-4) and do some food shopping while you're at it when a Dean and Deluca is too far to get to in your heels. Scrumptious varieties of low-fat muffins and danishes available fresh in the mornings ($1.70). Later, a selection of appealing sandwiches go for around $5. Open daily 7am-9pm. **Other locations:** 475 Park Ave. South, 245 W. 38th St., 333 Seventh Ave., and 30 Broad St. AmEx, V, MC.

WEST MIDTOWN

see map
pp. 332–333

Your best budget bets generally lie along **Eighth Ave.** between 34th and 59th St. in the area known as **Hell's Kitchen.** Within the past few years this area has prospered enough to open up a fantastically diverse array of restaurants. Those willing to spend more should try a meal on posh **Restaurant Row** on 46th St. between Eighth and Ninth Ave. The block caters to a pre-theater crowd, so arriving after 8pm will make it easier to get a table. Celebrities occasionally drift over to **Sardi's**, 234 W. 44th St. (☎221-8440), and take a seat on the plush red leather, surrounded by caricatures of themselves and their best friends. Traditionally, on the opening night of a major Broadway play, the main star makes an entrance at Sardi's following the show—to hearty cheers for a superb performance or polite applause for a bomb. Several of the city's finest have excellent *prix fixe* lunch deals, which include an appetizer, entree, and dessert. **Le Beaujolais**, 364 W. 46th St. (☎974-7464), is a charming French bistro with a $14.25 lunch special. Unless otherwise noted, all restaurants accept major credit cards.

🗹 **Hourglass Tavern,** 373 W. 46th St. between Eighth and Ninth Aves. (☎265-2060). A dark, crowded, two-floor triangular joint on Restaurant Row with a changing menu that regularly features fresh fish, filet mignon, New York select steak, and various pasta dishes. Servers flip an hour-glass at your table when you sit down; the 59-min. time limit is strictly enforced when crowds are waiting. Dramatized in John Grisham's *The Firm* as the covert meeting place for two cloak-and-dagger types. *Prix fixe* entrees ($12-16) include soup and salad. Open M-W 5-11:15pm, Th-F 5-11:30pm. AmEx, Disc., MC, V. **$$**

Manganaro's, 488 Ninth Ave. between 37th and 38th Sts. (☎563-5331 or 800-4-SALAMI). This classy Italian grocery and restaurant retains all the authentic flavor of pre-gentrified Hell's Kitchen. The staff will construct the sandwich of your dreams; or select one from their vast menu ($3-12). Mail order groceries available to the U.S., Canada, and the Carribbean. AmEx, Disc., Diner's, MC, V. Open M-F 8am-7pm, Sa 9am-7pm; Dec.-May also Su 11am-5pm. **$-$$**

Becco, 355 W. 46th St. between Eighth and Ninth Aves. (☎397-7597). Gourmet cuisine that makes you forget your budget. Their 70 wines priced at $18 a bottle allows the luxury of selectivity minus the guilt of dropping a c-note (or two) before a Broadway show. For a $17 *prix fixe* lunch (dinner $22) you can have a gourmet *antipasto* platter or caesar salad, plus unlimited servings of the 3 pastas of the day. Open daily noon-3pm and 5pm-midnight. **$$$**

Carnegie Delicatessen, 854 Seventh Ave., at 55th St. (☎757-2245). One of New York's great delis. Ceiling fans whir overhead as photos of famous and well-fed customers stare down from the walls. After waiting in line, eat elbow-to-elbow at long tables and chomp on free dill pickles. First-timers shouldn't leave without trying the cheesecake (oy, it's so good!) topped with strawberries, blueberries, or cherries ($6.95). Cash only. Open daily 6:30am-4am. **$$**

Original Fresco Tortillas, 536 Ninth Ave. between 39th and 40th Sts. (☎465-8898). This tiny 9-seater could be Taco Bell's humbler, more dignified father. Excellent homemade food at fast-food prices: fajitas and tacos $1-2, quesadillas $2-4, giant burritos $4-5. No artificial or chemical spices, no MSG, no preservatives, no kidding. AmEx, MC, V. Open M-F 11am-11pm, Sa-Su noon-10pm. **$**

Sapporo, 152 W. 49th St. between Sixth and Seventh Aves. (☎869-8972). A Japanese diner, with the grill partially obscured by rice paper walls. A favorite spot for Broadway cast members and corporate types. Items listed on the wall in Japanese (the menu explains in English). Filling portions and astounding flavors. The Sapporo ramen special is only $7.30. Open M-Sa 11am-11:30pm, Su 11am-10:30pm. **$-$$**

EAST MIDTOWN

see map
pp. 332–333

Keep in mind that in Midtown, cash is king. Here, CEOs run their corporate empires by wining and dining their clients, while socialite shoppers drop as much money on a late lunch as on a Fendi tote. Budget travelers don't despair—underpaid underlings all scour for cheap lunches here. The 50s on **Second Ave.** and the area immediately surrounding Grand Central Terminal contain good, inexpensive fare. Grocery stores offer a salad and hot food alternative to the mad deli rush. Numerous public plazas and parks invite you to picnic; try **Greenacre Park**, 51st St. between Second and Third Aves., or **Paley Park**, 53rd St. between Fifth and Madison Aves. If you do want to splurge, many top restaurants offer relatively reasonable *prix fixe* lunch menus that include an appetizer, entree, and dessert. Try **Aureole**, 34 E. 61st St. between Madison and Park Aves., one of the best restaurants in the city. (☎319-1660; reservations required. 2-2:30pm, three-courses $20.

Coldwaters, 988 Second Ave. between 52nd and 53rd Sts. (☎888-2122). This recently renovated restaurant makes quite a catch with its brunch and dinner deals. Brunch ($9; 11am-3pm) tempts daily with 2 drinks (alcoholic or non) and choice of entree, salad, and fries. Dinner entrees come with all-you-can-eat salad, fries or baked potato, and a basket of fresh garlic bread. Idaho Rainbow Trout $10, Cajun Catfish $12. Open daily 11am-3am. AmEx, Diner's Club, Discover, MC, V. **$$**

◪ Dosanko, 423 Madison Ave. between 48th and 49th Sts. (☎688-8575). A welcome sanctuary from Midtown craziness, all is tranquil at this aromatic Japanese pit-stop. The *gyoza* ($4.50) is a favorite, as are the many varieties of *larmen* (Japanese noodle soup, $6-7). Cash only. Open M-F 11:30am-10pm, Sa-Su noon-8pm. **$$**

Fortune Garden, 845 Second Ave. between 45th and 46th Sts. (☎687-7471). Confucious say: You will go to a moderately overpriced Chinese restaurant. The food will be very good. You will consider getting take-out because it is cheaper. The specials ($6.25) will sound good to you. Open daily 11am-11pm. AmEx, MC, V. **$-$$**

Taipei Noodle House, 986 Second Ave. (☎759-7070). Great for a quick sit-down lunch, this house o' noodles will satisfy even the pickiest of eaters. Friendly, quick service. Entrees $6.50-9. The real deal is the weekday lunch special (M-Sa 11am-4pm) featuring entree, soup, rice, and egg roll for $4.75-6. Open M-Su 11am-midnight. AmEx, V, MC. **$-$$**

SHOPS

Food Emporium, 969 Second Ave. between 51st and 52nd Sts. (☎593-2224); **D'Agostino,** Third Ave. between 35th and 36th Sts. (☎684-3133); or **Associated Group Grocers,** 250 E. 65th St. (☎421-7673). Upscale supermarket chains with branches scattered throughout Manhattan. All feature reliable, well-stocked delis, fresh fruit and salad bars, ice cold drinks, gourmet ice cream, tons of munchies, and a storeful more. Standard prices.

Teuscher Chocolatier, 620 Fifth Ave., on the promenade at Rockefeller Center (☎246-4416). No Snickers or Kit-Kats here. A choco-holic's paradise, Teuscher offers the freshest chocolates flown in from Zurich weekly, and unfortunately have the prices to prove it. But don't let a little transatlantic overhead keep you from this experience—you can still savor a single piece for under $2. AmEx, V, MC.

UPPER EAST SIDE

see map
pp. 334–335

Meals on the Upper East Side descend in price as you move east away from Fifth Avenue's glitzy, mildly exorbitant museum cafes toward Lexington, Third, and Second Aves. Second and Third Aves., especially from the mid-70s to the mid-80s, boast *beaucoup* restaurants.

◪ Luncheonette, 1678 Third Ave. at 94th St. (☎831-1800). Enjoy big, tasty portions like "'Mom's Lovin' Meatloaf" ($11) in this restaurant full of dog paraphernalia, from the doghouse-shaped entrance to the pictures of celebrities and their hounds. Salads $5-9; sandwiches $6-8. Specials (M-F 5-7pm) come with soup or salad and dessert. Open daily 8am-11pm. **$-$$**

Candle Cafe, 1307 Third Ave., at 75th St. (☎472-0970). A vegan's delight, this restaurant manages to add a twist to organic ingredients, reinventing them into tasty dishes. Try the excellent Classic Caesar ($6) or Herbed Tofu Roller with grilled portabello mushrooms. Open M-Sa 11:30am-10:30pm, Su 11:30am-9:30pm. **$-$$**

EJ's Luncheonette, 1271 Third Ave., at 73rd St. (☎472-0600). Scrumptious fare, like the buttermilk pancakes ($6), served in hip 1950s diner-style decor, has gained the loyalty and devotion of many Upper Eastsiders. After all, what could be better than breakfast served all day? Open M-Sa 8am-11pm, Su 8am-10:30pm. **Other locations:** 477 Amsterdam Ave. between 81st and 82nd Sts. (☎873-3444); 432 Sixth Ave. between 9th and 10th Sts. (☎473-5555). **$**

El Pollo, 1746 First Ave. between 90th and 91st Sts. (☎996-7810). Providing authentic Peruvian cuisine and famous for its roasted, marinated, 7-flavored chicken, this restaurant also serves up delicacies like fried sweet plantains ($3) and papas con aji ($5). Half-chicken $6. Open M-F 11am-11pm, Sa-Su 12:30pm-10:45pm. **$-$$**

Hale and Hearty Soups, 849 Lexington Ave. between 64th and 65th Sts. (☎517-7600). Quick and friendly service, exciting daily specials served in filling portions with a slice of fresh bread or oysterettes. A mecca of over 40 different varieties of soup plus a "tossed-to-order" salad bar ($4-9). Great choices for vegetarians and diet-watchers. Cups $3-4, bowls $5, bread bowls $6. Half-sandwiches $4, whole $6. M-F 8:30am-8pm, Sa 10am-5:30pm, Su 11am-5pm. **$**

Jackson Hole Wyoming, 232 E. 64th St. between Second and Third Aves. (☎371-7187). Home of the famed 7oz. burger and offering over 25 different kinds of burgers and 25 chicken sandwiches, Jackson Hole is synonymous with grease, which is synonymous with TASTE! Burgers, chicken sandwiches, and platters $6-11. Open 10am-1am. **$-$$**

Luke's Bar and Grill, 1394 Third Ave. between 79th and 80th Sts. (☎249-7070). Start things off right with an order of chewy, breaded mozzarella sticks ($5), followed by their juicy 10oz. hamburger ($6). Known for very tasty, reasonably priced appetizers. Open M-F 11:30am-2am, Sa 10am-4am, Su 10am-1am **$-$$**

Papaya King, 179 E. 86th St., at Third Ave. (☎369-0648). Since 1972, New Yorkers have tolerated outrageously long lines, no seating, and tropical decor at this dive all for a taste of the "tastier than filet mignon" hot dogs ($1.50). It's hard to just have one, though, so you might opt for the special: 2 hot dogs and a 16-oz. taste of their famous tropical shakes for $4, a rare deal for the Upper East Side. Open Su-W 8am-midnight, Th-Sa 8am-1am. **$**

Viand, 673 Madison Ave., at 61st St. (☎751-6622). Given 4 stars by the *The New York Times*, *The Daily News*, and *New York Magazine*, Viand has locals, who claim that it has the best turkey sandwich ($7.50) in New York, singing high praises. Open M-Sa 6am-10pm, Su 6am-9pm. **$-$$**

BBQ, 1265 Third Ave., at 73rd St. (☎772-9393). Big portions, tasty rib and shrimp dishes, and pina coladas ($7) and daiquiris ($7) bigger than Texas itself. Open Su-Th 11:30am-midnight, F-Sa 11:30am-1am. **$-$$**

SHOPS

Ecce Panis, 1126 Third Ave. between 65th and 66th Sts. (☎535-2099). The name means "behold the bread" in Latin, and after sampling the delicious chocolate cupcakes or 1 of the 7 varieties of sweet *biscotti* in this baked-goods Mecca, that's exactly what you might do. Open M-F 8am-8pm, Sa-Su 8am-7pm.

Grace's Marketplace, 1237 Third Ave., at 71st St. (☎737-0600). Your tongue will be plastered to the counter's window once you see the cornucopia of fresh goodies this gourmet shop has to offer. Don't be ashamed...the Chanel-suited patrons already recognized you as an Outsider (or at least a West Sider) who must have slipped through security. Even if you can't afford a thing at this meticulous market, Grace's is a education in Upper East Side life. Open M-F, Sa 7am-8:30pm, Su 8am-7pm.

UPPER WEST SIDE

see map pp. 338–339

The Upper West Side offers restaurant choices that may be slightly pricey but wonderfully ethnic and unique. If you're not in the mood to dine fancy, check out the countless pizza shops and diners. Browse around Columbus Ave., Amsterdam Ave., and Broadway to find cute sidewalk cafes in the summer. **Gray's Papaya,** at 72nd St. and Broadway, can also satiate your hunger with amazing deals on hot dogs—their never-ending "recession special" sells 2 franks and 1 fruit drink (banana daiquiri, pineapple, piña colada, papaya) for a mere $1.95. Around 72nd St., from West End all the way to Columbus, kosher travelers can find the food they've forgone in other parts of the city.

🍽 **Ollie's,** 1991 Broadway between 67th and 68th Sts. (☎595-8181). Inside this big, seemingly un-Asian joint is one of NY's most well-known noodle shops. Just looking at the extensive menu of noodle soups ($6), fried rice (around $7), seafood ($10-14), and meat dishes ($8-10) will make you full. Great vegetarian options, too ($7-8). Lunch special M-F 11:30am-3pm $6 (entree, soup, and rice). Open M-Th and Su 11:30am-midnight, F-Sa 11:30am-1am. **$-$$**

🍽 **Big Nick's Pizza and Burger Joint,** 2173 Broadway, at 77th St. (☎362-9238). Serving the West Side's "compulsive noshers, weekend partyfolk, mellow-groovy happyfolk, dedicated loners, lovers after the afterglow." Tried-and-true pizza and burgers (and breakfast dishes) since 1962. They also have "diet delights," but why turn away a plate-sized burger? Also at 70 W. 71st at Columbus Ave. (☎ 799-4444). Free delivery. Open 24hr., "sometimes 25." **$**

Brother Jimmy's, 428 Amsterdam Ave. between 80th and 81st Sts. (☎501-7515). A bust of Elvis and Duke paraphernalia, as well as the hog decor, heartily beckon. This joint offers BBQ-ed meat (BBQ chicken and ribs $15, pulled pork $12), and other dishes southern style. M is for margarita (free margaritas with dinner), W is ladies' night (ladies $1 drinks at the bar). M-F 5-7pm is happy hour, $1 drafts and half-price drinks. Open daily 5pm-midnight. **$-$$**

Good Enough to Eat, 483 Amsterdam Ave. between 83rd and 84th Sts. (☎496-0163). New England has come to the Upper West in the form of Good Enough to Eat, a wonderfully homey cafe serving comfort food. Healthy salads (about $10) and vegetarian options abound (such as *vegetable napoleon*, various vegetables served on a bed of greens and griddled focaccia). Breads and desserts made on premises. Vermont cheddar and apple omelette with buttermilk biscuits $7.25; strawberry almond waffles with Vermont syrup $8.50. Breakfast M-F 8am-4pm; brunch Sa-Su 9am-4pm; lunch M-F noon-4pm; dinner M-Sa 5:30-10:30pm, Su 5:30-10pm. **$-$$**

La Caridad 78 Restaurant, 2197-2199 Broadway, at 78th St. (☎874-2780). A *packed* Chinese-Cuban hybrid. You could eat here 160 times and never have the same dish twice. The ebullient waiters charm in three languages. No elaborate decor, but the delicious homestyle cooking will remind you of your *abuelita*. Prices around (and often well below) $10. Lunch special M-F 11:30am-4pm $5. Open M-Sa 11:30am-1am, Su 11:30am-10:30pm. **$**

D+S Plaza, 182 Amsterdam Ave. between 68th and 69th Sts. (☎579-0808). We know that you've seen them all over the city: groceries/salad bars vending stuffed tofu, watermelon and cantaloupe slices, and pasta salad. We know these groceries hold near iconic status in NYC. But we *didn't* know that any of these salad bars had air-conditioned dining halls downstairs—so, we thought we'd tell you: some of these convenience store salad bars have air-conditioned dining halls downstairs. Vast, fresh, hot and cold salad bars $4.49 per lb. Open 24hr. **$**

The Lemongrass Grill, 2534 Broadway, at 95th St. (☎666-0888). Delicious culinary mainstay of the Upper West. Thai noodles and vegetables ($6-8) sate locals. $6 Lunch specials (M-F noon-3pm) include entree, rice, and additional delights. Great appetizers (spring rolls $3.25) and salads (*yum pla muk*, thai calamari salad, $7). Open Su-Th noon-11:30pm, F-Sa noon-12:30am. **$**

Tamarind, 424 Amsterdam Ave. between 80th and 81st Sts. (☎712-1900). Futuristic decor and velvety sofas put this Indian spot a step above the others. Entrees are served with rice. The vegetarian *saag paneer* (cheese and spinach, $7) is a delight, as is the chicken vindaloo (hot curry, $6.25). Most dishes are mildly spicy. Open Su-Th 11:30am-11pm, F-Sa 11:30am-midnight. **$**

Ivy's Cafe, 154 W. 72nd St. between Broadway and Columbus Ave. (☎787-3333 or 787-0165). Soon to open, this restaurant serves both Chinese and Japanese cuisine. The Chinese menu spans all sorts of meat and vegetable dishes, for not more than $10, and the Japanese menu has some healthy teriyaki and tempura choices that are only slightly more expensive. Sushi bar available ($13-16 for sushi platters). If you're in the mood for Asian food but don't know what kind, drop by Ivy's. Open M-Th 11am-midnight, F-Sa 11am-1am, Su noon-midnight. **$-$$**

CAFES

Café Lalo, 201 W. 83rd St. between Broadway and Amsterdam Ave. (☎496-6031). A wall of French windows allows live jazz (and the occasional *bon mot* from a suave *monsieur* within) to escape onto the street. Perfect cakes $5 per slice; full bar available. Wonderful ambiance, *sans blague*! Open M-Th 8am-2am, F 8am-4am, Sa 9am-4am, Su 9am-2am.

drip, 489 Amsterdam Ave. between 83rd and 84th Sts. (☎875-1032). Commercial culture decor, pastel interior, and comfy couches set the backdrop for students on laptops, young ladies lounging with complimentary magazines, and single Upper West Siders nervously eyeing each other over coffee. For the true lush, a full bar opens with the coffee shop. Beer $4; cocktails $4-9; coffee $1.25-2. Their **dating service** ($10 to sign up, $3 to request a date) has no fewer than 24,500 heart-sick participants in its database. **Psychic** readings M 7-11pm, $10. Open M-Th 8:30am-1am, F-Sa 8:30am-3am, Su 9am-midnight.

Café Mozart, 154 70th St. between Amsterdam and Columbus Aves. (☎595-9797). A relaxing, elegant spot. Sample gourmet coffee and one of over 50 desserts over the paper. Even check your email for free. Lunch special (M-F 11:30am-4pm) includes sandwich, quiches, or omelette

Here's your ticket to freedom, baby!

Airline Tickets | Hotel Rooms | Rental Cars
New Cars | Long Distance

Wherever you want to go, priceline.com can get you there for less. Our customers regularly save up to 40% or more off the lowest published airfares. But we're more than just airline tickets. At priceline.com, you can Name Your Own Price^{SM} and save big on brand-name hotels nationwide. Get great rates on all your long distance calls — without changing your long distance carrier. Even get the car of your dreams, at the price *you* want to pay. If you haven't tried priceline.com, you're missing out on the best way to save. **Visit us online today at www.priceline.com.**

with soda or coffee and dessert ($5). Generously proportioned salads ($4-10), large selection of sandwiches ($6-9), and pasta. Live music (usually classical or jazz piano) M-F 9pm-midnight, Su 1-4pm and 9pm-midnight. Open M-Th 8am-1am, F 8am-3am, Sa 10am-3am, Su 10am-1am.

Café La Fortuna, 69 71st St., at Columbus Ave. (☎724-5846). Delicious Italian pastries, coffees, and sandwiches served in an intimate grotto. A local favorite, boasts that it is the oldest cafe in the Upper West Side. Espresso $2.25; pies about $4; sandwiches $3-6; and salads $4.75-6.75. In the summer, they sell flavored ices out front ($1.35-4) in 8 delightful flavors. Open Su-Th noon-midnight, F noon-1am, Sa noon-2am; Student Advantage discounts.

SHOPS

Street Vendor

🔲 **Zabar's,** 2245 Broadway between 80th and 81st Sts. (☎787-2000). This Upper West Side institution often featured on TV's "Mad About You" sells everything you need for a 4-star meal at home. Cheese, salmon, beautiful bread, and droves of shoppers in this gourmet grocery store. The adjoining cafe serves pastries, sandwiches (panini $4.50, soup and sandwich combo $5.49, entree with 2 sides lunch special $6), and great coffee. Cafe open M-Sa 7:30am-7pm, Su 8am-6pm; store open M-F 8am-7:30pm, Sa 8am-8pm, Su 9am-6pm.

H&H Bagels, 2239 Broadway, at 80th St. (☎692-2435). H&H has fed Upper West Siders for years with cheap bagels (75¢) that hold a reputation for being the best in Manhattan. Dozen $9. Send a dozen home to mom—they'll ship anywhere in the world on command. Open 24hr.

MORNINGSIDE HEIGHTS

see map pp. 340-341

Pizza!

Morningside Heights caters mostly to Columbia students, faculty, and their families. This usually means that hours run late and the price range fits that of a starving student. If you walk along Broadway, you'll find everything from old-fashioned coffee shops and new-age diners to romantic Italian restaurants and quick-service Chinese food. There is, without a doubt, a restaurant on Broadway to represent each type of cuisine and ethnicity found on the seven continents. Major credit cards are accepted unless noted.

Street Vendor

Amir's Falafel, 2911A Broadway between 113th and 114th Sts. (☎749-7500). Low-priced Middle Eastern staples like *shawarma*, *baba ghanoush,* and *musakaa* (cold eggplant salad) for vegetarians and meat-lovers alike. Sandwiches ($3-5) and vegetarian platters ($5) made with care. Cash only. Open daily 11am-11pm. **$**

Koronet Pizza, 2848 Broadway, at 110th St. (☎222-1566). Huge slices for $2.25. Also Jamaican beef patties, lasagna, and calzones. Cash only. Open Su-W 10am-2am, Th-Sa 10am-4am. **$**

Mama Mexico, 2672 Broadway, at 102nd St. (☎864-2323). Wonderful Mexican food, if a bit pricey. With colored lanterns, a *loud* mariachi band, and a vivacious crowd, Mama promises a lively dinner. Amazing margaritas in 14 tropical flavors $6. Entrees $11-20. Reservations strongly recommended. Open Su-Th noon-midnight, F-Sa noon-2am. **$$**

Massawa, 1239 Amsterdam Ave., at 121st St. (☎663-0505). Wash your hands before heading to this restaurant specializing in Ethiopian and Eritrean cuisine—traditional finger food. Veggie dishes ($5-7) served with spongy *ingera* bread or rice. M-F 11:30am-2pm they offer a great luncheon buffet ($7), not to mention lunch specials like lamb stew and collard green/potato platters ($6-7). Wine (by the glass) around $4, imported beer $3-4. Open daily 11:30am-midnight. **$-$$**

Mill Korean Restaurant, 2895 Broadway, at 112th St. (☎666-7653). The Mill offers traditional Korean food at reasonable prices. They take special pride in their *bi bim bap,* a Korean rice dish with meat and assorted vegetables ($7). For a couple extra dollars get it in a hot, stone pot where the rice at the bottom cooks at your table to a candy-like crisp. Lunch specials M-F 11am-3pm ($6-7). Complete dinners with side dishes like *kim chee* (Korean pickled vegetables) for $7-10. Open daily 11am-11pm. **$-$$**

La Rosita Restaurant, 2809 Broadway between 108th and 109th Sts. (☎663-7804). Simple, genuine Spanish/Cuban cuisine. Daily specials $5-6. Try the *caldo gallega* soup, made with white beans ($2-3), or the *carne guisada* beef stew ($6). Most dinners come with a heaping portion of rice and beans. Excellent *cafè con leche* (espresso with milk) $1.10. Domestic beer $2, imported $3; cocktails $3.50. Open daily 7am-midnight. Bar opens at 6pm. **$$**

Obaa Koryoe, 3143 Broadway between Tiemann and La Salle, near 125th St. (☎316-2950). Excellent West African food in a laid-back, elegant setting. Try the bean stew and fried plantains, with *jollof* rice ($9) or chicken, bean stew, *wachey,* and *gari* ($10). Indulge in a bottle of "budget" South African wine ($8-19). Lunch specials 11:30am-4pm. Open daily 11am-midnight. **$$**

Tom's Restaurant, 2880 Broadway, at 112th St. (☎864-6137). Immortalized as the storefront featured in *Seinfeld,* this diner is about as cheap and average as it gets. Offers luxurious milkshakes. Greasy, but tasty, burgers ($3-8), excellent fries ($2), and entrees ($6-8). Cash only. Open Th-Su 6-1:30am, F-Sa 24hr. **$**

Toast, 3157 Broadway between La Salle and Tiemann, near 125th St. (☎662-1144). Offering a huge variety of sandwiches ($4-9), this new-age, funkadelic cafe provides the perfect setting for a relaxed and tasty meal. Daily lunch special ($7.50) includes half-sandwich, soup, and pint of soda. Check weekend brunch specials. Live jazz W 9-11pm. Beer on tap $4. Happy Hour daily 5-7pm. Open M-F 11am-midnight, Sa-Su 9am-midnight.**$-$$**

Emily's, 1325 Fifth Ave., at 111th St. (☎996-1212). Rumored to serve "the best ribs in New York," Emily's features an all-you-can-eat buffet M-Tu 3pm-midnight. Th 7-11pm enjoy live jazz as you eat. Fully-stocked bar (mixed drinks $6-10) and late-night menu. Excellent gospel brunch Su (11am-2pm) and infamous chicken and waffles ($10). Open M-Tu 11am-midnight, W and F-Sa 11am-3am, Th 11am-2am, Su 9am-midnight.**$$**

SHOPS

The Hungarian Pastry Shop, 1030 Amsterdam Ave., at 111th St. (☎866-4230). If you don't know the difference between Fila and *phyllo,* lace up the former and head over here to experience the latter. Plain, friendly pastry shop. Eclairs, cake slices, and other goodies for around $2. Pleasant outdoor seating. Cash only. Open daily 8:30am-10:30pm.

HARLEM

see map pp. 340–341

In Harlem, the food is as diverse and colorful as the people. Ethnic food is *everywhere*, with various Latino foods in Spanish Harlem and some of the most delicious and exciting examples of black cuisine—ranging from East and West African, to Caribbean, Creole, and some of the best soul food north of the Mason-Dixon Line—along Lenox Ave. between 116th and 135th Sts. Near 135th St., especially, there are a number of affordable, excellent restaurants like **Pan Pan** (☎926-4900) and **Joseph's Food Basket** (☎368-7663). Major credit cards are accepted unless otherwise noted.

🔳 **Copeland's,** 547 W. 145th St. between Broadway and Amsterdam Ave. (☎234-2357). Excellent soul food accompanied by live music in an elegant dining room. Entrees pricey ($11-26), so you may want to check out Copeland's "cafeteria" next door—same food, more options, entrees

$4-11. Popular mid-week jazz buffet (all-you-can-eat for $15) Tu, W, and Th 4:30-10:30pm. Gospel brunch Su with live jazz, all-you-can-eat buffet, and complimentary champagne; $17. Open Tu-Th 4:30-11pm, F-Sa 4:30pm-midnight, Su noon-9:00pm; cafeteria M-F 8am-11:30pm, Sa 8am-12:30am, Su 8am-1am. **$$**

🔲 **Sylvia's,** 328 Lenox Ave., at 126th St. (☎996-0660). This soul food has enticed New Yorkers for close to 40 years; now European tour groups arrive in buses. Sylvia, the proclaimed "Queen of soul food," accents her "World-Famous Talked-about BBQ Ribs Special" with "sweet spicy sauce" and a side of collard greens and macaroni and cheese ($11). Lunch special of salmon croquette, pork chop, fried chicken leg, collard greens, and candied yams ($7). Free live jazz and R&B F 6-9pm. Gospel Brunch Su. Open M-Sa 7:30am-10:30pm, Su 11am-8pm. **$$**

🔲 **Manna's Too!!,** 486 Lenox Ave. between 134th and 135th Sts. (☎234-4488). This recently opened restaurant and deli might just be the best thing in Harlem. The variety of soul food options are unbelievable and the salad bar is as fresh as they come. Simply put, the food speaks for itself. And the sweet aroma coming from the bakery in back is quite hard to ignore. Homemade cakes $2.50; peach cobbler $3. Cash only. Open M-Sa 7am-8pm, Su 10am-7pm. **$**

La Marmite, 2264 Frederick Douglass Blvd. between 121st and 122nd Sts. (☎666-0653). For authentic French and African cuisine, try this Senegalese restaurant. Beware the bite of some of the spices. Popular dishes on the lunch menu (noon-4pm) include *thiebou djeun*, which is fried rice served with fish and vegetables, and patrons rave about the dinner menu's *dibi* and *poisson grille* (served 4pm-6am). Open M-S 9-6am. **$-$$**

Sisters, 47 E. 124th St. between Madison and Park Aves. (☎410-3000). You won't be inundated by tourists or ambience at this small family restaurant, just good Caribbean food. Fried chicken and most other entrees range from $5-7. Open M-W 8am-8pm, Th-Su 8am-9pm. **$**

La Fonda Boricua, 169 E. 106th St. between Lexington and Third Aves. (☎410-7292). Traditional Puerto Rican cuisine served in a friendly, relaxed, artistic atmosphere. Lots of seafood options, like the popular seafood shrimp salad (small $7, combo $10). Dinner entrees $7-10. Daily luch specials $5-8. Open M-Sa 10am-8pm. **$**

Jamaican Hot Pot, 2260 Adam Clayton Powell Blvd./Seventh Ave. between 134th and 135th Sts. (☎491-5270). For the ultimate in Caribbean cuisine, look no farther. This restaurant cooks up a mean oxtail stew ($10) and hot, spicy jerk chicken ($10) that keeps locals begging for more. Open Su-Th 11am-1am, F-Sa 11am-2am. **$-$$**

SHOPS

🔲 **Fairway,** 2328 12th Ave., at W. 132nd St., on the Hudson River. (☎234-3883). This super super-market offers a ridiculous selection of food at wholesale prices. From the fresh bakery and gourmet cheeses to the huge variety of fruits and deli options, Fairway is synonomous with quality and selection. Accepts all major credit cards. Open daily 8am-11pm.

BROOKLYN

CENTRAL BROOKLYN

Because of its growing chic, **Park Slope** has become home to artsy coffee shops and chi-chi restaurants around **Seventh Ave.**, while other areas of Central Brooklyn remain a haven for international specialties. **Eighth Ave.** in **Sunset Park** is the heart of Brooklyn's Chinatown, and **Church Ave.** in **Flatbush** is the spot for West Indian eateries.

see map pp. 342-343

Gia Lam, 5402 Eighth Ave., at 54th St., in Sunset Park. (☎718-854-8818). Subway: N to Eighth Ave. This popular Vietnamese restaurant in Brooklyn's Chinatown serves large portions at low prices. The squid with lemongrass on rice ($3.75) is an excellent lunch choice. Lunches $3-5, dinner entrees $7-10. Open daily 10:30am-10:30pm. Cash only. **$-$$**

Monika Restaurant, 643 Fifth Ave. between 18th and 19th Sts. (☎718-788-6930). Subway: N, R to Prospect Ave., then one block west and several blocks south. This tiny joint serves numerous varieties of Slavic soups (including yummy cold fruit *compote*) for $1-2. Kielbasa, dumpling, and meat entrees $4-5. Open daily noon-8pm. Cash only.**$**

Roy's Jerk Chicken, 3125 Church Ave. (718-826-0987), between 31st and 32nd St. in Flat-bush. Subway: #2 or 5 to Church Ave. and 2 blocks east. Jerk chicken is a delicious Jamaican specialty—crispy chicken roasted with a sweet and very peppery marinade and served either hot or cold. You can also sample one of the many other enticing entrees ($6-7). Open M-Th 9am-2am, F-Su 24hr. Cash only. **$**

SHOPS

Hammond's Finger Lickin' Bakery, 5014 Church Ave., at Utica Ave. in Flatbush (☎ 718-342-5770). Subway: 3, 4 to Utica Ave.; then 2 blocks east. West Indian pastries $1-2, including car-rot cake ($1.25). Open M-F 8:30am-8pm, Sa-Su 8:30am-9pm. Cash only.

DOWNTOWN BROOKLYN

Fulton St. around the **Fort Greene** area has a variety of cafes and ethnic food joints, while **Atlantic Ave.** offers a plethora of Middle Eastern restaurants and food shops.

Brooklyn Moon, 745 Fulton St., at Lafayette St., in Fort Greene (☎ 718-243-0424). Subway: G to Fulton St.; C to Lafayette Ave. Comfy couches and local art on ochre sponge-painted walls. Salmon burger $6.50; apple salad $4.25. But what the Moon boasts are readings held on F open mic night at 10:30pm, when aspiring bards from all over NYC hold forth. Occasional perfor-mances and readings by authors like Jamaica Kincaid and Amiri Baraka. The preferred method of applause (at least by the upstairs neighbors) is to snap your fingers. Open Tu-Th 11am-10pm, F 11am-1am, Sa-Su 11am-10pm. **$**

Caravan, 193 Atlantic Ave. between Court and Clinton Sts., in Brooklyn Heights (☎ 718-488-7111). Subway: 2, 3, 4, 5, M, N, R to Borough Hall; then walk 4 blocks on Court St. to Atlantic Ave. One of Atlantic Ave.'s Middle Eastern offerings, Caravan prides itself on its couscous and tandoori oven-baked bread. *Prix fixe* dinner M-F ($12) includes an entree, hummus and baba ghnoush, soup or salad, dessert, and morrocan coffee. Belly-dancing Sa at 8:45pm. Open M-Th 11am-10pm, F 11am-11pm, Sa 11:30am-midnight, Su 11:30am-10:30pm. AmEx, V, MC. **$$**

Fountain Cafe, 183 Atlantic Ave. in Brooklyn Heights. (☎ 718-624-6764). Subway: 2, 3, 4, 5, M, R to Borough Hall; then walk 4 blocks on Court St. Named for the rumbly little fountain in its center, this eatery serves inexpensive and filling Middle Eastern food. *Shawarma* or *shish kebab* sandwich $4.65, falafel sandwich $3.30. Open M-Th 11am-10:30pm, F-Sa 11am-11pm. AmEx, V, MC. **$**

Fresco Tortilla Plus, 113 Court St. between Schermerhorn and State Sts., in Brooklyn Heights. (☎ 718-237-8898). Subway: 2, 3, 4, 5, M, N, R to Borough Hall; then head 2 blocks down Court St. A Tex-Mex express restaurant with tasty grit served swiftly. The grilled steak burrito is one of the most expensive things on the menu at only $5. Open M-F 11am-10:30pm, Sa-Su 11:30am-10pm. **$**

Grimaldi's, 19 Old Fulton St. between Front and Water Sts. (☎ 718-858-4300). Subway: A, C to High St. Delicious thin crust brick-oven pizza with wonderfully fresh mozzarella, sold only by the pie. Come admire the all-Sinatra decor and hear Ol' Blue Eyes on the jukebox. Small pies $12, large $14; toppings $2 each. Open M-Th 11:30am-11pm, F-Sa noon-midnight, Su noon-11pm. Cash only. **$**

Junior's, 386 Flatbush Ave. extension, at De Kalb St. (☎ 718-852-5257). Subway: 2, 3, 4, 5, B, D, Q, M, N, R to Atlantic Ave. Touted by *New York Magazine* as the home of "the world's finest cheescake ($4.25)," this is diner-land Brooklyn-style. Come bask in the fab glow of orange diner-light and eat roast beef and brisket to your heart's delight. 10oz. steakburgers start at $5.95. AmEx, V, MC, Discover. Open Su-Th 6:30am-12:30am, F-Sa 6:30am-2am. **$**

Keur N'Deye, 737 Fulton St. at S. Elliott Pl., in Fort Greene (☎ 718-875-4937). Subway: G to Ful-ton St.; C to Lafayette Ave. Even in New York's culinary melting pot, there aren't many Senegalese restaurants. *Thiou kandje dieun* (bluefish with vegetables stewed in a tomato sauce) is Senegal's most popular dish ($9). Open Tu-Su noon-10:30pm. **$**

Petite Crevette, 127 Atlantic Ave. between Henry and Clinton Sts., in Brooklyn Heights. (☎ 718-858-6660). Subway: 2, 3, 4, 5, M, N, R to Borough Hall; then walk 4 blocks on Court St. Half fish market, half restaurant, this small place serves tasty seafood dishes. Lunch special (soup/grilled chicken or vegetable sandwich) $6. Sandwiches $4-6; entrees $7-14. Open M-Th 11am-10:30pm, F-Sa 11am-11pm, Su 5-10:30pm. Cash only. **$-$$**

SHOPS

Sahadi Importing Company, 187 Atlantic Ave. between Court and Clinton Sts. (☎ 718-624-4550). Subway: 2, 3, 4, 5, N, R to Borough Hall-Court St. A Middle Eastern emporium that stocks everything from spices and seasonings, dried fruits, a variety of olives, and an array of spreads and dips like hummus and baba ghanoush. Open M-F 9am-7pm, Sa 8:30am-7pm.

Damascus Bakery, 195 Atlantic Ave. in Brooklyn Heights (☎ 718-625-7070). Subway: 2, 3, 4, 5, M, R to Borough Hall; then walk down 4 blocks on Court St. Friendly bakery serving up all kinds of baked goods, Middle Eastern and otherwise. Package of fresh pita bread 50¢; superior baklava $1.50; spinach and feta pies $1.35; pistachio turkish delights $8/lb. Open daily 7am-7pm.

Latticini-Barese, 138 Union St. between Columbia and Hicks Sts., in Red Hook (☎ 718-625-8694). Subway: F, G to Carroll St. Neighborhood cheese shop sells mouth-watering homemade mozzarella for only $5 per lb. Worth popping in for a slice of Italian culture. Open M-Sa 8am-6pm.

NORTH BROOKLYN

Bliss, 191 Bedford Ave. between 6th and 7th Sts. (☎ 718-599-2547). Subway: L to Bedford Ave. Full of blissed-out herbivores, this almost-vegan (they use eggs and cheese) hotspot serves up tasty specialties like a marinated-tofu sandwich with horseradish sauce ($6). BYOB. Open Su-Th 8am-11pm, F-Sa 6am-11pm. **$**

Oznot's Dish, 79 Berry St., at N. 9th St. (☎ 718-599-6596). Subway: L to Bedford Ave; then walk west to Berry St. and head north. Beautiful ambiance and good food. The lunch *meze platter* of pita, hummus and olives ($7) is a healthy option. Weekday dinner special with entree, soup or salad, and dessert $20. Garden out back. Open daily 11am-4:30pm and 6pm-midnight. **$-$$**

Planet Thailand, 115 Berry St. (☎ 718-599-5758). Re-opened on Berry St. and re-incarnated in a sassy, trendy, high-ceilinged space. Thai entrees remain reasonably priced ($8); new Japanese menu is a bit pricier (dinner box around $10, sushi deluxe dinner $14). DJ every night at 9pm. Open Su-W 11:30am-1am, Th-Sa 11:30am-2am. **$$**

Squeeze, 198 Bedford Ave. (☎ 718-782-9181). A juice bar offering freshly squeezed juice ($2.50-3.50), smoothies ($4.45), and supplements. Pick up organic blueberry granola, and while you're at it, peruse the fresh flowers ($5-8) and flyers announcing local events. **$**

L Café, 189 Bedford Ave. (☎ 718-388-6792). Subway: L to Bedford Ave. A colorful, funky joint that embodies Williamsburg cool. Check out the flyers up front and the nice garden out back. Beers $3.25; veggie burger $5.50. Sandwiches named after artsy revolutionary types like Joni Mitchell and Leonard Cohen ($4.50-8). Open M-F 9am-midnight, Sa-Su 10am-midnight. **$**

Ferdinando's, 151 Union St. between Columbus and Hicks Sts. (☎ 718-855-1545). This 95-year-old *focacceria* continues to serve Sicilian specialties. House specialty is the *arancini* (breaded, fried rice balls filled with meat, peas, and sauce; $2.50 each). Open M-Th 10:30am-6pm, F-Sa 10:30am-9pm. **$**

Miyako, 143 Berry St., at N. 6th St., in Williamsburg (☎ 718-486-0837). Subway: L to Bedford St.; go south on Bedford St. and turn west onto N. 6th. Where Manhattanites migrate, there too goeth the sushi; even has a special Williamsburg Roll ($6.50). Affordable sushi; most entrees under $10. Open M-F 11:30am-11pm, Sa 3:30-11:30pm. **$**

Stylowa Restaurant, 694 Manhattan Ave. between Norman and Nassau Aves., in Greenpoint. (☎ 718-383-8993). Subway: G to Nassau Ave. Cheap and filling Polish cuisine; sample *kielbasa* (Polish sausage) with fried onions, sauerkraut, and bread ($4.50). Excellent potato pancakes $3. All other entrees ($2.75-7.25) served with a glass of *compote* (pink, apple-flavored fruit drink). Open M-Th noon-9pm, F noon-10pm, Sa 11am-10pm, Su 11am-9pm. **$**

Vera Cruz, 195 Bedford Ave. between 6th and 7th Sts., in Williamsburg (☎ 718-599-7914). Subway: L to Bedford Ave. Only open for dinner, don't miss the "Mexican styled corn," corn on the cob covered in Mexican cheese and sprinkled with lime and chili powder ($2.50); also great margaritas and garden. Happy Hour M-F 4-7pm. Open M 4-11pm, Tu-Th 4-11:30pm, F-Sa 4pm-midnight, Su 11am-midnight. **$-$$**

SOUTH BROOKLYN

The shores of Brooklyn present a welcome culinary quandary: endless choices. Try Russian knishes (heated, flaky dough with a choice of filling) on **Brighton Beach Ave.**, Italian calamari (fried squid) in spicy marinara sauce along **Emmons Ave.** in Sheepshead Bay, or frankfurters on **Surf Ave.** in the amusement park area of Coney Island. Eat until you feel ill—it won't make a dent in your wallet.

▨ **Nathan's,** 1310 Surf Ave. between Stillwell and 15th Sts., in Coney Island (☎718-946-2202). 74 years ago, Nathan Handwerker became famous for underselling his competitors on the boardwalk: his hot dogs cost a nickel, theirs a dime. His crunchy dogs have since become famous world-over. A classic frank now sells for $1.95; cheese-fries $2.19-2.59. Sauerkraut available in winter, fried onions in summer. Open M-Th 6am-2am, F-Su 6am-4am. **$**

▨ **Primorski Restaurant,** 282 Brighton Beach Ave. between Brighton Beach 2nd and 3rd Sts. (☎718-891-3111). Populated by Russian-speaking Brooklynites, this restaurant serves Ukrainian *borscht* ($3.50) in an atmosphere that is best described as Sinatra-meets-Russian-wedding-hall. Eminently affordable lunch special (M-F 11am-5pm, Sa-Su 11am-4pm; $4) is one of NYC's great deals—your choice of 3 soups and about 15 entrees, bread, salad, and coffee or tea. Buffet available—a feast complete with a bottle of vodka and cold and hot dishes (M-Th $22 per person, F-Su $30 per person, Sa $35 per person). Russian music and disco M-Th 8pm-midnight, F-Sa 9pm-2am, Su 8pm-1am. Open daily 11am-2am. **$**

Taste of Russia, 219 Brighton Beach Ave. (☎718-934-6167). This Russian deli stocks everything from fresh-baked delicacies to mango soda. Favorites include the stuffed cabbage and the blintzes (both $4 per lb.). Great selection of fresh pickles (including pickled watermelon and tomatoes) and cole slaw. Open daily 8am-10pm. **$**

Totonno Pizzeria Napolitano, 1524 Neptune Ave. between 15th and 16th Sts. (☎718-372-8606). A Coney Island legend, this joint serves pizza by the pie that vies for the coveted title of finest pizza in New York. Pies $13-14.50. No slices. Open W-Su noon-8:30pm. **$**

SHOPS

▨ **Efe International,** 243 Brighton Beach Ave. (☎718-891-8933). Tantalizing dry goods store that vends every kind of nut, spice, seed, fruit, and gummy candy that you could possibly desire. Prices below $4 per lb.; apricots and various candies are only 99¢ per lb. Open daily 8am-9pm.

▨ **Philip's Confections,** 1237 Surf Ave., at the entrance to the B, D, F, N train, in Coney Island. (☎718-372-8783). Famous salt-water taffy 95¢ per ¼ lb.; candy or caramel apple 95¢; cotton candy $1; lime rickeys 65¢. Open Su-Th 11am-3am, F-Sa 11am-4am.

Sea Lane Bakery, 615 Brighton Beach Ave. between 6th and 7th Sts. (☎718-934-8877). Subway: D, Q to Brighton Beach. The best Jewish bakery in Brighton. Then again, you can't go wrong with 99¢ danishes or strudel with mixed fruit ($4). Open daily 6am-9pm.

QUEENS

This oft-overlooked borough offers visitors some of the best and most reasonably-priced ethnic cuisine in town, including Greek fish, Indian *daal*, Italian Ice, and Jamaican beef. Every neighborhood has affordable and safe street food.

ASTORIA

see map pp. 346–347

This neighborhood specializes in discount shopping and cheap eats and has many open produce markets such as **United Brothers Fruit Market,** 32-24 30th Ave., at the corner of 33rd St. (☎718-932-9876). You can also find bounty around **Steinway St.** (G, R to Steinway St. and Broadway). Greek and Italian restaurants proliferate around the elevated station at Broadway and 31st St.

▨ **Elias Corner,** 24-02 31st St., at the corner of 24th Ave. and 31st St. (☎718-932-1510). Subway: N to Astoria Boulevard. With no menus, outdoor dining, and fresh everything, this fantastic restaurant has a distinctly European character. Principally a fish restaurant, the waiter will explain which catches are fresh that day (whole grilled fish $7-14). Try the delicious *Tsatziki,* calamari, or grilled octopus as appetizers ($3-6 depending on plate size). Often crowded. No reservations. Open daily 4-11pm or midnight. AmEx, V, MC. $

▨ **Galaxy Pastry Shop,** 37-11 30th Ave. (☎ 718-545-3181). Subway: N to 30th Ave.-Grand Ave.; make a right on 30th Ave. and walk east to 37th St. A hangout for young locals, the Galaxy offers great pastries to ruin your diet. The baklava ($1.20) tastes like the answer to a Dionysian prayer. Relax in outdoor cafe seating during summer. Open daily 6:30am-3am. $

Uncle George's, 33-19 Broadway, at 33rd St. (☎ 718-626-0593). Subway: N to Broadway, then 2 blocks east; G, R to Steinway St., then 4 blocks west. Crowded, noisy, and friendly, this popular restaurant serves hearty Greek fare around the clock. All entrees under $12. Diehard fans feed on roast leg of lamb with potatoes ($9) or octopus sauteed with vinegar ($7). Open 24hr. $

FLUSHING
In Flushing you'll find excellent Chinese, Japanese, and Korean eateries. Restaurants here often make use of rarely seen ingredients like skatefish, squid, and tripe, which more Americanized Asian restaurants tend to avoid.

Kum Gang San, 138-28 Northern Blvd. (☎ 718-461-0909). Subway: 7 to Main St.; walk north on Main St. and take a right on Northern Blvd. (about 10min.). Good Korean food in an elegant setting with marble floors and dark wood tables. A complete lunch special can get you chicken teriyaki with salad, noodles, a California roll, and a dumpling all for $6-9. Open 24hr. AmEx, V, MC. $

JACKSON HEIGHTS
Come for great Indian food; even the cheap cafeterias serve tasty Indian fare. The one next to Anand Bhavan has luscious snacks. This is a great place to buy spices in bulk.

▨ **Jackson Diner,** 37-47 74th St., Jackson Heights, at 37th Ave. (☎ 718-672-1232). Subway: E, F, G, or R to Jackson Heights/Roosevelt Ave.; 7 to 74th St./Broadway, then walk 2 or 3 blocks north toward 37th Ave. Possibly the best Indian food in New York. Savor the *saag ghost* (lamb with spinach, tomato, ginger, and cumin; $10), and don't forget the samosas ($2.50). Lunch specials $6-7.50. Open M-F 11:30am-10pm, Sa-Su 11:30am-10:30pm. $

Anand Bhavan, 35-66 73rd St. (☎ 718-507-1600). Subway: F, G, H, R, 7 to 74th St.-Broadway; then walk 2 blocks down 73rd St. Tasty vegetarian South Indian restaurant. Picant lunch specials (noon-4:30pm) $6-8. The Anand Bhavan special, a 4-course meal ($13), includes *sambar* (spicy lentil soup) and a choice of *iddly* (rice crepe with peppers and onions) or *vada* (stuffed lentil dough). Foreign and domestic beers, $3-5. Open daily noon-9:30pm. AmEx, V, MC, Discover. $

CORONA
▨ **The Lemon Ice King of Corona,** 52-02 108th St., at Corona Ave. (☎ 718-699-5133). Subway: 7 to 111th St.; a healthy walk back 1 block to 108th and south 10 blocks. Keep walking—it's worth it. One of the most famous sites in Queens, on par with the Unisphere. The Emperor of Cool scrapes up juicy frozen treats outdoors. Every flavor you could want, including bubblegum, blueberry, cantaloupe, cherry, and, of course, lemon ($1-1.50). In the small park across the street, watch old Italian men play *bacci* in the summer. Open daily 10am-midnight. $

FOREST HILLS
▨ **Nick's Pizza,** 108-26 Ascan Ave. between Austin and Burns St. (☎ 718-263-1126). Subway: E, F, G, R to Forest Hills/71st Ave.; then walk 3 blocks on Queens Ave. (the numbers should be going up) and take a right on Ascan Ave. Suburban establishment serves up some of the best pizza in Queens. Flaky crust and delectable sauce and toppings ($11-12, toppings $2 extra). Open M-Th 11:30am-9:30pm, F 11:30am-11:30pm, Sa 12:30-11:30pm, Su 12:30-9:30pm. $

Più Bello, 70-09 Austin St. (☎ 718-268-4400). Subway: E, F to 71st Rd.-Continental Ave.; walk west on Queens Blvd. past 70th Rd. to 70th Ave., then take a left. A slick, family-owned restaurant where the neighborhood's cool kids hang out. The Argentine expatriate owners make their smooth *gelato* and delicious cakes on the premises. Entrees $7-8. Individual pizzas from $4. More than 20 *gelato* flavors ($6). Open daily 9am-1am. AmEx, V, MC. $

Eddie's Sweet Shop, 105-29 Metropolitan Ave., at 72nd Rd. (☎ 718-520-8514). Subway: E, F to 71st Rd.-Continental Ave.; then take the Q23 to Metropolitan Ave. or a 15min. walk through the suburbs. Selling homemade ice cream ($2), savory cappuccino ($3), junky brass horse sculptures ($90), and porcelain wares for 30 years. Decor evokes parlors of the 1950s and Swensen's of the 1980s. Open Tu-F 1-11:30pm, Sa-Su noon-11:30pm. **$**

JAMAICA

In Jamaica and other West Indian neighborhoods to the southeast, you can get cheap fast food like Jamaican beef patties or West Indian *rito* (flour tortillas filled with potatoes, meat, and spices). Jamaica Ave., in downtown Jamaica, and Linden Blvd., in neighboring St. Albans, boast many restaurants specializing in this type of cuisine. Jamaica also holds a **farmer's market,** 159-15 Jamaica Ave., where a few farmers offer their bounty next to a food court featuring Caribbean and Carolina-Southern eateries. Market: ☎ 718-291-0282. Open M-Sa 7am-7pm. *(To get to Jamaica: E, J to Jamaica Center; from there the Q4 bus goes to Linden Blvd. in St. Albans.)*

BAYSIDE

The nightlife area of Queens offers cheap appetizers and specials at bar/restaurants.

First Edition, 41-08 Bell Blvd., at 41st Ave. (☎ 718-428-8522). Subway: 7 to Main St.-Flushing; then the Q12 bus (catch it in front of Stern's Department Store, next to the station) along Northern Ave. to Bell Blvd., then walk north 3 blocks. Neon animal-print bar/restaurant has cheap, filling food specials and costly drinks. Entrees $8-14. Daily ½-price appetizer specials. Lively singles scene at night. Open Su-Th noon-11pm, F-Sa noon-2am; bar noon-3am. V, MC. **$-$$**

THE BRONX

⚑ *To get to the heart of the culinary Bronx,* **Arthur Ave.:** *subway C, D to Fordham Rd. and walk 5 blocks east; or subway 2 to Pelham Pkwy., then bus Bx12 two stops west.*

The cuisine of the Bronx reflects its diverse make-up, but the local Italian fare is the culinary magnet of the borough. The neighborhood of **Belmont** brims with pastry shops, streetside *caffè*, pizzerias, restaurants, and mom-and-pop emporiums vending Madonna 45s and imported espresso machines, without the touristy frills of Little Italy.

see map pp. 348-349

▨ Dominick's, 2335 Arthur Ave., near 186th St. (☎ 718-733-2807). Always packed, this small family-style Italian eatery sports an extra bar upstairs. Waiters seat you at a long table and simply ask what you want. No menu here and no set prices—locals are happy to give advice. Linguine with mussels and marinara ($7), marinated artichoke ($7), and veal *francese* ($12) are all house specials. Arrive before 6pm or after 9pm, or expect a 20min. wait. Open M and W-Sa noon-10pm, F noon-11pm, Su 1-9pm. **$-$$**

▨ Emilia's, 2331 Arthur Ave., near 186th St. (☎ 718-367-5915). Delicious food in large portions. The *calamari fra diavolo* ($15) is especially good. Appetizers $5-10; pasta $10; entrees $13-18. Lunch special $10. Open M-F and Su noon-10pm, Sa noon-11pm. **$$**

Pasquale's Rigoletto, 2311 Arthur Ave. (☎ 718-365-6644). Pasquale's will soothe you with luscious arias; if you have a favorite in mind, ask to have it played—or sing it yourself on amateur night (Sa). Favorite customer Joe Pesci's pictures adorn the front door. Pasta $13; meat dishes $15 and up; poultry $15; seafood $17. Open Su-F noon-9:30, Sa noon-10:30. **$$**

Reef Restaurant (a.k.a. Johnny's Reef), 2 City Island Ave. (☎ 718-885-2086). Surrounded by squawking seagulls and grease, Johnny's serves up cheap, fresh seafood, steamed or fried. Fish and chips $8. Open Su-Th 11am-midnight, F-Sa 11am-1am. **$**

SHOPS

Egidio Pastry Shop, 622 E. 187th St., at Hughes (☎ 718-295-6077). A neighborhood tradition. Since 1912, Egidio has baked up mountains of Italian pastries and cakes. The colorful cases display over 100 different fresh-baked goodies. The ever-popular cannoli ($1.25) tastes divine with a steaming cappuccino ($2.75). Homemade ices 75¢-$2.50. Open daily 8am-8pm.

STATEN ISLAND

see map p. 350

Cargo Cafe, 120 Bay St., near the SI Chamber of Commerce, away from the Ferry Terminal (☎ 718-876-0539). A painted exterior and open windows with iron fencing cut at different heights give this bar/restaurant a dark funky feeling. Art on walls and board games add to the chill atmosphere. Lunch special (daily special and beer) $4.95, dinner entrees about $8. **Open mic** M 9:30pm-midnight, **acoustic live** Sa 11pm-2am. Open daily noon-4am.

Nezzerman, 40 Bay St., at the start of Bay St. (☎ 718-815-3366). Swanky and dark, this lounge serves lunch and dinner and is open late. Dark blue speckled walls in the diner-esque dining room meld with the cabaret-feel of the bar and lounge area. Visit the bathroom where a screw is painted on one door, a nut on the other. **80's Night** Tu, **live jazz** W, **Different Thursdays** (deep tribal funk), F/Sa **live band/DJ** F and Sa. No cover. M 11am-3pm, Tu-Sa 11am-4am, M-F happy hour 4-7pm.

Nightlife

A city like this one makes me dream tall and feel in on things.
—Toni Morrison, *Jazz*

When that insomniac empress, Gotham, loosens her corset, takes down her hair, and retires her bustle, so should you. See performance art; witness avant-garde comedy; hear live hip-hop; sip a highball; work it at a drag show; and absolutely learn to salsa. Do whatever, so long as you keep up with your hungry hostess, the city herself. In New York's night kitchen, you could easily cook up a different feast for the senses every evening of your life and never repeat. Whether you prefer Times Square's blinding lights or a Harlem jazz club, a smoky Borough bar or a Lower East Side be-seen-ery, allow yourself to succumb to the city's dark side. At the end of it all, a 4:30am cab ride home through empty streets with the windows down will inevitably make your spirits soar. A number of publications print daily, weekly, and monthly nightlife calendars; try *Time Out: New York*, the *Village Voice*, *New York* magazine, *The New York Free Press*, and *The New York Times* (particularly the Sunday edition). The monthly *Free Time* calendar ($1.25) lists free cultural events throughout Manhattan. You can also tap endlessly knowledgeable salespeople at record stores (see **Shopping,** p. 137) for cultural information about music scenes in New York; if *Let's Go* doesn't list it, ask them to help you find that one club that spins "Cubo-funk-trip-indie-ambient" on a Tuesday evening. For gay and lesbian nightlife options see **Gay and Lesbian Life,** p. 221.

BARS

No one bar scene defines NYC in the way that pubs define Ireland or cruisy Hollywood bars define Los Angeles. NYC doesn't merely have every type of bar, but does them all

FLYERS! GET YOUR FRESH FLYERS!

Too good for our recommendations? Keep your eyes peeled as you travel the city by day to find nighttime options. Although NYC doesn't have the flyer culture that other big cities do, there are plenty of places to pick up party, club, or concert ads. Here are a few good stores to look into if you're around the neighborhood. And if it's a special type of music you're into, ask around at record stores—smaller, specialized stores generally have in-the-know staff.

Etherea, 66 Ave. A. Flyers for house/loungecore/techno events.

8th St. Lab, 69 E. 8th St. Huge selection of club flyers and the coveted *Flyer* monthly mag.

Dance Tracks, corner of First Ave. and E. 3rd St. Flyers for house music and techno events.

Throb, 211 E. 14th St. Techno event flyers.

Metropolis, 43 Third Ave. Club flyers.

A-1 Record Shop, 439 E. 6th St. Various flyers for hip-hop as well as techno club flyers.

House of Trance, 122 St. Mark's Pl. Trance/ambient event flyers.

Store, 325 E. 9th St. Mostly techno club flyers.

well. Bars listed by neighborhood are loosely ranked, but personal preference depends on your own social or alchoholic slant.

SOHO AND TRIBECA

Naked Lunch Bar and Lounge, 17 Thompson St., at Grand St. (☎343-0828). Adorned with the roach-and-typewriter motif found in the novel and movie of the same name. The after-work crowd has no qualms about dancing in the aisle alongside the bar. Unbeatable martinis like the Tanqueray tea ($8). Free BBQ hamburgers and hot dogs served W. All beers $6. Sometimes a $7 cover F and Sa after 10pm. Take $2 off all drinks during Happy Hour Tu-F 5-9pm. Open Tu-F 5pm-4am, Sa 9pm-4am.

Milady's, 160 Prince St., at Thompson (☎226-9069). A rough in the overbearing diamond mine that is SoHo. Down-to-earth neighborhood haunt that claims the only pool table in SoHo (not exactly accurate) and a cast of affable regulars. Milady's is a fun joint to shuck off local pretense and have a good time. Everything (even martinis) under $6. Good, inexpensive food served Su-Th 11am-midnight, F-Sa 11am-1am. Open daily 11am-4am.

NV and 289 Lounge, 289 Spring St., near Varick St. (☎929-6868). Gothic playground meets post-industrialism and results in a web of ceiling pipes over the curtain-laden, sconce-enhanced chambers. Two bars and dance floors. As long as the club remains up 'n' coming, you can enter the iron gates without too much bouncer inspection. Mixed drinks are club priced ($8-10) and the cover ($10-20) could be much more substantial for a night of pure fun. W and Su nights feature great R&B, hip-hop, and reggae vibes. Happy Hour W-Th 6-10pm. Open W-Su 10pm-4am.

Lucky Strike, 59 Grand St., at W. Broadway (☎941-0772). The people here are beautiful, but don't let that stop you. They're too secure to be pretentious, so all are welcome. Lovely food and divine drinks ($4 and up). The vanilla shanti ($8) tastes like a carnival in a martini glass. Open Su-W noon-3am, Th-Sa noon-4am.

MercBar, 151 Mercer St., between Prince and Houston Sts. (☎966-2727). Trendy bar with a good-looking crowd. Cozy couches and dim lighting set a relaxing mood. Looking for love? Maybe the drink will suffice ($11). All beers $6; mixed drinks start at $6. Open M-Tu 5pm-1:30am, W 5pm-2am, Th-Sa 5pm-3:30am, Su 6pm-1:30am.

Circa Tabac, 32 Watt St., between Sixth Ave. and Thompson St. (☎941-1781). Claims to be the first, and perhaps only, cigarette lounge in the world. As the war against smoking has become entrenched even in downtown NY, Circa Tabac remains a haven for cigarette-lovers. Enhancing its atmosphere of taboo, Tabac's trendy decor recalls a Prohibition-era speakeasy, with protective curtains and Art Deco pieces. State-of-the-art air purifiers and odor killers keep the air clear and sweet-smelling. 160 different kinds of cigarettes ($5-12); a few glam cigs perched on slender holders are always available. Domestic beers $5, imported $6; "champagne cocktails" $9-12. Open Su-W 5pm-2am, Th-Sa 5pm-4am.

X-R Bar, 128 Houston St., at Sullivan St. (☎674-4080). Comfortable joint sports couches and glowing marble behind a bar pumping true blues. Su-W quality live music focusing on acoustic sound with a gospel/bluesey lining; Th-Sa DJ. Beers $3-5; drinks $4-6. Happy Hour daily 3-7pm; all drinks $1 off. Open M-Sa 3pm-4am, Su 4pm-4am.

Cafe Noir, 32 Grand St., at Thompson St. (☎431-7910). Cool in so many ways. The patrons, the bartenders, and the street-front windows (open in summer), all provide this bar/lounge/restaurant with a classy but unpretentious feel. Draft beers $5-6. Entrees $19. Open daily noon-4am.

Fanelli's, 94 Prince St., at Mercer St. (☎226-9412). Established in 1847 in a beautiful building of black cast iron. A casual neighborhood hangout, where it always feels like it's late. Offers a full menu with great burgers ($8). Standard bar fare, cheap brew ($4 for domestic drafts, $4.50 for imports and microbrews), and a quick-witted waitstaff. Pick up a complimentary copy of their official history by the door. Open M-Th 10am-1:30am, F-Sa 10am-2:30am, Su 11am-1:30am.

Denizen, 73 Thompson St., between Broome and Spring Sts. (☎966-7299; 226-9858). This elegant and sexy bar/restaurant features some of the best flavored cosmos this city has to offer ($9). Check out the rock wall bathrooms. Restaurant open daily 5pm-2am; bar stays open until 4am.

Bar 89, 89 Mercer St., between Spring and Broome Sts. (☎274-0989). Upscale bar/restaurant serving American fare to a stylish crowd. Salads $7-11; sandwiches $7.50-10. All-American Grilled Cheese ($7.50) worth trying. The main attraction, however, is the unisex bathroom, which features glass doors that only become opaque when latched precisely. Open daily noon-1:15am.

GREENWICH VILLAGE

▧ **The Whitehorse Tavern,** 567 Hudson St. at W. 11th St. (☎243-9260). Dylan Thomas drank himself to death here, pouring 18 straight whiskies through an already tattered liver. Boisterous students and locals pay homage to the poet. Great jukebox. Outdoor patio. Beer $3-5. Open Su-Th 11am-2am, F-Sa 11am-4am.

▧ **The Village Idiot,** 355 W. 14th St., between Eighth and Ninth Aves. (☎989-7334). No Dostoevksy here. New York's infamous honky-tonk bar has reopened in the Village, and the beer is still cheap ($1.25 mugs of MGD), the music still loud (and still country), and the ambience still as close to a roadhouse as this city gets. As if the customers' drunken antics weren't enough, the (female) staff occasionally dances on the bar and gives out free shots. Open daily noon-4am.

Automatic Slims, 733 Washington St., at Bank St. (☎645-8660). Simple bar with an excellent selection of blues and soul. Decorated with pictures of the Velvet Underground. 20-somethings sit at tables with classic vinyls under glass. Weekends pack a more diverse crowd. American cooking served 6pm-midnight. Entrees $7.50-14. Open Tu-Sa 6pm-4am.

Moomba, 133 Seventh Ave. S., betweeen W. 10th and Charles Sts. (☎989-1414). Hip, candlelit lounge with a mellow mood. Come for cocktails ($8-15) or Karoake (M; cover $5). Supposedly Madonna and Prince come here—but that's such a NYC bar claim. Open daily 6pm-3am; Su brunch 11:30am-4pm.

Bar 6, 502 Sixth Ave., between 12th and 13th St. (☎691-1363). Subway: #1, 2, 3 to 14th St.; or A, E, B, or D to Sixth Ave./8th St. French-Moroccan bistro by day, sizzling bar by night. Live DJ spins (primarily house) F-Su nights. Beers on tap ($4-5 per pint) usually from local Brooklyn Brewery. Kitchen open Su-Th noon-2am, F-Sa noon-3am; bar stays open later.

Kava Lounge, 605 Hudson St., between Bethune and W. 12th Sts. (☎989-7504). Done in stylish brass and tans, Kava is a few blocks removed from the colorful center of the West Village. The bar prides itself on its vast selection of Aussie and New Zealander wines. 2-for-1 Happy Hour M-F 5-7pm. Open Su-W 5pm-1am, Th-Su 5pm-4am.

Panaché Brasserie, 470 Sixth Ave., between 11th and 12th Sts. (☎243-2222). This austere bar and café invites the posturing of failed poets and philosophers, cigarette and chalice in hand. Even if you can't resist the urge to strike a pose, indulge in the people-watching, '60s avant-garde music (think Nico. . . solo), and delicious crepes ($3.25-5). Open Su-M 11am-2am, Tu-F 11am-4am.

Peculiar Pub, 145 Bleecker St. (☎353-1327). 500 brews (25 on tap) priced from $3.25 (the usual American suspects) to $13 (limited-edition Belgian über-ales), including such obscure labels as Cyprus' smooth, Keo lager, distinguish this underground beer hall. Open Su-W 5pm-2am, Th-Sa 5pm-4am.

Nell's, 246 W. 14th St., between Seventh and Eighth Aves. (☎675-1567). Declining legendary hot spot; the faithful hang on for mellow schmoozing and soulful music upstairs and phat beats below. Racially diverse crowd. Free comedy M nights. Beer $6. Cover Su-W $10, Th-Sa $15. No sneakers or jeans. Open M 7pm-1am, W 9pm-3am, other nights 10pm-4am.

The Slaughtered Lamb Pub, 182 W. 4th St., at Jones St. (☎627-5262). A somewhat sinister-looking English Pub dedicated to the werewolf, with surprisingly appealing results. Patronized by a fond NYU crowd. More than 150 types of beer ($5-25 per bottle) and yards of ale. $3 special on rotating beers. Open Su-Th noon-2am, F-Sa noon-4am.

Rose's Turn, 55 Grove St (☎366-5438). Mixed piano bar with open mic and perhaps the most musically talented barstaff in New York. Bar is packed F-Sa; Su provides a small-to-medium crowd for a pleasant balance of liveliness and intimacy. Come F-Su 9pm-4am to hear singer Terri White (who also tends bar)—her voice is one of the city's undiscovered wonders. Beer $4.50-5.50. Drinks $5-6. Open daily 4pm-4am.

LOWER EAST SIDE

bOb Bar, 235 Eldridge St. between Houston and Stanton Sts. (☎777-0588). Comfy and laid-back, with a hip-hop-inclined crowd and DJs that spin anything they can get their hands on. Happy Hour F 7-10pm $2 beers. While Tu alternates between Latin, reggae, and hip-hop (free), Th is strictly hip-hop ($5 cover after 10pm) in this small but happening bar. Open daily 7pm-4am.

Idlewild, 145 E. Houston St., between Eldridge and Forsyth Sts. (☎477-5005). This eclectic spot is still hip. Taking JFK airport's former name and running with it, the spot lifts the theme bar to new heights (get it?) with a fuselage-shaped interior, reclining airplane seats with tray tables, and a boarding ramp. Th is a chill drum'n'bass night (free). Beer $4-5. Drinks $7-10. Open Su-W 8pm-3am, Th-Sa 8pm-4am.

Orchard Bar, 200 Orchard St., between Houston and Stanton Sts. (☎673-5350). A long, narrow haunt frequented by hip Lower East Side scene-sters. The lack of a sign out front should clue you in to the fact that you needn't mention that you heard about it in a travel guide. DJ after 10pm on some weekend nights. F is proper house with one of NY's best DJs, Rob Salmon (free). Beer $4-5. Other drinks $5-6. Open daily 6pm-4am.

Fun, 130 Madison St., at Pike St. (☎964-0303). In-the-know hipsters hang at this "never a cover, never a guest list" hangout, and so can you. Its whimsical decor (complete with hydraulic lifts for the bartenders and wall video projections) merit the self-titled "integrated sound and video environment." VJs and DJs rotate nightly. Tu playstation nights. Drinks start at $9 but are worth the phunne. Open daily 8pm-4am.

Max Fish, 178 Ludlow St., at Houston St. (☎529-3959). Aggressively hip bar draws big crowds of cool people Th-Sa, and small crowds of cool people on other days. Easily the best jukebox in town, playing everything from the Fugees to the Stooges. Keeps all the great things about a bar: pinball, pool tables, and relatively inexpensive drinks. Beer $2.75. Open daily 5:30pm-4am.

Baby Jupiter, 170 Orchard St. (☎982-2229). Everything you could want in a single locale—including local art and a metal shark. Delicious food with a Southern flair, like the blackened catfish ($13). Brunch Sa 11am-4pm, Su 11am-5pm. Entrees $10+. Beers $4, cocktails $6-8. Bar hosts music, comedy, and performance art. Comfy couches in the back room let you curl up as you digest. Music acts every night, with a different act almost every hour. Occasional $5 cover. Open Su-Th 11am-midnight, F-Sa 11am-1am; shows start at 8pm.

EAST VILLAGE

Tribe, 132 First Ave., at St. Mark's Pl. (☎979-8965). Behind the frosted glass windows lies a chic, friendly bar with colorful but subtle back lighting, complete with comfortable lounging areas. DJ nightly: M live music and DJ, Tu Salsa/Latin. Beer $5; cocktails $5-10. Open daily 5pm-4am.

Bbar (Bowery Bar), 40 E. 4th St., at the Bowery (☎475-2220). Bbar has long held court on Bowery as a flagship of cooler-than-thou-ness. While newer spots challenge its cachet, this white and blue building—with garden patio—and its frequenters have still got more than enough attitude to give you a healthy sense of self-worth for going there. $5 beers. Tu night is "Beige," Erich Conrad's wonderfully flamboyant gay party. Open Su-Th 11:30am-3am, F-Sa 11:30am-4am.

Izzy Bar, 166 First Ave., at 10th St. (☎228-0444). Izzy Bar is a chic, wooden-decor-laden, votive-glowing hangout that happens to also spin progressive sets of drum'n'bass, funky house, and other "ful-feeling music" in its two floors. Drinks are pricey (Corona $5) but worth it for the atmosphere. Cover up to $7. Open daily 7pm-4am.

Coup, 509 E. 6th St., between Aves. A and B (☎979-2815). Wood, silver beams, and capsule-esque lights create a futuristic modern bar. Beer $5; wine $7. Open daily 4pm-4am.

Simone, 134 First Ave., at St. Mark's Pl. (☎982-6665). Step into this lushly-decorated oriental temple-meets-cabaret for espresso, wine, and food. Its windows open onto First Ave., making for great people-watching. Open daily noon-4am.

Yogi's Bar

d.b.a., 41 First Ave., between 2nd and 3rd Sts. (☎475-5097). It could mean "drink better ale" or "don't bother asking." Peruse the drink menus written meticulously on chalk boards. With 19 premium beers on tap (Corona $5), well over 100 bottled imports and micro-brews, classy bourbons and whiskeys ($6), wines ($5), and 45 different tequilas, this extremely friendly space lives up to its motto—"drink good stuff." Beers debut here, and tastings are held monthly. Mellow jazz and a sassy crowd. Outdoor beergarden open until 10pm. Open daily 1pm-4am.

Beauty Bar, 231 E. 14 St., between Second and Third Aves. (☎539-1389). Unless you knew this was a bar, you would think it was a regular beauty parlor. Both the exterior and interior retain its original outfit, and its customers seem well primped in a slightly punk style. Beer $3-4.50, during happy hour (M-F 5-8pm) $1 off. Crowded with East Village natives all week. Open Su-Th 5pm-4am, F-Sa 7pm-4am.

Naked Lunch Bar

Korova Milk Bar, 200 Ave. A, between 12th and 13th Sts. (☎254-8838). A tribute to the recently deceased Stanley Kubrick's twisted vision, this mockup of little Alex's "moloko plus" bar in *A Clockwork Orange* is replete with sultry naked female mannequins, lusciously shaped couches, Kubrick's movie playing on various screens, and an anarchist atmosphere. Drink specials and no cover F 7-10pm. Open daily 5pm-4am.

McSorley's Old Ale House, 15 E. 7th St., at Third Ave. (☎473-9148). Their motto is, "We were here before you were born," and unless you're 146 years old, they're right. Since its 1854 opening, McSorley's has played host to such luminaries as Abe Lincoln, the Roosevelts (Teddy and Frankie) and John Kennedy; women were not allowed in until 1970. A crowd respectful of the pervasive sense of history comes to share in each other's company. Only 2 beers: light and dark. Two-fisters take note: mugs come 2 at a time ($3 for 2). Open M-Sa 11am-1am, Su 1pm-1am.

Sake Bar Decibel, 240 E. 9th St., off Second Ave. (☎979-2733). All things Japanese are seriously fashionable in the East Village, and *sake* (Japanese rice wine) is no exception. Downstairs bar imitates Japanese architectural simplicity. Very Japanese clientele. Over 60 kinds of *sake* $4-6 per glass. Minimum order $8 per person during busy weekend hours. Open M-Sa 8pm-3am, Su 8pm-1am.

Knitting Factory

WELCOME TO THE JUNGLE

Early in the 90s, black Londoners spawned jungle, a frantic urban music style that has adapted well to New York City. NYC is the original urban jungle, although here the crowd is comprised mostly of white post-ravers. Jungle incorporates the slow, dubby basslines of reggae with sped-up hip-hop breakbeats and recombinant sampling strategies, stewed thick and fast with inflections of techno. The result is edgy, experimental, and futuristic. New York now offers a few jungle club nights a week. **Konkrete Jungle** (☎604-4224) is the most established, while **Jungle Nation** (☎802-7495) throbs with a more serious crowd. The legendary, though mainstream, Limelight hosts a Global Bass party once a summer; call for date and details. (660 6th Ave., at 20th St. ☎807-7780. $20 advance tickets, $25 at the door.) For slightly more drum 'n' bass-oriented clubbing, try Thursday nights at **Aria**, 539 W. 21st St., presented by DJ Cassien and friends. ($8 before midnight, $10 after; 21+ only.) DJs to look for include Dara, Delmar, Soulslinger, DB, Cassien, and Peshay. Smaller music stores probably offer the best resource for finding jungle nights, with flyers and knowledgeable staff.

La Linea, 15 First Ave., between 1st and 2nd Sts. (☎777-1571). A long narrow bar with three rooms. The first opens onto the street and is a friendly, lantern-laden bar room. The middle room is a comfortable lounge area, and the back room is a blue grotto. Beer $4; happy hour (daily 3-9pm) $1 off. M is Sexual Chocolate night: DJ, no cover, $3 margaritas after 9pm. Open daily 3pm-4am.

Lucky Cheng's, 24 First Ave. between 1st and 2nd Sts. (☎473-0516). One of New York's better-known drag clubs, with an Asian twist. Upstairs restaurant and downstairs bar decorated in over-the-top Asian kitsch, serviced by gorgeous "girls" (who are more of a draw than the food). Tempura salmon rolls ($9) and other dimsum delights. Drag shows Su-W 8pm, 10pm, and 11:30pm; Th 8:30pm, 11pm, and 12:30am; F-Sa 7:30pm, 12:30am, and 1:30am. F night "trans-fem-ation" party: cover for "girls" $10, boys $15. Bar open Su-Th 6pm-midnight, F-Sa 6pm-3am.

Tenth Street Lounge, 212 E. 10th St., between First and Second Aves. (☎473-5252). An unassuming door opens up a world of swank. Chic village hangout with a matching clientele. Gorgeous place for an early-evening drink. $4-5 beers. Occasional $10 cover F-Sa evenings; no cover in summer. Call ahead to be put on the guest list. Open M-Sa 5pm-3am, Su 3pm-2am.

KGB, 85 E. 4th St., at Second Ave. (☎505-3360). Formerly a meeting place for the Ukrainian Communist Party, this dark red hangout for literati and Slavophiles retains its original furnishings, including the Lenin propaganda banner and candle-illuminated photos of factories. Furtive entrance that harks upon its revolutionary past. Occasional readings. Over 20 different kinds of Stoli ($3 per shot). Open daily 7:30pm-4am.

Joe's Bar, 520 E. 6th St., between Aves. A and B (☎473-9093). An eclectic, typically East Village neighborhood crowd makes up most of the regulars. Very laid-back. Pilsner, Bass, and Fosters on tap. Beers $2-3 a mug. Serious pool on M nights. Open daily noon-4am.

Doc Holliday's, 141 Ave. A, at 9th St. (☎979-0312). Expect a raucous clientele, cheap beer ($1.75 cans of Pabst Blue Ribbon), lots of cowboy boots affixed to the walls and ceiling, and country music blaring from the jukebox. Coronas $4, Bud $3.50. Happy hour daily 5-8pm with 2-for-1 drinks. Open daily noon-4am.

MIDTOWN: CHELSEA, UNION SQ.

Coffee Shop Bar, see **Food & Drink,** p. 192.

Billiard Club, 220 W. 19th St. (☎206-7665). Thirsty for pool? $7 per hr. 11am-7pm; $12 per hr. after 7pm. Opens M-F 11am, Sa 1pm, Su 2pm; closes late everyday.

Lemon, 230 Park Ave. South, above Union Sq. Park (☎614-1200). A unique version of a Hard Rock Cafe, this restaurant-bar sells magazines on the main floor. Relaxing—a good place to go for drinks and a chat. Open M-W and Su 11:30am-midnight, Th-Sa 11:30am-3am.

Old Town Bar and Grill, 45 E. 18th St. between Park Ave. and Broadway (☎529-6732). A quiet, dark, 104-year-old hideaway nestled among furniture and interior decoration shops, with wood, brass, and a mature clientele to match. Seen on the old "Late Night with David Letterman" opening montage. Beware of perpetual after-work and weekend mobs. Beer on tap $4, Heineken $3.75. Open M-Sa 11:30am-1am, Su 3pm-midnight. AmEx, V, MC.

Passerby, 436 W. 15th St. between Ninth and Tenth Aves. (☎266-7321). Adjacent to owner Gavin Brown's gallery, Passerby's mirror and neon floor panels create a dizzying space-age-meets-70s-disco optical illusion on the outskirts of the meat-packing district. Most drinks $8. Open Su-M 6pm-1am, Tu-W 6pm-2am, Th-Sa 6pm-4am.

Heartland Brewery, 35 Union Sq. W., at 17th St. (☎645-3400). Packed, loud, and friendly brew pub with a "down home" American menu ($13-15) and an after-work corporate crowd. Daytime family feel gives way to swinging singles' scene at night. Draught beers $5. Open M-Th noon-11pm, F-Sa noon-midnight, Su noon-10pm; bar closes 2 hours later. AmEx, V, MC, Transmedia.

Peter McManus, 152 Seventh Ave., at 19th St. (☎WA9-9691). Made famous by a *New York Times* article on the timeless appeal of ordinary bars, of which this is the epitome. Ordinary drinks, ordinary clientele, and ordinary prices. The carved mahogany bar and leaded glass windows add to the ordinary pub charm. A smattering of video games and a jukebox. Dinner specials $6-8 until midnight. Draught beers $2-4.50. Open daily 10:30am-3am.

B.M.W. Bar, 199 Seventh Ave. between 21st and 22nd Sts. (☎229-1807). A funky dive with local art and unique objects adorning the walls. Serves Beer, Music, Wine ($4-6), and Coffee, an option that didn't make it into its name. Happy hour M-F 4-8pm: house wine and beer $3. Open mic Tu from 10pm-late. Live music. Open daily 4pm-4am.

Tramps, 51 W. 21st St. between Fifth and Sixth Ave. (☎727-7788). One of the best places to hear your favorite band if they've got a gig here. Screaming violins and clattering washboards pack the intimate space. Indie rock, disco, hip-hop, Louisiana zydeco, blues, and reggae bands. Box office open M-F 11am-7pm, Sa noon-7pm, extended on night of show. Sets usually M-Th 8pm, Sa-Su 9pm. Doors open 1hr. before shows. Cover $5-20.

UPPER WEST SIDE

Amsterdam Ave. between 86th and 68th Sts. is lined with bars, mostly of the rambunctious, sports bar variety, but there are also bars for martini-drinking, high-heeled patrons. If you don't like where you are, just walk next door.

🏅 **Potion Lounge,** 370 Columbus Ave. between 77th and 78th Sts. (☎721-4386). Step into this silvery-blue lounge complete with local art on the walls, bubbles rising through pipes in the windows, and velvety sofas. Order a colorful layered drink ("potions" around $10) and watch a chemical miracle take place before your eyes. The Potion Lounge is NY at its hippest...and friendliest. Boys, an icy surprise awaits you, if you so choose, in the bathroom. DJs on weekends. Open M-Th 6pm-midnight, F-Sa 6pm-4am.

🏅 **The Evelyn Lounge,** 380 Columbus Ave., at the corner of 78th St. (☎724-2363). Swanky bar for the after-work set. Great live music Tu-Th 9:30pm-1:30am. Drinks ($9 martinis) are a bit pricey but cover the cost of comfy couches colonized by cultured cliques. Enticing bar menu $7-14. Open daily 6pm-4am.

Hi-Life Bar and Grill, 477 Amsterdam Ave., at 83rd St. (☎787-7199). Step into the 1950s at this chic, sleek hangout with a friendly waitstaff and late-night menu. Sushi and raw bar ½-price M-Tu, big bowls of pasta $8 W and Su, fajitas $8.50 Th and Sa. Other early dinner specials daily 5-7:30pm. DJ Th-Sa. Open M-F 4:30pm-late, Sa-Su 10:30am-4pm for brunch and 4:30pm-late.

Merchants, 521 Columbus Ave. between 85th and 86th Sts. (☎721-3689). Intimate tables by the fireplace in winter and a happening sidewalk scene in the summer makes Merchants perennially popular. Swank singles scene. Draughts $5; cocktails $5-9. Open daily 11:30am-4am.

Yogi's, 2156 Broadway, at 76th St. (☎873-9852). Three attributes place this bar in the booze stratosphere: a constant stream of Elvis and country faves from the jukebox; bartenders' and customers' predilection to dance on the bar; and, most importantly, seriously cheap beer. The bar's namesake bear greets outside. Pitchers $5; shots from $1.50. Open daily noon-4am.

◼ ▐ ◨ ▨ ▥ ▦ ◧ ▞ ◰ ◩ ▨ ◪ ◓ ◩ ▞ ◨ ◧ ▨

UPPER EAST SIDE

Ozone, 1720 Second Ave. between 89th and 90th Sts. (☎860-8950). Dim and elegant, Ozone's front room holds a classy bar, while the back has a mellow and comfortable lounge. Wear black and walk in with an attitude—you'll fit right in. Large selection of imported ($4) and domestic ($3) beers. Happy Hour daily 4-7pm; live DJ spinning the latest in funk, jazz, and hip-hop F-Sa. Open Su-W 4pm-2am, Th-Sa 4pm-4am.

Match, Uptown, 33 E. 60th St. between Madison and Park Aves. (☎906-9177). Sleek and elegant bar in a nouveau-Asian restaurant. Dim lighting and a sophisticated crowd dressed-to-impress make this a NY hotspot. Beer $5, cocktails $7-8, dim sum rack $9.50. Open daily 11:30am-midnight. **Downtown:** 160 Mercer St. between Houston and Prince Sts. (☎343-0020).

Mo's Caribbean Bar and Grille, 1454 Second Ave., at 76th St. (☎650-0561). Lively, friendly bar with the island touch. Big screen TV invites raucous and rapt attention to sporting events. Sign onto website for 2 free drinks. Beer, imported and Caribbean, $4.50; domestic $4.00. Try the mixed drinks, like the famous Mo' Betta Colada ($6). Happy Hour 4-7pm. Open M-F 4pm-4am, Sa-Su noon-4am.

Auction House, 300 E. 89th St. between First and Second Aves. (☎427-4458). Don't be intimidated by the name of the bar or its seemingly calculated "antique" appearance. Inside this classy establishment are rooms of ornately-carved, comfortable wood chairs, gilt oil paintings of naked women, and crimson velvet curtains. Sit back and watch the young elite mingle and drink. Beers $5. Open Su-Th 7:30pm-2am, F-Sa 7:30pm-4am.

Brother Jimmy's Carolina Kitchen BBQ, 1461 First Ave., at 76th St. (☎545-7427). The sign advertises "BBQ and booze," and this greasy-chops Carolina kitchen serves up plenty of both. Ribs are a bit pricey ($17), but the bar is where the action is—light weights, watch out. Lots of original drinks; "Swampwater" comes with a toy alligator. Ladies' night M-W serves margaritas and drafts for $1. Happy Hour M-F 5-7pm. Open M-F 5pm-midnight, Sa-Su noon-midnight. Bar stays open until 4am M-Sa, Su until 1am.

Spancill Hill, 1715 First Ave., at 89th St. (☎410-6301). Brand-spankin' new and named after a little horseracing town in Ireland, the relaxing and friendly atmosphere of this bar, with its colorful murals and red candle-lighting, is sure to impress and delight. Imported beer $4.50, domestic $4, draft $4.50-5. Open daily 11pm-4am.

American Trash, 1471 First Ave. between 76th and 77th Sts. (☎988-9008). Cavernous barroom hung with "trash" (read: twisted metal bits) from NASCAR go-carts to Molly Hatchet posters. Have a wild 'n' crazy time celebrating lowbrow culture. Drink specials change nightly. Live music Su (JJ and the All-American-Trash band), live DJ M. Known for their wide variety of beers (domestic $4, imported $4.50). Happy hour M-F noon-7pm, Sa-Su 5-7pm. Open daily noon-4am.

BROOKLYN

Montero's Bar & Grill, 73 Atlantic Ave., at Hicks St., in Brooklyn Heights (☎718-624-9799). Subway: 2, 3, 4, 5, M, N, R to Borough Hall; then 4 blocks on Court St. Heavily bedecked with nautical paraphernalia, this friendly dive still looks like the longshoremen's bar it once was. Beer $3. Open M-Sa 10am-4am, Su noon-4pm.

Waterfront Ale House, 155 Atlantic Ave. between Henry and Clinton Sts. (☎718-522-3794). Subway: 2, 3, 4, 5, M, N, R to Borough Hall; then walk 4 blocks on Court St. Friendly neighborhood joint is a great spot to go for beer and burgers. 15 beers on tap change seasonally. Specials like mussels in a *weiss* beer broth broaden the definition of pub grub. Family eatery by day, offers live blues W nights and jazz on Th nights from 10:30pm. Happy Hour M-F 4-7pm. Open daily noon-11pm; bar open until 3 or 4am.

Brooklyn Ale House, 103 Berry St., at N. 8th St. (☎718-302-9811). Across the street from Teddy's. A friendly neighborhood joint that welcomes everyone. Has interesting theme nights: M is "Cheese Night" with 5-6 types of free *fromage* from Murray's Cheese Shop in the East Village; On Tu there is a good pool tournament. Open daily 3pm-4am.

Teddy's, 96 Berry St., at N. 8th St., in Greenpoint (☎718-384-9787). Subway: L to Bedford Ave. An eclectic mix of artists and wizened Brooklynites—many of them regulars—visits Teddy's for its great jukebox and friendly atmosphere. Great, big Bloody Marys that "bloom" with vegetables ($5). Occasional 1970s lounge night. Tu honky tonk and go go dancin'. Monthly DJ party on one Sa Nov.-Mar. Jazz on Th. Brunch Sa-Su 11am-5pm. Cheap drinks $1-3. Happy hour M-F 4-7pm. Open Su-Th 10am-2:30am, F-Sa 11am-4am.

Montague Street Saloon, 122 Montague St., near Court St. (☎718-522-6770). Subway: 2, 3 to Clark St.; take Henry St. to Montague. The yuppie crowd congregates here to eat, drink, and be merry on this fashionable street in Brooklyn Heights. Open M-Tu 11:30am-1am, W-Su 11:30am-2am.

THE BRONX

The Boat Livery, Inc., 663 City Island Ave., at Bridge St. (☎718-885-1843). Subway: 6 to Pelham Bay Park, then bus Bx29 to City Island Ave. and Kilroe. The place to come if you want cheap beer, bloodworms, or fishing tackle. This is the real deal, the sort of place you can only find on City Island. You can even rent a skiff ($20 per hr.). Bud $1. Boat rental open 5am-4:30pm; bait shop open 5am-8:30pm; bar open 5am-midnight.

SOBs

QUEENS

BAYSIDE

Bell Blvd., out east near the Nassau border, is the center of Queens nightlife for the borough's young and semi-affluent, with many blocks of restaurants, bars, and clubs lining the Boulevard. The best way to deal with this upscale street is to jump from bar to bar to find your niche, be it Irish pub, hoochie-mama rock club, or Jazz bar. The **Bourbon Street** 40-12 Belle Blvd. (☎718-224-2200), has a noisy pub-like atmosphere with frequent live jazz, and **Victorian Lounge** (47-39 Belle Blvd., ☎718-229-0167), clad in gothic curtains and sporting low red and black lighting, are two good options.

Ozone

HOBOKEN, NEW JERSEY

Right across the Hudson River, Hoboken is a small-town (yet still hip and *filled* with bars) alternative to NYC nightlife. See **Daytripping,** p. 230 for listings.

DANCE CLUBS

A wilderness of human flesh
Crazed with avarice, lust and rum
New York, thy name's Delirium.
—Byron R. Newton, "Ode to New York"

Carefree crowds, hype music, unlimited fun, massive pocket book damage—these foundations of the New York club scene make it an unparalleled institution of boogie. The simplest route to fabulosity entails asking around record stores (especially the smaller ones), where salespeople are usually in the know and often have flyers for discount admission. Some of the best parties stay underground, advertised only

BOB Bar

KILLER NIGHTS

The number of deaths at New York City clubs has skyrocketed over the last year. Not since the days of Studio 54 has the New York club scene been so racked with tragedy. Who's to blame? The press seems to be focusing on a tiny pill called Ecstasy. What heroin was to the 70s and cocaine was to the 80s, so ecstasy is to clubbers today. Called "X," "E-ball," or simply "E," it is the drug of the moment. In the summer of 2000, there were several ecstasy-suspected deaths at NYC clubs. An amphetamine, the clinical name for ecstasy is MDNA, and it is categorized as a hallucinogen. Intitally it was considered the ideal drug, as it seemed to have many benefits and few side-effects. But in the last few years, studies have proven that the drug is, in fact, very dangerous. Although the verdict is not out, long-term effects seem to be quite severe, including extreme depression, anxiety attacks, confusion, paranoia and back pain. For more information on Ecstasy, check out www.ecstasy.org.

by word of mouth, or by flyer. Many clubs move from space to space each week, but hard-core clubbers know where to find them.

The rules are simple. Door people, the clubs' fashion police, forbid anything drab or conventional. Like, don't wear khaki shorts and a purse across your chest, for crying out loud. Above all, just look confident—attitude is at least half the battle. Come after 11pm unless you crave solitude. In fact, you're pretty uncool if you show up before 1 or 2am. A few after-hours clubs keep gettin' busy until 5-6am, or even later. Careful, though: even the best clubs are only good on one or two nights a week.

Let's Go has ranked the following according to fun and value. The suggestions could well have changed by the summer of '01, as New York hip is an elusive commodity. Call ahead to make sure that you know what (and whom) you'll find when you arrive.

101 on Seventh, 101 Seventh Ave., 1 block south of Christopher St. (☎620-4000). Featuring live R&B, funk, soul, and old-school hip-hop seven nights a week, this jumping spot is hard to walk past. Happy Hour 6-9pm, all drinks half-price. Open Su-Th 6pm-3am, F-Sa 6pm-4am. No cover. 1 drink min. Beer $6. Mixed drinks $6-8.

Arlene Grocery, 95 Stanton St. between Ludlow and Orchard St. Subway: F to Second Ave or J, M, Z to Essex St. (☎358-1633; www.arlenegrocery.com). Every night Arlene Grocery puts on at least 3 rock, punk, indie, or hip-hop bands back-to-back. Big names like Bob Dylan are known to come by and play in this intimate space. No cover. Doors open at 6pm. Stop by next door at the **Butcher Bar** where the bands sometimes play an impromptu acoustic set. Cover for featured events $5.

Centrofly, 45 W. 21st. St. between Fifth and Sixth Aves. (☎627-7770). This is where the beautiful people come to dance to the latest House and Techno. Although the patrons rave about the martinis ($11), it's the psychedelic lights and funky decor that put the "fly" in Centrofly. Cover $20. Mixed drinks $8-10. Open M-Sa 10pm-5am. Call for weekly schedule of events and DJ's.

Cheetah, 12 W. 21st. St. between Fifth and Sixth Aves. (☎206-7770). Cheetah-print sofas and greenery create the setting for this club. A self-consciously trendy crowd struts it. Beers $6. Cover charge usually $20-25. Th is Clique, female DJ rotation with open bar 10-11pm. F is Great British House with open bar 10-11pm. Sa is Cherchez La Femme, hip hop and R'n'B with open bar 10-11pm. Open 10pm-4am.

Kilimanjaro, 95 Leonard St., at Broadway. (☎343-0957). Featuring the latest in hip-hop, reggae, and R&B, this club will take you to new heights of dancing enjoyment. Themed F always crowded, sweaty, and worth every minute. Cover: women $5 before midnight, $10 after; men $10-15. Drinks $7. Open F-Sa 11pm-4:30am.

Nell's, 246 W. 14th St. between Seventh and Eighth Ave. Subway: #1, 2, 3, or 9 to 14th St. (☎675-1567;

www.nells.com). A legendary hot spot in slight decline; the faithful stay for mellow shmoozing and soulful music upstairs and phat beats below. Diverse crowd. No sneakers, jeans, or workboots. Cover M-W $10, Th-Su $15. Open Th-Su, Tu 10pm-4am, M 8pm-2am, W 9pm-3am.

Ohm, 16 W. 22nd St. between Fifth and Sixth Aves. (☎229-2000). This warehouse-style space, housing three bars and a restaurant, is one of the hottest clubs in the city. F is House and Trance, Sa hears latest Latin and International on the main floor, with hip-hop DJ Louie Passion keeping you on your feet downstairs. Open W-Sa 10pm-4am. Cover $20. Mixed drinks $8-16.

Spa, 76 E. 13th St. between Broadway and Fourth St. (☎388-1062). Don't be intimidated by the elegance of the crowd or the Herculean-sized bouncers. Just wear black and walk in with attitude. "Rock and Roll W;" other nights have hip-hop, house, and R&B to get you in the dancing groove. Th is a very popular gay night. Open Tu-Sa 10pm-4am. Cover F-Sa $20-25.

Tunnel, 220 Twelfth Ave. at 27th St. Subway: #1, 9, or C, E to 23rd St. (☎695-7292 or 695-4682). The premier scene in the late 80s and early 90s, this warehouse club has seen better days, but it still attracts anyone and everyone. With five rooms, lounges, glass-walled live shows, and cages for dancing, crowd is diverse, with celebrities, drag queens, and hip-hop heads alike. F and Sa feature techno, house, R&B, hip-hop, and other genres; Su is hip hop. Dress clean and casual. Cover $20 for women, $25 for men. State-issued ID required. Open F-Su 10pm-4am.

Twilo, 503 W. 27th St. between Tenth and Eleventh Aves. (☎268-1600). Perhaps the best of the widely-known NYC clubs, this warehouse-like complex features cavorting glam boys and their mixed friends. **Junior Vasquez** heats it up on Sa. Parties often run well past noon. Cover $20-25. Doors open around 11pm.

Webster Hall, 125 E. 11th St. between Third and Fourth Ave. Subway: #4, 5, 6, N, or R or L to Union Sq./14th St. 3 blocks south and a block east. (☎353-1600). Popular club offers 4 floors dedicated to R&B/hip hop, 70s and 80s/Top 40, house/techno/trance, and Latin. Sportsbar and coffeebar to boot. Psychedelic Thursdays often feature live bands and Ladies Nights mean all ladies get in free. Open Th-Sa 10pm-4am. Cover F-Sa $25, Su-Th $20.

MISCELLANEOUS HIPSTER HANGOUTS

New York is a sucked orange.
  —Ralph Waldo Emerson

A New York night is filled with attractions and events that defy categorization, from performance art to renegade parties to poetry slams. Many hot spots don't have defined locations: mobile parties like **Giant Step** and **Soul Kitchen** move from club to club with an ardent crowd of followers, drawn in by the innovative amalgamations of jazz, funk, and hip-hop beats. The cover varies from show to show. Check the papers for upcoming locations.

A2i's, 248 W. 14th St., between Seventh and Eighth Aves. (☎807-1775). Two metallic floors—one at street level, one below—throbbing to urban beats laid down by a rotating crew of DJs. Booming BTUs and midriffs are the rule. To get through the velvet rope, come looking the part. Reggae M-Su; Hip Hop and House W-Sa. Cover $5-15. Drinks $6-12. Open W-M 11pm-4am.

BC No Rio, 156 Rivington St., near Clinton St. (☎254-3697; schedule info ☎539-6089). Subway: B, D, Q to Essex St. Walk a block north and then 3 blocks east. A non-profit, community-run space featuring lots of hardcore and punk-related genres, as well as occasional poetry readings, art exhibitions, etc. No alcohol served. All ages. Cover $2-5.

Absolutely 4th, 228 W. 4th St., at Seventh Ave. S. (☎414-4345). A new, sexy splash in the murky puddle that is West Village nightlife. The loungish bar's plush, high-backed, fan-shaped booths are constantly rearranged for a new feel every night. Jazz W, Improv comedy Su. Drinks $5-10. Open daily 4pm-4am.

The Anyway Café, 34 E. 2nd St. at Second Ave. (☎533-3412). Sample Russian-American culture at this dark, relaxed, leopard-spotted hangout. Numerous literary readings during the week, as well as jazz F and Sa nights, and Russian folk on Su. Music of sorts every night from 9pm. Friendly and free of pretension. A great place to kick back with homemade sangria and sample gourmet Russian specialties ($8-12). Open M-Th 5pm-2am, F-Sa 5pm-4am, Su noon-1am.

Astor Bar and Restaurant, 316 Bowery, at Bleecker St. (☎253-8644). Downstairs Moroccan cave-like lounge plays loud R&B and Top 40 (Sa) for late-20s/early-30s business set enjoying their weekend. Shots around $6. Bar until 4am. Restaurant open usually 5-11pm or midnight. Sa-Su brunch 11:30am.

⬛ **Bowlmor,** see **Sports,** p. 173, for info. An after-hours lights-out bowling alley with glowing pins where DJs spin jungle, trip-hop, and house. Beer $2.50.

Chelsea Bar & Billiards, 54 W. 21st St., between Fifth and Sixth Aves. (☎989-0096). A swanky place for cocktails and pool. Cocktails $10, beers cheaper ($5-6). Pool: $5-14 per hr. for first 2 hr., $2-4 per additional hr., high end are on weekend nights. Open daily 11am-4am.

Collective Unconscious, 145 Ludlow St., south of Houston St. (☎254-5277). A performance space collectively (and unconsciously) run by 21 local artists who put up their own shows and provide a venue/studio/rehearsal/you-name-it space for the downtown artistic community. Frequent open-mic events, including Rev. Jen's Anti-Slam (W). Call for events schedule. Friendly, artsy people and usually something interesting. Aug. brings New York's International Fringe Festival. No alcohol or other refreshments served, but BYOB is A-OK. Cover $3-9.

The Elbow Room, 144 Bleecker St., between Thompson St. and LaGuardia Pl. (☎979-8434). Features 3-6 live bands a night playing jazz, blues, and rock to a room that fits 500. Karaoke W 11am-4am. Call for nightly schedule. Cover usually $7. Closed most Su.

Galapagos, 70 N. 6th St., between Kent and Wythe Sts., in Williamsburg, Brooklyn (☎718-782-5188; www.galapagosartspace.com). Subway: L to Bedford St.; go south along Bedford and then west along N. 6th St. A bit deserted at night; go with a friend. Once a mayonnaise factory, this space is now one of the hipper cultural spots in the city. Puts up parties, as well as **Ocularis,** their weekly film series (Su 7pm and 9:30pm, M 8:30pm; $5 cover). The people here *are* the Williamsburg arts scene; ask them what's up in this kinetic community. Great bar in an interesting futuro-sleek decor makes for a funky hangout. DJ's every Tu-Sa. Events sometimes charge $5 cover. Happy hour M-Sa 6pm-8pm. Open Su-Th 6pm-2am, F-Sa 6pm-4am.

Halcyon, 227 Smith St., in Brooklyn. Subway: F or G to Garden's neighborhood (☎718-260-9299). The hippest Brooklyn hangout south of Flatbush Ave. Avant-garde combinations of classical art and contemporary design on the projection screen play backdrop for house DJs who spin skewed trance and hip-hop. Smoking in the back garden, BYOB, coffee and snacks on sale, as well as records (Quentin Tarantino stocks his charger here) and old, forgotten board games like Twixt. No cover. Open Su-Th 8pm-midnight, F-Sa 9pm-3am.

Halo, 49 Grove St., between Seventh Ave. S. and Bleecker St. (☎243-8885). Exclusive lounge and restaurant where DJs set the tone with hip-hop and house. The kitchen serves a few carefully crafted and dearly priced New American dishes. Reserve in advance, dress to kill, or somehow find your way onto the owner's guest list. Open daily 9pm-4am.

Hell, 59 Gansevoort St., south of Hudson St. between Greenwich and Washington (☎727-1666). A lounge with red velvet curtains, this small bar has photos of famous people graffitied with red horns and mustaches, making them look like devils. Hard-to-find but worth the trip. Open Sa-Th 7pm-4am, F 5pm-4am.

Joe's Pub, 425 Lafayette St. between 4th St. and Astor Pl. (☎539-8776; ☎539-8777 for info/reservations; ☎539-8778 for cover charge). This swank space hosts events and performances. Late night events are usually DJ-spun, M is Benefit (downtown music), W is Fever (reggae), Th and Su varied. Beers $5. Open daily 6pm-4am.

Lola, 30 W. 22nd St., between Fifth and Sixth Aves. (☎675-6700). Although entrees are expensive (around $30), the bar hosts an elegant after-work crowd. Beers $5. M is Mellow Dramatic, Tu has jazz, W-Sa R'n'B. Open Su-Th 11am-3pm and 6pm-midnight, F-Sa 6pm-1am.

Nuyorican Poets Café, 236 E. Third St., between Ave. B and Ave. C. Subway: F to Second Ave. Walk 3 blocks north and 3 blocks east. (☎505-8183). New York's leading joint for "poetry slams" and spoken-word performances; several regulars have been featured on MTV. A mixed bag of doggerel and occasional gems. If you don't like the poets, don't worry—there's likely to be a heckler in the house. Workshops for your inner poet, DJ-enhanced parties, and occasional risque acts like "Erotic words en Español." Cover $10-12.

The Point, 940 Garrison Ave., in the Bronx, at the corner of Manida in Hunt's Point. (☎718-542-4139). Subway: 6 to Hunts Point. On the fringe of one of NY's poorest neighborhoods, The Point houses a growing artistic community and is home to dancer/choreographer Arthur Aviles. Monthly Latin jazz and hip-hop performances are offered, as well as studio facilities, a theater, and classes in art and self-defense. Community-based efforts like the South Bronx Film and Video Festival enable Hunt's Point to call itself "the artistic capital of the Bronx." Call for schedule of events.

Soundlab (☎726-1724). Locations vary. Cultural alchemy in the form of an illbient happening, nomadic style. Expect a smart, funky, racially mixed crowd absorbing smart, funky, radically mixed sound. Call to find where the next Lab goes down; past locales include the base of the Brooklyn Bridge, the 15th floor of a Financial District skyscraper, and a Chinatown park.

Scharmann's, 386 West Broadway (☎219-2561). Mismatched sofas and a high ceiling make this a nice space for the art on its walls. Classy and loungy. Beer $4. Open Su-W 10am-1am, Th-Sa 10am-3am.

Smoke, 2751 Broadway, between 106th and 105th Sts. (☎864-6662). This new sultry cocktail lounge has excellent jazz seven nights a week in an intimate and lively setting. Jam sessions M at 10pm and Tu at midnight. Also Funk W and Latin Jazz Su. Happy Hour 5-8pm. M-W no cover; Th-Su $10-20. $10 drink min. Open daily 5pm-3:30am.

◪ **Sugar Shack,** 2611 Frederick Douglass Blvd/Eighth Ave., at 139th St. (☎491-4422). Sexy lounge and soul food restaurant (entrees $10-12), with phenomenal daiquiries and smoothies ($6-12). M comedy night, W poetry series, Th 70s, F 6-10pm smooth jazz, and Sa groove to the latest R'n'B, hip-hop, and reggae. Ladies, don't miss Ladies' Night Tu with $3 drinks. Cover: M $5 ladies, $7 gents; W $5. 2 drink min. Reservations recommended. Open M-Th 5pm-midnight, F-Sa 5pm-3am, Su brunch all you can eat buffet ($14) 11am-5pm. V, MC.

Wild Lily Tea Room, 511-A W. 22nd St., between Tenth and Eleventh Aves. (☎691-2258). Sparse menu is full of Asian ingredients like shiitake mushrooms and mesclun greens. Order an jasmine or green mattcha iced tea ($5—but it's a tall glass!). Wax philosophical within its Asian minimalist Tea Room, featuring a circular pond complete with koi fish and floating flowers. Open Tu-Su 11am-10pm.

COMEDY CLUBS

Comic Strip Live, 1568 Second Ave., between 81st and 82nd Sts. (☎861-9386). Subway: 4, 5, 6 to 86th St. Sunday comics' characters Dagwood and Dick Tracy line the 4-color walls of this well-established pub-style club. Former regulars include just about everyone in the post-SNL pantheon. Usually a 2-drink minimum. Su and Tu-Th $10 cover; F-Sa $14 cover. Make reservations, especially for weekends. Shows Su-Th around 8pm, additional shows on weekends.

Dangerfield's, 1118 First Ave. between 61st and 62nd Sts. (☎593-1650). Subway: N, R to Lexington Ave. Rodney's respectable comic-launching pad. HBO specials featuring Roseanne Barr and Jerry Seinfeld have been taped at the club. Be prepared for a surprise—the line-up is only available the day of the show, and unannounced guest comedians appear occasionally. Cover Su-Th $12.50, F-Sa $15, Sa 10:30pm show $20. Su-Th shows at 8:45pm; F shows at 9pm and 11:15pm; Sa shows at 8pm, 10:30pm, and 12:30am; doors open 1hr. before 1st show.

Gotham Comedy Club, 34 W. 22nd St. between Fifth and Sixth Aves. (☎367-9000). Subway: 1, 9 to 23rd St. One of the more upscale comedy clubs, it also serves American cuisine. Usually a 2-drink minimum. Su-Th $8 cover, F-Sa $12. Shows Su-Th 8:30pm, F-Sa 8:30pm and 10:30pm.

Upright Citizens Brigade Theater, 161 W. 22nd St. between Sixth and Seventh Aves. (☎366-9176). Subway: 1, 9 to 23rd St. Funny, offbeat sketch and improv comedy. 2-3 shows per night except M, usually 8pm and 9:30pm. Tickets up to $5.

The Queer Apple

New York has been a major center for American gay life since the 19th century, when an open bohemian lifestyle flourished in Greenwich Village. During the 1920s and 30s, the fledgling community found its way uptown to Harlem, where the clubs were more tolerant and the scene vibrant and creative. Gay life throughout the mid-20th century was nonetheless an underground affair, existing in secret societies and private "bottle clubs." Persecution was common: gay establishments were routinely raided and their patrons harassed or arrested. It was during one such police raid of the Stonewall Inn in Greenwich Village, on June 27, 1969, that tensions erupted. In the now-legendary incident, the bar's transsexual, gay, and hustler patrons spontaneously fought the police as they were being led to the paddy-wagon. This singular act of rebellion ignited the community and set off four days of protest, as hundreds of gay men and lesbians took to the streets of NYC to combat injustice. The incident has since become known as the **Stonewall Riot,** and is often credited as the inspiration for the modern gay rights movement.

In the decades since Stonewall, the gay community of New York has grown into a vital and varied community, with a remarkable ability to celebrate itself and respond to adversity. In 1981, in the face of AIDS and the frustration associated with an excess of media hype and lack of helpful action, gay New Yorkers founded the **Gay Men's Health Crisis (GMHC),** the first medical organization dedicated to serving those with AIDS. When the political and medical establishment persisted in its silence about AIDS, activists formed **The AIDS Coalition to Unleash Power (ACT-Up),** a "leaderless" gay militant group whose aggressive actions have spurred the development of effective treatments for the disease and that continues to stage political events throughout the city and nation.

Gay pride is celebrated in late June every year, when hundreds of thousands turn out for the **Pride Parade,** which wends its way down Fifth Avenue and into Greenwich Village. This ecstatic event is jam-packed with juggling drag queens, jubilant confetti-tossers, and cheering throngs toting the banners of gay organizations as varied as the gay volley-ball league to **Dykes on Bikes.** The scent of hairspray fills the air on Labor Day weekend during **Wigstock,** the *fabulous* day-long celebration of cross-dressing, during which New York's astounding variety of drag queens cinch, pad, and strut their stuff. (At Pier 54 in the West Village; call ☎800-494-TIXS for tickets and information.)

Today, gay and lesbian neighborhoods thrive in New York. An established and well-heeled contingent still clusters around **Christopher Street** in the West Village (see p. 22), while the center of gay life has shifted uptown a few blocks to **Chelsea** (see p. 23). Here, buff boys waltz from gym to juice-bar, and rainbow flags fly over dry cleaners and taxi dispatch centers. An edgier, often younger, group rocks out in the **East Village** on First and Second Avenues, south of East 12th Street (see p. 21). A large lesbian community in **Park Slope** has lent the neighborhood the moniker "Dyke Slope" (see p. 178).

RESOURCES AND SHOPS

The **Lesbian and Gay Community Services Center,** 208 W. 13th St. between Seventh and Eighth Aves. (☎620-7310; www.gaycenter.org), provides information and referral ser-vices, while hosting myriad programs, groups, and social activities of interest to the gay community. (Subway: A, C, E, F to 14th St. Open daily 9am-11pm.) The Center also houses the **National Museum and Archive of Lesbian and Gay History** (open daily 6-9pm), as well as a famous bathroom on the second floor, every surface of which has been bril-liantly and provocatively painted by the artist, Keith Haring. Recent renovations to the Center should be finished by December 2000, but until they're finished it has relocated to 1 Little W. 12th St. between Ninth and Hudson Aves.

There are numerous publications dedicated to the gay and lesbian community of New York. *HomoXtra* (*HX* and *HX for Her*) and *Next* both have listings of nightlife and activities, and are available free at gay hangouts around the city. The free *LGNY* (no, that's not *Let's Go NY*, but *Lesbian-Gay NY*) and the *New York Blade News* are com-munity broadsheets and are distributed throughout the boroughs. The nationally distrib-uted *Advocate* magazine has a New York section; also check out the *Village Voice*, which details events, services, and occasional feature articles of interest to gays and les-bians. In addition, some websites will give you info that the printed rags don't reveal. Check out www.gmad.org, a resource for gay men of African descent, and www.pridelinks.com, a no-holds-barred **queer search engine.**

The helpful **Gayellow Pages,** P.O. Box 533, Village Station, New York, NY 10014 (☎674-0120; fax 420-1126; email gayello@banet.net; gayellowpages.com), has a special New York edition ($16) that lists accommodations, organizations, and services in the city.

HEALTH AND SUPPORT SERVICES

Callen-Lorde Community Health Center, 356 W. 18th St. between Eighth and Ninth Aves. (☎271-7200; www.callen-lorde.org). Subway: A, C, E to 14th St. Comprehensive general health services for the queer community, plus counseling and a health resource department. Callen-Lorde offers a sliding-scale fee structure for individuals without insurance coverage, and no one is turned away. Open M 12:30-8pm, W 8:30am-1pm and 3-8pm, Tu and Th-F 9am-4:30pm.

Gay Men's Health Crisis (GMHC), 119 W. 24th St. between Sixth and Seventh Aves. (☎367-1000). Subway: 1, 9, F to 23rd St. Health care, support groups, physician referrals, and counsel-ing for men and women with HIV and AIDS. Walk-in counseling M-F 11am-8pm. GMHC's **Geffen Center** provides confidential (not anonymous) HIV testing (☎367-1100). **Hotline:** ☎800-243-7692 or 807-6655 (open M-F 10am-9pm, Sa noon-3pm).

Gay and Lesbian Switchboard (☎989-0999; glnh.@glnh.org). Information, peer counseling, or referrals for the gay or lesbian traveler. Open M-F 6-10pm, Sa noon-5pm. 24hr. recording.

BOOKSTORES

A Different Light, 151 W. 19th St., at Seventh Ave. (☎989-4850). Subway: 1, 9 to 18th St. This fabulous bookstore offers an amazing selection of lesbian and gay readings—everything from the latest queer sci-fi thriller to anthologies of transgender theory. The store really shines with its frequent readings by prominent names in les-bi-gay literary circles and small gallery featuring local artists. Open daily 11am-10pm.

Oscar Wilde Gay and Lesbian Bookshop, 15 Christopher St., near Sixth Ave. (☎255-8097). Subway: 1, 9 to Christopher St. This cozy little shop has the distinction of being the world's first gay and lesbian bookstore. Usual readings in queer literature, and a number of rare and first edition books. Open M-Sa 11am-8pm, Su noon-7pm.

RELIGIOUS SERVICES

Church of St. Paul and St. Andrew, on 86th St., at West End Ave. (☎362-3179). Subway: 1,9 to 86th St. United Methodist Church dating from 1897. Check out the octagonal tower and the angles in the spandrels. Gay-friendly services Su 11am.

Congregation Beth Simchat Torah, 57 Bethune St. (☎929-9498; www.cbst.org). Synagogue catering to the NY lesbian and gay community. Services F at 8pm at the **Church of the Holy Apostle,** at 9th Ave. and 28th St.

Metropolitan Community Church of New York, 446 W. 36th St. between 9th and 10th Sts. (☎629-7440). Subway: A, C, E to 34th St. Christian Church of the queer community. Services Su 10am, 12:30pm (in Spanish), 7pm; and W 7pm.

ACCOMMODATIONS

If you're moving to New York and want help finding a gay, lesbian, bi- or transsexual roommate, it might be worthwhile to pay a visit to **Rainbow Roommates,** 268 W. 22nd St., near Eighth Ave. For $150, Rainbow Roommates provides you with a four-month subscription to personalized listings matching the roommate criteria you have requested. (☎627-8612. www.rainbowroommates.com. Open Tu-Sa noon-6pm.) You may also want to try **DG Neary Realty,** 57 W. 16th St., on the corner of Sixth Ave., which hosts **"G.R.I.N."**— the Gay Roommate Information Network. (☎627-4242. Fax 989-1207. Registration fee $50. Open Su-F 10am-6pm.) Here are some more B, G, L, T accommodation options.

Colonial House, 318 W. 22nd St. between Eighth and Ninth Aves., in Chelsea (☎800-689-3779 or 243-9669; fax 633-1612). Subway: C, E to 23rd St. Very comfortable B&B in a classy Chelsea brownstone. All rooms have cable TV, A/C, and phone; some have bath and fireplace. Sun deck with a "clothing optional" area. 24hr. desk and concierge service. Continental breakfast (8am-noon) included. Check-in 3pm. Check-out noon. Reservations are encouraged and require one night's deposit within 10 days of reservation. Double bed "economy" room $80-99; queen-size bedroom $99-125, with private bath $125-140.

Incentra Village House, 32 Eighth Ave. between W. 12th and Jane Sts., in Greenwich Village (☎206-0007; fax 604-0625). Subway: A, C, E to 14th St. Lovely brick landmark townhouse, built in 1941, with a cozy double Victorian parlor, antique furnishings, and a 1930s baby grand piano. Rooms are uniquely decorated, most have fireplace and kitchenette. Profits are held in a trust benefiting various AIDS service organizations. Check-in 2pm. Check-out noon. Reservations encouraged. Studios: single $99, double $149, triple $179, quad $209; suites: single $129, double $179, triple $209, quad $239.

Chelsea Pines Inn, 317 W. 14th St. between Eighth and Ninth Aves., near Greenwich Village (☎929-1023; fax 620-5646). Subway: A, C, E to 14th St. The ultimate in fabulous stays. Friendly, amenity-laden haven of cozy rooms decorated with vintage film posters. Gorgeous garden and "greenhouse" out back. A/C, cable TV, refrigerator, and washing facilities in all rooms. 3-day min. stay on weekends. Continental breakfast included, with fresh homemade bread. Reservations are essential. Rooms with private showers and shared toilet $99-119; queen-size bed with private bath $119-139, with breakfast area $139. $20 for extra person.

Chelsea Savoy Hotel, 204 W. 23rd St. between Seventh and Eighth Aves., in Chelsea (☎929-9353; fax 741-6309). Subway: 1, 9, C, E to 23rd St. Alhough this definitely feels like a hotel and it's not exclusively gay, the Chelsea Savoy hosts a great many of the *fabulous* set and is right in the middle of Chelsea. Cable TV, A/C. Singles $99-115; doubles $145-155; quads $145-185.

HANGOUTS AND RESTAURANTS

For general restaurant information, see **Food,** p. 175. For those looking to dine among the friends of Judy, one need not look farther than any of the well-adorned restaurants on Eighth Avenue between 14th and 23rd Sts., all of which are swarmed every night. Below are some particularly groovy hangouts and a real bargain or two.

Big Cup, 228 Eighth Ave. between 21st and 22nd Sts., in Chelsea (☎206-0059). Bright, campy colors and comfy velvet chairs make this a great place to curl up with a cup of joe ($1.30) and cruise for cute Chelsea boys who will happily wink back. Sandwiches $6.50. Tarot readings Tu at 9pm. Opens M-F 7am, Sa-Su 8am. Closes Su-Th 1am, F-Sa 2am.

Caffe Raffaella, 134 Seventh Ave S., north of Christopher St., in Greenwich Village (☎929-7247). Serves Italian food to a largely gay, male clientele. Intimate, unpretentious atmosphere with a touch of subdued, Old World decadence. Sip steamed milk with *orzata* (sweet almond syrup, $3) while reclining in the embrace of an overstuffed chair. Sandwiches $6.50-8; pizza $8-10; pasta $9-11. Open daily 10am-2am.

Bendix Diner, 219 Eighth Avenue, at 21st St., in Chelsea (☎366-0560). Thai-American chow; packed with hungry locals and easy on the charge card. Grab a window seat and watch the neighborhood parade by. Pad Thai $6.95; meatloaf $6.45. Open daily 8am-1am.

Lips, 2 Bank St., off Greenwich Ave., in Greenwich Village (☎675-7710). The Hard Rock Café of drag. Impromptu performances from a saucy high-heeled staff. Italian-Continental cuisine. Entrees $12-22. Open Su-Th 5:30pm-midnight, F-Sa 5:30pm-2am; Su brunch 11:30am-4pm.

NIGHTLIFE

Following is a list of clubs (some of them dance-oriented, others geared toward conversation and drinking) at the center of gay and lesbian nightlife. Some of these clubs are geared exclusively toward lesbians or gay men, and may frown on letting in hopefuls of the opposite sex. If you and a friend of the opposite sex want to go to any of these clubs together, it might be wise to avoid behaving like a heterosexual couple, especially in front of the bouncer. To find out where the next dykerrific dance party is being held, lesbians should call the **Sheescape Danceline** (☎686-5665). **Her/She Bar** (☎631-1093 or 631-1102) and **Lovergirl** (☎631-1000) also throw female fetes; call to find out current locations. Also keep in mind **Hot: The NYC Celebration of Queer Culture,** Vineyard 26, 309 E. 26th St., at Dixon Pl. After Pride warms everyone up in July, Hot steps in to fill the gay culture void (like there could ever be one) with artsy performances and off-beat happenings. (Subway: 6 to 28th St. ☎532-1546; www.dixonplace.org.) In addition, there is always a great deal of excellent **gay theater** off-off- and off-Broadway, and the **New York Gay and Lesbian Film Festival** opens its celluloid closet every year in June (keep your eyes peeled in *HX*, *Next*, and the *Village Voice* for listings).

GREENWICH VILLAGE AND BELOW

🏳️ **Stonewall,** 53 Christopher St., in Sheridan Sq. (☎463-0950). Subway: 1, 9 to Sheridan Sq. Legendary bar of the Stonewall Riots (see p. 221). Check out the gallery of articles detailing the events and toast the brave drag queens who fought back. These days the Stonewall is not the mafia-run hole-in-the-wall of yore, but rather a spiffed-up den for pilgrims & locals. Upstairs, the Club at Stonewall has a dance floor. 2-for-1 Happy Hour M-F 3-9pm. $2 frozen margaritas Sa-Su 2:30-9pm. Open daily 2:30pm-4am.

🏳️ **Clit Club,** at Mother, 432 W. 14th St., at Washington St. (☎366-5680). Subway: A, C, E to 14th St. The grandmother of NY dyke clubs, every F night in the Bar Room. Tu nights the same space becomes **Queen Mother** (☎366-5680). Mother closed right before publishing—at that time these nights had no plans to move elsewhere. Try calling for info.

The Lure, 409 W. 13th St. between Ninth and Tenth Aves. (☎741-3919). Subway: A, C, E to 14th St. One of the world's great leather bars, located in the meat-packing district. W night is Pork, a more diverse, less uniformly leather evening than other nights, featuring live S/M and fetish performances. Pork opens at 10pm. Leave the sneakers and button-downs at home. Weekend dress code is strictly leather, Levis, tees, rubber, and uniforms. Open daily 8pm-4am.

Trannie Chaser and **Living Legends,** at Nowbar, 22 Seventh Ave. S., at Leroy St. (☎802-9502). Glorya Wholesome hosts hot parties for "ladies, trannies, gentlemen, gay, straight, lesbian, conservative, liberal, blue collar, white collar, big boned, and anorexics and their admirers!" Expect a more specific crowd of trannies, go-gos, and lap dancers. Legends Sa, Trannie Th; both 10pm-4am. Cover $5 for trannie/drag queens, $10 for ladies, $15 for men.

Body & Soul, at Vinyl, 6 Hubert St., at Hudson St. (☎330-9169). Su evening throngs pack this place to wiggle-n-jiggle amid the lights and house music. A New York must. Doors open at 4pm, but things really grind 5pm-midnight. $14 for nonmembers, $10 for members.

The Duplex, 61 Christopher St. (☎255-5438). Subway: 1, 9 to Sheridan Sq. Renowned piano bar always abuzz with performances by the talented waitstaff and filled with merry theatrical throngs who can recite every lyric from *On the Twentieth Century,* and will. Cabaret performance room upstairs. Open daily 5pm-4am.

Bar d'0, 29 Bedford St. (☎627-1580). The coziest lounge with the most sultry lighting in the city. Superb performances by drag divas Joey Arias and Raven O (Tu and Sa-Su nights 10:30pm, $5). Even without the fine chanteuses, this is a damn fine place for a drink. M night is "Pleasure" for women. The bar packs a glam night of drag kings. Go early for the atmosphere, around midnight for the performances, and 2am to people-watch/gender-guess. Don't try to leave in the middle of a show, or you'll be in for a nasty tongue-lashing. Cover $3. Opens at 10pm.

Chi Chiz, 135 Christopher St., at Hudson St. (☎462-0027). Subway: 1, 9 to Sheridan Sq. *The* Manhattan hot spot for men of color. Open M-Sa 5pm-4am, Su noon-4am.

The Cubbyhole, 281 W. 12th St., at W. 4th St. (☎243-9041). Subway: A, C, E, L to 14th St. This bar has a low ceiling from which hang fantastically cute flowers and fish to give the bar a relaxed, intimate feeling. Very low-key, but definitely queer. Happy hour M-Sa until 7pm. No cover. Open M-F 4pm-3am, Sa 2pm-4am, Su 3pm-4am.

Henrietta Hudson, 438 Hudson St. between Morton and Barrow St. (☎243-9079). Young, clean-cut lesbian crowd. Mellow in the afternoon, packed at night and on the weekends. Very neighborhood-girl bar, it's also gay male friendly. Try the Henrietta Girlbanger or the Girl Scout ($6.50). Happy hour (2-for-1) M-F 5-7pm. Sa is Beautiful Girl, a fierce dance party (doors open 9pm, $3-5). Su is Girl Parts, a cover band highlighting lesbian-friendly music. Open daily 3pm-4am.

Crazy Nanny's, 21 Seventh Ave. S., near LeRoy St. (☎366-6312). Subway: 1, 9 to Houston St. Glamour dykes and the women who love them come here to shoot some pool, play video games, and just hang out. Dancing nightly in the two-floored, two-bar space. 2-for-1 Happy Hour M-Sa 4-7pm. Karaoke W 8pm; free. F is Sweat, a go-go dance party; doors open 9pm, $8. Sa is Mixer, a party for gay men and women; doors open 9pm, $5. Open daily 4pm-4am.

CHELSEA, WEST MIDTOWN, AND UPPER WEST SIDE

🏳️ **Splash,** 50 W. 17th St. between Fifth and Sixth Aves. (☎691-0073). Subway: 1, 9 to 18th St.; F to 23rd St. One of the most popular gay mega-bars. Enormous bar complex on two floors, packed on weekends with muscular boys who love to flirt. Cool, almost sci-fi decor provides a sleek backdrop for a very crowded scene, with a dance floor that completes the evening. Cover varies, peaking at $7. Drinks $4-7. Open Su-Th 4pm-4am, F-Sa 4pm-5am.

🏳️ **g,** 223 W. 19th St. between Seventh and Eighth Aves. (☎929-1085). Subway: 1, 9 to 18th St. Glitzy, popular bar shaped like an oval racetrack—somehow an appropriate architectural metaphor, given the well-exercised, pumped-up Chelsea boy clientele that speeds around this circuit trying to win glances. Fortunately, the famous frozen Cosmos satisfy the thirst of those logging their miles. No cover. Open daily 4pm-4am.

🏳️ **La Nueva Escuelita,** 301 W. 39th St., at Eighth Ave. (☎631-0588). Subway: A, C, E to 42nd St. Queer Latin dance club that throbs with merengue, salsa, soul, hip-hop, and arguably the best drag shows in New York. Largely Latin crowd. F, starting at 10pm, is Her/She Bar, with go-go gals, performances, and special events. (Her/She: ☎631-1093; $8 before midnight, $10 after.) Open Th-Sa 10pm-5am, Su 7pm-5am. Cover Th $5; F $10; Sa $15; Su 7-10pm $5, after 10pm $8.

Barracuda, 275 W. 22nd St., at Eighth Ave. (☎645-8613). Subway: C, E to 23rd St. Brimming with ripped Chelsea boys of all shapes and sizes. 1950s decor, complete with sofas, a pool table, and a dazzling collection of kitsch furniture, makes for a cozy hangout in the back, while the determined mobs in front seem to have something else on their minds. Drinks $4-7. 2-for-1 Happy Hour M-F 4-9pm. Open daily 4pm-4am.

The Roxy, 515 W. 18th St. (☎645-5156). Currently *the* place to be on Sa nights. Hundreds of gay men dance and drink in the Roxy's gigantic, luxurious space. Upstairs, lounge/bar provides a different DJ and more intimate setting. Downstairs, high ceilings, a beautiful dance floor, and lounge space give hedonists plenty of room to play. Busy nights boast beautiful go-go boys. Beer $5. Drinks $6+. Cover $20. The Roxy starts late: prime hours are midnight-6am.

The Big Apple Ranch, at Dance Manhattan, 39 W. 19th St. between Fifth and Sixth Aves., 5th fl. (☎358-5752). Subway: F, N, R to 23rd St. A friendly crowd of urban cowboys and girls welcomes all to a romping evening of gay and lesbian two-stepping. $10 cover includes lesson. Sa only 8pm-1am; lessons 8-9pm.

King, 579 Sixth Ave., at 16th St. (☎366-5464). Cruisy place with bartenders who are refreshingly low on bad attitude. Draws a multi-ethnic mix of patrons. Weekends are a good bet. Drinks $4-7. Open daily 4pm-4am.

Chase, 255 W. 55th St. between Broadway and Eighth Aves. (☎333-3400). Subway: 1, 9, C, E to 50th St. New Hell's Kitchen watering-hole for Midtown residents. Trendy and chic, Chase brings a li'l bit of Chelsea to Hell's Kitchen, drawing in well-groomed party boys and the neighborhood theatrical community. Open daily 3pm-4am.

The Works, 428 Columbus Ave., at 81st St. (☎799-7365). Subway: C to 81st St. Upper West Side hangout for the Banana Republic set. The Works packs them in Th and Su, when aspiring guppies seek genuine bargains in $1 frozen margaritas and cosmos (Th 8pm-2am) and the $5 all-you-can-drink Beer Blast (Su 6pm-1am). Open daily 4pm-4am.

The Spike, 120 Eleventh Ave., at W. 20th St. (☎243-9688). Subway: C, E to 23rd St. Caters to an adventurous crowd of leather-clad men (and some women) who know how to create a spectacle. Drink specials F-Sa 9pm-midnight. Open daily 9pm-4am.

EAST VILLAGE AND ALPHABET CITY

The Cock, 188 Avenue A, at 12th St. (☎946-1871). Subway: N, R, 4, 5, 6 to Union Square/14th St. Busy rock-n-sleaze boy bar with a full offering of nightly gay diversions. Foxy Saturday asks the patrons to multiple their "Foxy dollars" through a gamut of risqué challenges. Call for the nightly change of entertainment fare. Open daily 9:30pm-4am.

Aspara, at the Gemini Lounge, 221 Second Ave. between 13th and 14th Sts. (☎254-5260). A seriously sexy party with gorgeous ladies trying to outdo each other on the wild tip. Come to dance hard, play hard, and strut your stuff. Cover $8, with flyer $6. Every other Su 10pm-4am.

Boiler Room, 86 E. 4th St. between First and Second Aves. (☎254-7536). Popular locale catering to alluring alternative types, NYU college boys, and eager refugees from the sometimes stifling Chelsea clone scene. Terrific jukebox gives the evening a democratic spin. Open daily 4pm-4am.

Wonder Bar, 505 E. 6th St. (☎777-9105). On a strip crowded with bars, Wonder Bar stands out. Done up in zebra chic and laid back neutrals, frequented by a chill bohemian crowd and the occasional curious breeder. Open daily 6pm-4am.

DAYTRIPPING TO FIRE ISLAND

🔊 *For transportation info, see* **Daytrips,** *p. 238.*

A countercultural enclave during the 1960s and home to a thriving 1970s disco scene, Fire Island heads into the millennium partying loud and queer. Two prominent Fire Island resort hamlets, **Cherry Grove** and **The Pines,** host largely gay communities. Queer-filled streets border spectacular Atlantic Ocean beaches, and the fabulous scene rages late into the night. Weekdays provide an excellent opportunity to enjoy the beauty and charm of the island in a low-key setting, with Thursdays and Sundays offering an ideal balance of sanity and scene—Friday and Saturday see mounting crowds and prices.

Most vacationers buy a summer share, a Long Island tradition of sardine-esque accommodation. Meanwhile, both towns host establishments that advertise themselves as "guest houses." Be aware that some of these may not be legally accredited (due to such things as fire code violations), and that some may not be lesbian-friendly. **The Cherry Grove Beach Hotel** (☎631-597-6600) is a good bet, located on the Main Walk of Cherry Grove and close to the beach. Rooms feature double beds, kitchenettes, and balconies, and start at $70 (but can cost up to $400 for the best rooms during peak seasons). Weekday prices are lower (full price the first night and $30 each additional night). Reservations are required. The hotel is open May to October. Another options is **Holly House** (☎631-597-6911), which is on the Holly Walk, right behind the Ice Palace; it offers beds in clean rooms for reasonable prices (unless it's the weekend and peak season). For real luxury, try the **Belvedere** (☎631-597-6448). Themed rooms and a beautiful building make this all-male establishment a popular place. Even at its cheapest, however, expect to pay at least $100 for a night.

Fire Island's restaurant life generally entails unspectacular eats at astounding prices. One pretty good option is **Rachel's at the Grove** (☎631-597-4174), on Ocean Walk at the beach. Patio seating overlooks the Atlantic. A standard American meal will cost you $9-12. Reservations are recommended for dinner. (Open M-F 8:30am-midnight or 2am, Sa-Su 8:30am-3am or 4am.)

NIGHTLIFE

There is a very established schedule to gay nightlife in Fire Island. Everyone is there for the same thing, and they all know where to go. Both towns are not very big—the best thing to do is just ask around, either at your hotel or restaurant.

CHERRY GROVE. In this more commercial of the two resort towns, narrow, raised boardwalks line the roadless area and lead to small, uniformly shingled houses that overflow with men, although lesbian couples make up the majority of the town's population. A night in Cherry Grove usually begins early at the **Ice Palace** (☎516-597-6600), attached to the Cherry Grove Beach Hotel. You can disco till dawn here, or follow the locals to Kiss or a new club "where the old Monster used to be." Most go to the Pines for late-night partying; you can catch a water taxi from the docks at Cherry Grove.

THE PINES. A 10-minute walk up the beach from Cherry Grove, the Pines has traditionally looked down its nose at its uninhibited neighbor. Houses here are spacious and often stunningly modern, with an asymmetric aesthetic and huge windows. Here, naughtiness cloaks itself in darkness. You may want to bring along a flashlight to navigate the often poorly lit boardwalks here. The Pines' active, upscale nighttime scene, unfortunately has a bit of a secret club feel to it—you need to be in the know or somehow be able to look like you know the schedule. **Low Tea,** from 5-8pm, is at the bar/club next to the Botel (big hotel). Move on to disco **High Tea** at 8pm at the Pavilion, but make sure you have somewhere to disappear to during "disco nap" time (after 10pm). Around 1:30am you can emerge unabashedly to dance till dawn at the **Island Club and Bistro** (☎631-597-6001), better known as the Sip and Twirl. The Pavilion also becomes hot again late-night on weekends, including Sundays during the summer. To finish off your night in true Fire Island style, find a local to bring you to the woods or down to the Harbor... *(For more information on Fire Island, see **Daytripping**, p. 238.)*

QUICKY MALE SEX. In the wooded area between the Pines and the Grove is a loosely-bounded area that those in the know call the **Meat Rack.** There are lots of walkways leading in myriad directions, and this is where things go down—Gay Men's Health Crisis actually puts condoms in the trees to keep everyone safe. Another similar cruising location has recently sprung up on Harbor between Fire Island Boulevard and Ocean Walk—just ask for **Dick Dock.**

Daytripping

Tired of the hustle and bustle of the City? Can't fake the funk? You need a break. Unfortunately, most people who live in the areas surrounding NYC spend as little time in their home towns as possible and would rather drive to the city—for a reason. But we at *Let's Go* have picked what potable berries we could from the sour selection. Included are Hoboken, NJ (bars bars bars) and Long Island (frightful hair and the Hamptons), but don't worry—NYC will still be there when you come running back.

HOBOKEN, NJ

see map
p. 351

Right across the Hudson River from downtown Manhattan, Hoboken's proximity to New York (10min. and $1 away via the PATH train) makes it both accessible and enjoyable. Known primarily as a party town by outsiders, its 1.3 square miles hold culinary surprises and fashionable boutiques while boasting a bevy of bars. The thriving "scene" and cheap commute have drawn all types of New Yorkers who appreciate stylish living and friendly charm. Furthermore, all types of residents share a respect for the town's notorious history as the original home of Frank Sinatra and baseball. A walkable neighborhood composed of colorful buildings with unique storefronts and a fantastic view of Manhattan prove to be well worth an afternoon or evening jaunt to Hoboken. If you get tired of walking, taxis list prices as low as $3 for city limits (☎201-420-1480).

ORIENTATION

Take **subway** lines B, D, F, N, Q, or R to 34th St., then take the **PATH train** ($1) to the first stop in Hoboken. The PATH train also leaves from the F stations at 23rd and 14th Sts., and the PATH stations at 9th St./Sixth Ave., Christopher St./Greenwich Ave., and WTC.

GO DOWN, MOSES

Robert Moses, New York's most influential builder, executed his first projects on the barren sandbars of Long Island. Moses freed up huge areas of land for public recreation and established the power base from which he would eventually build $27 billion worth of public works. Before Moses took over the Long Island Parks Commission, New Yorkers had nowhere to take their first automobiles—only a few strips of beaches lay open to them, and it took up to four dust-choked hours to get there from downtown Manhattan. Moses finagled $14 million from a graft-ridden state budget, built tree-lined highways (Northern State and Southern State Parkways), and developed Jones Beach, a recreaton area with lavish facilities and a Disney-like attention to detail. To wrest right-of-way and parkland from its owners, Moses attacked the rich, who owned most of the island; failing to win their cooperation, he rerouted his plans, obliterating small farmers. To keep his beaches "clean," he had the bridges over the parkways built too low to accomodate city buses, blocked the Long Island Railroad from building a stop, and made it nearly impossible for charter companies carrying African-Americans to get permits for Jones Beach. Those who could not pay parking fees were directed to "poor lots" far from the beach. With Long Island a precedent was set for grand public works projects, accommodation of a large and mobile middle class, and institutional racism and classicism, with which Moses would revolutionize public building.

To get to Hoboken's main drag, **Washington St.,** walk along Hudson Pl. from the PATH station to Hudson St., make a right, walk one block to Newark St., turn left, walk two blocks to Washington St., and turn right. **NJ Transit bus** 126 runs along Washington St.

On the far east side of the city, **Frank Sinatra Dr.** curves along the coast from 4th St. to 11th St. The **Hoboken City Hall,** at 1st and Washington, can provide you with an excellent map. Washington St. houses most of the action in Hoboken; **Hudson St.** and **Hudson Pl.** near the PATH station also bustle with activity.

For nearby **hotels** on the New Jersey shoreline, see **Accommodations,** p. 408.

SIGHTS

Before getting caught up in the alcoholic frenzy of Hoboken nightlife, you may want to indulge in charms not served in a frosty mug. On Hudson Pl., in front of the NJ Transit train terminal, is **Erie-Lackawanna Train Plaza,** where in the summer months the city hosts the free **Movies under the Stars.** (☎ 201-420-2207 for schedule. W at dusk.)

On the far eastern side of 8th St., walking uphill and across the grass until reaching a cannon, is **Castle Point** (on the campus of the Stevens Institute of Technology). There, *voilà,* you'll happen upon a spectacular vista of Manhattan's West Side.

Amid the brownstones on the eastern side of Hoboken resides a handful of parks sporting the mayor's slogan, "More than a city…we're a neighborhood." **Church Square Park** interrupts Park Ave. between 4th and 5th Sts. with its frolicking children, relaxing seniors, and gazebo commemorating classical music masters. A more recent musical monument, **Frank Sinatra Park,** sits on the eastern waterfront at Frank Sinatra Dr. between 4th and 5th Sts. Baseball supposedly began in **Elysian Park** (10th and 11th Sts. on Hudson St.), in an 1846 game between the "New Yorks" and the "Knickerbockers."

Church Square Park, Elysian Park, and Sinatra Park all are hosts to various cultural events, part of Hoboken's impressive effort to showcase local culture. The **Hudson Shakespeare Company** kicks off its summer season at Church Square Park and Sinatra Park. Sinatra Park and Elysian Park also host a **summer music concert festival.** (Shakespeare shows at 7pm throughout June; concerts June-Aug. at Elysian Park Tu 7pm, at Sinatra Park Th 7pm. All events free.) May through September, the **Art and Music Festival** hits Washington St. with a unique Hoboken flair. For more information inquire at the **Cultural Office.** (☎ 201-420-2207. City Hall, 2nd fl.)

FOOD

While Hoboken may not have the same culinary diversity and distinction as its larger cousin across the Hudson, there are a growing number of good establishments with funky ambiences. Unfortunately, the majority of these cater to the city's wealthier clientele. Bars, or the small cafes, are possible eating options (see **Nightlife,** below).

The Hoboken Gourmet Company, 423 Washington St. (☎201-795-0110). Offering healthy salad options and fresh sandwiches ($5-6), and sporting local art on its walls, it's "gourmet" perfectly priced. Pretend you're a local and stop in to enjoy breakfast until 2pm. Open M-F 6:30am-9pm, Sa-Su 6:30am-7pm. **$**

Bagels on the Hudson, 802 Washington St. (☎201-798-2221). This is the place to pick up a picnic for Castle Point. Bagels are a mere 50¢ in this convenience store-esque joint. Ask for their free button magnets as a souvenir. Open 24hr. 7 days a week. **$**

La Isla, 104 Washington St. (☎201-659-8197). Cuban food aficionados will love this charming take-out-turned-sitdown restaurant. Daily lunch specials range from $5-9. The large servings are mostly under $8. Adventurous vegetarians might try the *yuca,* a tasty Caribbean potato-like vegetable. Bring your own booze. Open M-Sa 7am-10pm, Su brunch 11am-4pm. **$**

Amanda's, 908 Washington St. (☎201-798-0101). Although its regular menu starts around $16, enjoy a full meal of New American fare with the fantastically-priced early dinner special ($20 for 2 or $10 per person). Open M-Th 5-10pm, F-Sa 5-11pm, Su 5-9pm; Sa-Su brunch 11am-3pm, early dinner special M-Sa 5-6pm. **$**

Flip's, 320 Washington St. A window of heaven opens on to Washington, offering 40 flavors of Italian ices ($1.25 for a single "flip"), 15 flavors of gelato ($2.50 for single), and 12 flavors of ice cream ($1.50). Take home all sizes—from a single "flip" to full quarts (quarts $6-12). Open Su-Th 11am-11pm, F-Sa 11am-2am. **$**

NIGHTLIFE

8th Street Tavern, 800 Washington St. Claiming to be one of Hoboken's "original bars," this bar boasts friendly clientele and relatively cheap beer ($2.50 Coors). As Frank, the bartender, says: "We've no phone, we like people to drop in." He's there M-Th 10am-2am, F-Sa 10am-3am.

Maxwell's, 1039 Washington St. (☎201-798-0406, for show info 201-653-1703; www.nj.com/maxwells). A great hangout that features strong underground acts in all-age shows. Cover up to $16 (average $6-8). Shows sometimes sell out, so get tix in advance from Maxwell's or Ticketmaster (☎201-507-8900 or 212-307-7171). Beer is relatively cheap ($3 for Rolling Rock, $3.50 for Budweiser on tap), and bar food is available for less than $10 in its saloon/lounge-like restaurant. Happy hour Tu-F 5-8pm; $1 off drinks. Open Tu-Su 5pm-late.

Planet, 16-18 Hudson Pl., in front of the PATH train station (☎201-653-6888). Complete with a Cadillac hanging upside down from the ceiling. Happy hour W-F from 4pm; free "Las Vegas-style buffet" 5-8pm. F 9-11pm all beer $1. **Fatal Fury** (Th) promises trance for "trendsetters and fashion gurus." Open W-F 4pm-last entrance 2am, Sa-Su 8pm-last entrance 2am.

Cadillac Bar, 34-42 Newark St., off Hudson St. (☎201-659-4860 or 201-659-0223). A complex of bars that begins at the Cadillac Bar. Features power hour ($1 drinks) M-Th 9-10:30pm. Th sees the dance floor turned into **Space** (no cover, $2 drinks for women). **Boo Boo's Funkadelic Lounge** at Cadillac is always no cover. Open M-Th 5pm-2am, F-Sa 5pm-3am.

Miss Kitty's Saloon and Dance Hall Floozies, 94-98 Bloomfield St., at 1st St. (☎201-792-0041). Howdy! and welcome to a Wild West bar saloon. Moderately-priced food and $3-5 beers. Open M-Th 4pm-2am, F 4pm-3am, Sa-Su 6pm-2am, Sa-Su brunch noon-4pm.

SHOPPING

Shopping in Hoboken is more of a look-don't-touch experience. Specializing in boutiques carrying the hottest new London imports, it's exciting but inaccessible. If you still want to shop, take advantage of the **Free Shopper Shuttle** that runs Sa-Su 11am-5pm on Washington St. and Willow Avenue (☎201-222-1100 for info).

Hand Mad, 106 Washington St. (☎201-653-7276). Selling everything from gag gifts ("handy hindu" finger puppets $1) to handmade vegetable glycerin soaps ($6), utility bags to wigs, and Japanese lacquer dishes to tin windup toys, this store has great selection for any kind of gift. Open M-F noon-8pm, Sa 11am-9pm, Su noon-6pm.

LONG ISLAND

Long Island's nose (tactfully shaved off by a local plastic surgeon) nuzzles the tip of Manhattan. Technically, this 120 mile-long island includes Queens and Brooklyn, but you'll see that the true Long Islander (natives would say "Lawn-GUY-lander") would happily let piggybacking boroughs sink into the Atlantic—as long as their bridges to Manhattan remained intact. Largely a land of sport utility vehicles and carpools, landscape "artists" and snow-blowers, boob-jobs and climate control, Long Island's voice is nasal and irritating, yet strangely comforting. Despite its profusion of Avon products, "Strong Island" has drawn millions of city expatriates eastward in search of a little bit of grass and fresh air (although most continue to commute to "money-makin'" Manhattan for work and play).

Long Island is a pleasant, if inconvenient, place to visit, and deserves a daytrip if you want to find out how a population flourishes with Kool Aid flowing through its veins. Stereotypes aside, LI isn't all poufed bangs and blue contact lenses. There's new money, old money, and no money spread from Hicksville (no joke) to the Hamptons.

Miles of sandy beaches, scenic harbors, and lush parks lured New York millionaires, who built country homes on the rocky north shore. Thus arose the exclusive "Gold Coast" captured in its 1920s heyday by F. Scott Fitzgerald's *The Great Gatsby*. Later emigrés moved east to the resort towns of Montauk and the Hamptons. The 1950s brought a turning point for the island: cars became more affordable, and young couples enjoying postwar prosperity sought houses for their baby-boom families. This comfortable ideal, however, appears dimmer through the lenses of artists such as David Lynch, Eric Fischl, and John Cheever. Much of Long Island is firmly developed today. Resort towns prosper and the small offshore islands provide relaxation.

TRANSPORTATION AND PRACTICAL INFORMATION

Trains: Long Island Railroad, LIRR (automated info ☎ 718-217-5477 or 516-822-5477; TDD ☎ 718-558-3022; lost and found ☎ 212-643-5228, open daily 7:20am-7:20pm). Long Island's main public transportation trains leave from **Penn Station** in Manhattan (34th St. at Seventh Ave.; subway: 1, 2, 3, 9, A, C, E; see **Once in NYC**, p. 35) and meet in **Jamaica, Queens** (subway: E, J, Z) before proceeding to "points east." LIRR also connects in Queens at the 7 subway **Hunters' Point Ave., Woodside, Jamaica,** and **Main St.-Flushing** stations, and in Brooklyn at the **Flatbush Ave.** station (subway: 2, 3, 4, 5, D, Q to Atlantic; B, M, N, R to Pacific). Most Long Island towns are served by LIRR; call for info. Fares vary daily and by "zone." Rush hour "peak" tickets (Manhattan-bound 5am-9am, outbound 4-8pm) cost $4.75-15.25. Off-peak fares are up to $5 cheaper. Tickets can be purchased aboard trains, but you will be surcharged if the station ticket office is open. The LIRR offers various expensive but convenient **day tours** May-Nov. ($15-58).

Buses:

MTA Long Island Bus (☎ 516-766-6722; open M-Sa 8am-5pm). Daytime bus service in eastern Queens, Nassau, and western Suffolk. Service runs along major highways, but the routes are complex and irregular—confirm your destination with the driver. Some buses run every 15min., others every hr. Fare $1.50; crossing into Queens from Nassau County costs an additional 50¢; transfers 25¢, free with MetroCard. Disabled travelers and senior citizens pay half fare. Serves Jones Beach daily during summer; every 25-40min. from the LIRR station in Freeport.

Suffolk Transit (☎ 631-852-5200; open M-F 8am-4:30pm). Runs from Lindenhurst to the eastern end of Long Island. The 10a, 10b, and 10c lines make frequent stops along the South Fork. No service Su. Fare $1.50; seniors and the disabled 50¢; transfers 25¢; under 5 free. Buses run in summer from the LIRR station in Babylon to Robert Moses State Park on Fire Island, hourly M-F and more frequently on the weekends.

Hampton Jitney (☎ 800-936-0440 or 631-283-4600; www.hamptonjitney.com). The luxury bus. Two lines servicing destinations in the Hamptons. More expensive, but more comfortable and comprehensive than other buses or the LIRR. Departs from various Manhattan locations; most buses depart on the hr., although some more frequently. One-way $22, round-trip $40. Reservations required; call in advance, especially on weekends.

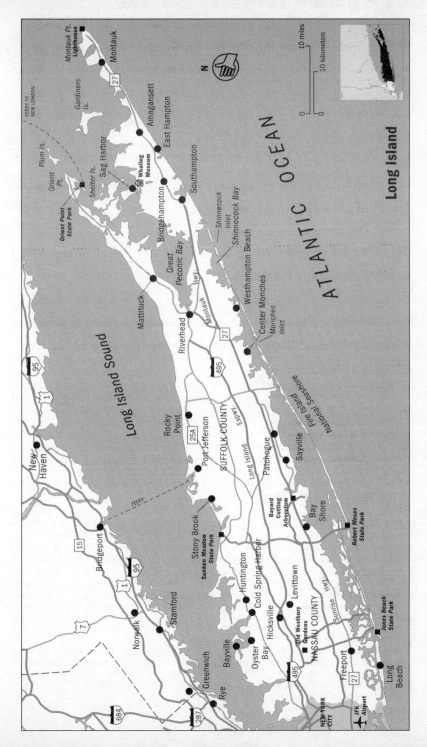

Long Island

Sunrise Express (☎800-527-7709, in Suffolk 631-477-1200). "NY Express" runs a few times daily from Manhattan to the North Fork ($15, round-trip $29). Call for schedule. Buses go directly to River-head, then stop at almost all villages on the North Fork to Greenport. Catch buses on the southwest corner of 44th St. and Third Ave. or in Queens (LIE Exit 24 to Kissena Blvd., in front of Queens College's Colden Ctr., at the Q88 bus stop). Bicycles ($10) and pets ($5) allowed. Kids (under 5) on laps ride free. Reservations recommended. Cash only.

Taxis: Most local cab companies have cars at train stations. At stations where this is not the case or at other places, consult a phone book or call 411. As in New York City, Long Island taxis are expensive, but sometimes necessary. **Long Island Taxi and Transportation** has cabs in North Hempstead (☎516-621-1111), Levittown (☎516-520-0555), and Deer Park (☎631-254-4464). In the Hamptons, try **Hampton Bays Taxi** (☎631-288-5533). Many companies ask you to pay double the metered fare, because the drivers must spend time and money on the return trip.

Visitor Information: Long Island Convention and Visitors Bureau (☎631-951-2423; www.licvb.com). On the eastbound side of the Long Island Expwy. between Exits 51 and 52 (in Deer Park), the eastbound side of the Southern State Pkwy. between Exits 13 and 14 (in Valley Stream), and in Tanger Outlet Mall in Riverhead. Information on how to order free brochures and maps for Long Island and the Hamptons, including a free Lodging Guide. Open May Th-Su 9am-5pm; June-Aug. daily 9am-7pm; Sept.-Oct. daily 9am-5pm.

Area Code: 516 (Nassau); 631 (Suffolk).

SHOPPING IN LONG ISLAND

If the iridescent lighting of the Manhattan Mall has you craving that suburban sprawl, hightail it out to the mecca of malls: Long Island.

Roosevelt Field Shopping Center, in **Hempstead,** was the airstrip where Amelia Earhart began her famous voyage in 1928. Too bad she didn't go down in style, in digs from the Armani Exchange with shoes by Steve Madden. (☎516-742-8000. Roosevelt Field has its own exit, M2, off the Meadowbrook Pkwy., just south of the Northern State Pkwy. Open M-Sa 10am-9:30pm, Su 11am-7pm.)

Tanger Outlet Centers, in **Riverhead,** is for the shopper with more time and less money. Designer duds at Off Fifth Avenue (Saks), Corningware at Corning Revere, boxers at Calvin Klein, orange socks at the Gap Outlet, and cross trainers at Nike. (☎631-369-2732 or 369-6255. At the very end of the LIE. Accessible with Sunrise Express buses. Open Apr.-Dec. M-Sa 10am-9pm, Su 10am-7pm; Jan.-Mar. Su-Th 10am-7pm, F-Sa 10am-9pm.)

Walt Whitman Mall, in **Huntington Station.** A brand-spanking new Saks Fifth Avenue and Bloomingdales will put this mall on the designer map. (☎516-271-1741. Intersectio of Rte. 110 and Jericho Tpke, take 49N off the LIE. Open M-Sa 10am-9:30pm, Su 11am-7pm.)

NASSAU COUNTY

Nassau County, the western half of the island, is a tale of two identities—the North "fro-yo is less fattening" Shore and the South "yo, I like gold chains" Shore, with a neatly ordered web of suburbia in between. South Shore is the home of young-lovin' Joey Buttafuoco, iridescent jogging suits, and muscled men with rattails dusting their necks. North Shore daughters wear U. Penn sweatshirts, talk on the Lexus car phone, and smoke slim cigarettes, the healthy alternative. Amid the cookie-cutter residential architecture, Nassau offers peaceful beaches quiet garden estates, and historical preserves. The LIRR and buses access the following sites (call ahead as bus schedules vary daily).

JONES BEACH

🚩 *Reachable from **Freeport.** ☎516-785-1600. **Directions:** LIRR to Freeport; shuttle bus stops every 30min. In the summer, the LIRR runs a package deal for the trip ($11 from Manhattan, June 29-Sept. 7). Both the Meadowbrook Pkwy. and the Wantagh Pkwy. lead directly to Jones Beach; if you drive, you will have to pay for parking ($7 before 4pm, free after 4pm; open till sundown, Lot 4 until midnight).* ***Hours:*** *Park closes at midnight, except for those with special fishing permits.*

Although the water is not the bluest nor the sun the strongest, the 6½ miles of Jones Beach State Park still attracts a small army of beach-goers, due to its wealth of attractions and proximity to Manhattan. Only 40 minutes from the city, barely a patch of sand shows under all the umbrellas and blankets in the summertime. Along the 1½-mile **boardwalk** you can find two Olympic-sized pools, softball fields, roller-skating, mini-golf, a fitness course, basketball, and nightly dancing. The **Marine Theater** inside the park often hosts big-name rockers such as Pearl Jam, the Beach Boys, and Def Leppard.

NASSAU COUNTY MUSEUM OF ART

◪ *1 Museum Dr., in Roslyn Harbor,* **Roslyn.** ☎*516-484-9338.* **Train:** *LIRR to Roslyn Station (50min., round-trip $9) from there take a taxi (approx. $5).* **Car:** *LIE to Exit 39N (Glen Cove Rd. North); go 2 mi. to Northern Blvd. (Rte. 25A), and turn left. At the second light, turn right into the museum.* **Admission:** *$4; students and children $2; seniors $3.* **Open:** *Tu-Su 11am-5pm.* **Tours** *given free Tu-Sa 2pm. Admission to* **Miniatures Museum** *included; same hours as main museum.*

The Nassau County Museum's rich collection is housed in a Georgian mansion that was previously part of the Frick family's Long Island estate. The permanent collection has works from masters such as Bonnard, Braque, Rauschenberg, and Vuillard. The gorgeous 145-acre **grounds** and an impressive **sculpture park** with works that include Botero and Calder, are exceptional. Also on the grounds is the fascinating **Tee Ridder Miniatures Museum,** boasting tiny intricate representations of our designed world.

OLD WESTBURY GARDENS

◪ *In* **Old Westbury.** ☎*516-333-0048.* **Train:** *LIRR to Westbury and then call a taxi.* **Car:** *LIE to Exit 39S, Glen Cove Rd. Take a left on Willets Rd. Drive east until Old Westbury Rd. The entrance to the gardens is up to the left.* **Open:** *W-M 10am-5pm. Last ticket sold 4pm.* **Admission:** *$8, seniors $6, ages 6-12 $3; house and garden $10, seniors $8, ages 6-12 $6.*

Now obscured by car dealerships and chain restaurants, a ghost of the luxury life is alive at the Old Westbury Gardens. Once the home of a Gold Coast millionaire, the huge, elegant manor house roosts comfortably amid acres of formal, flower-filled gardens, replete with lakes and gazebos. Children will love the full-sized **playhouse** in the Cottage Garden. Wednesday evening classical concerts are occasionally performed by Juilliard students in May, June, September, and October (free with regular admission).

OYSTER BAY

Oyster Bay, a town on the monied North Shore, is an example of Long Island at its most pictoresque, with big, beautiful houses lining a shining seashore.

SAGAMORE HILL

◪ ☎*516-922-4447 or 516-922-4788.* **Train:** *LIRR to Oyster Bay and call a taxi.* **Car:** *LIE to Exit 41 North, take the road toward Oyster Bay and follow signs to Sagamore Hill.* **Visitors' Center** *open daily 9:30am-4pm; off-season W-Su 9:30am-4pm. $5, under 16 free.* **Tours** *of the house every 30min. Come early; only 200 tickets available each day.*

Perhaps the most precious jewel in the crown of Oyster Bay is this estate on Sagamore Hill Rd. This National Historic Site was once the summer presidential residence of Theodore Roosevelt. In 1905 Roosevelt met here with envoys from Japan and Russia to begin negotiations that would end of the Russo-Japanese War. The house is packed with memorabilia; the collection of antlers reflects Teddy's interest in "preserving" wildlife.

PLANTING FIELDS ARBORETUM

◪ ☎*516-922-0061.* **Train:** *LIRR to Oyster Bay or Locust Valley, then call a taxi.* **Car:** *North Hempstead Tpke. to Mill River Hollow Rd.; take a left on Glen Cove Rd. and another left on Planting Fields Rd. Parking on the grounds 9am-5pm; $5. Main greenhouse* **open** *daily 9am-5pm.* **Admission** *free.* **Coe Hall:** ☎*516-922-0479. Open daily May-Sept. noon-3:30pm. $5; students and seniors $3.50; 7-12 $1.*

Nestled among the sportscar-filled grounds of Oyster Bay affluence, the massive arboretum is 409 of some of the most valuable acres in the New York area. The flowers bloom during the unlikely months of December, January, and February, when most city-dwellers have begun to forget what flora looks like. Other quirky highlights include a "synoptic garden" of plants obsessively alphabetized according to their Latin names. The **Fall Flower Show,** held for two weeks in October, attracts huge crowds. The arboretum hosts a summer concert series; past seasons have seen Joan Baez, the Indigo Girls, and Tito Puente. Insurance magnate William Robertson Coe once counted his coins at **Coe Hall** on the grounds of the arboretum. Constructed in 1921 in the Tudor Revival style, the mansion has rows upon rows of mind-boggling windows.

LONG BEACH

⚑ Directions: Take the LIRR (orange line) to Long Beach, the last stop; you may have to transfer at Jamaica. 50min. Round-trip: $9.50-14. **Beach:** Follow the crowds heading straight south for about 5 blocks. Beach pass $5 per day; 10-visit pass $25. **Combination Ticket** (LIRR and beach pass) $12; must be purchased at either Penn Station in Manhattan or Flatbush Station in Brooklyn.

Each summer the sleepy suburb of Long Beach transforms into a blissful beach town. Teenagers wax surf boards and whip out the peroxide; mothers pop open the iced tea mix; local drugstores run out of flip-flops and sunscreen. Since going topless in New York is now legal for both sexes, you can work on eradicating that farmer's tan. Most city folk head straight to **National Beach,** the beach directly parallel to the train station. **Volleyball** nets cluster on National, Edwards, and Riverside Beaches.

Restaurants cluster around **Park Street,** parallel to the beach. **Gino's Pizzeria,** across from the train station on Park St., sells great pizza. (☎ 631-432-8193. Regular slices $1.50, gourmet slices $2.35. Open M-Th and Su 11am-midnight, F-Sa 11am-1am.) A down-to-earth scene thrives nightly in the many **bars** that dot the small streets of Long Beach's west end. To get to the west end from the train station, head toward the beach to Beech St., make a right onto Beech, and walk about eight blocks. If you want to stay and drink in Long Beach, remember that the LIRR runs with limited service as the night wears on.

SUFFOLK COUNTY

The eastern half of Long Island, including its small islands, makes up Suffolk County. Far from the frenzy of Manhattan, the communities are so small that many are self-proclaimed villages. Residents hang American flags from the porches of paint-chipped farmhouses, and weekend activity is mostly antique shopping and barn sales.

WALT WHITMAN'S BIRTHPLACE

⚑ 246 Old Walt Whitman Rd., **South Huntington.** ☎ 516-427-5240. **Directions:** LIRR to Huntington and catch the S1 bus to Amityville; get off at the Walt Whitman Mall. The museum is diagonally across from the Mall. The S1 does not run on Su. **Open:** Summer M and W-F 11am-4pm, Sa-Su noon-5pm; winter W-F 1-4pm, Sa-Su noon-4pm. **Admission:** $3; students and seniors $2; ages 7-13 $1; under 7 free.

Walt Whitman's Birthplace State Historic Site and Interpretive Center is a simple memorial to the American poet whose 1855 *Leaves of Grass* introduced a free-verse style infused with a democratic spirit. The Whitmans moved to Brooklyn when the poet-to-be was only four years old, but the house provides interesting commentary on his life. A new visitor's center has a copy of the only known recording of Whitman.

THE HAMPTONS

The most famous region of Suffolk County is the cluster of communities along the South Fork collectively known as The Hamptons. It is home to wealthy summering Manhattanites and displaced West Coast stars. Artists and writers have made the sufficiently sexy Hamptons their home for decades. The area peaks in July, when traffic is horrific. The rich and famous often bypass this line-up by helicoptering into their monstrous estates.

Each Hampton has its own stereotype: Westhampton is new money, Southampton is old money, and East Hampton is artists; Bridgehampton connects the last two. All have main streets with rows of resort-style stores (read: beachware, art galleries, and glazed pottery vendors). The side streets hide myriad castle-like complexes. It's hard to find an entrance to the quiet, perfect beach that borders the Hamptons, as residents have stacked their well-guarded pleasure palaces in a tight row along the ocean; going through Amagansett and Montauk is easier.

SOUTHAMPTON AND WATER MILL

🚂 Directons: *From the Southampton LIRR station, head right out of the parking lot along Railroad Plaza to North Main St.; turn left onto N. Main and walk to the stop sign; bear left and keep walking as N. Main becomes Main St. and takes you to the center of town (about a ½-mile altogether).*

Southampton has several museums and homes worth visiting, making it a nice daytrip. Most of the sites lie within walking distance of each other. Established in 1640 as the first English colony in the future New York State, Southampton is a beautiful town of vast 19th-century houses that grow larger closer to the ocean. You can glimpse houses designed by Stanford White and other luminaries of the late 19th-century through their surroundng hedges. Most **beaches** are difficult to reach, and the few open to the public (look for signs) lack changing facilities and bathrooms.

At the corner of Main and Meeting House Ln. is the **Southampton Historical Museum,** where you'll find a collection of buildings and exhibits, including a one-room schoolhouse, whaling and farming equipment, and local Native American artifacts. (☎631-283-2494. Open June 12-Sept. 15 Tu-Su 11am-5pm; by appointment in winter. $3; seniors $2; children 6-12 $1; under 6 free.) The Venetian-style **Parrish Art Museum** is next door. Here, a modern gallery houses a permanent collection concentrating on American artists, particularly those (like William Merritt Chase and Fairfield Porter) who lived and worked near Southampton. (☎631-283-2118. Open June-Sept. M-Sa 11am-5pm, Su 1-5pm. Suggested donation $2, seniors $1, students free. Wheelchair accessible.)

EAST HAMPTON AND AMAGANSETT

East Hampton is fast becoming the playground of the area's elite. The center of town is home to more art galleries, clothing stores, and colonial memorabilia outlets than one would care to imagine, but the town is great for strolling, window-shopping, and whiling away the hours. Many artists have found inspiration and refuge here—most prominently Jackson Pollock. The studio/home he shared with Lee Krasner has since been dubbed the **Pollock-Krasner House and Study Center,** 830 Fireplace Rd., a museum of sorts. None of the artists' major works is on display. Visitors must tread around the home in foam slippers so as not to damage any of the paint splotches on the floor. (☎631-324-4929; www.pkhouse.org. Open by appointment May-Oct. Th-Sa 11am-4pm. $5.)

Nearby **Amagansett** is little more than a tiny Main St. that offers some great live music. **The Stephen Talkhouse,** 161 Main St., hosts performers such as Marianne Faithfull and Judy Collins, as well as lesser-known acts. (☎516-267-3117; www.stephentalkhouse.com. Performances begin at 9pm. Tickets $5-10.)

SAG HARBOR

🚂 Directions: *The LIRR does not stop at Sag Harbor, but the town is accessible via Suffolk County Transit bus: take the LIRR to the Southampton station and catch the S92, which runs 9 times a day.*

Out of the South Fork's north shore droops Sag Harbor. Founded in 1707, this port used to be more important than New York Harbor; at its peak, this winsome village was the world's fourth-largest whaling port. James Fenimore Cooper began his first novel, *Precaution,* in a Sag Harbor hotel in 1824. Rounding off Sag Harbor's dazzling and captivating history, during Prohibition the harbor served as a major meeting place for smugglers and rum-runners from the Caribbean.

Sag Harbor's former grandeur survives in the second-largest collection of Colonial buildings in the US and in the cemeteries lined with the gravestones of Revolutionary soldiers and sailors. Check out the **Sag Harbor Whaling Museum** in the Masonic Temple at the corner of Main St. and Garden St. A huge whale rib arches over the front door. (☎631-725-0770. Open May-Sept. M-Sa 10am-5pm, Su 1-5pm. $3; seniors $2; ages 6-13 $1. Tours by appointment; $2.)

8 8

MONTAUK

⚑ Directions: *LIRR to Montauk and head to the right out of the train station along the 4-lane road. This is Edgemere Rd., which leads straight to the village green, a 10-15min. walk. M-F the only trains back to the city leave at 10:36pm and 12:52am, Sa-Su there are several afternoon and evening trains; the Hampton Jitney makes a dozen trips daily.*

As the easternmost point of the South Fork, Montauk offers an unobstructed view of the Atlantic Ocean. Despite the slightly commercialized tourist/hotel areas and the three-hour trip, the peaceful salt air is worth the effort. The 110-foot **Montauk Point Lighthouse and Museum,** off Rte. 27., went up in 1796 by special order of President George Washington. The first public works project in the newly formed United States, it helped guide many ships into the harbor, including the schooner *La Amistad*. It is now fully attached to the mainland. Lungs willing, you should climb the 137 spiraling steps to see across the Long Island Sound to Connecticut and Rhode Island. Try to spot the *Will o' the Wisp*, a ghostly clipper ship sometimes sighted on hazy days with a lantern hanging from its mast. Experts claim that the ship is a mirage resulting from the phosphorus in the atmosphere, but what do they know? (☎ 631-668-2544. Open June-Sept. M-F and Su 10:30am-6pm, Sa 10:30am-7:30pm; other times call for info. $4; seniors $3.50; under 12 $2.50.)

If tower climbing has made you hungry, stop at **Lobster Roll,** on Hwy. 27 (the Montauk Pkwy.), in the Napeague Stretch. The restaurant's featured dish, a flaky, lobster salad-stuffed treat ($10.75), is worth every penny. (☎ 631-267-3740. Open daily 11:30am-10pm.)

If you prefer to catch your own chicken of the sea, try a half-day fluke-fishing cruise with **Viking** (☎ 631-668-5700; $32, children $15, including equipment; departs 8am and 1pm; no reservations necessary). Viking also runs whale-watching cruises (July-Aug. Th-Su 10:30am; $36, seniors $31, children $18).

FIRE ISLAND

This, southern Long Island's barrier against the temperamental Atlantic, developed in the early 20th-century, when middle-income families began to acquire beachfront property en masse. Some towns retain their original layout of closely packed bungalows without yards. The amazingly influential urban planner Robert Moses himself could not build a road across the island because citizens fought so fiercely to retain their quiet plots of land. Since then, the state has protected most areas of Fire Island by declaring them either a state park or a federal "wilderness area." Still, 17 summer communities have managed to forge distinct niches on Fire Island, visiting amongst themselves by water taxi. The distance has kept the towns diverse—providing homes for middle-class clusters, openly gay communities (see **The Queer Apple,** p. 221), and vacationing stars.

GETTING THERE

Traveling from Fire Island from Manhattan involves multiple modes of transportation. **Trains** from Penn Station depart almost every hour to one of the three ports that will lead you to the island. However, sometimes you must transfer trains to get there. After your train arrives at **Bay Shore** ($9.50) or **Sayville** ($9.50), you must take a taxi to the port. The train to **Patchogue** ($10.75) takes longer and only leads to several of the ports on Fire Island but does not necessitate a taxi. Ferries from Bay Shore (☎ 516-665-3600), go to Kismet, Saltaire, Fair Harbor, Atlantic, Dunewood, Ocean Beach, Seaview, and Ocean Bay Park (round-trip $11.50, under 12 $5.50). Ferries from Sayville (☎ 631-589-8980) go to Sailors' Haven (round-trip $9), Cherry Grove, and Fire Island Pines (round-trip $11, under 11 $5). Ferries from Patchogue (☎ 516-475-1665) go to Davis Park and Watch Hill (round-trip $10, under 12 $5.50). To get from one town to the other, call one of many water taxi companies like the aptly named **Water Taxi** (☎ 516-665-8885). Prices range from a couple of bucks to $35 depending on how far you are going.

BEACHES AND COMMUNITIES

Ocean Beach is the largest and most publicly accessible community. Signs throughout the city warn visitors that they must act respectfully: no drinking in public; no walking around town without a shirt; no "discourteous" public displays. Ocean Beach's main street is lined with gray wooden buildings with thick shingles, restaurants, small groceries, and beachware shops. Grab a delightful bite to eat at **Michael's Pizzeria** (sandwiches $5-8, pizza and pasta $10-14; open M-F 8am-midnight, Sa-Su 6am-noon). Save room for a soft, chewy oatmeal raisin cookie ($1.75) from **Rachel's Bakery** (open daily 7am-10pm). **The Alligator** (☎613-583-8896) is a barely adorned bar that concentrates instead on drinks ($2-5) and a big-screen TV (Sa cover $5; open M-F 4pm-4am and Sa-Su noon-4am).

Take any side street (perpendicular to the main drag) all the way across the island to arrive at miles and miles of coastline. Once there, you can walk along the shore to see the beachfront homes; the largest homes are located about two miles away in posh **Saltaire** (a completely residential community), followed closely by the up-and-coming town of **Fair Harbor**. If you walk in the other direction just over 2½ mi., you will arrive at the bungalows and raised boardwalks of **Cherry Grove** and the colossal homes of **Fire Island Pines,** two predominantly gay communities (for more see **The Queer Apple,** p. 221).

Those in the know travel by water taxi to nearby **Ocean Bay Park,** a community that grew tired of the restrictions in Ocean Beach. **Flynns** (☎631-583-5000) proves the local lore nightly; the bar rocks every weekend (open Su-Th noon-11pm, F-Sa noon-2am).

Ferries run late into the night, but if you want to spend the night, shack up at **Gregg's Hotel,** which has clean rooms and a friendly, knowledgeable staff. Room prices vary according to season, number of vacancies, and days of the week. Doubles can cost anywhere from $60 on a weekday to $220 on a peak-season weekend.

PARKS AND SIGHTS

The **Fire Island National Seashore** (☎516-289-4810 for the headquarters in Patchogue) is the official moniker for the stretches of coastline that hug the island. This is Fire Island's biggest draw, and the daytime hotspot for summertime fishing, clamming, and guided nature walks. The facilities at **Sailor's Haven** (just west of the Cherry Grove community) include a marina, a nature trail, and a famous beach. Similar facilities at **Watch Hill** (☎631-597-6455) include a 26-unit campground, where reservations are required.

The **Sunken Forest,** so called because of its location behind the dunes, is another of the island's natural wonders. Located directly west of Sailor's Haven, its soil supports an unusual and attractive combination of gnarled holly, sassafras, and poison ivy. Some of the forest's specimens are over 200 years old.

Planning Your Trip

WHEN TO GO

New York is expensive to visit in any season, but coming in the off season may leave you more comfortable, less overwhelmed by crowds, and slightly less at the mercy of price-gouging establishments. In May and September the weather improves, waves of tourists recede, and prices descend. Most facilities and sights stay open all winter—after all, New York is the city that never sleeps, and it certainly doesn't hibernate. Here are some preliminary tips to help you through, whatever the time of year.

First of all, consider your address book a supplementary travel guide; staying with relatives, friends, or enemies greatly alleviates the cost of living in New York. Keep an eye out for news of special events. New York has a special talent for impressive annual celebrations—see the Discover chapter for a table of annual holidays and events that occur in New York, with the dates for late 2000 and all of 2001 given. But New York is more than just famous places and annual celebrations. There are always local and underground concerts, gallery openings, dance performances, plays—whatever your desire, NYC will provide if you keep your eye out for flyers and newspaper or magazine listings.

CLIMATE

New York's weather is the worst of both worlds: summers are hot and sticky, while winters compete with neighboring New England for cold and snow. Winter snowfalls are common, but the city clears streets immediately (sidewalks are a different matter). In spring and fall, frequent impromptu showers make carrying an umbrella a good idea.

The US uses the Fahrenheit temperature scale rather than Celsius. To convert Fahrenheit to Celsius temperatures, subtract 32, then multiply by 5 and divide the result by 9. See the inside back cover for more detailed Farenheit and Celsius conversions.

JANUARY	APRIL	JULY	OCTOBER: 3.4"
RAINFALL 3.2"	RAINFALL 3.8"	RAINFALL 3.8"	RAINFALL 3.4"
HIGH 38 LOW 26	HIGH 61 LOW 44	HIGH 92 LOW 68	HIGH 66 LOW 50

DOCUMENTS AND FORMALITIES

AMERICAN EMBASSIES & CONSULATES ABROAD

Contact the nearest US embassy or consulate to obtain information on visas and passports to the US. The US **Bureau of Consular Affairs** provides contact information for US overseas stations, which can be found at **http://travel.state.gov/links.html.** You can find websites, email addresses, further contact info, and hours for US embassies and consulates worldwide. For consular services in New York, see **Service Directory,** p. 290.

US Embassies: In **Australia,** Moonah Place, Canberra, ACT 2600 (☎02 6214 5600; fax 6214 5970); in **Canada,** 490 Sussex Dr., Ottawa, ON K1N 1G8 (☎613-238-5335); in **Ireland,** 42 Elgin Rd., Ballsbridge, Dublin 4 (☎01 668 7122); in **South Africa,** 877 Pretorius St., Arcadio 0083; P.O. Box 9536, Pretoria 0001 (☎012 342 1048; fax 342 2244); in the **UK,** 24/31 Grosvenor Sq., London W1A 1AE (☎020 7 499 9000; fax 7 409 1637).

US Consulates: In **Australia,** MLC Centre, 19-29 Martin Pl., 59th fl., Sydney NSW 2000 (☎612 9373 9200; fax 9373 9125); 553 St. Kilda Rd., Melbourne, VIC 3004 (☎03 9526 5900; fax 9525-0769); 16 St. George Terr., 13th fl., Perth, WA 6000 (☎08 9231 9400; fax 9231 9444); in **Canada,** 490 Sussex Dr., Ottawa, ON K1N 1G8 (☎613-238-5335 or 800-283-4356); 360 University Ave., Toronto, ON M5G 1S4 (☎416-595-1700; fax 595-0051); 615 Macleod Trail S.E., Room 1000, Calgary, Alberta, T2G 4T8; P.O. Box 65, Postal Station Desjardins, Montréal, QC H5B 1G1 (☎514-398-9695; fax 398-0973); 2 Place Terrasse Dufferin, B.P. 939, Québec, QC G1R 4T9 (☎418-692-2095; fax 692-4640); 1095 W. Pender St., Vancouver, BC V6E 2M6 (☎604-685-4311); in **New Zealand,** General Bldg. 4th fl., 29 Shortland St., Auckland, Private Bag 92022 (☎09 303 2724; fax 366 0870); in **South Africa,** Monte Carlo Building, 7th Fl., Heerengracht Foreshore; PO Box 6773, ROGGEBAAI, 8012, Capetown (☎021 421 4280; fax 425 3014); 1 River St., Killarney; PO Box 1762, HOUGHTON 2041, Johannesburg (☎011 644 6800; fax 646 6916); in the **UK,** Queen's House, 14 Queen St., Belfast, N. Ireland, BT1 6EQ (☎0123 232 8239; fax 224 8482); 3 Regent Terr., Edinburgh, Scotland EH7 5BW (☎0131 556 8315; fax 557 6023).

PASSPORTS

REQUIREMENTS
Citizens of Australia, Ireland, New Zealand, South Africa, and the UK need valid passports to enter the US and to re-enter their own country. The US does not allow entrance if the holder's passport expires in less than six months; returning home with an expired passport is illegal, and may result in a fine.

LOST PASSPORTS
If you lose your passport, immediately notify the local police and the nearest embassy or consulate of your home government. To expedite its replacement, you will need to know all information previously recorded and show identification and proof of citizenship. In some cases, a replacement may take weeks to process, and it may be valid only for a limited time. Any visas stamped in your old passport will be irretrievably lost. In an emergency, ask for immediate temporary traveling papers that will permit you to re-enter your home country.

NEW PASSPORTS

All applications for new passports or renewals should be filed several weeks or months in advance of your planned departure date—remember that you are relying on government agencies to complete these transactions. Demand for passports is highest in most nations between January and August, so apply as early as possible around these months. A backlog in processing can spoil your plans. Most passport offices do offer rush passport services for an extra charge. Citizens residing abroad who need a passport or renewal should contact their nearest embassy or consulate.

Australia: ☎ 13 12 32; email passports.australia@dfat.gov.au; www.dfat.gov.au/passports. Apply for a passport at a post office, passport office (in Adelaide, Brisbane, Canberra, Darwin, Hobart, Melbourne, Newcastle, Perth, or Sydney), or overseas diplomatic mission. Passports AUS$128 (32-page) or AUS$192 (64-page); valid for 10 yrs. Children AUS$64 (32-page) or AUS$96 (64-page); valid 5 yrs.

Canada: Canadian Passport Office, Department of Foreign Affairs and International Trade, Ottawa, ON K1A 0G3 (☎613-994-3500 or 800-567-6868; www.dfait-maeci.gc.ca/passport). Applications available at passport offices, Canadian missions, and post offices. Passports CDN$60; valid 5 yrs. (non-renewable).

Ireland: Get application at a *Garda* station or post office, or request one from a passport office. Then apply by mail to the Department of Foreign Affairs, Passport Office, Molesworth St., Dublin 2 (☎01 671 1633; fax 671 1092; www.irlgov.ie/iveagh), or the Passport Office, Irish Life Building, 1A South Mall, Cork (☎021 27 25 25). Passports IR£45; valid 10 yrs. Under 18 or over 65 IR£10; valid 3 yrs.

New Zealand: Send applications to the Passport Office, Department of International Affairs, P.O. Box 10526, Wellington, New Zealand (☎0800 22 50 50 or 4 474 8100; fax 4 474 8010; www.passports.govt.nz). Standard processing time: 10 working days. Passports NZ$80; valid 10 yrs. Children NZ$40; valid 5 yrs. 3 day "urgent service" NZ$160; children NZ$120.

South Africa: Department of Home Affairs. Passports issued only in Pretoria, but all applications must still be submitted or forwarded to nearest S. African consulate. Processing time is 3 months or more. Passports around SAR80; valid for 10 yrs. Under 16 around SAR60; valid 5 yrs. For more info: http://usaembassy.southafrica.net/VisaForms/Passport/Passport2000.html.

UK: ☎0870 521 0410; www.open.gov.uk/ukpass/ukpass.htm. Get an application from a passport office, main post office, travel agent, or online (for UK residents only) at www.ukpa.gov.uk/forms/f_app_pack.htm. Then apply by mail to or in person at a passport office. Passports UK£28; valid 10 yrs. Under 15 UK£14.80; valid 5 yrs. The process takes about 4 weeks; faster service (by personal visit to the offices listed above) costs an additional £12.

VISAS AND WORK PERMITS

As of August 2000, citizens of South Africa and most other countries need a visa—a stamp, sticker, or insert in your passport specifying the purpose of your travel and the permitted duration of your stay—in addition to a valid passport for entrance to the US. To obtain a visa, contact the nearest US embassy or consulate.

ESSENTIAL INFORMATION

ENTRANCE REQUIREMENTS

Passport (p. 242). Required for all visitors to the US and Canada.

Visa In general a visa is required for visiting the US and Canada, but it can be waived. (See p. 243 for more specific information.)

Work Permit (p. 243). Required for all foreigners planning to work in Canada or the US

Driving Permit. Required for all those planning to drive.

AIDS (p. 249) HIV-positive persons are not allowed to immigrate permanently to the US.

VISITS OF UNDER 90 DAYS

Citizens of Andorra, Argentina, Australia, Austria, Belgium, Brunei, Denmark, Finland, France, Germany, Iceland, Ireland, Italy, Japan, Liechtenstein, Luxembourg, Monaco, the Netherlands, New Zealand, Norway, Portugal, San Marino, Singapore, Slovenia, Spain, Sweden, Switzerland, the UK, and Uruguay can waive US visas through the **Visa Waiver Pilot Program.** Visitors qualify if they are traveling only for business or pleasure (*not* work or study), are staying for fewer than 90 days, have proof of intent to leave (e.g., a return plane ticket), an I-94W form (arrival/departure certificate attached to your visa upon arrival), and are traveling on particular air or sea carriers.

VISITS OF OVER 90 DAYS

All travelers planning to stay more than 90 days (180 days for Canadians) need to obtain a visa. For more information on procuring a long-term visa, see **Living in the City,** p. 279.

IDENTIFICATION

When you travel, always carry two or more forms of identification on your person, including at least one photo ID. A passport combined with a driver's license or birth certificate usually serves as adequate proof of your identity and citizenship. Many establishments, especially banks, require several IDs before cashing traveler's checks. Never carry all your forms of ID together.

STUDENT AND TEACHER IDENTIFICATION

While less widely recognized in the US and Canada than in Europe, the **International Student Identity Card (ISIC)** is still the most widely accepted form of student identification. Flashing this card can often procure you discounts for sights, theaters, museums, transportation, and other services. You must present an ISIC card to purchase reduced-rate student airplane tickets. Cardholders can access a toll-free 24-hour ISIC helpline whose multilingual staff can provide assistance in medical, legal, and financial emergencies overseas (☎ 877-370-ISIC in the US and Canada; elsewhere call collect ☎ 1-715-345-0505).

Many student travel agencies around the world issue ISICs, including STA Travel in Australia and New Zealand; Travel CUTS in Canada; USIT in Ireland and Northern Ireland; SASTS in South Africa; Campus Travel and STA Travel in the UK; Council Travel, STA Travel, and via the web (www.counciltravel.com/idcards/default.asp) in the US (see Budget Travel Agencies in **Service Directory,** p. 290). When you apply for the card, request a copy of the *International Student Identity Card Handbook*, which lists some of the available discounts in the US and Canada. You can also write to Council for a copy. The card is valid from September of one year to December of the following year and costs AUS$15, CDN$15, or US$22. Applicants must be at least 12 years old and degree-seeking students of a secondary or post-secondary school. Because of the proliferation of phony ISICs, many airlines and some other services require additional proof of student identity, such as a signed letter from the registrar attesting to your student status that is stamped with the school seal or your school ID card. The **International Teacher Identity Card (ITIC)** offers similar but limited discounts. The fee is AUS$13, UK£5, or US$22. For more info on these cards, contact the **International Student Travel Confederation (ISTC),** Herengracht 479, 1017 BS Amsterdam, Netherlands (☎ 31 20 421 28 00; fax 421 28 10; email istcinfo@istc.org; www.istc.org).

YOUTH IDENTIFICATION

The International Student Travel Confederation also issues a discount card to travelers who are 26 years old or younger, but not students. This one-year card, known as the **International Youth Travel Card (IYTC),** formerly GO25, offers many of the same benefits as the ISIC, and most organizations that sell the ISIC also sell the IYTC. To apply, you will need either a passport, valid driver's license, or copy of a birth certificate, and a passport-sized photo with your name printed on the back. The fee is US$22.

CUSTOMS

Upon entering the US or Canada, you must declare certain items from abroad and pay a duty on the value of those articles that exceed the allowance established by the US or Canada's customs service. Keeping receipts for purchases made abroad will help establish values when you return. It is wise to make a list, including serial numbers, of any valuables that you carry with you from home; if you register this list with customs before your departure and have an official stamp it, you will avoid import duty charges and ensure an easy passage upon your return. Be especially careful to document items manufactured abroad, and don't try to bring perishable food over the border.

Upon returning home, you must declare all articles acquired abroad and pay a **duty** on the value of articles that exceed the allowance established by your country's customs service. Goods and gifts purchased at **duty-free** shops abroad are not exempt from duty or sales tax at your point of return; you must declare these items as well. "Duty-free" merely means that you need not pay a tax in the country of purchase. For more specific information on customs requirements, contact the following information centers:

Australia: Australian Customs National Information Line (in Australia ☎ 01 30 03 63, from elsewhere ☎ +61 2 6275 6666; www.customs.gov.au).

Canada: Canadian Customs, 2265 St. Laurent Blvd., Ottawa, ON K1G 4K3 (☎ 800-461-9999 (24hr.) or 613-993-0534; www.revcan.ca).

Ireland: Customs Information Office, Irish Life Centre, Lower Abbey St., Dublin 1 (☎ 01 878 8811; fax 878 0836; www.revenue.ie/customs.htm).

New Zealand: New Zealand Customhouse, 17-21 Whitmore St., Box 2218, Wellington (☎ 04 473 6099; fax 473 7370; www.customs.govt.nz).

South Africa: Commissioner for Customs and Excise, Privat Bag X47, Pretoria 0001 (☎ 012 314 9911; fax 328 6478; www.gov.za).

UK: Her Majesty's Customs and Excise, Passenger Enquiry Team, Wayfarer House, Great South West Rd., Feltham, Middlesex TW14 8NP (☎ 020 8910 3744; fax 8910 3933; www.hmce.gov.uk).

MONEY

In Boston they ask, How much does he know? In New York, How much is he worth?
—Mark Twain

Accommodations in NYC start around $22 for dorm-style living and $60 for a hotel single. A simple sit-down meal can be had for around $10, and even a decent meal at a hip eatery can be had for under $20. But with NYC's astronomical transportation costs and exciting activities, plan on spending a minimum of $70-120 per day. No matter how cheap you are, you won't be able to carry all your cash with you, and keeping large sums in a money belt is even risky. Non-cash reserves are a necessary precaution in the big bad city. Unfortunately, out-of-state personal checks aren't readily accepted in NYC, even at banks. If you plan to travel for more than a few days, carry a credit card.

CURRENCY AND EXCHANGE

The main unit of currency in the US is the **dollar** (symbol $; also known as a 'buck'), which is divided into 100 **cents** (symbol ¢). Dollars circulate almost exclusively as paper money. The green bills come in denominations of $1, $5, $10, $20, $50, and $100. US coins come valued at 1¢ (penny), 5¢ (nickel), 10¢ (dime), and 25¢ (quarter). Additionally, there are coins worth a dollar, confusingly only slightly larger than quarters, some of them gold, and rare sightings of the John F. Kennedy fifty-cent coin.

The currency chart below is based on August 2000 exchange rates between US dollars (US$), Canadian dollars (CDN$), British pounds (UK£), Irish pounds (IR£), Australian dollars (AUS$), New Zealand dollars (NZ$), South African Rand (ZAR), and European Union euros (EUR€). Check a large newspaper or the web (e.g. finance.yahoo.com or www.bloomberg.com) for the latest exchange rates.

THE GREENBACK (THE US DOLLAR)

CDN$1 = $0.67	US$1 = CDN$1.49
UK£1 = $1.50	US$1 = UK£0.66
IR£1 = $1.15	US$1= IR£0.87
AUS$1 = $0.59	US$1= AUS$1.70
NZ$1 = $0.46	US$1 = NZ$2.19
SAR1=$0.14	US$1 = SAR6.97
EUR€=$0.90	US$1=EUR€1.10

Convert your currency infrequently and in large amounts to minimize exorbitant exchange fees. As a general rule, it's cheaper to convert money once you arrive in New York than in your home country. However, it's important to have enough US currency to last for the first 24 to 72 hours in the city in case you arrive after banking hours or on a holiday. Try to buy traveler's checks in US dollars so that you won't have to exchange currency in the process of cashing them. Be sure to observe commission rates closely and check newspapers to get the standard rate of exchange. A good rule of thumb is to go only to places that have a 5% margin between their buy and sell prices. Anything more and they are making too much profit. Be sure that both prices are listed. Most banks will not cash personal checks unless you open an account with them, a time-consuming affair (see **Service Directory: Currency Exchange,** p. 291).

BANKS

Banks generally have better rates than tourist offices or exchange kiosks. ATM cards with low international transaction fees may actually offer the best exchange rates on withdrawals in US currency—**ATM withdrawals** are also most convenient. New York **banks** are usually open Monday through Friday 9am to 5pm; some open Saturdays from 9am to noon or 1pm. All banks, government agencies, and post offices are closed on **legal holidays:** New Year's Day (January 1), Martin Luther King, Jr. Day (January 17), Presidents' Day (February 15), Memorial Day (May 29), Independence Day (July 4), Labor Day (September 3), Columbus Day (October 9), Veterans' Day (November 11), Thanksgiving Day (November 22 in 2001), and Christmas Day (December 25). For information on opening a bank account in New York, see **Living in the City,** p. 285.

TRAVELER'S CHECKS

Traveler's checks are one of the safest and least troublesome means of carrying funds, since they can be refunded if stolen, and they are widely accepted in NYC. Several agencies and banks sell them, usually for face value plus a small percentage commission. **American Express** and **Visa** are the most widely recognized. If you're ordering checks, do so well in advance, especially if you are requesting large sums.

In order to collect a **refund for lost or stolen checks,** keep your check receipts separate from your checks and store them in a safe place or with a traveling companion. Record check numbers when you cash them, leave a list of check numbers with someone at home, and ask for a list of refund centers when you buy your checks. Never countersign your checks until you are ready to cash them.

American Express: Call ☎800 251-902 in Australia; in New Zealand ☎0800 441 068; in the UK ☎0800 52 13 13; in the US and Canada ☎800-221-7282. Elsewhere, call US collect ☎1-801-964-6665; www.aexp.com. American Express traveler's checks are available in US (but not Canadian) dollars. Checks can be purchased for a small fee (1-4%) at American Express Travel Service Offices, banks, and American Automobile Association offices. AAA members (see p. 261) can buy the checks commission-free. American Express offices cash their checks commission-free (except where prohibited by national governments), but often at slightly worse rates than banks. *Cheques for Two* can be signed by either of two people traveling together.

Citicorp: Call ☎ 800-645-6556 in the US and Canada; in Europe, the Middle East, or Africa, call the UK office at ☎ 44 020 7508 7007; from elsewhere, call US collect ☎ 1-813-623-1709. Traveler's checks in 7 currencies. Commission 1-2%. Guaranteed hand-delivery of traveler's checks when a refund location is not convenient. Call 24hr.

Thomas Cook MasterCard: From the US, Canada, or Caribbean call ☎ 800-223-7373; from the UK call ☎ 0800 622 101; from elsewhere, call ☎ 44 1733 318 950 collect. Available in 13 currencies. Commission 2%. Offices cash checks commission-free.

Visa: Call ☎ 800-227-6811 in the US; in the UK ☎ 0800 895 078; from elsewhere, call ☎ 44 1733 318 949 and reverse the charges. They can tell you the location of their nearest office.

CREDIT CARDS

In NYC, you are your credit rating. There are so many opportunities to get that *one* thing you've *always* wanted, that you're going to want as much money at your disposal as possible. Few establishments in the city reject all major cards, but you'll probably come across at least one establishment that only takes cold, hard cash. But credit cards are invaluable in an emergency—an unexpected hospital bill or the loss of traveler's checks—which may leave you temporarily without other resources. Major credit cards such as **MasterCard** and **Visa** can be used to extract cash advances in dollars from associated banks and teller machines throughout NYC for wholesale (e.g. very good) exchange rates. **American Express** cards also work in some ATMs, as well as at AmEx offices and major airports. All such machines require a **Personal Identification Number (PIN).** Ask your credit card company for a PIN before you leave; without it, you will be unable to withdraw cash with your credit card outside your home country. If you already have a PIN, make sure it will work in the US. Credit cards often offer an array of other services, from insurance to emergency assistance; check with your company. **Visa** (☎ 800-336-8472), **MasterCard** (☎ 800-307-7309), **American Express** (☎ 800-843-2273), and the **Discover Card** (☎ 800-347-2683; outside US 1-801-902-3100) are all popular and widely recognized in the US.

CASH CARDS

Cash cards—popularly called **ATM** (Automated Teller Machine) cards—are everywhere in NYC. You can access any US and most foreign banks through them. Check your card to see which international money networks it uses, then look for ATM machines using the same (most machines will use all). The two major international money networks are **Cirrus** (US ☎ 800-424-7787) and **PLUS** (US ☎ 800 843-7587). **NYCE** is a major US network. ATMs often offer superior exchange rates—up to 5% better than the retail rate used by banks and other currency exchange establishments. Typically the ATM you use will add a $1-1.50 surcharge and your home bank may charge $1-5 per withdrawal. A $200-500 daily cash withdrawal limit is generally imposed by your home bank (check before you leave). Be sure to memorize your PIN code in numeric form since machines often don't have letters on their keys. Also, if your PIN is longer than four digits, ask your bank whether you need a new number. If you're coming to NYC to stay for a while, open a savings account at one of the local banks and get an ATM card, which you can use at any time all over the city (see **Living in New York**, p. 285).

Visa TravelMoney (for customer assistance ☎ 800-847-2911) is a system allowing you to access money from Visa ATMs (check www.visa.com/pd/atm). You deposit an amount before you travel (plus a small administration fee), and you can withdraw up to that sum. The cards, which give you the same favorable exchange rate for withdrawals as a regular Visa, are especially useful if you plan to travel through many countries. Check with your local bank to see if it issues TravelMoney cards. **Road Cash** (US ☎ 877-762-3227; www.roadcash.com) issues cards in the US with a minimum US$300 deposit.

GETTING MONEY FROM HOME

AMERICAN EXPRESS. Cardholders can withdraw cash from their checking accounts at any of AmEx's major offices and many representative offices (up to US$1000 every 21 days; no service charge, no interest). AmEx "Express Cash" withdrawals from any AmEx ATM in the US or Canada are automatically debited from the cardholder's checking account or credit line. Green card holders may withdraw up to US$1000 in any seven-day period (2% transaction fee; minimum US$2.50, maximum US$20). To enroll in Express Cash, cardmembers should call ☎800-227-4669 in the US; outside the US call collect ☎+1 336-668-5041.

WESTERN UNION. Travelers from most of the world can wire money to and form their home country or state through Western Union's money transfer services. In the US, call ☎800-325-6000; in Canada, ☎800-235-0000; in the UK, ☎0800 833 833. Manhattan has five Western Union send/payout offices, all around TriBeCa. To wire money within the US using a credit card (Visa, MasterCard, Discover), call ☎800-CALL-CASH (225-5227). The rates for sending cash are generally US$10-11 cheaper than with a credit card, and the money is usually available at the place you're sending it to within an hour. To find the nearest Western Union location online, consult www.westernunion.com.

HEALTH

For more information on long-term health care and insurance in NYC, see **Living in New York,** p. 286. For lists of doctors, hospitals, pharmacies, and emergency numbers, see **Service Directory,** p. 289.

BEFORE YOU GO

Before you leave, check if your insurance policy covers medical costs incurred while traveling (see **Insurance,** p. 251). Always have proof of insurance and policy numbers with you. If you risk traveling without insurance, you may have to rely on public health organizations and clinics that treat patients without demanding proof of solvency—use the emergency numbers in the **Service Directory,** p. 291 in this case. If you require **emergency treatment,** call ☎911 or go to the emergency room of the nearest hospital.

MEDICAL CONDITIONS

Those with medical conditions (e.g., diabetes, allergies to antibiotics, epilepsy, heart conditions) may want to obtain a stainless steel **Medic Alert** identification tag ($35 the 1st year, and $15 annually thereafter), which identifies the condition and gives a 24-hour collect-call information number. Contact the Medic Alert Foundation, 2323 Colorado Ave., Turlock, CA 95382 (☎800-825-3785; www.medicalert.org). Diabetics can contact the American Diabetes Association, 1660 Duke St., Alexandria, VA 22314 (☎800-232-3472), to receive copies of the article "Travel and Diabetes" and a diabetic ID card that describes the carrier's diabetic status in 18 languages. The *MedPass* from **Global Emergency Medical Services (GEMS),** 2001 Westside Dr., #120, Alpharetta, GA 30004, USA (☎800-860-1111; fax 770-475-0058; www.globalems.com), provides 24-hour international medical assistance, support, and medical evacuation resources.

AIDS AND HIV

Acquired Immune Deficiency Syndrome (AIDS) is a growing problem around the world. In December 1998, it was estimated that out of every 100,000 people in NY State, almost 50 have AIDS. The easiest mode of HIV transmission is direct blood-to-blood contact with an HIV-positive person; *never* share intravenous drug, tattooing, or other needles. The most common mode of transmission is sexual intercourse. *Use latex condoms in all sexual encounters*—these are readily available *everywhere;* see Birth Control, below.

If you are **HIV positive,** contact the Bureau of Consular Affairs, #4811, Department of State, Washington, D.C. 20520 (☎202-647-1488; fax 647-3000; http://travel.state.gov). According to US law, **HIV positive persons are not permitted to enter the US.** However, HIV testing is required only for those planning to immigrate permanently. Travelers from areas with particularly high concentrations of HIV positive persons or persons with AIDS may be required to provide more information when applying.

For more information on AIDS, call the **US Centers for Disease Control's** 24-hour hotline at ☎800-342-2437, or contact the **Joint United Nations Programme on HIV/AIDS (UNAIDS),** 20 av. Appia 20, CH-1211 Geneva 27, Switzerland (☎+41 22 791 36 66; fax 791 41 87). Council Travel's brochure, *Travel Safe: AIDS and International Travel,* is available at their offices and on their website (www.ciee.org/lsp/safety/travelsafe.htm).

BIRTH CONTROL

Although reliable contraception is easily obtainable in New York City, women taking **birth control pills** should bring enough to allow for extended stays and should bring a copy of their prescription, since forms of the pill vary a good deal. **Condoms** can be found in any pharmacy, either behind the main counter or right on the shelves. Many of the city's pharmacies, conveniently, stay open all the time, and every corner grocery and 24-hour store will be sure to have condoms near the cashier.

WOMEN'S HEALTH

Abortion is legal in New York state; if you are in the New York area and need an abortion, contact the **National Abortion Federation,** a professional association of abortion providers. Call its toll-free hotline for information, counseling, and the names of qualified medical professionals in the area. (☎800-772-9100. Open M-F 9am-7pm.) The NAF has informational publications for individuals and health-care clinics alike. Clinics they recommend must maintain certain safety and operational standards. In New York, the NAF will refer you to the Planned Parenthood clinics (or call directly: ☎212-274-7200).

INSURANCE

Travel insurance generally covers four basic areas: medical/health problems, property loss, trip cancellation/interruption, and emergency evacuation. Although your regular insurance policies may well extend to travel-related accidents, you may consider purchasing travel insurance if the cost of potential trip cancellation/interruption is greater than you can absorb. Prices for travel insurance purchased separately generally run about $50 per week for full coverage, while trip cancellation/interruption may be purchased separately at a rate of about $5.50 per $100 of coverage.

Medical insurance (especially university policies) often covers costs abroad; check with your provider. **Homeowners' insurance** (or your family's coverage) often covers theft during travel and loss of travel documents (passport, plane ticket, etc.) up to $500.

ISIC and **ITIC** provide basic insurance benefits, including $100 per day of in-hospital sickness for up to 60 days, $3000 of accident-related medical reimbursement, and $25,000 for emergency medical transport (see **Identification,** p. 244). Cardholders can access a toll-free 24-hour helpline whose multilingual staff can help in medical, legal, and financial emergencies overseas (☎877-370-4742 in the US and Canada; elsewhere call the US collect ☎1-713-342-4104. **American Express** (☎800-528-4800) grants most cardholders automatic car rental insurance (collision and theft, but not liability) and ground travel accident coverage of $100,000 on flight purchases made with the card.

INSURANCE PROVIDERS. Council and **STA** (see p. 253 for complete listings) offer plans that can supplement your insurance coverage. Other private insurance providers in the **US** are: **Access America** (☎800-284-8300); **Berkely Group/Carefree Travel Insurance** (☎800-323-3149 or 516-294-0220; email info@berkely.com); **Globalcare Travel Insurance** (☎800-821-2488); and **Travel Assistance International** (☎800-821-2828 or 202-828-5894; email wassist@aol.com). Providers in the **UK** include **Campus Travel** (☎018 6525 8000) and **Columbus Travel Insurance** (☎020 7375 0011). In **Australia,** try **CIC Insurance** (☎02 9202 8000).

GETTING THERE

BY PLANE

If you're planning to fly into New York, you will have to choose not only a carrier but an airport as well. Three airports serve the New York metropolitan region. The largest, **John F. Kennedy Airport,** or JFK (☎718-244-4444), is 12 mi. from midtown Manhattan in southern Queens and handles most international flights. **LaGuardia Airport** (☎718-533-3400), 6 mi. from midtown in northwestern Queens, is the smallest, offering domestic flights as well as hourly shuttles to and from Boston and Washington, D.C. **Newark International Airport** (☎973-961-6000), 12 mi. from Midtown in Newark, NJ, offers both domestic and international flights at budget fares often not available at the other airports (although getting to and from Newark can be expensive).

DETAILS AND TIPS

Timing: Airfares to the US peak mid-June to early September; holidays are also expensive times to travel. Midweek (M-Th morning) round-trip flights run $40-50 cheaper than weekend flights, but the latter are generally less crowded and more likely to permit frequent-flier upgrades. Return-date flexibility is usually not an option for the budget traveler; traveling with an "open return" ticket can be pricier than fixing a return date when buying the ticket and paying later to change it.

Fares: Round-trip fares from Western Europe to NYC range from US$100-400 (during the off-season) to US$200-550 (during the summer); from Australia the cost ranges from US$700-1000; New Zealand US$900-1300; South Africa US$1300-2200.

Commuter Shuttles to New York: The Delta Shuttle and the US Airways Shuttle are a relatively inexpensive mode of transportation between Washington D.C., Boston, and NYC (in any variation). The USAir Shuttle, which leaves every hour on the hour, is slightly cheaper than the Delta Shuttle, which

leaves every hour on the half hour, under most circumstances. The cheapest fare offered by USAirways is a $85 one-way weekend fare, available from 12:01am Sa to 3pm Su. For both airlines, look for youth or student fares when buying more than one round-trip.

BUDGET AND STUDENT TRAVEL AGENCIES

Students and under-26ers with **ISIC and IYTC cards** (see **Identification,** p. 245), respectively, qualify for big discounts from student travel agencies. Most flights from budget agencies are on major airlines, but in peak season some sell seats on less reliable charter planes.

usit world (www.usitworld.com). Over 50 **usit campus** branches in the UK (www.usitcampus.co.uk), including: 52 Grosvenor Gardens, **London** SW1W 0AG (☎0870 240 1010); **Manchester** (☎0161 273 1721); and **Edinburgh** (☎0131 668 3303). Nearly 20 **usit now** offices in Ireland, including 19-21 Aston Quay, O'Connell Bridge, **Dublin** 2 (☎01 602 1600), and **Belfast** (☎02890 327 111). Offices also in Athens, Auckland, Brussels, Frankfurt, Johannesburg, Lisbon, Luxembourg, Madrid, Paris, Sofia, and Warsaw.

Cheap Tickets (☎800-377-1000; www.cheaptickets.com) offers cheap flights around the US.

Council Travel (www.counciltravel.com). US offices include: Emory Village, 1561 N. Decatur Rd., **Atlanta,** GA 30307 (☎404-377-9997); 273 Newbury St., **Boston,** MA 02116 (☎617-266-1926); 1160 N. State St., **Chicago,** IL 60610 (☎312-951-0585); 931 Westwood Blvd., Westwood, **Los Angeles,** CA 90024 (☎310-208-3551); 254 Greene St., **New York,** NY 10003 (☎212-254-2525); 530 Bush St., **San Francisco,** CA 94108 (☎415-566-6222); 424 Broadway Ave E., **Seattle,** WA 98102 (☎206-329-4567); 3301 M St. NW, **Washington, D.C.** 20007 (☎202-337-6464). **For US cities not listed,** call ☎800-2-COUNCIL (226-8624). In the UK, 28A Poland St. (Oxford Circus), **London,** W1V 3DB (☎020 7437 7767).

CTS Travel, 44 Goodge St., **London** W1 (☎020 7636 0031; fax 7637 5328).

STA Travel, 6560 Scottsdale Rd. #F100, **Scottsdale,** AZ 85253 (☎800-777-0112; fax 602-922-0793; www.sta-travel.com). A student/youth organization with over 150 offices worldwide. Ticket booking, insurance, railpasses, and more. US offices include: 297 Newbury St., **Boston,** MA 02115 (☎617-266-6014); 429 S. Dearborn St., **Chicago,** IL 60605 (☎312-786-9050); 7202 Melrose Ave., **Los Angeles,** CA 90046 (☎323-934-8722); 10 Downing St., **New York,** NY 10014 (☎212-627-3111); 4341 University Way NE, **Seattle,** WA 98105 (☎206-633-5000); 2401 Pennsylvania Ave., Ste. G, **Washington, D.C.** 20037 (☎202-887-0912); 51 Grant Ave., **San Francisco,** CA 94108 (☎415-391-8407). In the UK, 11 Goodge St., **London** WIP 1FE (☎020 7436 7779 for North American travel). In New Zealand, 10 High St., **Auckland** (☎09 309 0458). In Australia, 366 Lygon St., **Melbourne** Vic 3053 (☎03 9349 4344).

Travel Avenue (☎800-333-3335; www.travelavenue.com) searches for best available published fares and then attempts to find better consolidator fares. They also offer package deals to many places.

FLIGHT PLANNING ON THE INTERNET

The Web is a great place to look for travel bargains—it's fast, it's convenient, and you can spend as long as you like exploring options without driving your travel agent insane.

Many airline sites offer special last-minute deals on the Web. Other sites do the legwork and compile the deals for you—try www.bestfares.com, www.onetravel.com, www.lowestfare.com, and www.travelzoo.com.

STA (www.sta-travel.com) and **Council** (www.counciltravel.com) provide quotes on student tickets, while **Expedia** (msn.expedia.com) and **Travelocity** (www.travelocity.com) offer full travel services. **Priceline** (www.priceline.com) allows you to specify a price, and obligates you to buy any ticket that meets or beats it; be prepared for antisocial hours and odd routes. **Skyauction** (www.skyauction.com) allows you to bid on both last-minute and advance-purchase tickets, but you may not get your first-choice dates.

Just one last note—to protect yourself, make sure that the site uses a secure server before handing over any credit card details. Happy hunting!

Travel **CUTS** (Canadian Universities Travel Services Limited), 187 College St., **Toronto,** ON M5T 1P7 (☎416-979-2406; fax 979-8167; www.travelcuts.com). 40 offices in Canada. Also in the UK, 295-A Regent St., **London** W1R 7YA (☎020 7255 1944).

COMMERCIAL AIRLINES

The commercial airlines' lowest regular offer is the **APEX** (Advance Purchase Excursion) fare, which provides confirmed reservations and allows "open-jaw" tickets. Generally, reservations must be made 7 to 21 days in advance, with 7- to 14-day minimum and up to 90-day maximum-stay limits, and hefty cancellation and change penalties (fees rise in summer). Book peak-season APEX fares early, since by May you will have a hard time getting the departure date you want. Although APEX fares are probably not the cheapest possible fares, they will give you a sense of the average commercial price, from which to measure other bargains. Specials advertised in newspapers may be cheaper but have more restrictions and fewer available seats.

Popular carriers to NYC include:

American, ☎800-433-7300; www.americanair.com.

Continental, ☎800-525-0280; www.flycontinental.com.

Delta, ☎800-241-4141; www.delta-airlines.com.

Northwest, ☎800-225-2525; www.nwa.com

TWA, ☎800-221-2000; www.twa.com.

United, ☎800-241-6522; www.ual.com.

US Airways, ☎800-428-4322; www.usairways.com.

OTHER CHEAP ALTERNATIVES

AIR COURIER FLIGHTS

Couriers help transport cargo on international flights by guaranteeing delivery of the baggage claim slips from the company to a representative overseas. Generally, couriers must travel light (carry-ons only) and deal with complex restrictions on their flight. Most flights are round-trip only with short fixed-length stays (usually one week) and a limit of a single ticket per issue. Most of these flights also operate only out of the biggest cities. Generally, you must be over 21 (in some cases 18), have a valid passport, and procure your own visa, if necessary. Groups such as the **Air Courier Association** (800-282-1202; www.aircourier.org) and the **International Association of Air Travel Couriers,** 220 South Dixie Hwy., P.O. Box 1349, Lake Worth, FL 33460 (561-582-8320; email iaatc@courier.org; www.courier.org) provide their members with lists of opportunities and courier brokers worldwide for an annual fee.

CHARTER FLIGHTS

Charters are flights a tour operator contracts with an airline to fly extra loads of passengers during peak season. Charters can sometimes be cheaper than flights on scheduled airlines, some operate nonstop, and restrictions on minimum advance-purchase and minimum stay are more lenient. However, charter flights fly less frequently than major airlines, make refunds particularly difficult, and are almost always fully booked. Schedules and itineraries may also change or be canceled at the last moment (as late as 48 hours before the trip, and without a full refund), and check-in, boarding, and baggage claim are often much slower. As always, pay with a credit card if you can, and consider traveler's insurance against trip interruption. **Discount clubs** and **fare brokers** offer members savings on last-minute charter and tour deals. Study their contracts closely; you don't want to end up with an unwanted overnight layover.

STANDBY FLIGHTS

To travel standby, you will need considerable flexibility in the dates and cities of your arrival and departure. Companies that specialize in standby flights don't sell tickets, but rather the promise that you will get to your destination (or near your destination) within a certain window of time (anywhere from 1-5 days). You may only receive a monetary refund if all available flights that depart within your date-range from the specified region are full, but future travel credit is always available. Carefully read agreements with any company offering standby flights, as tricky fine print can leave you in the lurch. To check on a company's service record, call the Better Business Bureau of New York City (☎212-533-6200). It is difficult to receive refunds, and clients' vouchers will not be honored when an airline fails to receive payment in time.

Airhitch, 2641 Broadway, 3rd fl., New York, NY 10025 (☎800-326-2009 or 212-864-2000; www.airhitch.org), and Los Angeles, CA (☎888-247-4482). In Europe, the flagship office is in Paris (☎+33 01 47 00 16 30), and the other one is in Amsterdam (☎+31 20 626 32 20). Offers one-way flights to and from Europe to the Northeast (US $159).

AirTech.Com, 588 Broadway #204, New York, NY 10012 (☎212-219-7000; email fly@airtech.com; www.airtech.com). AirTech.Com also arranges courier flights and regular confirmed-reserved flights at discount rates.

TICKET CONSOLIDATORS

Ticket consolidators, or **"bucket shops,"** buy unsold tickets in bulk from commercial airlines and sell them at discounted rates. The best place to look is in the Sunday Travel section of any major newspaper, where many bucket shops place tiny ads. Call quickly, as availability is typically extremely limited. Not all bucket shops are reliable establishments, so insist on a receipt that gives full details of restrictions, refunds, and tickets, and pay by credit card. For more information, check the website **Consolidators FAQ** (www.travel-library.com/air-travel/consolidators.html).

kids

in the city

camp
new york city

New York City is just as fascinating for children as it is for adults—skyscrapers, fast cars, FAO Schwartz, the Bronx Zoo, Central Park...your child will never be bored. But you may have to slow your pace, and you must plan ahead. Make sure your accommodations are child-friendly, when renting a car ask for a car seat for younger children, and always set up a reunion spot in case of separation when sight-seeing.

Discounts abound for children: always ask for them at restaurants, museums, attractions, and even when buying airline tickets.

Kid-friendly activities are highlighted in boxes like this throughout *Let's Go: NYC*.

TRAVELING WITHIN THE US AND CANADA. Travel Avenue (☎ 800-333-3335; www.travelavenue.com) rebates commercial fares to or from the US (5% for over US$550) and will search for cheap flights from anywhere for a fee. **NOW Voyager,** 74 Varick St., #307, New York, NY 10013 (☎ 212-431-1616; fax 219-1793; www.nowvoyagertravel.com) arranges discounted flights both within the US and internationally. Other consolidators worth trying are **Interworld** (☎ 305-443-4929; fax 443-0351); **Pennsylvania Travel** (☎ 800-331-0947); **Rebel** (☎ 800-227-3235; email travel@rebeltours.com; www.rebeltours.com); **Cheap Tickets** (☎ 800-377-1000; www.cheaptickets.com); and **Travac** (☎ 800-872-8800; fax 212-714-9063; www.travac.com). Consolidators on the web include the **Internet Travel Network** (www.itn.com); **Surplus-Travel.com** (www.surplustravel.com); **Travel Information Services** (www.tiss.com); **TravelHUB** (www.travelhub.com); and **The Travel Site** (www.thetravelsite.com). Keep in mind that these are just suggestions to get you started in your research; *Let's Go* does not endorse any of these agencies. As always, be cautious, and research companies before you hand over your credit card number.

TRAVELING FROM THE UK, AUSTRALIA, AND NEW ZEALAND. In London, the **Air Travel Advisory Bureau** (☎ 020 7636 5000; www.atab.co.uk) can provide names of reliable consolidators and discount flight specialists. From Australia and New Zealand, look for consolidator ads in the travel section of the *Sydney Morning Herald* and other papers.

BY BUS

Getting in and out of New York can be less expensive and more scenic by bus or train than by plane. The hub of the Northeast bus network, New York's **Port Authority Terminal,** 41st St. and Eighth Ave. (☎ 212-435-7000; subway: A, C, E to 42nd St.-Port Authority; 1, 9, 2, 3, 7, S, N, R to 42nd St.-Times Square), is a tremendous modern facility with labyrinthine bus terminals. The Port Authority has good information and security services, but the surrounding neighborhood is somewhat deserted at night, and it pays to be wary of pickpockets and to call a cab. Exercise caution in the terminal's bathrooms.

Greyhound (☎ 800-231-2222; www.greyhound.com) operates the largest number of lines, departing from **Boston** (4½hr.; $39, $74 round-trip), **Philadelphia** (2hr.; $20, $39 round-trip), **Washington, D.C.** (4½hr.; $39, $74 round-trip), and **Montreal** (8hr.; $70, $103 round-trip). The fares listed require no advance purchase, but discounts off these fares can be had by purchasing tickets 14 days in advance. Ask about the 3-day adavance purchase two-for-one deal, which is sometimes available. Some buses to these cities take longer (anywhere from 1-3 hrs. more) due to additional stops or time of travel. A number of **discounts** are available on Greyhound's standard-fare tickets: students ride for 15% off with the Student Advantage Card (☎800-962-6875 to purchase), senior citizens ride for 10% off, children under 11 ride for half-fare, and children under 2 ride for free in the lap of an adult (one per adult). A traveler with a physical disability may bring along a companion for free after clearing them by calling ☎800-752-4841, and active and retired US military personnel and National Guard Reserves (and their spouses and dependents) may take a round-trip between any two points in the US for $169 or a one-way for $99.

BY TRAIN

The locomotive is still one of the cheapest ways to travel in the US. You can save money by purchasing your tickets as far in advance as possible, so plan ahead. You must travel light on trains; not all stations will check your baggage. **Amtrak** (☎800-USA-RAIL/872-7245; www.amtrak.com) is the only provider of intercity passenger train service in the US. The informative web page lists up-to-date schedules, fares, and arrival and departure info. You can reserve tickets on the web page. Many qualify for discounts: senior citizens (10% off); students (15% off) with a Student Advantage Card (call ☎800-96-AMTRAK/962-6872 to purchase the $20 card); travelers with disabilities (15% off); children 2-15 accompanied by a parent (50% off); children under age two (free); current members of the US armed forces, active-duty veterans, and their dependents (25% off). "Rail SALE" offers online discounts of up to 90%; visit the Amtrack web site for details and reservations. Amtrak's trains connect NYC to most other parts of the country through **Penn Station.**

Penn Station, 33rd St. and Eighth Ave. (subway: 1, 2, 3, 9, A, C, E to 34th St.-Penn Station), deals with longer routes. The major line is **Amtrak** (☎800-872-7245). To Boston 4-6hr., $50-71 one-way; to Washington, D.C., 3-4½hr., $67-118 one-way; to Philidelphia 1½hr., $43-77 one-way. Penn Station also handles the **Long Island Railroad (LIRR)** (☎718-217-5477 or 516-822-5477; fares range $4-11 with service extending to the eastern tip of the island and including Belmont and Shea Stadium; see **Daytripping,** p. 229) and the **NJ Transit** service to New Jersey (☎973-762-5100; in NJ 800-772-2222). **PATH** trains (☎800-234-7284) operate between Newark, NJ and various locations in downtown New York, including the World Trade Center and 33rd St. and 6th Ave., near Penn Station.

Grand Central Terminal, 42nd St. and Park Ave. (☎212-340-3000). Subway: 4, 5, 6, 7, S to 42nd St.-Grand Central. Serves the three **Metro-North** (☎800-638-7646; in NYC 212-532-4900) commuter lines to Connecticut and New York suburbs (Hudson, Harlem, and New Haven lines).

BY CAR

There are several major paths leading to New York. From New Jersey there are three choices, each costing $4 a pop (you can pay by credit card at E-Z Pass booths). The **Holland Tunnel** connects to lower Manhattan, exiting into the SoHo area. From the NJ Turnpike you'll probably end up at the **Lincoln Tunnel,** which exits in Midtown in the West 40s. The third, and arguably easiest, option is the **George Washington Bridge,** which crosses the Hudson River into northern Manhattan, offering access to either Harlem River Drive or the West Side Highway. If you are coming from New England or Connecticut on I-95, follow signs for the **TriBoro Bridge.** From there get onto the FDR Drive, which runs along the east side of Manhattan and exits onto city streets every 10 blocks or so. Or look for the Willis Avenue Bridge Exit on I-95 to avoid the toll, and enter Manhattan farther north on FDR Drive. The **speed limit** in New York State, as in most other states, is 55 miles per hour. As in most other states, wearing a seat belt is required by law. For information on renting a car, see **Once in NY,** p. 37.

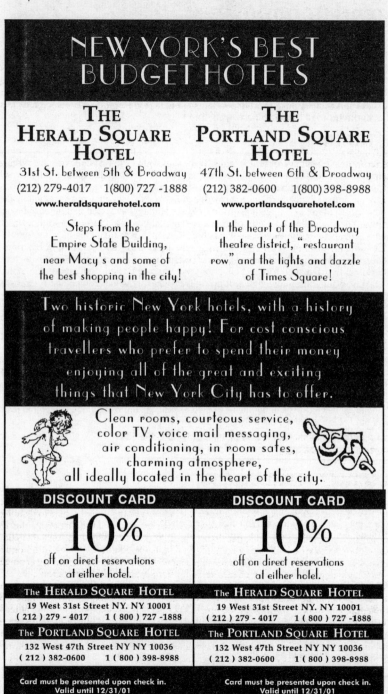

SPECIFIC CONCERNS

WOMEN TRAVELERS

Women exploring NYC on their own inevitably face additional safety concerns. In general, NYC by day is safe, but from evening to morning some neighborhoods are definitely dangerous—always trust your instincts: if you'd feel better somewhere else, move on. Always carry extra money for a phone call, bus, or taxi. Stick to centrally located accommodations and avoid late-night treks or subway rides.

Excercise caution when using public transportation. On the subway, don't stand too close to the tracks, and choose the middle car where the conductor is—you'll see his face from the platform. Falling asleep is never a good idea, which is why you should avoid traveling during the night. Perverts also come out to play in the subways; if you are pinched, grabbed, or squeezed, make your discomfort understood **loudly;** everyone will look, and you will not be the one who is embarrassed.

Look as if you know where you're going (even when you don't) and consider approaching women or couples for directions if you're lost or feel uncomfortable. Your best answer to verbal harassment is no answer at all. Don't hesitate to seek out a police officer or a passerby if you are being harassed.

The look on your face is the key to avoiding unwanted attention; have a New Yorker's attitude. These warnings should not discourage women from traveling alone—NYC women manage just fine.

For general information and for information on rape crisis centers and couseling services, contact the **National Organization for Women (NOW),** 105 W. 28th St., #304, **New York, NY** 10010 (☎212-627-9895; fax 627-9891; www.nownyc.org).

OLDER TRAVELERS

Senior citizens are eligible for a wide range of discounts on transportation, museums, movies, theaters, concerts, restaurants, and accommodations throughout New York City. If you don't see a senior citizen price listed, it's certainly worth it to ask—it can be 15% or more. Agencies for senior group travel are growing in enrollment and popularity. For example, seniors now have access to a reduced fare MetroCard. Here are a few helpful options for the older traveler in New York City.

New York City Department for the Aging Infoline: ☎212-442-1000.
The MTA Reduced Fare Line: ☎718-243-4999, M-F 9am-5pm.

DISABLED TRAVELERS

Particularly since President George Bush signed the Americans with Disabilities Act in 1990, New York City has slowly but surely removed many of the impediments to disabled travel. The city's **buses** all have excellent wheelchair access. Call the Transit Authority Access (☎718-596-8585) for information on public transit accessibility. Access-A-Ride door-to-door service is available for some; call to apply (see number above). In general it is advisable to inform airlines and hotels in advance of a disability when making arrangements for travel; some time may be needed to prepare special accommodations.

Arrange transportation well in advance to ensure a smooth trip. Hertz, Avis, and National **car rental agencies** have hand-controlled vehicles at some locations. In the US, both **Amtrak** and major airlines will accommodate disabled passengers if notified at least 72 hours in advance. Hearing-impaired travelers may contact Amtrak using teletype printers (☎800-872-7245). **Greyhound** buses will provide free travel for a companion; if you are without a fellow traveler, call Greyhound (☎800-752-4841) at least 48 hours before you leave and they will make arrangements for you.

Elevators and escalator accessibility hotline: ☎1-800-734-6772, 24hr.
Access-A-Ride: ☎1-877-337-2017. (For public transportation.)

USEFUL RESOURCES

Moss Rehab Hospital Travel Information Service (☎215-456-9600 or 800-CALL-MOSS; email netstaff@mossresourcenet.org; www.mossresourcenet.org). An information resource center on travel-related concerns for those with disabilities.

Society for the Advancement of Travel for the Handicapped (SATH), 347 Fifth Ave., #610, New York, NY 10016 (☎212-447-7284; www.sath.org). An advocacy group that publishes the quarterly travel magazine *OPEN WORLD* (free for members, US$13 for nonmembers). Also publishes a wide range of info sheets on disability travel facilitation and destinations. Annual membership US$45, students and seniors US$30.

TOUR AGENCIES

Directions Unlimited, 123 Green Ln., Bedford Hills, NY 10507, USA (☎914-241-1700 or 800-533-5343; www.travel-cruises.com). Specializes in arranging individual and group vacations, tours, and cruises for the physically disabled.

The Guided Tour Inc., 7900 Old York Rd., #114B, Elkins Park, PA 19027, USA (☎800-783-5841 or 215-782-1370; www.guidedtour.com). Organizes travel programs for persons with developmental and physical challenges around the US.

DIETARY CONCERNS

Vegetarians won't have any problem eating cheap and well in New York. Excellent vegetarian restaurants abound, and almost every non-vegetarian place offers non-meat options (see **Food,** p. 175). For information about vegetarian travel, contact the **North American Vegetarian Society,** P.O. Box 72, Dolgeville, NY 13329 (518-568-7970), which publishes the *Vegetarian Journal's Guide to Natural Food Restaurants in the US and Canada* ($12).

Travelers who keep **kosher** should call a New York synagogue for information about kosher restaurants; your own synagogue or college Hillel office should have lists of NYC Jewish institutions. ChaBad houses (centers for Lubavitch Hassidim and out-

reach) should also be able to either provide kosher food or direct you to it. NYU's Cha-Bad is at 566 La Guardia #715 (☎ 212-998-4945), and the Upper East Side's ChaBad *shuckles* at 311 E. 83rd St., Ste. B (☎ 212-717-4613). They also provide general infomation, help, classes, and matchmaking for religious visitors.

Muslim travelers seeking **halal** foods should check the local *Yellow Pages* listings under "halal."

GAY AND LESBIAN TRAVELERS

New York City is perhaps as queer-friendly as it gets in the US—see **The Queer Apple** (p. 221) for details.

INTERNET RESOURCES

American Automobile Association (AAA) Travel Related Services (www.aaa.com). Provides maps and guides free to members. Offers emergency road and travel services and auto insurance (for members). For emergency road services or to become a member, call ☎ 800-222-4357.

Big World Magazine (www.bigworld.com). A budget travel 'zine with a web page with great links to travel pages.

Council on International Educational Exchange (CIEE), 205 East 42nd St., 14th fl., New York, NY 10017-5706 (☎ 888-COUNCIL/268-6245; fax 212-822-2699; www.ciee.org). Council administers work, volunteer, academic, internship, and professional programs around the world. They also offer identity cards (including the ISIC) and a range of publications, among them the useful magazine *Student Travels* (free). Call for further information.

Expedia (www.expedia.com). Everything budget for trips.

Shoestring Travel (www.stratpub.com). A budget travel e-zine, with feature articles, links, user exchange, and accommodations information.

TravelHUB (www.travelhub.com). A great site for cheap travel deals.

Travelocity (www.travelocity.com). More marvelous travel info and deals.

Yahoo (www.yahoo.com/Recreation/Travel). Better organized search engine with travel links.

Let's Go (www.letsgo.com). Find our newsletter, information about our books, travel, and other fun stuff. There's also a message board and forum for talking about your journeys and for asking questions.

Village Voice (www.villagevoice.com). Known city-wide for its lengthy real estate listings—the place to find apartment swaps, sublets, and rentals.

New York Today (www.newyorktoday.com). The New York Times provides webcrawlers with in-depth entertainment info daily; also Food, Accommodations, and every other category of info.

Accommodations

If you know someone who knows someone who lives in New York, get that person's phone number and ask to stay with them. The cost of living in New York can rip the seams out of your wallet. At true full-service establishments, a night will cost at least $125, with an additional hotel tax of 13.4%. Many reasonable choices are available for about $70 a night, but it depends on your priorities. People traveling alone may want to spend more to stay in a safer neighborhood. The young and the outgoing may prefer a budget-style place crowded with students; honeymooning couples may not.

Hostels offer fewer amenities than hotels, yet manage to preserve a greater feeling of camaraderie. Cheap YMCAs and YWCAs offer another budget option, but miss the social life of a hostel. All of these places advise you to reserve in advance—even once you get to New York you should call to make sure your rooms are available prior to making the trek there with your bags.

Crime-free neighborhoods in the city exist only in dreams; never leave anything of value in your room if you are staying in budget accommodations. Many places have safes or lockers available, some for an extra fee. Don't sleep in your car, and never, ever sleep outdoors anywhere in New York. The city has a hard enough time protecting its vast homeless population—tourists simply would not stand a chance.

The internet often expedites finding New York accommodations. Many of the accommodations listed below have websites and some offer discounts for internet reservations—ask when calling. There are also a number of online sites that list accommodations. **New York City Reference** (www.panix.com/clay/nyc/query.cgi?H3), the **Hotel Guide** (www.HOTELGUIDE.com), and **New York citysearch.com** (www.newyork.citysearch.com/New_York/Visiting_the_City/Hotels/). For long-term accommodations, see **Living in the City,** p. 284.

HOSTELS

Hostels are generally dorm-style, with large rooms and bunks where sexes are separated. Wihtout much luxury and privacy, beds can cost as little as $14 per night. Guests must often rent or bring sheets or "sleep sacks" (two sheets sewn together); sleeping bags are usually not allowed. Kitchens, storage, and laundry facilities are sometimes available for guest, and you can sometimes get a more private room for more money.

If you're traveling extensively in the rest of the US or Canada, you should consider joining **Hostelling International-American Youth Hostels (HI-AYH),** the leading organization of hostels. There are over 300 HI-AYH-affiliated hostels throughout North America; these are usually of a higher standard than private hostels, although they tend to be more institutional. HI-AYH runs an excellent hostel in New York, with much space and many amenities (see below). Yearly **HI-AYH membership** is $25 for adults, $10 for those under 18, $35 for families, and $15 for those over 54. **Nonmembers** usually pay $3 extra per night, which can be applied toward membership. For more information, contact HI-AYH, 733 15th St. NW, #840, Washington, D.C. 20005 (☎202-783-6161, ext. 136; fax 202-783-6171; email hiayhserv@hiayh.org; www.hiayh.org), or inquire at any HI-affiliated hostel.

Although you might not be as enthusiastic as the Village People, don't overlook the **Young Men's Christian Association (YMCA)** or the **Young Women's Christian Association (YWCA).** Slightly more expensive than hostels but usually much cleaner, singles average $45-61 per night, and rooms include use of a pool and other facilities. However, you may have to share a room and bath or shower. Some YMCAs in New York (listed below) accept women and families as well as men. Reserve at least two weeks in advance and expect to pay a refundable key deposit of about $10. For information and reservations, write or call **The Y's Way,** 224 E. 47th St., New York, NY 10017 (☎212-308-2899).

A very friendly alternative to hostels is **Homestay New York,** 630 E. 19th St., Brooklyn (☎/fax 718-434-2071; email helayne@homestayny.com; homestayny.com). Travelers are placed in homes of New York City residents, all within 30min. of central Manhattan. Rates from $90 per day for a standard single to $130 for a deluxe double and include some meals; call or email for reservations at least 10 days ahead.

DORMITORIES

Miss that two-by-four dorm ambience? Some colleges and universities open their residence halls to conferences and travelers, especially during the summer. You may have to share a bath, but rates are often low and facilities are usually clean and well maintained.

Columbia University, 1230 Amsterdam Ave., at 120th St. (☎678-3235; fax 678-3222). Subway: 1, 9 to 116th St. Whittier Hall sets aside 10 rooms year-round, all equipped with full beds. Rooms are clean, max. 4 people. Generally tight 24hr. security. Not the safest neighborhood, but well-populated until fairly late at night. Reserve in Mar. for May-Aug., in July for Sept.-Dec. 1-week max. stay. Credit card deposit required—AmEx, V, MC, and Discover accepted. Singles $55; doubles with A/C and bath (some with kitchen) $75.

New York University, 14a Washington Pl. (☎998-4621; www.nyu.edu\housing\summer). NYU summer school students get priority and lower rates, and housing is only available for individuals, not families or couples. Housing options in the Village as well as near South Street Seaport. Min. age of 17, unless an approved summer school student. Max. stay 11-12 weeks. Min. stay 3 consecutive weeks. Reception M-Tu 9am-5pm, W-Th 9am-7pm, Su 9am-2pm. Call for prices.

HOTELS

A single in a cheap hotel should cost $45-65. Most hotel rooms can (and should) be reserved in advance. Ask if the bathroom is communal or private. Most hotels require a key deposit when you register. You may be able to store your gear for the day even after vacating your room, but most proprietors will not take responsibility for the safety of your belongings. Some hotels require a *non-refundable* deposit for reservations.

BED AND BREAKFASTS

Bed and Breakfasts (private homes that rent out one or more spare rooms to travelers) are a great alternative to impersonal hotels. Many don't have phones, TVs, or showers with their rooms. Reservations should be made long in advance, usually with a deposit, and most have two-night minimums. Most B&B agencies list accommodations in boroughs other than Manhattan; these can be an excellent budget alternative. Prices generally run singles $70-100; doubles $80-135, but call for specifics. **Urban Ventures** (☎594-5650; fax 947-9320) is the oldest and most established agency in the city. **New World Bed and Breakfast** (☎675-5600 or toll-free from the U.S. and Canada, ☎800-443-3800; fax 675-6366) specializes in short-term furnished apartments, and **Bed and Breakfast of New York** (☎645-8134) offers weekly and monthly rates.

ACCOMMODATIONS BY PRICE

$40 AND UNDER
Aladdin Hotel	(p.274)
Big Apple Hostel	(p.274)
Chelsea Center Hotel	(p.273)
Chelsea Star Hotel	(p.271)
Gershwin Hotel	(p.269)
International Student Center	(p.275)
International Student Hospice	(p.271)
Jazz on the Park	(p.275)
Manhattan Youth Castle	(p.275)
New York International HI-AYH Hostel	(p.275)
Sugar Hill International House	(p.276)
Uptown Hostel	(p.276)

$41-60
Chelsea International Hotel	(p.271)
Hayden Hall	(p.275)
Herald Square Hotel	(p.273)
Malibu Studios Hotel	(p.275)
New York Bed and Breakfast	(p.276)
Senton Hotel	(p.269)
YMCA-Flushing	(p.277)

$61-80
Amsterdam Inn	(p.275)
Big Apple Hostel	(p.274)
Carlton Arms Hotel	(p.269)
Chelsea Star Hotel	(p.271)
Crystal's Castle Bed and Breakfast	(p.276)
De Hirsch Residence	(p.274)
Laarchmont Hotel	(p.269)
Pickwick Arms Hotel	(p.273)

$61-80
Pioneer Hotel	(p.269)
Murry Hill Inn	(p.271)
On the Ave	(p.275)
The Suite Sound of Comfort Inn	(p.274)
West Side Inn	(p.275)
West Side YMCA	(p.276)
West End Studios	(p.276)
YMCA-McBurney	(p.273)
YMCA-Vanderbilt	(p.273)

$81-100
Aladdin Hotel	(p.274)
Broadway Inn	(p.274)
Chelsea Inn	(p.271)
Hotel 17	(p.271)
Hotel Belleclaire	(p.275)
Hotel Stanford	(p.273)
Madison Hotel	(p.271)
St. Mark's Hotel	(p.269)

$101-120
Chelsea Savoy Hotel	(p.271)
Gershwin Hotel	(p.269)
Hotel Grand Union	(p.269)
Hotel Wolcott	(p.273)
ThirtyThirty	(p.271)
Union Square Inn	(p.271)

$121 AND UP
Akwaaba Mansion	(p.277)
Bed and Breakfast on the Park	(p.277)
Washington Square Hotel	(p.269)

ACCOMMODATIONS BY NEIGHBORHOOD

Let's Go lists prices excluding tax, unless otherwise noted. The following accommodations are the best hostels, YMCA/YWCAs, hotels, and B&Bs in New York; all are ranked according to quality, value, price, safety, and location.

LITTLE ITALY

Pioneer Hotel, 341 Broome St. between Elizabeth St. and the Bowery. (☎226-1482; fax 266-3525). Subway: N, R to Canal and walk north to Broome. In a 100-year-old building, the Pioneer is a good, no-frills place to stay, and close to the nightlife of SoHo and the East Village. All rooms have TV, sinks, and fans. Rooms with private bath have A/C. Generally tight security at night. Check-out 11am. Reservations recommended at least 6 weeks in advance. AmEx, Diner's Club, Discover, MC, V. Singles $62; doubles $70, with bath $82; triples with bath $138.

see map
pp. 318–319

GREENWICH VILLAGE

Washington Square Hotel, 103 Waverly Pl., at MacDougal St., in Greenwich (☎777-9515 or 800-222-0418; fax 979-8373). Subway: A, B, C, D, E, F, Q to W. 4th St. The lobby's marble and brass match the fantastic location. A/C, cable TV, key-card entry to rooms. Clean and comfortable, all rooms have private bath. Friendly, multilingual staff. C3 is the hotel's trendy restaurant/bar. 24hr. excercise room. 10% ISIC discount. Continental breakfast included. Reserve 2 months in advance for weekend, 1 month for weekdays. AmEx, JCB, MC, V. Singles $121-142; doubles $142-160; queen-size bed or two twins $160-174; quads $174-205. Rollaway bed $20.

see map
pp. 322–323

Larchmont Hotel, 27 W. 11th St., between Fifth and Sixth Aves., in Greenwich (☎989-9333; fax 989-9496). Subway: N, R, L, 4, 5, 6 to 14th St./Union Sq. Spacious, clean rooms in a white-washed brownstone on a quiet block. A/C, TV, desks, closets, and wash basins in all rooms. Shared bath. Continental breakfast included. Reserve 5-6 weeks in advance. Singles $70-95; doubles $90-115; queen-size bed $109-125.

EAST VILLAGE

St. Mark's Hotel, corner of St. Mark's Pl. and Third Ave. (☎674-2192). Recently renovated, this hotel offers perhaps the most exciting location in the city. Call ahead for reservations. Cash or travelers checks only. Doubles with private bath and cable TV $100.

UNION SQ., GRAMERCY PARK, MURRAY HILL

☒ Carlton Arms Hotel, 160 E. 25th St., between Lexington and Third Aves. (☎679-0680). Subway: 6 to 23rd St. Each room is decorated by a different artist; pop into one room to indulge in childhood fantasies with stuffed animals and blackboard walls. All 54 rooms have sinks. $6-8 discounts for students and foreign travelers. Pay for a week up front and get 10% off. Check-out 11:30am. Reserve for summer 2 months in advance; confirm 10 days in advance. MC, V. Singles $63, with bath $75; doubles $80, $92; triples $99, $111; quads $105, $117.

see map
pp. 328–329

☒ Gershwin Hotel, 7 E. 27th St., between Fifth and Madison Aves. (☎545-8000; fax 684-5546). Subway: 6, N, R to 28th St. Full of pop art, random furniture, and artsy twenty-somethings; offers spaces for poetry, comedy, concerts, and open-mic nights. Internet $1 per 4min. 21-night max. stay. Check-out 11am. Reception 24hr. AmEx, V, MC. 8-12 bed dorms $30 per bed, with TV and phone $50; 4-bed dorms $40; 2-bed dorms $60 (tax not included). Private rooms (single or double occupancy) $99-169; triples and quads add $10 per person.

Hotel Grand Union, 34 E. 32nd St., between Madison and Park Aves. (☎683-5890; fax 689-7397). Subway: 6 to 33rd St. Centrally-located hotel offering newly-remodeled rooms with cable TV, phone, A/C, mini-fridge, and full bathroom. 24hr. security. AmEx, DC, Discover, JCB, MC, V. Wheelchair accessible. Singles and doubles $110; triples $125; quads $150.

Senton Hotel, 39-41 W. 27th St., between Sixth Ave. and Broadway (☎684-5800; fax 545-1690). Subway: R to 28th St. Comfortable beds in spacious quarters. A/C, cable TV, VCR, and

refrigerators in every room. The hotel is renovating. Security 24hr. Singles $57.20; with private bath $67.60; doubles $78; 2-room suites with 4 double beds $83.20. Tax not included.

Murray Hill Inn, 143 E. 30th St., between Lexington and Third Aves.,(☎683-6900 or 888-996-6376). Subway: 6 to 28th St. Clean, floral-print rooms at reasonable prices. 5 floors—no elevator. All rooms have sink, A/C, cable TV, and phone. 21-day max. stay. Check-in 2pm. Check-out noon. Singles $75, private bath $115; doubles $95, private bath $125. Extra bed $10.

Hotel 17, 225 E. 17th St., between Second and Third Aves. (☎475-2845; fax 677-8178). This historic site served as the setting for Woody Allen's *Manhattan Murder Mystery;* Madonna even had her portrait done in these eccentric accommodations. Mostly foreign crowd enjoys beautiful, high-ceilinged rooms with sink and A/C. Check-out noon. Singles $81.28; doubles $109.59; triples $171. (Tax included.) If staying for 5 days in a triple, $160 per night.

ThirtyThirty, 30 E. 30th St., between Park and Madison Aves. (☎689-1900; fax 689-0023; www.thirtythirty-nyc.com). To be completed by fall 2000, this place promises to be luxurious. Prime location at relatively budget costs. All rooms have color TV, A/C, iron, hair dryer, and phone. Current renovation rates $99-115. Expected normal rates: singles $125; doubles $175.

Madison Hotel, 21 E. 27th St., at Madison Ave. (☎532-7373 or 800-9MADISON; fax 686-0092). Subway: 6, N, R to 28th St. For budget rates, these rooms are a bargain—color TV, A/C, and private bath. Breakfast included. $5 cable deposit; $40 phone deposit. 14-night max. stay. Check-in noon. Check-out 11am. AmEx, Discover, MC, V. Singles $99; doubles $121; rooms for 2-4 with 2 double beds $145.

Union Square Inn, 209 E. 14th St. between Second and Third Aves. (☎358-0720; fax 358-0778). Subway: 4, 6 to 14th St. Set to open in Sept. 2000, this 5-floor walk-up promises 40 renovated rooms, all with cable TV and A/C. Reception 24hr. Check-in 2pm. Check-out noon. Tentative prices for singles and doubles: $105-155, plus tax.

HOSTELS

International Student Hospice, 154 E. 33rd St., between Lexington and Third Aves. (☎228-7470). Subway: 6 to 33rd St. Up a flight of stairs in a brownstone with a brass plaque saying "I.S.H." Better resembles a house full of bric-a-brac than a hostel. Rooms for 1-4 people and tiny hall bathroom. Call ahead. $28 per night including tax.

CHELSEA

see map pp. 328–329

🖼 **Chelsea Inn,** 46 W. 17th St., between Fifth and Sixth Aves. (☎800-640-6469; 645-8989; fax 645-1903). Subway: F, R to 23rd St. Charmingly mismatched antiques in spacious rooms with kitchenettes, reminiscent of Parisian hotels. Worth the splurge. Reception 9am-11pm. Check-in 3pm. Check-out noon. Reservations recommended. Guest rooms with shared bath $89-129; studios $149-169; 1-bedroom suites $179-199; 2-bedroom suites $199-259.

Chelsea Savoy Hotel, 204 W. 23rd St., between Seventh and Eighth Aves. (☎929-9353; fax 741-6309). Subway: 1, 9, C, E to 23rd St. Clean, functional rooms. All with private bath, TV with cable, A/C, irons and boards, and hair dryers. Reception 24hr. Check-in 3pm. Check-out 11am. Reservations recommended. Singles $99-115; doubles $125-155; quad $145-185.

Chelsea Star Hotel, 300 W. 30th St, at Eighth Ave. (☎244-7827; fax 279-9018). Subway: A, C, E to 34th St.-Penn Station. Stay in one of the theme rooms where Madonna reportedly lived when she was a struggling artist. Clean and coveted walk-up. Reception daily 8am-midnight. Residents get keys. Safe deposit box $5. Max. stay 21 days. Check-in noon. Check-out 11am. Reserve at least one month in advance. 20 rooms, 4 per bath. Prices do not include tax. Dorm bed $29.99; single $70; double $90; triple $112; quad $120.

HOSTELS

Chelsea International Hostel, 251 W. 20th St. between Seventh and Eighth Aves. (☎647-0010; fax 727-7289). Subway: 1, 9, C, E to 23rd St. Scandinavians with dreads characterize the clientele of this hostel. The congenial staff offers pizza Wednesday night. All rooms have windows and

a sink. Kitchens and laundry. Internet access. Key deposit $10. Check-in 8am-6pm. Reservations recommended. 4- and 6-person dorms $25; private rooms $60.

Chelsea Center Hostel, 313 W. 29th St. between Eighth and Ninth Aves. (☎643-0214; fax 473-3945). Subway: 1, 2, 3, 9, A, C, E to 34th St. To enter, ring the labeled buzzer on door. Gregarious, knowledgable, multi-lingual staff will help you out. Room for 22 in this residence–turned-hostel, 16 of whom stay in a spacious basement room. 5 others stay in a bedroom on the main floor. 2 showers. Light breakfast and linen included. 2-week max. stay. Check-in 8:30am-10:30pm. Flexible lockout 11am-5pm. Cash and traveler's checks only. Dorm beds $28.

YMCA–McBurney, 206 W. 24th St., between Seventh and Eighth Aves. (☎741-9226; fax 741-8724). Subway: 1, 9, C, E to 23rd St. No-frills, clean rooms. Mix of elderly locals, students, and other travelers. All rooms have TV. Free access to pool and athletic facilities. Key deposit $5. 25-day max. stay. 24hr. door security. Reception 8am-11pm. Check-out noon. Usually has vacancies, but reservations are advisable. Wheelchair accessible. Singles $59-71; doubles $72-82; triples $94-104; quads $105-115; with A/C add $5.

HERALD SQUARE

see map
pp. 328–329

🏨 **Hotel Stanford,** 43 W. 32nd St., between Fifth Ave. and Broadway (☎563-1500 or 800-365-1114; fax 629-0043). Subway: B, D, F, N, R to 34th St. Located in NY's Korean district, this glitzy hotel's lobby glitters. Adjoins the **Pari Pari Ko Bakery,** which serves up Korean delicacies and pastries. Rooms are impeccably clean, with firm mattresses, plush carpeting, cable TV, A/C, small refrigerators. Continental breakfast included. Check-out noon; fee for late checkout. Reservations recommended. AmEx, JCB, MC, V. Singles $90-110; doubles and triples $120-150.

Herald Square Hotel, 19 W. 31st St., at Fifth Ave. (☎279-4017 or 800-727-1888; fax 643-9208). Subway: B, D, F, N, R to 34th St. In the Beaux-Arts home of the original *Life* magazine. Magazine covers grace the hallways and the small, pleasant rooms. Rooms have undergone recent renovations; all include cable TV, safe, phone, voicemail messaging, and A/C. Reserve 2-3 weeks in advance. 10% discount for international students. AmEx, DC, JCB, MC, V. Singles $60, with bath $85; doubles $115; twins $130; triples $140; quads $150.

Hotel Wolcott, 4 W. 31st St. between Fifth Ave. and Broadway (☎268-2900; fax 563-0096). Subway: B, D, F, N, R to 34th St. The building boasts a history as rich as its decor: here, in the early 1900s, Titanic survivors wrote letters and, decades later, 50s rock-and-roll legend Buddy Holly recorded two hit albums in now-defunct studios upstairs. Now rooms are simpler and include A/C, cable TV, and voicemail. Internet $1 for 4min. Safety deposit boxes. Self-service laundry. AmEx, JCB, MC, V. Singles and doubles $99-140; triples $115-160.

EAST MIDTOWN

see map
pp. 332–333

Pickwick Arms Hotel, 230 E. 51st St. between Second and Third Aves. (☎355-0300 or 800-742-5945). Subway: 6 to 51st St.; or E, F to Lexington/Third Ave. Business types congregate in this well-priced, mid-sized hotel. Chandeliered marble lobby contrasts with tiny rooms and tinier hall bathrooms. Roof garden and airport service available. A/C, cable TV, phones, and voicemail in all rooms. Check-in 2pm. Check-out 1pm. A credit card to guarantee room. Accepts AmEx, Diner's Club, MC, V. Singles $70, with bath $100; doubles with bath $130; studios with double bed and sofa for 2 people $150; for 4-person family $170. Additional person in room $25.

HOSTELS

YMCA–Vanderbilt, 224 E. 47th St. (☎756-9600; fax 752-0210), between Second and Third Ave.s Subway: 6 to 51st St.; or E, F to Lexington/Third Ave. Convenient, with reasonable security. Clean, brightly-lit lobby bustles with international visitors. Small rooms have A/C and cable TV; usually enough bathrooms to go around. Free use of well-equipped gym and safe-deposit boxes.

Five shuttles per day to the airports. Key deposit $10. 25-night max. stay. Check-in 3pm. Check-out 11am; luggage storage until departure $1 per bag. Make reservations 2-3 weeks in advance and guarantee with a deposit. AmEx, V, MC. Singles $68; doubles $81, with sink $83.

WEST MIDTOWN

Broadway Inn, 264 W. 46th St., at Eighth Ave. (☎997-9200 or 800-826-6300; fax 768-2807). Subway: 1, 2, 3, 9, 7, N, R, S to 42nd St.-Times Square. Clean rooms have the dignity of a European B&B . TV, dataport jack, private bath, and A/C in all rooms. Continental breakfast included. No wheelchair access. AmEx, Discover, Diner's, V, MC. Singles $95-115; doubles $135-195 (high-end includes jacuzzi); suites (for 2 adults and 2 children 6-12 or 3 adults) $195-225.

see map
pp. 332–333

HOSTELS

Aladdin Hotel, 317 W. 45th St., between Eighth and Ninth Aves. (☎246-8580; fax 246-6036). Subway: 1, 2, 3, 9, A, C, E, N, R to 42nd St.-Times Sq. Purple, yellow, green, and red decor makes its lobby and smoking lounge look like a club or a circus. Lots of international travelers on rooftop garden. Internet access $1 per 3min. Lockers of various size $3-5. Laundry facilities. Reserve at least one week in advance. No wheelchair access. AmEx, Diner's, Discover, JBC, MC, V. 4-bed dorms $35 per bed; singles and doubles with shared bath $87-99.

Big Apple Hostel, 119th W. 45th St., between Sixth and Seventh Aves. (☎302-2603; fax 302-2605). Subway: 1, 2, 3, 9, A, B, C, D, E, F, N, Q, R to 42nd St.-Times Sq. Centrally located, this hostel has clean, carpeted rooms, kitchen with refrigerator, luggage room, big back deck with grill, and laundry facilities. Americans need out-of-state photo ID or other convincing proof that they're tourists. Reception 24hr. Safe deposit 25¢. Internet access $1 per 5min. No reservations Aug.-Sept., but they'll hold a bed after 11:30am, same-day; advance reservations accepted Oct.-June through website or by fax—send your credit card number. No curfew. No wheelchair access. MC, V. Bunk in dorm-style room with shared bath $30; singles and doubles $80.

UPPER EAST SIDE

HOSTELS

De Hirsch Residence, 1395 Lexington Ave., at 92nd St. (☎415-5650 or ☎800-858-4692; fax 415-5578). Subway: 6 to 96th St. Affiliated with the 92nd St. YMHA/YWHA, De Hirsch has some of the larger, cleaner hosteling in the city. Huge hall bathrooms, kitchens, and laundry machines on every other floor. Single-sex floors, strictly enforced. 24hr. access and security. Access to the many facilities of the 92nd St. Y, including 75 ft. swimming pool, and reduced concert rates. Organized activities such as walking tours of New York. All have A/C. Rents only on monthly basis. Wheelchair accessible. Single $945 per month; shared room $655-765 per person per month.

see map
pp. 334–335

The Suite Sound of Comfort Inn, 1596 Lexington Ave between 101st and 102nd Sts., in the same building as the Youth Castle, below (☎831-4440). 4 recently-renovated private suites, with themes like "Titanic" and "Madonna." All have private bathrooms, cable TV, refrigerator, and microwave. Rates $70-100 for one person and $100-120 for two, tax not included.

HOSTELS

Manhattan Youth Castle, 1596 Lexington Ave. between 101st and 102nd Sts. (☎831-4440; fax 722-55746). Subway: 6 to 103rd St. Small and affordable accommodation in the friendly and unique environment bordering Spanish Harlem and the Upper East Side. Helpful staff offers special themed tours of the city. 3-week max. stay. Reservations recommended. Call two months in advance for summer, otherwise 2 weeks is sufficient. Passport ID required. V, MC, AmEx. Key deposit $5. $20-30 per person per day; $120-180 per person per week.

UPPER WEST SIDE

see map
pp. 338–339

Malibu Studios Hotel, 2688 Broadway, at 103rd St. (☎222-2954; fax 678-6842). Subway: 1, 9 to 103rd St. Clean rooms; sink for those with shared bath. Reception 24hr. Reservations required. Ask about student, off-season, and weekly/monthly discounts. No wheelchair access. Singles $49; doubles $69; triples $85; quads $99. Deluxe rooms include private bath, A/C, and TV: singles and doubles $99; triples $129; quads $139.

Amsterdam Inn, 340 Amsterdam Ave., at 76th St. (☎579-7500; fax 579-6127). Subway: 1, 9 to 79th St. Safe and well-located, the 25 rooms are small but renovated and clean. 2-fl. walk up to the first floor. All rooms have A/C and color TV. Check-in 3pm. Check-out 11am. Singles $75; doubles $95; with private bath $115-125.

Hayden Hall, 117 W. 79th St., off Columbus Ave. (☎787-4900; fax 496-3975). Subway: B, C to 81st St. Great location, but dingy. Good weekly rates. Reservations recommended. Singles and doubles with shared bath $50; 2- to 3-person room with private bath $90; 4-person room $100; 2-room suite for up to 4 $125.

Hotel Belleclaire, 250 W. 77th St., corner of Broadway. (☎362-7700; 877-HOTELBC). Reservations recommended. Previously a hotel, now a nice budget-priced hotel. Check-in 3pm. Check-out noon. Economy (shared bath) room $99; queen bed $169; two double beds $189.

On the Ave, 2178 Broadway, at 77th St. (☎362-1100). Currently being built, it has pre-opening rates until finished. Hurry and enjoy full hotel amenities before the rates go up to the standard prices. Pre-opening rates: $75 students; double with queen bed $155, with king bed $175.

West Side Inn, 237 W. 107th St. between Broadway and Amsterdam Aves. (☎866-0061; 866-0062). Subway: 1, 9 to 110th St. Decent and clean private rooms with shared kitchenettes and bathrooms on each floor. Check-in 2pm. Check-out 11am. Internet access $1 per 4min. Call 2-3 weeks in advance. Prices $75-109, depending on number of people in room, tax not included; call for off-season rates.

HOSTELS

New York International HI-AYH Hostel, 891 Amsterdam Ave., at 103rd St. (☎932-2300; fax 932-2574). Subway: 1, 9, B, C to 103rd St. In a block-long, landmark building, resides the mother of all youth hostels—the largest in the US, with 90 dorm-style rooms and 624 beds. Shares site with the **CIEE Student Center** (☎666-3619) and a **Council Travel.** Soft carpets and spotless bathrooms. Members' kitchens and dining rooms, laundry ($1), communal TV lounges, and a large garden. Walking tours and outings. Internet access. Key-card entry to individual rooms. Linen and towels included. Secure storage area and individual lockers. 29-night max. stay, 7-nights in summer. Credit card reservations a must; 1-night deposit needed to confirm reservations. Open 24hr. Check-in any time. Check-out 11am (late check-out fee $5). No curfew. Wheelchair access. Nov.-Apr.: 10- to 12-bed dorms $27; 6- to 8-bed dorms $30; 4-bed dorms $33. May-Oct. dorms $2 more. Non-members $3 more. Groups of 4-9 may get private rooms with bathroom ($120); groups of 10 or more definitely will.

Jazz on the Park, 36 W. 106th St., at Central Park W. (☎932-1600). Subway: B, C to 103rd St. New to the scene, the Jazz riffs to the tune of clean, newly renovated hostel-dom. Chic, modern decor. Lockers and A/C make you a real cool cat. Internet access. Java bar hosts live bands and other assorted hepcats. Taxes, linens, towels, and breakfast included. Check-out 11am. No curfew. No wheelchair access. 12- to 14-bed dorms $30; 4-bed dorms $34.

Central Park Hostel, 19 W. 103rd St., near Manhattan Ave. (☎678-0491). Subway: B, C to 103rd St. Slightly away from the heart of Manhattan, this hostel makes up for it with its renovated cleanliness. Shared bathrooms. Linen/towels provided. Lockers available. A/C. 2-week max. stay. No curfew. Dorm $25; private double $75.

International Student Center, 38 W. 88th St., between Central Park W. and Columbus Ave. (☎787-7706; fax 580-9283). Subway: B, C to 86th St. Open only to foreigners aged 18-30; you must show a foreign passport or valid visa. An aging brownstone on a tree-lined street noted for frequent celebrity sightings. No-frills, livable dorms include showers and linens. Single and mixed-sex rooms available. Large basement TV lounge with kitchen, fridge, and affable atmosphere. Key deposit $10. 7-night max. stay (flexible in winter). No curfew. Reception daily 8am-11pm. No reservations, and generally full in summer, but call after 10:30am on the day you wish to stay to check for availability. No wheelchair access; lots of stairs. 8- to 10-bed dorms $15.

West Side YMCA, 5 W. 63rd St., near Central Park W. (☎875-4273 or 875-4173; fax 875-1334). Subway: A, B, C, D, 1, 9 to 59th St. Highly institutionalized atmosphere behind its impressive Moorish façade. Access to facilities (pool and fitness center), in-house cafe, and central location make this a good choice. All rooms have A/C and cable TV. Shuttle buses to airports available ($14 to LaGuardia, $16 to JFK). Luggage storage. Check-in 2:30pm. Check-out noon. 25-day max. stay. Deposit required to hold reservation. Wheelchair access. Singles $72, with bath $105; doubles (bunk beds) $84, with bath (double bed) $120. Membership fees included.

West End Studios, 850 West End Ave. between 101st and 102nd Sts. (☎749-7104; fax 865-5130). Subway: 1, 9 to 103rd St. Very well-situated, but rooms are small and only ok. All have A/C, refrigerator, and satellite TV. Reserve at least 3 weeks in advance. Check-in 3pm. Check-out noon. Valid ID required. Single bed $79; double bed $89; deluxe room (4-5 people) $119.

HARLEM

see map pp. 340–341

BED AND BREAKFASTS

New York Bed and Breakfast, 134 W. 119th St., between Lenox and Adam Clayton Powell Aves. (☎666-0559; fax 663-5000). Subway: 2, 3 to 116th St. or 125th St. Run by Gisèle of the Uptown Hostel (see below), this B&B has a double *and* single bed in every light and airy room, coffee, juice, and danishes for breakfast, and an aloof black cat, Harlem. 2-night min. stay. Check-in 1-7pm. Summer reserve 1 month in advance. Right next door, Gisèle also owns **another B&B** featuring the same rates and conditions, but without any pets. Sept.-May doubles $55, triples $75; June-Aug. doubles $65, triples $85.

Crystal's Castle Bed & Breakfast, 119 W. 119th St. between Lenox/Malcolm X Ave. and Adam Clayton Powell Blvd. (☎865-5522; fax 280-2061). Subway: 2 to 125th St. and Lenox Ave. Two neat rooms in a comfy brownstone belonging to Crystal and her family of professional musicians. Continental breakfast included. 25% deposit required. Check-out 1pm. Call at least 2 months in advance in summer; 1 month ahead in off-season. 1-week cancellation notice required. MC, V. Singles $76; doubles $97; both $409 per week (plus tax).

HOSTELS

▨ **Sugar Hill International House,** 722 St. Nicholas Ave., at 146th St. (☎926-7030). Subway: A, B, C, D to 145th St. Reassuring, lively neighborhood, across from subway. Brownstone with enormous rooms (25-30 beds total). Rooms for 2-10 people. All-female room available. Internet access $1 per 10min. Has kitchen and library. Key deposit $10. 2-week max. stay. Check-in 9am-10pm. Check-out 11am. No reservations accepted July-Sept. Reserve 1 month earlier otherwise. Passport ID required. No smoking. Just up the street the owners of Sugar Hill also run the 4-floor **Blue Rabbit Hostel,** 730 St. Nicholas Ave. (☎491-3892). Similar to Sugar Hill, but with more doubles and more privacy. Friendly kitty-cats, common room, and kitchen. Rooms $25-30.x

Uptown Hostel, 239 Lenox/Malcolm X Ave., at 122nd St. (☎666-0559; fax 663-5000). Subway: 2, 3 to 125th St. Run by the knowledgeable and friendly Gisèle. Bunk beds in clean, comfy rooms. Spacious hall bathrooms. Wonderful new common room and kitchen add to the family atmosphere. Key deposit $10. Check-in 11am-8pm. Lockout June-Aug. 11am-4pm. Call as far in advance as possible in summer, 2 days in advance the rest of the year. Sept.-May singles $17, doubles $23; June-Aug. singles $20, doubles $25.

BROOKLYN

see map pp. 342–343

BED AND BREAKFASTS

Akwaaba Mansion, 347 MacDonough St., in Bedford-Stuyvesant. (☎718-455-5958; fax 718-774-1744). Subway: A, C to Utica Ave.; turn to Stuyvesant Ave., make a left, and walk four blocks to MacDonough St. The B&B won an award from the New York Landmarks Preservation Society, and photographers come here to do fashion and advertising shoots. Each of the 18 rooms is decorated in African cultural decor. Library, TV room, tree-shaded patio, wrap-around sun porch, and breakfast in an elegant dining room. Rooms comfortably fit 2. All include private bath and A/C. Check-in 4-7pm. Check-out 11am. F jazz and Su brunch with Southern/African cuisine ($10). Call at least a month in advance to reserve a room. Rooms $120-135; weekends $135-150.

Bed & Breakfast on the Park, 113 Prospect Park W., between 6th and 7th Sts., in Prospect Park (☎718-499-6115; fax 718-499-1385). Subway: F to Seventh Ave./Park Slope; then 2 blocks east and 2 blocks north. A magnificently restored brownstone, its furnishings (rococo armoires, oriental carpets) are museum-quality. Gourmet breakfast in sumptuous common room. Get out of Manhattan and splurge. 8 doubles (2 with shared bath), each in a different style, $125-300.

QUEENS

see map pp. 346–347

HOSTELS

YMCA—Flushing, 138-46 Northern Blvd. between Union and Bowne Sts., in Flushing, Queens (☎718-961-6880; fax 718-461-4691). Subway: 7 to Main St.; from there walk 10min. north on Main St. (the avenue numbers should get smaller), and turn right onto Northern Blvd. The area towards Flushing's nearby shopping district is lively and well populated, but the neighborhood deteriorates north of Northern Blvd. Carpeted, small, clean rooms with TV and A/C. Bathrooms and public telephones in the hall. Daily maid service provided. Gym and swimming facilities included. Free breakfast vouchers at local diner. 25-night max. stay (longer stays possible with advance arrangements). Key deposit $10. Photo ID required. Reserve at least a month in advance for summer, one week otherwise. AmEx, V, MC. Singles $50; doubles $70; triples $80. <

Living in NYC

Long after the days when the Statue of Liberty ushered hopeful immigrants into the land of opportunity, foreigners and US citizens alike continue to flood the streets of NYC, looking for fame and fortune. The Big Apple is the center of many industries, from business to publishing, Broadway to Lincoln Center. Every year thousands of college grads swarm to Wall St., millions of actors come to wait tables, and packs of well-dressed beautiful people fight over Diana Vreeland and Donna Karen's legacy. Welcome to the center of it all; you'll get all the immediate excitement and opportunity you're looking for, and you may even find that this city could be the place for you.

VISAS AND WORK PERMITS

LONG-TERM VISAS

All travelers planning to stay more than 90 days (180 days for Canadians) need to obtain either a non-immigrant (for temporary stay) or immigrant (for permanent stay) visa. Most travelers need a **B-2**, or "pleasure tourist," visa. Those planning to travel to the US for a different purpose—such as students or temporary workers—must apply for a different visa in the appropriate category (see **Study and Work Visas,** below). Be sure to double-check entrance requirements at the nearest US embassy or consulate, or consult the **Bureau of Consular Affairs** web page (http://travel.state.gov/visa_services.html#niv).

SIX-MONTH TOURIST VISAS. Visa applications should generally be processed through the American embassy or consulate in the country of your residence (see **Planning Your Trip,** p. 242). Or, the **Center for International Business and Travel (CIBT),** 23201 New Mexico

Ave. NW #210, Washington, D.C. 20016 (☎202-244-9500 or 800-925-2428), can secure B-2 visas to and from all possible countries for a variable service charge (6-month visa around $45). If you lose your I-94 form, you can replace it at the nearest **Immigration and Naturalization Service (INS)** office (☎800-375-5283; www.ins.usdoj.gov), although it's unlikely that the form will be replaced during your stay. **Visa extensions** are sometimes attainable with a completed I-539 form; call the forms request line (☎800-870-3676). HIV-positive individuals cannot get a visa to enter the US. B-2 applicants must prove that they do not intend to immigrate by demonstrating that the purpose of their trip is for business, pleasure, or medical treatment; that they plan to remain for a limited period; and that they have a residence outside the US.

STUDY AND WORK VISAS

Working and studying are the only means of staying in the US for longer than six months. Unfortunately, separate visas are required for both. Holders of B-2 visas and those who have entered the US visa-free under the Visa Waiver Pilot Program cannot enter into full-time study or paid employment.

STUDY VISAS. Two types of study visas are available: the **F-1,** for **academic studies** (including language school), and the **M-1,** for **non-academic and vocational studies.** In order to secure a study visa, you must already be accepted into a full course of study at an educational institution approved by the Immigration and Naturalization Services (INS). F-1 applicants must also prove they have enough readily-available funds to meet all expenses for the first year of study; M-1 applicants must have evidence that sufficient funds are immediately available to pay all tuition and living costs for the entire period of intended stay. Applications should be processed through the American embassy or consulate in your country of residence (see **Planning Your Trip,** p. 242).

WORK PERMITS. In typical bureaucratic style, there are dozens of employment visas, most of which are nearly impossible to get. There are three general categories of work visas/permits: **employment-based visas,** generally issued to skilled or highly educated workers that already have a job offer in the US; **temporary worker visas,** which have fixed time limits and very specific classifications (for instance, "artists or entertainers who perform under a program that is culturally unique" or "persons who have practical training in the education of handicapped children"); and **cultural exchange visas,** which allow for employment by participants in either fellowships or reciprocal work programs with the aim of promoting cultural and historical exchange. For more on the requirements for each type of visa, visit http://travel.state.gov/visa_services.html#niv. While the chances of getting a work visa may seem next to impossible, there is hope: the **Council on International Educational Exchange (CIEE)** facilitates a **work/study/intern exchange** program between the US and citizens of Australia, China, France, Germany, Italy, Japan, Spain, Taiwan, and the UK. For a fee, CIEE will guide university students and recent graduates through the red tape of the visa application process; once in the US, they can also help you find employment (see **Finding Work,** p. 280). For more information, contact your local Council Travel office (see **Planning Your Trip,** p. 253) or visit the CIEE web site (www.ciee.org).

FINDING WORK

Hordes of young folk flock to this city of opportunity in their post-college years to just "*be*in the city." And while *be*-ing is a noble profession, still there are bills to pay. So, these *be*-ings will invariably intern, wait tables, serve as bike couriers, act, model, bartend, read manuscripts for a publishing firm, work in "the biz" (whatever the "biz" may be), and wait tables some more. Competition is steep in NYC, but jobs do exist, particularly in the city's current booming economy (unemployment is around an outstandingly low 5%). Keep your chin up and your resume handy, and you're sure to find some gainful employment.

Minimum wage in NYC is very low ($5.15/hr.) considering the exorbitant cost of living. In order to afford life as a New Yorker, you'll need to make at least $10 an hour, and even then, you'll still only be gazing longingly at most of the city's restaurants, shops, and clubs. When you are hired you will have to fill out **W-2 and I-9 tax forms** that authorize the government to take out state, federal, and Social Security taxes from your paycheck; in addition, New Yorkers pay city income tax (living outside the five boroughs, however, eliminates city tax). The combined income taxes in New York can be anywhere from 20 to 60%, so plan accordingly when budgeting your pay. Paycheck withholdings do not include government **health insurance;** only full-time, year-round jobs provide insurance, and then through a private provider. The standard work week is 40 hours; if you work more than this, you are entitled to **overtime pay,** usually 150% of your hourly wage. In an eight-hour workday, most jobs allow you to take a lunch break, although whether it is paid or unpaid varies.

RESOURCES

When finding a job in New York, the **Internet** will be your best friend; numerous websites are devoted to placing folks like you in swank joints throughout the city (see **Job Hunting on the Internet,** right). While technology has eliminated some of the pavement-pounding, many jobs are still found only through old-fashioned leg work. Check the **classifieds** of New York's newspapers, particularly in the *Village Voice, New York Press,* and the Sunday edition of the *New York Times.* Also check **bulletin boards** in local coffee shops, markets, libraries, and community centers for help wanted posters (for a list of community centers, see **Community Resources,** p. 286). In addition, all of New York's colleges and universities have **career and employment offices;** even if you can't get into the office itself (some may require a school ID to enter), most have bulletin boards outside (for a list of colleges and universities in New York, see **Studying in New York,** p. 282). Sometimes a restaurant or store will post a sign in the window—keep your eyes peeled. As a last resort, it can be fruitful to **go door-to-door with your resume** and a cover letter, particularly if you're targeting a type of establishment that is concentrated in a given area (this works well in an area like SoHo, for example, for someone interested in finding work at a gallery).

OPTIONS FOR WORK

CHILDCARE

Childcare can be a lucrative field, as babysitters and nannies are always in demand (and sometimes can be paid under the table). Make sure you know what you're getting into, though, as some parents think you should also do housework. If you go through an agency, make sure you research the company thoroughly, as many of them make a killing on fees while providing little service or support to you (some also have a limit on what you can be paid by the family, and some don't do the background checks on the families that they claim to do).

FOOD SERVICE

The highest-paid food service employees are generally **waiters** and waitresses. Waitstaff make less than minimum wage, but their salary is supplemented with **tips,** which can average

ESSENTIAL
INFORMATION

JOB HUNTING ON THE INTERNET

Putting the keywords "New York" and "jobs" into any good search engine yields hundreds of thousands of results. Here are a few that stand out.

www.careerpath.com promises "the Web's largest number of the most current job listings."

www.ci.nyc.ny.us/html/ filmcom/pdf/tech.pdf gives info on productions being filmed in NY on a weekly basis.

www.freelancers.com specializes in "creative" jobs in design, photo, illustration, and fine arts.

www.monster.com helps find jobs and internships through the help of trendy cartoon icon Thwacker. Very comprehensive.

www.ny.yahoo.com/ Employment has great links to agencies in NY. The omniscient search-engine can find you a job, baby!

newyorkjobs.net specializes in high-tech, high-power jobs. Allows you to post your resume free of charge.

newyork.preferredjobs. com is similar to a recruitment firm—they match applicants with potential employers. You can also post a resume, search listings, and read company profiles.

www.summerjobs.com is a great site for finding, you guessed it, a summer job. Links to a varied, if small, selection of quality jobs in NYC and Long Island.

upwards of $15 per hour. Since tipping is 15-20% of the bill, the more expensive the restaurant, the more tips for the waitstaff (although higher-class restaurants want experienced staff). If you are working as a **cashier** or **host,** you won't make much in tips and your salary will be close to minimum wage. **Bartenders** make great tips, but they work late and usually need certification and previous experience.

HEAD HUNTERS

The following agencies work to find companies that special employee, and you that special job. These are *not* temp agencies: companies and employees should both be looking for a long-term match.

Seven Staffing, 36 E. 12th St. (☎254-8600; fax 358-7524; www.sevenstaffing.com). Places proud computer geeks in choice jobs.

Wall Street Services, 11 Broadway, Ste. 930 (☎509-7200; fax 509-1673; www.wallstservice.com). Finds opportunities in the financial sector.

INTERNSHIPS AND VOLUNTEERING

New York City headquarters just about every industry and nonprofit sector imaginable, with the exception of government (and even then, there's the high-profile Mayor's Office and City Hall). In particular, NYC is the primary American home for publishing, advertising, theater, television, finance, fashion, and museum curating; it also houses offices for most international and nationwide nonprofit organizations. In other words, if you want it, it's here. While it's difficult to get paying, short-term positions at these offices, most are eager for interns; however, even interning and volunteering in the Big Apple is fiercely competitive. Be sure to contact your organization of choice early (around three to six months before you plan to arrive) and be prepared for an extensive application process. Manhattan College (see **Colleges and Universities,** p. 282) sponsors an internship program for foreign students.

TEMPORARY WORK

One of the easiest (and most mindless) ways to earn money is as a temp worker. Offices often hire employees for short periods (anywhere from a few days to several months) through temp agencies, massive clearinghouses of unemployed but oh-so-skilled workers. Most jobs are secretarial in nature: data entry, filing, answering phones, etc. Often, agencies can place you in full-time work after only a few weeks; if they do, health insurance is often included.

National Association of Temporary Staffing Services, New York Chapter (☎646-435-6350; www.natss.org/ny). Large organization with branches in NYC, Westchester, and Long Island.

Oliver Staffing Inc., 350 Lexington Ave. (☎634-1234). Temporary employment agency serving the gay and lesbian business community.

Paladin Staffing Services, 270 Madison Ave. (☎545-7850; fax 689-0881; email newyork-recruiter@paladinstaff.com; www.paladinstaff.com). Specializing in marketing, advertising, communications, and creative temporary placements.

STUDYING IN NYC

The following is a select list of colleges, universities, and specialty schools in New York. For a complete list of academic institutions in the city, visit the official New York City website at www.ci.nyc.ny.us.

COLLEGES AND UNIVERSITIES

Barnard College, Columbia University, Office of Admissions, 3009 Broadway, New York, NY 10027 (☎854-2014; fax 854-6220; email admissions@barnard.edu; www.barnard.columbia.edu). Hosts a pre-college summer program for high school girls. Office of Pre-College Programs, Barnard College, Columbia University, 3009 Broadway, New York, NY 10027 (☎854-8866; fax 854-8867; e-mail pcp@barnard.edu; www.barnard.edu/pcp/).

City University of New York (CUNY), Office of Admissions, 1114 Ave. of the Americas, 15th Fl., New York, NY 10036 (☎997-2869; www.cuny.edu). Serves all CUNY campuses, including community colleges throughout the city and Brooklyn College, City College, Hunter College, John Jay College, and Queens College.

Columbia University, Student Services, 203 Lewisohn Hall, Mail Code 4111, 2970 Broadway, New York, NY 10027; Office of Admissions, 3009 Broadway, New York, NY 10027. (Services: ☎854-2820; fax 854-7400; email summersession@columbia.edu; www.columbia.edu. Admissions: ☎854-2014; fax 854-6220.) School of Continuing Education includes a high school program, summer school, visiting students program, and special courses, including creative writing.

Fordham University, Office of Undergraduate Admission, Thebaud Hall, 441 East Fordham Rd., New York, NY 10458 (☎800-FORDHAM, Rose Hill campus ☎718-817-4000, Lincoln Center campus ☎636-6710; fax 718-367-9404 to Rose Hill, 636-7002 to Lincoln Center; email enroll@fordham.edu; www.fordham.edu). Campuses in the Bronx (Rose Hill) and Manhattan (Lincoln Center). Summer programs for undergrads and graduate students.

Joggers in Central Park

Manhattan College, Office of Admissions, Manhattan College Parkway, Riverdale, New York 10471 (☎800-MC2-XCEL and 718-862-7200; fax 718-862-8019; email admit@manhattan.edu; www.manhattan.edu). Sponsors the New York City Semester for college students; contact Susan Hannon, the program coordinator (☎718-862-7476; email shannon@manhattan.edu).

New School University, Office of Admissions and Student Services, 66 W. 12th St., New York, NY 10011 (☎229-5600; www.newschool.edu). This avant-garde and intellectually rigorous university has over 20,000 continuing education students enrolled in everything from its Educated Citizen Project to the Dial Cyberspace Campus.

New York University, Office of Summer Sessions, 7 E. 12th St., 6th Fl., New York, NY 10003 (☎998-1212; fax 995-4103; www.nyu.edu/summer). Welcomes visiting students to its massive summer school.

SPECIALTY SCHOOLS

Chinatown grocery shopping

The Cooper Union for the Advancement of Science and Art, Cooper Square, New York, NY 10003 (general info ☎353-4000; adult education ☎353-4195; www.cooper.edu). Large, inexpensive adult education program in architecture, art, and engineering.

Fashion Institute of Technology, Office of Admissions, Room C139, Seventh Ave. at 27th St., .New York, NY 10001 (☎217-7775; www.fitnyc.suny.edu). Offers extremely competitive semester for visiting students.

French Culinary Institute, Office of Admissions, 462 Broadway, New York, NY 10013 (☎219-8890 and 888-FCI-CHEF; fax 431-3054; www.frenchculinary.com). Very expensive courses (2 to 9 months) for the budding chef or the serious amateur.

The Juilliard School, Evening Division, 60 Lincoln Center Plaza, New York, NY 10023 (☎799-5040; email juilliardatnight@juilliard.edu; www.juilliard.edu). Evening programs for adults aged 18-88, with or without artistic talent. Intensive summer courses also available.

Algonquin Hotel

LONG-TERM ACCOMMODATIONS

So you're one of millions looking for an apartment in NYC (competition is so fierce that city slickers joke about *NYTimes* obituaries: "Joe Schmo died yesterday, leaving his wife, two children, and a spacious 4-bdrm. on the West Side with river view"); the market is extremely tight, rents are high, brokerage fees exorbitant, and most landlords will not rent without a guarantor on the lease and all potential tenants present when the decision to rent is made. However, this isn't the impossible dream (although you'll probably need a cell phone, call waiting, and eight hours a day to make this dream reality); like everything else here, finding housing is possible with a little perseverence, ingenuity, and luck.

APARTMENTS

TIPS. Unless you are planning on permanently relocating to New York, **subletting** an apartment for a limited period of time is your best bet. When New Yorkers feel the need to escape, they will rent out their (usually furnished) apartments for a month or more. For longer stays, it is easier to become a **roommate** in someone's apartment than to find your own lease. When apartment hunting in NYC, **act fast.** If you find something suitable (but perhaps not your dream apartment), take it immediately; it *will* be gone when you call back, and you're *not* going to find your dream place. However, do not rush your search: always thoroughly investigate the apartment and surrounding neighborhood to make sure you feel comfortable living there. Finding an apartment in Brooklyn or Queens will be **cheaper and less competitive** than Manhattan, and not that inconvenient. Hoboken, West New York, and Weehawken, across the Hudson, also offer more for your money, a view of the Manhattan skyline, and a quick $1 (cheaper than the subway) commute to the center of everything.

RESOURCES. Word of mouth can be the best way to find a place in NYC. Ask friends if they know of vacancies; ask your friends' friends if they know of vacancies. If you are staying at the **Uptown Hostel** (see **Accommodations,** p. 276), Gisèle will often help you find a cheap apartment. Check the **Village Voice** for listings early Wednesday mornings (the day it comes to press). Their website (www.villagevoice.com) is another resource that can get the information to you a night before those poor, misguided seekers who wait in line at Astor Pl. the next morning for a hard copy. The **New York Times** also has a helpful classified section with real estate options (online at www.nytimes.com). There are also myriad **websites** devoted to finding roommates, subletters, and apartments throughout the city; type "New York" and "apartments" in and watch your search engine go crazy. And, seriously: check the **NYTimes obituary** section. If your search is too frustrating and exhausting, turn to a **realtor.** Be warned, however, that brokerage fees are extremely high. For realtors and websites listing sublets and rentals, see **Room for Rent,** opposite page.

OTHER OPTIONS

DORMS

Many universities in New York rent out their vacant dorms to summer visitors. The length of stay varies depending on the school, but often you can stay for the entire summer. The two largest dormitory options are at **New York University** (see **Accommodations,** p. 265) and at **Long Island University,** Brooklyn Campus, 1 University Plaza, Brooklyn, New York 11201 (Main ☎718-488-1011; Resident Hall Director ☎780-1552), in downtown Brooklyn. Rates at LIU average $50 per night, but vary depending on your length of stay. For a more complete list of colleges and universities in New York, see **Studying in New York,** p. 282, or www.ci.nyc.ny.us.

HOME EXCHANGE AND RENTAL

For shorter stays, home exchange and rental can be cost-effective options, particularly for families with children. Home rentals, as opposed to exchanges, are much more expensive, although they are remarkably cheaper than an extended stay at a comparably serviced hotel. In New York, most home exchanges and rentals come with kitchen, cleaning lady, telephones, and TV. Unfortunately, it can be difficult to arrange an exchange or rental for more than one month. Both home rentals and exchanges are organized by the following exchange services. A great site listing many other home exchange companies is at www.aitec.edu.au/~bwechner/Documents/Travel/Lists/HomeExchangeClubs.html.

HomeExchange.com, P.O. Box 30085, Santa Barbara, CA 93130 (☎805-898-9660; email admin@HomeExchange.com; www.home-exchange.com).
The Invented City: International Home Exchange, 41 Sutter St., Ste. 1090, San Fransisco, CA 94104 (☎800-788-2489 in the US, 415-252-1141 elsewhere; email invented@aol.com; www.invented-city.com). For $75, your offer is listed in 1 catalog and you have access to a database of thousands of homes for exchange.

HOSTELS

Although many of New York's hostels have maximum stay limits, some do allow long-term stays. If a hostel doesn't have a maximum stay limit, ask, and perhaps you shall receive. Otherwise, hostels that do have limits usually hover between 25 and 30 days; for a two- or three-month stay, it's always possible to stay at two or three different hostels, in singles, for the duration of your trip. For a list of hostels, see **Accommodations By Neighborhood,** p. 267. The **DeHirsch Residence,** on the Upper East Side, rents rooms by the month for stays over two months (see p. 274). In addition, **YMCA-Flushing** allows long-term stays with advance notice (see p. 277).

MONEY MATTERS
BANKING

If you don't have an account at one of the city's mega-banks, it might be worth your while to open a new checking account. New York is expensive and you'll be withdrawing money frequently; unfortunately, ATM fees are as expensive as everything else in NYC. The largest banks are **Citibank** (☎800-627-3999), **Chase Manhattan** (☎800-935-9935), and the **Bank of New York** (☎888-LINK-BNY). These three clamor over one another to have an ATM on every corner. While this makes ATM withdrawals inexpensive, those savings are often made up for by expensive monthly account fees. Smaller, local banks might be cheaper and friendlier, albeit less ATM convenient.

To open a checking account, you'll need a social security number, local address, and minimum deposit (for the cheapest accounts, it's usually around $100-200). Foreign visitors will find it near impossible to open a checking account; consider opening a savings account instead. Call your bank of choice about their requirements for foreign account holders; usually, you will need to register for a social security number first.

CUTTING CORNERS

It may seem impossible to live on a budget in the Big Apple, but with planning and self-restraint, it can happen. The largest

ᔿ ESSENTIAL
INFORMATION

ROOM FOR RENT!

Gamut Realty Group
301 E. 78th St. (☎879-4229; fax 517-5356). Assists in finding sublets and short- and long-term rooms and apartments. Open M-F 9am-6pm, Sa-Su 10am-4pm.

Gay Roommate Information Network
(☎627-4242) matches gay roommates.

Manhattan Lodgings
(☎677-7616) is a network that puts visitors in contact with New York apartment tenants who want to rent out their respective pads for a few days or weeks.

New York Habitat
307 Seventh Ave., Ste. 306 (☎255-8018; fax 627-1416; email rent @nyhabitat.com; www.nyhabitat.com). Finds sublets (www.nyhabitat-sublet.com), roommates (www.nyhabitat-roommate.com), and apartment rentals.

WESITES LISTING SUBLETS, RENTALS, AND SWAPS:

www.relocationcentral.com Helps with everything from apartment hunting to renting a moving van.

www.roomiematch.com is a "quick and amusing" search engine that helps young New Yorkers find flatmates.

www.roommatelocator. com/form.asp

www.roommatebbs.com

www.summerexchange. com

expense is undoubtedly housing. The cheapest option is to live in Hoboken or other nearby areas of NJ, where rent is cheap and commuting costs negligible ($1 to Midtown). The outer boroughs also have less expensive rents, and are much, much cooler than NJ, but cheap housing in Queens or Brooklyn may be in less safe neighborhoods. City transportation is very expensive ($1.50 per ride), especially if you need to commute to work/school/play every day. Buying a 30-day MetroCard is by far the cheapest option, because cars are either too expensive, too inconvenient, or too much of both. Food is no more expensive in NYC than anywhere else, especially since large supermarkets (not the nice, gourmet type—stay away from those money-eaters) are within walking distance to almost everything. What will *really* hurt your finances quickly—without you noticing—is entertainment. The city abounds with tempting concerts, shows, good restaurants, bars, and clubs. Most of these things are worth the splurge, but there are ways of getting around high prices if you know where to look. Free events happen all the time, and, especially during the summertime, extremely famous DJs, bands, theater groups, and dance companies offer free entertainment. If you skim the *NYTimes*, *Village Voice*, or *New York* every now and then, you should have plenty of cheap options.

MEDICAL CARE

Should you require medical attention while in NYC, clinics and emergency rooms are the best places to be treated. Both accept walk-ins and spare you the hassle of having to choose a doctor and go through an initial screening. Medical care is expensive, so health insurance is advisable; for foreign visitors, arrange health insurance before you arrive in the US, as it is notoriously impossible (not to mention expensive) to procure. Both clinics and emergency rooms in public hospitals will treat the non-insured. For a list of clinics, hospitals, and pharmacies, see **Service Directory,** p. 289.

COMMUNITY RESOURCES
COMMUNITY CENTERS

The following are umbrella organizations for community centers throughout the five boroughs. Contact them for a list of centers in your neighborhood.

United Neighborhood Houses of New York (UNH), 70 W. 36th St., 5th Fl. (☎967-0322; fax 967-0792; www.unhny.org). Partnerships with community centers throughout the 5 boroughs; check their web page for a complete list.

United Community Centers, 613 New Lots Ave., Brooklyn (☎718-649-7979). Similar to UNH.

GAY AND LESBIAN RESOURCES

For information on gay and lesbian resources in New York, see the **Queer Apple,** p. 221.

ETHNIC RESOURCES

For more resources, see **Cultural Institutes,** p. 163.

Chinese American Planning Council, 150 Elizabeth St. (☎941-0925).

Jewish Community Center, 15 W. 65th St., 8th Fl. (☎580-0099; fax 799-0254; www.jccny.org).

Instituto Cervantes, 122 E. 42nd St., Ste. 807 (☎689-4232; fax 545-8837). A cultural center for Spanish-speakers.

Schomburg Center for Research in Black Culture, 515 Malcolm X Blvd. (☎491-2200; www.nypl.org/research/sc.sc.html). Has information on African, African-American, and West Indian community and cultural centers.

WOMEN'S RESOURCES

In addition to the women's centers listed below, the **National Organization for Women** has an office in New York (☎627-9895).

Barnard College/Columbia University Women's Center, 3009 Broadway (☎854-4907).
Brooklyn College Women's Center, 227 New Ingersoll Hall, Brooklyn (☎718-780-5777).
Hunter College Women's Center, 695 Park Ave., Box 368.
NYU Women's Center, 21 Washington Pl., Box #179.

WORKING OUT

GYMS

Membership at most of NYC's swank gyms is high-priced. Cheaper alternatives include public fitness centers and YMCA/YWCAs. **Public fitness centers,** or recreation centers, are run by the city government and feature most of the amenities, classes, and equipment of the brand-name gyms. Membership is an astounding $10-25 per *year* and there are over 30 branches throughout the city. In Manhattan, gyms include Asser Levy, E. 23rd St. (☎447-2020), between 1st and FDR Dr.; Carmine, (☎242-5228), on 7th Ave. at Clarkson St.; East 54th St., 358 E. 54th St. (☎397-3154); and West 59th St. (☎317-3159), at 10th Ave. and 59th St. Another affordable option are the city's **YMCAs, YWCAs, and YM-YWHAs.** Facilities at the following locations are high quality (call the Vanderbilt Y for other locations): Vanderbilt YMCA, 224 E. 47th St. (☎756-9600); 92nd St. YM-YWHA, 1395 Lexington Ave. (☎415-5729), at 92nd St.; and YWCA, 610 Lexington Ave. (☎735-9753), at 53rd St.

JOGGING

If you plan to jog along the street, be prepared to dodge pedestrians and to break your stride at intersections. A better alternative to the sidewalk are paths along the rivers or in Central Park—most are pavement, but there is a 1.58 mi. cinder loop that circles the **Jacqueline Kennedy Onassis Reservoir** (between 84th and 96th St.). Joggers pack this path from 6-9am and 5-7pm on weekdays and all day on weekends. If you can, run between 9am and 5pm to avoid the night-time crime and rush-hour collisions on the narrow strip. For information on running clubs, call the **New York Roadrunner's Club,** 9 E. 89th St. (☎860-4455), between Madison and Fifth Ave.

Service Directory

ACCOMMODATION AGENCIES

See also **Realtors,** p. 293.

Homestay New York, 630 E. 19th St., Brooklyn (☎718-434-2071).

YMCA, 224 E. 47th St. (☎212-308-2899).

AIRLINES

Major airlines have numerous Manhattan offices; call for the closest location.

American, ☎800-621-8489.

Continental, ☎800-525-0280.

Delta, ☎800-221-1212.

Northwest, ☎800-225-2525

TWA, ☎800-221-2000.

United, ☎800-241-6522.

US Airways, ☎800-428-4322.

AIRPORTS

John F. Kennedy Airport (JFK), ☎718-244-4444. In Queens.

LaGuardia Airport, ☎718-533-3400. In Queens.

Newark Int'l Airport, ☎973-961-6000. In NJ.

AIRPORT TRANSPORT

Gray Line Air Shuttle, ☎800-451-0455. Serves JFK and LaGuardia.

JFK Flyer, ☎516-766-6722.

New York Airport Service, ☎800-769-7004, 718-706-9658.

Olympia Trails Coach, ☎212-964-6233. Serves Newark.

AUTO RENTAL

AAMCAR Rent-a-Car, 315 W. 96th St., between West End Ave. and Riverside Dr. (☎212-222-8500). Open M-F 7:30am-7:30pm, Sa 9am-5pm, Su 9am-7pm.

Dollar: at JFK ☎718-656-2400; at LaGuardia ☎718-244-1235.

Enterprise, ☎800-566-9249.

Nationwide, 241 W. 40th St., between Seventh and Eighth Ave. (☎212-867-1234). Open M-F 7:30am-6:30pm.

BICYCLE RENTAL

Pedal Pushers, 1306 Second Ave. between 68th and 69th Sts. (☎288-5592). 3-speeds $4 per hr., $10 per day, $12 overnight; 10-speeds $5 per hr., $14 per day, $14 overnight; mountain bikes $6 per hr., $17 per day, $25 overnight. Overnight rentals require $150 deposit on a major credit card, regular rentals only need major credit card, passport, or a NY state driver's license deposit. Open F-M 10am-6pm, W 10am-7pm, Th 10am-8pm. Helmet extra $2 per day.

Loeb Boathouse, mid-park at 75th St., in Central Park (☎861-4137; 717-9048). 3-speeds $8 per hr., 10-speeds $10, tandems $15. Valid ID and $100 cash or credit card deposit required. Open Apr.-Sept. daily 10am-5pm, weather permitting.

Metro Bicycle Stores, Lexington Ave. at 88th St. (☎427-4450). Seven convenient locations throughout the city. $7 per hr., $35 per day, $45 overnight. Daily rentals due back 30min. before store closes and overnight rentals next day at 10am. $250 cash or credit card deposit and valid ID required. Helmet rental $2.50 per bike. Open F-Tu 9:30am-6:30pm, W-Th 9:30am-7:30pm.

BUDGET TRAVEL AGENCIES

Council Travel, 254 Greene St. (☎212-254-2525; www.counciltravel.com).

STA Travel, 10 Downing St. (☎212-627-3111).

BUSES

See also **Metro Transit,** p. 293.

Green Bus Lines, ☎718-995-4700. Serves Jamaica and central Queens.

Greyhound, ☎800-231-2222.

Jamaica Buses, Inc., ☎718-526-0800. Serves Jamaica and Rockaway.

Liberty Lines Express, ☎718-652-8400. Serves the Bronx.

MTA/Long Island Bus, ☎516-766-6722.

New York Bus Service, ☎718-994-5500. Serves the Bronx.

Port Authority Terminal, ☎212-435-7000.

Queens Surface Corp., ☎718-445-3100.

TriBoro Coach Corp., ☎718-335-1000. Serves Forest Hills, Ridgewood, and Jackson Hts.

CONSULATES

Australia, 150 E. 42nd St., 34th Fl. (☎212-351-6500). No visa services.

British Commonwealth, 800 Second Ave (☎212-599-8478).

Canada, Main Concourse Level, 1251 Avenue Of The Americas (☎212-596-1700).

France, 934 Fifth Ave. (☎212-606-3600). Visa services, 10 E. 74th St. (☎212-472-8110).

Ireland, 345 Park Ave. (☎212-319-2555).

Israel, 800 Second Ave. (☎212-499-5000).

New Zealand, 780 Third Ave., Suite 1904 (☎212-832-4038).

South Africa, 333 E. 38th St., 9th Fl. (☎212-213-4880).

UK, 845 Third Ave. (☎212-745-0200).

CRISIS AND HELP LINES

See also Emergency, p. 291; Hospitals, p. 292; Medical Clinics, p. 293; and Women's Health, p. 294.

AIDS Information, ☎212-807-6655. Open M-F 10am-9pm, Sa noon-3pm.

AIDS Hotline, ☎212-447-8200. Open daily 9am-9pm; 24hr. recording.

Alcohol and Substance Abuse Info Line, ☎800-274-2042. 24hr. info and referrals.

Crime Victims' Hotline, ☎212-577-7777. 24hr. counseling and referrals.

Gay and Lesbian Switchboard, ☎989-0999; glnh.@glnh.org. Open M-F 6-10pm, Sa noon-5pm. 24hr. recording.

Help Line, ☎212-532-2400. Crisis counseling and referrals. Open daily 9am-10:30pm.

National Abortion Federation, ☎800-772-9100. Open M-F 9am-7pm. Poison Control Center, ☎212-764-7667. Open 24hr.

Roosevelt Hospital Rape Crisis Center, ☎212-523-4728. M-F 9am-5pm.

Samaritans, ☎212-673-3000. Suicide prevention. Open 24hr.

Sex Crimes Report Line, ☎212-267-7273. NYPD-related. 24hr. information and referrals.

Venereal Disease Information, ☎212-427-5120. Open M-F 8am-4pm.

CURRENCY EXCHANGE

American Express, American Express Tower, 200 Vesey St. (☎212-640-2000), near the World Financial Center. Open M-F 8:30am-5:30pm. Other branches include:

Macy's Herald Square, 151 W. 34th St. (☎212-695-8075), at Seventh Ave., on Macy's balcony level. Open M-Sa 10am-6pm.

420 Lexington Ave. (☎212-687-3700), at 43rd St. Open M-F 9am-6pm.

822 Lexington Ave. (☎212-758-6510), near 63rd St. Open M-F 9am-6pm, Sa 10am-4pm.

374 Park Ave. and 53rd St. (☎212-421-8240). Open M-F 9am-5pm.

1185 Sixth Ave. and 47th St. (☎212-398-8585). Open M-F 9am-6pm.

111 Broadway (☎212-693-1100), near Pine St. Open M-F 8:30am-5:30pm.

200 Fifth Ave. (☎212-691-9797), at 23rd St. Open M-F 8:30am-5:30pm and Sa 10am-4pm.

Bank Leumi, 579 Fifth Ave. (☎917-542-2343), at 47th St. Open M-F 9am-3pm.

Cheque Point USA, 1568 Broadway (☎212-869-6281), at 47th St. Other branches throughout the city; call for locations. Open daily 8am-9:30pm.

Thomas Cooke, 29 Broadway (☎800-287-7362), at Morris St. Open M-F 8:30am-4:30pm.

DENTISTS

Emergency Dental Associates, ☎800-439-9299. 24hr.

NYU College of Dentistry, ☎212-998-9800. Open M-Th 8:30am-6:45pm, F 8:30am-4pm.

DISABLED RESOURCES

Access-A-Ride, ☎1-877-337-2017. For public transport.

Directions Unlimited, 123 Green Ln., Bedford Hills (☎914-241-1700, 800-533-5343).

Elevators and Escalator Accessibility, ☎1-800-734-6772. 24hr.

Moss Rehab Hospital Travel Information Service, ☎215-456-9600, 800-CALL-MOSS.

Society for the Advancement of Travel for the Handicapped (SATH), 347 Fifth Ave., #610, (☎212-447-7284).

Transit Authority Access, ☎718-596-8585.

DRY CLEANERS

Midnight Express Cleaners, ☎212-921-0111. Open M-F 8am-8pm, Sa 9am-1pm; closed Sa July-Aug. Picks up laundry.

EMERGENCY

In an emergency, dial 911. See also Crisis and Help Lines, p. 291; Hospitals, p. 292; Medical Clinics, p. 293; and Women's Health, p. 294.

Ambulance: ☎212-988-8800.

Fire: ☎212-999-2222.

Police (non-emergency): ☎212-374-5000.

TDD Police: ☎212-374-5911.

ENTERTAINMENT INFO

See also **Ticket Services**, p. 294.

Parks & Recreation Special Events Hotline, ☎212-360-3456. 24hr.

MoviePhone, ☎777-FILM/3456.

NYC/ON STAGE Hotline, ☎212-768-1818.

New York City On Stage Hotline, ☎212-768-1818.

HOSPITALS

See also **Crisis and Help Lines,** p. 291; **Emergency,** p. 291; **Medical Clinics,** p. 293; and **Women's Health,** p. 294.

Bellevue Hospital Center, 462 First Ave. (☎212-562-4141), at 27th. St. Adult ER ☎562-3015; pediatric ER ☎562-3025.

Beth Israel Medical Center, First Ave. at E. 16th St. (☎212-420-2000). Adult ER ☎420-2840; pediatric ER ☎420-2860.

Bronx-Lebanon Hospital Center, 1650 Grand Concord (☎718-590-1800). 2 ERs: 1650 Grand Concord (☎718-518-5120), 1276 Fulton Ave. (☎718-960-8700).

Brooklyn Hospital Center, 121 DeKalb Ave. (☎718-250-8000). ER ☎718-250-8075.

Columbia-Presbyterian Medical Center, 622 W. 168th St. (☎212-305-2500). ER ☎305-6204.

Interfaith Medical Center, 555 Prospect Pl., near Franklin St., Brooklyn (☎718-935-7000).

2 ERs: St. Marks (☎718-935-7110), Atlantic Ave. (☎718-604-6110).

Jacobi Medical Center, 1400 Pelham Parkway South, Bronx. ER ☎718-918-5000.

Jamaica Hospital Medical Center, 8900 Van Wyck Expressway (☎718-206-6000), in Jamaica, Queens. ER ☎718-206-6066.

Mount Sinai Medical Center, Fifth Ave. and 100th St. (☎212-241-6500). ER ☎241-7171.

New York University Medical Center, 560 First Ave., between 32nd and 33rd St. (☎212-263-7300). ER ☎263-5550.

New York University Downtown Hospital, 170 William St., between Spruce and Beekman Sts. (☎212-312-5000).

IN-LINE SKATE RENTAL

Blades, over eight stores in the Metropolitan area (☎888-55-Blades). Open M-Sa 11am-8pm, Su 11am-6pm.

Peck and Goodie Skates, 917 Eighth Ave., between 54th and 55th St. (☎212-246-6123). Open M-Sa 10am-8pm, Su 10am-6pm.

INTERNET ACCESS

Canal Jean Co., 504 Broadway, between Spring and Broome St. (☎212-226-3663), in SoHo. Free. Open daily 9:30am-9pm.

alt.coffee, 139 Ave. A, between 8th and 9th St. (☎212-529-2233). Open Su 11am-1:30am, M-Th 8:00am-1:30am, F-Sa 8:00am-3am.

Cybercafe, 273 Lafayette St. (☎212-334-5140), at the corner of Prince St. Open M-F 8am-11pm, Sa-Su 11am-10pm.

Kinko's. Over 30 locations; call ☎800-254-6567 for the one you want. Open 24hr.

LIBRARIES

Bronx Reference Center, 2556 Bainbridge Ave. (☎718-579-4200).

Brooklyn Public Library, Grand Army Plaza, Brooklyn (☎718-230-2100).

Donnell Library Center, 20 W. 53rd St., between Fifth and Sixth Ave. (☎212-621-0618). Across the street from the Museum of Modern Art. Open M, W, and F 10am-6pm; Tu and Th 10am-8pm; Sa 10am-5pm.

Mid-Manhattan Library, 455 Fifth Ave. (☎212-340 0849), at 40th St. Open M and W 9am-9pm, Tu and Th 11am-7pm, F-Sa 10am-6pm.

New York Public Library, 11 W. 40th St. (☎212-930-0830, 869-8089), entrance on Fifth Ave. at 42nd St. Open M and Th-Sa 10am-6pm, Tu-W 11am-7:30pm.

New York Public Library for the Performing Arts (☎212-870-1630). Relocated to Mid-Manhattan Library until Feb. 2001; at Lincoln Center after Feb. 2001.

Queensborough Public Library, 89-11 Merrick Blvd., Jamaica, Queens (☎718-990-0700).

Schomburg Center for Research in Black Culture, 515 Lenox Ave./Malcolm X Blvd. (☎212-491-2200), on the corner of 135th St. Library open M-W noon-8pm, Th-Sa 10am-6pm; archives open M-W noon-5pm and Th-Sa 10am-5pm.

St. George Library Center, 5 Central Ave., Staten Island (☎718-442-8560).

MEDICAL CLINICS

See also **Crisis and Help Lines,** p. 291; **Dentists,** p. 291; **Emergency,** p. 291; **Hospitals,** p. 292; **Pharmacies,** p. 293; and **Women's Health,** p. 294.

Callen-Lorde Community Health Center, 356 W. 18th St., between Eighth and Ninth Aves. (☎212-271-7200). Serves the queer community. Open M 12:30-8pm, Tu and Th-F 9am-4:30pm, W 8:30am-1pm and 3-8pm.

D*O*C*S, 55 E. 34th St. (☎212-252-6000), at Park and Madison Aves. Also at: 1555 Third Ave. (☎212-828-2300), at 88th St.; 202 W. 23rd St. (☎212-352-2600).

Doctors Walk-in Clinic, 55 E. 34th St., between Park and Madison Ave. (☎212-252-6001, ext. 2). Open M-Th 8am-8pm, F 8am-7pm, Sa 9am-3pm, Su 9am-2pm.

Gay Men's Health Crisis-Geffen Clinic, 119 W. 24th St., between Sixth and Seventh Aves. (☎212-367-1100). Open M-F 10am-9pm, Sa noon-3pm.

METRO TRANSIT

See also **Airport Transport,** p. 289; **Buses,** p. 290; and **Trains,** p. 294.

Bus Info, ☎516-766-6722.

General Info, ☎718-330-1234 in English, ☎718-330-4847 for other languages.

MetroCard Info, ☎800-638-7622.

Reduced Fare Info, ☎718-878-7294, ☎718-878-0165 TDD.

PHARMACIES

See also **Medical Clinics,** p. 293.

Duane Reade, 224 57th St., at Broadway (☎212-541-9708). Open 24hr. Other locations: 2465 Broadway, at 91st St. (☎212-799-3172); 1279 Third Ave., at 74th St. (☎212-744-2668); 378 Sixth Ave., at Waverly Pl. (☎212-674-5357).

Love Drug, 209 E. 86th St., between Second and Thrid Aves. (☎212-427-0954). Open M-Sa 8am-midnight, Su 9am-midnight.

POSTAL SERVICES

US Postal Service Customer Service Assistance Center, ☎212-967-8585 (M-F 8:30am-6pm), ☎800-725-2161 (24hr.).

Central Post Office, 0421 Eighth Ave. (☎212-330-2902), occupying the block between Eighth and Ninth Ave. and 33rd and 32nd St.

Federal Express, ☎800-247-4747.

MailBoxes, Etc., 1173A Second Ave., between 61st and 62nd Sts. (☎212-832-1390). Open M-F 9am-7pm, Sa 10am-5pm.

REALTORS

See also **Accommodation Agencies,** p. 289.

DG Neary Realty, 57 W. 16th St., on the corner of Sixth Ave. (☎627-4242; fax 989-1207). Open Su-F 10am-6pm.

Gamut Realty Group, 301 E. 78th St. (☎212-879-4229). Open M-F 9am-6pm, Sa-Su 10am-4pm.

Manhattan Lodgings, ☎212-677-7616.

New York Habitat, 307 Seventh Ave., Ste. 306 (☎212-255-8018).

Rainbow Roommates, 268 W. 22nd St., near Eighth Ave. (☎627-8612; www.rainbowroommates.com). Open Tu-Sa noon-6pm.

SALONS

Astor Place Hair Designers, 2 Astor Pl., at Broadway (☎212-475-9854). Open M-Sa 8am-8pm, Su 9am-6pm. Cuts start at $11.

Ginger Rose on Bleecker, 154 Bleecker St., between Thompson St. and LaGuardia Pl. (☎212-677-6511). Open M-Sa 10am-8pm, Su noon-6pm. Cuts start at $11.

Jean Louis David, 1180 Sixth Ave., at 46th St. (☎212-944-7389). Open M-F 10am-7pm. Cuts around $23.50.

TAXIS

All City Taxis, ☎718-402-2323.
Bell Radio Taxi, ☎212-206-1700.
Tri-State, ☎212-777-7171.
Tel Aviv, ☎212-777-7777.
Taxi Commission, 40 Rector St. (☎212-221-8294). Open M-F 9am-5pm.

TICKET SERVICES

See also **Entertainment Info,** p. 292.
Discount Tickets, ☎212-221-0885.
Tele-Charge, ☎212-239-6200 (24hr.).
Ticket Central, ☎212-279-4200. Daily 1-8pm.
Ticketmaster, ☎212-307-4100.
TKTS, ☎212-768-1818.

TOURIST INFORMATION

See also **Accommodation Agencies,** p. 289.
New York Convention and Visitors Bureau, 810 Seventh Ave., at 53rd St. (☎212-484-1222).
New York State Department of Economic Development, 633 Third Ave., between 40th and 41st St. (☎212-803-2200, 800-CALL-NYS). Open M-F 9am-8:30pm.

Staten Island Chamber of Commerce, ☎718-727-1900.

Times Square Visitors Center, 1560 Broadway, between 46th and 47th St. (☎212-869-5453; fax 997-4021). Open daily 9am-6pm. Other locations: Grand Central terminal, south side of the main concourse; Penn Station terminal, south side of the Amtrak rotunda; at 34th St., between Seventh and Eighth Ave.; Manhattan Mall info booth at 33rd and 6th St.

Lower East Side Visitors Center, 261 Broome St., between Orchard and Allen (☎888-VAL-UES-4-U). Open Su-F 10am-4pm.

Travelers' Aid of NY & NJ, at JFK Airport (☎718-656-4870), in Terminal 4W. Open daily 9am-8pm.

TRAINS

See also **Metro Transit,** p. 293.
Amtrak, ☎800-872-7245.
Grand Central Station, ☎212-340-3000.**Long Island Railroad (LIRR),** ☎718-217-5477, 516-822-5477.
NJ Transit, ☎973-762-5100, 800-772-2222 in NJ.
PATH, ☎800-234-7284.
Metro-North Commuter Lines, ☎800-638-7646.

WOMEN'S HEALTH

See also **Crisis and Help Lines,** p. 291; **Hospitals,** p. 292; and **Medical Clinics,** p. 293.

Eastern Women's Center, 44 E. 30th St. (☎212-686-6066), between Park and Madison Ave. Exams by appointment only; walk-in pregnancy testing.

Planned Parenthood, Margaret Sanger Center, 26 Bleecker St. (☎212-274-7200). Also in Brooklyn, 44 Court St., and the Bronx, 349 E. 149th St. and Cortland St.

Women's Health Line, New York City Department of Health (☎212-230-1111). Open M-F 8am-6pm.

Index

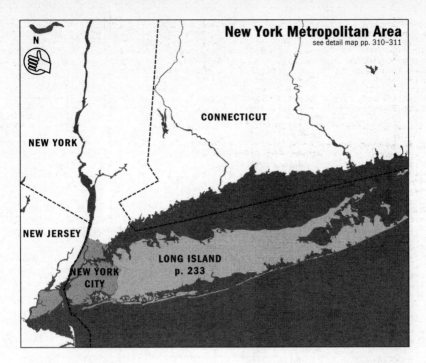

New York Metropolitan Area
see detail map pp. 310–311

N

CONNECTICUT

NEW YORK

NEW JERSEY

NEW YORK
CITY

LONG ISLAND
p. 233

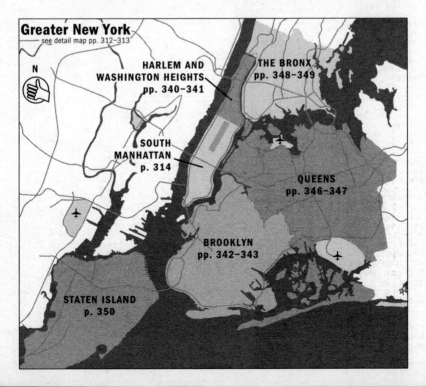

Greater New York
see detail map pp. 312–313

N

HARLEM AND
WASHINGTON HEIGHTS
pp. 340–341

THE BRONX
pp. 348–349

SOUTH
MANHATTAN
p. 314

QUEENS
pp. 346–347

BROOKLYN
pp. 342–343

STATEN ISLAND
p. 350

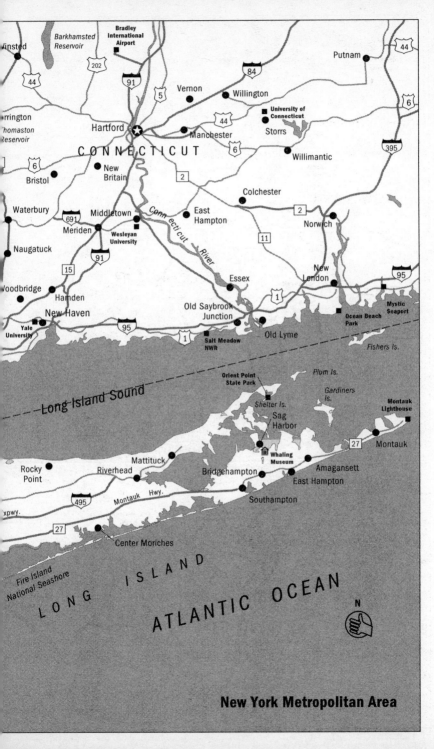

New York Metropolitan Area

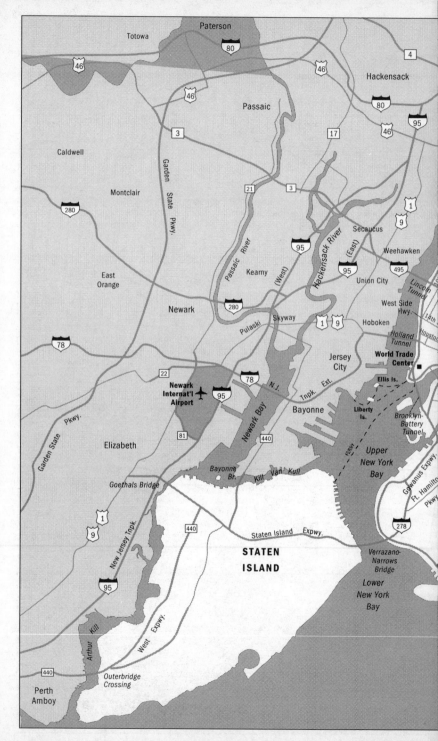

Long Island Sound

Yonkers

Mount Vernon

BRONX

George Washington Bridge

Cross

Yankee Stadium

MANHATTAN

Central Park

Metropolitan Museum of Art

Queensboro Bridge

United Nations

Queens-Midtown Tunnel

Hempstead Bay

Sands Point

Port Washington

City Island

Throgs Neck Bridge

Bronx-Whitestone Br.

Rikers Is.

LaGuardia Airport

QUEENS

Great Neck

Manhasset

Manhasset Bay

Little Neck Bay

Northern

Blvd.

State

Floral Park

Bellerose

Long Island

Elmont

Hempstead Tnpk.

Brooklyn-Queens Expwy.

Interborough

Atlantic Ave.

Eastern

Linden Blvd.

BROOKLYN

Southern State Pkwy.

Valley Stream

Sunrise Hwy.

Belt Pkwy. (Southern Pkwy.)

John F. Kennedy Internat'l Airport

Cedarhurst

Inwood

Lawrence Beach

Jamaica Bay

ATLANTIC OCEAN

N

0   2 miles

0   2 kilometers

Greater New York

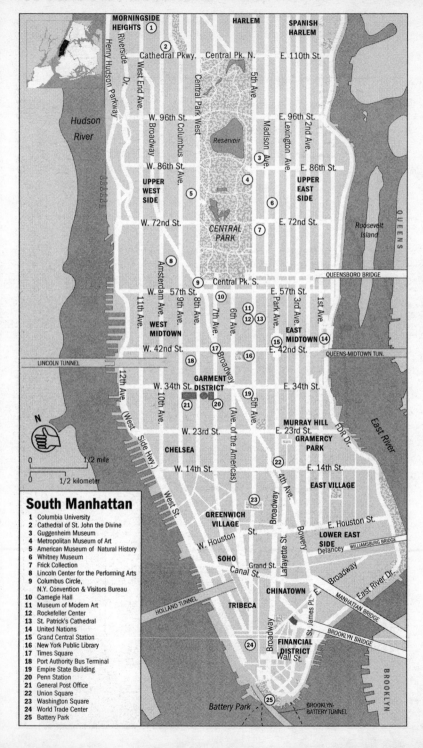

MORNINGSIDE HEIGHTS ①
②
Cathedral Pkwy.
HARLEM
SPANISH HARLEM
Central Pk. N. E. 110th St.
5th Ave.
Central Park West

Hudson River

West End Ave.
Broadway
Columbus Ave.
5th Ave.
W. 96th St. E. 96th St.
Lexington Ave.
2nd Ave.
Madison Ave.

Reservoir

③
W. 86th St. E. 86th St.
④ E. 86th St.
UPPER WEST SIDE
⑤
UPPER EAST SIDE
⑥
W. 72nd St. E. 72nd St.
⑦
CENTRAL PARK

Roosevelt Island

QUEENS

⑧
Amsterdam Ave.
11th Ave.
⑨ Central Pk. S.
QUEENSBORO BRIDGE
W. 57th St. E. 57th St.
⑩
9th Ave.
8th Ave.
7th Ave.
6th Ave.
⑪ ⑫ ⑬
3rd Ave.
Park Ave.
1st Ave.
WEST MIDTOWN
EAST MIDTOWN ⑭
⑮
W. 42nd St. ⑰ E. 42nd St. QUEENS-MIDTOWN TUN.
⑱ ⑯
LINCOLN TUNNEL
GARMENT DISTRICT
12th Ave. (West Side Hwy.)
10th Ave.
W. 34th St. E. 34th St.
⑲
⑳ 5th Ave.
㉑
W. 23rd St. E. 23rd St.
MURRAY HILL
GRAMERCY PARK
N
CHELSEA
4th Ave.
FDR Dr.
East River
0 1/2 mile
0 1/2 kilometer
W. 14th St. ㉒ E. 14th St.
EAST VILLAGE

South Manhattan
㉓
West St.
(Ave. of the Americas)
Broadway
Broadway
Bowery
Lafayette St.
 1 Columbia University
 2 Cathedral of St. John the Divine
 3 Guggenheim Museum
 4 Metropolitan Museum of Art
 5 American Museum of Natural History
 6 Whitney Museum
 7 Frick Collection
 8 Lincoln Center for the Performing Arts
 9 Columbus Circle, N.Y. Convention & Visitors Bureau
10 Carnegie Hall
11 Museum of Modern Art
12 Rockefeller Center
13 St. Patrick's Cathedral
14 United Nations
15 Grand Central Station
16 New York Public Library
17 Times Square
18 Port Authority Bus Terminal
19 Empire State Building
20 Penn Station
21 General Post Office
22 Union Square
23 Washington Square
24 World Trade Center
25 Battery Park

GREENWICH VILLAGE
W. Houston St.
E. Houston St.
LOWER EAST SIDE
SOHO
Delancey WILLIAMSBURG BRIDGE
Grand St.
Canal St.
East River Dr.
CHINATOWN
St. James Pl.
MANHATTAN BRIDGE
HOLLAND TUNNEL
TRIBECA
BROOKLYN BRIDGE
FINANCIAL DISTRICT
㉔ Wall St.
BROOKLYN
Broadway
Battery Park ㉕
BROOKLYN-BATTERY TUNNEL

Henry Hudson Parkway
Riverside Dr.
Central Park North

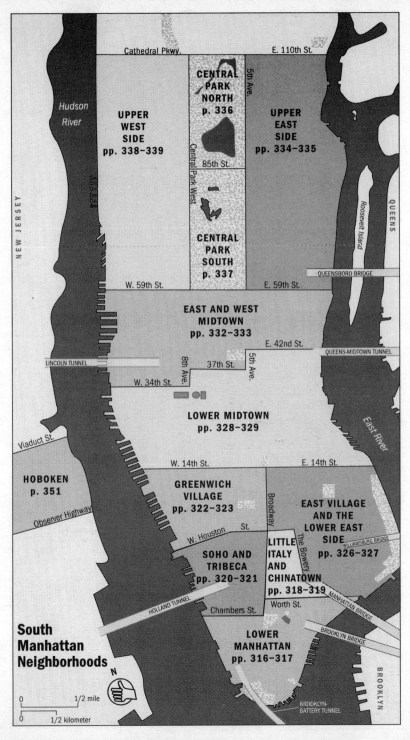

Hudson River

NEW JERSEY

Cathedral Pkwy.

E. 110th St.

CENTRAL PARK NORTH p. 336

5th Ave.

UPPER WEST SIDE pp. 338–339

Central Park West

85th St.

UPPER EAST SIDE pp. 334–335

Roosevelt Island

QUEENS

CENTRAL PARK SOUTH p. 337

W. 59th St.

E. 59th St.

QUEENSBORO BRIDGE

EAST AND WEST MIDTOWN pp. 332–333

E. 42nd St.

QUEENS-MIDTOWN TUNNEL

LINCOLN TUNNEL

8th Ave.

37th St.

5th Ave.

W. 34th St.

East River

LOWER MIDTOWN pp. 328–329

Viaduct St.

W. 14th St.

E. 14th St.

HOBOKEN p. 351

GREENWICH VILLAGE pp. 322–323

Broadway

EAST VILLAGE AND THE LOWER EAST SIDE pp. 326–327

Observer Highway

W. Houston St.

WILLIAMSBURG BRIDGE

SOHO AND TRIBECA pp. 320–321

LITTLE ITALY AND CHINATOWN pp. 318–319

The Bowery

MANHATTAN BRIDGE

HOLLAND TUNNEL

Chambers St.

Worth St.

BROOKLYN BRIDGE

South Manhattan Neighborhoods

LOWER MANHATTAN pp. 316–317

BROOKLYN

N

0   1/2 mile

0   1/2 kilometer

BROOKLYN BATTERY TUNNEL

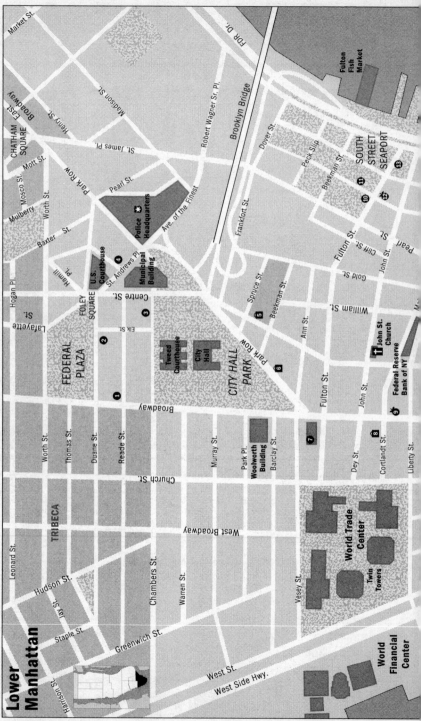

Lower Manhattan

Market St.

East Broadway

CHATHAM SQUARE

Madison St.

Henry St.

St. James Pl.

Mott St.

Mosco St.

Mulberry

Worth St.

Baxter St.

Hogan Pl.

Hamill Pl.

Lafayette St.

Park Row

Pearl St.

Police Headquarters

Ave. of the Finest

FDR Dr.

Brooklyn Bridge

Robert Wagner Sr. Pl.

Dover St.

Peck Slip

Fulton Fish Market

SOUTH STREET SEAPORT

Beekman St.

⑬

⑪

⑩

⑫

Frankfort St.

U.S. Courthouse

St. Andrews Pl.

④

Municipal Building

Centre St.

③

Spruce St.

Beekman St.

⑤

Ann St.

William St.

Cliff St.

Gold St.

John St.

Pearl St.

John St. Church

🕇

FOLEY SQUARE

Elk St.

②

FEDERAL PLAZA

①

Tweed Courthouse

City Hall

CITY HALL PARK

Park Row

⑥

Fulton St.

John St.

Federal Reserve Bank of NY

Broadway

Worth St.

Thomas St.

Duane St.

Reade St.

Murray St.

Park Pl.

Woolworth Building

Barclay St.

⑦

Dey St.

Cortlandt St.

⑧

Liberty St.

⑨

Church St.

World Trade Center

Twin Towers

TRIBECA

Leonard St.

Hudson St.

1st St.

Staple St.

Harrison St.

West Broadway

Chambers St.

Warren St.

Vesey St.

Greenwich St.

West St.

West Side Hwy.

World Financial Center

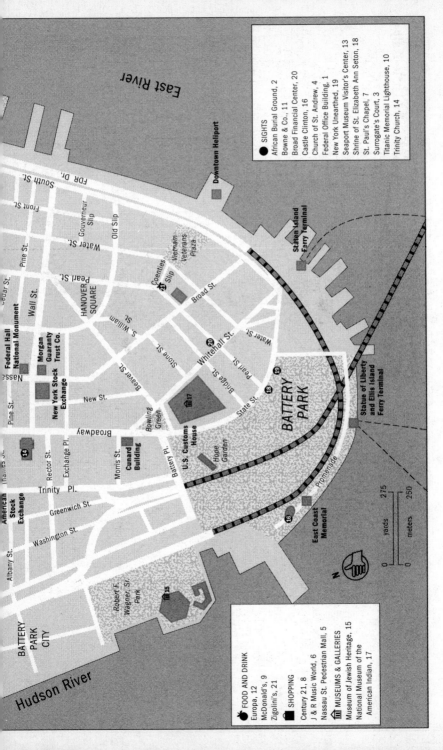

East River

Hudson River

FDR Dr.

South St.

Front St.

Gouverneur Slip

Pine St.

Water St.

Old Slip

Cedar St.

Wall St.

Pearl St.

HANOVER SQUARE

Coenties Slip

Vietnam Veterans Plaza

Broad St.

Downtown Heliport

Federal Hall National Monument

Nassau St.

Morgan Guaranty Trust Co.

S. William St.

Pine St.

New York Stock Exchange

New St.

Stone St.

Whitehall St.

Water St.

Staten Island Ferry Terminal

Beaver St.

Bridge St.

Pearl St.

Broadway

Bowling Green

Exchange Pl.

Rector St.

Trinity Pl.

Morris St.

Cunard Building

Battery Pl.

State St.

BATTERY PARK

Statue of Liberty and Ellis Island Ferry Terminal

American Stock Exchange

U.S. Customs House

Hope Garden

Albany St.

Greenwich St.

Washington St.

Promenade

East Coast Memorial

BATTERY PARK CITY

Robert F. Wagner, Jr. Park

N

yards   0   275

meters   0   250

SIGHTS
African Burial Ground, 2
Bowne & Co., 11
Broad Financial Center, 20
Castle Clinton, 16
Church of St. Andrew, 4
Federal Office Building, 1
New York Unearthed, 19
Seaport Museum Visitor's Center, 13
Shrine of St. Elizabeth Ann Seton, 18
St. Paul's Chapel, 7
Surrogate's Court, 3
Titanic Memorial Lighthouse, 10
Trinity Church, 14

FOOD AND DRINK
Europa, 12
McDonald's, 9
Zigolini's, 21

SHOPPING
Century 21, 8
J & R Music World, 6
Nassau St. Pedestrian Mall, 5

MUSEUMS & GALLERIES
Museum of Jewish Heritage, 15
National Museum of the
    American Indian, 17

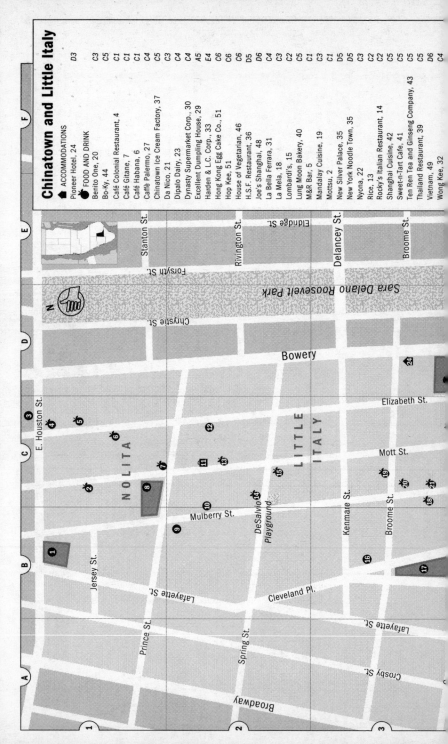

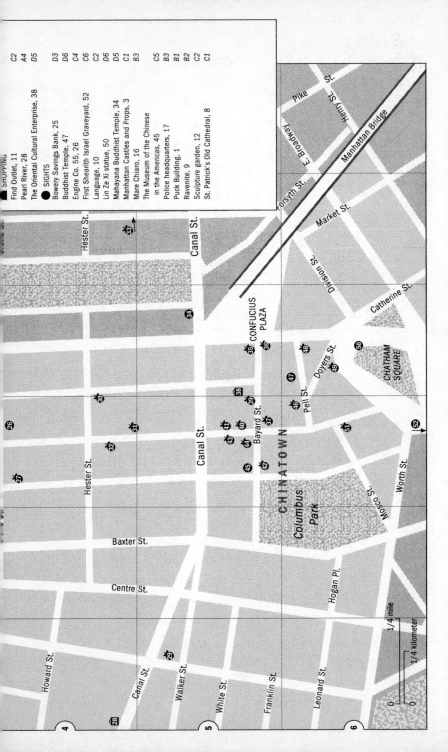

SoHo and TriBeCa

🍎 FOOD AND DRINK

Bar Odeon, 61	B6
Brisas del Caribe, 38	D3
Bubby's, 58	B5
Dean and Deluca, 27	D2
El Teddy's, 66	C5
Gourmet Garage, 40	D3
Jerry's, 17	D2
Kelley and Ping Asian Grocery and Noodle Shop, 14	C2
Le Gamin Cafe, 3	B2
Lucky's Juice Joint, 7	C1
Lupe's East L.A. Kitchen, 52	B3
Pakistan Tea House, 63	C7
Penang, 35	D2
Space Untitled, 15	C1
Uptown Juice Bar, 62	C7
Yaffa's Tea Room, 60	A6

🛍 SHOPPING

A Photographer's Place, 29	D2
Agnès B., 13	C2
Anna Sui, 16	C2
Armani, 24	D2
Betsey Johnson, 9	C2
Canal Jean Co, 37	D3
Cynthia Rowley, 12	C2
Dolce & Gabbana, 33	D2
Final Home, 32	D2
Girlprops.com, 5	C2
INA, 25	
Joseph, 16	C2
K. Trimming, 36	D3
Miu Miu, 13	C2
Sephora, 30	D2
Todd Oldham, 10	C2
Universal News and Cafe Corp, 39	C1
Untitled, 4	C2

🏛 MUSEUMS & GALLERIES

Artists Space, 41	C4
Deitch Projects, 42	C3
Dia Center for the Arts, 8	C2
Drawing Center, 45	C3
Exit Art/The First World, 31	D2
Guggenheim Museum SoHo, 22	D2
Illustration House, 34	D2
Museum for African Art, 21	D1
New Museum of Contemporary Art, 23	D2
New York City Fire Museum, 55	A3
POP, 6	C1
Printed Matter, Inc., 48	C3
Shakespeare's Fulcrum, 46	C3
Staley-Wise, 26	D2
Thread Waxing Space, 20	D1
Tony Shafrazi, 11	C2
Wooster Projects, 43	C2

♪ ARTS & ENTERTAINMENT

Angelika Film Center, 19	D1
Film Forum, 1	A1
Knitting Factory, 65	C6
SoHo Repertory Theater, 67	C5
SoHo Think Tank Theater, 47	C3
Wetlands Preserve, 57	A5

● SIGHTS

TriBeCa Grill, 59	A6

🍷 NIGHTLIFE

Cafe Noir, 53	B4
Circa Tabac, 51	B3
Fanelli's, 28	D2
Kilimanjaro, 64	D6
Lucky Strike, 44	C4
MercBar, 18	D1
Milady's, 49	B2
Naked Lunch Bar and Lounge, 54	B4
NV and 289 Lounge, 56	A3
Scharmann's, 50	C3
X-R Bar, 2	B1

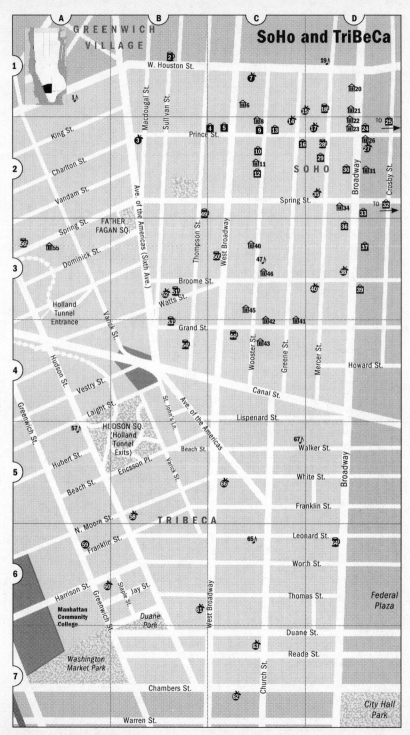

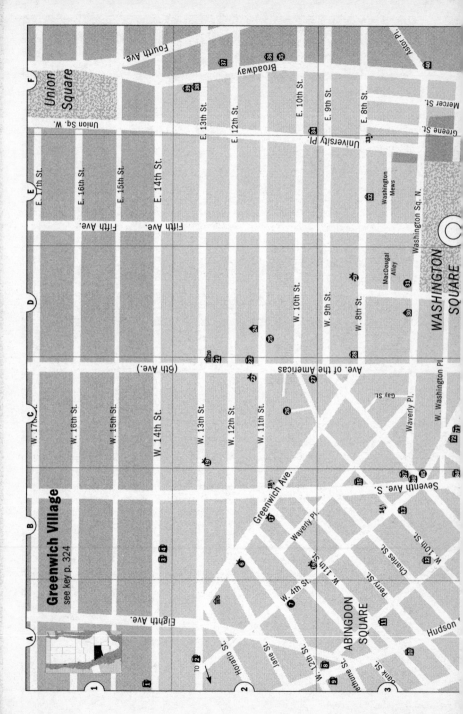

Greenwich Village
see key p. 324

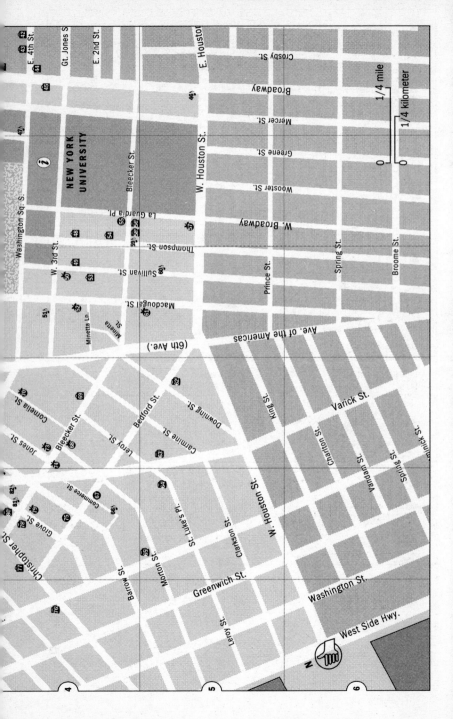

Greenwich Village

see map pp. 322–323

East Village and Lower East Side
see map pp. 326–327

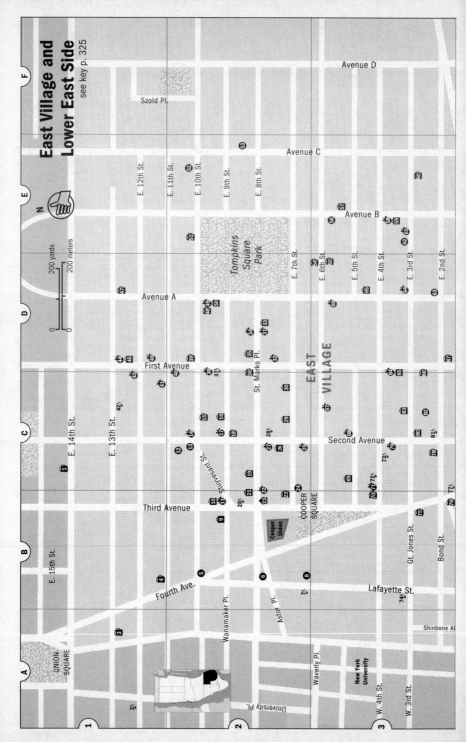

East Village and
Lower East Side

see key p. 325

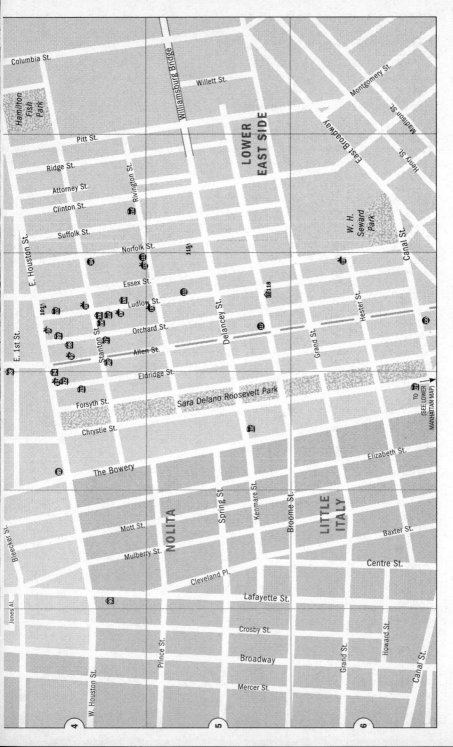

Columbia St.

Hamilton Fish Park

Willett St.

Williamsburg Bridge

Montgomery St.

Madison St.

Pitt St.

Ridge St.

East Broadway

Attorney St.

Henry St.

LOWER EAST SIDE

Clinton St.

Rivington St.

Suffolk St.

W. H. Seward Park

E. Houston St.

Norfolk St.

115

Canal St.

Essex St.

118

Hester St.

E. 1st St.

Ludlow St.

Delancey St.

101

Orchard St.

Grand St.

117

Stanton St.

Allen St.

Eldridge St.

TO 32 (SEE LOWER MANHATTAN MAP)

Forsyth St.

Sara Delano Roosevelt Park

Chrystie St.

Elizabeth St.

The Bowery

NOLITA

Spring St.

Kenmare St.

Broome St.

LITTLE ITALY

Baxter St.

Mott St.

Bleecker St.

Mulberry St.

Centre St.

Cleveland Pl.

Jones Al.

Lafayette St.

Crosby St.

Prince St.

Broadway

Grand St.

Howard St.

Canal St.

W. Houston St.

Mercer St.

4

5

6

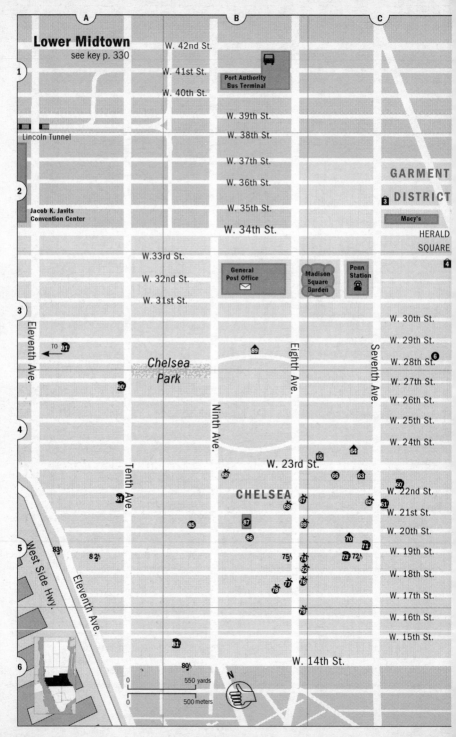

Lower Midtown
see key p. 330

W. 42nd St.
W. 41st St.
W. 40th St.

1

Port Authority
Bus Terminal

Lincoln Tunnel

W. 39th St.
W. 38th St.
W. 37th St.
W. 36th St.
W. 35th St.
W. 34th St.

2

Jacob K. Javits
Convention Center

GARMENT

DISTRICT

3

Macy's

HERALD

SQUARE

4

W.33rd St.
W. 32nd St.
W. 31st St.

General
Post Office

Madison
Square
Garden

Penn
Station

3

Eleventh Ave.

TO **31**

Chelsea
Park

89

Eighth Ave.

Seventh Ave.

W. 30th St.
W. 29th St.
W. 28th St.
W. 27th St.
W. 26th St.
W. 25th St.
W. 24th St.

6

90

4

Ninth Ave.

65
64

W. 23rd St.

88
66 **63**

CHELSEA

60

Tenth Ave.

84

67
68

62
61

W. 22nd St.
W. 21st St.

87
85
86

69

W. 20th St.

70
71

5

West Side Hwy.

83

82

75
74
73 **72**
92
78 **77** **76**

W. 19th St.
W. 18th St.
W. 17th St.

Eleventh Ave.

79

W. 16th St.
W. 15th St.

31

80

W. 14th St.

6

0 ———— 550 yards

0 ———— 500 meters

N

D   E   F

Bryant Park

New York Public Library

E. 42nd St.

E. 41st St.

American Standard Building

E. 40th St.

E. 39th St.

MURRAY

1

E. 38th St.

HILL

E. 37th St.

(VEHICULAR TUNNEL BELOW STREET)

2♪

Pierpont Morgan Library

E. 36th St.

E. 35th St.

Madison Ave.

18

17

Park Ave. S.

Empire State Building

E. 34th St.

FDR Dr.

19

Lexington Ave.

E. 33rd St.

5

20

E. 32nd St.

16

15

21

E. 31st St.

Fifth Ave.

22

Third Ave.

Second Ave.

First Ave.

E. 30th St.

Broadway

14

13

23

E. 29th St.

7

E. 28th St.

8

12

E. 27th St. **24**♪

9

11

E. 26th St. **25**

GRAMERCY

E. 25th St.

Madison Square

26

PARK

E. 24th St.

10

E. 23rd St.

Avenue of the Americas (Sixth Ave.)

59

58

53

52

E. 22nd St.

E. 21st St.

Gramercy Park

57

27 28

E. 20th St.

56

54

55

51

44

E. 19th St.

43

E. 18th St.

29

30

50

49

45

42

40♪

E. 17th St.

31

48

47

46

Union Square

38♪

37

39

Irving Pl.

E. 16th St.

Stuyvesant Square

33♪

E. 15th St.

36

34♪

32

E. 14th St.

35♪

W. 13th St.

E. 13th St.

Lower Midtown
see map pp. 328–329

🏠 ACCOMMODATIONS

Carlton Arms Hotel, 26	E4
Chelsea Center Hostel, 89	B3
Chelsea Inn, 48	D5
Chelsea International Hostel, 70	C5
Chelsea Savoy Hotel, 63	C4
Gershwin Hotel, 9	D4
Hotel 17, 31	F5
Hotel Grand Union, 16	E3
International Student Hospice, 20	E3
Madison Hotel, 12	E4
Senton Hotel, 8	D4
ThirtyThirty, 14	D3
YMCA–McBurney, 64	C4

🍴 FOOD AND DRINK

Basta Pasta, 49	D5
Bendix Diner, 68	B5
Blue Moon Mexican Café, 76	B5
Caesar's, 62	C5
Candela, 39	E6
Chat 'n' Chew, 47	D5
Coffee Shop Bar, 46	E5
Food Bar, 77	B5
Guy & Gallard, 19	E2
Intermezzo, 69	B5
Jai-Ya, 23	E3
Kitchen, 67	B5
La Chinita Linda Restaurant, 92	B5
Mary Ann's, 79	C6
Moonstruck, 21	F3
Negril, 88	B4
Pete's Tavern, 29	E5
Soups on Seventeen, 78	B5
Spring Joy, 74	B5
Sunburnt Espresso Bar, 30	E5
Tibetan Kitchen, 22	E3
Zen Palate, 36	E6

🛍 SHOPPING

Books of Wonder, 50	D5
The Complete Traveller Bookstore, 17	E2
Kikko Import, Inc., 7	D3
Lord and Taylor, 1	D1
Manhattan Mall, 4	C3
Midnight Records, 65	C4
Nobody Beats the Wiz, 5	D3
Reminiscence, 59	D4
Revolution Books, 55	D5
Rock and Soul, 3	C2
Throb, 32	F6
Weiss and Mahoney, 51	D5

🏛 SIGHTS

69th Regiment Armory, 25	E4
Andy Warhol's Factory, 15	D3
Church of the Incarnation, 18	E2
Church of the Transfiguration, 13	D3
Cushman Row, 85	B5
Flatiron Building, 52	D4
Flower District, 6	C3
General Theological Seminary, 86	B5
Hotel Chelsea, 66	C4
Metropolitan Life	
Insurance Tower, 10	E4
National Arts Club, 27	E5
New York Life Insurance Building, 11	E4
The Player's Club, 28	E5
St. Peter's Church, 87	B5
The Theodore Roosevelt	
Birthplace, 44	E5
Union Square Savings Bank, 57	E6

🍺 NIGHTLIFE

B.M.W. Bar, 61	C5
Billiard Club, 73	C5
Centrofly, 56	D5
Cheetah, 57	D5
Chelsea Bar and Billiards, 54	D5
Gotham Comedy Club, 50	D4
Heartland Brewery, 45	E5
Lemon, 42	E5
Lola, 58	D4
Ohm, 53	D4
Old Town Bar and Grill, 43	E5
Passerby, 81	B6
Peter McManus, 71	C5
Tramps, 59	D5
Tunnel, 91	A3
Twilo, 90	A4
Upright Citizens Brigade Theater, 60	C4
Wild Lily Tea Room, 89	A5

♪ ARTS & ENTERTAINMENT

Bowlmor, 35	E6
Chelsea Piers, 83	A5
The Cooler, 80	B6
Dance Theater Workshop, 72	C5
De La Guarda, 38	E6
Irving Plaza, 33	E6
Joyce Theater, 75	B5
The Kitchen, 82	A5
Repertorio Español, 24	E4
Ricki Lake Show, 2	D2
Union Square Theater, 40	E5
Vineyard Theater Company's	
Dimson Theater, 34	E6

East and West Midtown
see map pp. 332–333

🏠 ACCOMMODATIONS

Aladdin Hotel, 72	B4
Big Apple Hostel, 56	C4
Broadway Inn, 65	F3
Pickwick Arms Hotel, 35	C3
Portland Square Hotel, 54	C3
YMCA–Vanderbilt, 37	F3

🍎 FOOD AND DRINK

Aureole, 16	E1
Becco, 70	B4
Carnegie Delicatessen, 5	C2
Coldwaters, 33	F3
Dosanko, 43	E5
Food Emporium, 34	F3
Fortune Garden, 38	F4
Hourglass Tavern, 71	B4
Le Beaujolais, 70	B4
Manganaro's, 75	B5
Original Fresco Tortillas, 74	B5
Sapporo, 52	C3
Sardi's, 62	C4
Taipei Noodle House, 33	F3
Teuscher Chocolatier, 45	D3

💼 SHOPPING

Asahiya Bookstore, 42	E4
Bergdorff-Goodman, 18	D2
Coliseum Book, 2	C2
The Counter Spy Shop, 44	D3
The Drama Book Shop, 53	C3
Dollar Bills, 41	D4
F.A.O. Schwarz, 17	D2
Fine Line, 29	E2
Gotham Book Mart, 48	D3
Hacker Art Books, 14	D2
Hammacher Schlemmer, 27	E2
Nike Town, 23	D2
Saks Fifth Avenue, 46	D3
Tiffany & Co., 22	D2
Warner Bros. Studio Store, 21	D2

🏛 MUSEUMS & GALLERIES

American Craft Museum, 11	D3
Christie's, 47	D3
Fuller Building, 26	E2
International Center of Photography, 58	D4
Japan Society, 36	F3
Museum of Television and Radio, 12	D3
Pace Gallery, 25	E2

🎵 ARTS & ENTERTAINMENT

Birdland, 68	B4
Carnegie Hall, 6	C2
City Center, 7	C2
Lamb's, 57	C4
Late Show with David Letterman, 3	C2
Manhattan Theater Club, 8	C2
NBC Studios, 50	D3
Playwrights Horizons, 73	B4
Primary Stages, 67	B4
Roseland, 4	C3
Samuel Beckett Theater, 73	B4
Shubert Theater, 64	C4
Swing 46, 69	B4
Ziegfeld, 10	C2

⚫ SIGHTS

The Algonquin Hotel, 59	D4
Central Synagogue, 30	E2
Citicorp Center, 31	E2
City Center Theater, 9	C2
Crown Building, 19	D2
The Dramatists Guild, 60	C4
GE Building, 49	D3
Guardian Angel Headquarters, 66	B3
The James A. Farley Building, 76	B6
John Jay College of Criminal Justice, 1	A2
Madison Lexington Venture Building, 28	E2
The New York Times, 61	C4
Pulitzer Fountain, 15	D1
Radio City Music Hall, 51	D3
Schubert Alley, 63	C4
Sony Plaza, 24	D2
St. Bartholomew's Church, 32	E3
Times Square Visitors' Center, 55	C4
Trump Tower, 20	D2
Tudor Park, 40	E4
Unicef House, 39	F4
University Club, 13	D2

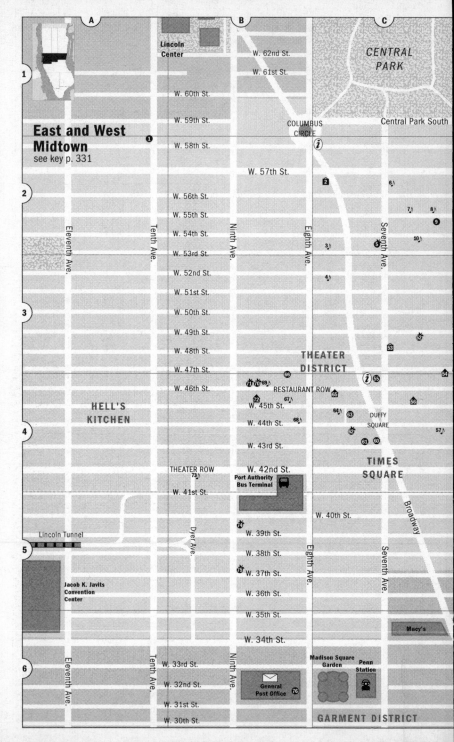

East and West Midtown
see key p. 331

CENTRAL PARK

Lincoln Center

W. 62nd St.
W. 61st St.
W. 60th St.
W. 59th St.
W. 58th St.
W. 57th St.
W. 56th St.
W. 55th St.
W. 54th St.
W. 53rd St.
W. 52nd St.
W. 51st St.
W. 50th St.
W. 49th St.
W. 48th St.
W. 47th St.
W. 46th St.
W. 45th St.
W. 44th St.
W. 43rd St.
W. 42nd St.
W. 41st St.
W. 40th St.
W. 39th St.
W. 38th St.
W. 37th St.
W. 36th St.
W. 35th St.
W. 34th St.
W. 33rd St.
W. 32nd St.
W. 31st St.
W. 30th St.

COLUMBUS CIRCLE

Central Park South

Eleventh Ave.
Tenth Ave.
Ninth Ave.
Eighth Ave.
Seventh Ave.
Broadway

THEATER DISTRICT

RESTAURANT ROW

HELL'S KITCHEN

TIMES SQUARE

DUFFY SQUARE

THEATER ROW

Port Authority Bus Terminal

Dyer Ave.

Lincoln Tunnel

Jacob K. Javits Convention Center

Macy's

Madison Square Garden

Penn Station

General Post Office

GARMENT DISTRICT

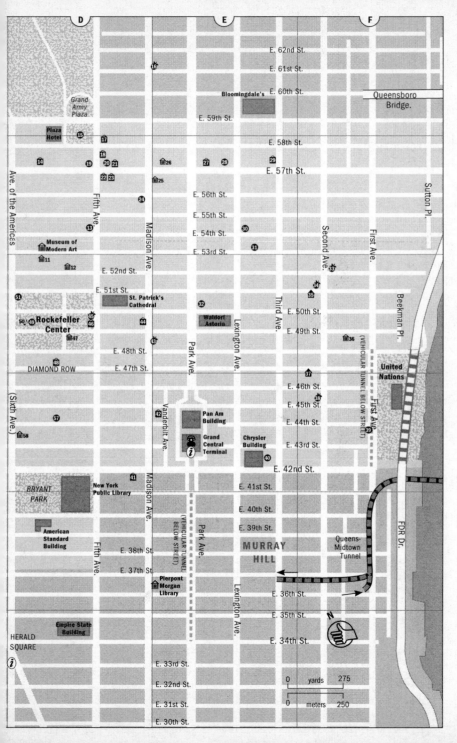

D E F

E. 62nd St.
E. 61st St.
E. 60th St.
Queensboro
Bridge.

Grand
Army
Plaza

Bloomingdale's
E. 59th St.

Plaza
Hotel 15 17
E. 58th St.

14 18
19 20 21 26 27 28 29
E. 57th St.
22 23 25

24
E. 56th St.

E. 55th St.

13
E. 54th St. 30

E. 53rd St. 31

Museum of
Modern Art
11 12
E. 52nd St.

51
E. 51st St.
St. Patrick's
Cathedral 32
34
35
50 49 Rockefeller
Center E. 50th St.

47 44
49 E. 49th St.

DIAMOND ROW 45
43 E. 48th St. 36

48 E. 47th St. 37
United
Nations
E. 46th St.

57 E. 45th St. 38

42 Pan Am
Building E. 44th St. 39

58 Grand
Central
Terminal Chrysler
Building E. 43rd St.

40 E. 42nd St.

41 New York
Public Library E. 41st St.

BRYANT
PARK E. 40th St.

E. 39th St.

American
Standard
Building MURRAY
HILL Queens-
Midtown
Tunnel

E. 38th St.
E. 37th St.
Pierpont
Morgan
Library E. 36th St.

E. 35th St.
N

Empire State
Building E. 34th St.

HERALD
SQUARE
E. 33rd St.

E. 32nd St.
0 yards 275

E. 31st St.
0 meters 250

E. 30th St.

Ave. of the Americas
Fifth Ave.
Madison Ave.
Second Ave.
First Ave.
Sutton Pl.
Beekman Pl.
Lexington Ave.
Third Ave.
Park Ave.
Vanderbilt Ave.
(Sixth Ave.)
Fifth Ave.
(VEHICULAR TUNNEL BELOW STREET)
Lexington Ave.
FDR Dr.
(VEHICULAR TUNNEL BELOW STREET)

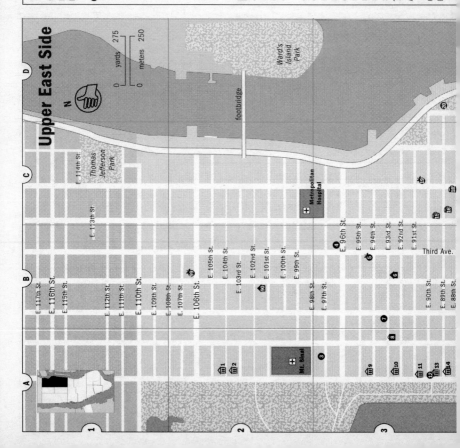

Upper East Side

▲ ACCOMMODATIONS
DeHirsch Residence, 16 · B3
Manhattan Youth Castle, 4 · B2
The Suite Sound of Comfort Inn

⚬ FOOD AND DRINK
Barking Dog Luncheonette, 15 · B3
BBQ, 43 · B5
Candle Café, 38 · B5
Ecce Panis, 57 · B6
EJ's Luncheonette, 42 · B5
El Pollo, 21 · C3
Grace's Marketplace, 44 · B5
Hale and Hearty Soups, 58 · B6
Jackson Hole Wyoming, 59 · B6
La Fonda Boricua, 1 · B2
Luke's Bar and Grill, 34 · B4
Papaya King, 24 · B4
Viand, 69 · A6

🛍 SHOPPING
Argosy Bookstore, 64 · B5
Barneys NY, 70 · A6
Bloomingdale's, 62 · B6
Chick Darrow's Fun Antiques
 & Collectibles, 61 · C6
Corner Bookstore, 8 · A3
Crawford Doyle, 30 · A4
Diesel, 63 · B6
Encore, 28 · A4
Game Show, 27 · B4
HMV, 25 · B4
Michael's, 32 · A4
Rita Ford Music Boxes, 55 · A6
Star Magic, 26 · B4

🏛 MUSEUMS
Asia Society, 48 · B5
Asia Society (temporary), 66 · B6
Cooper-Hewitt, 11 · A3
El Museo del Barrio, 2 · A2

♪ ARTS & ENTERTAINMENT
Dicapo Opera Theater, 39 · B5
Cultural Institutes:
Alliance Française, 66 · B6
Americas Society, 52 · B6
China Institute, 56 · B6
Goethe Institute, 29 · A4
Italian Cultural Institute, 50 · B5
Spanish Institute, 51 · B5

● SIGHTS
Campbell Funeral Chapel, 31 · A4
Gracie Mansion, 22 · D3
Henderson Place Historic District, 23 · D4
Hunter College, 47 · B6
Houses of Worship:
Christ Church, 67 · A6
Emanu-El, 54 · A6
Heavenly Rest, 12 · A3
Holy Trinity, 19 · C4
Islamic Cultural Center, 6 · B3
Russian Orthodox Church, 7 · B3
St. Jean Baptiste, 40 · B5
St. Nicholas Russian Orthodox
 Cathedral, 5 · A3
Old Boys Clubs:
Groller, 67 · B6
Knickerbocker, 71 · A6
Lotos, 53 · A6
The Metropolitan, 72 · A6
Union, 46 · B5

🎭 NIGHTLIFE
American Trash, 35 · C5
Auction House, 18 · C3
Brother Jimmy's Carolina
 Kitchen BBQ, 36 · C5
Comic Strip Live, 33 · B4
Dangerfield's, 60 · C6
Match, Uptown, 68 · A6

Upper East Side

N

0 yards 275

0 meters 250

*Ward's
Island
Park*

footbridge

Thomas
Jefferson
Park

Metropolitan
Hospital

Mt. Sinai

E. 117th St.
E. 116th St.
E. 115th St.

E. 114th St.
E. 113th St.

E. 112th St.
E. 111th St.
E. 110th St.

E. 109th St.
E. 108th St.
E. 107th St.
E. 106th St.

E. 105th St.
E. 104th St.
E. 103rd St.
E. 102nd St.
E. 101st St.
E. 100th St.
E. 99th St.

E. 98th St.
E. 97th St.

E. 96th St.
E. 95th St.
E. 94th St.
E. 93rd St.
E. 92nd St.
E. 91st St.

E. 90th St.
E. 89th St.
E. 88th St.

Third Ave.

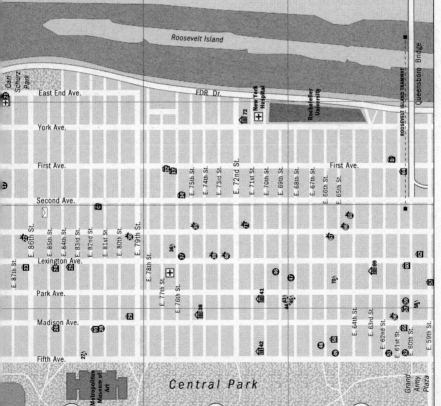

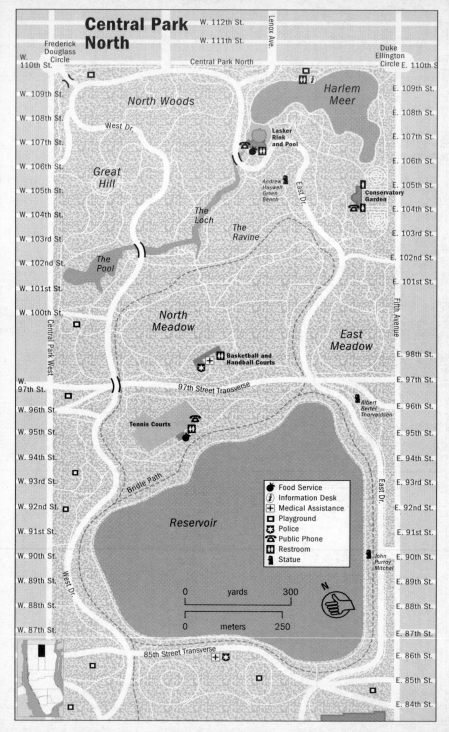

Central Park North

W. 112th St.

W. 111th St.

Lenox Ave.

Frederick Douglass Circle

Central Park North

W. 110th St.

Duke Ellington Circle E. 110th St

W. 109th St.

E. 109th St.

North Woods

Harlem Meer

W. 108th St.

E. 108th St.

West Dr.

W. 107th St.

Lasker Rink and Pool

E. 107th St.

W. 106th St.

E. 106th St.

Great Hill

W. 105th St.

Andrew Haswell Green Bench

East Dr.

Conservatory Garden

E. 105th St.

W. 104th St.

The Loch

E. 104th St.

W. 103rd St.

The Ravine

E. 103rd St.

W. 102nd St.

The Pool

E. 102nd St.

W. 101st St.

E. 101st St.

W. 100th St.

North Meadow

Fifth Avenue

W.

Central Park West

East Meadow

E. 98th St.

Basketball and Handball Courts

W. 97th St.

97th Street Transverse

E. 97th St.

W. 96th St.

Albert Bertel Thorvaldsen

E. 96th St.

W. 95th St.

Tennis Courts

E. 95th St.

W. 94th St.

E. 94th St.

W. 93rd St.

Bridle Path

E. 93rd St.

W. 92nd St.

Reservoir

E. 92nd St.

W. 91st St.

E. 91st St.

W. 90th St.

John Purroy Mitchel

E. 90th St.

W. 89th St.

West Dr.

East Dr.

E. 89th St.

Legend

🍴 Food Service
ℹ️ Information Desk
✚ Medical Assistance
☐ Playground
✿ Police
☎ Public Phone
🚻 Restroom
🗿 Statue

W. 88th St.

0   yards   300

E. 88th St.

W. 87th St.

0   meters   250

N

E. 87th St.

85th Street Transverse

E. 86th St.

E. 85th St.

E. 84th St.

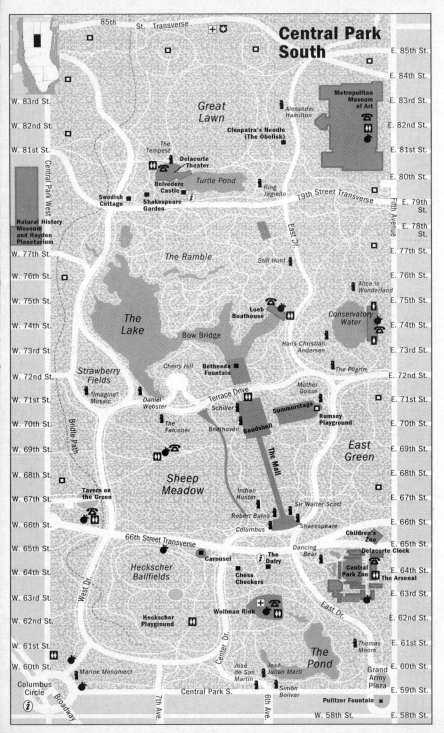

Central Park South

85th St. Transverse

E. 85th St.

E. 84th St.

W. 83rd St.

Great Lawn

Metropolitan Museum of Art

E. 83rd St.

Alexander Hamilton

W. 82nd St.

E. 82nd St.

Cleopatra's Needle (The Obelisk)

W. 81st St.

The Tempest

E. 81st St.

Delacorte Theater

E. 80th St.

Belvedere Castle

Turtle Pond

King Jagiello

Swedish Cottage

79th Street Transverse

E. 79th St.

Shakespeare Garden

Natural History Museum and Hayden Planetarium

E. 78th St.

Central Park West

East Dr.

W. 77th St.

The Ramble

W. 76th St.

Still Hunt

E. 77th St.

E. 76th St.

Alice in Wonderland

W. 75th St.

Loeb Boathouse

E. 75th St.

Conservatory Water

W. 74th St.

The Lake

E. 74th St.

Bow Bridge

W. 73rd St.

Hans Christian Andersen

E. 73rd St.

Cherry Hill

Bethesda Fountain

The Pilgrim

W. 72nd St.

Strawberry Fields

E. 72nd St.

"Imagine" Mosaic

Daniel Webster

Terrace Drive

Mother Goose

W. 71st St.

Schiller

Summerstage

E. 71st St.

The Falconer

Beethoven

Bandshell

Rumsey Playground

W. 70th St.

E. 70th St.

Bridle Path

The Mall

East Green

W. 69th St.

E. 69th St.

W. 68th St.

Sheep Meadow

E. 68th St.

Tavern on the Green

Indian Hunter

W. 67th St.

E. 67th St.

Sir Walter Scott

W. 66th St.

Robert Burns

Columbus

Shakespeare

Children's Zoo

66 Street Transverse

E. 65th St.

Delacorte Clock

W. 65th St.

Carousel

The Dairy

Dancing Bear

Central Park Zoo

West Dr.

Heckscher Ballfields

Chess Checkers

E. 64th St.

The Arsenal

W. 64th St.

W. 63rd St.

E. 63rd St.

Wollman Rink

W. 62nd St.

Heckscher Playground

Center Dr.

East Dr.

Thomas Moore

E. 61st St.

W. 61st St.

The Pond

W. 60th St.

Marine Monument

Jose de San Martin

Jose Julian Marti

Grand Army Plaza

E. 60th St.

Columbus Circle

Simón Bolivar

E. 59th St.

Broadway

7th Ave.

Central Park S.

6th Ave.

Pulitzer Fountain

W. 58th St.

E. 58th St.

Upper West Side

▲ ACCOMMODATIONS

The Amsterdam Inn, 36	C4
Central Park Hostel, 5	D2
Hayden Hall, 38	C4
Hotel Belleclaire, 34	C4
International Student Center, 17	D3
Jazz on the Park, 4	D1
Malibu Studios Hotel, 7	C2
New York International HI-AYH Hostel, 6	C2
On the Ave., 37	C4
West End Studios, 9	C4
West Side Inn, 2	B2
West Side YMCA, 59	C1
	D6

● FOOD AND DRINK

Big Nick's Pizza and Burger Joint, 33	C4
Brother Jimmy's, 26	C4
Café La Fortuna, 44	D5
Café Lalo, 22	C4
Café Mozart, 51	C5
D+S Plaza, 52	C5
drip, 21	C4
Good Enough to Eat, 21	C4
Gray's Papaya, 46	C5
H&H Bagels, 30	C4
Ivy's Cafe, 45	C5
La Caridad 78 Restaurant, 32	C4
The Lemongrass Grill, 12	C2
Ollie's, 53	C5
Tamarind, 26	C4
Zabar's, 29	C4
Mama Mexico, 8	C2

● SHOPPING

Allan and Suzi, 27	C4
Applause Theater and Cinema Books, 47	C5
Gryphon Bookshops, 28	C4
Gryphon Record Shop, 48	C5
Maxilla & Mandible, 25	C4
Murder Ink, 13	C3
Ordning & Reda, 43	D5

Upper West Side

Central Park

Central Park North (W. 110th St.)

W. 112th St.
W. 111th St.
Cathedral Pkwy.
W. 109th St.
W. 108th St.
W. 107th St.
W. 106th St.
W. 105th St.
W. 104th St.
W. 103rd St.
W. 102nd St.
W. 101st St.
W. 100th St.
W. 99th St.
W. 98th St.
W. 97th St.
W. 96th St.
W. 95th St.
W. 94th St.
W. 93rd St.
W. 92nd St.
W. 91st St.
W. 90th St.
W. 89th St.
W. 88th St.
W. 87th St.
W. 86th St.
W. 85th St.

Broadway
Amsterdam Ave.
Broadway

Riverside Park

Henry Hudson Pkwy.

Hudson River

MUSEUMS & GALLERIES

The Children's Museum of Manhattan, 23 — C4
New York Historical Society, 41 — D4

ARTS & ENTERTAINMENT

Beacon Theatre, 50 — C5
Bloomingdale School of Music, 1 — B1
Claremont Stables, 15 — C3
Live with Regis (WABC), 56 — D5
Mannes College of Music, 20 — C3
Merkin Concert Hall, 54 — C5
Symphony Space, 11 — C2
The View (ABC), 55 — B5
at Lincoln Center:
Alice Tully Hall, 63 — C6
Avery Fisher Hall, 62 — C6
Metropolitan Opera House, 67 — C6
New York Public Library for
the Performing Arts, 66 — C6
New York State Theater, 61 — C6
Vivian Beaumont Theater, 65 — C6
Walter E. Reade Theater, 64 — C6

● **SIGHTS**

Ansonia Hotel, 49 — C5
Apthorp Apartments, 31 — C4
Bib e House, 60 — D6
Dakota Apartments, 42 — D5
El Dorado Apartments, 18 — D3
Hotel des Artistes, 57 — D5
Lotus Garden, 10 — B2
New York Convention Center and
Visitors Bureau, 69 — D6
New York Society for Ethical Culture, 58 — D6
Soldiers and Sailors Monument, 14 — B3
Trump International Hotel and Towers, 68 — D6
West Side Community Garden, 16 — C3

📷 **NIGHTLIFE**

Eve yn Lounge, 39 — C4
Hi-Life Bar and Grill, 24 — C4
Merchants, 19 — C3
Potion Lounge, 40 — C4
Yog's, 35 — C4
Smoke, 3 — B1

Harlem and Washington Heights

🏠 ACCOMMODATIONS

Crystal's Castle Bed & Breakfast, 46	E6
New York Bed and Breakfast, 47	E7
Sugar Hill International House, 10	D4
Uptown Hostel, 44	E6

🍎 FOOD AND DRINK

Amir's Falafel, 29	C7
Copeland's, 7	C4
Emily's, 49	E7
Fairway, 20	C5
The Hungarian Pastry Shop, 33	C7
Jamaican Hot Pot, 19	D5
Koronet Pizza, 31	C7
La Marmite, 38	D6
La Rosita Restaurant, 32	C7
Manna's Too!!, 17	E5
Massawa, 27	D6
Mill Korean Restaurant, 34	C7
Obaa Koryoe, 22	C6
Sisters, 43	E6
Sylvia's, 41	E6
Toast, 23	C6
Tom's Restaurant, 30	C7

🛍 SHOPPING

Liberation Bookstore, 18	E5
Sugar Hill Thrift Shop, 9	D4

🏛 MUSEUMS & GALLERIES

Audubon Terrace Museum Group, 6	C3
Cloisters, 1	A2
Studio Museum, 40	E6

♪ ARTS & ENTERTAINMENT

Apollo Theatre, 37	D6
Cotton Club, 21	C6
Lenox Lounge, 42	E6
Londel's, 14	D5
Manhattan School of Music, 24	C6
Showman's Café, 36	D6
St. Nick's Pub, 8	D4

● SIGHTS

The Abyssinian Baptist Church, 15	E5
Audubon Ballroom, 4	C3
Barnard College, 28	C7
Cathedral of St. John the Divine, 35	D7
City College, 12	D5
Grant's Tomb, 25	C6
Hale House, 45	E6
Hamilton Grange, 11	D4
Masjid Malcolm Shabazz, 48	E7
Morris-Jumel Mansion, 5	D3
Overlook Terrace, 2	A3
Riverside Church, 26	C6
The Schomburg Center for Research in Black Culture, 16	E5
Teresa Hotel, 39	E6
Yeshiva University, 3	B3

☕ NIGHTLIFE

Sugar Shack, 13	D5

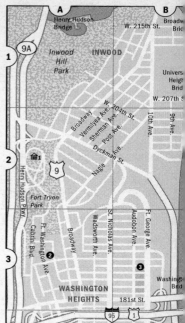

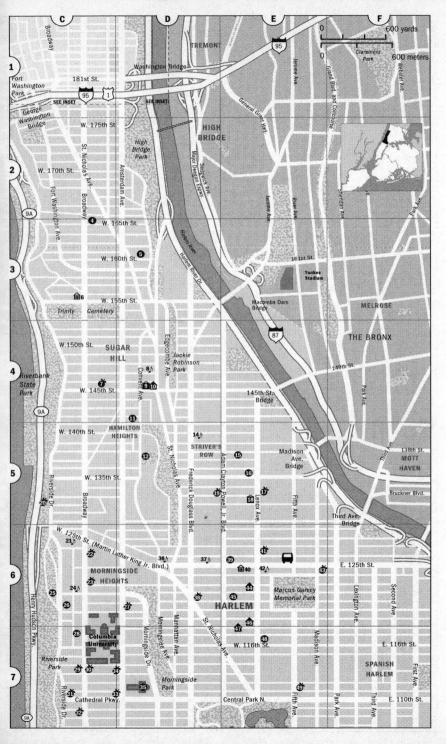

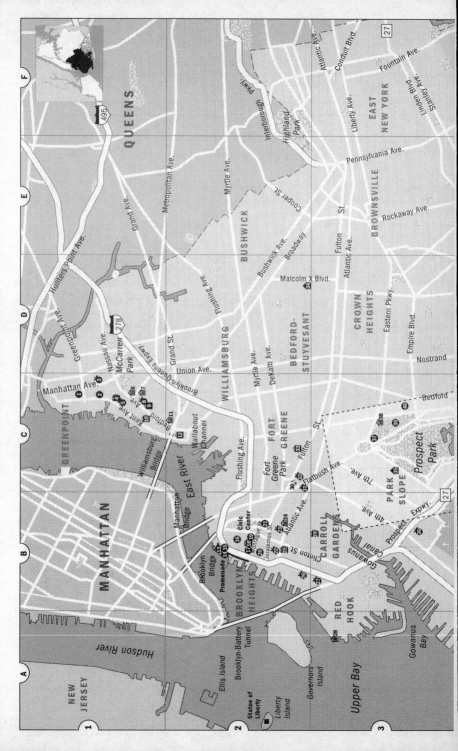

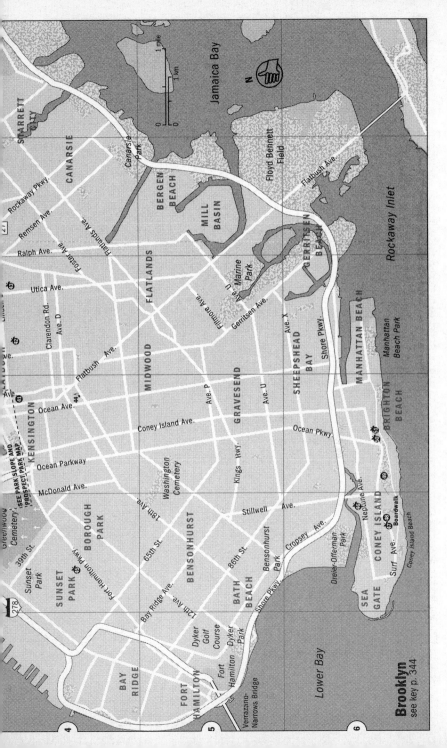

Brooklyn
see key p. 344

Jamaica Bay

STARRETT CITY

CANARSIE

Canarsie Park

Rockaway Pkwy.

Remsen Ave.

Ralph Ave.

Flatlands Ave.

Foster Ave.

Utica Ave.

Clarendon Rd.

Ave. D

Flatbush Ave.

Ocean Ave.

Coney Island Ave.

Ocean Parkway

McDonald Ave.

39th St.

Sunset Park

SUNSET PARK

BOROUGH PARK

Fort Hamilton Pkwy.

65th St.

Bay Ridge Ave.

12th Ave.

13th Ave.

18th Ave.

Washington Cemetery

BENSONHURST

Kings Hwy.

Stillwell Ave.

86th St.

Ave. P

Ave. U

BATH BEACH

Bensonhurst Park

Shore Pkwy.

Cropsey Ave.

Dreier-Offerman Park

SEA GATE

Surf Ave.

Neptune Ave.

Boardwalk

CONEY ISLAND

Coney Island Beach

BRIGHTON BEACH

Ocean Pkwy.

SHEEPSHEAD BAY

Ave. X

GRAVESEND

MIDWOOD

FLATLANDS

BERGEN BEACH

MILL BASIN

Marine Park

Fillmore Ave.

Gerritsen Ave.

GERRITSEN BEACH

MANHATTAN BEACH

Manhattan Beach Park

Shore Pkwy.

Flatbush Ave.

Floyd Bennett Field

Rockaway Inlet

Shore Pkwy.

Lower Bay

BAY RIDGE

FORT HAMILTON

Fort Hamilton

Dyker Park

Dyker Golf Course

Verrazano-Narrows Bridge

Greenwood Cemetery

KENSINGTON

SEE PARK SLOPE AND PROSPECT PARK MAP

278

1 mile

1 km

N

4

5

6

17

Brooklyn
see map pp. 342–343

🛏 ACCOMMODATIONS

Akwaaba Mansion, 34	D2
Bed & Breakfast on the Park, 35	C3

🍎 FOOD AND DRINK

Bliss, 8	C1
Brooklyn Moon, 32	C2
Caravan, 22	B2
Damascus Bakery, 22	B2
Efe International, 50	C6
Ferdinando's, 26	B2
Fountain Cafe, 22	B2
Fresco Tortilla Plus, 23	B2
Gia Lam, 45	B4
Grimaldi's, 13	B2
Hammond's Finger Lickin' Bakery, 43	D4
Junior's, 31	C2
Keur N'Deye, 32	C2
L Café, 8	C1
Latticini-Barese, 27	B3
Miyako, 5	C1
Monika Restaurant, 36	B3
Nathan's, 47	B4
Oznot's Dish, 5	C1
Petite Crevette, 22	B2
Philip's Confections, 47	C6
Planet Thailand, 5	C1
Primorski Restaurant, 51	C6
Roy's Jerk Chicken, 42	D4
Sahadi Importing Company, 22	B2
Sea Lane Bakery, 51	C6
Squeeze, 8	C1
Stylowa Restaurant, 3	C1
Taste of Russia, 50	C6
Totonno Pizzeria Napolitano, 46	C2
Vera Cruz, 8	C1

🛍 SHOPPING

Clovis Press, 9	C1
Domsey's, 12	C2
Fulton Mall, 33	C2
Girdle Factory, 9	C1

🏛 MUSEUMS & GALLERIES

Brooklyn Museum of Art, 38	C3
Eyewash, 7	C1
New York Transit Museum, 24	B2
Pierogi 2000, 6	C1
Waterfront Museum, 28	A3
The Williamsburg Art and Historical Center, 11	C2

🎵 ARTS & ENTERTAINMENT

Brooklyn Academy of Music (BAM), 30	C2
Brooklyn Center for Performing Arts, 44	C4

● SIGHTS

Borough Hall, 21	B2
Brooklyn Botanic Gardens, 39	C3
Brooklyn Brewery, 2	C1
Brooklyn Historical Society, 17	B2
Brooklyn Public Library, 37	C3
Coney Island Amusement Parks, Circus Sideshow, Museum, 48	B6
DUMBO, 15	B2
The Eagle Warehouse and Storage Co., 14	B2
Ebbets Field, 40	C3
Erasmus Hall Academy, 41	C4
Grace Church, 20	B2
Greenpoint Historic District, 1	C1
New York Aquarium, 49	C6
St. Ann and the Holy Trinity Episcopal Church, 19	B2
Willow Street, 16	B2

🍺 NIGHTLIFE

Brooklyn Ale House, 4	C1
Galapagos, 10	C1
Halcyon, 29	B2
Montague Street Saloon, 18	B2
Montero's Bar & Grill, 25	B2
Teddy's, 4	C1
Waterfront Ale House, 25	B2

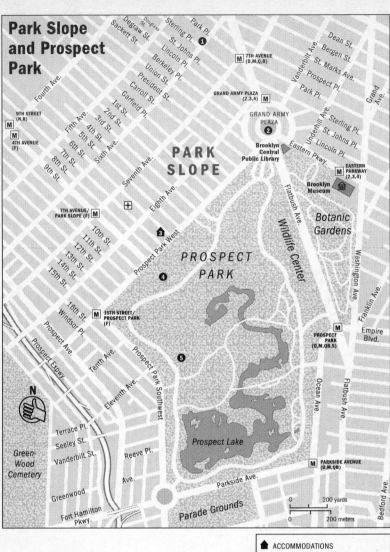

Park Slope and Prospect Park

Douglass St.

Degraw St.

Sackett St.

Sterling Pl.

St. Johns Pl.

Lincoln Pl.

Berkeley Pl.

Union St.

Carroll St.

President St.

Garfield Pl.

1st St.

2nd St.

3rd St.

4th St.

5th St.

6th St.

7th St.

8th St.

9th St.

10th St.

11th St.

12th St.

13th St.

14th St.

15th St.

16th St.

Fourth Ave.

Fifth Ave.

Sixth Ave.

Seventh Ave.

Eighth Ave.

Prospect Park West

Windsor Pl.

Prospect Ave.

Tenth Ave.

Eleventh Ave.

Prospect Expwy.

Park Pl.

🅜 **7TH AVENUE**
(D,M,Q,B)

Dean St.

Bergen St.

St. Marks Ave.

Prospect Pl.

Park Pl.

Vanderbilt Ave.

Underhill Ave.

Sterling Pl.

St. Johns Pl.

Lincoln Pl.

Grand Ave.

GRAND ARMY PLAZA
(2,3,4) 🅜

**GRAND ARMY
PLAZA**
❷

Eastern Pkwy.

**Brooklyn
Central
Public Library**

🅜 **EASTERN
PARKWAY
(2,3,4)**

**Brooklyn
Museum**

**9TH STREET
(N,R)**
🅜

🅜 **4TH AVENUE
(F)**

**PARK
SLOPE**

**Botanic
Gardens**

Washington Ave.

Franklin Ave.

Bedford Ave.

✚

🅜 **7TH AVENUE/
PARK SLOPE (F)**

❸

**PROSPECT
PARK**

Wildlife Center

Flatbush Ave.

❹

🅜 **15TH STREET/
PROSPECT PARK
(F)**

❺

🅜 **PROSPECT
PARK
(D,M,QB,S)**

Ocean Ave.

Flatbush Ave.

Empire
Blvd.

🖐 **N**

Prospect Park Southwest

Terrace Pl.

Seeley St.

Vanderbilt St.

Reeve Pl.

Ave.

**Green-
Wood
Cemetery**

Prospect Lake

🅜 **PARKSIDE AVENUE
(D,M,QB)**

Greenwood

Fort Hamilton
Pkwy.

Parkside Ave.

Parade Grounds

0	200 yards
0	200 meters

🏠 ACCOMMODATIONS
Bed & Breakfast on the Park, 3
● SIGHTS
Bandshell, 4
Friends Cemetary, 5
Memorial Arch, 2
St. Augustine's Church, 1

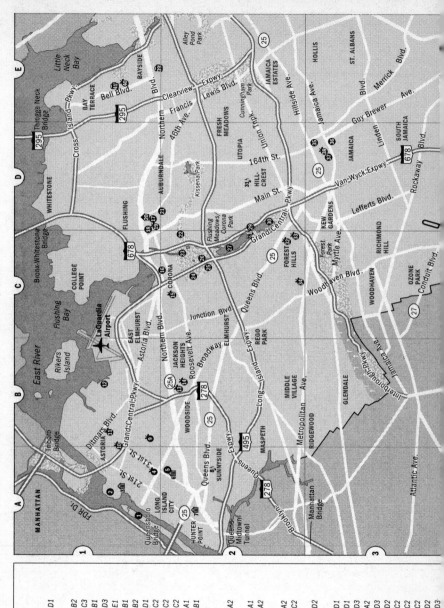

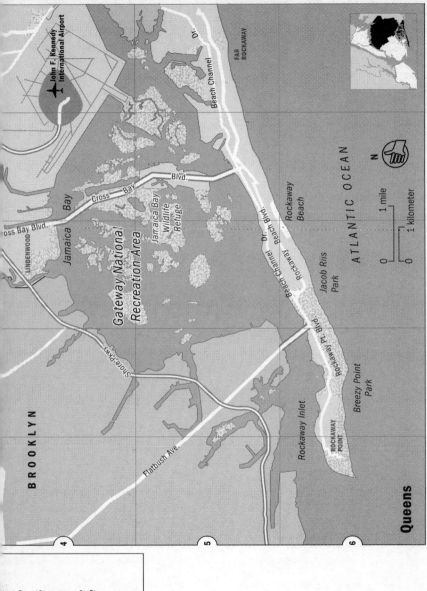

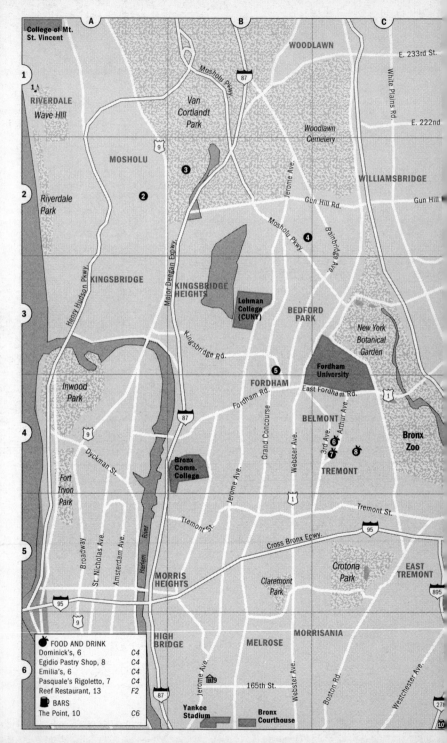

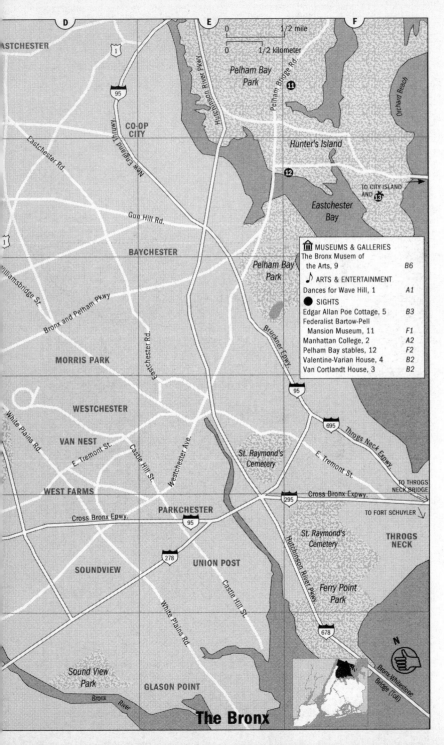

The Bronx

EASTCHESTER

CO-OP CITY

Eastchester Rd.

Williamsbridge St.

Gun Hill Rd.

BAYCHESTER

Bronx and Pelham Pkwy.

MORRIS PARK

White Plains Rd

WESTCHESTER

Eastchester Rd.

VAN NEST

E. Tremont St.

Castle Hill St.

WEST FARMS

Westchester Ave.

PARKCHESTER

Cross Bronx Epwy.

SOUNDVIEW

UNION POST

Castle Hill St.

White Plains Rd.

Sound View Park

Bronx River

GLASON POINT

Pelham Bay Park

Hutchinson River Pkwy.

Pelham Bridge Rd.

Hunter's Island

Orchard Beach

Eastchester Bay

TO CITY ISLAND AND 13

Pelham Bay Park

Bruckner Epwy.

St. Raymond's Cemetery

E. Tremont St

Throgs Neck Expwy.

Cross Bronx Expwy.

TO THROGS NECK BRIDGE

TO FORT SCHUYLER

St. Raymond's Cemetery

THROGS NECK

Hutchinson River Pkwy.

Ferry Point Park

Bronx-Whitestone Bridge (Toll)

N

🏛 MUSEUMS & GALLERIES
The Bronx Musem of
the Arts, 9   B6

♪ ARTS & ENTERTAINMENT
Dances for Wave Hill, 1   A1

● SIGHTS
Edgar Allan Poe Cottage, 5   B3
Federalist Bartow-Pell
  Mansion Museum, 11   F1
Manhattan College, 2   A2
Pelham Bay stables, 12   F2
Valentine-Varian House, 4   B2
Van Cortlandt House, 3   B2

0   1/2 mile
0   1/2 kilometer

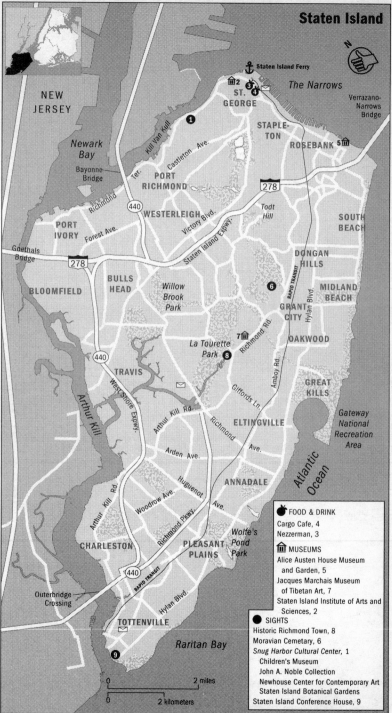

Staten Island

⚓ Staten Island Ferry

NEW JERSEY

The Narrows

🏛2
3
4 ✉
ST. GEORGE

Verrazano-Narrows Bridge

Newark Bay

①

STAPLE-TON

ROSEBANK 5🏛

Kill Van Kull

Bayonne Bridge

Ter.

Castleton Ave.

PORT RICHMOND

278

Richmond

WESTERLEIGH

Todt Hill

SOUTH BEACH

Goethals Bridge

Forest Ave.

PORT IVORY

Victory Blvd.

Staten Island Expwy.

DONGAN HILLS

278

BULLS HEAD

Willow Brook Park

RAPID TRANSIT

⑥

MIDLAND BEACH

BLOOMFIELD

Hylan Blvd.

GRANT CITY

OAKWOOD

440

La Tourette Park

7🏛

Richmond Rd.

⑧

TRAVIS

West Shore Expwy.

✉

Amboy Rd.

GREAT KILLS

Arthur Kill

Giffords Ln.

Richmond

ELTINGVILLE

Ave.

Gateway National Recreation Area

Arden Ave.

ANNADALE

Atlantic Ocean

Arthur Kill Rd.

Woodrow Ave.

Huguenot

Richmond Pkwy.

Ave.

Wolfe's Pond Park

🍎 **FOOD & DRINK**
Cargo Cafe, 4
Nezzerman, 3

CHARLESTON

PLEASANT PLAINS

440

RAPID TRANSIT

🏛 **MUSEUMS**
Alice Austen House Museum
   and Garden, 5
Jacques Marchais Museum
   of Tibetan Art, 7
Staten Island Institute of Arts and
   Sciences, 2

Outerbridge Crossing

Hylan Blvd.

✉

TOTTENVILLE

⑨

Raritan Bay

● **SIGHTS**
Historic Richmond Town, 8
Moravian Cemetary, 6
Snug Harbor Cultural Center, 1
   Children's Museum
   John A. Noble Collection
   Newhouse Center for Contemporary Art
   Staten Island Botanical Gardens
Staten Island Conference House, 9

0 ———— 2 miles
0 ———— 2 kilometers

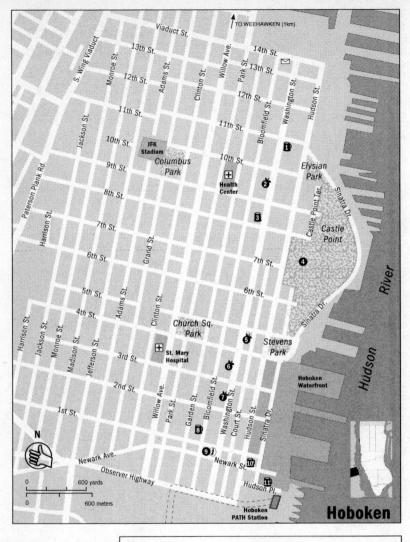

TO WEEHAWKEN (1km)

Viaduct St.

13th St.

S. Wing Viaduct

Monroe St.

12th St.

Adams St.

11th St.

Clinton St.

Willow Ave.

Park St.

14th St.

13th St.

Washington St.

12th St.

Hudson St.

Jackson St.

11th St.

11th St.

10th St.

JFK Stadium

10th St.

Columbus Park

9th St.

Bloomfield St.

❶

Elysian Park

Paterson Plank Rd.

8th St.

✚ **Health Center**

❷

Castle Point Ter.

Sinatra Dr.

Harrison St.

7th St.

❸

6th St.

Grand St.

Castle Point

5th St.

7th St.

❹

4th St.

Adams St.

6th St.

Sinatra Dr.

Harrison St.

Jackson St.

Monroe St.

Madison St.

Jefferson St.

Clinton St.

Church Sq. Park

✚ **St. Mary Hospital**

3rd St.

❺

Stevens Park

❻

2nd St.

Willow Ave.

Park St.

Garden St.

Bloomfield St.

❼

Washington St.

Court St.

Hudson St.

Sinatra Dr.

Hoboken Waterfront

1st St.

❽

N

👍

Newark Ave.

❾ *i*

Observer Highway

Newark St.

❿

| 0 | 600 yards |

| 0 | 600 meters |

⓫

Hudson Pl.

Hoboken PATH Station

Hoboken

Hudson River

🍅 **FOOD AND DRINK**
Amanda's, 2
Flip's, 6
The Hoboken Gourmet Company, 5
La Isla, 7

● **SIGHTS**
City Hall, 9
Overlook Point, 4

🍺 **NIGHTLIFE**
8th Street Tavern, 3
Cadillac Bar, 10
Maxwell's, 1
Miss Kitty's Saloon and Dance Hall Floozies, 8
Planet, 11

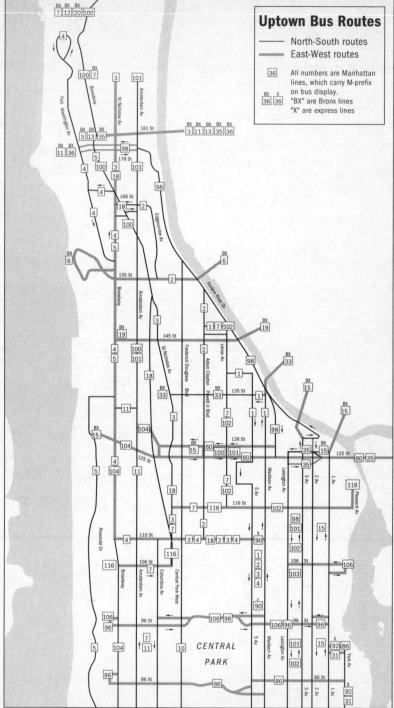

Uptown Bus Routes

—— North-South routes

—— East-West routes

All numbers are Manhattan lines, which carry M-prefix on bus display.
"BX" are Bronx lines
"X" are express lines

Downtown Bus Routes

—— North-South routes

∿∿∿ East-West routes

15 All numbers are Manhattan lines, which carry M-prefix on bus display.

15 15 15 "Q" are Queens lines; "B" are Brooklyn lines "X" are express lines

www.lowealpine.com
If I had my life
to live over again,
I would relax. I would limber up. I would take more chances.
I would take more trips.
I would climb more mountains, swim more rivers, and watch more sunsets.
I would go places and do things and travel lighter than I have.
I would ride more
merry-go-rounds.
Excerpt from Nadine Stair, 85 years old / photo> John Norris
Lowe alpine®
technical packs & apparel

Will you have enough stories to tell your grandchildren?

Yahoo! Travel

Do You YAHOO!?

Find Yourself. Somewhere Else.

Don't just land there, do something. Away.com is the Internet's preferred address for those who like their travel with a little something extra. Our team of travel enthusiasts and experts can help you design your ultimate adventure, nature or cultural escape. Make Away.com your destination for extraordinary travel. Then find yourself. Somewhere else.

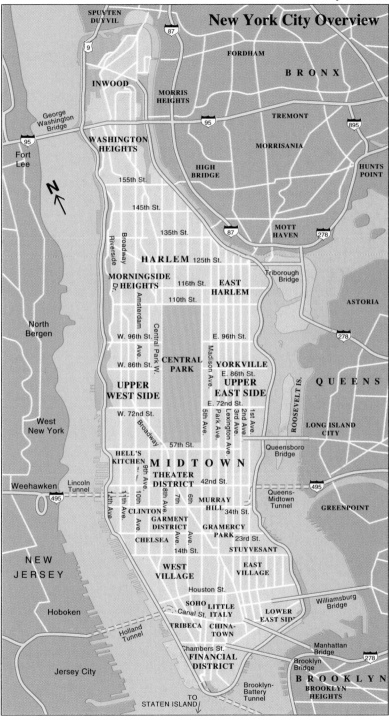

New York City Overview

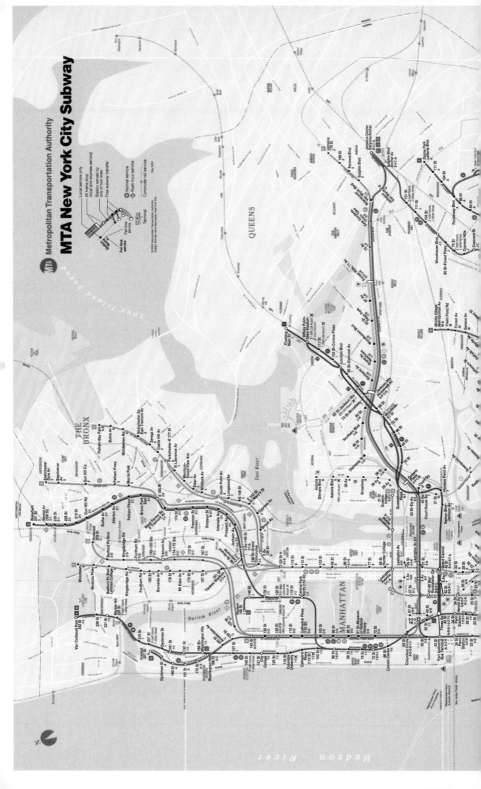

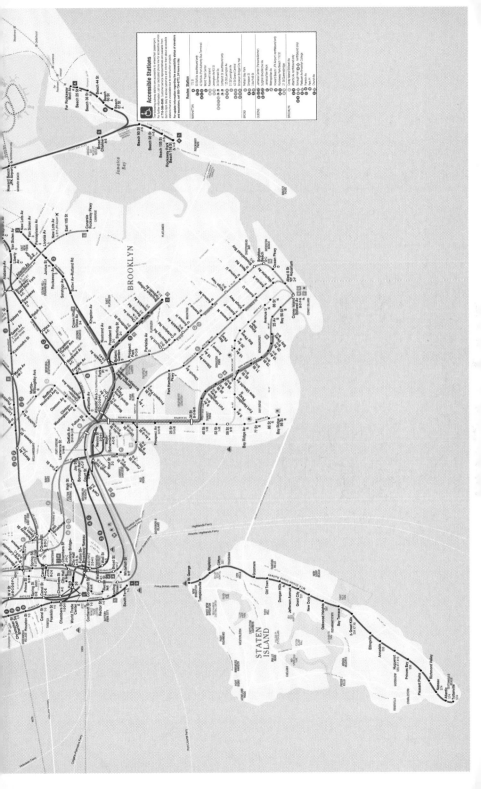

Downtown Manhattan

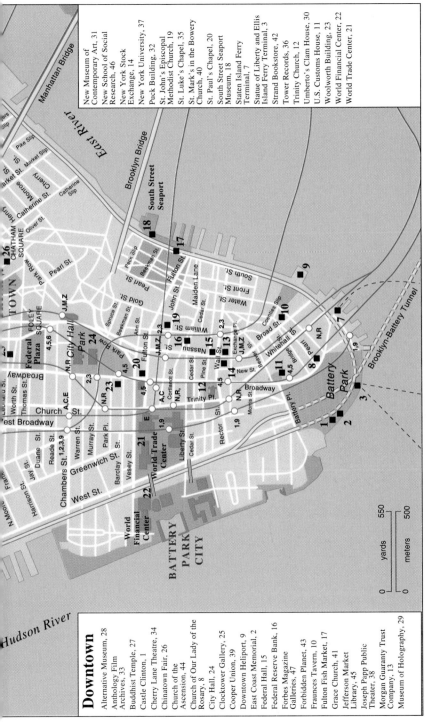

Downtown

Midtown Manhattan

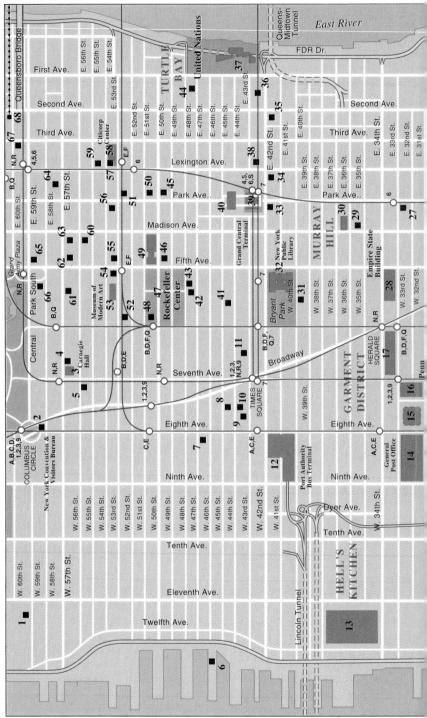

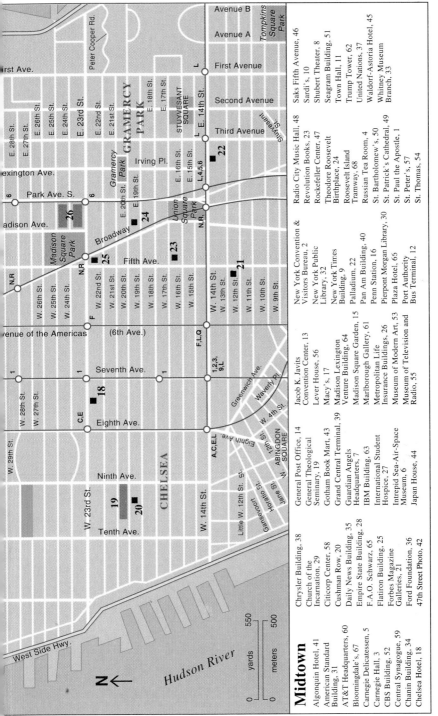

Midtown

Algonquin Hotel, 41
American Standard Building, 31
AT&T Headquarters, 60
Bloomingdale's, 67
Carnegie Delicatessen, 5
Carnegie Hall, 3
CBS Building, 52
Central Synagogue, 59
Chanin Building, 34
Chelsea Hotel, 18

Chrysler Building, 38
Church of the Incarnation, 29
Citicorp Center, 58
Cushman Row, 20
Daily News Building, 35
Empire State Building, 28
F.A.O. Schwarz, 65
Flatiron Building, 25
Forbes Magazine Galleries, 21
Ford Foundation, 36
47th Street Photo, 42

General Post Office, 14
General Theological Seminary, 19
Gotham Book Mart, 43
Grand Central Terminal, 39
Guardian Angels Headquarters, 7
IBM Building, 63
International Student Hospice, 27
Intrepid Sea-Air-Space Museum, 6
Japan House, 44

Jacob K. Javits Convention Center, 13
Lever House, 56
Macy's, 17
Madison Lexington Venture Building, 64
Madison Square Garden, 15
Marlborough Gallery, 61
Metropolitan Life Insurance Buildings, 26
Museum of Modern Art, 53
Museum of Television and Radio, 55

New York Convention & Visitors Bureau, 2
New York Public Library, 32
New York Times Building, 9
Palladium, 22
Pan Am Building, 40
Penn Station, 16
Pierpont Morgan Library, 30
Plaza Hotel, 65
Port Authority Bus Terminal, 12

Radio City Music Hall, 48
Revolution Books, 23
Rockefeller Center, 47
Theodore Roosevelt Birthplace, 24
Roosevelt Island Tramway, 68
Russian Tea Room, 4
St. Bartholomew's, 50
St. Patrick's Cathedral, 49
St. Paul the Apostle, 1
St. Peter's, 57
St. Thomas, 54

Saks Fifth Avenue, 46
Sardi's, 10
Shubert Theater, 8
Seagram Building, 51
Town Hall, 11
Trump Tower, 62
United Nations, 37
Waldorf-Astoria Hotel, 45
Whitney Museum Branch, 33

Uptown

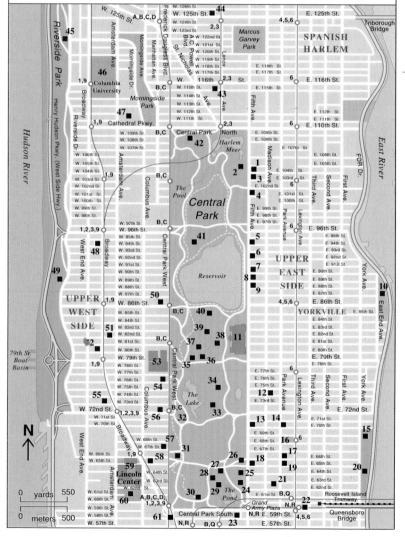